What Others Are Saying

Schooling in America has, over decades, become worse—worse for children's mental and physical health, creativity, critical thinking, and meaningful academic understanding. A major cause is the increased centralized, hierarchical control of schools, which ignores the real needs of children and families in favor of the perceived needs of those at the top of the power hierarchy. In Transforming Education, Frank Dixon shows brilliantly how an understanding of our nation's schooling requires us to view it within the context of the entire corporate, economic, political structure of the nation. I recommend it to anyone concerned with the nation's future.

—Peter Gray, Ph.D., Boston College Research Professor of Psychology and Neuroscience, Author of Free to Learn: Why Unleashing the Instinct to Play Will Make Our Children Happier, More Self-Reliant, and Better Students for Life

Transforming Education is a comprehensive account of how coercive anti-educational standard schools have a symbiotic relationship with coercive dehumanizing societal institutions—including alienating workplaces and a mental health system that routinely pathologizes normal reactions to coercion and alienation. Moreover, Frank Dixon provides a comprehensive solution that will make perfect sense to anti-authoritarian readers who have rebelled against their coercive socialization, retained their critical thinking, and rejected the idea that life is supposed to suck.

—Bruce E. Levine, Ph.D., Clinical Psychologist, Author of A Profession Without Reason: The Crisis of Contemporary Psychiatry—Untangled and Solved by Spinoza, Freethinking, and Radical Enlightenment

The knowledge-fragmenting "core" curriculum that has organized most of the secondary level school day since 1893 ignores important new fields of study, ignores how all fields of study fit together, and ignores how they interact to create a whole far greater than their sum. Transforming Education's whole system approach respects and capitalizes on the seamless way the brain perceives and processes information and puts it to practical, real-world use.

—**Marion Brady, Professor, Education Researcher, Author of What's Worth Learning?, Introduction to Systems, and Investigating World History: A Systems Approach**

TRANSFORMING EDUCATION

A WHOLE SYSTEM APPROACH TO EMPOWERING YOUNG PEOPLE AND ACHIEVING SUSTAINABLE SOCIETY

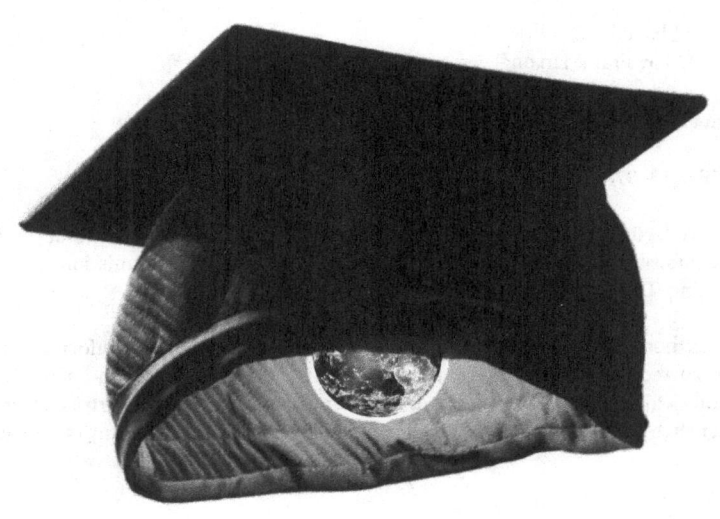

Transforming Education
A Whole System Approach to Empowering Young People and Achieving Sustainable Society

Global System Change Book Series, Volume 6 of 7

by Frank Dixon

First Edition, published 2023
Copyright © 2023 by Frank Dixon

Cover Design and Interior Layout by Reprospace, LLC

Paperback ISBN-13: 978-1-952685-67-5

All rights reserved. No portion of this book may be reproduced in any form without permission from the publisher, except as permitted by U.S. copyright law. For permissions contact: Kitsap Publishing, Telephone 360-626-0241.

Although the author and publisher have made every effort to ensure that the information in this book was correct at press time, the author and publisher do not assume and hereby disclaim any liability to any party for any loss, damage, or disruption caused by errors or omissions, whether such errors or omissions result from negligence, accident, or any other cause.

20220126

KITSAP
PUBLISHING

Published by Kitsap Publishing
P.O. Box 572
Poulsbo, WA 98370
www.KitsapPublishing.com

Dedication

Children and Future Generations

Humanity's innate love for children perpetuates our species. Teaching young people to cooperate effectively and follow their inner wisdom empowers them to reach their fullest potential, live satisfying lives, and create sustainable society. This book describes how to implement a sustainable education system that honors and empowers young people.

Acknowledgment

Rosalind Morley, my dear friend who provided extensive editing and inspirational support for all of the *Global System Change* books.

Evelyn Brandin, my lifelong friend and spiritual ally.

Francis J. Dixon and Carol J. Dixon, my wonderful parents.

Contents

Foreword
Introduction i
Education Funding 1
Privatization 12
    Education Reform Programs 12
    Charter Schools 17
    Degrading the Teaching Profession 20
    Teach for America 24
    Public Deception 33
    Manufactured Crisis 39
    Harming Children 51
Public Funding of Religion 56
Business Influence of Education 76
Authoritarianism 82
Hitting Children 103
Competitive Grading 118
    Self-Esteem 121
    Social Skills 124
    Inaccurate Measurement 128
    Motivation 130
    Productivity 131
    Teacher-Student Relationships 132
    Suppression of Minorities 133
    Misconceptions and Deceptions 134
    Effective Assessment 137
    Protecting Children 143
Boredom 145
Psychiatric Drugs 153
    Complexity and Lack of Knowledge 155
    Brain Chemical Imbalance Theory and Depression 157
        Depression Research 159
        Causes of Depression 163
        Adverse Effects of Antidepressants 169
        The Placebo Effect and Beliefs 172
        Public Deception 177
    Diagnosis of Mental Disorders 181
        Pathologizing Normal Human Behavior 182

- DSM Diagnostic Method 189
- Drug Company Influence 193
- Inadequate Psychiatric Training 196
- Alternative Diagnostic Methods 196

Stimulants and ADHD 200
Antipsychotics and Bipolar Disorder 215
- Bipolar Disorder 216
- Antipsychotic Drugs 217
- DSM Changes 221
- Psychiatric Drugs Causing Mental Illness 224
- Drug Company Influence of Government 227
- Growing Off-Label Use 227
- Rushing Drugs to Market 229
- Suppressing Disruptive Behavior 230
- Non-Addictive Qualities 231
- Growing Institutional Use 232
- Patent Extensions 233
- Drug Company Influence of Research 234
- Drug Company Influence of Doctors 237
- Similarity of Symptoms Between Mental Disorders 238
- Insurance Reimbursement Practices 238
- Prescription in Primary Care Settings 239
- Drug Company Marketing 240
- Difficulty Holding Drug Companies Responsible 242
- Alternative Approaches 243

The Vulnerability of Children 249
Psychiatric Drug Solutions 252
- System Change 255
- Healthcare Reform 257
- Improve Psychological Diagnosis 259
- Require Full Disclosure 265
- Improve Psychiatric Education 265
- Focus Treatment Guidelines on Non-Drug Solutions 266
- Restrict Prescription of Psychiatric Drugs 266
- Restrict Drug Company Marketing 267
- Restrict Psychiatric Drug use among Children and Teenagers ... 269
- Restrict Compulsory Psychiatric Drug Use 269
- Require Long-term, Independent Drug Research 269
- Hold Drug Companies Fully Responsible 270
- Restrict Off-Label Drug Use 271
- Emphasize Psychotherapy 271
- Effectively Address Addictive and Compulsive Behavior 275

    Consider Spiritual Solutions............................. 276
    Establish Support Networks............................. 277
    Expand Parent Support and Training..................... 278
    Research and Expand Alternative Treatments............. 280
    Incentivize Recovery, Not Treatment.................... 281
    Encourage Following Intuitive Wisdom................... 281
    Encourage Service and Activism......................... 282
    Promote Rational Thought, Not Skepticism............... 284
    Face Negative Emotions................................. 287
    Encourage Meditation................................... 288
    Empower People... 288
  Psychiatric Drugs Conclusion............................. 290

Higher Education 294
  Rapid Tuition Growth.................................... 297
  High Student Debt....................................... 299
  Declining Class Mobility................................ 300
  Bloated University Administrations...................... 302
  Expanding For-Profit Colleges........................... 304
  Expanding Online Education.............................. 306
  Business Control of University Research................. 319
  Suppression of Professors............................... 321
  Suppression of Critical Thinking........................ 324
    Objectivism and Atlas Shrugged......................... 326
    Libertarianism... 346
      Rule of Law.. 348
      Limited Government................................. 351
      Individualism and Individual Rights................ 359
      Spontaneous Order.................................. 361
      Free Markets....................................... 365
      Virtue of Production............................... 368
      Natural Harmony of Interests....................... 370
      Hypocrisy.. 372
      Same-Sex Marriage.................................. 375
      Public Deception................................... 384
  Limited Job Opportunities for Graduates................. 395
  Unfair Student Debt Terms............................... 397
  Higher Education Solutions.............................. 402

Education Solutions.. 414
  Clarify Purpose... 416
  Clarify Method.. 418
  Teach Whole System Thinking and Intuitive Wisdom........ 419
  Teach Critical Thinking................................. 430

Whole System Strategy 431
End Business Control of Education 433
Fully Fund Public Education 434
Fully Fund Preschool and Daycare 438
Hold Charter Schools Accountable 440
Prohibit Public Funding of Religious and other Private Schools 445
Freedom-Based Education 447
    Benefits of Self-Directed Education 452
    Concerns about Freedom in Education 458
    Transition to Freedom-Based Education 474
Eliminate Competitive Grading 480
Improve Measurement and Accountability 482
Honor and Empower Teachers 487
Refocus Online Education 493
Prohibit 'Zero-Intelligence' Discipline 499
Prevent Bullying 509
Prohibit Physical Punishment 521
Prohibit Compulsory Psychiatric Drug Use 522
Protect Student Privacy 524
Teach the Whole System Mind 526
Teach and Model Cooperation 533
Promote Co-Education 537
Reduce Segregation 540
Teach Clear Communication 542
Teach Healthy Living 544
Provide Daily K-12 Physical Education 545
Ensure Adequate Recess 546
Increase Outdoor Education 546
Minimize Homework 547
Encourage Civic Responsibility and Community Service 548
Educate Parents 548
Improve Adult Education 551
Engage Elderly People in Education 552
Engage Communities in Education 553
Improve Business Education 555
Optimize Developing Country Education 558
Emulate Finland 560

Education Conclusion 566
Endnotes 574
Index 595

Foreword

by Garry Jacobs

Education is the most powerful instrument humanity has created to support conscious social advancement and individual progress. Yet in spite of remarkable achievements over the past century, new problems seem to be outpacing solutions to existing ones. In this age of complexity and very rapid change, education has been unable to keep pace. The time warp between past knowledge and pedagogy and the need to prepare future generations is only widening. All our educational achievements are inadequate to address our needs.

Frank Dixon is a visionary thinker who views every dimension of modern society through a whole system perspective. This very important book on education applies this whole system approach to examine in breadth and depth the weaknesses of our present system and the enormous potential for consciously transforming education to meet the needs of the 21st Century. It illuminates the link between prevailing failures in our social, economic and political systems and our incapacity to fully harness the progressive power of education. It views education in the context of future needs rather than past achievements and calls for concerted efforts to accelerate progress in education as a driver for accelerating social evolution.

American education has long been the model and standard for the rest of the world to emulate. Today it is acquiring some of the characteristics long associated with societies that cling to outmoded beliefs and seek to impose them on an unwilling population. Like authoritarian regimes, the US increasingly appears to view education as a weapon for political power, rather than a powerful tool for promoting enlightened thinking, human development, and social harmony.

The book seeks to found our future education system on freethinking and the highest human values, rather than ritualized political and social dogma. It illuminates the root causes of present problems and proposes many practical solutions. It shifts the focus from education as an instrument for economic advancement to education as a catalyst for the development of a freethinking mind and mature personality in each student. Therein lies the greatest potential for the future flourishing of America.

Garry Jacobs, President & CEO, World Academy of Art & Science, Executive Chairman, UN Global Security for All campaign

Introduction

Protecting children and future generations is the primary obligation of humanity. Providing outstanding education is one of the most important aspects of this. It broadly benefits society, in large part by empowering children, teenagers and young adults to live successful, fulfilling lives.

The United States education system fails on this most important obligation. It severely degrades young people and society. Academic performance is not the most important output of education. Young people forget much of what they learn in K-12 education. But this usually has little impact on their ability to succeed in life.

The most important qualities needed for life success include high self-esteem, strong social and emotional skills, critical thinking ability, and empowerment to build one's life around their unique skills and passions. The forced education system, with its competitive grading and standardized curriculums, suppresses these qualities, and thereby severely inhibits young people's ability to prosper in life.

COVID-19 substantially disrupted K-12 and higher education. But there were deep, fundamental problems in US education before the pandemic. This book analyzes these problems and describes how to evolve education systems into empowering, sustainable forms. Many US examples are given. But the broader solutions presented here apply to nearly all countries.

Two main themes of this book are: education follows society and education creates society. Education follows society in the sense that it usually evolves to serve the goals of society. The US education system strongly reflects the US focus on economic growth, shareholder returns and business well-being. As the focus shifts to maximizing the well-being of all current and future citizens (i.e. abiding by the US Constitution), we will implement a substantially different education system. Education also creates society in the sense that it teaches young people how to think and act in the world they one day will control.

Transforming Education is part of the *Global System Change* book series. The books are based on whole system thinking. Human society reflects human thinking. All major aspects of society are connected. But considering everything at once is complex. As a result, we often study the economy, education system, and other parts of society without adequate reference to the whole system that contains them.

This reductionistic thinking produces flawed economic and political systems that cause unintended consequences, such as widespread environmental and social degradation. Reductionism is the root cause of all major challenges facing humanity. As Einstein said, resolving these challenges requires higher-level, whole system thinking. The Global System Change books use this thinking to provide systemic solutions for all major areas of society.

Transforming Education puts education in a whole system context. It uses whole system thinking to address root causes and provide effective education solutions. A whole system approach is essential because the most important causes of education decline lie outside the education area. As a result, *Transforming Education* often refers to other *Global System Change* book sections.

Focusing only on improving education will help, but not come close to establishing empowering, sustainable education. To illustrate, poverty is the main cause of poor education performance in the US, and has been for over 100 years. Education reform approaches implemented over the past 40 years usually did not adequately address this root cause. As a result, they failed to substantially improve education performance.

Another root cause of US education decline is the shifting focus of US society. As business control of government increased in the 1980s, the education reform movement was initiated. The stated goal was to improve education. But this was not the effectively measured and managed goal. Education 'reform' approaches were implemented that strongly benefited business and enhanced shareholder returns, but degraded young people, education and society. These include privatization, standardized testing, and many other processes discussed in this book.

Prior to the 1980s, the US was more broadly focused on promoting the general welfare of society. This contributed to the US being a world leader in K-12 and higher education in the 1950s and 1960s. From the 1930s to the

1970s, wages largely rose with economic growth. Those who benefited the most from society paid fair taxes. We had the largest middle class in the world. The Fairness Doctrine required media to present both sides of controversial issues (i.e. tell the truth).

However, beginning in the late 1970s, campaign finance laws largely were dismantled. Wealthy citizens and companies are now allowed to anonymously spend unlimited amounts on political campaigns. This gave them strong control of government and both major political parties. Largely as a result, nearly all economic and stock market growth since the 1980s has been concentrated at the top of society. Inflation-adjusted wages have been nearly flat for 40 years. Taxes on wealthy individuals and corporations were substantially reduced.

Business-controlled government removed the Fairness Doctrine in 1987. Since then, media often provides dishonest, one-sided coverage that divides society into debating factions (i.e. conservatives and liberals). As the people are divided, they are conquered. They lose their ability to control government and ensure the public wealth is used to equally and fairly benefit of all citizens. Education follows society. The growing US focus on business well-being drove the implementation of an education system that strongly benefits business in the short-term.

Finland and other world education leaders use strong, well-funded public education and honored, well-compensated teachers and college professors to achieve world-leading performance. The US used this approach to achieve education leadership 60 years ago.

However, this proven strategy largely was abandoned under business-focused education reform. Vested interests misled citizens into thinking that privatizing and standardizing public education would improve education performance. But US performance relative to other developed countries substantially declined in several areas over the past 40 years.

This book discusses many strategies for improving K-12 and higher education. They could be segregated into two broad categories. First, reestablish US education leadership. And second, go beyond it. The first broad strategy largely involves reversing education reform. The purpose of education should be to benefit young people and society, not businesses and shareholder returns. The US should emulate world leaders and reestablish the systems that enabled us to be a global education leader long ago.

Once we reestablish strong public education and the dignity of the teaching profession, we should go beyond it. Modern education is a legacy of the Protestant Reformation and Industrial Revolution. The goals were and largely still are indoctrination and obedience training.

Competitive grading makes the large majority of students feel inadequate during 13 of the most formative years of their lives. Standardized curriculums often teach them that their unique interests and talents have little value. Forced education suppresses critical thinking, in part by emphasizing what to think instead of how to think. It conditions young people to not question injustices in society, such as business control of government, degradation of environmental life support systems, and unfair concentration of public wealth.

Forced education teaches young people to endure boring jobs and control by authorities for the rest of their lives. This perpetuates unjust, unsustainable economic and political systems and facilitates ever-increasing shareholder returns. But it severely degrades society and violates our primary obligation to protect children.

Thomas Jefferson, John Adams and several other US Founders said that a freethinking, well-educated population was essential for democracy. The US was born in the Age of Enlightenment and Reason. Rational thinking and science triumphed over irrational blind faith in dogma. Education reform benefited business, but degraded society. It is a main cause of the US entering a New Dark Age.

Suppressed wages and job benefits, and reduced job and retirement security since the 1980s, made life more difficult for many people and drove frustration and discontent. This combined with 40 years of suppressed critical thinking made citizens vulnerable to deception and division. Many people blindly believe deceptive media positions, rather than think for themselves. They often are manipulated into attacking false enemies (liberals, conservatives) and ignoring major problems (democracy decline, corporate welfare). The dumbing down of US society under education reform and deceptive media since the 1980s bloomed into the election of a grossly unqualified president, attack on the US Capitol, and degradation of democracy and fair elections.

A generation ago, logic usually was the entry point for public discussion and debate. People who made illogical or factually incorrect statements usually were ignored or dismissed. This enabled people to engage in the often difficult work of finding practical solutions within the realm of logic.

However, these logical conversations frequently threatened ever-increasing shareholder returns. As a result, vested interests and deceptive media often used irrational, emotional arguments to block logical conversation. Well-educated citizens would see through these deceptions and think for themselves. Dumbing down US education protected vested interests in the short-term and the unsustainable systems that benefit them. A Second Enlightenment is needed in the US and many other countries. This book describes how to implement an empowering, sustainable education system that strongly supports this Enlightenment.

Transforming Education introduces the concept of Freedom-Based Education. Going beyond current education requires transforming forced education into freedom-based education. Young people should not be ranked against each other and forced to study subjects they find boring and irrelevant. This degrades self-esteem, weakens social skills (by teaching them to see peers as obstacles to success), often causes them to think their unique skills and interests are worthless, and teaches them to seek external validation rather than trust their inner wisdom. Freedom-based education does the opposite. It strongly promotes the most important qualities needed for life success and achieves superior retention of important information.

As is the case in all of the *Global System Change* books, the purpose here is not to criticize business, political and education leaders. Flawed economic and political systems routinely compel well-intentioned leaders to take actions that harm society, such as putting shareholder returns ahead of the well-being of children. These systems, and the reductionistic thinking that created them, are the main enemies of education and society overall. The purpose here and in all the *Global System Change* books is to use whole system thinking to improve flawed education and other human systems.

Reductionistic economic and political systems do not hold companies fully responsible for negative environmental and social impacts. This unintentionally compels harm. If companies voluntarily try to stop harming the environment and society, costs increase and they ultimately go out of business. This is not sustainable. Destructive systems inevitably will change through voluntary or involuntary means. Throughout history, all flawed human systems changed, usually by collapsing quickly (e.g. American and French revolutions, end of US slavery and USSR communism).

Humanity almost certainly has entered another phase of rapid system change, as indicated by rapidly growing, often unprecedented environmental, social, economic and political problems (e.g. COVID-19, Ukraine invasion, Capitol attack, democracy decline, climate change). Improving flawed economic and political systems before they collapse is essential for protecting society. Empowering young people to think critically, logically and objectively will help to resolve major challenges and protect the long-term well-being of business and society.

Transforming Education facilitates system change by assessing and linking all major education areas. A whole system approach places education in the context of larger environmental, social, economic and political systems. Complex issues are summarized in easy to understand terms. With over 700 endnotes, *Transforming Education* serves as a comprehensive education reference book. The book discusses many problems and whole system solutions in K-12 and higher education, including the following.

The Education Funding section discusses the immense societal benefits of investing in public education and the poor academic performance and other problems caused by the inequitable US funding system. Students from low-income communities usually require greater support in school. The majority of developed countries provide more funding for disadvantaged students. The US is one of only three developed countries that provide less. This strongly contributes to poor academic performance in low-income community schools.

The Privatization section discusses how public deception and business influence of government drove extensive privatization of US public schools and degradation of US education. Issues discussed include No Child Left

INTRODUCTION

Behind and other education reform laws, degrading the teaching profession through the Teach for America program and other means, and lack of accountability and other problems with charter and private schools. The section describes how a false crisis was manufactured in US education to justify privatization.

The Public Funding of Religion section discusses problems with this type of education funding, including lack of accountability, discrimination, increased taxes, degradation of public education, and lack of public support. The US Founders strongly opposed taxpayer funding of religious education. Separation of church and state is established in the US Constitution. Thirty-six state constitutions prohibit public funding of religion. Nearly every public referendum on the subject opposed it. However, business influence of judicial appointments contributed to legal decisions that allow taxpayer funding of religious education, for example, through vouchers and tax credits. As a result, taxpayers of one religion are being forced to pay to teach religions that are different than their own. Some Christian textbooks teach that God created the world 6,000 years ago, gay people are equivalent to rapists, and the purpose of environmentalism is to destroy the economy. Citizens should not be forced to pay to teach children these irrational and harmful ideas.

The Business Influence of Education section discusses growing business influence of K-12 and higher education over the past 40 years. Privatizing public education was seen as a good business opportunity for the corporate and financial sectors. As a result, politicians who accepted money from education and other companies strongly promoted privatization. Reduced public funding compelled many K-12 schools and universities to seek private funding and support. This enabled companies to place advertising in schools, restrict teaching of climate change and other subjects that threaten shareholder returns, and suppress academic research that shows corporate products to be harmful.

The Authoritarianism section discusses growing authoritarianism in US education and society. This protects vested interests by suppressing logical freethinking. Authoritarianism makes it easier to divide and disempower citizens, concentrate wealth, and perpetuate unjust, harmful systems. Issues discussed include zero-tolerance discipline, standardized testing, surveillance, drug testing, incarceration, compiling student databases, declining liberal arts, student debt, screen viewing, religious fundamentalism, attacking intellectuals, and public deception.

The Hitting Children section discusses the extremely harmful nature of hitting children and other forms of physical punishment. Over 100 countries prohibit hitting children in schools. Thirty-two countries prohibit it in all settings, including homes. However, all 50 US states allow parents to hit their children. Nineteen states allow hitting in schools. Over 60 percent of US families physically punish their children. Overwhelming research shows that hitting children often causes severe mental health problems. Hitting is prohibited in prisons and nearly all other settings in the US. The only people we are allowed to hit are those who are the smallest, weakest, most vulnerable and defenseless, least likely to understand why they are being hit, most likely to be severely psychologically harmed by hitting, and the ones we say we love the most. This is absurd. Children should receive the most protection from hitting, not the least. This section discusses the severe harm caused by hitting, rationalizations use to justify it, religious influence, parental self-awareness and control, more effective forms of discipline, and how other countries banned physical punishment.

The Competitive Grading section discusses the harmful nature of competitive grading and suggests more effective and empowering assessment alternatives. Competitive grading degrades the most important qualities needed for life success to measure less important factors (i.e. academic performance). It suppresses the motivation to learn, creates innately adversarial relationships between teachers and students, and shifts the focus of education from learning to judgment. As discussed throughout the *Global System Change* books, the overwhelming force in nature is cooperation. To survive and prosper, humanity must substantially increase cooperation in society. Competitive grading teaches young people competition. This facilitates authoritarianism and perpetuates unjust systems. Issues discussed in this section include self-esteem, social skills, motivation, productivity, teacher-student relationships, suppression of minorities, and effective student assessment.

INTRODUCTION

The Boredom section discusses widespread boredom in US education and the many problems this causes. Humans evolved to learn by freely doing what interests them. However, education systems in the US and many other countries are not based on how children learn most effectively. They are based on history. The classroom model of education was developed during the Protestant Reformation. Education was intended to break the will of children and teach dogma. The Industrial Revolution added standardization, centralization and passive worker compliance. Education reform increased boredom by emphasizing standardized curriculums and reducing fun and interesting activities, such as physical education, recess, music, art, shop and team sports. Children often are forced to sit passively in sterile environments for several hours per day listening to adults talk to them. Boring education conditions them to endure boring jobs for the rest of their lives.

The Psychiatric Drugs section provides a comprehensive discussion of psychiatric drugs, in large part because young people often are encouraged or compelled to take these drugs in school. The boring, judgmental, grossly flawed US education system inevitably produces large amounts of inattention, hyperactivity, depression, anxiety, disruptive behavior and other psychological problems. The solution is not to drug children so they comply with the deeply flawed US education system. It is to fix the system. This section discusses the complexity of the mind, problems with the current method of diagnosing mental disorders, harm caused by widespread use of psychiatric drugs, factors driving high growth in psychiatric drug use, and alternative approaches for diagnosing and addressing psychological problems.

The Higher Education section discusses the many societal benefits of higher education, growing business influence, and related problems. Resolving major challenges requires objective, whole system thinking. Colleges and universities are main places where this can and should occur. Enlightened thinking often threatens vested interests. Growing business influence of higher education protects them by suppressing higher-level thinking. It also creates many other problems, including rapid tuition growth, high student debt, declining class mobility, bloated university administrations, expanding for-profit and online education, business influence of academic research, suppression of professors and critical thinking, and replacing true higher education with vocational education (i.e. courses that benefit business). This section suggests several higher education solutions, including fully fund public higher education, greatly reduce student debt, reduce business influence, ensure independent academic research, reestablish the dignity and independence of professors, and restore true higher education.

Transforming Education concludes with a comprehensive Education Solutions section. The 38 solutions subsections describe many systemic and specific education solutions, including teach whole system thinking and cooperation, equitably fund public education, hold charter and private schools to the same standards as public schools, eliminate competitive grading, honor and empower teachers, prohibit physical punishment and compulsory psychiatric drug use, protect student privacy, provide daily physical education, and implement freedom-based education.

Whole system thinking is essential. Education follows society. The current education system nearly perfectly supports the primary focus of society – maximizing economic growth and shareholder returns. Shifting the focus to maximizing the well-being of all citizens, especially children, will shift the focus of education.

Much can be done under current economic and political systems to improve education. The solutions discussed in this book will strongly promote the freethinking, well-educated population the US Founders said was essential for democracy. Providing empowering, sustainable education will drive the evolution of human society and systems into sustainable forms and most effectively empower young people to live successful, satisfying lives.

Education Funding

Investing in public preschool, primary education (kindergarten through 5th grade), secondary education (6th grade through 12th grade), and higher education (undergraduate and graduate) is one of the most important and effective investments that citizens can make in a civilized society. Possibly as much or more than any other factor, public education provides equal opportunity to children of all socioeconomic backgrounds. It often enables children from low-income families to make it into the middle class or higher.

On a national level, public education provides very large benefits to society. Having a well educated population and workforce greatly improves international competitiveness and promotes the advancement of science and technology. Citizens are the ultimate leaders in a democracy. Teaching children to critically examine ideas and be independent, freethinkers greatly enhances democracy.

As discussed in the Crime section of Global System Change, investment in high quality public education is a major component of preventing crime. For example, the extra cost of providing small class sizes, well-qualified teachers, and excellent educational facilities and materials often will be far more than offset by lower incarceration and social welfare costs. Reducing crime by investing in public education also provides extensive intangible benefits, such as enhanced public safety, spirit and well-being.

In general, investments in public education are highly cost-effective. For example, college graduates in the US earn about 65 percent more than high school graduates.[1] By enabling many low and middle-income students to receive college educations, low-cost public higher education strengthens the economy and increases tax revenues. From 1944 to 1956, the G.I. Bill enabled over two million veterans to attend college, and nearly seven million more to receive some type of training.[2] It is estimated that the G.I. Bill returned nearly seven dollars to the economy for every one dollar invested in it.[3]

Education illustrates the importance of adopting a whole system perspective. Children are not taught in a vacuum. They are educated in whole systems, such as communities and society overall. The situation for children outside of school has a major impact on performance in school. If conditions outside of school decline, performance in school also often will decline, even if education spending increases.

From the 1930s to 1980, conditions for children improved substantially in the US. Social Security, Medicare, and other social well-being programs facilitated the establishment of a large and stable middle-class. Increased union protections drove fair wages and often enabled one parent to stay home and raise children. Child labor laws, child abuse laws, civil rights protections, and family courts improved children's protections and quality of life. Birth control enabled parents to control the number and timing of children. This increased family prosperity and stability. The Women's Rights movement encouraged fathers to take a more active role in raising children. Childhood lifestyles often provided abundant time for play, sports and other physically stimulating activities.

These programs and societal actions provided safe, stable, healthy living environments for many children outside of school. This combined with substantial investments in public education enabled the US to achieve among the best educational performance in the world.[4] In the 1950s and 1960s, the US was a world-leader in K-12 public education.[5]

However, as discussed in the Finance and Capital Markets section of *Global System Change*, in the early 1980s, large companies and wealthy business owners increased their influence of government and drove reductions of social well-being programs that threatened ever-increasing shareholder returns. This freed up more taxpayer wealth to be used for corporate welfare. In 1980, the top one percent of US households received 10 percent of the nation's pre-tax income. By 2000, this grew over 21 percent.[6] Shifting substantial public funds from social welfare to corporate welfare caused extensive societal degradation, including in the education area.

Shifting production offshore and weakening unions frequently reduced the availability of high-quality jobs and compelled both parents to work. Overwhelming advertising targeted children, lowered self-esteem, and often produced materialistic and inaccurate ideas about how to achieve life satisfaction. As discussed in the Crime section of *Global System Change*, substantial reductions of social welfare and other programs intended to protect low-income families and communities contributed to increased crime, family instability, and other problems. Very high, world leading incarceration rates for nonviolent crimes frequently degraded families and communities. It also diverted substantial funds from public education.

Shifting extensive public wealth from social welfare to corporate welfare over the past 40 years of plutocracy (i.e. control of government and society by the wealthy) greatly reduced opportunity and economic mobility in the US. Largely as a result, the poor got poorer, the middle class stagnated, and the wealthy got wealthier. The US was once considered to be a land of opportunity. But in many ways, this no longer is the case.

Many studies have shown that the US has less equality of opportunity than nearly all other developed countries. For example, fewer people move from lower-income to middle or upper-income segments of society in the US than in most of Europe and all of Scandinavia.[7] Further indicating lack of opportunity in the US, the life prospects of a US citizen are more dependent on the income and education of parents than in nearly all other developed countries.[8] In other words, shifting public wealth from all citizens to the small group of wealthy citizens that controls government has greatly increased class stratification and lack of opportunity in the US.

As the focus of the US over the past 40 years of plutocracy shifted from maximizing the well-being of all citizens to maximizing the well-being of the small group that gives the most money to politicians, conditions for children, especially those from low-income families, often declined substantially. This strongly contributed to declining US educational performance relative to other countries.

The US ranks 24th in the world on reading, 39th on math and 24th on science.[9] The World Economic Forum ranked the quality of the US primary education system as 38th in the world. The overall US education system was ranked 28th.[10] The US ranks 27th in the percentage of college students who obtain degrees in science or engineering and 48th in the quality of our math and science education.[11] In the late 1990s, 50 percent of high school seniors in the US did not know in which century the Civil War occurred, 60 percent could not say how the US came into existence, and 60 percent could not name the three branches of the US government.[12]

The College Board, the nonprofit organization that administers the SATs, found that 57 percent of high school graduates who took the SATs did not have the skills needed to succeed in college or a career.[13] In 2011, more than 50 percent of public school students and over 75 percent of African American and Hispanic students could not read or do math at grade level in the 4th and 8th grades.[14] About 30 percent of students fail high school each year. Only about 50 percent of African American and Hispanic students graduate from high school. Roughly 50 percent of all students who are eligible to go to college actually go.[15] And less than 50 percent of those who go to college graduate (i.e. the worst performance among developed countries).[16]

Partly to support cuts in public education programs that might increase taxes and threaten ever-increasing shareholder returns, businesses and their allies often stated that public education expenditures increased over the past 40 years, but educational performance declined. They often argued that this proves or implies that spending more on public education does not improve performance. This rationale makes it easier to cut funding for public education and use more taxpayer funds for corporate welfare.

But this position is highly deceptive. A study by the Heritage Foundation found that expenditures per student on K-12 public education increased by 49 percent from 1984 to 2004 adjusted for inflation.[17] Average expenditures per student on K-12 public education were about $13,000 in 2020.[18] This is among the highest expenditure levels in the world. However, this macro-level assessment hides several underlying problematic trends.

Public K-12 education expenditures are about $670 billion per year.[19] About 49 percent of this funding is provided by state governments, 43 percent by local property taxes, and eight percent by the federal government.[20] On average, about half of property taxes in the US are used to fund K-12 public education. This system creates wide variations in education funding. In wealthy school districts, up to 90 percent of school budgets are funded by local property taxes. In the poorest school districts, as little as six percent of funding comes from property taxes. As a result, some wealthy school districts spend over $25,000 per student per year, while the poorest school districts often spend less than one-third that amount.[21]

As with incarceration, the US is an outlier state in the education funding area. The majority of developed countries provide more funding for disadvantaged students.[22] Among the 34 OECD countries, only the US, Israel and Turkey provide fewer resources. Rather than heavily relying on inequitable property tax funding systems, 54 percent of K-12 education funding in other developed countries on average is provided by the federal government.[23]

Providing more funding for disadvantaged students is logical because children from wealthier families often have more learning opportunities. In the US, children from lower-income families enter kindergarten knowing about 67 percent fewer words than children from wealthier families. These children often have higher stress levels, which can strongly interfere with learning. Their families frequently face higher unemployment, evictions and homelessness. They also often face greater exposure to environmental toxins.[24] Spending more to educate low-income children would provide many financial and non-financial benefits, such as reduced crime and incarceration.

The position that increased education funding in the US did not improve educational performance appears to ignore the wide variations in education funding at the community level. Prior to the financial collapse of 2008, real estate prices often rose rapidly. This frequently drove increased property tax revenue, especially in upper-income and upper-middle-income communities. This often enabled increased public education funding in wealthier communities. The system of partly funding education with property taxes in the US strongly contributed to increased public education spending as real estate prices rose. But much of this increase was concentrated in wealthier communities. Higher spending there increased US average educational expenditures relative to other countries. But high average expenditures hide the fact that education spending in poor communities often is substantially lower.

While average education funding often increased over the past 40 years, certain types of funding frequently declined. For example, in low and middle-income communities, increased emphasis on standardized testing caused many schools to reduce funding for physical education, art, music, shop, foreign languages and other classes. Reflecting reduced funding in lower-income communities, class sizes have been growing in many schools in these areas.[25]

Cuts in public education funding have expanded since the 2008 recession. In nearly two-thirds of states, K-12 education funding per student was lower in 2012 than in 2008. Over one-third of states cut funding by more than 10 percent. A 2012 assessment of US public schools found that over 50 percent increased class sizes, nearly one-third reduced elective classes such as foreign languages and social sciences, nearly 30 percent eliminated field trips, 29 percent reduced extracurricular activities, and 22 percent eliminated summer school.[26] Reflecting reduced funding and growing class sizes, about 300,000 teaching positions were eliminated in the US from 2008 to 2013.[27] Art, music and other non-core programs continued to decline through 2020.[28]

The dilapidated state of US K-12 public schools is one of the strongest indicators of inadequate public education funding. A report by the National Center for Education Statistics found that upgrading US K-12 public school buildings to "good overall condition" would cost about $200 billion. The average age of the main instructional building at US public schools is 44 years. Over half of public schools must spend about $4.5 million per school on repairs, renovations and modernizations to put them in good condition.[29]

Most states provide less funding for schools in lower-income areas. Only 14 states provide more. Reduced state funding combined with lower property tax funding causes schools in low-income communities to often be in worse condition than schools in wealthier communities. For example, schools in low-income communities in New Jersey often have extensive mold, asbestos insulation and rodent droppings. Los Angeles public schools frequently are in poor condition, with problems including broken sinks, broken computers and insect infestations. New York State facilitates charter school development by providing fewer resources for schools in low-income communities than in wealthier communities. Like most other states, New York State underfunds low-income public schools. This often lowers academic performance. The State then frequently criticizes poor performance in these schools and promotes the expansion of charter schools.[30]

Perhaps the most deceptive aspect of the vested interest statement that increased education funding does not improve educational performance involves myopia. The statement implies that children are educated in a vacuum. But as noted, they are not. If conditions for children outside of school decline, performance in school also often will decline, even if education expenditures increase. As discussed in the Crime section, if the basic needs of children are not being met and if they do not feel safe in their communities, it frequently will be very difficult for children to focus on schoolwork and do well in school.

Under plutocracy since the 1980s, trillions of dollars of taxpayer wealth have been shifted from social welfare to corporate welfare. This made life more difficult for millions of middle and low-income families. Degraded living conditions, especially in low-income communities, are the main cause of declining educational performance over the past 40 years. Indicating the link between poverty and academic performance, the income and education level of parents is the most reliable predictor of academic performance in the US.[31]

To further illustrate this link, for over 100 years, the high school dropout rate for the 40 percent lowest income group in the US has been over 60 percent. This group traditionally was comprised of African Americans and immigrants. Academic performance in the low-income segment of society always has been below average. But as programs to provide jobs and other support to low-income citizens were cut, academic performance got even worse. For example, as social welfare was reduced and corporate welfare increased, the academic performance gap between rich and poor children increased by 30-40 percent from 1976 to 2001.[32]

If the 40 percent low-income group is excluded, the 60 percent highest income segment of society achieves academic performance that is near the best in the world.[33] US schools where less than 10 percent of children live in poverty are number one in the world in reading. Schools where more than 75 percent of children live in poverty achieve academic performance that is similar to developing countries.[34] In other words, much of the poor academic performance in the US occurs in lower-income communities.

This is not meant to be critical of low-income families. Many low-income parents do an outstanding job of raising their children well. But as discussed above, low-income families face many challenges that wealthier families do not. These challenges often make it more difficult for children from these families to do well in school. Also, while many low-income families have excellent, loving parents, low-income sometimes indicates problems that make it difficult for parents to earn a living and raise children well, such as mental or physical health problems.

Proposals to improve educational performance by cutting teachers unions, increasing standardized testing or privatizing schools largely will not work because the main cause of poor educational performance lies outside of schools. The main cause in the US is poverty.[35] The greater emphasis on shareholder returns and economic growth relative to other developed countries is a main cause or the main cause of poverty in the US. This focus often drives manufacturing and high quality jobs offshore. It also results in implementation of a much weaker social safety net than most other developed countries.

The relatively greater emphasis on the well-being of business instead of the well-being of society causes the US to have near the highest childhood poverty rate in the developed world. Among 35 developed countries, the US was ranked 34th. Only Romania has a higher childhood poverty rate.[36] The childhood poverty rate in the US is about five times higher than the average of OECD countries. About 26 percent of US children live in poverty. The rate is well under 10 percent in most other developed countries.[37] In many Southern and Western US regions, a majority or near majority of children live in poverty. Illustrating the link between poverty and educational performance, Finland is considered to have the best or near the best educational performance in the world. However, Finland also has among the strongest social safety nets. As a result, the child poverty rate in Finland is five percent versus 26 percent in the US (41 percent among children of color).[38] [39]

The greatest equity in US education funding occurred during the War on Poverty and Great Society period in the 1960s and 1970s. More federal funding was provided to urban and poor rural school districts. Other programs reduced unemployment in low-income communities. In 1975, for the first time, the rates of African American, Latino and white students going to college were equal. But most of the programs intended to improve education, employment and other critical factors in low-income communities were eliminated or greatly reduced in the 1980s.[40] Shifting public funds from social welfare to corporate welfare since the 1980s has greatly increased poverty and raised income inequality to the highest level in the past 100 years.[41] This shift of wealth to the small group that controls government is the main factor driving declining education performance in the US.

The strategy for improving educational performance in the US is myopic. Adopting a whole system perspective shows that the most important action needed to improve performance is to end the redistribution of public wealth to the top of society through corporate welfare. As this occurs, the wealth of this great nation can be used to fairly benefit all citizens, in large part by implementing a social safety net that is comparable to other developed countries.

Another deceptive aspect of the vested interest position that increased education funding will not improve educational performance involves logic. In essence, the position is illogical. In nearly all other areas, spending more money often produces superior outcomes. All other things being equal, people usually will get a higher quality product or service if they spend more money. For example, someone probably could buy a better car if they spent $30,000 instead of $1,000.

In the education area, states that spend the most on education, such as Connecticut, Massachusetts and Vermont, usually have the highest academic performance. States that spend the least, such as California, Mississippi and Louisiana, usually have the lowest performance. California once was an education leader. But the state has substantially lowered education funding over the past 30 years, while increasing funding for incarceration. As California lowered education funding, it put itself among Southern states as having the worst academic performance in the country. At the community level, wealthier communities often spend three to four times more per student than low-income communities.[42] These communities nearly always have higher graduation rates, better test scores and superior academic performance in general.[43]

Vested interests attempt to mislead the public into believing the irrational statement that spending more money on public education will not improve educational performance. This deception helps to free up more public wealth for corporate welfare. In many public schools in low-income communities, classes often have 40 students or more, while class sizes in wealthier schools often are 25 or less.[44] In low-income communities, schools frequently are old, dilapidated and poorly maintained compared to the higher quality schools in wealthier communities. Books, computers and other school supplies often are lower quality and less available than in wealthier schools. Vested interests frequently argue that we already have spent too much money on public education. Don't throw more money at it, they often say. But if one were to walk into many public schools in low-income communities, it quickly would become obvious that the problem is inadequate, not excessive, spending.

As discussed in the Misleading the Public section of *Global System Change*, it is inappropriate to use the deceptive and derogatory statement, don't throw money at it, in reference to public education. As discussed in the Finance and Capital Markets section, it would be appropriate to use this statement when low and middle-income taxpayer funds are used to cover the losses of wealthy speculators who made highly risky investments, as occurred with the bank bailouts. As discussed in the Governance section, it also would be appropriate to say, don't throw money at it, when spending far more money on the US military than any other country, in large part to support hundreds of military facilities in other countries that apparently are used mainly to protect US business interests rather than national security. But it is not appropriate to use the statement, don't throw money at it, when discussing our most sacred obligation – protecting and supporting our children. There probably is inefficiency and waste in public education that can and should be eliminated. But this is not the only solution.

The increase in public education funding creates the illusion that the US commitment to public education has increased over the past 40 years. But it has not. As business control of government increased, the focus of government and society in general shifted from maximizing the well-being of society to maximizing the well-being of business. This drove a large general disinvestment in social well-being programs and frequent disinvestment in public education in low and lower-middle-income communities. This great shifting of public wealth from social welfare to corporate welfare, and the increased difficulty it caused for low and middle-income families, is the main reason that US public educational performance fell from near the best in the world in the 1950s and 1960s to poor compared to many other developed countries.

The decline in the US commitment to education since the 1980s is indicated by a study of high school and college graduation rates. Among 55 to 64-year-olds, the US ranks number one in the world on high school graduation and number three on college completion. But among 25 to 34-year-olds, the US ranks 10th and 13th, respectively.[45] Further indicating the declining commitment to education relative to other countries, a study of OECD countries found that "the US is the only nation where young adults are less educated than the previous generation".[46] This disinvestment in US society will continue to degrade the US economy and society until citizens wake up, end the vested interest-driven civil war between conservatives and liberals, and halt the theft of our wealth and power.

We have a paramount obligation to protect our children, in part by investing in them when necessary. As discussed below, increased funding of public education, especially in low-income communities, and increased investment in programs that support children outside of school is critical to improving educational performance in the US.

Privatization

The privatization of public education represents one of the most tragic and destructive trends in the US. This section discusses the negative impacts of privatization and other businesslike practices being implemented in the US education system. It should be noted up front that the negative impacts of privatization obviously do not result from an intention to harm children or degrade the education system. Instead, the sincere intention often is to help children and improve US education. As occurs in many other areas, negative impacts are unintended consequences of failing to see the big picture and blindly adhering to the philosophy that placing the well-being of business before all else maximizes the well-being of society.

Education Reform Programs

Not surprisingly, the trend toward education reform through privatization and increased businesslike practices began in the 1980s when business influence of government substantially increased. A 1983 report, called *A Nation at Risk*, claimed that the US education system was failing to educate children well and that this would hurt US competitiveness. The report made many recommendations, including suggesting increased focus on core subjects and standardized testing. The report helped to initiate many local, state and federal reform initiatives that emphasized businesslike practices, such as establishing goals, measuring performance, and using penalties and incentives to achieve goals. The *Nation at Risk* report catalyzed what has been referred to as the Accountability Movement in US education.

The increased emphasis on standardized testing was codified by the No Child Left Behind Act (NCLB) of 2002. NCLB required all public schools receiving federal funding to administer statewide standardized tests to all students in certain grades each year. Schools with students who were not proficient in core skills, such as reading and math, were required to achieve adequate yearly progress on student test scores. Increasingly severe actions or penalties were required if schools failed to make adequate progress. Actions included publicly labeling schools as failing, allowing students to transfer to other schools, requiring free tutoring, and replacing staff. If poor performance continued, schools could be privatized, taken over by the state or closed.

In 2015, NCLB was replaced by the Every Student Succeeds Act (ESSA). ESSA transfers some control of education from the federal to the state level. But the most important (and as discussed below, harmful) aspects of NCLB are continued in ESSA. For example, states still are required to use standardized tests to test students in grades three through eight and once in high school. As with public education funding, the US is an outlier on standardized testing. Few countries use standardized tests, especially before high school.[47] As problems with standardized testing (discussed below) became more obvious, many parents prohibited their children from taking the tests. ESSA limits the ability of parents to opt out of standardized tests by requiring 95 percent participation.[48] This protects the companies that profit from standardized testing and give large amounts of money to politicians. ESSA also promotes private sector initiatives in public schools and other activities that benefit wealthy campaign donors.

ESSA removes the federal requirement that teacher evaluations be based on student test scores. But it leaves evaluations of schools in place. Under ESSA, states must intervene in the lowest performing five percent of schools, high schools with graduation rates below 67 percent, and schools where subgroups, such as minorities, consistently underperform.[49] Intervention can include taking over schools or converting them to charter schools. This requirement protects the shareholder returns of companies that profit from privatization, for example, by establishing charter schools and implementing other businesslike processes in public schools.

While ESSA transfers some education authority to states, the federal government maintains an oversight role. States are required to submit accountability plans to the US Department of Education. Under NCLB, states sometimes sought to evade stringent performance requirements by using more subjective measures, such as parent/teacher involvement. ESSA limits the ability of states to do this by requiring that accountability be based more on factors such as standardized test scores and graduation rates.[50]

ESSA was compromise legislation that addressed some concerns about federal control of education. But like NCLB, ESSA strongly promotes and protects key aspects of the US approach to education reform, such as standardized testing and privatization. While some authority is shifted from the federal to the state level, the approach remains top-down. Teaching methods and student evaluation approaches often are not chosen by local schools and teachers, as they are in many countries that lead the world in education performance. Instead, they frequently are imposed by state governments. Like NCLB, ESSA strongly protects the large companies and wealthy citizens who substantially control government and education policy in the US.

Beyond NCLB/ESSA, other education reform initiatives include Common Core standards, value-added modeling and the Race to the Top program. Common Core seeks to harmonize diverse state academic curricula by encouraging states to adopt a common set of core standards. Value-added modeling often involves linking teacher evaluations and pay to student test scores. The Race to the Top program sought to spur innovation and reforms by providing increased funding to states for implementing programs such as promoting charter schools and privatization. Due to these and other programs, many states began linking teachers' pay and evaluations to standardized test scores.[51]

Various reform programs that directly or indirectly promote privatization have led to the opening of many private and charter schools, as well as contributed to the conversion of some public schools to charter schools. Programs that promote privatization include voucher programs being implemented by some states and municipalities. Under these programs, parents often receive taxpayer-funded vouchers that can be used to pay for private schools.

Trigger laws being implemented in some regions also promote privatization. These laws frequently allow a majority of parents to sign a petition that triggers options such as firing staff, closing schools or turning them over to private school companies. Further promoting privatization, Georgia amended its constitution to allow the state to create private, for-profit schools as part of the public education system. Other states are considering similar measures.[52]

Adopting Common Core standards also strongly drives the privatization of public education and creates many opportunities for education companies. Over 40 states adopted the standards. Kentucky was the first state to adopt them. When students were tested using these new standards, elementary and middle school students considered to be proficient or better in reading and math dropped by one-third.[53] The decline in proficiency when tested with the new standards is expected to be even greater in several other states.

As a result of the Common Core standards, parents who previously had been told that their children and schools were doing well were told that they were failing. This sudden relabeling of many students and schools as failing compelled many schools to buy products and services from for-profit companies in an effort to improve performance. Business opportunities were created for lesson plans, test preparation, educational software, and many other products and services.

Common Core standards further increase business profits by facilitating economies of scale. Common standards enable education companies to sell the same products in many states, rather than developing customized products for each state. Also, relabeling many public schools as failing increased business profits by strongly promoting privatization of these schools.[54]

NCLB required that all students be proficient in reading and math by 2014. This was an impossible goal. (As noted, about half of students were not proficient in reading and math in 2011.) Achieving the goal is impossible in large part because the US emphasis on the well-being of business is driving ongoing cuts in social welfare programs. This exacerbates the primary driver of poor academic performance – poverty. The NCLB proficiency goals probably cannot be achieved until the emphasis of the US government and society is switched from the well-being of business to the well-being of society. Due to unachievable goals, the federal government allowed many states to opt out of NCLB in return for adopting programs, including those that promote privatization.[55] ESSA eliminates the requirement that all students be proficient in reading and math.

Privatizing public schools and implementing increased businesslike practices in public education have been strongly promoted by many Republican and Democratic politicians. But there are several problems with these approaches. For example, white students often outperform African American and Hispanic students. One goal of NCLB was to reduce this achievement gap. However, extensive data and research showed that the increased accountability and high stakes testing either increased the achievement gap or had no impact on it. This occurred mainly because accountability does not address the primary cause of the achievement gap – poverty.[56]

Students in Finland take nearly no standardized tests. But they achieve the highest or near the highest scores in the world in reading, math and science.[57] Education reform based on increased accountability and standardized testing has increased over the past 40 years. But these approaches existed for over 100 years. A century's worth of evidence showed that increased accountability and standardized testing not only do not improve academic performance. They often lock in or exacerbate problems that cause poor performance.[58]

To illustrate, under NCLB, schools that failed to make adequate progress on test scores faced reduced funding and other punishments.[59] This would be like telling a child whose hunger was causing them to underperform in school, if you do not improve performance, we will give you even less food. Poor academic performance often occurs in underfunded schools with large class sizes in low-income communities. It is not rational to think that taking funds away from these schools, labeling them as failures, and punishing them in other ways will improve performance. Instead, it frequently will reduce it.

When NCLB/ESSA and other programs label a school as failing, proactive parents often attempt to take their children out of the school. Highly motivated parents and students frequently do not like the stigma of attending a 'failing' school. Students with absent or less proactive parents often are left in these schools. This process of labeling schools as failing and giving parents the option to remove children from them drove substantial reductions in funding for public education. Through voucher and other programs, many states reduced funding for public education, but increased public funding for charter schools, cyber schools and other private schools.[60]

Basing teacher pay, school funding and other rewards on student test scores drove extensive cheating, corruption and gaming of education systems by school districts and states. For example, some states lowered test standards to improve test scores and protect funding.[61] The focus on testing also often compelled teachers and schools to teach subjects and skills that improve test scores, while inadequately teaching other important subjects and skills.

The accountability approach to public education appears to be based largely on magical or myopic thinking. It seems to ignore the obvious fact that unemployment, family instability, divorce, unsafe communities, illness, poverty and other factors outside of school can affect performance in school. The approach magically, irrationally and incorrectly implies that more testing and accountability can overcome external factors, including poverty—the largest driver of poor educational performance.

Charter Schools

Charter schools represent a primary means of privatizing K-12 education in the US. The growing use of these schools creates many potential problems. The first US charter school opened in 1992. Charter schools often are publicly funded, but not controlled by local school districts. They have greater autonomy over curriculum, instruction and operations. Charter schools originally were established to promote greater innovation and experimentation in education. They were intended to support and collaborate with public schools, rather than undermine and compete with them. These schools frequently were intended to recruit the weakest students and develop more effective ways of teaching them.[62]

Charter schools run by nonprofit organizations with educational missions often provide high quality education. However, a growing number of charter schools are run by for-profit, publicly traded companies, often referred to as educational management organizations (EMO's). For example, about 80 percent of the charter schools in Michigan are run by EMOs.[63] Even though charter schools frequently are nonprofit, there usually are many profit-making opportunities related to them. For example, for-profit companies often provide real estate, consulting, accounting, legal, food, transportation and other services to these schools.

Charter school advocates frequently argue that the businesslike focus of schools run by for-profit companies can lower costs and improve academic performance. However, extensive research refutes these positions. Charter schools often are heavily subsidized by private donations.[64] When this funding is combined with public funding, these schools sometimes cost more than traditional public schools.[65]

In addition, overwhelming evidence shows that charter schools do not outperform traditional public schools and frequently underperform. For example, studies by the US Department of Education, John Hopkins University, the RAND Corporation[66], the University of California, the Economic Policy Institute and the policy research firm Mathematica found that charter schools do not outperform traditional public schools.[67] A large Stanford University study found that 46 percent of charter schools achieve the same level of performance as traditional public schools, 37 percent underperform traditional public schools, and 17 percent outperform.[68]

An updated version of the Stanford study found that charter school performance had improved to be about the same as traditional public schools. However, about one-third of the performance improvement was due to the closing of schools that underperformed in the earlier study. Also, charter school enrollment policies can produce misleading performance research results. As discussed below, charter schools often discourage the enrollment of lower-performing students as well as push out students with low test scores. This can create the illusion that charter schools are teaching more effectively, when in reality they simply are focused on enrolling higher-performing students. A study of a large charter school chain (KIPP) found that their students outperformed traditional public school students. But the study was called into question by some experts because funding for the study was provided by an organization that also provides substantial funding to KIPP.[69]

Charter schools are less transparent and accountable to parents and communities than public schools. Parents, communities and states often have less control over charter schools than traditional public schools. For example, some states require charter schools to be nonprofit. But for-profit companies still can establish charter schools and effectively run them. This frequently is done by establishing boards of local residents who allow for-profit companies to run the schools with little or no interference.

To illustrate, the CEO of a charter school company advised senior staff to make sure that local boards understood that they were not responsible for making decisions about budgets, hiring principals, school policies and other matters. The CEO said, "It is our school, our money, our risk, not theirs."[70] Reflecting hypocrisy, charter schools often emphasize their public nature when seeking public funds, but then emphasize their private nature when seeking to avoid labor laws and other societal protections by which public schools must abide.

Students are assigned to traditional public schools. But students and parents choose charter schools. Many charter schools have waiting lists and assign places by lottery. Better students with more proactive parents often apply to the schools. Charter schools usually strive to achieve high test scores. As a result, many charter schools only accept a limited number of students with disabilities and low English language skills. The schools also sometimes force out students with low test scores.[71] This emphasis on accepting higher-performing students often causes charter schools to be more segregated along racial and income lines than traditional public schools.[72]

Opening charter schools frequently weakens traditional public schools by taking resources from them. This often compels traditional public schools to cut teachers and programs. Charter school discrimination further weakens public schools. As noted, charter schools often refuse to take children with disabilities or limited English language skills as well as push out underperforming students and send them back to traditional public schools. As discussed in the Crime section of *Global System Change*, for-profit prisons often refuse to take prisoners with high healthcare costs and send prisoners back to public prisons when they become seriously ill. For-profit schools frequently essentially do the same. Concentrating students who are more expensive to educate in traditional public schools often lowers funding available for other students. This can reduce traditional public school performance and promote further privatization.[73]

Another problem with charter schools involves fragmenting the education system. Using taxpayer funds to pay for two sets of public schools (traditional and charter) often reduces economies of scale and increases redundancy and administrative costs. Taxpayer funds frequently are distributed to for-profit companies rather than invested in education. Public funds often are used to pay high executive compensation that would not be allowed in public school systems.[74] The need to provide superior investor returns, high executive compensation and other factors can cause administrative costs of for-profit schools to be substantially higher than traditional public schools. As discussed in the Healthcare section of *Global System Change*, administrative costs in the largely for-profit US healthcare system are about twice as high as those in the public Canadian healthcare system.

Charter schools represent about five percent of public schools. Privatization is driving rapid growth of for-profit charter schools. Most of these schools are located in cities and other low-income areas.[75] Rapid growth of charter schools is substantially degrading public education by taking funds away from traditional public schools. Taxpayer funds frequently are being transferred to for-profit schools. As discussed below, the requirement to provide ever-increasing shareholder returns will drive ongoing education quality degradation and rising education costs.

Degrading the Teaching Profession

One of the main problems with privatization is degradation of the teaching profession. In other developed countries such as Finland, being a teacher is a high status profession, comparable to being a lawyer or doctor. Nearly all developed countries protect teachers with unions. For example, 98 percent of teachers and principals in Finland belong to the educators union.[76] Good pay, benefits and job security attract highly qualified people to the teaching profession. This is completely appropriate. Children often spend about half of their waking lives in school. Caring for our children is the most important obligation of humanity. As a result, teaching probably is the most important job in society. Therefore, we must provide the pay, benefits, job security and academic freedom needed to attract the best teachers.

But this is the opposite of what is happening in the US. Through privatization and implementing businesslike practices, businesses, politicians paid by them and other business allies are attempting to standardize and commoditize education. Ensuring that children are taught the same curriculum and take the same tests will make it easy for a few large education companies to provide standardized education products and achieve high sales.

But standardizing and commoditizing education is extremely ignorant, myopic, irresponsible and incorrect. Children are human beings, not machines. Each child is different. Attempting to grind our children through standardized education mills that produce proficient test-takers is the height of idiocy. The best teaching styles vary from child to child and teacher to teacher. Some children learn better through one teaching approach versus another. Some teachers are more effective when using a particular approach. The idea that all children should be forced to learn in one particular way and all teachers forced to teach in a certain way is ignorant in the extreme.

Teaching is as much or more an art than a science. Teaching occurs on many levels, not just intellectual. Effective teachers must be able to discern the emotional and psychological needs of children and teenagers, as well as intellectual needs. This is a main reason why teaching is such an honored profession in many developed countries that outperform the US in the education area. Teachers must have the flexibility to determine which approach works best for a particular child in a particular situation. They also must have the flexibility to teach in ways that emphasize their particular strengths. Effective teaching requires wisdom, compassion and good judgment as much or more than intellectual knowledge.

A sophisticated, effective education system would recognize that each student and teacher is a unique human being with particular strengths and weaknesses. The system would be flexible and honor the uniqueness of each student and teacher. But this wise recognition of reality would severely impede the standardization, commoditization and privatization of education in the US.

Teachers unions were a major component of superior US education performance in the past. Unions ensured teachers received the pay, benefits and job security commensurate with the honored and important position of teaching in society. Unions also helped to ensure that teachers had the academic freedom to tailor their approaches in ways that work best for individual students and take advantage of teacher strengths. Good pay and benefits along with academic freedom enabled the teaching profession to attract many highly talented individuals.

As noted, under deregulation since the 1980s, business-controlled government cut many social welfare programs. This allowed corporate welfare to be increased. But in spite of cuts in other areas, education spending often increased, at least in wealthier communities. Unions frequently protected teachers from pay cuts that were being imposed in other social well-being areas. This contributed to increased education spending.

To facilitate the commoditization and privatization of education and enable the cost-cutting needed to provide ever-increasing shareholder returns, it was essential that teachers unions be weakened or eliminated. This occurred to a large degree over the past 30 years. Teachers' rights in the areas of tenure, academic freedom, due process and unionization often have been severely eroded.[77] Teacher strikes are banned in 37 states. Teachers frequently are not honored and respected the way they used to be.[78]

Vested interests used many public deceptions to degrade and weaken unions and the teaching profession in general. For example, teachers and unions often were blamed for declining education performance. But this is dishonest. As noted, poor academic performance has existed in low-income communities for over 100 years. But teachers were not blamed for this in the past. The obvious main cause of poor performance was and is poverty, not teachers, unions or failure to implement a standardized curriculum.[79] Vested interests also argued that US teachers are overpaid and under-worked. This also is dishonest. An OECD report found that US teachers work longer hours and receive relatively less pay than teachers in nearly all other developed countries.[80]

Privatization and the growing use of charter schools run by for-profit companies has been a major driver of degradation of teachers unions and the teaching profession in general. Charter schools often lay off or do not hire unionized, more experienced teachers.[81] They usually have less experienced teachers and higher teacher turnover rates.[82] In general, privatization and implementing increased businesslike practices greatly increased teacher turnover in US schools. In the 1987-88 school year, the largest group of teachers had 15 years of experience. This fell to one year by the 2007-08 school year.[83]

The weakening of unions, reduction of teacher status and academic freedom, and lowering of pay and benefits made the teaching profession much less attractive. As a result, fewer people are pursuing teaching careers. Among those who enter the profession, many leave teaching and seek higher-paying jobs that enable them to live a reasonable quality of life. Between 40-50 percent of people entering the teaching profession leave within five years.[84] Education reform-driven degradation of the teaching profession is causing teacher shortages at school districts across the US.[85]

This degradation is the expected outcome of privatization. As noted, charter schools run by nonprofit organizations can provide outstanding education because this is the goal of those organizations. But the goal of for-profit companies running charter schools is to provide outstanding shareholder returns. This often conflicts with providing high-quality education.

Honoring teachers and providing them with academic freedom and superior pay and benefits will attract talented individuals who provide excellent education to our children. For nearly all of human history, businesses only were required to earn reasonable profits that might not grow every year. But as discussed in *Global System Change*, since the 1980s, a suicidal business model dominated the economy. This myopic model demands that profits and shareholder returns always grow, regardless of how much it degrades society. To achieve this, for-profit education companies usually must continuously increase revenues and/or reduce costs. This model will place ongoing downward pressure on teacher pay and benefits. This in turn will severely inhibit the ability of the education system to attract talented teachers and provide children with the high-quality education they deserve.

Teach for America

An organization called Teach for America (TFA) also contributes to degradation of the teaching profession and privatization of public schools. Established in 1990, TFA recruits high-achieving college graduates to teach for two years in low-income urban and rural schools. A goal of TFA is to help close persistent achievement gaps between white and minority children, and between children from low-income and middle/upper income families. TFA participants complete a five-week summer training program before beginning their two-year teaching commitment.

TFA is like the Peace Corps in the sense that participants receive minimal training, work for two years, and then usually move on to other fields. About 89 percent of TFA participants do not intend to make teaching a lifelong career. About 88 percent have no teacher education or training before taking their five-week TFA training course. About 56 percent of TFA participants leave the school in which they were placed after two years. After five years, 72 percent of those who enter TFA no longer are teaching.[86] Several other studies found that over 80 percent of TFA participants are not teaching after three to five years.[87] As noted, the five-year turnover rate among other types of teachers is 40 to 50 percent. This was substantially lower before education reform largely degraded the attractiveness of the teaching profession.

The TFA approach is problematic in several ways. For example, regular teachers often get bachelor's and/or master's degrees in education. They usually intend to pursue a career in teaching. They frequently work as teachers' aides or student teachers and get substantial supervised classroom experience before teaching on their own. Also, depending on the state, they often are required to pass rigorous testing and certification requirements. These people are far better prepared and qualified to teach than TFA participants. TFA participants often have expedited, less stringent certification requirements. As noted, they also usually do not plan to pursue teaching careers and have no teacher training or experience before their five-week training course.

The differences between real teachers and TFA participants are especially important at schools in low-income communities. (It would be inappropriate to call TFA participants teachers because they usually lack the education, training, experience, rigorous skills certification and long-term commitment of actual teachers.) Students in low-income schools often are the most difficult to teach because they frequently face the greatest problems outside of school. They sometimes are being abused, do not have basic needs met, or face more violence in their communities. As a result, it often is more difficult for them to pay attention in class. People who receive education degrees and in-classroom training will be far more effective in these difficult learning environments than people who receive only a five-week summer training course.

Experienced, committed teachers frequently remain in schools for many years. They often get to know the parents and siblings of students. They frequently understand community needs, problems and available resources. These teachers provide stability and familiarity to schools and students. The TFA approach causes cycling of young, inexperienced quasi-teachers through schools. This creates instability for schools and students. Even if TFA participants teach well, students can feel abandoned because teachers to whom they might have become attached often leave. Unfortunately, children in low-income schools frequently face instability or abandonment outside of school. TFA brings this abandonment and lack of stability into schools. At times, it might make sense for schools to hire young, inexperienced teachers. But this works best when teachers plan to stay for many years. With the TFA approach, the training and experience provided by schools is regularly lost. Schools must repeatedly start over with the next round of new, inexperienced quasi-teachers.

From the perspective of improving education and helping low-income children, the TFA model seems questionable. Well-trained, experienced teachers who meet rigorous certification requirements and are committed to the teaching profession nearly always could do a better job of teaching than virtually untrained, college graduates with no teaching experience, little or no commitment to the teaching profession, and expedited or perfunctory certification.

However, from the perspective of maximizing the well-being of business, the benefits of TFA are much clearer. TFA and affiliated organizations play major roles in weakening teachers unions, closing or privatizing so-called failing public schools, expanding charter schools, and tying teachers' pay and job security to student test scores.[88] TFA supports the privatization of public schools and expansion of charter schools in several ways.

For example, in 2008, TFA established a political organization, called Leadership for Educational Equality (LEE). LEE helps TFA alumni get elected to local school boards and attain other policy, advocacy and educational leadership roles. The organization supports TFA alumni who advocate privatization and opening charter schools once they get elected to local school boards. LEE helps TFA candidates to win local elections by providing consulting, website development and fundraising assistance.[89]

TFA also facilitates privatization and charter school expansion through it First Placement policy. TFA requires that members accept the first teaching position offered to them. TFA participants often are not allowed to negotiate with charter and other schools about wages and benefits. Also, TFA participants have no union protection. As a result, schools can fire them at any time for any reason. Knowing that TFA participants only commit to work for two years, many schools overwork them, and then replace them with new TFA participants.[90]

Suppressing teachers makes TFA highly attractive to charter school companies. For example, a large charter school network (Rocketship) gets about 75 percent of its teachers from TFA. Further indicating strong links between TFA and charter schools, the founder of TFA is married to the president of KIPP, one of the largest charter school networks in the US.[91]

TFA could be thought of as an anti-labor union. Labor unions protect workers by collectively bargaining for fair wages, benefits and working conditions. TFA does the opposite. It often essentially forces participants to accept lower wages and benefits and poor working conditions. TFA participants usually work for lower pay and accept fewer healthcare and pension benefits than actual teachers.[92] TFA provides easy access to a pool of low-cost, inexperienced teacher replacements. This greatly facilitates laying off unionized teachers and privatizing public schools. Privatizing a public school often shifts the focus from providing outstanding education to providing outstanding shareholder returns. This generally requires an ongoing focus on cost reduction. Replacing well-paid unionized teachers with low-cost TFA participants strongly facilitates cost reduction, and thereby greatly benefits for-profit education companies.

Thousands of unionized inner-city teachers are being laid off and replaced by TFA participants. For example, the city of Chicago is closing 48 public schools, laying off 850 teachers and hiring 350 TFA participants.[93] TFA receives substantial funding and donations from businesses and wealthy business owners.[94] This strongly indicates that the organization provides many benefits to business and is heavily influenced by business.

An analysis of peer-reviewed studies about the teaching effectiveness of TFA participants produced the obvious and expected outcome. The analysis found that students taught by credentialed beginning teachers performed substantially better in reading and math than those taught by TFA novices. In other words, people who studied to become teachers and received rigorous certification taught more effectively than those who only received the five-week TFA training. As TFA participants gained teaching experience, their effectiveness improved.[95] But as noted, about 80 percent of TFA participants leave teaching within three to five years. As a result, this experience is regularly lost. TFA participants who become effective teachers routinely are replaced with ineffective TFA novices.

While nearly all studies find the expected outcome (i.e. more training, experience and commitment produces more effective teachers), one study found that students taught by TFA participants did slightly better on math and the same on reading compared to students taught by actual teachers.[96] Studies that produce unexpected outcomes such as this often require closer examination. To illustrate by expanding differences, if a study found that five-year-old children did quantum physics better than people with PhD's in quantum physics, one might suspect bias or other study problems.

In the same way, one would expect that experienced, well-trained, rigorously certified, committed teachers would teach more effectively than college graduates with no experience, little training and no long-term commitment to teaching. As discussed throughout this book, when independent studies show companies' products to be unsafe, companies often attempt to refute or discredit independent research by funding or influencing studies that, not surprisingly, show their products to be safe and effective. No suggestion is being made here that the above study contained business bias or influence. However, in general, one probably should consider the possibility of business influence when studies produce unexpected outcomes that benefit business.

Beyond business influence, other factors could impact or distort studies that show TFA to be effective. For example, the above study examined academic performance. But as discussed below, effective teaching involves more than good test scores. Other important benefits of good education include developing strong critical thinking and social skills and enhancing self-esteem. As a result, accurate assessments of teaching effectiveness would examine more than test scores.

In addition, education reform often has made teaching more difficult and stressful. Dealing with growing class sizes, declining resources and expanding standardized testing requirements can cause long-term teachers to become burned out or emotionally drained. Young, energetic, well-motivated TFA participants who have no intention of remaining in education might be more enthusiastic and engaging during their two-year teaching stint. They will not have to tolerate the oppressive, dispiriting teaching conditions caused by education reform for long. As a result, they might be able to help students get higher test scores in some cases.

But this does not mean that actual teachers should be replaced by a constantly changing pool of inexperienced TFA participants. As discussed below, the honor, dignity, pay, benefits and job security of teachers should be returned to the level that it was when the US was a world leader in K-12 public education. In addition, K-12 teachers should be allowed to take periodic sabbaticals. K-12 teaching can be emotionally draining, especially in low-income schools because children often require extra compassion and attention. Enabling teachers to periodically recharge their batteries, so to speak, without fear of losing their jobs, could substantially enhance teacher effectiveness.

Some experts have criticized the TFA approach for being elitist, arrogant, irrational, myopic and/or naïve.[97] Minority children in low-income inner-city schools are treated like indigenous children in developing country villages. As in the Peace Corps, frequently white, upper-middle-class bright young people come in to 'rescue' poor children of color from presumably incompetent teachers and schools. Doing the good deed of helping poor children for a couple of years looks good on resumes. It often helps young people to get into graduate school or find better jobs. But this approach is wrong in many ways.

As discussed, poor academic performance in the US occurs most often in low-income communities. The main cause of this poor performance is not bad teachers or schools. It is poverty. US inner-city schools are not developing country villages. Inner-city children deserve to be taught by well-trained, committed, professional teachers. Replacing real teachers with a constantly rotating pool of inexperienced young people who have no long-term commitment to teaching makes a mockery of inner-city children and their education. Educating inner-city children should not be seen as a brief detour made by bright young people on their way to better careers.

The TFA model is irrational. It implicitly assumes that people with knowledge of a subject, such as math or English, and a willingness to be around children can teach effectively with little teacher training and experience.[98] But this generally is not true. In addition to knowledge of certain academic disciplines, effective teaching usually requires extensive training about the psychology of how children learn, alternative teaching methods, and other important teaching skills. Supervised classroom experience prior to independent teaching also enhances teaching effectiveness.

Consistency and stability are critical for effective education, especially in inner-city environments where these often are lacking at home. TFA will not achieve its mission of closing income and racial achievement gaps. It often will make these gaps larger by providing children in low-income communities with lower quality, unstable teaching. As noted, children are the most important people in society. This makes teaching one of the most important, if not the most important job in society. All children deserve to be taught by well-trained, committed, professional teachers.

Education companies and their paid political servants often attempt to mislead the public by blaming teachers for poor academic performance in low-income communities. They often imply that teachers are lazy, incompetent and overpaid. TFA implicitly supports this deception. The TFA approach implies that bright, energetic young people can teach more effectively than well-trained, experienced teachers. This approach supports the idea that inner-city teachers are incompetent and easily replaceable. This is a gross disservice to teachers and students. These teachers work in many of the most difficult teaching environments. Their jobs have been made more difficult by declining resources, increased class sizes and expanded standardized testing. In reality, these teachers often are heroes. TFA does not improve inner-city education by strongly facilitating the removal of committed, heroic teachers.

It is important to note that TFA is being implemented in low-income, frequently minority communities. This approach probably often would not be tolerated in wealthier white communities. In most or nearly all cases, upper-middle-class and wealthier parents probably would not tolerate having their children taught by transient, inexperienced, minimally trained young people who see teaching as a stepping stone to something better. If the TFA approach is not good enough for children from wealthy, white families, it is not good enough for any children.

In some ways, TFA is tragic for participants. TFA participants are high-achieving, bright young people who probably nearly always sincerely want to help disadvantaged children and teenagers. Many of them probably form close bonds with some of the children they teach. Working with children can be very rewarding. As a result, many TFA participants probably will cherish their memories of teaching children. Many participants also probably would have chosen to pursue teaching careers if the profession had not been so severely degraded by education reform. As a result, bright young people who would have made excellent, committed teachers frequently are compelled to pursue other careers that provide a more reasonable standard of living.

Heavy TFA promotion probably often gives young people a distorted or myopic view of reality. At times, TFA participants probably do not fully understand the big picture. They probably do not see that they frequently are being used as pawns in a larger strategy that is mainly focused on weakening or eliminating teachers unions and privatizing K-12 public education.

Teachers with years of experience in education often see the problems caused by the standardized curriculums and tests being promoted by education companies and politicians who accept money from them. As a result, they might resist actions that they know will degrade education. But lack of experience and perspective frequently make TFA participants unable to see the degradations caused by standardization, privatization and other so-called education reform approaches. Business-influenced training might teach them that these approaches improve, rather than degrade education. As a result, they often will quickly comply with standardization, privatization and other actions that help business, but degrade education. This can put pressure on actual teachers to also comply with new approaches, or risk losing their jobs.

Even if TFA participants do see problems, they often will not be around long enough to do anything about them. TFA participants probably virtually always want to be part of the solution to education problems in the US. Probably nearly all of them believe that they are benefiting children and improving the education system. This occasionally might be true on a short-term or micro-level. But at a macro or big picture-level, TFA is part of the problem because it strongly facilitates the firing of experienced teachers and privatization of public schools. As a result, TFA participants unintentionally contribute to the degradation of US education.

Nearly all TFA participants probably are good, well-meaning young people. But we should not be recruiting young people into education who have no long-term commitment to teaching. TFA participants often might be distracted or preoccupied with what comes after TFA, such as finding better-paying jobs or getting into law school, medical school or some other type of graduate program outside of the education field.

Many TFA participants have criticized the program. They often say that five weeks of training does not adequately prepare them to teach. In particular, participants frequently say that TFA training leaves them ill-prepared to teach in lower-income communities because children there often have learning and/or behavioral problems. TFA participants mainly are trained to help students pass tests. They receive little training on more important aspects of teaching, such as fostering the development of social skills, self-esteem and critical thinking skills. Many TFA participants worry that the inadequate TFA training and approach are causing them to do more harm than good.[99]

From 1990 to 2012, about 28,000 college graduates completed their two-year TFA commitments. This is relatively small compared to 3.2 million public school teachers in the US. But privatization is contributing to TFA growth. In 2012, the organization received 48,000 applications, from which 5,800 new TFA participants were selected. With assets of $350 million in 2011, TFA is having a large negative impact in Chicago and many other urban areas by replacing well-trained, experienced, committed teachers with inexperienced, minimally trained, uncommitted college graduates and by facilitating privatization, which, as noted, shifts the emphasis of schools from providing outstanding education to providing outstanding profits.[100]

TFA charges schools about $3,000 to $5,000 per instructor per year. Rather than spending taxpayer funds outside of school districts, communities often would be better off investing funds locally, for example, by paying more money to hire well-trained actual teachers who are committed to working in local schools for many years.

TFA substantially helps business, but harms children by degrading the quality of their education. The focus of education should be on maximizing the well-being of children, not business. But the business-focused US government allows public funds to be used to pay for TFA quasi-teachers who have inadequate training, certification and commitment to teaching. As US education is refocused on the well-being of children, instead of business, school districts should be prohibited from using public funds for TFA. All children should be taught by well-trained, certified and committed teachers.

If TFA shifts its focus and begins providing actual teachers, perhaps it could once again receive public funds.

Teaching children is one of the most satisfying and rewarding professions. Many highly talented young people probably would pursue teaching careers if the degradations imposed under education 'reform' were reversed. Instead of continuing to degrade the teaching profession with TFA, privatization and other approaches, we should emulate world education leaders such as Finland. In these countries, teaching is an honored profession with attractive pay and benefits, as it used to be in the US.

Public Deception

A key question about US education reform is, why did we pursue privatization, standardization and other businesslike approaches as a means of reform? This strategy implies that declining US educational performance was caused by the absence of these approaches. But even in the 1980s, it was obvious that this was not the case. As discussed, the strong link between income and academic performance was obvious over the previous 70 years. Poverty was the main cause of poor academic performance, not the lack of businesslike efficiencies and processes in schools.

The flaws of the US education reform approach became even clearer as we proceeded with privatization and standardization. Many other developed countries were outperforming the US. Virtually all of them had well-funded public education systems with strong teachers unions. In other words, countries that were outperforming the US were using the same approach that the US used in the 1950s and 1960s to achieve world-leading educational performance. We proved that strong support for public education and teachers unions can produce superior educational performance, as current world leaders continue to prove.

Another potentially puzzling aspect of US education reform involves the requirement under NCLB/ESSA that education policy be based on robust research and evidence.[101] However, as discussed below, overwhelming evidence and research show that standardization and privatization do not improve academic performance. The failure to modify reform approaches based on this evidence indicates that US education reform is not based on robust evidence and research. Instead, it appears to be based on the ideology or philosophy that placing the well-being of business before all else maximizes the well-being of society.

But using philosophy to explain US education reform is unnecessarily complex. There is a much simpler explanation. Privatization and implementation of businesslike practices in US education largely reflect the great extent to which business influences or controls politicians from both political parties.

The financial community is continuously looking for new investment opportunities. Several forecasters project slow economic growth, sluggish consumer spending and government cost-cutting.[102] Privatization of public education represents an attractive investment opportunity for the financial community. As a result, many business and financial leaders have been active in the privatization movement for several years, for example, by sitting on the boards of charter school companies.[103]

Privatizing public education by investing in charter schools is attractive to the financial community for several reasons. For example, education is a stable, largely recession proof industry. Risk is low because government (i.e. taxpayers) pays the bills. Labeling many traditional public schools as failing contributes to high demand for charter schools. In 2012, there were about two million students in 5,600 charter schools throughout the US. About 600,000 children were on waiting lists for charter schools.[104] Roughly 500 charter schools are being opened each year. In total, the privatization and commoditization of US public education is estimated to represent a $500 billion investment opportunity for the financial community.[105] Privatizing public education will enable the creation of new equity, debt and derivative securities. In addition, a 39 percent federal tax credit for charter school construction can double investor returns in seven years.[106]

Another attractive financial aspect of privatization is the ability to suppress unions. As discussed in the Labor section of *Global System Change*, about 75 percent of the net increase in profits of S&P 500 companies from 2000 to 2007 resulted from cutting employee wages and benefits. As a result,

US labor compensation is at a 50-year low relative to company sales and US GDP.[107] Unions are a main factor blocking ongoing use of this profit-enhancing strategy. As noted, charter schools often employ less experienced, lower-cost, non-unionized teachers.

To drive privatization, financial sector companies, charter school companies and other businesses that benefit from privatization have been giving money to politicians and aggressively influencing all levels of government in other ways for many years. As discussed in the Influencing the Supreme Court section of *Global System Change*, Republican politicians generally do whatever large companies request with few restrictions. Privatization strongly benefits business. As a result, Republicans often strongly support privatization of education and many other government functions. Much of the government influence activity has been focused on Democratic politicians because Republicans already usually support privatization. If Democratic politicians wish to receive money from businesses and financial sector companies, they often must promise to support privatization and charter schools.[108]

As discussed extensively throughout this book, two main strategies used by businesses to achieve ever-increasing shareholder returns are inappropriate government influence and misleading the public. Extensive public deception has been used to mislead citizens into believing that privatization, standardization and commoditization will improve the US education system. Common deceptions include unions hurt educational performance, unions reduce teacher flexibility and control, competition will improve the performance of traditional public schools, privatization is the best way to improve educational performance, and school choice benefits students.

Regarding unions hurting performance, states with the strongest teachers unions usually have the highest test scores.[109] However, this correlation results more from poverty than unions. Less unionized states generally have higher poverty, as one might expect in lower wage states. Poverty is the main cause of low test scores. Vested interests often argue that unions limit teacher flexibility and control. But this is deceptive. A main strategy of for-profit school companies is to standardize curricula and teaching methods. This will increase sales of standardized education products. But it also means that non-unionized teachers in charter schools run by for-profit companies frequently will have substantially less control over curricula and other factors than traditional public school teachers.

The idea that competition will improve the performance of traditional public schools also is deceptive. Competition based on standardized test scores essentially ignores factors outside of school that cause poor performance, such as poverty. Using competition to label public schools as failing and justify lower funding often reduces the performance of traditional public schools.

The idea that privatization is the best way to improve educational performance also is highly deceptive. No other developed country is privatizing its education system nearly to the extent of the US. Many other developed countries are outperforming the US by strongly supporting unionized public education systems. The obviously superior approach is to do what worked in the past in the US and what continues to work in other developed countries.

Privatization in general has been a major public deception since deregulation began in the 1980s. Businesses, politicians paid by them and other business allies have convinced many citizens to blindly believe the irrational idea that the private sector always can provide higher quality, lower cost services than the public sector. As discussed extensively, this is irrational for several reasons. The public sector has several major competitive advantages, such as economies of scale, that enable it to frequently provide higher quality, lower cost services than the private sector.

One of the most important public-sector advantages is the lack of the profit motive. As discussed in the For-Profit Prisons and other sections of *Global System Change*, for-profit companies often can lower costs initially by cutting wages and other expenses. But over time, the requirement to provide ever-increasing shareholder returns frequently creates pressure to increase prices and lower service quality. As a result, privatization frequently causes taxpayers to pay higher prices for lower quality services, especially over the longer-term.

Many studies and examples have shown that government often provides lower costs and higher quality than the private sector. For example, overhead costs of Medicare are far lower than those of private health insurance companies. The federal government frequently pays private contactors nearly twice as much as government employees for the same tasks.[110] Several state and local governments have taken back control of privatized services due to poor quality and cost performance.

State and local governments also increasingly are opening bidding processes to public workers. Eliminating the requirement to provide high profits often enables the public sector to provide lower costs and higher quality services. For example, public service workers outbid the private sector to provide fleet, facilities and street maintenance in Tulsa, landfill management in San Diego, and highway lane stripe painting in Minnesota.[111] In addition to frequently raising costs and lowering service quality, privatization often imposes intangible costs and degradations on governments, such as loss of operational control, reduced access to cost and operational data, and loss of in-house expertise.

School choice is one of the most important deceptions used to trick citizens into supporting privatization of public education. Advocates of education privatization apparently want citizens to blindly believe that increased choice always will improve quality and lower costs. But this position is irrational. Rational thought and observations of reality show that increased choice *sometimes* improves quality, lowers costs and provides other benefits. But at other times, it lowers quality, increases costs and reduces benefits.

For example, choice of products often stimulates competition and innovation, which can lead to improved quality and reduced price. But education is more complex than a simple, nonliving product. One goal of education is to prepare young people to succeed in life. Many qualities are needed to achieve this. These qualities have intellectual, social, emotional, physical and moral aspects. Privatization shifts the focus of education from providing outstanding education to providing outstanding profits. As discussed below, this type of education often degrades many of the most important qualities and characteristics needed for success in life.

Also, K-12 education is a public good. It should not be seen as an independent product that parents choose and buy. Choice often is not the best way to provide public goods. For example, with public safety, citizens usually would not benefit by choosing from several for-profit police companies. The same is true of roads, parks, sewers and many other public goods. In these cases, increased choice often would cause redundancy, inefficiency and reductions in service quality. Education is a public good because it benefits whole communities, including citizens who do not have children in school. Without schools, wild, misbehaving, uneducated children often would be running around town. Public schools produce educated, better behaved children. They benefit local businesses by educating future employees. Public schools also benefit communities by training young people to become working adults who will carry the load when current adults retire.

Every other developed country sees education as a public good. It also was seen as a public good when the US was a world leader in K-12 education. As discussed, poor education performance in the US does not result from lack of school choice. Poor performance mainly results from a weak social safety net and underfunding public schools in low-income communities. The solution to poor education performance is not to offer parents more school choices. It is to do what every other country that leads the world in education does – ensure that virtually all parents can send their children to high quality, local public schools.

But the US is not doing this. Instead, we are degrading public schools by diverting taxpayer funds to private and less accountable charter schools. Taxpayer funds traditionally have not been used for religious and other private schools in the US. But citizens have been misled into supporting this. Increased school choice helps some parents who are lucky enough to get their children into limited high-quality charter and private schools. But for most parents, especially low-income parents, the choice is to keep children in defunded and degraded public schools or try to get them into charter or private schools that pay teachers less money, are less accountable to parents and taxpayers, and provide fewer services than public schools.

As noted, increased school choice has not improved academic performance. To illustrate, Pennsylvania strongly supports charter schools. Charter school performance there is the third worst in the nation. Every charter school in the state failed to meet its Adequate Yearly Progress goal in 2013.[112] Rational thought shows that school choice often will degrade communities, in the same way that choice of police, roads, parks, sewers and other public goods frequently would do so.

An international assessment of educational performance found that the countries with the best academic performance (i.e. Finland and South Korea) had the lowest levels of school choice.[113] We know from past US actions and current education leaders that increasing school choice is not the best way to improve overall academic performance. Why then would we pursue this goal? The answer of course is that increased school choice benefits businesses and increases shareholder returns. Large companies and their wealthy owners largely control government and society in the US. As a result, we often do what is best for business, even when it degrades society.

Manufactured Crisis

One of the most important strategies for maximizing shareholder returns is to manufacture or stimulate demand for business products and services. The Advertising, Media and Culture section of *Global System Change* discussed how extensive advertising is used to create demand, for example, by making people feel inadequate without advertised products. Another version of this strategy is to create the illusion that a crisis exists, and then mislead citizens into thinking that business products and services are the solution to the non-existent crisis. This approach has been used extensively, probably often unintentionally or unconsciously, in the education reform area.

This is not to suggest that a crisis does not exist in US education. As discussed, children from low-income families and communities have been underperforming for over 100 years. Even without research, the main cause of this crisis or problem is obvious when one employs rational thought. Children who face greater violence and stress at home and in their communities and who do not have basic needs met usually will perform worse than children who have basic needs met and live in safe, peaceful homes and communities. In addition, children who attend underfunded schools with large class sizes and poor facilities and learning materials usually will perform worse than children in well-funded schools with small class sizes and adequate facilities and learning materials.

The US education crisis exists largely in low-income communities and schools. It is caused mainly by poverty and inadequate public school funding. But solving this crisis could increase taxes and reduce the amount of public wealth that could be used for corporate welfare. To protect shareholder returns, businesses and their paid political servants must turn citizens' attention away from solutions that actually would solve or greatly relieve the US education crisis, such as strengthening the social safety net and adequately funding public schools in low-income communities. Instead, businesses, politicians and other business allies must deceive citizens about the nature of the US education crisis. They must trick them into thinking that factors which restrict shareholder returns, such as teachers unions, are the cause of the crisis, and that factors which help shareholder returns, such as standardized testing and privatization, are the solution.

In effect, businesses and their allies turn citizens' attention away from the real crisis and actual solutions, to a false crisis and false solutions. The deception involves claiming or implying that poor education performance results mainly from the lack of accountability, standardized testing and other businesslike processes. This implies that business products and services should be a main component of education solutions. In other words, businesses, politicians and other business allies essentially portray the crisis as the lack of business products, services and processes in the education area. This is a false crisis. It does not exist. Expanding businesslike processes in education often will harm children, degrade society and worsen academic performance. In other words, it is a false solution. It often will help business, but harm children and society.

Lack of widespread public opposition to increased standardized testing and other accountability efforts strongly indicates the ease with which non-expert citizens can be misled. Citizens often lack full information because they do not have the time needed to gather and analyze it. Instead, they frequently rely on vested interests that provide false, misleading or incomplete information. If citizens reviewed independent research and efforts in other countries, it would become clear that standardized testing and the accountability movement in the US have failed. Over 30 years of increased accountability efforts have failed to improve education performance or close performance gaps between white and minority children and low-income and middle-income children. The large majority of independent research shows that standardized testing, basing teacher pay on student test scores, privatization, charter schools, Teach for America, trigger laws, online education and voucher programs do not improve academic performance.[114][115]

Countries that lead the world in education performance largely are not using these approaches. Instead, they usually rely on well-funded public education and strong teachers unions. As discussed extensively, the primary public deception is to divide the public into debating, acrimonious factions. This often blocks rational thought. For example, privatization advocates frequently characterize criticisms of the accountability movement as liberal opinions. When this occurs, many conservatives who dislike liberals simply ignore or discount the criticisms, rather than rationally consider the logic, research and results being presented.

Comments by the US Secretary of Education and other privatization advocates illustrate how the public is misled about education reform. Like virtually all other international rankings, the Program for International Student Assessment (PISA) recently found that US education performance lags behind many other developed countries.[116] At a conference discussing the findings, the Secretary argued that the results prove that the US should do even more standardized testing, privatization and other businesslike approaches. The moderator pointed out that none of the top scoring nations in the PISA rankings were using the approaches being advocated in the US, such as evaluating teachers based on student test scores and promoting charter schools. World leaders in education, such as Finland and South Korea, do not have charter schools, for example.[117]

The secretary essentially ignored the comment and repeated a vague, but familiar talking point about the need for "accountability for student learning".[118] Simply repeating dogma or philosophies, such as the idea that greater accountability will improve academic performance, misleads many citizens. The term accountability as it is used in US education reform is vague and misleading. Privatization proponents often mislead citizens by saying or implying that those who oppose the privatization and accountability movements are against accountability in education. This is irrational, deceptive and even ridiculous. Teachers, schools and the education system in general can be held accountable for many different factors in many different ways. Standardized testing of core subjects is not the only way to hold teachers and schools accountable. Other countries prove that there are far more effective accountability approaches.

Privatization proponents are defining accountability in ways that help business, but often harm students and society. Schools teach children many things and provide many valuable services, especially in low-income communities where basic needs sometimes are not adequately met at home. As discussed below, the most important skills and traits learned in school, in terms of promoting life success and satisfaction, include social skills, self-esteem and critical thinking skills. In addition, schools also frequently provide nutrition, health, counseling, mentoring and physical fitness services that help children to prosper. But standardized tests generally do not assess whether these critical services and skills are being provided or taught effectively.

As discussed below, standardized testing and other competitive grading approaches often degrade the most important skills and factors needed to achieve a successful and satisfying life. When people oppose the accountability movement in US education, it does not mean that they are opposed to accountability in general. It virtually always means that they oppose the specific accountability approach being employed. Instead, they usually advocate holding schools and teachers accountable for factors, services and learning that actually benefit children and society. This type of accountability movement would be very different from the one employed in the US. It frequently would look more like those being used in nations that lead the world in education performance.

US privatization advocates often incorrectly imply that world leaders in education are not holding schools and teachers accountable. This implies that these countries do not care about education performance. This is irrational. These countries prove that they care by outperforming the US. They care about performance and expect results. They achieve them by employing more effective accountability methods than those used in the US.

To illustrate, 40 years ago, Finland had average education performance. Now they are a world leader. The Finns obviously care about good teaching and education. But they do not burden teachers with standardized testing and rank teachers based on students' standardized test scores. Instead, Finland provides attractive wages and benefits and gives teachers honored status in society. This enables the country to attract talented young people into the teaching profession. Finland requires rigorous masters-level teacher training. After this high-level training, teachers are given far more freedom than US teachers to teach in ways that they feel are most effective.[119] The wisdom of this approach is proven or strongly indicated by Finland's performance. As discussed below, standardized testing lowers the performance and enthusiasm of teachers and students. Finland and other leading countries prove that there are far more effective ways to maximize education performance than the flawed accountability approaches being employed in the US.

But US education, like US society in general, increasingly is not focused on maximizing the well-being of children and society. It largely is focused on maximizing the well-being of large companies and their wealthy owners. As a result, business-controlled politicians and government promote education reform approaches that benefit business, but often harm children and society.

NCLB, ESSA and the Common Core standards illustrate how standardized testing is used to create a false crisis for which business products and services are presented as the optimal solution. NCLB/ESSA requires public schools in all 50 states to test students every year. Prior to NCLB, only 19 states conducted annual statewide tests. Under NCLB, schools were measured against benchmarks that no schools had ever met. After 10 years of NCLB testing, over half of the public schools in the US were listed as failing. Many of the others were near failing.[120]

Standardized testing under NCLB did not improve academic performance or close racial and income related academic performance gaps. High school dropout rates increased for nearly ten years following NCLB implementation.[121] In other words, more children were left behind by the No Child Left Behind Act. This illustrates the deceptive terminology frequently used by business-influenced politicians. For example, as discussed in the Misleading the Public section, the deceptively named Clear Skies initiative increased air pollution by weakening and lengthening electric utility compliance deadlines.

After declining for several years, high school graduation rates increased from 2011 to 2015. NCLB required states to improve graduation performance or risk losing funding. This compelled states to take several actions to increase graduation rates. Enhanced academic programs accounted for some improvement. But much was caused by deceptive practices. For example, many states weakened graduation standards and/or eliminated state graduation exams. Many states also began offering different types of high school diplomas. Some have low standards that do adequately prepare graduates for work or college. In addition, many states implemented online credit recovery programs that allow students to make up for failed courses. Several experts have said the programs frequently have questionable or lax grading practices that pass underperforming students.[122]

Rising graduation rates in the US largely do not reflect improved academic performance. Average ACT and SAT scores are declining.[123] Young people often are less well prepared for work and college. Rising graduation rates result in large part from deception and gaming the system.

US high school graduation rates peaked in the late 1960s when the US was a global education leader. The US public K-12 education system was focused on maximizing the well-being of young people and society. As a result, high school graduates usually were well prepared for post-high school life. But the focus of the increasingly privatized US education system often is not on helping young people. It mainly is on helping shareholders. Increased graduation rates help education companies. As a result, actions are taken to achieve this objective. But young people frequently receive lower quality education and are less well prepared to succeed in life.

When one considers the big picture and uses rational thought, it becomes obvious that NCLB/ESSA would often fail to improve the academic performance of public schools. The NCLB/ESSA strategy could be described as test and punish. As noted, taking resources away from schools and publicly labeling them as failing frequently will lower academic performance, not raise it. If the goal of NCLB/ESSA actually were to help improve the performance of public schools, greater resources and other assistance would be provided to schools with low academic performance. In other words, we would have employed a test and help strategy, instead of test and punish.

But as noted, the goal of business-controlled government often is not to help children, public schools or society in general. It is to help business. From this perspective, the test and punish approach of NCLB/ESSA is the obvious and expected outcome. NCLB/ESSA strongly facilitates a narrative of failure in the US. Many schools that had been performing well or adequately suddenly were labeled as failing. This helped to create the perception of an education crisis. Most importantly from a business perspective, NCLB/ESSA greatly facilitates increased privatization of public schools, opening of charter schools, and sales of business products and services.

Based on the test and punish strategy employed and the business benefits gained, the actual goal of NCLB/ESSA apparently is not to help public schools improve academic performance. It was to help business, often by shutting down or privatizing public schools. Strongly indicating how US education reform is focused on helping business instead of public education, from 2008 to 2013, the number of charter schools grew by about 50 percent, while nearly 4,000 public schools were closed.[124]

Many business leaders and politicians paid by business probably sincerely believe that NCLB/ESSA helps children and US education. Financial bias and myopia probably often prevent them from seeing the harmful nature of the test and punish approach. NCLB/ESSA is another example of how flawed systems frequently compel business and government to put the well-being of business ahead of the well-being of society. It is another example of how our myopic, flawed systems often compel good, well-meaning business and political leaders to take actions that degrade society.

The Common Core standards greatly expand the NCLB/ESSA narrative of failure. This further benefits business by increasing privatization of public schools and sales of business products and services. The Common Core standards sometimes are referred to as Common Core State standards. But this is deceptive. The standards are national, not state level. The federal government is prohibited by law from controlling curriculum or instruction in public schools. But the federal government was able to circumvent this prohibition by essentially forcing states to adopt the Common Core standards.[125] As noted, states essentially were required to adopt national standards to receive funds under the Race to the Top program. This federal mandate contributed to over 40 states adopting the Common Core standards.[126] Under ESSA, the federal government is prohibited from encouraging states to adopt the Common Core. But many states still use the standards.

The development of the Common Core strongly indicates the great degree to which businesses influence education reform in the US. Development of the standards was funded in large part by a wealthy business owner in the software sector. The standards were developed mainly by assessment and testing experts, many of whom had financial ties to testing companies. Few teachers and school administrators and no parents were involved in development.[127] The standards were not field-tested before implementation. There was no evidence to indicate that they would improve academic performance or close racial and income-related performance gaps. Proponents claim that the standards would ensure that all students would graduate from high school "college and career ready". But there was no research or experience to support this claim.[128]

The Common Core standards are substantially more difficult than many of the standards used under NCLB. This greatly increased the number of students and schools that were labeled as failing. One expert estimated that about 80 percent of students would fail Common Core tests in many schools.[129] In New York State, 69 percent of third to eighth grade students failed the Common Core English tests. Failure rates were 97 percent among students who spoke English as a second language, 95 percent among disabled students, and over 80 percent among African American and Hispanic students. Results on the Common Core math tests were only slightly better.[130] Several Common Core advocates argued that the Common Core should become the standard for high school graduation. If this occurs, it almost certainly will increase the high school dropout rate.[131]

The Common Core tests frequently caused stress, anger and anxiety among students and parents, in part because students often were tested on material that they had not been taught.[132] Teachers frequently claimed that they were not given the training and resources needed to teach the Common Core.[133] The testing process does little to help teachers and schools teach and evaluate students. Schools do not receive test questions before the tests. They also do not receive test results until many months after the tests. By then, students often have moved on to other classes.[134]

The Common Core substantially increases school costs (and business revenues). For example, Common Core tests must be taken on computers, which many schools do not have. Los Angeles plans to spend about $1 billion on tablet computers to facilitate Common Core preparation and testing.[135] Increased Common Core expenditures often will divert funds from teacher salaries, facilities maintenance, educational materials and other critical education expenditures.

The Common Core standards supposedly are intended to help children and teenagers by ensuring that they are ready for college and careers when they graduate from high school. But the standards are heavily influenced by business and strongly benefit business. As discussed below, the standards do not promote the type of education that would maximize young people's ability to achieve successful and satisfying lives. They supposedly emphasize critical thinking skills. But forcing students to memorize information and answer multiple-choice test questions is not the best way to promote the development of these skills. Regularly taking multiple-choice tests often does not foster the skills and confidence that students need to formulate their own complex opinions and interpretations.[136]

NCLB showed that millions of students were not meeting academic standards. The implied Common Core solution to this dilemma was to make standards even more difficult. From the perspective of helping students in public schools, this is not rational. The test and punish strategy was shown to be ineffective by NCLB. Expanding test and punish with the Common Core standards will be even less effective. But as noted, the apparent goal of the heavily business-influenced Common Core standards is not to benefit students in public schools. It is to benefit business. From the perspective of helping business even if it hurts children in public schools, the Common Core standards will be extremely effective. As noted, the standards will expand charter schools, privatization, and sales of business products and services. Education companies and their paid political servants often advocate rapid implementation of the Common Core standards.[137] This is not surprising given the tremendous business benefits that will result from the standards.

An excellent article by Diane Ravitch, PhD, called *"Why so many parents hate Common Core"*, discusses the Common Core standards.[138] As noted, about 70 percent of New York State students failed the Common Core English tests. Dr. Ravitch noted that the state set unrealistic passing marks. State education administrators knew in advance that this would cause about 70 percent of students to fail the tests. One might ask, why would government education administrators implement tests that sometimes unfairly test students on information they have not been taught and establish passing grades that cause many students to fail? This would lower student self-esteem. It also often would cause stress, anger and anxiety among students, parents and teachers.

By now, the answer to this question should be obvious. Implementing unfair and difficult standardized tests helps business. Government education administrators overseen by politicians who accept large amounts of money from businesses essentially become business agents. Unfair, difficult standardized tests greatly accelerate the privatization of public schools. This severely harms society, but helps the education and other companies that strongly influence or control government.

Turning public education into a business by privatizing it requires replacing an academic model with a business or economic model.[139] A main purpose of public education is to teach young people in ways that maximize their ability to achieve successful and satisfying lives as well as to maximize the well-being of society over the long-term. These largely are qualitative, subjective, long-term factors. They are difficult to measure. But businesses need a value proposition. They generally must measure outputs or success in the short-term.

Standardized test scores provide short-term measurable outputs. Standardized testing turns children and their test scores into commodities. Test scores become the 'currency' of education.[140] Having standardized, measurable outputs greatly facilitates running education like a business. It creates many opportunities to profit from the education of our children. It provides a way to measure the 'effectiveness' of virtually all education expenditures, including teacher salaries, operating budgets and government funding. It provides a justification for lowering teacher salaries and other expenditures that are not producing the desired output.

But this approach is irrational. Turning education into a business essentially turns schools into factories and students into commoditized outputs. Accurately measuring production efficiency and output quality is critical for business success. But children are not machines or commodities. They are infinitely more complex. Assuming that high standardized test scores means that children are being educated well is irrational. As discussed in the Competitive Grading section below, this type of testing often degrades the most important qualities needed to achieve a successful and satisfying life, including self-esteem, social skills and critical thinking skills. Finland and other education leaders use little or no standardized testing. Standardized testing obviously is not needed to maximize academic performance. But it is needed to maximize business performance.

Accurately measuring the true effectiveness of education is difficult and perhaps impossible. As noted, the true measures of success (individual life satisfaction and success, long-term well-being of society) are qualitative, subjective and long-term. Using standardized test scores to measure education effectiveness is irrational not only because it ignores the most important education outputs, but also because it degrades them. As discussed below, the process of standardized testing harms children in the short-term and long-term, and therefore also harms society in general. This once again shows the truly tragic and suicidal nature of our grossly flawed economic and political systems. Economic growth and shareholder returns always must increase, regardless of how much this degrades children and society.

Commoditizing education through the use of standardized test scores creates many opportunities for business. A report by a leading consulting firm estimated that gathering and utilizing student academic performance data represents an annual $1.2 trillion economic opportunity worldwide ($400 billion in the US).[141] Student test scores can be used to produce many types of business products and services, such as customized teaching materials. Student test data also could be used to screen students for college and employment opportunities. But utilizing this data could create many problems. For example, the process attempts to render complex human beings down to a few numbers. Humans are vastly more than their test scores. Many people who were successful in business and other areas did poorly in school. Overly relying on student test data often will cause discrimination and inaccurate, counterproductive screening.

The software billionaire who heavily funded the Common Core standards also funded an organization that gathers and utilizes student test data.[142] These investments were partly done as philanthropy. But business philanthropy often turns out to be business development. Producing, gathering and utilizing student test scores provides very large business opportunities in the software, hardware, data management and related industry sectors. This philanthropy supposedly was intended to benefit children. But instead it strongly benefits business, frequently at the expense of children. Commoditizing education through standardized testing also provides many opportunities for financial and business speculation. For example, investors might fund the education of a bright student in exchange for 20 percent of their future earnings.[143]

A main problem with education reform in the US is that it largely is being driven by business for the benefit of business. Businesses and wealthy business owners are using inappropriate government influence and public deception to convert US public education into a lucrative business opportunity. As discussed in the Misleading the Public section, if logical arguments are not available to protect shareholder returns, businesses and their allies often are compelled to use illogical arguments. Comments made by the Secretary of Education noted above illustrate this deception technique. The Secretary argued that poor US academic performance proves that even more accountability, standardized testing, charter schools and privatization are needed. Unfortunately, it often is easy to mislead non-expert citizens into believing this illogical argument, especially when they have been divided, conquered and caused to dislike or hate each other.

Research, results and experience in other countries largely show that the opposite of what the Secretary of Education said is true. The results of the accountability movement prove that this form of accountability does not work. It does not achieve the stated goal of improving academic performance and closing racial and income related performance gaps. Expanding the US test and punish approach to education reform with the Common Core standards will further degrade US education, not help it. As discussed below, education is far more than teaching core subjects. But even if this were the only goal of education, standardized testing, privatization and other accountability approaches being employed in the US are not the best way to maximize learning of these subjects.

US education reform largely is transferring control of education from communities and states to the federal government and large corporations. Businesses and their paid political servants are using standardized tests to create or manufacture a false crisis. Arguing that more business products, services and processes are needed to improve US education implies that the crisis is caused by the lack of these things. But this is a false crisis. It does not exist. Businesses should not be controlling US education. Once the people regain control of government in the US, we can put the focus of education where it once was and again should be – on the well-being of children and society.

Harming Children

Privatizing public education is one of the most tragic and destructive trends in the US. Protecting and caring for our children should be the top priority of society. But our suicidal economic and political systems demand that shareholder returns take priority over children and all else. To achieve ever-increasing shareholder returns, companies often face strong pressure to take over government functions. But businesses do not have a divine right to grow forever or take over whatever sectors they choose. The priority of society should be the well-being of society, not the well-being of business. We must objectively determine which options maximize societal well-being, rather than blindly adhere to the irrational philosophy that maximizing business well-being is what's best for society. Companies must be placed in service of society, not vice versa.

Businesses often can do many things better than government. But education is not one of them. The profit motive is incompatible with educating children well. Our children should not be seen as investment opportunities. They also should not be seen as little machines that can be standardized and processed into proficient test-takers.

Privatization of public education is tragic in part because we are on the verge of creating the same disaster we caused in the healthcare area. Every other developed country sees healthcare as a public good and basic right of citizens. They provide this public good through nonprofit, government-owned or government-managed healthcare systems. All other developed countries provide vastly superior coverage at a much lower cost, often with superior healthcare outcomes. The profit motive is the main reason why the US has the highest cost, worst coverage healthcare system in the developed world. The focus of for-profit companies is on providing superior profits, not superior healthcare or education performance.

The high cost, poor coverage and mediocre results of the US healthcare system will occur in the US education system if we continue with privatization. As seen in the healthcare area, for-profit education companies will face strong pressure to continuously increase prices and/or reduce costs. This will drive ongoing reductions in the quality of US education, especially in low-income communities, and rapid growth in education costs.

To illustrate, a report by the Economic Policy Institute analyzed the impact of privatization on the quality of education in low-income communities. It found that charter schools and other privatized schools often provide inferior education. The report discussed a large chain of charter schools called Rocketship. The chain operates primarily in low-income communities. It cuts costs in many ways. For example, it uses large class sizes and inexperienced, low-cost teachers. (As noted, about 75 percent of Rocketship teachers are provided by TFA.)

The chain further cuts staff costs by using blended learning, an approach that replaces teachers with computers. Students are taught by a 'blend' of inexperienced teachers and computers. Rocketship usually provides no gym classes, art classes, librarians, or significant science or social studies education. The curriculum is focused almost completely on math, reading and passing standardized tests. Yet in spite of this near exclusive focus on standardized testing, Rocketship schools frequently fail to make adequate yearly progress on test scores.[144] The stripped-down, extremely low quality education provided by Rocketship illustrates how privatization is degrading education quality.

Wisconsin has been a leader in school privatization for many years. The state frequently closes public schools and replaces them with Rocketship and other types of charter schools. To accelerate privatization, legislation was introduced that would require closure of public schools with failing grades after three years. However, charter schools would be allowed to have failing grades for nine years before being forced to close.[145] This is the type of legislation that one would expect from politicians who received large amounts of money from charter school and other education companies. Charter school executives and supporters often speak enthusiastically about the quality of charter school education, but then send their children to wealthy public or private schools that provide small class sizes and abundant personalized attention from teachers.[146]

Online education represents another problematic charter school trend. Several companies have established online charter schools. Children in these schools often do not attend regular schools. Instead, they learn online. In addition to operating online schools, online charter school companies also frequently provide online education courses to physical charter and other schools. As discussed in the Higher Education section below, online education is inferior to traditional classroom education in many ways.

This is especially true for K-12 school students in low-income communities. These children often face high stress outside of school. They usually need the most one-on-one attention from teachers. But with online charter schools, students get little or no face-to-face interaction with teachers and other students. Teachers usually communicate with students by e-mail and other electronic means. Middle-income and wealthier parents frequently would not tolerate having their children taught in this suboptimal manner. But most online charter schools, like regular charter schools, are focused on serving low-income, often minority children. Parents of these children usually complain less, partly because they frequently are seeking alternatives to underfunded traditional public schools.

Online charter schools often are highly profitable. They frequently charge nearly as much as traditional public schools. But they do not have physical school buildings and many other expenses. Also, they usually pay teachers substantially less than traditional public schools.[147] Online charter schools perfectly illustrate how privatizing public education will grossly degrade education quality, especially for low-income, minority children.

Privatization of public education will drive the same ghettoization seen in the public housing and hospital areas. Proactive parents often will put their children into wealthier charter schools or other private schools. Children with absent or less proactive parents, frequently children from low-income families, often will be left in public schools (or perhaps transferred to low budget charter schools like those described above if public schools are closed). As children with proactive parents are removed from traditional public schools, pressure to adequately maintain the quality of education in these schools will decline. Traditional public schools will become the equivalent of public housing projects.[148]

Beyond being morally reprehensible, this ghettoization or segmentation of education is financially irrational. Low-income children abandoned in underfunded, low-quality public schools or dehumanized, low-budget charter schools are the ones most likely to engage in crime and other destructive activities. As they grow up, these children are the ones we most often will be paying $50,000 per year to incarcerate. From a purely financial perspective, it makes overwhelming good sense to spend at least as much to educate these children as is spent to educate children in wealthier communities.

Having a strong public education system is critical to the ongoing success of the US. Our formerly world-leading unionized public education system produced many excellent scientists, doctors, engineers, teachers and other professionals. It strongly contributed to the success of this country. We must not allow ourselves to be deceived into believing that privatizing public education will benefit society.

Privatization is occurring rapidly in the US. As occurred with the implementation of genetically-engineered crops, giving money to politicians and misleading the public often enables businesses to rush the implementation of new approaches before citizens fully understand negative consequences. Once much of our public education system is privatized and the remainder is ghettoized for low-income students, it will be difficult to turn back. Therefore, we must stand up and protect our children now. Schools are not factories. Children are not products that require standardized processing. Children are the most precious and sacred beings in society.

Public Funding of Religion

Diverting taxpayer funds from public education to religious and other private schools, for example through voucher programs, is a significant and growing cause of degradation of public education in the US. About 86 percent of K-12 students in the US attend public schools, 11 percent attend private schools and three percent are homeschooled. Religious schools represent about 80 percent of private school students and 76 percent of private schools.[149]

Using taxpayer funds (i.e. public funds) to pay for religious education is a gross violation of the principles upon which the US was founded. As discussed in the Population section of *Global System Change*, many people came to North America to escape religious persecution in Europe. The US was a product of the Age of Reason and Enlightenment. Several Founders were strongly influenced by the philosophy of Deism, including George Washington, Benjamin Franklin, John Adams, Thomas Jefferson and James Madison. They believed that the existence of God could be rationally deduced by observing the nearly infinite sophistication and beauty of nature. They further believed that humans must abide by the laws of nature, including the moral laws of equality and fairness.

The Founders greatly valued rational reasoning and science. As indicated in George Washington's Farewell Address, many of the Founders strongly believed in the importance of abiding by religious principles, such as treating other people with kindness and respect, helping the needy, and protecting God's creation, including nature and all life. These principles are common to virtually all of the world's great religions.

However, as noted in the Population section, George Washington, Benjamin Franklin, John Adams, Thomas Jefferson and many other Founders did not believe in superstition, miracles, or religious dogma, such as the divinity of Jesus, the divine origin of the Bible, the Virgin birth, the resurrection and many other Christian dogmata that could not be supported by rational thought. Dogmatic religious ideas often vary among religions. Disagreement about these unprovable, often irrational ideas was a major cause of religious persecution and suffering in Europe during the Dark and Middle Ages and throughout human history. To avoid this persecution and suffering, the Founders structured the US in ways that prohibit religious dogma from having any influence on government.

At the time the US Constitution was written, several states had laws that supported particular religions. But the Founders specifically prohibited government from favoring or supporting any religion. In 1777, in response to a proposal that would have taxed Virginians to pay for Christian teaching in public schools, Thomas Jefferson wrote the Virginia statute for religious freedom (discussed in the Population section). Enacted in 1786, the statute guaranteed citizens' religious freedom. It also served as a template for separating church and state in the US Constitution.[150] Article VI prohibits religious tests or requirements for political office. The First Amendment prohibits passing laws that establish or favor a particular religion or block the free exercise of religion. The US government was required to remain neutral on religion. The US was established as a country of religious freedom. The Founders strongly believed that each citizen should be free to live according to their own religious or moral beliefs.

Benjamin Franklin, Thomas Jefferson, James Madison and many other Founders strongly opposed taxation to support religious education and other religious activities. Instead, they believed that religious activity should be supported by voluntary contributions. Benjamin Franklin said, "When a Religion is good, I conceive that it will support itself; and when, it cannot support itself, and God does not take care to support, so that its Professors are obliged to call for help of the Civil Power, 'tis a sign, I apprehend, of its being a bad one."[151]

Using taxpayer funds to pay for religious education would compel citizens of one religion to pay for the teaching of a different religion. President Theodore Roosevelt said, "I hold that in this country there must be complete severance of Church and State; that public moneys shall not be used for the purpose of advancing any particular creed; and therefore that the public schools shall be non-sectarian and no public moneys appropriated for sectarian schools."[152]

Throughout US history, the Supreme Court and the rest of the US government have maintained the strong wall between church and state that was established by our Founders and enshrined in the US Constitution. However, as discussed in the Influencing the Supreme Court section, businesses and their owners apparently paid politicians to appoint pro-business justices to the Supreme Court. As shown in *Citizens United*, *Heller* and other cases, these judges used irrational arguments to support a so-called conservative ideology. In *Citizens United*, they implied that corporations were equivalent to human citizens and deserve the same rights. The Founders obviously did not believe this given how corporations were restricted in the early US. As discussed in the Crime section, in *Heller*, the five conservative justices changed the meaning of the Constitution by effectively ignoring the preamble to the Second Amendment and overturning 200 years of legal precedent.

Through several bitterly divided decisions, the Supreme Court used irrational arguments to violate the First Amendment, weaken the separation between church and state, and say that taxpayer funds could be used to pay for religious education. For example, in a 2002 case, *Zelman v. Simmon-Harris*, by a 5-4 decision, the Supreme Court said that an Ohio voucher law did not violate the First Amendment because parents, not government, were directing taxpayer funds to religious schools. In this case, 96 percent of students using the vouchers were attending religious schools, nearly all Christian.[153] But since parents had the option of using the vouchers for nonreligious private schools, the Supreme Court majority said that the voucher program did not constitute establishment or support of religion.

However, as noted by dissenting justices, this argument ignores the obvious fact that taxpayer funds are paying for religious education. The mechanism by which this occurs is irrelevant.[154] As a result of this decision, Jewish citizens are being forced to pay for Christian education. Christian citizens potentially are being forced to pay for the teaching of radical Islam and other religious or spiritual creeds that they often would oppose. Many citizens would feel that being forced to pay for the teaching of a religion different than their own interferes with their free exercise of religion. This interference is prohibited in the First Amendment. Also, using nearly all voucher funds to support Christian education strongly establishes or supports Christianity. The First Amendment prohibits this favoritism or establishment of religion. Passing taxpayer funds through a third-party (parents) does not make public funding of religion constitutionally acceptable.

In a 2007 case, *Hein v. Freedom From Religion Foundation*, through another bitterly divided 5–4 decision, the majority found that use of taxpayer funds by the executive branch to support religion, in part by funding conferences that allegedly promote religion, did not violate the First Amendment. The majority essentially found that the First Amendment and legal precedent prohibit the Legislative branch from taking these actions, but not the Executive branch. But this is ridiculous. As noted by dissenting justices, the First Amendment applies to all of government, not just the Legislative branch.[155] It is absurd to suggest that the Founders would have allowed the Executive branch, but not the Legislative branch, to establish or support religion.

A 2011 case, *Arizona Christian School Tuition Organization v. Winn*, further weakens the separation between church and state. In addition to the US Constitution, about 36 state constitutions have provisions that separate church and state.[156] For example, the Arizona Constitution specifically forbids public funding of religious schools or religious education.[157] In an effort to get around this constitutional prohibition, the state implemented a program that gives tax credits to parents who send children to religious schools.

In *Winn*, through another bitterly divided 5–4 decision, the majority found that the Arizona tax credit program did not violate the First Amendment. They argued that a tax credit is not a direct appropriation of public funds, and therefore does not constitute establishment or support of religion. But as noted by dissenting justices, this is irrational. A tax credit for religious education lowers government revenues. This must be made up through increased taxes and/or reduced spending. In other words, a tax credit for religious education has essentially the same tax raising impact as a direct appropriation. As in *Zelman*, the mechanism is irrelevant. Citizens of one religion effectively are being forced to pay for the teaching of different religions.

These decisions show the danger of allowing a small group of wealthy business owners to strongly influence or control Supreme Court appointments. As discussed in the Influencing the Supreme Court section, when businesses strongly influence Supreme Court appointments, justices probably are not selected based on their wisdom, fairness and commitment to upholding the Constitution. The primary selection criterion appears to be willingness to put business interests before all else, including the Constitution and general welfare of society.

As shown in *Citizens United, Heller, Connick v. Thompson* (discussed in the Crime section), *Zelman, Hein* and *Winn*, so-called conservative justices often used complex precedents and obscure logic that many average citizens would not understand. However, if one cuts through the biased, frequently deceptive arguments, steps back and looks at the big picture, it becomes clear that the final result often is unfair and unconstitutional. For example, *Zelman* and *Winn* essentially said that public funding of religious education is acceptable if it occurs through certain mechanisms. But the Founders almost certainly would have said that this public funding never is acceptable. This could create many problems.

To illustrate, most religious schools in the US are Christian. As a result, most public funds given to religious schools would be used to support Christian education. There might be a reluctance to support other religions. For example, some Louisiana legislators were unwilling to support a voucher program because an Islamic school would have received funding. But once the Islamic school withdrew its funding request, the legislators approved the program.[158] This illustrates giving preference to one religion over another. It grossly violates the religious freedom and separation of church and state principles upon which the US was founded.

Government support or funding of religion inevitably will produce many problems. That is why the Founders strongly opposed it. As noted, leading US Founders believed that religious activity should be funded through voluntary contributions, not public funds.

Hein in particular shows the danger of appointing business-biased justices to the Supreme Court. The logic of *Hein* (i.e. effectively saying that the Executive branch can promote religion, but not the Legislative branch) is absurd. The justices appear to act like dictators in an oppressive regime. They loudly proclaim that two plus two equals five. Citizens can do nothing about it because the Supreme Court appears to be the highest authority. But it is not. As discussed throughout *Global System Change*, the people are the highest authority. They have the power to compel the Supreme Court to uphold the Constitution and promote the general welfare. As discussed in the Judicial Branch section of *Global System Change*, one of the most important ways to do this is to impose term limits on the Supreme Court, as the US Constitution allows Congress to do, as Thomas Jefferson strongly advised, and as every other developed country does.

By breaking down the wall between church and state established by our Founders, the Supreme Court is severely degrading public education and creating many other problems. Some people argue that the federal government already provides funding to religious hospitals and some charities. Funding religious schools is the same, they say. But it is not. Religious hospitals and charities that help the poor, for example, usually impose no religious requirements on users. Hospital patients are not required to study religion or attend religious services. However, religious school students usually are required to do these things. In addition, religion frequently is integrated into nonreligious subjects, such as science.

Regarding funding religious hospitals and charities, this would be less necessary if the US were focused more on the well-being of society, than on the well-being of business. Every other developed country considers healthcare to be a basic right. Citizens collectively provide healthcare to everyone through their agent government, always at a much lower cost and frequently with better healthcare outcomes. As discussed in the Misleading the Public section, NGOs and religions often strive to meet public needs when the business-focused US government fails to do what governments in nearly every other developed country do.

A major problem with public funding of religious education is that taxpayers sometimes are forced to pay for the teaching of irrational, anti-science ideas. The US is a product of the Age of Reason. The Founders greatly valued rational reasoning and strongly opposed the influence of religious dogma on government. This practical focus on reality and science has served the US well. Throughout US history, publicly funded education taught children and teenagers to focus on reality and think rationally. Religions often contain unprovable ideas that sometimes are refuted by science. Children were taught these dogmatic ideas outside of public schools, frequently in privately funded religious schools. But the Supreme Court has allowed public funds to be used to teach religious dogma, such as creationism.

Creationism often holds that the Biblical creation story in Genesis is literally true (i.e. that God created the Earth and humans about 6,000 years ago). Some Christian schools teach that creationism is true and the scientific theory of evolution is false, or highly uncertain. These positions are grossly irrational. There is overwhelming scientific evidence that the Earth was formed about 4.5 billion years ago and life began about 3.8 billion years ago. There also is overwhelming evidence that the theory of evolution is correct. Among biologists, the scientific validity of evolution is as well established as the existence of gravity or the germ theory of disease.[159] Claiming that creationism is true and evolution is false essentially is the same as claiming that the Sun revolves around the Earth.

Federal courts have found that creationism is theology based on a literal interpretation of the Bible. Creationism is irrational religious dogma because it is disproven by science. It is unconstitutional to teach creationism in public schools because using taxpayer funds to teach children religious dogma violates the freedom of religion provision of the First Amendment.[160]

Religious groups and their allies sometimes use irrational or deceptive arguments to promote teaching creationism in public schools. For example, some religious groups and politicians argue that teaching the controversy of evolution promotes critical thinking among students. This position is irrational because it implies that evolution and creationism are about equally valid. But critical, rational thinking would show that evolution is scientifically proven. It is based on observations of reality. Creationism, on the other hand, is scientifically disproven. It violates observations of reality.

Critical thinking shows that creationism is no more valid than any other creation myth. In other words, critical, reality-based thinking shows that evolution is valid and real, while creationism is a scientifically invalid myth. Teaching children that this myth is as valid as real science is the opposite of promoting critical thinking. It teaches children to ignore reality and science. This strongly suppresses critical thinking.

Proponents of creationism also sometimes argue that academic freedom should allow teachers to teach creationism. Academic freedom is important in college. But it generally is not allowed at the high school level because teenagers are impressionable. As a result, courts have found that school officials and boards have a right to reign in teachers who stray too far from accepted curriculum.[161] Giving high school teachers academic freedom would empower them to teach other irrational, destructive ideas, such as Holocaust denial or racism.

As discussed in the Environmental Sustainability Principles section of *Global System Change*, thousands of creation myths have been developed throughout human history. These myths sought to explain how the Earth and humans were created to simple, unscientific and often superstitious people hundreds or thousands of years ago. Genesis and other creation myths are not based on science or rational thinking. They are the equivalent of childhood fairytales. They were developed to comfort the mind by providing an explanation for creation. It is not rational to believe that Genesis is more valid than any other creation myth.

Creationism usually is taught by more dogmatic Christian schools. However, many Christians do not believe that Genesis is literally true. The Catholic religion, for example, often is considered to be within the more conservative wing of Christianity. But the Catholic religion takes a more practical and rational view of science and creation. Catholics and other more rational Christians frequently promote the theory of intelligent design. This view essentially holds that the nearly infinite complexity of nature strongly indicates the presence of a creator or God. This is what many of the Founders believed. The existence of God cannot be disproven. Therefore, intelligent design is not irrational. The theory often holds that God created life, which then developed through the process of evolution. Science cannot explain how life originated. Therefore, it is not irrational to believe that God created life. But this idea cannot be proven. Therefore, it is not scientific.

Taxpayer funds should not be used to teach children irrational, anti-science ideas such as creationism. As noted, this suppresses critical thinking by teaching children to ignore reality and science. It is the same as teaching them that any other creation myth or childhood fairytale is literally true. Intelligent design is less offensive to rational reasoning. However, taxpayer funds probably should not be used to teach this idea because it is unprovable, and therefore unscientific. If students ask a teacher how life originated, the teacher could say, science cannot answer that question. But your parents or religious leaders could speak with you about how life might have been created.

Some dogmatic religious schools teach ideas that are grossly irrational and offensive to civilized society. For example, a widely used set of Christian textbooks says that humans and dinosaurs definitely existed on Earth at the same time, gay people have no more claim to special rights than rapists and child molesters, and the goal of environmentalists is to destroy the economies of developed countries.[162] Perhaps it is legal to teach children these ignorant, harmful and hateful ideas in religious schools. But citizens should not be forced to pay to teach them in publicly funded schools.

Nearly all citizens would strongly oppose using taxpayer funds to teach radical Islamic ideas to US children. The majority of citizens in the US are Christian. But forcing all citizens to pay for the teaching of Christian dogma to children also is wrong. The majority might oppose teaching Islam to US children. But the minority has an equally valid basis to oppose paying to teach Christianity to US children. No citizen should be forced to pay for the teaching of a religion that is different than their own. When government and taxpayers fund religion, discrimination is bound to occur (as it did in the Louisiana example cited above). Government must not be placed in the position of having to determine which religious ideas are appropriate to teach children. The Founders well understood the dangers and abuse that result from mixing religion and government. That is why they firmly and clearly prohibited it.

Teaching religious principles, such as those supported by the Founders, probably would be highly beneficial. As noted, these religious or moral principles include treating people with kindness, love and respect, caring for the needy, and protecting the environment and all life. These principles essentially are laws of nature. They are universally applicable and universally beneficial. Teaching children these ideas to a much greater degree would strongly counteract the frequently selfish, materialistic and unintentionally harmful messages of advertising and media. Teaching religious or moral principles in public education would be highly beneficial, especially for children who are not learning these ideas at home. However, as the Founders intended, citizens never should be forced to pay to teach children religious dogma.

Additional problems related to public funding of religious education include lack of accountability, failure to improve academic performance, failure to help low-income families, increased taxes and costs, degradation and segregation of public education, distraction from real solutions that actually would improve overall educational performance, and lack of public support.

Regarding accountability, religious and other private schools are far less accountable than public schools. Parents and government have even less control over religious schools than they do over charter schools. Religious schools often are not required to test students, publish curriculum or meet other standards by which public schools must abide. They also are free to impose religious requirements on teachers and fire them for marrying someone of a different faith, getting divorced, being gay, or taking public stands that conflict with religious views.

Private schools also are allowed to discriminate against students based on religion, disability, economic background, academic record, English language ability and disciplinary history.[163] Illustrating possible discrimination at religious and other private schools, private schools serve 11 percent of K-12 students in the US, but only one percent of disabled students. In public schools, 43 percent of students are from minority families, compared to 24 percent at private schools.[164] Teacher and student discrimination might be legal in private schools. But taxpayers should not be forced to pay for it.

Lack of accountability also can force taxpayers to fund substandard schools. Many substandard religious schools sought or received voucher (i.e. taxpayer) funding. One school was housed in a windowless building with no playground.[165] Another was housed in a dilapidated building with inadequate heat and no fire alarms. Another taught children by having them watch videos all day. When states attempted to mandate accountability standards for religious schools that accepted vouchers, the schools sometimes did not comply.[166] In addition, legislators often hesitate to hold religious schools accountable because this could be seen as interfering with religious education. But if religious schools receive public funds, they should abide by the same standards as public schools. Taxpayers must be assured that their funds are paying for valid education.

Regarding performance, studies of voucher programs in Milwaukee, Cleveland and Washington DC found that students who use vouchers to attend private schools do not perform better in reading and math than public school students. The Washington DC study also found that students using vouchers to attend private schools do not engage in extracurricular activities, do homework or voluntarily read more often. Private school students also were tardy to the same degree and may have been absent more frequently.[167]

Regarding low-income families, vouchers often fail to help them. Vouchers frequently do not cover the full cost of private school tuition and other mandatory fees. In Cleveland, for example, the majority of families who were granted vouchers did not use them because they could not afford the additional private school fees. Many low-income students remain in public schools that are degraded as voucher programs siphon off funding.[168]

Regarding increased education costs and taxes, as students use vouchers to leave public schools, these schools often cannot lower fixed costs. School funding frequently is based partly on the number of students. As students leave, funding often declines. But costs frequently do not decline by the same amount. In addition, there are costs to administer voucher programs. The cost of these programs often cannot be fully deducted from public education funding. As a result, total taxpayer-funded education costs frequently increase. As with charter schools, using vouchers to pay for private schools lowers economies of scale and potentially increases administrative and other costs because costs are spread over a greater number of schools. After implementing a voucher program, the city of Milwaukee had to raise property taxes several times to pay increased education costs.[169]

Another potential cause of increased education costs relates to for-profit private schools. Voucher and other privatization programs are driving the development of more for-profit private schools, such as cyber schools. Some politicians have argued that voucher expenditures can be reduced over time because for-profit schools will use increased efficiency, suppression of unions and teacher pay, and other means to lower costs. However, experience in the healthcare area shows that the opposite outcome is more likely.

For-profit school companies are required to provide ever-increasing profits and shareholder returns. Cutting costs helps to achieve this goal. But the ability to cut costs often is limited. For example, it probably would not be practical or possible to pay teachers less than minimum wage. As a result, as occurred in the healthcare area, for-profit school companies frequently will face strong pressure to increase tuition and other fees to achieve ever-increasing shareholder returns. This often will mean that taxpayers will have to pay more to fund voucher programs, which could increase total taxpayer-funded education costs.

Regarding degradation and segregation of public education, increased use of charter schools and private schools is reducing funding available for traditional public schools. Wealthier or more proactive parents often put their children in charter or private schools. Lower-income children frequently are left in increasingly segregated and degraded public schools. Vouchers drive this trend and potentially reduce the expectation that all children deserve a good education in the US. As noted, it is more likely that for-profit private schools will increase tuition and other fees. But it often will be difficult for politicians to increase voucher amounts. Instead, they may face great pressure to lower voucher amounts as private school costs increase. This will force parents who wish to avoid degraded public schools to pay a greater share of education expenses.

Virtually every other developed country believes that all children should have access to high-quality public education. Many people still believe this in the US. But we are moving towards the same situation seen in the healthcare area. It appears that expectations are changing or possibly being managed in the US. It seems that we are moving toward a situation where parents no longer can expect high quality education from traditional public schools. If they want their children educated well, they increasingly will have to pay for it directly, rather than through taxes.

Eliminating or greatly reducing public education will increase total education and other costs, reduce overall education performance, and severely degrade society. In many cases, society can receive much better services at far lower costs by pooling its resources. This often occurs in transportation, defense, education and many other areas. Reducing or eliminating public education will increase crime and cause many other problems in society. This probably will increase incarceration and other costs by far more than is saved on education. In addition, it will severely degrade society, for example, by lowering productivity and the quality of the US workforce. It also will greatly reduce opportunity in the US because high quality education will be provided mainly to children from wealthier families.

Regarding distractions from real solutions, much of the current implied education reform strategy is irrational. The implied or advocated solution to declining educational performance in public schools often is privatization. In other words, the implied solution, or solution actually being implemented, seems to be abandon public education. But this will not work. As noted, about 86 percent of K-12 students in the US attend public schools. It is not practical to think that all or most of these students can be transitioned to private schools or less accountable charter schools. The solution to declining public education is not to abandon it. It is to improve it. The model for achieving high quality education for all or nearly all students is well established and proven. The US used this model in the past to achieve world-leading educational performance. Current education leaders continue to use it. The model is a well-funded public education system with honored and unionized teachers.

Instead of using trillions of dollars of public wealth each year to pay for corporate welfare, we should use it to fairly benefit all citizens, especially children. We should ensure that all children have the option to attend high-quality public schools with reasonable class sizes and well-qualified, well-paid teachers. Public schools in wealthier communities usually already have this and achieve good academic performance. The problem occurs mainly in underfunded schools in low-income areas. The solution in these schools is not to pull out the few students with wealthier or more proactive parents and abandon the rest. It is to provide the same high quality education that children receive in wealthier public schools.

Using taxpayer funds to pay for religious and other private schools is a major distraction. It is not the solution to education problems. The real solution is to fix public education, not abandon it. Some people argue that the goal of education reform through increased accountability and standardized testing is to improve public education. This may be the intention. But it often is not the result. Accountability and standardized testing frequently lead to reduced public education funding, which lowers performance and drives privatization. If the goal actually were to improve public education, when performance declined, we would increase funding and help public schools in other ways. We would not harm them by reducing funding and removing students. As discussed in the Manufactured Crisis section, if the actual goal of education reform were to help public schools improve performance, we would use a test and help, rather than test and punish approach.

The education reform strategy actually being implemented implies and often states that teachers are a main problem in education. This enables suppression of teachers unions and teacher pay and benefits. It also facilitates privatization and earning ever-increasing shareholder returns. But this position largely is irrational. Especially in low-income communities, teachers often must deal with growing class sizes, declining educational materials and resources, and inattentive or misbehaving students. As discussed in the Teach for America section, these teachers largely are saints, not scoundrels. There are some bad teachers. But the overwhelming majority are good or excellent. It is unfair and irrational to largely blame increasingly stressed teachers for poor academic performance. Main causes are poverty and declining funding for public education in low-income schools.

Regarding lack of public support, many polls have shown that the large majority of citizens do not support using taxpayer funds to pay for religious education. When citizens are given the opportunity to vote on vouchers and other forms of taxpayer support for religious education through ballot referendums, they virtually always reject this use of public funds. Since 1967, voters in 23 states have rejected vouchers and other taxpayer support of religious education, usually by wide margins.[170]

However, despite widespread public opposition in the past, there appears to be limited opposition more recently. This probably partly relates to the Supreme Court. Justices violated the Founders' intentions and effectively ignored the Constitution apparently to implement their so-called conservative philosophy. Many citizens probably feel that they could do nothing about this clear constitutional violation because the Supreme Court appears to have absolute power. But it does not.

Another possible factor limiting opposition is a vocal minority who support using taxpayer funds to pay for religious education. Three groups in this minority include parents who wish to send their children to religious schools, religious school administrators who wish to reverse declining enrollment, and religious leaders who wish to impose their will on society. The intention of the first two groups is understandable and worthy of empathy. The intention or goal of the third group is completely unacceptable.

Many good, devout parents wanted to send their children to religious schools, but could not afford private school tuition. Mechanisms such as vouchers and tax credits can enable them to do so. These parents have a financial bias that might cause them to turn a blind eye toward constitutional violations. From the perspective of these parents, throughout US history, it was unfortunate that taxpayer funds could not be used to help them. But this is a price that we pay to live in a democracy that guarantees religious freedom. Parents who could not afford to send their children to religious schools had and continue to have other options. For example, children can learn religion at home, in church, at Sunday school and in other venues. Also, many religious schools offer scholarships and financial aid.

Catholic schools represent the largest segment of the private school sector. About half of elementary private school students and three-quarters of secondary private school students attend Catholic schools. Catholic school enrollment peaked in the 1960s and declined through the 1990s. Several factors drove declining Catholic and other private school enrollment, including migration to suburbs, rising tuition costs, stagnating wages, and expanding charter schools.[171] To reverse declining enrollment, Catholic and other private schools usually strongly supported voucher programs.

Some religious schools address declining enrollment by converting to charter schools. Charter schools must maintain separation between church and state. But religious groups can set up separate nonprofit organizations that run charter schools and receive public funds. There often is heavy overlap between religious groups and affiliated charter schools. Religious charter schools often teach much of the same Biblical and other religious dogma that is taught in private religious schools.[172] As with voucher funding of private religious schools, religious charter schools violate the Constitution because public funds frequently are used to pay for religious education.

Some well-intentioned religious leaders and citizens believe that many problems in society result from lack of religion or godliness. This group also might turn a blind eye toward constitutional violations related to taxpayer funding of religious education. Our suicidally-flawed economic and political systems enable a small group of wealthy citizens to essentially steal the wealth and power of average citizens. As this occurs, life becomes increasingly difficult for many low and middle-income citizens. Frustration and anger grow. This makes people more vulnerable to deception. They often are told that solutions lie in the past, such as getting back to old ways or more religious ways. As discussed in the Misleading the Public section, religious leaders and citizens sometimes are absolutely certain that they are correct. They blindly believe religious dogma and frequently feel that society would be better if more people did the same.

Many religious leaders say that public schools teach secular humanism and that this degrades society. Secular humanism is an outgrowth of the 1700s Enlightenment.[173] The philosophy embraces rational reasoning, science, ethical and moral behavior, and social justice. It rejects dogma and superstition. It holds that all religious and political ideologies must be thoroughly and rationally examined, rather than blindly accepted or rejected on faith. This is the same philosophy that was embraced by our most important Founders.

In an enlightened and rational world, this is exactly what we should be teaching our children. But teaching them to be critical thinkers will make them less likely to blindly accept religious, economic or other dogma. People who believe that their dogma is absolutely correct often are threatened by critical thinking. Their dogma sometimes tells them that they will be damned to an eternity of suffering if they question dogma. Some religious leaders and citizens might believe that making religious education more widely and easily available will help to counteract the critical thinking that is frequently taught in public schools. As a result, this group might strongly support taxpayer funding of religious education.

In addition to promoting religious schools, some Christian groups are aggressively promoting their dogma in public schools. Adult religious leaders are not allowed to proselytize to children in public schools during school hours. But these leaders and churches often are training children to proselytize in public schools and providing extensive support for these efforts. The goal of one Christian group is to proselytize every student in every public school in the US.[174]

Dogmatic Christian groups sometimes defend their efforts to promote religious schools and proselytize public schools by saying that the US was established as a Christian country. Therefore, children should be taught Christian beliefs or dogma. But as discussed in the Population section, this is exactly incorrect. It is the opposite of what the Founders intended. George Washington, Benjamin Franklin, John Adams, Thomas Jefferson, James Madison and many other Founders would strongly disagree with the idea that the US was established as a Christian nation. The US was established as a nation of religious freedom. Our country was intended to be a refuge from the religious dogma and persecution that was widely seen in Europe during the Dark and Middle Ages.

Using taxpayer funds to pay for religious education strongly violates the religious freedom upon which this country is founded. Allowing extensive, well-organized Christian proselytizing efforts in public schools also violates religious freedom. This inevitably will lead to religious discrimination. For example, the Christian group noted above often organizes events where students openly pray around flagpoles at public schools.[175] Some Christians might support this. But what if Muslim students were praying around flagpoles at public schools? Many citizens probably would find this highly offensive and unacceptable. If it is unacceptable for one religion to proselytize in public schools, it is unacceptable for any religion to do so.

Another example of promoting Christianity in public schools occurred in Texas. A 2007 state law requires public schools to teach the Old and New Testament. The law requires that the Bible be taught in an academically sound manner. But this largely is not enforced.[176] As a result, some schools teach the Bible with a fundamentalist Christian bias. For example, some Bible courses in Texas public schools teach students that the US was established as a Christian nation and that the Bible provides scientific proof that the Earth was formed 6,000 years ago.[177] Other public schools use Biblical scripture to justify homophobia, slander of African Americans and Jews, and denial of climate and evolutionary science.[178] In several schools, the Old Testament is taught from a Christian perspective. At least one public school taught that racial diversity among humans resulted from a curse placed on Noah's son in the Biblical flood story.[179]

The Texas representative who co-authored the law that requires teaching the Bible in public schools said, "I don't believe there's such a thing as the separation of church and state."[180] Some high schools and colleges teach comparative religion courses. These courses often teach young people about all of the world's major religions. This provides valuable, mind-opening perspective and insight. Courses such as these do not violate the First Amendment because they do not promote one particular religion. However, requiring public school students to study the Bible, but no other religious books or religions, strongly promotes Christianity, especially when the Bible is taught from a Christian rather than a Jewish, Muslim or non-denominational perspective. Parents are free to teach their children religion. But taxpayer funds should not be used to teach Christianity in public schools.

Some Christian groups oppose teaching yoga in public schools, in part because the practice came from Hinduism. This illustrates giving preference to one religion. Yoga classes taught in public schools have no expressed or implied religious content.[181] The courses usually involve stretching to improve flexibility, holding poses to improve balance and strength, and controlled breathing for relaxation and meditation. These all are highly beneficial activities, especially given high levels of obesity, stress and depression among young people.

Fundamentalist Christian groups sometimes oppose teaching these nonreligious activities, but support teaching their own religion in public schools, for example, by requiring that the Bible be taught. Christians might argue that it is acceptable to teach the Bible in public schools because the majority of people in the US are Christian. But this is unfair. James Madison and other Founders often spoke of protecting the minority from the tyranny of the majority. Children from non-Christian families should not be forced to learn Christianity or the Bible in public schools. The Founders established the First Amendment to ensure that this did not happen. If the Bible is taught in public schools, non-Christian citizens can legitimately demand that their religious books also be taught. To avoid this problem, no religion should be taught in public schools, except perhaps through comparative religion courses that do not give preference to any religion.

The First Amendment prohibits government from establishing or favoring a particular religion. It also guarantees that citizens have the right to freely exercise their religion. A major component of this freedom is the right of parents to teach children their own religion. Parents have a right to determine which religion their children will be taught. Forcing non-Christian children to study the Bible, but no other religious books, in public schools obviously interferes with parents' right to control their children's religious education. Forcing non-Christian citizens to pay for the teaching of Christianity, for example through vouchers or tax credits, also violates the ability to freely exercise religion.

The fact that US citizens often tolerate laws and court decisions such as these clearly indicates the Founders' greatest concern about democracy – the ease with which non-expert citizens could be divided and misled by vested interests. Forcing non-Christian children to study the Bible and compelling non-Christian citizens to pay for Christian school tuition obviously is unconstitutional. But the people have been so effectively divided, deceived and turned against each other that they frequently tolerate these obvious violations of our Constitution.

As discussed in the Population section, the US was experiencing great change and turmoil after the Civil War. During these stressful times, many people claimed that the US was established as a Christian nation and tried to integrate Christian dogma into government. Similar actions appear to be happening today in response to growing stress and problems in society. But this approach is as misguided today as it was after the Civil War. Our solutions largely do not lie in the past. We must move forward to greater enlightenment, not backward to the ignorance, anti-science and religious dogma of the Dark Ages.

The main problem in society is not lack of religious dogma. Lack of the religious or moral principles that are common to all major religions is a problem. But this problem is driven in large part by an even larger problem – the US focus on the well-being of business instead of the well-being of society. As discussed in the Advertising, Media and Culture section, the goal of advertising and for-profit media companies is maximizing shareholder returns, not maximizing the well-being of society. Advertising and media often overwhelm society with deceptive messages that strongly promote selfishness and materialism. This degradation of society is not intentional. It is the unintended consequence of placing the well-being of business ahead of the well-being of society.

Trying to impose religious dogma on citizens will not improve society. It will make it worse, as occurred during the Dark Ages. A main solution is to end business control of government and refocus our country on the general welfare, as our Constitution demands. Then we can establish the true democracy that our Founders intended. We can limit emotionally deceptive and harmful advertising and place media primarily in service of society, rather than shareholders. We can use the wealth of this great nation to fairly benefit all citizens, in large part by once again establishing a world-leading, non-sectarian public education system.

Business Influence of Education

Business influence is a main factor driving the degradation of public education in the US. Our flawed economic and political systems demand that shareholder returns and economic growth always increase, regardless of how much this degrades society. If continuing public education or teaching children to be critical, freethinkers interferes with ever-increasing shareholder returns, companies often will face strong pressure to suppress these activities. As discussed in the Privatization section, many education, financial and other companies see privatization of public education as a good investment opportunity. As a result, businesses and their owners frequently give large amounts of money to politicians, who then work aggressively to privatize public education.

Businesses frequently seek to influence K-12 and college education in several other ways. As noted, funding of public K-12 and higher education is declining in many states. This makes public schools highly vulnerable to business influence. For example, to supplement declining public funding, many colleges seek corporate and other private funding. This often gives businesses substantial influence over higher education. In exchange for providing funding, companies sometimes require colleges to teach conservative philosophy and are given the ability to influence the hiring of professors.[182]

Perhaps most importantly, providing funding to universities often gives companies the ability to influence or suppress research that threatens shareholder returns. Universities frequently conduct independent research that shows various corporate products or processes to be harmful to the environment, public health or society in general. By giving money to universities, businesses often can structure or bias studies in ways that hide or fail to disclose harm. In the K-12 area, several public school systems are seeking corporate sponsors to supplement declining public funding. This can give companies the ability to market or promote their products in public schools.[183]

One of the most important areas of inappropriate business influence of public education involves climate change. As discussed in the Climate Change section of *Global System Change*, energy companies and many other publicly traded companies often essentially are structurally required to oppose actions that threaten shareholder returns, such as restrictions on carbon dioxide emissions, even if these actions greatly benefit society. Two main strategies for blocking actions are inappropriate influence of government and misleading the public. The primary strategy for misleading the public frequently involves blocking rational thought by dividing society into debating, acrimonious factions, such as conservatives and liberals. By building up animosity or hatred for the other side, businesses and their allies can block actions that threaten shareholder returns by labeling them conservative or liberal. This approach has been used very effectively in the climate change area.

As discussed extensively in the Climate Change section, there is no debate in the scientific community about the major components of climate change. Virtually all scientists who are not directly or indirectly paid or influenced by energy and other companies find that climate change is occurring, human society is significantly contributing to it, and climate change already is and will continue to have substantial negative impacts on humanity. Yet in spite of this overwhelming consensus in the nonbusiness-influenced portion of the scientific community, many people in the US believe that climate change is not occurring or is not a major threat to humanity. This is a testament to the ease with which non-expert citizens can be misled, the Founders' primary concern about democracy.

Energy and other companies often hire scientists who, not surprisingly, find that climate change is not happening or that it is not a threat to humanity. Businesses and their allies also frequently label climate change as a liberal conspiracy to harm the economy. Animosity for the other side often causes many conservative citizens to blindly believe these biased vested interest positions. It frequently is easy to mislead adults this way because they watch extensive biased media and are not studying science. However, it often is more difficult to mislead children and teenagers about climate change because they are learning science and critical thinking in public schools.

They also frequently spend much less time watching or reading news and related media.

Teaching young people about the reality of climate change could substantially hurt the shareholder returns of energy and other companies. To minimize this harm, businesses and their owners often fund so-called conservative think tanks that seek to promote climate skepticism in public schools, for example, by providing free 'educational' materials that promote climate skepticism to cash-strapped schools. They also give money to politicians who propose or pass laws that require public schools to teach the 'controversy' about climate change. Several states have passed or are considering such laws.[184]

Religious organizations often work with businesses to promote these anti-science agendas. As discussed, some radical religious groups seek to suppress the teaching of evolution because it threatens irrational, dogmatic ideas about creationism. These business and religious anti-science efforts often are deceptively labeled as promoting critical thinking. But they do the opposite.

As discussed in the Climate Change section, within the realm of logic, it is not possible to argue that humanity should not be taking aggressive action to address climate change. Believing that climate change is not real requires believing the following ideas – that thousands of leading independent climate scientists are lying or mistaken, that the strong correlation between temperature and atmospheric carbon concentrations that has existed for at least 800,000 years will magically end, and that emitting many types of known greenhouse gases into the atmosphere at vastly higher than natural emissions rates will have little or no impact on climate. Even if there were uncertainty about climate change, we should not wait for near certainty before acting. The priority is protecting our children and future generations, not the shareholder returns of energy and other companies. Once we reach perhaps 10 to 20 percent certainty that children are at risk, we must act. We probably reached this level of certainty about climate change more than 20 years ago.

Opposition to addressing climate change shows the suicidal nature of our economic and political systems. Well-meaning business and political leaders are forced to take actions that place humanity at grave risk. Some business and religious groups are attempting to compel public schools to teach that the science of climate change and evolution is highly uncertain. But these ideas are lies. They ignore reality. Teaching the 'controversy' about climate change or evolution would be like teaching children that the idea that the Sun revolves around the Earth is as valid as the idea that the Earth revolves around the Sun.

Our suicidal systems are driving great deception, division and degradation of society. Some religious and business groups promote harmful ideas that are intended to protect religious dogma and shareholder returns. One large coalition of religious groups states that climate change is a "dangerous expansion of government control over private life." It also claims that the environmental movement is "unbiblical – indeed, a new and false religion."[185] These ideas are not rational. Democratic government is the manifestation of the people's desire to protect themselves. Governments establish laws and regulations to protect current and future generations. Saying that climate change restrictions represent a dangerous expansion of government control over private life is like saying that murder laws are a dangerous and unwarranted government intrusion into people's private lives.

Arguing that the environmental movement is a new and false religion also is ridiculous. The Bible commands believers to respect and protect God's creation, including the environment. There is no life without an environment that is clean and stable enough to keep us alive. Protecting the environment is the most important aspect of protecting life because the environment is the foundation of all life. Saying that protecting our life-sustaining environment is unbiblical or unreligious is irrational in the extreme.

When religious leaders make obviously incorrect statements such as these, it can lead one to believe that business is strongly influencing religion in the same way that it strongly influences government and education. Requiring businesses to not degrade environmental life support systems can restrict shareholder returns. Our flawed systems often require publicly traded companies to oppose return-restricting actions. To turn the public against environmental protection, it is possible that businesses give money to religious groups in exchange for saying or implying that environmental protection is unreligious or unbiblical. Business and religious leaders can take advantage of the animosity that conservatives frequently have for liberals by labeling environmental protection a liberal idea. This animosity often compels some conservatives to blindly believe these irrational and suicidal ideas without rationally considering them.

Beyond religion, business groups also are attempting to promote dangerous ideas in public education. For example, a large business-funded coalition is attempting to promote climate skepticism and other harmful ideas in public schools, in part by providing free educational materials that promote these ideas. A presenter at one of the group's conferences said, "If we're not careful, we will end up with a full generation of secular humanists, of multiculturalists – with kids who don't know real American values."[186]

As discussed, secular humanism promotes rational reasoning, critical thinking, ethical and moral behavior, and social justice. Multiculturalism is the peaceful coexistence of different cultures. These are main values and beliefs of our most important Founders. They are the values upon which this country was established. This is what we should be teaching our children. The opposite of multiculturalism is racism. The opposite of secular humanism is promotion of unethical or immoral behavior, suppression of rational thought, and blind faith in often irrational, unintentionally harmful ideas. These are not American values. Opposing secular humanism and multiculturalism violates the principles upon which the US was founded and will greatly harm our country.

Blind faith religious, business and political leaders sometimes mistakenly think that anything different from their ideas is immoral or wrong. But morality largely is not defined by ideas. It ultimately is defined by actions. For example, treating other people with kindness, love and respect is the highest form of morality. It does not make someone immoral to not believe in religious dogma or God. Actions are key. The ideas that drive good, beneficial actions often vary from person to person. The belief that only one set of ideas, such as Christian dogma, defines morality is ignorant and harmful.

Our suicidal economic and other systems demand that anything which threatens shareholder returns, such as critical, rational thinking, must be pushed aside. But we must not allow this. We must not allow business to promote its society-degrading, shareholder-protecting ideas, such as climate skepticism, in public schools. We must place business in service of society. We must replace suicidal business structures that are required to grow forever with ones that are focused on maximizing the well-being of society.

One of the most important actions needed to end inappropriate business influence of education is to adequately fund public K-12 and higher education. Inadequate funding can make schools desperate and compel them to seek business funding. Instead of spending trillions of dollars of public wealth on corporate welfare, we should spend some of this money on public education and other services that benefit all citizens.

Authoritarianism

Misleading the public is one of the most important issues discussed in *Global System Change*. Citizens collectively are the most powerful force in society. But they cannot effectively exercise their power if they are not able to freely and objectively consider major problems and solutions, and then work together in areas of common interest, such as ensuring the survival and prosperity of our children and future generations. This free, rational, objective thinking often would threaten vested interests that are required to grow forever. To protect these groups, many people must be conditioned to not think freely and not question authority. They must be taught to believe what those in power tell them, and to cynically and irrationally criticize anything that differs from it.

Authoritarianism could be defined as blind submission to authority, as opposed to freedom of thought and action by individuals. In government, authoritarianism refers to a political system that concentrates power in the hands of a leader or small elite group that is not constitutionally responsible to the people. Using this definition, an authoritarian government has been established in the US over the past 40 years of deregulation as a small group of wealthy business owners gained strong control of government.

Education is key to building an authoritarian society that does not question this small group of unconstitutional rulers. Education can be used to teach young people to think for themselves, determine right from wrong, and stand up for what they believe. Alternatively, it can be used to crush critical, freethinking and condition young people to not question authority. As discussed below, many factors indicate that the US education system is well down this authoritarian path. This is not to suggest that there is a coordinated effort to mold our children into unthinking automatons who do what they are told and attack ideas that are different from what authorities say. However, this dumbing down of young people nevertheless occurs in many ways. It results from many related and unrelated factors.

The movement toward an authoritarian society partly results from differing worldviews. An excellent article by Sara Robinson, called *How the*

Conservative Worldview Quashes Critical Thinking -- and What That Means For Our Kids' Future, summarizes these conflicting views.[187] Some dogmatic conservative and religious groups believe that people are inherently flawed, fallen or evil. Strong discipline and strict rules are needed to force people to do the right things. Without this, people will succumb to their inherently flawed nature and society will decline. Under this worldview, critical thinking is seen as extremely dangerous. It could lead to rebellion, or at least questioning or opposing authority. As people leave the path laid out by authorities, society will decline, according to this worldview.

Opposing this worldview, many others believe that most people are inherently good and moral. They can be trusted to make the right decisions for themselves. Under this worldview, young people are taught and encouraged to think for themselves and find their own path in life. This position is critical for effective democracy. When people think and do what they are told by the small group that controls government, democracy does not exist. People are not thinking freely and exercising their collective power. They have been intellectually neutered by authoritarianism.

The rise of authoritarianism is the expected, even inevitable, outcome of our grossly flawed economic and political systems. Our suicidal systems demand that a small group of wealthy citizens gets continuously wealthier. Anything that threatens this suicidal growth, such as freethinking and democracy, must be suppressed.

An excellent article by psychologist Bruce Levine, called eight *Reasons Young Americans Don't Fight Back: How the US Crushed Youth Resistance*, discusses many factors that suppress young people and critical thinking in the US.[188] Dr. Levine points out that young people traditionally drove many rebellions and other efforts to improve society, such as the democracy movements in the Middle East. In the 1960s and early 1970s, widespread demonstrations by college students and other young people hastened the end of the Vietnam War. But youth resistance and questioning of authority has been greatly reduced since then. The Occupy Wall Street movement (OWS) is one exception. But as described in the Privacy section of *Global System Change*, OWS efforts often were brutally suppressed. As a result, the movement had far less impact than the Vietnam War, civil rights and other protests in the 1960s and 1970s.

There probably is no coordinated effort to suppress critical thinking among young people in the US. But this effect nevertheless strongly occurs. Factors that promote the rise of authoritarianism and suppress critical thinking include widespread standardized testing, zero-tolerance disciplinary policies in schools, extensive drug testing, privatization and expanding charter schools, world-leading youth and adult incarceration, increased surveillance in schools, forming databases of student psychological and other personal information, widespread psychiatric drug use, declining liberal arts education, rising college costs and debt, extensive screen viewing (TVs, computers, cell phones), widely available fattening and depressing foods, consumerism, fundamentalist religions, IQ variations, attacking intellectuals, and coercion.

Standardized Testing. Standardized testing or testing in general teaches children that their value is based on external assessment (i.e. someone else's opinion of them). It fosters lifelong dependence on external authority. Standardized testing suppresses curiosity, self-assessment, critical thinking and questioning authority. It forces teachers and students to focus on the demands of test creators. It implies that education primarily is about acquiring a body of knowledge, rather than learning to think for oneself, solve problems, and rationally analyze theories and other information and knowledge.[189]

Zero-Tolerance Discipline. Zero-tolerance programs in schools have been growing since deregulation began in the 1980s.[190] These programs provide swift and harsh punishments for misbehavior. Indicating growing intolerance, many school districts are implementing increasingly punitive disciplinary policies. For example, the use of suspension and expulsion often has grown. Across all grade levels, African American students are suspended at about three times the rate of white students.[191] About 20 percent of African American boys and 12 percent of African American girls are suspended each year in the US, compared to six percent of white boys and two percent of white girls. About 95 percent of suspensions are for non-violent offenses, such as tardiness, dress code violations or talking back to teachers.[192]

Over three million students are suspended each year in the US. Many studies have shown that suspensions are an ineffective method of changing behavior. Suspensions double the likelihood that students will dropout or wind up in jail.[193] They also cause academic delays. Students often cannot learn when they are out of school on suspension. As a result, they frequently fall behind. Even one suspension increases the chance that students will dropout. Suspensions disproportionately affect students of color. As a result, they increase the performance gap between white students and students of color.[194]

Many schools increasingly are relying on police and juvenile courts to address misbehavior that used to be handled in schools.[195] For example, many school districts across the US use the criminal justice system to address truancy. Parents and students often receive large fines and are threatened with jail time. Schools sometimes receive a percentage of fines levied by courts. This increases the incentive for schools to use the court system to punish children.[196]

Until recently, truancy in Texas was a misdemeanor. This meant that children could be tried as adults for missing school. Texas adult courts handled about 100,000 truancy cases per year. Students who were charged with truancy often were removed from schools in handcuffs and held in jail for several days. They were not provided with legal counsel in court. Students must pay court fees, even if they are found not guilty. This discouraged them from exercising their right to a full hearing. Truancy defendants often were encouraged to plead guilty and pay fines to avoid going to trial, paying additional court fees and risking jail time.[197]

The use of armed police in schools has grown rapidly across the US. About 68 percent of schools have a police officer on campus.[198] Zero-tolerance policies often take disciplinary discretion out of the hands of teachers and school administrators and place it in the hands of police officers. They frequently have little or no training in child psychology, mediation and anger management. Police sometimes are given financial incentives to make more arrests in schools. These policies have greatly increased arrests for minor infractions that used to be handled by school authorities. For example, in Florida, about 12,000 students were arrested in 2012. About 67 percent of arrests were for misdemeanors or other minor offenses such as fistfights, dress code violations and talking back to teachers. African American students comprise 21 percent of Florida youth, but accounted for 46 percent of arrests.[199]

In New York City, 77 percent of police interventions in schools were for minor offenses, such as having food outside the cafeteria, having a cell phone or being late. Only four percent of police interventions were for major crimes against persons.[200] In Texas in 2010, police officers in schools issued about 300,000 criminal citations to students as young as six years old. Citations were issued for violations including wearing perfume, talking back to teachers, profanity, flatulence and making loud noises. To address citations, students must skip class, appear in court, pay fines and engage in community service, probation or other punishment programs. If students fail to appear in court or parents cannot afford to pay fines, a warrant often is issued for the student's arrest when they turn 17. This frequently has the same discriminatory impact as a criminal conviction. It must be reported on job, college and other applications.[201]

Especially in lower-income schools, students regularly endure hallway stops, locker and backpack searches, full-body pat-downs, and drug-sniffing dogs. In Florida, a six-year-old girl was handcuffed, arrested and charged with a felony and two misdemeanors for having a tempter-tantrum in her kindergarten class. In Mississippi, children as young as ten routinely are arrested for offenses including wearing the wrong color socks and flatulence in class.[202] Taking teenagers away from school in handcuffs can have major psychological impacts. Even if charges are dismissed, for the rest of their lives, young people often must answer yes when asked if they were arrested on job and other applications. As discussed in the Crime section, students who are convicted of drug and other felonies can be legally discriminated against for life in areas including housing and college benefits.

Zero-tolerance policies and using the criminal justice system to handle minor infractions that formerly were handled by schools have established what many experts call the school-to-prison pipeline. This pipeline is used disproportionately on African American children. These children are being arrested and given criminal records for minor infractions, such as talking back to teachers or disrupting classes. Children in the school-to-prison pipeline often face stress and turmoil at home and in their communities. Exposing them to the criminal justice system for minor school infractions expands their frequently existing psychological problems. The school-to-prison pipeline creates an underclass of African American and other children who can be legally discriminated against for life. It frequently ruins their lives before they have a chance to get started.[203]

A study by the American Psychological Association found that zero-tolerance policies are ineffective at preventing misbehavior and do not make schools safer.[204] This occurs in part because answering abuse or problems at home with harsh treatment in schools often makes students worse. It frequently increases the likelihood that young people will engage in misbehavior or criminal activity. The more effective approach often is to wisely (i.e. not naïvely) provide the compassion and understanding that is lacking at home. Zero-tolerance policies also degrade schools in other ways. For example, across the US, many schools are increasing police, surveillance and other disciplinary expenditures, while reducing spending on teacher salaries, books, computers, school counselors and building maintenance.

Zero-tolerance approaches reflect a profound lack of wisdom and compassion in society. Professional educators usually understand that the children causing the most problems in schools often are receiving the most abuse at home or in neighborhoods. Misbehavior frequently is the only way that children know to get attention or help. Giving children the same lack of compassion they receive at home often will further harm them and increase the likelihood they will wind up in jail. There are far more effective and compassionate ways to deal with misbehaving students. These approaches were used more widely when the US was a world leader in public education. But the rise of authoritarianism is forcing wisdom and compassion out of our schools.

As noted, many studies strongly linked high suspension rates to poor academic performance, low graduation rates and increased involvement with the criminal justice system. Schools' adherence to zero-tolerance policies is the second strongest predictor (after poverty) of poor performance on standardized tests.[205] In other words, suspensions and other zero-tolerance policies usually do not work. They put children on paths of increased delinquency and lifelong failure. Suspensions essentially say to children, You're garbage. We don't want to deal with you. Leave.

Suspensions are used in part because they often are less expensive than other disciplinary approaches. It frequently is cheaper to send children away rather than try to help them. Increasingly severe disciplinary policies in schools reflect the growing level of division, animosity and unwillingness to tolerate any questioning of authority in the US. It also shows the destructive nature of our economic and political systems. The need to provide ever-increasing shareholder returns often degrades all other aspects of society, including funding for public education. As this funding is reduced, schools frequently cannot afford to help disruptive children. It usually is cheaper to essentially throw them in the garbage (i.e. suspend them). From a whole system perspective, this is irrational. It would be far less expensive to help troubled children while they are young rather than incarcerate them for many years when they become adults. It also would vastly improve the quality and spirit of society.

Drug Testing. Drug testing programs further illustrate growing authoritarianism and zero-tolerance policies in US schools. Nearly 30 percent of high school students are subjected to drug testing, often as a requirement for participating in sports or other extracurricular activities. Many studies have shown that drug testing does not lower drug use. Several studies have shown that it often encourages students to switch to more dangerous drugs. Marijuana residues can remain in the body for several days. But residues from cocaine, heroin and several other more dangerous drugs often exit the body in a few hours. To avoid detection, students sometimes switch to more dangerous drugs.[206]

Warrantless drug testing without suspicion of drug use violates the privacy rights of students. It is humiliating, invasive and ineffective. It undermines relationships and trust between students and school staff. It violates the Constitutionally-guaranteed presumption of innocence by assuming that students are guilty until they prove otherwise.[207] Widespread drug testing demeans young people and conditions them to tolerate inappropriate privacy intrusions from authorities.

Privatization and Charter Schools. Privatization and expanding charter schools also often facilitate authoritarianism and suppress critical thinking. As noted, charter schools mostly are established in low-income areas. These schools often employ education and disciplinary policies that would not be tolerated by middle-income and wealthier parents. Charter schools in low-income communities frequently implement strict, zero-tolerance policies. Children who do not comply with behavior and other standards often are quickly punished or expelled.

To illustrate, a large charter school chain (KIPP) often required students to walk through hallways in military-type silence, sit with limbs arranged a certain way, and keep their eyes constantly locked on teachers. At one KIPP school, misbehaving children were confined to a padded, windowless, closet-sized room for up to 20 minutes.[208] Public shaming often was used to control behavior at KIPP schools. Children who misbehaved were forced to sit at a special table at lunch, wear their school shirts backwards, or engage in other humiliating actions. At one school, misbehaving African American children were forced to sit on a bench and wear signs that said "CRETIN" around their necks. At another school, children were forced to crawl on hands and knees and bark like a dog. Strict bathroom policies sometimes cause children to have accidents or vomit on themselves in class.[209]

At KIPP schools, children often were forced to sit on the floor for a week and 'earn' their right to sit at desks. They frequently were required to do assignments perfectly. If they made one mistake, they often had to do the entire assignment over. Teachers at these and other charter schools often are taught mainly how to discipline children and help them pass tests. They usually receive little training about how to get to know children and treat them like unique human beings.[210]

KIPP schools used a behavior training technique called "slant". Children are required to sit up straight, listen, ask questions, nod, and track the speaker with their eyes.[211] This authoritarian approach reflects a lack of understanding about child psychology. When children do not look at or pay attention to teachers and other adults, it usually is not because they are being rude or impolite. It often is because they are not interested in what adults are saying or they are not being respected by adults. It also frequently indicates that children feel afraid, insecure, inadequate or confused. Alternatively, they might be hungry or not have other basic needs met. Using zero-tolerance policies to force children to pay attention when they are not interested can teach them to be inauthentic or phony. This ignorant authoritarian approach attempts to force troubled children to behave a certain way without considering why children are misbehaving or not paying attention in the first place.

Wise and compassionate teachers treat children with respect and teach them in an interesting and engaging manner. Children often yearn for positive attention from adults, especially when they are not getting it at home. They usually will naturally make eye contact with and pay attention to teachers and other adults who give them the dignity and respect they deserve, teach interesting material, and present it in an engaging manner. Failure to pay attention or make eye contact would not be seen as misbehavior that warrants punishment. Instead, it might be seen as a call for help that requires more personalized attention. But the goal of business-influenced education systems is not to honor children and help them to become empowered, freethinking adults. It is to help business. As a result, charter and other schools often use harsh zero-tolerance policies that force children to be compliant.

Incarceration. One of the strongest indicators of US authoritarianism is our world-leading incarceration rates. As discussed in the Crime section, the US incarceration rate is six times higher than the median rate of all other countries. With less than five percent of the world population, we have about 25 percent of the world's prisoners. The US also leads the world in youth incarceration. The US youth incarceration rate is five times higher than the next highest country.

The US approach to crime is extremely expensive and counterproductive. The goal of our criminal justice system appears to be punishment, rather than rehabilitation and maximizing the well-being of society. As George Washington warned in his Farewell Address, this type of hatred, vengeance and intolerance is what happens when vested interests divide countries into acrimonious factions. By incarcerating young people at far higher rates than any other country and using police and juvenile courts to address problems in schools, children see where they often will be sent if they fail to obey. This instills fear and unwillingness to question authority.

Surveillance. Many schools are using electronic surveillance to monitor and track the location of students. For example, schools often issue student ID cards with radio frequency identification (RFID) tags embedded. Schools also frequently use GPS tracking software in computers and CCTV video camera systems to track and monitor students.[212] Some schools have issued computers that enable school authorities to spy on students by secretly turning on webcams and taking screenshots. In one case, school spying was discovered when a school attempted to punish a 15-year-old student for behavior in his bedroom.[213] Surveillance technologies often remove students' senses of privacy and freedom. Young people must submit to constant monitoring by authorities. This conditions them to a lifetime of being monitored and controlled by authorities.

Student Databases. As discussed in the Manufactured Crisis section, a software billionaire heavily funded the development of the Common Core and related student data gathering activities. Part of the Common Core involves assembling profiles of each student that contain up to 400 data points.[214] In addition to academic performance data, the profiles often contain extensive psychological and other personal information about students and their families. Information gathered can include Social Security numbers, mother's maiden name, psychological problems, criminal and antisocial behavior, disciplinary and truancy records, personality traits, behavior patterns, sexual behavior and attitudes, religious beliefs and affiliations of students and their families, family voting status, family income, medical history, and fingerprints.[215]

Student information can be gathered through screening, evaluations, testing and surveys.[216] It could be obtained through direct questions. Alternatively, academic and other questions can be structured in ways that indirectly elicit personal information. In some cases, students are attached to sensors while taking tests. The sensors measure factors including facial expression, posture and/or biofeedback, such as pulse and galvanic skin response (i.e. the skin conductivity measured by lie detectors). Students essentially can be hooked up to lie detectors while being asked direct or indirect questions about sexual orientation, political beliefs and religious affiliations. Parental consent usually is not required to gather personal information from students.[217]

The federal government is not allowed to establish student databases. But it gets around this prohibition by compelling states to establish databases through the Common Core program. This essentially establishes a national student database that is shared among states and the federal government.[218] Many states are implementing student databases that contain personal information.[219] States and private organizations that manage student databases often argue that confidential student information will not be disclosed. But this is deceptive. Various loopholes allow private student data to be shared with state and federal agencies as well as private companies.[220] Parents generally are not informed about how their children's private information is being distributed and used.[221]

Proponents of gathering personal student data frequently argue that this information could be used to develop more effective education products and strategies, measure social and emotional skills, and intervene with at-risk students. This might be true in some cases. But the risks and costs of assembling profiles of personal student information vastly outweigh the benefits. These profiles often will be maintained for life. As discussed in the Privacy section, data brokers assemble profiles on nearly all US citizens. Gathering personal student information could enable the development of far more detailed profiles begun at a much earlier age.

This information could be used to unfairly discriminate against people. For example, probably millions of young people have difficult childhoods that compel them to misbehave and/or do poorly in school. But many of them improve and go on to have successful lives. Permanent records of youthful mistakes and poor academic performance could limit adults' ability to find work and succeed in other areas.

Assembling profiles of citizens' psychological and other personal information greatly facilitates authoritarianism. It enables government to more effectively monitor and suppress those who might oppose corporate welfare and business control of government. It also helps businesses to maximize shareholder returns by facilitating more effective marketing and screening approaches. But this privacy violation is an outrage. Government and the private sector have no right to gather personal information about law-abiding citizens, especially children and teenagers. Government is the servant, not the master of society. Once the people regain control of government, we can end this and other privacy violations.

Psychiatric Drugs. As discussed in the Psychiatric Drug section below, psychiatric drugs are one of the most tragic and potentially harmful means of controlling young people. Many schools strongly encourage or even require that parents place children who are misbehaving or not paying attention on psychiatric drugs. Drugging children often causes them to abide by rules and not question authority. But the price of achieving this compliant good behavior frequently is too high. As discussed in several sections, many studies show that antidepressants and other psychiatric drugs are ineffective and potentially harmful. The long-term consequences of these drugs largely are unknown. Children are being massively over-medicated to gain compliance in a system that increasingly will tolerate no questioning of authority.

Declining Liberal Arts. Eliminating or suppressing liberal arts education and courses represents another important authoritarian mechanism. Liberal arts subjects include logic, philosophy, rhetoric, literature, anthropology, sociology, world religions, foreign languages, history, art and music. As discussed by Sara Robinson in the article cited above, a liberal arts education develops strong critical thinking skills, mental flexibility and deep perspective. Studying liberal arts teaches young people to better express themselves persuasively and be better innovators and problem solvers. It also teaches them to exercise foresight, make better decisions, act in an ethical and moral manner, consider their impacts on others, be better team players, and make a difference in the world. A liberal arts education can produce more effective leaders because it gives people the mental perspective and competence needed to better deal with uncertainty, adapt to a rapidly changing world, recognize and seize opportunities, marshal and manage resources, develop and implement strategic plans, and collaboratively guide teams.[222]

However, by developing strong critical thinking skills, a liberal arts education also better enables young people to identify and understand public deception and injustice in society. It often would cause them to question and oppose business control of government and theft of the public wealth through corporate welfare. By suppressing liberal arts, expanding standardized testing, and emphasizing core subjects that are useful for lower-level business activities, the education system can condition the large majority of young people to obey authority and become good, compliant employees.

The increased emphasis on core subjects is causing many public schools to reduce or eliminate liberal arts courses. As a result, the children of low and middle-income citizens often are receiving less liberal arts education. However, the small group of wealthy citizens that largely controls government frequently sends their children to elite private schools that teach classic liberal arts education. This prepares them to take over the leadership roles of their parents and rule over a compliant flock of well-conditioned citizens.

Thomas Jefferson said, "Preach, my dear Sir, a crusade against ignorance; establish and improve the law for educating the common people. Let our countrymen know that the people alone can protect us against these evils [of tyranny], and that the tax which will be paid for this purpose is not more than the thousandth part of what will be paid to kings, priests and nobles who will rise up among us if we leave the people in ignorance."[223] President Jefferson believed that failing to provide publicly funded education would enable the establishment of an oppressive oligarchy (i.e. rule by a small group of people) that deceives, manipulates and abuses the ignorant majority.

This is exactly what is happening. Increasing authoritarianism in the US education system will enable ongoing public deception and plutocracy. In this rapidly changing world, we should be teaching young people how to think, not what to think. This is essential for democracy. Liberal arts education strengthens critical thinking and morality. But this threatens vested interests. Partly as a result, liberal arts are being suppressed in the US.

Student Debt. High levels of student debt also suppress questioning of authority. As Dr. Levine points out in the article cited above, youth often is a time when people are best able to resist authority because they do not have family responsibilities yet. But having high levels of debt can cause young people to worry about resisting authority, losing their jobs, and being unable to pay off debt. In the 1960s and 1970s, many colleges in the US were low-cost or free. Young people frequently could get bachelor's and even master's degrees without incurring debt. This lack of student debt facilitated protests in the 1960s and 1970s. Many public colleges in the Middle East are free. This absence of pacifying student debt facilitated widespread pro-democracy protests by young people in several Middle Eastern countries.[224] As discussed in the Higher Education section below, college costs and student debt have risen rapidly under deregulation since the 1980s. This discourages many young people from protesting against injustices in society.

Screen Viewing. Extensive screen watching also suppresses youth and questioning of authority. US children watch screens (TVs, computers, cell phones) for an average of eight hours per day (not including school-related use).[225] For many young people, this represents nearly all of their waking time outside of school. As discussed in the Advertising, Media and Culture section, extensive violence in media and disempowering advertising create widespread fear and senses of inadequacy in society. This isolates people and makes them less likely to join together to resist authorities. Screen watching is a pacifying activity. Watching TV slows brain waves and inhibits critical thinking. Dr. Levine points out that many boys and young men experience their only potency while playing video games. This virtual potency is no threat to authorities.[226]

Fattening Foods. Widespread availability of unhealthy foods represents another factor suppressing youth in the US. As discussed in the Food section of *Global System Change*, childhood and teenage obesity have grown rapidly. This is due in large part to the widespread availability of fat, sugar, salt and MSG-laden foods that have little nutritional value. Eating these foods often promotes obesity, depression and passivity. This inhibits critical thinking and questioning of authority.

Consumerism. Widespread consumerism is one of the strongest factors suppressing youth and questioning of authority in the US. As discussed extensively in the Advertising, Media and Culture section, the US focus on economic growth causes the primary job of citizens to be buying things. Overwhelming advertising is used to increase consumption. Ads nearly always strongly imply that happiness, success and acceptance by others are gained through consumption. People buy things, but only find temporary satisfaction. As a result, they often keep consuming in a fruitless effort to find true life satisfaction.

In a consumerist society, such as the US, citizens are seen as passive, conditionable objects. This culture legitimizes advertising and manipulation of people. They are conditioned to be dependent on businesses for their happiness. This dependence makes them less likely to question authority. In addition, as people are conditioned to accept the manipulative and deceptive advertising and media culture, they become more vulnerable to deceptions that divide society and create animosity. This makes people less likely to trust others and work together to address injustices in society.

Religious Fundamentalism. Religious fundamentalism is another factor suppressing critical thinking and questioning of authority. Strict, dogmatic or conservative religions often strongly encourage absolute, unquestioning belief in and adherence to dogma. Members are encouraged to believe and not question the supposed word of God communicated by others (rather than listen to the actual word of God or intuitive wisdom available to every person within). Members are warned that questioning dogma or authority could cause eternal damnation and suffering. But blindly abiding by dogma produces eternal bliss with God in Heaven, they are told. Fundamentalist religions often castigate secular humanism because the philosophy encourages critical thinking and questioning dogma.

Dogmatic religions frequently are good allies for the small group of wealthy business owners that largely controls the US government. As discussed, businesses influence education in many ways, including by promoting standardized testing. This suppresses critical thinking and questioning of authority. Dogmatic religion further suppresses these factors. This suppression promotes the development of a compliant workforce that does not question authority. It helps to increase economic growth and shareholder returns. But it severely degrades society.

IQ Variations. The well-being of society demands that we teach young people to think for themselves. We must not condition them to be unquestioning drones for corporations. It is especially important to teach the young to think for themselves because some people are highly vulnerable to authoritarianism. Several studies have shown that people with lower IQs tend to gravitate to more conservative, right-wing ideologies and hold more prejudiced attitudes.[227] IQ partly measures critical thinking and analytic ability. Conservative philosophies often emphasize hierarchy, resistance to change, and obeying authorities. They offer structure and order. These ideologies can appeal to people who have more difficulty understanding the complexity of society. But as discussed in the Suppression of Critical Thinking section below, conservative philosophies sometimes contain grossly oversimplified views of reality. As a result, they frequently produce unintended negative impacts in society.

Regarding prejudice, overcoming racism often requires adopting another person's point of view. This can be difficult for people with less analytic ability. As a result, it might be more intellectually comfortable to adopt or retain prejudiced views.

Discussing links between IQ, political philosophies and racism is a highly sensitive issue. But studies that link IQ to political philosophies have little value at the individual level. There are millions of brilliant conservatives and millions of less than brilliant liberals. In addition, as discussed below, IQ is a flawed and myopic measure of a human being. Everyone has unique interests that excite them on a deep level. Identifying this excitement or passion and building one's life around it produces the highest level of life satisfaction and true success. Each person probably often has the unique abilities needed to pursue their passion, or bliss as Joseph Campbell says.

People who are good analytic thinkers probably frequently enjoy analytic thinking. Following their excitement probably requires this particular skill. People who have lower analytic thinking ability probably are less interested in it. They are more interested in other skills that are necessary to pursue their unique excitement in life. In other words, lower ability to think analytically probably mostly results from lack of interest, not lack of competence. This is one reason why IQ is such a poor measure of the whole human being.

While analytic thinking ability only is one aspect of a human, it is important. People with less interest in analytic thinking often are more vulnerable to authoritarianism. Conservative philosophies frequently stress respect for authority and suppress critical thinking. To illustrate, in 2012, the published platform of the Texas Republican Party stated, "We oppose the teaching of Higher Order Thinking Skills (HOTS) (values clarification), critical thinking skills and similar programs that are simply a relabeling of Outcome-Based Education (OBE) (mastery learning) which focus on behavior modification and have the purpose of challenging the student's fixed beliefs and undermining parental authority."[228]

In other words, this conservative group specifically opposes teaching young people to think critically. It also is against challenging fixed beliefs. Fixed or unswerving beliefs often refer to dogmatic religious ideas that authorities say should not the questioned. In terms of undermining parental authority, many parents probably want their children to learn to think for themselves and find their own path in life. Parents love and understand their children probably better than anyone else. But children grow into young, independent adults. No one, including parents, ultimately knows what is best for another person. Everyone ultimately must determine this for themself. Parents and other wise people can provide highly beneficial guidance to young people. But they cannot see into their child's heart or mind. Discouraging young people from thinking freely and finding their own unique path in life can produce an unsuccessful and unsatisfying life.

Attacking Intellectuals. Another form of suppressing critical thinking involves attacking intellectuals. These people frequently spend considerable time logically analyzing reality. Nearly all technological, medical and similar advances in society result from rigorous, reality-based analysis. This type of analysis often enables intellectuals to identify deception and injustices in society. Logical thinking by intellectuals can threaten vested interests, for example, by exposing corporate welfare and business control of government.

To protect these interests and unjust systems, intellectuals often are irrationally attacked.

Many years ago, intellectuals frequently were killed in China because they posed a threat to abusive, authoritarian leaders. Intellectuals sometimes are attacked by saying they have their heads in the clouds. People who do not question authority or think critically might blindly believe this irrational assessment. But intellectuals, such as Benjamin Franklin, Thomas Jefferson, James Madison and many other Founders, often are the people who most logically and accurately assess reality. Those criticizing intellectuals frequently are attempting to prevent citizens from thinking rationally and seeing the harm caused by vested interests.

Coercion. Coercion is an important defining characteristic of authoritarianism. It takes people's freedom away. Coercion involves compelling citizens to act in certain ways by using subtle or blatant threats, intimidation, or other types of force. In the US, the people's wealth, power and freedom essentially are being stolen through corporate welfare and business control of government. Hundreds of millions of low and middle-income citizens must continuously sacrifice so that a small group of wealthy citizens can get continuously wealthier. Average citizens would not tolerate this if they understood what was happening. As a result, public deception and coercion are widely used to perpetuate this injustice. Coercion is omnipresent in US society. It is so widespread that many people take it for granted or do not recognize it.

An excellent article by Dr. Bruce Levine, called *The More a Society Coerces Its People, the Greater the Chance of Mental Illness*, describes extensive coercion in US society and contrasts this to many indigenous societies.[229] Mental illness was rare in indigenous societies, in large part because people were not forced to do what they did not want to do. But the US economy is focused on maximizing the well-being of the small group that strongly influences government. As a result, employees often are forced to do more work for lower pay and benefits. As discussed below, this causes about 70 percent of employees to dislike or not feel engaged with their jobs. People frequently essentially are forced to take jobs that they do not like to survive. If our economy and government were focused on the well-being of the many instead of the few (as the Constitution requires), jobs frequently would be more interesting and employees would be fairly compensated for their hard work.

The US political system also is coercive. In a majority rule system, citizens in the minority often are forced to go along with government policies and programs that they do not support. Seeking consensus frequently is more time-consuming. But it can enhance society by producing less coercion and resentment.

Beyond employment and politics, coercion is widespread in K-12 education. As discussed below, continuously ranking students on subjects that they often find boring makes many young people unhappy with school. But they frequently are told that they cannot succeed without education. Young people often essentially are forced to endure education that they find boring or disempowering. Coercion also is widespread in parenting. With the best of intentions, parents often force their children to do things that they have little interest in doing. Once people are coerced, it frequently becomes easier to coerce others.

Dr. Levine describes how coercion often leads to resentment, anxiety, depression and rebellion. It frequently causes widespread problems in relationships. As discussed in the Psychiatric Drugs section below, coercion is a main cause of widespread and growing mental illness in the US. People often engage in addictive or compulsive behavior to escape the psychological pain caused by our coercive society. Coercing young people in education and other areas greatly suppresses critical thinking and teaches them to not question authority.

It is imperative that all young people be taught to think for themselves. Suppressing critical thinking through authoritarianism enables and perpetuates gross injustices in society, such as corporate welfare and business control of government. It also enables harmful legislation and Supreme Court decisions, such as the Patriot Act and *Citizens United*. In addition, suppressing critical thinking enables gross public deceptions.

To illustrate, as discussed in the Finance and Capital Markets section, in the early 1980s, businesses increased their influence of government and compelled politicians to remove regulations that protected society but threatened ever-increasing shareholder returns. A main strategy for achieving this was to turn citizens against Government. They were encouraged to blindly believe the irrational idea that government was bad and society would be better off with less of it.

To mislead the public, politicians sometimes sarcastically joked, "The nine most terrifying words in the English language are: I'm from the government, and I'm here to help." The illogical implication is that government degrades society and cannot do anything right. But government is not inherently good or bad. It is a tool. Government is an expression of the people. It is as good as we demand that it be or as bad as we allow it to be. Government is essential for civilization, at the current level of human development. But government regulations that protect society often limit ever-increasing shareholder returns. As a result, vested interests frequently attempt to trick citizens into blindly believing that government always is bad. This is one reason why teaching young people to think for themselves is so important.

When citizens think critically, they would dismiss irrational and sarcastic statements such as "I'm from the government and I'm here to help". For example, when firemen put out a burning home, police arrest an armed robber, or municipal workers repair a bridge, these people effectively are saying to citizens, I'm from the government and I'm here to help. The irrational vested interest position implies that citizens should tell firemen, police officers and municipal workers to leave because they are not interested in help from the government. If young people were taught to think rationally, politicians making idiotic statements like this would be laughed or booed off the stage.

The dogmatic religious view that humans are inherently flawed, and therefore need structure, discipline and authority to prosper, is incorrect. It is not based on reality. It is impossible to prove that God did not create humans and the environment. While God may have created humans (assuming that God exists), the actual vehicle for creation was nature. Humans literally came from nature. We are not separate from it. No other species in nature is inherently flawed. It is irrational to assume that only humans are. Observing reality, probably over 99 percent of human actions are good or at least civilized. Based on observations of reality, humans are inherently good, as are all other creations of nature.

Enlightened society (i.e. democracy) is based on the innate goodness, competence, morality and freedom of people. To maximize the well-being of society, we must teach independence and freethinking, not suppress them. We also should honor our young people by asking them what they want. Do they want to be unthinking automatons who blindly obey authorities? Or do they wish to be freethinkers who are encouraged and empowered to do what they believe is right? Obviously, children want the latter. This is their destiny and our obligation. As a result, we must end authoritarianism in the US and establish true democracy.

It should be emphasized that this section is not intended to be critical of religious, business or political leaders. This book takes the position that leaders are good people who intend to benefit society. But as discussed extensively, our grossly flawed ideas and systems often compel good people to do bad things, such as blindly believe in irrational, unintentionally harmful economic and religious dogma, seek infinite growth in a finite system, and use authoritarianism to suppress critical thinking and democracy.

Hitting Children

Hitting, spanking and other forms of physical (i.e. corporal) punishment enable and strongly support growing authoritarianism in the US. Physically hurting and humiliating children teaches them that disobeying authorities can be painful and harmful. Hitting and other types of physical punishment are prohibited in schools in over 100 countries.[230] Thirty-two countries, including Israel, Kenya and most European countries, prohibit hitting and other physical punishment of children in all settings, including homes.[231] Sweden was the first country to prohibit physical punishment of children. Swedish law states, "Children are entitled to care, security and a good upbringing. Children are to be treated with respect for their person and individuality and may not be subjected to corporal punishment or any other humiliating treatment."[232]

However, in the US, all 50 states allow parents to hit their children and physically punish them in other ways. Nineteen states allow hitting of children in schools.[233] About 220,000 children are hit by teachers and school administrators each year in the US. African American students are hit more than twice as often as white students.[234] Hitting students is most common in the South and Midwest. For example, over 28,000 children were hit by teachers and administrators in Georgia schools in 2008.[235]

Beyond hitting, other forms of physical punishment in schools include physically restraining children and isolating them in rooms (often called scream rooms) against their will. Nearly all experts say that these approaches should not be used. But many schools in the US nevertheless use physical punishments, such as pinning uncooperative children facedown on the floor, locking them in dark closets, or tying children up with straps, handcuffs, bungee cords or duct tape. Three-quarters of restrained students have physical, emotional or intellectual handicaps.[236]

These practices are illegal in most hospitals and psychiatric centers. But schools often are allowed to use them in the authoritarian US. Schools reported restraining or isolating students against their will more than 267,000 times in 2012. However, use of these practices probably occurs much more frequently. Many child advocates and government officials say that schools often do not report the use of physical punishment. Parents frequently are unaware that their children have been restrained or isolated against their will because many states do not require schools to notify parents.[237]

Schools often defend these practices by saying they are needed to protect students and teachers. But many schools use these practices when students pose no risk to themselves or others. For example, schools frequently restrain or isolate students for having tantrums or failing to follow directions.[238] These forms of physical punishment are humiliating and extremely counterproductive. Wiser teachers and school administrators use more compassionate and effective means of calming disruptive students and securing compliance.

In addition to physical punishment in schools, over 60 percent of families in the US hit their children or physically punish them in other ways.[239] The UN Convention on the Rights of the Child is an international treaty that prohibits all forms of physical or mental violence against children. The US and Somalia are the only two countries that have not ratified the Convention.[240] Somalia has not had a central government for over 20 years.

Many parents in the US hit their children because it often is the easiest and fastest way to force children to stop misbehaving. Hitting children effectively gains compliance in the short-term. But extensive research shows that it is harmful to children in the long-term. Many schools and health organizations strongly recommend that physical punishment of children in schools be prohibited. Organizations opposing this practice include the National Congress of Parents and Teachers, the National Education Association, the National Association of Elementary School Principals, the National Association of State Boards of Education, the American Medical Association, the American Academy of Pediatrics, and the American Academy of Child and Adolescent Psychiatry.[241] Many mental health and medical organizations, including the American Psychoanalytic Association and American Academy of Pediatrics, strongly recommend that physical punishment of children be prohibited in the US in all settings, including homes.[242]

Hitting people is not allowed in prisons, the military and mental health institutions. Due to the overwhelming evidence of long-term harm, many experts say that hitting children also should not be allowed. (The term spanking is misleading because it does not adequately reflect the violence and long-term harm imposed on children when they are hit. As a result, to improve accuracy and minimize public deception, this section uses the term hitting instead of spanking.)

Many studies have been conducted on the impacts of hitting children and using other types of physical punishment. The studies often compare groups of teenagers or adults who were hit as children to those who were not hit. As with other statistically valid research, the studies often adjust or control for other factors that might influence results. Virtually no study found that hitting children provides any benefit beyond short-term compliance. Nearly all studies show or indicate that physical punishment causes harm that often lasts a lifetime. For example, in a review of 80 studies, no study found any long-term benefit from physical punishment.[243] The most common finding is the children who are hit become more aggressive over time. Children who are not hit become less aggressive over time.[244]

Children often admire and seek to emulate their parents. If a child sees parents solving problems with violence, they often will do the same. Hitting children teaches them that violence is acceptable behavior. Many studies have shown that hitting substantially increases the likelihood that children will become bullies, use violence against siblings, abuse their spouses or children later in life, or engage in violence or criminal activity.[245]

Many studies also have shown that hitting children can cause mental health problems in childhood and later in life. For example, a study published in the journal Pediatrics linked physical punishment of children to increased anxiety disorders, mood disorders, personality disorders, depression and substance abuse.[246] Hitting children often causes them to feel distress, anger, fear, shame and disgust. It frequently increases delinquency and antisocial behavior.[247] Some studies indicate that hitting children can reduce cognitive ability and inhibit the ability to regulate stress and emotions. Hitting often teaches children to lie to avoid being hit.[248] It also frequently teaches them to avoid the hitter, not the bad behavior.[249] Hitting another person frequently would harm the relationship with that person. It is the same with children. Many studies have shown that hitting children reduces trust and damages relationships between parents and children.[250]

A study of 34,000 adults found that people who were physically punished as children were 24 percent more likely to be obese and 35 percent more likely to have arthritis than those who were not physically punished.[251] As discussed in the Food section, people often use overeating and other addictive or compulsive behaviors to suppress unpleasant emotions. Low self-esteem, depression and other psychological problems caused by physical punishment during childhood can produce unpleasant emotions that people attempt to suppress with overeating.

Several studies also have shown that hitting children in schools is harmful. Peers often know when a student is being physically punished in school. Children sometimes are hit in front of peers. This can cause intense embarrassment and humiliation that might leave lifelong psychological damage. Various studies have shown that hitting in school reduces self-esteem and academic performance. It also is linked to increased truancy, dropout rates, violence and vandalism.[252]

Beyond overwhelming evidence that hitting children causes psychological harm, logic and a basic understanding of psychology can be used to illustrate how hitting children is harmful. Children probably are born with some elements of personality and character. This is strongly indicated by the fact that many siblings who were raised in the same way grow up to be very different. But it nevertheless is widely understood that some of the most important elements of personality and character are developed in early childhood. The child is like a nearly blank slate. As discussed in the Psychiatric Drugs section below, core values and beliefs learned in childhood largely determine the quality of a person's life. Once basic needs are met, quality of life is determined almost completely by perceptions of what is happening in life, rather than by what actually is happening. Many people have few resources and face struggles but nevertheless are happy, while many others appear to have everything but are miserable.

Core values and beliefs largely are learned through experiences and emotions, not intellectual processes. To young children, parents and the home largely are the whole world. Deep, unconscious beliefs that children learn in this family world will strongly influence their perceptions of the rest of the world throughout their lives. In early childhood, children learn the most important things needed to have a satisfying life. For example, they learn, is the world safe or unsafe? Will my needs be met? Can I trust other people? Will those I love and depend on love me in return or hurt me? Beliefs such as these form the foundation of people's personalities. They largely are not formed through intellectual processes. They function in the background. People often are not aware of them. But these core beliefs strongly influence how life is perceived and experienced.

If children are consistently loved and nurtured and if their needs are met, they usually will grow up believing that the world is a safe place, their needs will be met, they can trust others, and those they love will love them in return. While experiences later in life may pose challenges, having these types of core beliefs gives a person resilience. It strongly enables them to have a satisfying life, regardless external circumstances.

However, if children do not receive consistent love and nurturing and if their needs are not met, they frequently will grow up with a more problematic set of core beliefs. They might believe that the world is not a safe place, their needs will not be met, they cannot trust others, and those they love will hurt or reject them. Again, these beliefs usually are not conscious, unless one works to make them so, for example through psychotherapy. But these beliefs largely govern how people interpret situations and act in life. Someone who believes that the world largely is safe and other people can be trusted will act one way, while someone who believes that the world is unsafe and others are untrustworthy often will act a different way.

When the people a child loves and depends on for survival (i.e. parents) hit the child, it can cause deep psychological wounds. Young children have little or no frame of reference. They largely do not know what happens in other families or in the rest of the world. They mostly only know their own family. Children and people in general have strong survival instincts. For example, children in war zones who lost parents often will do amazing things to survive. If a child is hit by parents, they frequently will adapt to survive. The intention of the parent and the words said around the hitting largely are irrelevant. Children often cannot think in a more rational or abstract manner until about eight years old. Younger children learn the most important things through actions, experiences and emotions, not words or parental intentions.

Children often are not able to recognize or understand if their parents have problems. In addition, they depend on parents to survive. As a result, to protect themselves, children usually would not assume that parents are flawed. Instead, they frequently will assume on a deep, non-intellectual level that they are flawed. When parents hit children and cause physical pain and negative emotions, even if no physical injury occurs, children learn that the world is not safe. People who they love and depend on cannot be trusted. At some point, these people will harm the child.

The child might remain affectionate to parents because they need the parents for survival. But on a deep unconscious level, their ability to trust has been wounded. When the love and trust between parents and children is wounded through hitting, the child often goes into survival mode. They realize that if they wish to receive love from parents and avoid harm, they must act a certain way. They frequently become hyper-focused on parents' moods or behavior, for example. They learn that it is not safe to express who they are. Survival demands that they remain focused on pleasing someone else or meeting someone else's needs, rather than their own.

These kinds of experiences in early childhood can severely damage people in teenage years and adulthood, as shown by extensive research. Young children usually cannot understand parents' problems, moods or intentions. If they are hit or treated abusively, they often 'rationalize' (i.e. in a deep unconscious way) that they are flawed and deserve to be hit. They frequently grow up with unconscious beliefs, such as I am not a good person, I do not deserve to have my needs met, and people will harm me because that is what I deserve. Again, these ideas often are not conscious. Teenagers and adults frequently adopt survival mechanisms or inauthentic personalities (i.e. masks) to compensate for a deep, unconscious sense of unworthiness. These core beliefs might cause someone to be shy or become a loner. Alternatively, they might display bravado to mask inner unworthiness. People who act in a rude and arrogant manner often are compensating for a deep sense of unworthiness.

One of the main problems with hitting children or withholding love in other ways is that the child learns to expect less from life. Children who are hit or abused often wind up in abusive relationships. They frequently remain in jobs, relationships and other situations that make them unhappy because they believe on a deep unconscious level that they deserve no better. Hitting children often makes them very focused on obeying authority, not listening to their inner wisdom, and not following their bliss, excitement or own path in life. This is why hitting children is so beneficial for authoritarian leaders. It trains people to be compliant drones who tolerate boring jobs and gross injustices in society.

Degree is important in this area. Some children are hit frequently. Others are hit rarely, and only with the best of intentions. Children who are hit frequently are likely to suffer more negative impacts than those who are hit rarely. But even one hit from a parent can cause deep, long-lasting negative impacts. If an adult hit a friend or adult family member, it is unlikely that the hit would be easily forgotten. It might end the relationship or damage it for life. Children are more vulnerable and less able to understand hitting than adults. Their personalities and senses of security in the world still are forming. Therefore, it is highly likely that even one incident of hitting a child could cause far more damage than hitting an adult. Weakening the ability to trust a parent can damage the ability to trust all other people throughout life.

Core unconscious beliefs that people develop in childhood often are difficult to change. The way a person sees and deals with the world becomes their security blanket. It is their means of survival. Even if believing that other people are untrustworthy produces a painful life, this worldview is familiar. It also probably is unconscious. Once the pain of this worldview becomes too great, people sometimes are compelled to take action. They might seek the help of a psychotherapist. Through this process, unconscious harmful beliefs can be made conscious and changed. But this work requires courage. Getting honest about deep senses of unworthiness and fear of the world can be painful in the short-term (but highly beneficial in long-term).

Changing familiar ways of dealing with other people can be disconcerting and frightening. This is why many people never change the disempowering unconscious beliefs that they learned as children.

Hitting children is not rational. We do not allow other people to be hit. For example, employers are not allowed to hit employees when they make mistakes. If a waitress made several mistakes with an order, the customer would not be allowed to spank the waitress. The only people we allow to be hit in society are the smallest, weakest, most powerless and defenseless, most vulnerable, least likely to understand why they are being hit, most likely to be severely psychologically harmed by hitting, and the ones who we say we love the most. This is absurd. Probably the only time hitting is appropriate in society is for self-defense. But even this is not needed for children. If a young child is trying to hurt another child or an adult, the adult can restrain the child without hitting them.

Normally, hitting a smaller, weaker, defenseless person is seen as cowardly and abusive. But our culture makes this harmful, cowardly action acceptable. Rather than saying that it is not acceptable to hit anyone except children, we should say that it is not acceptable to hit anyone, especially children. Children are the most vulnerable and defenseless. Therefore, they should be given the most protection from hitting, not the least. A husband might say to his wife, I'm going to hit you because I love you. You made a mistake. It's for your own good. This approach would not help a marriage. It would harm it. Using the same rationalization and approach with children also is harmful and ignorant.

As noted, children often adapt to hitting or abuse by assuming they are unworthy and deserve to be harmed. This helps them to survive a physically and/or psychologically dangerous childhood. But this survival mechanism frequently produces an unhappy life in adulthood. For example, many wives stay with abusive husbands. If a woman was hit or abused by her father as a child, she might hold the unconscious belief that she deserves to be hit or does not deserve a good life. She might be unconsciously attracting abusive or unloving men like her father. The bottom line is that hitting a child can ruin or severely degrade a person's whole life.

Hitting children often says more about the parent than about the child. Many parents are well-adjusted and hit their children because they sincerely believe it will help them. But many other parents hit children due to anger, frustration and immaturity. As discussed in the Advertising, Media and Culture section, advertising and media in our materialistic culture frequently condition people to selfishly focus on meeting their own needs. These selfish, immature attitudes strongly contribute to widespread divorce in the US. (The US has the highest divorce rate in the world.) These attitudes also strongly contribute to bad parenting. Good parenting requires maturity and patience. Selfish and immature parents probably often resent having to give up time or freedom for a misbehaving or crying child. Hitting the child can quickly resolve the problem and allow the parent to do what they want. But this hitting was not done out of love. It was done out of frustration, immaturity and selfishness.

Parents also sometimes hit children because they do not know alternative, harmless, more effective methods of discipline. Hitting might be the only tool in their toolbox, so to speak. In addition, some parents hit their children because they mistakenly think the child is intentionally defying them. They take the misbehavior personally and incorrectly think that it is a battle of egos. They probably were not taught or do not understand the stages of child development. For example, defiance or misbehavior is normal at some stages of childhood. It has little or nothing to do with intentionally defying parents. Joan Durrant, child psychologist and lead author of a major study on the harmful impacts of hitting children, said, "Two-year-olds are the most aggressive people in the world. They don't understand the impact of their behavior and they can't inhibit themselves. So the more a child sees someone resolving conflict with aggression, the more aggressive they become."[253]

There are many public deceptions and misconceptions about hitting children. For example, some people say that hitting children has been done for a long time. Many parents do it. Therefore, it must be okay. But just because something has been done for a long time does not mean that it is not harmful. Society usually moves towards greater enlightenment. As we better understand the world, we sometimes realize that practices which once were thought to be beneficial actually are harmful. Overwhelming evidence shows that hitting children produces long-term, often severe psychological harm. Once we realize that an action is harmful, especially to children, the well-being of society demands that we end it.

Other people sometimes argue that, in the heat of the moment, for example when children are misbehaving and parents must focus on something else such as driving, hitting children is the only option. It quickly and effectively stops the misbehavior or emotional outburst. But this position is not rational. Millions of parents never hit their children. These nonviolent parents often face the same difficult, stressful situations as hitting parents. They prove that hitting children never is necessary, in the same way that hitting adults never is necessary in civilized society. Parents who think that hitting sometimes is necessary probably have not learned or applied alternative disciplinary techniques.

A major irrational component of the idea that hitting children sometimes is necessary involves benefits and costs. The short-term benefit of hitting children is obvious. It quickly ends misbehavior. But the long-term cost is vastly higher than the short-term benefit. Children who are hit are much more likely to rebel and get into trouble as teenagers. In exchange for a few minutes saved by hitting a child, parents might have to endure years of frustration during teenage years. Also, parents who hit their children often will have to endure the heartache of seeing their children have problems in adulthood, such as depression, addiction or failed marriages.

Another misconception involves parental intentions. As noted, many parents hit their children out of love and a sincere desire to help the child. They truly believe that hitting is in the best interest of the child. This is understandable because it has been done for generations, many parents still hit their children, and some experts still recommend it. But as discussed in other sections, many harmful actions are done with the best of intentions. The point here is not to blame or criticize loving, well-meaning parents. It is to raise awareness about the harmful effects of hitting children. Once loving parents understand this, they will use nonviolent, more effective means of disciplining children.

One of the most important deceptions or misconceptions related to hitting children involves the idea that government does not have a right to tell parents how to raise children. This is irrational in some ways. People form governments to protect themselves and society in general. Each person cannot be their own police force, for example. People protect themselves through their agent government by prohibiting harmful actions, such as murder. In a civilized society, parents do not have a right to raise children in ways that cause severe harm. For example, society would not allow a parent to punish a child by burning them with a cigarette butt. Once we know at a high level of certainty that hitting children frequently causes severe psychological harm, we must prohibit this action.

Another misconception related to hitting children involves parents saying, I was hit as a child and I'm okay. This also is irrational in some ways. For example, parents and other adults have little or no frame of reference on this issue. They cannot compare themselves to the version of them that was not hit because that person does not exist. Therefore, they are not able to determine how much better their life would be if they were disciplined without hitting. Also, there are tens of millions of adults in the US who are obese, depressed, have other mental illnesses, and/or are engaging in excessive, compulsive or addictive behaviors. Many, if not the large majority, of these people were hit as children. It does not appear that they are doing well.

Another misconception involves the idea that if I do not hit my children, I do not care about them. This is irrational. Not hitting does not mean not disciplining. As discussed below, there are many alternatives to hitting that are more effective and not harmful. Parents sometimes feel that if they do not hit their children, they implicitly are criticizing their parents who hit them. But again, society's ideas about what is beneficial and harmful often evolve over time. Parents who hit their children in older generations frequently did so out of love and good intentions. It does not insult or dishonor grandparents when parents use alternative disciplinary approaches once it becomes clear that these approaches are more effective.

One of the most important public deceptions about hitting children involves the idea that it would be difficult to change this practice in the US. As noted, over 60 percent of families sometimes hit their children or physically punished them in other ways. But as discussed with many other issues in this book, we must not let difficulty stand in the way of doing the right thing, especially for our children. It was not easy to end slavery. But it was the right thing to do.

Sweden provides a good model of how to end physical punishment of children. Prior to 1979 when physical punishment was prohibited, about half of children in Sweden were hit.[254] Since then, a whole generation of children has been raised with nearly no physical punishment. The Swedish approach was wise. Physical punishment was made illegal. But there are no criminal penalties if parents hit children. Instead, social service representatives visit parents and explain that physical punishment is illegal and harmful. They often provide support, such as links to parenting groups, child development information, assistance with childproofing homes, and explanations about alternative disciplinary methods. These methods include withholding privileges, using time-outs (i.e. requiring children to remain in a room for a period of time or until misbehavior ends), and offering consequences (i.e. if you throw your toy and break it, you won't be able to play with it anymore).[255]

To prevent misbehavior, parents are encouraged to reinforce positive behavior with praise and rewards and to emphasize words instead of actions. Children frequently are unable to articulate their anger or frustration. Parents are encouraged to speak with and listen to children and teach them how to articulate their feelings. This helps then to improve self-awareness and regulation of emotions. Parents also are encouraged to explain their reasons to children. This helps them to develop more effective decision-making capabilities. In addition, parents are reminded that children emulate them. Therefore, parents are encouraged to model the behavior that they wish to see in their children, such as nonviolence, compassion and understanding. Parents also are encouraged to use positive wording. For example, instead of saying, don't spill your drink, say, hold your cup carefully. The first statement places the idea of spilling a drink in the child's mind. The latter causes them to focus on holding the cup carefully.[256]

Perhaps the most important parental advice regarding hitting children involves increased self-awareness. As noted, hitting children often says more about the parent than the child. When parents are using violence on children or are about to use it, they frequently have lost control of themselves and the situation. They often are acting out of anger, frustration, selfishness or immaturity. Frustration is understandable given how difficult raising children frequently is. This is why self-awareness and maturity are so important. If parents let their emotions get the best of them and hit a child, frustration might be temporarily relieved. But they frequently will pay it back many times over in teenage and later years. Hitting a child never is wise or appropriate. Raising children is difficult. But the love and other benefits parents receive from this hard work is one of the greatest joys in the human experience. If the benefits did not vastly outweigh the costs, humanity might greatly decline or cease to exist.

One of the most urgent and important changes needed in the US is to end hitting and other forms of physical punishment in schools. Children have a right to be free from pain and embarrassment. Schools should model the behavior they wish to see in children. As noted above, hitting children in school is ineffective. It creates many problems. There are vastly more effective disciplinary approaches. These model and teach children conflict resolution and socially acceptable behavior. Hitting children in school models violence. It teaches them that violence is an appropriate way to deal with problems. This is ridiculous. School administrators should know better. They should not be acting worse than the children they are disciplining.

Hitting children should be prohibited in public and private schools, such as religious schools. Children used to be hit regularly in Catholic schools. But now most Catholic schools in the US prohibit physical punishment. Hitting children often occurs in fundamentalist Christian schools.[257] This once again shows the danger of blind faith adherence to religious dogma. Radical religious groups often believe that the Bible is absolutely and literally true. The Old Testament says that beating a child with a rod will save his soul (Proverbs 23:13-14).

Additional Biblical instructions for dealing with misbehaving children include, "If someone has a stubborn and rebellious son who does not obey his father and mother... his father and mother shall take hold of him and bring him to the elders at the gate of his town... Then all the men of his town are to stone him to death." (Deuteronomy 21:18-21) Regarding children who make prophesies or communicate what they hear God saying in their own hearts, the Bible commands, "And if anyone still prophesies, their father and mother, to whom they were born, will say to them, 'You must die, because you have told lies in the LORD's name.' Then their own parents will stab the one who prophesies." (Zechariah 13:3)

The Old Testament contains many violent, barbaric, tribalistic ideas that no longer apply in modern society, such as encouraging slavery and killing disobedient children. For Christians, the New Testament supersedes the Old Testament. The primary, paramount commandment of Jesus and Christianity is to love each other. As discussed in several other sections, people have access to the actual word of God (or intuitive wisdom) within. This is the highest authority. It takes priority over what someone else said God said thousands of years ago. It was this inner voice of wisdom that compelled humanity to end slavery and other abominations promoted by dogmatic, blind faith religions throughout history.

Hitting children, especially with a rod, is an abomination. The least amount of reflection on the love advocated by Jesus and the vulnerability of children shows this to be true. Given the great love that Jesus showed to children in the New Testament, it is virtually impossible to imagine him hitting a child. He was filled with love, compassion, understanding and forgiveness. The Bible says that Jesus got angry at adults who were misinterpreting or abusing God's teachings on rare occasions. But it is inconceivable that he would display anger or violence to children.

Radical Christian sects that promote hitting children are like radical Muslims who misinterpret their peaceful religion in ways that justify killing innocent people. Both of these groups appear to make anger and hatred the primary commandments of their religion. Blind faith in old dogma has closed their minds and hearts to the living word of God (or intuitive wisdom for those who do not believe in God).

Blind faith dogmatic Christians are good people who mean well. But their close-minded interpretation of dogma causes their good intentions to create harm in the world, in this case to children. As noted, blind faith religions that promote hitting children and other authoritarian measures are good allies for business vested interests who wish to suppress dissent and promote obedience to economic dogma, such as the idea that economic growth should take priority over all else.

We the People must stop allowing vested interests to divide us, take our power and wealth, and promote authoritarianism in the US. The survival and well-being of our children take priority over everything but our own survival. Our children are not animals. We must not treat them like animals by hitting them. (As discussed in the Food section, abusing animals also is not appropriate in a civilized society.) We must protect our children.

In the US, there often is a thin, vague line between physical punishment and physical abuse. Physical punishment causes pain but not physical injury. Therefore, it is not considered to be abusive or illegal. This creates many problems in schools. Teachers and administrators frequently are required to report child abuse to children's protective services or social services organizations. When this occurs, social service representatives might ask about the size of a bruise on a child. If the bruise is not large enough, the hitting that caused it might only be considered legal punishment, not illegal abuse.

This dichotomy is idiotic. Strong evidence shows that hitting children often causes severe psychological harm, even when there is no physical injury. In reality, there is no dichotomy or separation. All physical punishment potentially is psychologically harmful. Parents have no way of knowing in advance if their well-intentioned physical punishment will cause long-term psychological harm. But this type of punishment frequently causes low self-esteem, violent behavior and many other problems. Therefore, all physical punishment should be considered to be abusive. It never is acceptable. To protect our children, we must prohibit hitting and other physical punishment in all locations, including schools and homes.

Competitive Grading

Competitive grading and competition in general strongly indicate humanity's much lower level of intelligence, sophistication and wisdom compared to nature. The overwhelming force in a healthy human body, other healthy natural systems, and nature in general is cooperation. When the overwhelming force is competition, as in a body with terminal cancer, the system usually is declining or dying. The highest life forms, including humans, evolved to cooperate. A basic form of cooperation involves a mother caring for a child. But humans also evolved to form cooperative groups and communities. Those who did not gain the ability to cooperate probably often did not survive.

As discussed in the Well-Being of Society section of *Global System Change*, indigenous religions frequently were based on cooperation and unity with nature. This reality-based thinking enabled these groups to survive and prosper on Earth over the long-term. Humans often violated these religions when we pushed nature aside to build cities, domesticate animals and grow crops. Instead of ending the violations, new religions arose that said humans were separate from and above nature. But we are not separate from nature. We cannot survive apart from it.

As discussed in the Women's section of *Global System Change*, the illusion of separation produced fear that needs would not be met. This created the belief in the need for competition. In this environment, those with greater physical strength, aggressiveness and competitiveness (men) often were more highly valued. When power is defined this way, men innately have more power. Many studies show that women innately have more wisdom, when it is defined as cooperation, empathy, whole system thinking, multitasking, relationship skills and intuitive wisdom. (These generalizations are irrelevant at the individual level. Everyone is different. All men and women have power and wisdom. There are many wise men and powerful women.)

The belief in separation from nature and the need for competition are foundational components of our flawed economic and political systems. As discussed throughout *Global System Change*, achieving sustainability and real prosperity requires greatly enhanced cooperation and wisdom in society. Recognizing this will help to elevate women to a position of true equality with men. As noted, women innately manifest greater cooperation and wisdom than men. As a result, greater valuing of these qualities will cause greater valuing and honoring of women. While our flawed systems overemphasize competition, human society largely is cooperative. For example, in competitive team sports, the winning team often is the one that cooperates most effectively. A less skilled team that cooperates well frequently can beat a team with more skilled players who do not cooperate as well. The same is true in business. The most successful companies usually are the ones that are managed most effectively. Good management largely involves maximizing cooperation within the company, in the supply chain, and with customers and other stakeholders. In other words, even in competitive environments, the team, company or group that cooperates most effectively usually wins.

The idea that human society is competitive largely is an illusion. If each human interaction were labeled cooperative or competitive, probably over 99.99 percent of interactions would be cooperative. Even at a one percent level of competition, society quickly would descend into anarchy. For example, if each person hit every hundredth person they passed on the street or tried to rob every hundredth store they entered, society quickly would fall apart.

Social skills are the most important skills needed to succeed in life. Gaining these skills mainly involves learning to cooperate and get along with others. It also includes learning to understand and manage emotions. Good social and emotional skills not only are important for life success. They also enhance academic performance and the ability to learn. Anxiety, anger, fear and other negative emotions can strongly inhibit or block students' ability to focus and learn. As a result, many schools in the US have implemented social-emotional learning programs.[258]

Psychological or noncognitive skills and traits often are better predictors of life success than academic performance measures. They include self-awareness, self-restraint, persistence and the ability to cooperate effectively. These skills and traits sometimes are collectively referred to as emotional intelligence. Many studies have shown that people with higher noncognitive skills or emotional intelligence have longer marriages, more successful careers, better physical health, and fewer psychological problems.[259]

True success in life also often requires high self-esteem. This is gained in large part by having the sense that one is able to make a unique, positive contribution to society. As discussed below, competitive grading often substantially degrades social skills, self-esteem and the ability to find one's unique, most fulfilling path in life. To measure and rank children on less important skills (i.e. academic and intellectual), we severely degrade the most important qualities and skills needed for success in life. This is not rational.

Global System Change extensively discusses the essential need to evolve economic, political and social systems into sustainable forms to achieve sustainability and real prosperity. This largely means emulating nature by making systems more cooperative. If we teach children cooperation, we will strongly promote a more cooperative, sustainable and prosperous society. If we continue to teach them competition, we will help to perpetuate our competitive, unsustainable systems and the rapidly growing environmental and social problems that result from them.

However, teaching children cooperation and self-empowerment would threaten current fear-based, competitive, authoritarian systems. As discussed above, testing and competitive grading teach children that their value is based on someone else's opinion of them. Competitive grading often lowers self-esteem and conditions young people to depend on and obey authorities. This enables the perpetuation of gross injustices in society, such as business control of government and theft of the public wealth through corporate welfare.

Enhancing and protecting the well-being of children and society demands that we greatly lower competition and increase cooperation in education. Competitive grading definitely is not needed to educate children effectively. One could make a strong case that competitive grading makes it impossible to achieve truly effective education that maximizes the well-being of individuals and society.

This section summarizes problems caused by competitive grading and more effective ways of assessing student learning. Problems relate to self-esteem, social skills, inaccurate measurement, motivation, productivity, teacher-student relationships, suppression of minorities, and public deception.

Self-Esteem

High self-esteem is one of the most important qualities needed for success in life. It sometimes is inaccurately equated to self-delusion, selfishness or arrogance. But self-esteem does not involve pretending that one is perfect or focusing exclusively on self. Self-esteem is similar to self-compassion. People with high self-esteem compassionately acknowledge their mistakes, and then move on with life. They do not condemn themselves for being imperfect. Self-esteem or self-confidence enables people to focus more on others, rather than obsessively seek to meet their own needs, as people with strong senses of inadequacy or low self-esteem often do.

People with high self-esteem believe that they deserve a good life and generally will not settle for less. But those with low self-esteem, perhaps because they were hit as children, frequently feel that they do not deserve a good life. As a result, they often settle for less. They tolerate boring jobs, abusive or unloving relationships, and harmful behavior, such as overeating or other addictions.

Teachers and schools usually have a large impact on children's levels of self-esteem. As discussed in relation to IQ above, each person has unique interests and skills. Identifying these and building one's life around them usually produces the highest levels of self-esteem, satisfaction and true success in life. This is how individuals function in the virtually infinitely more sophisticated and sustainable systems of nature.

Each living component of nature is intuitively or instinctually guided to do what they are best adapted to do. This enables them to reach their fullest potential. When each individual is guided and coordinated by the virtually infinitely greater intelligence of nature, there is someone or something to do everything and everything gets done. This is indicated by the vast beauty, symmetry, coordination, efficiency, resilience and longevity of nature. In nature, all unique interests and skills implicitly are valued and utilized. But this is not what happens in our vastly less sophisticated human society.

Education follows society. Education systems are structured in ways that people believe will benefit society. Since the 1980s, deregulation and public deception largely have shifted the focus of US society from doing what is best for society to doing what is best for business and the economy. This is partly reflected by shifts in curriculums. As noted, under education reform, liberal arts and vocational courses often were reduced, while core subjects were emphasized. Competitive grading of core subjects identifies skills and traits that are important to business, such as problem solving, written communication, obeying authorities and ability to follow directions. Young people who do well in subjects often go to the best colleges, get the best jobs and have the most financial success in life.

The system of grading and ranking students has been in place for generations. Many people take it for granted. They often assume competitive grading is a good system that would be difficult to change. But if one steps back, looks at the big picture and considers unintended consequences, they see that competitive grading of a narrow set of core subjects severely degrades society in many ways.

The purpose of education primarily should be to benefit individuals and society, not businesses and the economy. The education system should encourage and help young people to identify their unique skills and interests, and then build their lives around them. As noted, all or nearly all skills implicitly are valued in nature. Teachers and the education system in general should help children to understand that each person is different. Everyone has strengths and weaknesses. This diversity of skills and interests makes human society beautiful and resilient. The education system never should create the impression that certain skills, and the people who possess them, are more valuable or important than other skills and people.

But this is exactly what our self-esteem degrading, competitive education system does. Competitive grading strongly teaches young people in emotional, often unconscious ways that some people are more talented and valuable. This small group deserves more success in life, competitive grading implies. This conditions young people to accept the gross financial inequality that exists in the US. As discussed in the Corporate Welfare and other sections of *Global System Change*, inequality largely does not result from fair allocations of wealth based on merit and hard work. It mainly results from unconstitutional business control of government and theft of the public wealth through corporate welfare.

Competitive grading implies that a certain set of skills is most important. Young people who are lucky enough to have these particular skills often have the most success in our business focused and dominated society. Many schools used to require students to walk up to the teacher's desk to get their tests. The student with the highest test score would walk in front of the class first, while the student with the lowest test score would walk in front of their peers last.

This process of ranking students strongly implies and teaches various expectations about individual value and place in life. The first students in front of the class are shown to be more talented in areas that society implicitly values. Young people often understand that these supposedly more intelligent students frequently will go to better colleges, get better jobs, earn more money and attain leadership positions. The students ranked in the middle can expect less success in life. They might be working for the better students someday. The students with the lowest test scores being paraded in front of their peers might be seen as the least competent and intelligent. One might expect that they often would hold the least desirable, menial jobs and have the least success in life in general.

Most schools probably have ended these grossly demeaning practices. But even when grades are less publicized, the process of grading and ranking students produces similar, destructive ideas about value, self-worth and life expectations among young people. Schools should be places where children, teenagers and young adults can experience the joy of learning. Instead, they often are places where young people go to be judged and ranked against their peers. These environments can be extremely destructive to self-esteem.

Competition creates a situation where one person's success is another person's failure. With academic testing, there often is one winner, while everyone else implicitly is judged to have varying degrees of incompetence. Even winning (i.e. getting high test scores) frequently does not produce authentic self-esteem. Beating someone else can create temporary satisfaction. But it often leads to fear of not winning in the future. Students' sense of self-worth is based on external judgment. This can create a sense of helplessness. Young people might feel that they must continue beating others to feel adequate. Competitive grading frequently creates an omnipresent fear of failure. Rather than providing self-esteem, winning provides temporary relief from feeling like a failure.[260]

Young people who often receive below average grades can become depressed and discouraged with school. Children with learning disabilities might fear going to school and experiencing inevitable failure. Competitive grading can be especially damaging to young children (i.e. grades K-3). At this age, children frequently are not able to separate themselves from competitive outcomes. Poor performance relative to peers can have deep, long-lasting negative impacts during a time when children's lifelong senses of self-worth and value in society are being formed.[261]

Competitive grading and education benefit competitive business systems. By damaging self-esteem, children often appear to expect less from life. They are conditioned to obey authorities and tolerate boring jobs. In a society such as the US that places the well-being of business before all else, this degradation of young people might seem beneficial. That is a main reason why business control of governments and society must be ended. We must educate our children in ways that build up their self-esteem, not tear it down.

Social Skills

As noted, social skills (primarily cooperating and getting along with others) probably are the most important qualities needed for success and satisfaction in life. Teachers and school administrators nearly always intend and take actions to ensure that school environments promote the development of positive social skills, foster learning, and encourage friendship and enjoyment among young people. These outcomes occur to some degree in competitive education settings. But competitive grading strongly limits these benefits and causes many unintended negative impacts.

School often is a child's first or most important exposure to society outside the family. Children's minds, values, and conscious and unconscious beliefs still are forming. In addition, children spend much of their waking time in school during these formative years. As a result, experiences in school strongly influence young people's understanding of and expectations about society. Schools often are intended to provide nurturing learning environments. But children frequently experience something very different. With competitive grading, children quickly learn that they are being forced to compete against their peers. They will be judged and ranked relative to peers. And they will be rewarded or punished based on their performance. On a deep, often unconscious level, children can learn that they enter school with little or no inherent value. Their value largely will be determined and assigned by external authorities.

Through the judgment, ranking and reward process, children learn that there is a hierarchy of value in school (and by implication in society because school strongly conditions worldviews). Children implicitly, though unintentionally, receive the powerful implied but unspoken message, "You are here to be judged and ranked. Get used to it. That's how the world works. Those who perform well implicitly are more valuable. They will be rewarded and probably have better lives. If your performance is average or below average, do not expect much from life. You must learn your place in the value hierarchy."

Schools are intended to be places of learning. But this often is not the primary or most powerful experience in a competitive grading environment. Through powerful emotional experiences, children frequently learn that the main function of school is to judge and rank students. This can produce high levels of fear and anxiety. Competitive grading makes schools seem like dangerous places for many young people.

Standardized testing further increases anxiety, stress, fear, frustration and anger among students. As noted above, NCLB/ESSA requires standardized testing beginning in third grade. Some school districts are expanding standardized testing to K-2 grades. But many parents and teachers oppose giving multiple choice tests to children as young as four years old. Several experts state that this serves no educative purpose. Instead, it is developmentally inappropriate, excessive and destructive.[262]

Of course, no one intends that competitive grading teaches children that they have little or no inherent value, their value or self-worth is based on performance, and if their performance is poor, their value is low. As with hitting children, these ideas are not spoken or intended. But the deepest, most powerful and often unconscious beliefs are not formed through words or teachers' intentions. The most powerful beliefs about self-worth are formed through emotions and experiences. The experience of being ranked poorly relative to peers can have a profound, lifelong negative impact on self-worth.

As discussed in the Hitting Children section, children frequently adapt to physically or psychologically harmful situations, such as competitive grading environments which teach them that their value is not intrinsic, but rather based on performance. Children usually have no frame of reference. They do not know what a noncompetitive educational environment is like. On an unconscious level, they often will assume, competition is the way of the world, I might as well try to make the best of it. They frequently will make friends, learn things and have some fun.

Many children probably learn good values at home, in church and in other locations. For example, they hopefully are being taught that all people are inherently equal, regardless of performance. But these good values can be overwhelmed by the destructive values learned in a competitive grading environment.

Grading and ranking young people is inherently counterproductive. It can degrade character and social skills in many ways. For example, competitive education teaches young people to see peers as obstacles to success (because one person's success often is another person's failure). The primary measured and managed goal of education often is to beat the other person and not be the loser. Competition can teach people that peers can be used to achieve goals. It makes people less likely to cooperate and share ideas and resources. It also tends to marginalize less skilled or intelligent people because they are not as useful for goal attainment.[263]

Learning to see other people as obstacles to success, means to achieving a goal, or valueless due to low competence can severely impede the ability to cooperate and get along with others (i.e. social skills). Competitive grades effectively are rewards (high grades) and punishments (low grades). Using rewards can degrade character. For example, several studies have shown that using rewards to motivate children causes them to be less cooperative, compassionate and generous.[264]

Some people argue that competition, for example in team sports, builds character. But this is misleading in some ways. For example, character building results in large part from learning teamwork. In other words, character development results largely from learning to cooperate, not compete, more effectively. Some people also say that competition builds character by teaching young people to win gracefully. This is better than winning arrogantly. But the process of segmenting society into winners and losers often is problematic. For example, an emphasis on winning can create false senses of superiority or inferiority. Masking one's sense of superiority behind graciousness does not enhance character. Competition also can create a desire or willingness to do whatever it takes to win. All of these results of competitive grading can substantially degrade character and social skills.

Many people go through competitive education systems and wind up as good, cooperative, highly ethical people. This largely reflects the complexity of humans and the human experience. Many internal and external factors determine how people will be affected by competitive grading.

As discussed below, all of the supposed benefits of competitive grading can be achieved more effectively through other forms of assessment. On balance, competitive grading is strongly negative. It creates senses of fear and inadequacy, even among 'winners' who might be beaten on the next test. It also lowers trust and makes people less likely to work together by conditioning them to see peers as obstacles to success. Degraded social skills caused by competitive grading leaves people less able to achieve a successful and satisfying life.

Inaccurate Measurement

Inaccurate measurement represents another problem with competitive grading. As business influence of government and education increased since the 1980s, there has been a greatly increased focus on quantitative measurement of students, for example through increased standardized testing. Quantitative measures of processes, inventory, costs and other metrics are critical for business success. But children are not products or inventory. They cannot be reduced to a few numbers or letter grades.

Emphasizing quantitative measurement creates many problems in education. For example, it focuses education on what can be easily measured, rather than on what is important. Education should emphasize and teach the most important skills, knowledge and character traits needed for success in life. As discussed, these skills and traits include high self-esteem, strong social skills, critical and creative thinking, ability to deal with complexity, and ethical and moral behavior. These most important skills and qualities largely are qualitative and subjective. As a result, they often are difficult to quantify and measure. For example, in assessing the quality of writing, it is easier to grade grammatical errors than to assess the degree to which writers evoke interest and excitement in readers.

Many tests emphasize memorization of facts and other information. It is easy to measure and grade memory retention. But this skill is far less important than other skills. For example, students often memorize information for tests that they will not need for the rest of their lives. After the test, the information frequently is quickly forgotten. Vast and growing amounts of information are available online. Access to this information already is easy. It will be even easier in the future. Rather than memorization, the far more useful skill is being able to locate and analyze information, and then draw rational, useful conclusions from it.

A qualitative assessment by a teacher who knows a student well can be far more accurate, complete, informative and useful than quantitative test results. Human beings are complex. We have qualitative and quantitative aspects. As noted, the far more important aspects are qualitative. Accurate qualitative assessments of complex humans only can be done by trained and experienced humans, such as teachers. This shows the high skill level and sophistication needed for effective teaching. The link between superior education performance and sophisticated, well-qualified teachers is strongly indicated by the fact that teachers generally are honored and well compensated in countries that lead the world in education performance, such as Finland.

However, a major focus or result of education reform in the US has been the suppression of teachers and teachers unions. Privatizing, standardizing and applying businesslike processes in education makes teachers less important and relevant. Emphasizing competitive grading and standardized testing often forces the qualitative and subjective out of education. In other words, it massively dumbs down academic assessment. Schools increasingly buy standardized teaching materials, tools and tests from education companies. Teaching frequently is rendered down to a simplified process of presenting and grading standardized material. This makes teachers expendable and more easily replaceable.

Current competitive grading and measurement systems help businesses by ranking students on qualities that benefit business. The process of ranking further benefits business by lowering self-esteem and conditioning young people to obey authorities and tolerate boring jobs. This once again shows the suicidal nature of our systems. To facilitate earning ever-increasing shareholder returns, businesses severely degrade education. This degrades society, which ultimately degrades business. To protect and enhance the well-being of society, we must shift the focus of measurement in education away from what benefits business and the economy to what benefits individuals and society. Ironically, shifting the focus from business well-being to the well-being of society is the best, and perhaps only, way to maximize the well-being of business.

Motivation

Many studies have shown that competitive grading substantially lowers the quality of thinking and motivation to learn. For example, external motivation, such as competitive grading, often creates fear of failure. This can lower internal motivation and interest in learning. Grading creates a preference for easier tasks to avoid failure. When no grades or rewards are offered, people frequently choose more complex, difficult or challenging tasks.[265]

Grading lowers the quality of thinking by shifting the focus from what one is doing (i.e. the task) to how one is doing (i.e. performance). Young people often focus only on what is needed for tests, rather than on the whole subject. Students who are not graded frequently have better retention because they consider issues more fully without fear and make more connections in their minds.[266]

Grading and rewards work best when tasks are boring. Offering rewards or grades often lowers performance when tasks are interesting and solutions are not obvious. Rewards frequently are used for behavior modification, such as forcing children to learn in school. Behavior modification strategies such as grading and offering rewards work best on people who are powerless, dependent, bored, infantilized and/or institutionalized.[267]

The incorrect position that grading is needed to promote learning appears to be based partly on a negative view of humanity. As discussed, some religious and conservative groups believe that humans are inherently flawed and lazy. Strict rules and structures are needed to force them to do the right things. This authoritarian view of reality apparently originated in religions that separated humans from nature, and then spread to business, education and other areas of society. The idea that people are flawed or lazy is used to justify strict discipline and controls. But as discussed, extensive research and observations of reality show this authoritarian worldview to be false.

Like every other creature in nature, humans have an innate desire to reach our fullest potential. This produces the highest level of life satisfaction, and therefore is a strong internal motivator. Saying or implying that people are flawed, lazy, incompetent or unable to reach their fullest potential through their own inner motivation severely stifles people, especially young people, because they are more vulnerable to these lies.

Children are naturally curious. They have a strong, innate desire to learn. Judging, grading and ranking students against peers will not increase the desire to learn. It will lower it. Grading often replaces the desire to learn with a desire to win. Young people who do well on tests might be motivated by the desire to win, in the same way that a gambling addict is motivated to play a game by winning money. The problem with motivating learning through grading is that this produces winners and losers. The losers often lose their motivation to learn. And the winners sometimes adopt the delusion that they are superior to others.

Competitive grading harms the overall motivation to learn among students. If interesting material is presented in an engaging manner, and if young people do not have major distractions or problems outside of school, they often will be more motivated to learn by the absence of grades.

Productivity

Reduced productivity is another problem frequently caused by competitive grading and competition in general. Many people believe that competition increases productivity. But extensive research shows that the opposite often is true. For example, many studies have analyzed links between competitiveness and achievement or productivity. Several studies analyzed competitiveness among business people, college students, airline reservation agents, and elementary school students. Each of these studies found that higher competitiveness was correlated with lower productivity or achievement. In a review of 122 studies, 65 studies found that cooperation promotes higher achievement. Only eight studies found that competition improves achievement.[268]

There are several reasons why competition can hurt performance. For example, competitive people often waste time and energy thinking about other people's performance or trying to prevent them from winning. Also, as noted above, cooperating with others effectively frequently is the most important requirement for maximizing productivity and achievement (i.e. winning). Perhaps the best example of how cooperation enhances productivity lies in nature. There is no waste in nature. Nature usually achieves nearly perfect efficiency and productivity. Productivity, creativity and virtually every other positive factor are essentially infinitely greater in nature than in human society. The overwhelming force in nature is cooperation. Therefore, to maximize the well-being of our children and humanity overall, we should strive to emulate the virtually infinitely more intelligent master that is all around us, within us and available through intuitive wisdom.

Teacher-Student Relationships

Competitive grading frequently damages teacher-student relationships. After parents, teachers often are the most important people in students' lives, especially young students who frequently spend the whole school day with one teacher. Children often spend more time with teachers than parents. Teachers frequently represent children's first exposure to authority outside the family. They strongly influence children's perceptions of authorities and society in general. Teachers are intended to be allies who facilitate student learning and psychological development. This frequently occurs.

However, competitive grading creates an inherent conflict between teachers and students. The job of the teacher often is to focus on the negative by finding fault or errors. The teacher is the judge of the child. Teachers implicitly determine students' value through grading and ranking. Competitive grading inevitably creates an adversarial relationship between teachers and students. Many good teachers work hard to overcome this and help children to succeed. But the requirement to judge and rank students can create fear of teachers and authorities in general.

Standardized testing makes the situation worse. Teachers often used to provide more qualitative assessments and constructive, nonjudgmental feedback to students. But the increased focus on standardized testing frequently lowers qualitative assessment. Students' performance largely is determined by grades. In effect, the complex, qualitative, subjective human being is reduced to a few numbers and grades. This further distances teachers from students.

Competitive grading or grading on a curve also can mask bad teaching. If a teacher does a good job of explaining a subject, all students learn the material and they do well on tests, this should be seen as ideal. But competitive grading implies that it is bad. Many high scores often are interpreted to mean that the class is too easy. This creates a strong incentive to ensure that some students do poorly. In some cases, many low scores are considered to be positive. It implies that a teacher is tough. When in reality, it probably often means that the teacher simply is bad. Poor teaching caused students to not understand material and get low grades.

Teacher-student relationships are critical for learning, especially with young children. Competitive grading inevitably damages these relationships by making them adversarial. Far more effective ways to assess students are discussed in the Education Solutions section below. We must implement assessment methods that strengthen teacher-student relationships, rather than build distrust and fear of teachers and other authorities.

Suppression of Minorities

Another huge negative impact of competitive grading relates to African American children and other minorities. As discussed, white children frequently received higher grades than African American children. White racists sometimes claim that this results from innate deficiencies in African Americans. But as noted, poor academic performance occurs mainly in low-income communities. The lower performance of African Americans nearly completely relates to factors outside of school, such as poverty, violence and not having basic needs met. It has nothing to do with lower intelligence or competence. White children often arrive at school with more reading and other skills and more stable home lives. This is why they often outperform, not because they are smarter.

African American young people sometimes do not try to perform well in school. This is understandable. Why should they submit themselves to the constant humiliation and degradation of being ranked less intelligent or less competent than white children, when the ranking has nothing to do with intelligence or competence? Even if it were better understood that poor academic performance relates more to home life than intelligence, this still could be humiliating. Why should African American children have to expose to their peers that their parents perhaps cannot find jobs in our white dominated society? If we did not shame African American and other minority children with competitive grading, they almost certainly would try harder in school.

Misconceptions and Deceptions

There are several misconceptions or deceptions that facilitate the continuation of competitive grading. For example, some people argue that, while the vast majority of human interactions are cooperative, society still is competitive in many ways. Therefore, competitive education prepares students for a competitive world. Some people might say that competitive grading better prepares students to compete for scarce jobs.

Effectively addressing and considering this issue illustrates the need for a whole system approach. Education, the economy and everything else in human society are interconnected parts of one overall system. Small problems in various parts of human society often can be effectively addressed in isolation. But effectively resolving large problems nearly always requires a whole system approach. Regarding effectively competing for scarce jobs, one could first ask the larger question, why are jobs scarce? As noted, large publicly traded companies are structurally required to grow forever. To achieve this, they often give money to politicians, who then implement rules and regulations that benefit large companies. This helps them to put small companies out of business and severely degrades local economies.

Also, to grow forever, companies often compel fewer people to do more work. Improving productivity lowers the number of employees needed. By improving labor productivity, sending jobs overseas and taking other actions, companies can create scarcity of jobs. Having more people looking for jobs than there are jobs available gives companies great power over current and prospective employees. When job opportunities are limited, companies can force employees to take lower wages and benefits, work longer and harder, tolerate tedium, and accept other suboptimal employment conditions. Job scarcity is not necessary. It exists in large part because scarcity of jobs helps companies to achieve ever-increasing shareholder returns.

Job scarcity can be ended once citizens stop allowing themselves to be deceived and divided into debating factions (such as conservatives and liberals), take back control of government from business, and refocus society on doing what is best for all citizens, rather than the small group of wealthy people that controls government. Once this occurs, several important changes can be made. As we emulate the vastly greater sophistication of nature, we will rebuild local economies, in part by holding companies responsible for all negative environmental, social and economic impacts. Holding companies fully responsible by integrating all real external costs into prices will improve pricing accuracy. As discussed in the Trade, Scale and Competitive Advantage section of *Global System Change*, accurate pricing often will show that local production is the low-cost option. This will create more local jobs and local business ownership.

Also, as the US uses its wealth to benefit all citizens, we will establish a social safety net that is comparable to other advanced democracies. For example, Germany and other manufacturing leaders provide healthcare, retirement and other benefits to all citizens through government. As US companies no longer are required to provide benefits that are provided by government in nearly all other developed countries, the pressure to lower benefit costs by having fewer employees doing more work will decline. As a result, companies will be able to have two employees working 30 hours per week, instead of one person working 60 hours, for example. As these sustainable economic changes are made, job supply can match demand and job scarcity can be virtually eliminated.

However, setting aside economic changes that provide employment for everyone who wants or needs a job, one could argue that competitive education does not best prepare young people for competitive job markets. There generally are two hurdles that applicants must overcome to get jobs – skills and compatibility. Compatibility (i.e. the ability to get along with supervisors and co-workers) often is the more important factor, assuming that candidates have basic required skills. Competitive education frequently degrades self-esteem and the ability to cooperate and get along with others. Students educated in a cooperative educational environment (i.e. no competitive grading) often have higher self-esteem, better social skills, and equal or better academic skills (partly because competitive grading lowers interest in learning).[269] As a result, young people educated in a cooperative environment frequently will be better prepared to compete for jobs in competitive labor markets. This applies in virtually all areas of human society. As discussed in the Implement Freedom-Based Education section below, cooperative education more effectively prepares students to achieve success and satisfaction in life.

Another misconception about competitive grading is the idea that it works. Competitive grading has been around for a long time. During this time, the US became a world leader in economic and other areas. This implies that competitive grading is an effective strategy. There are several deceptive aspects to this position. For example, student assessment often was more qualitative when the US was a world leader in education. Education reform has increased the emphasis on quantitative factors. Also, competitive grading enhances the economy and businesses by lowering self-esteem and making young people more compliant. But it degrades individuals and society in many ways. In addition, just because something apparently works does not mean that it cannot be largely improved, as is the case with competitive grading.

Another deception involves the idea that it would be difficult to change competitive grading because it has been around for a long time and many people are used to it. But we must not let difficulty stand in the way of doing what is right for children and society overall. As discussed below, many schools successfully educate children without competitive grading. Experts have been studying and writing about cooperative education for decades.

There are abundant models and experts to help implement an education system that does not put students in conflict with teachers and each other.

Effective Assessment

Ending competitive grading does not mean ending assessment of students. Assessment is critical. It helps teachers to engage with students, identify strengths and weaknesses, and ensure that students are gaining maximum benefit from the education experience. Identifying the optimal assessment approach cannot be done until the optimal education strategy is defined. This cannot be done until the optimal, or at least sustainable, society is defined.

As noted, education follows society. At a whole system level, the purpose of education should be to maximize the well-being of society. Currently, society implicitly makes the grossly false and suicidal assumption that maximizing the well-being of business and the economy maximizes the well-being of society. Following this incorrect assumption, education appears to be increasingly focused on maximizing the well-being of business and the economy. We must end the irrational assumption that maximizing business well-being maximizes social well-being. Instead, we must begin to actually measure the well-being of society. Economic growth supposedly is the means to the end of social well-being. But if we measure the means, they become the end goal of society.

The first requirement of a sustainable, prosperous society is survival (i.e. protecting life support systems). Without this, everything else is irrelevant. As discussed in the Well-Being of Society section, the next requirement is strengthening and protecting communities and social structures that enable individuals to prosper. From an educational perspective, this largely means ensuring that young people know how to get along with others and cooperate effectively (i.e. build strong social skills). Once environmental and social systems are addressed and protected, individual needs and well-being should be addressed. After basic needs are met, the most important component of maximizing individual well-being often is helping each individual to identify and develop their unique areas of interest and competence, and then built their lives around them. Along with building strong social skills, this probably is the most important aspect of a truly effective education system that maximizes the well-being of individuals and society.

All people are inherently equal. We all have varying strengths and weaknesses. As noted, the education system never should create the impression that one set of skills, and the people who have them, are more valuable or important than other skills and people. But this is exactly what our unintentionally destructive, competitive education system does. We implicitly honor and elevate skills that benefit business and other segments of society, while implicitly demeaning or devaluing other skills, and the people who have them.

Competitive grading is bad enough. But the takeover of public education by the private sector is far worse. As discussed in the Privatization section, the profit motive is incompatible with effectively educating children. Continued privatization, standardization and implementation of business-like measurement and ranking processes will create the same disaster in the education area that we have in the healthcare area. The well-being of children and society demands that we reverse the private sector takeover of public education. Children are not machines that can be measured and managed through mechanized, standardized processes. Once privatization of public education is reversed, we can begin to phase out competitive grading and replace it with far more effective and beneficial assessment processes.

The most important aspects of humans are qualitative, not quantitative. Qualitative aspects, such as self-esteem and social skills, often are difficult to measure. They generally cannot be assessed with standardized tests. Proxies sometimes can be used to estimate difficult to measure factors. But generally, the qualitative aspects of humans must be qualitatively assessed by another human, such as a teacher.

Many schools effectively use noncompetitive assessment approaches. Experts often help schools to implement them. An article by Alfie Kohn, called *The Case Against Grades*, describes some of these approaches.[270] One of the most common and effective is to replace letter and number grades with narrative assessments and conferences with students and parents.

Adding comments or narratives to grades frequently does not work. When grades are present, students often ignore comments. When only comments are present, students usually read them. When course grades are required, some teachers use an intermediate approach. Grades are not placed on daily assignments and tests. Only qualitative feedback is provided. In this way, students do not feel judged every day.

Another highly effective strategy discussed by Alfie Kohn involves allowing students to provide input on assessments and grades. For example, teachers often discuss the purpose of assessments and allow students to make suggestions about assessment strategies. This frequently gives them a sense of ownership about the process and greatly increases interest in learning. Also, when course grades are required, teachers sometimes allow students to provide input on what grade they should receive. Many teachers report that students almost always suggest the same grade that teachers would have chosen.[271]

High performing students sometimes do not like the elimination of competitive grading. This takes away their opportunity to beat other students in class. However, over time, they usually adapt and learn more because the pressure of grading is gone.[272]

Some people argue that competitive grading is needed for college admittance. But this often is not true. Many students from grade-free high schools get admitted to colleges based on narrative reports, recommendations, essays and interviews. This material provides a much fuller assessment of students than grade-point averages. Many colleges report that students from grade-free high schools are better prepared for college because they are more motivated and proficient learners.[273] In addition, even if some grading is used in high school to facilitate college admittance, competitive grading is not needed before high school in grades K-8.

Teachers who replace competitive grading with qualitative assessments report many benefits. For example, teacher-student relationships usually improve because the relationships become far less adversarial. For many students, writing ability improves more quickly and lessons are retained longer. Also, many teachers report that students are more enthusiastic about going to school. Instead of being judged, they can enjoy learning in a much lower stress environment.[274]

A book by John Schindler, Ph.D., called *Transformative Classroom Management: Positive Strategies to Engage All Students and Promote a Psychology of Success*, discusses competition and cooperation in the classroom. The book suggests many strategies for implementing more cooperative learning environments, and the large benefits that these approaches provide. Dr. Schindler also discusses how some competition, or at least discussion of competition, in the classroom can be beneficial. It can help young people to more effectively handle competitive situations outside of school.

Dr. Schindler notes, "Students should receive guidance to see that the feelings that competition brings out are normal and predictable but not necessary. Feelings such as worrying about losing, needing to win to feel good about oneself, needing the drama of the competition to feel interested, or being so worried about the outcome that one looses focus on the process are all normal but ultimately dysfunctional habits of mind. We must help students recognize these normal tendencies and replace them with more functional thinking to guide their choices and define their state of mind during a competitive experience."[275]

Robert Brooks, Ph.D., author of *The Self-Esteem Teacher*, is another leader in this field. Dr. Brooks has written extensively about how to establish more cooperative learning environments that promote self-esteem, motivation and resilience in students. He suggests several approaches in an article called *How Can Teachers Foster Self-Esteem in Children?*[276]

To ensure that classrooms are self-esteem enhancing environments, Dr. Brooks states that it is important to recognize that children learn differently. To maximize success, teaching and assessment approaches should be adjusted accordingly and accommodations made, especially for children with learning problems. To manage perceptions that giving easier assignments and assessments to some students is unfair, he advises discussing fairness up front with students. The teacher could explain that some people are better at math, reading or running, for example. People who are skilled in a particular area will have higher goals and expectations.

Dr. Brooks also emphasizes that it is important to give students a sense of ownership, control and responsibility for their success in school. This greatly increases motivation and commitment to learning. To provide a sense of control, if a student is having difficulty learning something, a teacher might ask the student which learning approaches might be most helpful, and then try these approaches. Another option for giving students greater senses of control is to provide, for example, six homework problems, but only require that four be done. This allows students to choose which problems they do.

To improve self-esteem, Dr. Brooks suggests giving students opportunities to contribute or help in some way. For example, older students might read to younger students. Children might care for plants, hang art in school, or paint murals. Teachers also might establish cooperative learning groups. This gives students opportunities to learn teamwork and make a contribution to the group.

Another important action involves minimizing fear and embarrassment resulting from making mistakes. Dr. Brooks suggests discussing this up front with students. Teachers could encourage students to see mistakes as learning opportunities. Also, rules could be established about how teachers and students should respond if a student does not know an answer.

In *The Self-Esteem Teacher*, Dr. Brooks discusses how competitive grading can harm self-esteem and social skills. He emphasizes that self-esteem is enhanced by helping students to find their unique areas of competence, and then helping them to succeed in these areas. As discussed in the Education Solutions section below, instead of degrading self-esteem and social skills through competitive grading, schools should promote the enhancement of these important skills by implementing more social-emotional learning programs.

One of the most empowering, effective and beneficial assessment approaches is to essentially rank students against themselves, rather than other students. To achieve this, teachers work with students to identify desired levels of performance in particular areas, and then help students to improve. How they perform relative to other students largely is irrelevant. The focus should be on ensuring they are improving and attaining competence in key areas. This approach mainly relies on internal motivation, which usually is far more effective than external motivation. (As noted, external motivators such as grades often lower the internal motivation to learn.) This approach frequently is used in adult education classes. Adults often are not ranked against each other. The focus is on ensuring that each student makes progress and attains competency.

Teacher expectations frequently are critical to student learning. Students are much more likely to make progress and attain goals if teachers very clearly let students know that they believe they can succeed. To achieve success, goals must be reasonable and achievable. Teachers should set goals that are appropriate for each student. As Dr. Brooks points out in the above article, this does not require substantial extra work. For example, teachers do not have to develop separate education plans for each student. The most important requirement is that teachers, students and parents understand that each child has strengths and weakness, and then develop common expectations, goals and strategies for achieving goals.

It often is easier to hold all students to the same standard. But this is counterproductive and unfair. Expecting a child with weak math skills and little interest in math to perform at the same level as a child who loves math and does well in it insults and demeans the child with lower math interest and skills. Adjusting expectations and goals based on each child's interests and skills allows them to make progress, successfully achieve goals, and build self-esteem.

Using qualitative, noncompetitive assessment approaches and adjusting individual goals based on student interest and competence often make teaching more difficult. It usually is faster to grade standardized tests. However, cooperative approaches will improve student-teacher relationships and frequently make education more satisfying for teachers and students. In addition to knowledge, effective teaching requires wisdom, compassion and empathy. As noted, caring for our children is the most important obligation of humanity. This makes teaching one of the most important jobs, if not the most important job, in society. Effective education requires ending the business-driven degradation of teachers and teachers unions. We must re-establish honor, dignity and attractive pay and benefits in the teaching profession. We also must ensure that class sizes are small enough so that teachers have enough time to qualitatively assess and assist each student.

Protecting Children

The self-esteem damaging impacts of competitive grading are compounded by the fact that grading occurs over many years during a time when young people's lifelong senses of self-worth are being formed. Many children go through K–12 education with the same students. Year after year, they see the same groups of children getting high, mid-level or low grades. After a while, average or below average students might think, I'm not as smart as the kids who always get good grades. This can strongly condition them to expect and accept less from life.

Competitive grading teaches children that they will be judged throughout life. It frequently creates fear and makes the world seem like a dangerous place. Fear often strongly suppresses rational thought. To feel safe in an unsafe world, people often blindly cling to religious, economic and other dogma. Fear makes people highly vulnerable to deception. They become afraid to question authorities and injustices in society. This helps the small group that controls government and deceives the public about climate change, corporate welfare and other issues. But it severely degrades society.

We must not breed fear into our children through competitive grading. It is wrong to strongly imply that the interests and skills of one child are more important than those of another. A child who loves art and wants to build their life around it should not be made to feel less valuable than a child who loves math and wants to pursue a career in that area.

We have no right to rank our children against each other. Doing this shows the intense stupidity of humanity compared to nature. Implicitly insulting a child's unique skills and interests is unintentionally horrible. Teachers can assess students in ways that provide information for college admittance, for example, but do not degrade self-esteem. A beautiful quote, often attributed to Albert Einstein, shows the irrational and highly destructive nature of competitive grading. "Everybody is a genius. But if you judge a fish by its ability to climb a tree, it will live its whole life believing it is stupid."

By honoring the uniqueness of each child, we will develop freethinking, confident and empowered adults. These young people will expect more from life. They will not settle for less. They will demand that government and the economy serve and benefit all citizens equally and fairly. Empowered young people might pose a threat to the small group of business owners that controls government. But this business group is unintentionally degrading society. For their own good, and the good of all people, we must end business domination of government, education and society. Empowering young people through the elimination of competitive grading is critical to maximizing the well-being of society.

It also ultimately will help to maximize the well-being of business. Eliminating competitive grading will create a more confident and competent pool of potential employees. Enhanced ability to think critically and systemically often will enable these young people to suggest and implement business changes that not only benefit business, but all other stakeholders.

Competitive grading does a poor job of preparing young people for the real world. It degrades self-esteem, social skills, the motivation to learn, the quality of thinking, and many other important factors. Competitive grading definitely is not needed to educate our children. It almost certainly is not possible to maximize the well-being of young people by educating them in competitive grading environments.

Our children are human beings, not machines. We must give them the dignity and respect they deserve by treating them like human beings. The essentially infinitely greater intelligence and wisdom of nature are based on cooperation. To maximize the well-being of children and society, we must eliminate or greatly reduce competitive grading in schools and replace it with wiser, more beneficial assessment approaches.

Boredom

Widespread boredom is a major problem in US education. Boredom greatly suppresses the desire to learn and contributes to psychological problems, including inattention, anxiety, depression and defiance. Several factors cause boredom in US schools, including the basic structure of education. An excellent book by Peter Gray, PhD, called *Free to Learn: Why Unleashing the Instinct to Play Will Make Our Children Happier, More Self-Reliant, and Better Students for Life*, discusses the history of education and problems caused by current education structures, including boredom.[277]

Dr. Gray notes that the current structure of education is not based on scientific assessments of how children learn most effectively. It is based on history. The basic classroom model of education was developed during the Protestant Reformation about 400 to 500 years ago. The approach was intended to teach children the Bible, compel them to believe Scripture without question, and teach them to obey authorities. The top-down approach involved teaching, testing, rewarding and punishing. This classroom model worked well for obedience training and indoctrination (i.e. teaching young people to blindly believe prevailing economic, religious and other ideas). When education was taken over by states and made compulsory, the basic top-down classroom model was retained. Many early founders of schools believed that the purpose of education was to break the will of the child. Willfulness often was seen as sinfulness.

We still use essentially the same basic model of education that was developed during the Protestant Reformation. In his book, Dr. Gray discusses how this approach is nearly the exact opposite of what maximizes learning. People learn most effectively when they are free to explore what interests them. The current approach to education is coercive and severely freedom-restricting. Young people often are forced to study subjects that they find boring and are not allowed to explore areas that they find interesting. This approach to education strongly suppresses curiosity and the desire to learn. Under our antiquated, authoritarian education system, young people frequently see learning as work that should be avoided whenever possible.

In addition to the Protestant Reformation, an excellent article by Marion Brady, called *Ten Things Wrong with What Kids Learn in School*, discusses how the current education system is a legacy of the Industrial Age.[278] He points out that the standardized core curriculum was adopted in the late 1800s. Education was modeled after industrial ideas that were popular at the time. These include the factory system, standardization of parts, mass production, centralized decision making, and passive worker compliance. This basic industrial model of education still is in use today. All children have different skills and interests. But the current factory-like education system largely ignores these differences. Children spend 13 years studying nearly the same standardized curriculum. They are taught to passively obey authorities. This strong suppression of uniqueness and free will severely impedes young people and often makes education extremely boring.

Education reform is making the situation worse. Children frequently are spending more time in school studying core courses and doing more homework. Many studies have shown that children are less happy in school than in any other setting. Unhappiness and negative attitudes towards learning increase as children progress to higher grades. When children report enjoying school, the reason usually is that they enjoy doing well on tests or school is where they see their friends.[279]

Flawed systems are another major cause of boredom in the education area. As discussed, our flawed economic and political systems make economic growth and shareholder returns more important than any other factor in society. This directly and indirectly creates many problems, including frequently high levels of boredom in workplaces, schools and society in general. The structural requirement to provide ever-increasing shareholder returns often compels companies to reduce employee wages, benefits and any other factor that threatens returns. Over time, employees frequently are required to do more work for less pay and benefits. Practices that make workplaces more enjoyable and fulfilling often are reduced. These include flexible work hours, freedom to deal with important family issues during work, team-building exercises, company-sponsored leisure events during and after work hours, customizing work based on employee interests, company-sponsored volunteering opportunities to help communities and schools, and funding of employee education and development.

Unnecessary job scarcity enables companies to force employees to endure more difficult and boring work environments. Suppression of unions, wages, benefits and labor in general since the 1980s frequently has increased boredom in the workplace.

Growing boredom in the workplace coincided with growing boredom in schools. The increased emphasis on standardized testing of core subjects often reduced many interesting and enjoyable activities, and thereby made schools more boring. As discussed, the emphasis on competitive grading increases boredom by lowering the internal motivation to learn. Competitive grading further increases boredom by shifting the emphasis of schools from learning to judgment. Young people who do well on tests might find beating other students interesting and enjoyable. But the majority of students receive average or below-average grades. Consistently being ranked average or below average relative to peers is not fun. It often makes school boring and depressing.

From a big picture perspective, the overall structure of education greatly increases boredom among young people. Throughout human history, children usually learned skills needed for survival from parents. They frequently learned by moving around and doing tasks. They mostly did not learn by sitting still while an adult talked to them. Children naturally have high energy levels. Humans evolved to be moving around and often playing while young. They did not evolve to sit in classrooms for 30 or more hours per week.

In some ways, schools appear to be designed to benefit adults, not children. Sending children off to school for most of the workday enables parents to work, usually away from home. In K-12 education, children often spend over 15,000 hours in school over a period of 13 years. Much of the information they learn is quickly forgotten and never needed in life. Most of what people need to know for work, for example, often is learned on the job.

Children probably do not need to spend anywhere near 35 hours per week in school for 12 years. The material they will need for success as adults probably could be taught in far fewer hours. In many ways, it appears that schools are being used as babysitters. Children apparently are being sequestered away from home for many more hours than actually are needed to learn necessary information. In other words, required time in schools seems to be expanded for the convenience of adults and the economy. Spending more time than is necessary in school can make schools boring.

Placing young people in boring educational settings can benefit vested interests. Our suicidal economic and political systems make financial returns to a small group of wealthy citizens more important than all else, including the survival of humanity. Creating work environments where adults are forced to work long, boring, difficult jobs to survive helps to maximize shareholder returns. Forcing children to spend seven hours per day in often boring educational settings strongly conditions them to tolerate boring jobs for the rest of their lives.

There almost certainly is no conscious effort to make education boring so that children will tolerate boring jobs later in life. Boring jobs largely result from the grossly flawed requirement to put the financial well-being of shareholders ahead of labor and all other stakeholders. Boring education partly results from the need to keep children away from home for long hours so that parents can work.

Education reform in the US often seems to have greatly increased boredom in schools. Declining school budgets and the increased focus on core subjects caused many schools to substantially reduce physical education, vocational classes, art, music, liberal arts, shop, home economics, team sports, recess and many other non-core subjects, classes and activities. These subjects often provide a more well-rounded, interesting and useful education.

One of the most damaging aspects of educational reform has been reduced physical education classes. In 1992, about 42 percent of public school students attended daily physical education classes. In 2012, only four percent of elementary schools, eight percent of middle schools and two percent of high schools provided daily physical education classes.[280] Incorporating physical activity into education is highly beneficial. Physical health is critical for life success. Providing opportunities for children to be physically active every day helps to build lifelong healthy habits and strongly counteracts growing childhood obesity. Physical education and activity helps children to burn off their naturally high energy. This helps them to focus better in classes. Several studies have shown that regular physical education classes improve academic performance.[281] Physical education also makes school far more enjoyable for many young people.

Music, art, shop and other creative, hands-on courses also make schools more interesting. These classes tend to develop the more creative right side of the brain, whereas core subjects often develop the more analytic left-brain. Providing a balanced curriculum relieves boredom in school and better prepares children for creative problem solving and other life needs.

Cutting vocational education also can increase boredom and degrade society. Vocational education supports and strengthens the middle class. It provides training for young people who want to become technicians, mechanics, craftsmen, service providers and small business owners. Reducing this type of education can make school boring for young people who are most interested in these areas.

Cutting liberal arts classes also can increase boredom in schools. As discussed in the Authoritarianism section, liberal arts classes open young people's minds and strongly promote the development of critical, big picture thinking. Standardized testing of core subjects, on the other hand, often promotes boredom. Preparing for these tests frequently involves memorizing information that will not be needed later in life. Teaching this information also often is boring for teachers.

Technology can further increase boredom inside and outside of school. As discussed, young people watch screens (TVs, computers, cell phones) for an average of eight hours per day (excluding school use). In 2010, children sent an average of 3,300 text messages per month and had an average of 440 friends on Facebook.[282] Both inside and outside of school, it often would be more interesting and beneficial to read books or engage with the real world, rather than staring at screens and interacting with the cyberworld.

Increased online education also often makes school boring. Teaching children with computers instead of human beings helps for-profit schools to make more money. It also helps public schools to deal with reduced funding. But as discussed above and below, students are complex human beings. They are not machines that can be taught by machines. Forcing students to stare at computers and attempt to learn from them frequently is boring and ineffective.

Conditioning children to sit still in class for many hours each day, listen to adults talk to them or stare at computers, and resist their natural inclination to move around and learn by doing is a form of behavior modification. Using rewards such as grades to motivate behavior works better when people are bored. When one examines the actual processes and outcomes of US publicly funded education, it can appear that the main purpose is behavior modification, indoctrination and obedience training, not learning. This should not be surprising because the top-down classroom model being used to educate our children was developed for these purposes.

Forcing students to mainly study core subjects, and then judging and ranking them on performance, often makes school boring. Children effectively are being conditioned to endure tedium and obey authorities. Businesses frequently view labor as units of production, rather than human beings. Current education systems condition young people to be compliant workers who will not expect much satisfaction from work. When the focus of society is on maximizing the well-being of business, this strategy might appear to be logical. But this should not be the focus of society.

In addition to being boring, Dr. Bruce Levine points out that traditional competitive education causes many psychological problems among children and teenagers.[283] Young people often are forced to study subjects that they find boring, do homework that appears to have little value, and spend much of their waking lives in buildings that seem sterile and suffocating. Some students believe authorities who say they will be unsuccessful in life if they do not do well in school. As a result, they often become depressed or anxious. Other students rebel against coercive and boring education. As discussed in the Psychiatric Drugs section below, when our boring and coercive education system causes students be inattentive, depressed, anxious or defiant, they frequently are labeled mentally ill and prescribed powerful, mind-altering drugs. But in reality, these young people usually are displaying normal responses to our grossly flawed education systems.

As citizens regain control of government and society, we can make changes that greatly relieve boredom in work, school and society in general. For example, economic changes discussed above can virtually eliminate job scarcity and thereby greatly reduce fear of survival. Sustainable business structures can be implemented that focus on the well-being of all stakeholders, including employees. This will greatly increase job satisfaction.

Many changes can be made in the education area to reduce boredom and greatly enhance the education experience. For example, schools should not be used as babysitters for young people. Children should not be forced to sit for much of the day and listen to adults talk to them. Few adults would want to do this. Instead, young people should be given more opportunities to utilize their natural inclination to learn by doing. Increased activities might include hands-on learning and exploration in nature, working on farms, volunteering and doing community service.

Activities in school should develop the body and whole mind. Physical education classes are very important. Daily physical education and exercise should be required in K-12 grades. Recess also is critical. Children are the same as adults in this area. After a lecture or class, people need time to process information. Recess is children's free time. It helps them to develop communication and cooperation skills. It balances time in class. Under education reform, many schools eliminated recess. This is extremely unwise. Schools in Japan provide ten minutes of free time for every 50 minutes in class.[284] US schools should have similar adequate recess time.

A report by the Institute of Medicine recommended that children in all K-12 grades be required to take physical education classes every day. In addition, students should engage in daily moderate to vigorous physical activity during recess, in classrooms and after school. For example, teachers should organize classroom activity that requires students to get up and move. The report found that children who are more active pay better attention, process information faster, and do better on standardized tests than children who are less active. The report recommended that physical education be made a core subject and that federal and state governments adopt policies that promote physical education, recess and after school sports and other activities. Taking away recess or other physical activity should not be used as a form of punishment because this often will make children more disruptive, inattentive and hyperactive.[285]

To further relieve boredom in schools, the emphasis on core subjects should be reversed. Liberal arts, vocational classes, art, music, shop, home economics and other non-core classes should be restored. These classes develop the whole mind and make the educational experience more interesting. They also often provide more practical and useful preparation for life. For example, most people will not need to do advanced math or science calculations as adults. However, it would benefit nearly everyone to know how to make basic repairs around the home, prepare a meal, effectively participate on a team, write an interesting note or report, and critically and creatively analyze ideas.

Ironically, scaling back the focus on core subjects probably often will improve performance in these areas. Overemphasizing standardized testing of core subjects frequently makes school boring. This often makes it difficult for young people to concentrate on core subjects and learn them well. Increasing physical education, free time and creative, non-core subjects will relax students and open their minds. This frequently will enable young people to learn core subjects more effectively, even if they are spending less time on them. The Emulate Finland section below illustrates how children and teenagers in Finland achieve world-leading performance on standardized tests while spending less time in school, doing less homework, and having a more balanced, compassionate and physically active curriculum.

Spending 35 hours per week in school does not have to be boring. As discussed below, many excellent schools provide well-balanced education that develops the body and whole mind. Spending most of the day studying core subjects can be boring. But if this is balanced with creative right-brain courses and activities, liberal arts, physical education, more hands-on learning, and more learning and other activities outside of school, education can be far more beneficial and fun.

Education follows society. Currently, US education prepares children for our business-dominated society. But this should not be the goal of education. The goal should be to maximize the well-being of young people and society. We have an obligation to ensure that education is interesting, empowering, practical and well-balanced. This will produce wise, empowered adults who help to resolve the great challenges facing humanity.

Psychiatric Drugs

Widespread use of psychiatric drugs represents a tragic, major problem in education and child rearing in general. The ongoing transfer of wealth from social welfare to corporate welfare causes the US to have a weaker social safety net than most other developed countries. It also makes life increasingly difficult for millions of citizens. This contributes to the US having among the highest rates of depression and other mental disorders in the world.

Increasingly difficult living conditions strongly contribute to high growth in psychiatric drug sales. US sales of these drugs in 2008 were over $40 billion (antipsychotics $15 billion, anticonvulsants/mood stabilizers $11 billion, antidepressants $10 billion, stimulants and other ADHD drugs $5 billion).[286] Children and adults are prescribed psychiatric drugs to a much greater degree than in most other countries. The US has the highest rates of illegal and prescription drug use in the world.[287] More than eight million children and teenagers between the ages of 2 and 18 years old take psychiatric drugs in the US.[288]

Millions of children are taking psychiatric drugs because they are depressed, hyperactive or not paying attention well enough. But a large percentage of these symptoms almost certainly result from our grossly flawed education system, rather than from brain chemical imbalances or other neurological problems. The flawed nature of education reform is causing increased psychological problems in children. Cutting physical education and recess can make it difficult for children to burn off their naturally high-energy. This could cause them to be hyperactive or inattentive in class. Cutting liberal arts, creative and hands-on courses, and increasing core courses can make school boring. Placing children in environments where they are constantly judged and frequently found to be inadequate can be depressing.

Education reform is making schools more factory-like. Children are expected to sit for extended periods of time, absorb information quickly, and rapidly comply with teacher instructions. Many children naturally are unable to do this at various stages of development.[289] Few adults would want to sit still for many hours every day and listen to teachers talk. Boredom, difficulty paying attention and unhappiness are natural, normal responses to our flawed, judgmental, factory-like education system.

The implied goal of the system largely appears to be preparing children to work in business and the economy. This partly requires that children be compliant and able to tolerate tedium. From this perspective, it might seem logical to attempt to change children with powerful psychiatric drugs, rather than change the education system. However, if the actual goal of our education system were to maximize the well-being of children and society, we would implement a system that develops the bodies and whole minds of children. This type of education system would be varied, stimulating, interesting and engaging. As a result, children would be far less bored, inattentive, depressed and hyperactive.

As discussed throughout this section, psychiatric drugs are greatly overprescribed in the US. Business influence of government and doctors are main causes of overprescription. Government is supposed to protect society, in part by prohibiting harmful or unnecessary use of psychiatric and other drugs. But drug companies give large amounts of money to politicians, rotate employees in out of regulatory roles, and inappropriately influence government in other ways. This often compels politicians and regulators to focus primarily on helping drug companies to earn ever-increasing shareholder returns, in part by allowing widespread psychiatric drug use.

Doctors are trained to first do no harm. They often take an oath to abide by this principle. But as discussed in the Food section, drug companies heavily influence doctors, medical education and the healthcare sector in general. They also strongly influence drug research and information provided to doctors and other healthcare professionals. One review found that only 51 percent of studies reviewed by the FDA found antidepressants to be effective. But 94 percent of studies published in medical journals showed them to be effective.[290] Actions such as these can mislead doctors into believing that psychiatric drugs are more effective and less harmful than they actually are.

In addition, drug companies provide extensive financial and nonfinancial support and inducements to doctors. This can cause them to overprescribe psychiatric drugs. One study found that doctors who accepted payments from drug companies were five times more likely to prescribe drugs to children than doctors who did not accept such payments.[291]

The concept of first do no harm implies that doctors should be biased towards initially suggesting the least risky treatments. Psychiatric drugs often have severe side effects, increased death risks, and usually unknown but probably substantial long-term negative impacts. Prescribing psychiatric drugs frequently is the most risky option and should be seen as a last resort. But doctors often are misled or induced into quickly prescribing them (i.e. using them as the first or preferred treatment option).

Inappropriate business influence strongly interferes with the ability of government and doctors to protect public health and well-being. In the psychiatric drug area, as in nearly every other business sector in the US, the fox is watching the henhouse. This situation is tragic. Our defenseless children pay a huge price for overprescription of psychiatric drugs.

This section discusses the complexity of the mind, problems with the current method of diagnosing mental disorders, harm caused by widespread use of psychiatric drugs, factors driving high growth in psychiatric drug use, and alternative approaches for diagnosing and addressing psychological problems.

Complexity and Lack of Knowledge

The fields of psychology and psychiatry are highly complex. They contain vast areas of uncertainty. The brain/mind is by far the most complex and least understood part of the human body. Substantial advances have been made in brain research. Scientists have identified which parts of the brain are associated with various thoughts, emotions and actions. Researchers also have evidence of how activities such as meditation, problem solving and being in relationships can cause connections to form in the brain and presumably strengthen the mind.

However, while we know a lot about the brain and mind, compared to all there is to know, we know almost nothing. To illustrate, key questions that are not fully or clearly answered include, what is a thought? Is it only an electrical impulse? Is there a nonphysical component? Where are thoughts stored? When someone forgets something, is the thought still physically present, perhaps like a file stored on a computer chip?

Many factors indicate that the mind might extend beyond the body. There are strong indications that thoughts or ideas exist outside the brain and can be picked up by the brain, like an antenna receiving a signal. Carl Jung and others wrote extensively about the collective unconscious. Case studies and extensive ESP research indicate that humans can receive ideas from outside the brain. Many people have experiences which indicate that thoughts are not restricted to the brain, such as thinking of someone and the phone rings or immediately knowing that a loved one has been hurt. Quantum physics shows that one particle can influence separate particles. All of these factors indicate that separate objects can communicate in ways that appear to be nonphysical through mechanisms that humans do not fully understand.

Belief in God further indicates this phenomenon. The large majority of people in the world believe that God or some type of transcendent consciousness exists. This often involves believing that their minds can receive guidance from this source. Many people have had tangible inner experiences that convince them beyond the shadow of a doubt that God or transcendent consciousness exists.

Some people might refuse to acknowledge the possibility that the mind extends beyond the brain or can receive ideas from perhaps nonphysical sources. They might claim that the above phenomena occur only within the brain. But this is impossible to prove. Therefore, stating it as a fact is irrational. Logic requires acknowledging the possibility of phenomena that humans do not fully understand, such as transcendent consciousness or the mind extending beyond the physical brain.

The mind is highly complex and largely unknown. Even if it only resides in the brain, it still largely is unknown. As noted, we cannot locate a particular thought in the brain. Scanners might detect certain parts of the brain reacting to a particular thought. But that does not prove that the thought is stored there. We largely do not know how thoughts are created or stored. The vast uncertainty of psychology causes some people to call the field an art, not science.

Nevertheless, proven useful therapeutic models have been developed over the past 100 years. For example, as discussed in the Hitting Children section, overwhelming research shows that hitting children often causes problems in teenage and adult years. Through psychotherapy, people can bring to consciousness disempowering beliefs that were formed while they were being hit. Once these harmful beliefs are made conscious, people can choose more empowering beliefs and act on them. This frequently alleviates psychological problems and enables people to have more successful and satisfying lives.

Therapeutic processes such as these have been shown to be effective in millions of cases over the past century. But therapy does not work for everyone. This can make psychology seem less scientific. The mind functions through various mechanisms. We know relatively little about them. Various theories and diagnostic processes have been developed that make psychology, psychiatry and the study of the mind in general seem more scientific, credible and reliable.

Brain Chemical Imbalance Theory and Depression

The theory that mental disorders such as depression are caused by brain chemical imbalances is one of the most important theories in the fields of psychology and psychiatry. Psychiatrists (i.e. medical doctors with psychology training, allowed to prescribe drugs) often appear to have a preference for physical or medical explanations or causes of mental disorders. In the 1930s, psychiatrists faced growing competition from psychologists (doctorate in psychology related area, usually not allowed to prescribe drugs), social workers and other nonmedical therapists.[292] Physical treatments, such as drugs and electroshock therapy, help to differentiate psychiatrists from nonmedical practitioners.

The mind is highly complex, largely unknown and difficult to measure. As a result, the field of psychiatry often lacks the high quality research seen in other areas of medicine (i.e. randomized, placebo-controlled, double-blind). This contributes to a US General Accounting Office report finding that psychiatry might be the least respected medical specialty.[293] The brain chemical imbalance theory potentially enhances the credibility of psychiatry by providing a physical explanation for mental disorders.

The use of psychiatric drugs substantially increased in the 1960s, in part because safer drugs such as Valium were developed and amphetamines were approved for use with children.[294] To justify rapidly growing use of psychiatric drugs, drug companies and other parties often strongly promoted the brain chemical imbalance theory. The theory states that neurochemical transmitters strongly influence mood and other mental activities. Imbalances in these neurotransmitters can cause mental disorders. Restoring brain chemical imbalances with drugs can alleviate or cure mental disorders, according to the theory.

Over 100 neurotransmitters have been identified.[295] Low levels of two of these chemicals, serotonin and norepinephrine, are alleged to cause depression, for example. Raising the levels of these chemicals with SSRIs (selective serotonin reuptake inhibitors) and SNRIs (serotonin and norepinephrine reuptake inhibitors) theoretically can reduce the symptoms of depression.

But this only is a theory. It is difficult to directly measure neurotransmitter levels in the brain. Techniques such as placing measurement devices in the brain are being developed. Levels of serotonin, for example, can be estimated by measuring byproducts of serotonin breakdown in the blood, urine and cerebrospinal fluid. But more than half of these byproducts come from organs other than the brain. As a result, there are concerns that these brain chemical estimates might be inaccurate.[296]

Depression Research

Antidepressants are the most prescribed drug in the US.[297] About 10 percent of men and 21 percent of women take them. Promoting the idea that brain chemical imbalances cause mental disorders helps drug companies to provide ever-increasing shareholder returns. But this idea only is a theory. No study has proven or strongly indicated that imbalances of serotonin or any other brain chemical causes depression or any other mental disorder.[298] [299] However, many peer-reviewed studies provide evidence which strongly refutes the theory that serotonin imbalances cause depression.[300] The *American Psychiatric Press Textbook of Clinical Psychiatry* calls the link between serotonin deficiency and mental disorders an unconfirmed hypothesis.[301]

In advertising and product descriptions, drug companies often use noncommittal statements which indicate that the link between brain chemical imbalances and mental disorders only is a theory. For example, one advertisement for an antidepressant states, "Depression is a serious medical condition that *may be* due to a chemical imbalance". Another promotion states, "Two neurotransmitters *believed to be* involved in depression are serotonin and norepinephrine." Taking drugs that increase the levels of these chemicals is "*believed to* relieve symptoms of depression over time."[302] [emphasis added] Scientists who receive money from drug companies might 'believe' the brain chemical imbalance theory. But many other scientists do not.

A book by psychology and neuroscience professor Elliott Valenstein, Ph.D., called *Blaming the Brain: The Truth About Drugs and Mental Health*, provides extensive evidence which shows that the brain chemical imbalance theory is simplistic, flawed and inaccurate.[303] For example, Dr. Valenstein provides evidence that strongly refutes the theory that depression is caused by low levels of serotonin and norepinephrine.

He notes that reducing levels of serotonin and norepinephrine does not produce depression in humans. Some drugs that alleviate depression have little or no impact on serotonin and norepinephrine levels. Drugs that increase serotonin and norepinephrine levels, such as amphetamines and cocaine, do not alleviate depression. Some depression patients have low levels of serotonin and norepinephrine. But most do not. A review of several studies found that only about 25 percent of depression patients have low levels of serotonin and norepinephrine. Some depressed patients have high levels of serotonin and norepinephrine. And some people with no history of depression have low levels of serotonin and norepinephrine.[304] These findings strongly indicate that depression is not caused by brain chemical imbalances, or at least not by imbalances of serotonin and norepinephrine.

Drug companies sometimes claim that 80 percent of people with depression can be successfully treated with antidepressants. But these claims are deceptive.[305] The large majority of antidepressant research shows this statement to be false. To protect shareholder returns, drug companies generally do not publish results of clinical trials that find antidepressants to be ineffective. About 40 percent of clinical trials are not published, apparently because they often show antidepressants to be no more effective than placebos.[306]

An excellent book by Dr. Irving Kirsch, called *The Emperors New Drugs: Exploding the Antidepressant Myth*, extensively examines antidepressant research.[307] For example, Dr. Kirsch assessed antidepressant trials reviewed by the FDA. Only 43 percent of trials for the six most popular antidepressants found the drugs to be more effective than placebos. In cases where antidepressants outperformed placebos, the advantage was slight, or as Dr. Kirsch stated, "clinically negligible".[308]

Another review of antidepressant trials submitted to the FDA found that antidepressants outperformed placebos in 51 percent of trials.[309] But these trials usually were influenced by drug companies. They often contained biases that favored antidepressants, such as using inactive placebos. These enable patients to tell that they are not taking real drugs. If biases were removed and true independent research were conducted, probably all or nearly all studies would find antidepressants to be no more effective than placebos.

To promote the idea that antidepressants are effective, drug companies and their allies sometimes reference the STAR*D study. STAR*D was a large study of antidepressant effectiveness in actual clinical practice funded by the US National Institute of Mental Health (NIMH). Depressed patients who were not helped by one type of antidepressant were given up to three other types. The study claims to have achieved a cumulative 67 percent depression remission rate. But many researchers stated that these results were deceptive.

The 67 percent claim did not include depression relapses or patients who dropped out of the study. Also, a more lenient measurement system was applied mid-study and people who were not depressed enough to meet baseline requirements for the study were included in the study. When relapse and dropout rates are included, only three percent of patients who began the study achieved sustained depression remission. In addition, STAR*D did not include a placebo control group. People taking placebos in similar studies attained about the same remission rates as those taking antidepressants in the STAR*D study. Furthermore, several of the researchers in the study had financial ties to the drug companies that sold the antidepressants used in STAR*D.[310]

When published and unpublished antidepressant trials are examined, Dr. Kirsch found that antidepressants are no more effective than placebos. He stated, "All antidepressants, including the well-known SSRIs, had no clinically significant benefit over a placebo."[311] Dr. Kirsch concluded that antidepressants are not effective treatments for depression. He also stated that the idea that depression is caused by brain chemical imbalances is a myth promoted by drug companies and doctors who accept money from them. Ronald Pies, editor of the Psychiatric Times, stated "In truth, the 'chemical imbalance' notion was always a kind of urban legend—never a theory seriously propounded by well-informed psychiatrists."[312]

In general, drug company influence of research is a major problem in the medical and psychological areas. Most clinical drug trials are funded by drug companies. Many studies have shown that drug company funded trials of their own products are much more likely to find favorable results than independent studies.[313] An excellent article by Doctors Amit Shah and Thomas Finucane, called *Commercial Influence of Psychiatric Drug Studies*, described how drug company funded studies often contain biases that favor their drugs. Biases include using doses outside the usual range, altering dosage schedules, using self-serving measurement scales, masking adverse effects, repeatedly publishing positive results, withholding negative results, emphasizing positive but insignificant differences, biased selection of study participants and trial duration, and hiding drug company funding or involvement.[314]

Drug companies often hire marketing companies to help promote their drugs. These companies frequently ghostwrite articles, and then find doctors who agree to be listed as authors. Drug company funded studies, articles and other promotional materials often are heavily marketed to doctors and the general public. Based on frequently conflicting scientific literature, doctors must weigh risks and benefits, and then decide when to prescribe drugs.[315] Since much of the information they review is biased, they often make suboptimal decisions, such as overprescribing antidepressants and other drugs.

Doctors might honestly believe that antidepressants are effective because they see the drugs work for some patients. But these doctors are not conducting research. If they had given their patients convincing placebos, the fake drugs usually would have been equally effective. In addition, doctors often have inaccurate ideas about the safety and effectiveness of antidepressants because drug companies frequently do not publish the many trials that show antidepressants to be ineffective.

A study published in the British Medical Journal found that only one in seven people benefit from antidepressants.[316] The National Institute for Health and Clinical Excellence in the UK has acknowledged the failure of antidepressants to provide clinically meaningful benefits to most depressed patients. As a result, the UK government has implemented plans for providing alternate treatments for depression.[317]

In terms of research, antidepressants and antibiotics are very different. Antibiotics are proven and known to be effective. But this is not the case with antidepressants. The physical causes of depression, assuming there are any, are unknown. We do not know if brain chemical imbalances cause depression, if depression causes brain chemical imbalances, or if the two are unrelated.

Causes of Depression

The brain chemical imbalance theory has been challenged in the scientific community as being simplistic and flawed.[318] But some people defend the theory by saying that no demonstrably superior hypothesis has been discovered. This is deceptive. There is a far more accurate, logical and reliable model for explaining depression and other mental disorders. Depression often is a natural response to life situations. Psychological pain, like physical pain, frequently is a gift. It often signals that there is a problem and changes are needed.

Probably the vast majority of mental illness or mental disorders are caused by past or present life circumstances and the disempowering beliefs that result from them. For example, it is obvious and known that child abuse and other trauma can cause depression, PTSD, anxiety, ADHD and other problems. Hitting children or abusing them in other ways can be particularly harmful because core beliefs and personalities are forming. Unconscious, disempowering beliefs resulting from hitting, such as the belief that one has little value and deserves to be abused, can cause problems later in life.

Flawed economic and political systems are another main cause of depression and other psychological problems. These systems inevitably will cause increasing mental illness and other problems in society. Depression and many other psychological problems are caused in large part by overwhelming emotional pain. Our flawed systems produce widespread, growing pain and life difficulties for millions of citizens. The following summarizes several system flaws and societal problems that create growing emotional pain for many people and strongly contribute to increasing psychological problems.

As discussed extensively, the measured and managed focus of the US economy, government and society essentially is that a small group of wealthy citizens get continuously wealthier. To achieve this, literally trillions of dollars of public wealth essentially are stolen from low, middle and upper-middle-income citizens each year and transferred to this group through many forms of corporate welfare. This transfer or theft is indicated by wide variations in income growth. To illustrate, from 1993 to 2011, income for the top one percent of earners rose by 58 percent, while income for all other citizens rose by only six percent.[319] Transferring public wealth from social welfare to corporate welfare unfairly concentrates wealth and severely degrades the middle class. Healthcare and many other expenses are rising faster than income. As a result, wealth is declining and life is becoming more difficult for millions of US citizens. Several studies have linked declining wealth to increased depression, other psychological problems and suicide.[320]

In addition, as discussed in the Advertising, Media and Culture section, to achieve never-ending growth in sales and profits, companies often bombard citizens with advertising. Advertisements usually contain the emotionally powerful, implied message that people are inadequate without the advertised product. Advertising and other media activities create a strong focus on external factors such as wealth, appearance and possessions. Our advertising and media saturated culture produces widespread senses of emptiness and inadequacy in society.

Growing authoritarianism in the US causes increased intolerance and pressure to conform, often to irrational economic and religious dogma. To keep the people misled and maintain control of government and society, large companies and their media and political allies frequently foment growing division and hatred among conservatives and liberals. In the labor area, the emphasis on never-ending growth of shareholder returns has greatly reduced or eliminated loyalty or commitment to employees. To help wealthy investors make more money, employees often are required to work longer hours for less pay and benefits. The growing degradation of labor causes about 70 percent of US workers to hate, dislike or not feel committed to their jobs.[321]

An increasingly boring and judgmental education system creates widespread dissatisfaction among students. A Gallup poll found that 80 percent of elementary school students felt engaged, committed to or interested in school. This drops to 40 percent by the time students reach high school.[322] As discussed below, reduced funding for public higher education is driving rapid growth in student debt levels. This often forces young people to seek less filling, but higher paying jobs, rather than pursue their unique vocational interests and passions.

Sending jobs overseas and replacing employees with technology is forcing many people onto public assistance and driving increased debt. Financial stress often causes depression. The depression rate among people on public assistance is three times higher than those who are not on it. In addition, people with mental illness are three times more likely to be in debt than those without mental illness.[323] Only about half of the people in the US who need mental health treatment can afford it.[324] Failure to treat mental illness frequently perpetuates and expands it.

Focusing the US economy on the well-being of the small group that is controlling government, instead of the well-being of all citizens, creates high levels of unemployment, especially when discouraged workers are included (i.e. people who are willing and able to work, but have given up looking, often because they cannot find jobs). Unemployment substantially increases the risk of mental illness and suicide. Declining wealth and long-term unemployment have contributed to the US suicide rate rising by 24 percent from 1999 to 2014.[325]

Growing division, anger, intolerance and inadequacy in society, along with spending more time in the cyberworld, are causing more people to feel alienated, isolated and lonely. A study published in the American Sociological Review examined citizens' networks of confidants (close friends or family members who people trust with personal information and use as sounding boards). People with close friends and confidants, friendly neighbors and supportive coworkers are less likely to be depressed or have other psychological problems. In 1985, ten percent of people in the US said that they had no confidants. By 2004, this had risen to 25 percent.[326]

A study of loneliness found that lonely people are nearly twice as likely to die prematurely as those who do not feel isolated. Loneliness can disturb sleep, raise blood pressure and lower immunity. Loneliness often is the core emotion that leads to anger, sadness, worthlessness, resentment, emptiness, vulnerability, pessimism and depression.[327]

Poor marriages or significant relationships, or the absence of significant relationships, are another common cause of depression. Our advertising-driven, selfish, childish, Me-First culture causes many problems in relationships. A study of unhappily married women who were diagnosed with depression found that 60 percent of the women believed that marital discord was the cause of their depression. Hundreds of studies have linked relationship problems to depression. One study found that the best predictor of depression relapse among married people was the response to the question, how critical is your spouse of you?[328] Depression in marriages and significant relationships can create a downward spiral. When a spouse or partner is depressed, the other person often becomes critical or unhappy. This can degrade the relationship and cause worse depression.

An excellent article by Dr. Bruce Levine, called *Why Life in America Can Literally Drive You Insane*, discusses the causes of growing depression and other mental illness in the US.[329] Depression rates are 10 to 20 times higher than they were 50 years ago. Rapid growth in depression contributes to antidepressant use growing by nearly 400 percent over the past 20 years. Antidepressants are the most frequently used class of drugs among 18 to 44-year-old people in the US.[330] As discussed below, a large portion of the growth in mental illness is not actual growth. It results mainly from drug company-influenced over-diagnosis and relabeling of normal behavior as mental illness. However, in addition to false growth, there also is substantial growth in actual mental illness in the US.

Flawed systems are severely degrading society, for example, by stealing citizens' wealth and power. In the past, people often rose up and fought injustice through activism and other efforts. But as discussed in the Privacy section, to protect the status quo of business control of government and corporate welfare, businesses and their allies frequently use influence of government to brutally suppress dissent. The OWS movement could have severely threatened the unjust status quo. As a result, the Patriot Act often was used to spy on, infiltrate and suppress OWS and other activist groups.

These groups mostly were exercising their constitutional right to peacefully protest. But our flawed systems demand that anything which threatens the status quo, including the Constitution, must be suppressed. Business influence of Supreme Court appointments drove the appointment of pro-business justices. This enabled brutal suppression of dissent through rulings that, for example, empowered police officers and jail officials to taser, arrest, incarcerate and conduct body cavity searches on citizens for minor infractions, such as not wearing a seatbelt or not having an audible bell on their bicycles.

Growing authoritarianism, intolerance, division, anger and brutal suppression of dissent prevent many people from fighting injustice and engaging in activism. The injustices, problems and system flaws discussed above, combined with frequent inability to do anything about them, cause many people in the US to feel isolated, helpless, hopeless, afraid, bored and/or dehumanized. These negative emotions strongly drive depression and other psychological problems. Many studies have linked mental illness to problems in society. Dr. Levine says that mental illness sometimes is an unconscious rebellion against growing injustice and oppression.[331]

When people cannot use their negative emotions in a positive, empowered way, for example by engaging in activism, they often turn them inward in a destructive way. For example, people frequently suppress the widespread emptiness and inadequacy caused by our unjust and oppressive society through addictive or compulsive behaviors, such as overeating. In a sense, mental illness is an inner rebellion. People often respond to our increasingly intolerant and oppressive society by becoming depressed, anxious, inattentive or hyperactive.

As discussed in the Authoritarianism section, Dr. Levine points out that coercion is a major cause of mental illness in the US and many other countries. Flawed economic and political systems cause US society to be focused on the well-being of the small group that strongly influences or controls government. To benefit this small group, the large majority of citizens often must be coerced or essentially forced to do things that they do not want to do. For example, millions of people are coerced into taking jobs they do not like to survive. Millions of students are coerced into enduring boring, competitive, demeaning education so that they can survive later in life. The majority-rule political system frequently coerces the minority into tolerating policies and programs that they do not want or support. Advertising often uses emotional dishonesty and manipulation to coerce people into buying things that they do not need.

Once people are coerced, they are much more likely to coerce others who have less power, such as employees, children, students and sometimes spouses. Coercion severely degrades relationships and happiness. Widespread coercion in US society takes away people's freedom. This strongly contributes to depression and other psychological problems.[332]

The above factors strongly indicate that the large majority of depression and other mental disorders are caused by life circumstances and resulting disempowering beliefs. How the mind or brain mediates or processes these life experiences is a separate issue. This mediation or processing is not the actual cause of mental disorders. Life experiences may cause brain chemical imbalances and/or other physical brain/mind changes. This processing of life experience serves as a feedback loop. It sends information back to the person, informing them that changes are needed.

It is grossly oversimplistic to say or imply that brain chemical imbalances are the cause of depression and other mental disorders in most or all cases. This ignores reality. It ignores the overwhelmingly obvious fact that life experiences affect people and cause psychological problems. Negative life experiences often cause negative psychological effects.

When a phone rings, people often pick it up and speak. Using brain chemical imbalance logic, one might say that hand movement (i.e. picking up the phone) caused someone to be speaking on the phone. But this is simplistic and shortsighted. The phone ringing was the main cause. Hand movement was a mediating factor or proximate cause. However, this example is simplistic because hand movement is known to be the mediating or proximate cause of being on the phone. But it is not known if brain chemical imbalances are mediating or proximate causes of depression or other mental disorders.

We can be highly certain or nearly positive that life circumstances and resulting disempowering beliefs are the actual cause of depression and many other mental disorders in most, if not the large majority, of cases. However, we largely do not know the mediating factors or proximate causes of mental disorders because little is known about the mechanics of the brain/mind (compared to all there is to know). Even if brain chemical imbalances are the mediating cause of depression and other mental disorders, trying to adjust brain chemicals without addressing the life circumstances that cause mental disorders can be dangerous and harmful.

The brain or mind is a sensing and processing organ. There are physical, neurological problems, possibly including brain chemical imbalances, which interfere with brain/mind function and cause mental disorders. But the fields of psychology and psychiatry apparently have shifted too far in this direction. Psychology and psychiatry used to function mainly under the much more logical belief that the vast majority of mental disturbances or disorders result from unique combinations of personality, character, upbringing, life experience, beliefs and other nonphysical factors. It was believed that only a small percentage of mental disorders resulted from actual physical neurological problems.[333]

But this has changed. Clients often no longer are seen as active participants in a collaborative process that seeks to achieve increased self-awareness and positive changes in beliefs, attitudes, behaviors and life situations. Instead, people with mental disorders frequently are seen as passive drug takers. This implies that mental disorders are not caused by psychological or social factors. Rather they are caused by genetic or other physical conditions that possibly cannot be changed, but can be managed with drugs. The widespread apparent abandonment of the obviously superior and more logical psychological model of mental disorders for the simplistic, reality-ignoring, unproven brain chemical imbalance theory is truly tragic, especially for children.

Adverse Effects of Antidepressants

As indicated by antidepressant research, the benefits of psychiatric drugs often are uncertain, but the harm caused by them frequently is well known. Psychiatric drugs often cause severe side effects. To illustrate, the adverse or side effects of antidepressants include sexual dysfunction, dry mouth, jitteriness, nausea, headaches, sweating, dizziness, lethargy, weight gain and inability to sleep. Antidepressants also can cause anxiety, agitation and mania. As discussed below, antidepressant side effects such as mania can lead to diagnosis and treatment for more severe psychological problems, such as bipolar disorder.[334]

Antidepressants also potentially can harm unborn children. One study found that women who took antidepressants in the last six months of pregnancy were 87 percent more likely to have a child later diagnosed with autism. Women who took more than one type of drug to treat depression were 400 percent more likely to give birth to an autistic child. Taking antidepressants increases the risk that women will give birth prematurely. Premature birth is a known risk factor for autism.[335]

Regarding sexual dysfunction, loss of interest in pleasurable activities such as sex is one symptom of depression. Therefore, drugs that reduce interest in sex potentially should not be called antidepressants (because they exacerbate a characteristic of depression, rather than relieve it). Antidepressant manufacturers often estimate that 2 to 16 percent of antidepressant users experience sexual dysfunction. But several studies found that about 60 percent of men and women experience it, including loss of sexual desire, inability of have an orgasm or erectile dysfunction. Antidepressant trials show that 30 to 40 percent of people get relief from depression (about the same percentage as those taking placebos). Some researchers have argued that the name antidepressant is misleading. If antidepressants cause sexual dysfunction in 60 percent of people, but relieve depression in less than 40 percent, the drugs might be more accurately named anti-aphrodisiacs.[336]

Antidepressants also often increase the risk of violent behavior. As a result of this and other negative impacts, antidepressant use by children has been restricted in the UK since 2003. But the business-dominated US government still allows extensive antidepressant use among children. In about 90 percent of school shootings in the US, the young people who killed others and sometimes themselves were taking psychiatric drugs. These drugs can make children more hostile and aggressive.[337] They often apparently are making children and adults worse, not better.

Suicidal thoughts and suicide attempts are symptoms of more severe depression. As with sexual dysfunction, drugs that increase the risk of suicide potentially should not be called antidepressants. An FDA analysis of antidepressant trials found that people taking antidepressants were twice as likely as those taking placebos to have suicidal thoughts or attempts (i.e. two percent of people taking placebos and four percent of those taking antidepressants experienced suicidal thoughts or attempted suicide). Antidepressants should lower the risk of suicide. If they increase the risk even slightly, the drugs perhaps should not be called antidepressants.[338] The FDA issues a black box warning that antidepressants increase suicide risk among people under the age of 25.[339]

Several factors could cause antidepressants to increase suicide risk. For example, psychological pain can be a life-enhancing gift. It often results from disempowering beliefs or unsatisfying jobs or relationships. When drugs numb this pain, people frequently no longer get the gift or message that it was trying to deliver. As a result, the actual cause of depression or other mental disorders is not addressed. As the old saying goes, when the messenger knocks, if someone does not answer, the messenger knocks louder the next time. One possible reason that antidepressants increased suicide risk is that psychiatric drugs can take away pain and motivation to change or solve problems. As the actual causes of depression are ignored, life can get worse. This can increase suicide risk.

Several studies have shown that antidepressants increase, rather than reduce, long-term depression. This should not be surprising. Bathing the brain in strong chemicals that are not meant to be there could cause long-term negative cognitive, emotional and other impacts. An NIMH study found that patients who take tricyclic antidepressants were more likely to have depression relapses than patients who took placebos.[340] A World Health Organization study found that long-term antidepressant use is associated with higher rates of long-term depression. Many studies have shown that people who stop taking SSRIs often experience worse depression than before they started taking the drugs.[341] SSRIs increase serotonin levels in the brain. The brain quickly compensates by reducing the number of serotonin receptors. As a result, higher dosages often are needed. Several researchers have said that reduced serotonin receptors resulting from long-term antidepressant use could increase vulnerability to depression.[342] This is another mechanism by which antidepressants could increase suicide risk.

In addition to adverse physical effects, antidepressants often cause negative emotional impacts. For example, antidepressants frequently reduce negative and positive emotions. Sadness and anger often are reduced. But excitement, enjoyment, happiness, love, affection, passion and enthusiasm also frequently are lowered. To friends and family, it often appears that people taking antidepressants have changed. Aspects of personality appear to be altered or missing. People on antidepressants frequently are emotionally incomplete, detached or apathetic. They often care less about themselves, other people and responsibilities.[343]

Few, if any, studies have shown that antidepressants, mood stabilizers, antipsychotics or anti-anxiety drugs substantially improve quality of life, mainly because these drugs usually make people numb and apathetic. People taking these drugs experience less unhappiness. But they also experience less happiness. Emotional highs and lows are removed. People frequently become shadows of their non-medicated selves.

Inducing a detached, emotionless and/or apathetic state is not a cure. It also usually would not be considered beneficial. Only in limited cases would this effect be helpful, such as in relieving extreme distress or preventing harm to self or others. Even among patients whose depression was reduced or relieved by antidepressants, one study found that nearly half of the patients said that they would not take antidepressants again due to unwanted psychological side effects such as narrowing of affect, not feeling like oneself, loss of creativity, and inability to cry or feel other emotions.[344]

The Placebo Effect and Beliefs

Placebo results in antidepressant and other psychiatric drug research strongly indicate one of the most important and empowering aspects of psychology – psychological problems mainly are caused by disempowering beliefs.

Researchers often use placebo-controlled studies to determine the benefits of drugs or other treatments. People sometimes heal on their own. Also, the belief that one is receiving a beneficial treatment sometimes promotes healing. In other words, expectations or the power of the mind causes healing. This response is called the placebo effect. Placebo-controlled studies frequently separate actual healing caused by drugs (drug group) from healing caused by expectations (placebo group) and natural recovery (no treatment group). Drugs often are considered to be effective if they substantially outperform placebos. As discussed, nearly all antidepressant research shows placebos to be as effective or nearly as effective as antidepressants. This strongly indicates or virtually proves that nearly all of the benefit of antidepressants results from the placebo effect (i.e. the expectation that drugs will be effective), rather than from the chemical effect of the drugs.

This is logical when one considers the characteristics of depression. Dr. Kirsch notes that clinical depression often is debilitating. People with severe depression frequently are unbearably sad and sometimes consider suicide. They often feel worthless, guilty or anxious. Some have insomnia, while others oversleep and have difficulty getting out of bed. Some people with depression have difficulty concentrating or lose interest in activities that once were pleasurable or meaningful. Hopelessness is one of the most important characteristics of depression. Depressed people frequently doubt that they can or will recover from depression. This often causes them to feel that life is not worth living.[345]

Relieving the sense of hopelessness is a critical component of effectively treating depression. Drugs and convincing placebos (i.e. drugs that patients believe are real) can provide hope that recovery from depression is possible. Virtually any treatment for depression, including false treatments, can work if people believe they will. Faith, belief, trust or expectations that depression treatments will work often cause the treatments to be effective.

In some studies, patients do not know if they are getting real drugs or placebos. This can create doubt among all study participants about the effectiveness of the treatment. This doubt can reduce the percentage of people who get relief from depression, even among people who are taking real drugs. To illustrate the importance of expectations, one study assessed how patient expectations impacted the effectiveness of an experimental antidepressant. Among patients who expected the drug to be very effective, 90 percent had a positive response. But among patients who thought the drug would be moderately effective, only 33 percent responded positively.[346]

As discussed below, many studies have shown that several other types of psychiatric drugs are no more effective than placebos. The effectiveness of placebos strongly indicates that depression and many other psychological problems are not caused by brain chemical imbalances or other physiological or neurological factors. As noted above, the brain/mind is a sensing and processing organ. It responds to life circumstances. Negative past or present life events often produce negative psychological responses and problems.

But life circumstances are not the ultimate cause of psychological problems. The root cause is perceptions or beliefs about life circumstances. All life events ultimately are neutral. We assign the meaning. This meaning ultimately determines the impact an event or life circumstance has on us, not the event itself. Many life events would be extremely difficult to label positive, such as losing a child or being tortured. But even these events ultimately are neutral. This is not intended to condone torture, abuse or other horrible actions. People must protect themselves, for example, by leaving abusive or unhealthy relationships, jobs or other situations. However, once basic safety and other needs are met, beliefs about past negative events can cause psychological problems, such as low self-esteem. These beliefs can be changed. We have the power or free will to interpret anything in a positive way, or at least find meaning in it.

To illustrate, some people are unable to overcome the loss of a loved one or other terrible event. It ruins their lives. But other people, after a period of grief or learning to accept new life circumstances, are able to move on and live successful and satisfying lives. The difference between these people almost certainly is not a brain chemical imbalance or other physical characteristic. The primary difference is their beliefs or evolving interpretations of life.

This illustrates why psychotherapy usually is one of the most effective treatments for depression and other psychological problems. Skilled, compassionate therapists often help clients to better understand conscious and unconscious disempowering beliefs. Once people become aware of disempowering beliefs, such as the belief that they are unworthy and do not deserve a good life, they can choose new, more empowering ones. These usually produce new actions, which in turn produce a more successful and satisfying life.

However, core beliefs often are difficult to change, even when they produce depression and other life problems. People's worldviews and core beliefs about themselves and others are like security blankets. Attempting to change beliefs can produce uncertainty and fear. As a result, many people hang on to disempowering beliefs, even when good therapists help to make them conscious. This is a main reason why psychotherapy does not work for some people. They are not able to honestly admit and change their disempowering beliefs and behaviors.

The knowledge that beliefs about life circumstances largely determine quality of life is highly empowering. People often cannot change other people or past, present or future life circumstances. Sometimes they must remain in jobs they do not like to support their families, for example. But people have the ability to change their beliefs and perceptions about life and themselves. Even if external conditions remain the same, life satisfaction increases when people choose to love and accept themselves as they are, appreciate the good things they already have, and strive to find positive meaning in circumstances they once labeled negative.

As this inner transformation occurs, outer life also often improves. But even if it does not, it frequently does not matter because people are choosing to make the most of what they have. As President Lincoln said, people are about as happy as they choose to be. While it may not be clear at first, depression and other psychological problems mainly result from inner beliefs, choices and perceptions about reality. As people choose to change their beliefs and perceptions, psychological problems often disappear and life improves.

For example, poor relationships are a main cause of depression. But the root cause of depression, and possibly poor relationships, probably nearly always is disempowering beliefs. Our materialistic, advertising driven culture produces widespread senses of emptiness and inadequacy in society. This could cause people to believe at a deep, unconscious level that they are unworthy and do not deserve to have a good relationship. Hitting children or abusing them in other ways also could cause this sense of unworthiness. People often say that seeing is believing. But the opposite usually is true – believing is seeing. In other words, people use their beliefs to interpret life events. They see what they believe they will see.

To illustrate, someone might unconsciously believe that they are unworthy of a good relationship. Then, when their spouse or partner makes a mistake, they interpret it as confirmation that the person does not love them. This could cause overreaction, which in turn could cause stress and problems in relationships. In other words, the belief that one does not deserve a good relationship becomes a self-fulfilling prophecy. As the relationship gets worse, depression can increase.

Through psychotherapy or other acts of self-honesty, people can become aware of disempowering beliefs. This enables them to choose and act on more empowering ones, such as the idea that all people are inherently good and worthy of good lives. As self-esteem improves, people are able to see life more objectively. A mistake made by their spouse simply is a mistake, rather than a confirmation of unworthiness. People stop irrationally expecting others to be perfect or selfishly expecting spouses to make them happy. Growing self-esteem enables people to accept imperfection in themselves and others. It also better enables them to appreciate the good things they have in relationships and other areas. This can heal depression and improve relationships. It also can empower people to leave an abusive or otherwise inappropriate relationship.

Taking antidepressants and other psychiatric drugs often is like trying to turn on the air conditioning in a burning house. One says, I feel hot. I must find a way to cool down. In the same way, people taking antidepressants essentially are saying, I feel depressed. I must take something to relieve my depression. The person in the burning house should look around, see why they feel hot, and exit the house. It often is the same with depression and other psychological problems. Depression does not just show up with no cause. Resolving psychological problems usually requires identifying the actual cause, and then doing something about it, such as changing beliefs and life situations when possible.

Placebos often work for psychological, nonphysical problems because they change beliefs – the ultimate cause of probably nearly all psychological problems. The former belief was hopelessness (i.e. depression will not end). The new belief is hope (i.e. I can change, depression will end, life will improve). Placebos also often work for physical problems. This shows the power of the mind. A positive attitude can promote physical healing. But it especially promotes non-physical, psychological healing. Psychological problems mainly result from disempowering beliefs. Therefore, changing them, and the actions caused by them, frequently resolves psychological problems.

Public Deception

Public deception is a major issue in the psychiatric drug area. Millions of citizens have been misled into believing that antidepressants and other psychiatric drugs are safer and more effective than they actually are. This deception causes extensive overprescription of psychiatric drugs.

The brain chemical imbalance theory is one of the most deceptive aspects of psychiatry. Many citizens have been misled into believing that the theory is proven and valid. This facilitates the more important public perception that many or most psychological problems are caused by physical factors, such as brain chemical imbalances, and therefore can be effectively treated with physical solutions, such as psychiatric drugs.

But the brain chemical imbalance theory is simplistic and unproven. Extensive research strongly indicates that depression is not caused by brain chemical imbalances and not effectively treated with antidepressants. If the brain chemical imbalance theory were valid and antidepressants were effective, the drugs would substantially outperform placebos. But they do not.

Factors causing overprescription of psychiatric drugs are discussed in the following sections. Regarding public deception, issues that mislead the public and promote overprescription relate to drug company influence, the vulnerability of people with psychological problems, inadequate drug trials, 'treatment resistance', and risk-benefit profiles of psychiatric drugs.

Drug Company Influence. This is a major factor causing public deception and overprescription of psychiatric drugs. These drugs provide billions of dollars of revenue for drug companies. The companies often give money, stock options, vacations and other financial and nonfinancial inducements to doctors. Many studies show that doctors who receive more attention from drug company representatives and more money from drug companies prescribe more drugs. Business control of government frequently makes the FDA the ally of drug companies in promoting widespread psychiatric drug use.

Vulnerability of People with Psychological Problems. This is one of the most tragic reasons for widespread psychiatric drug use. Several studies have shown that people who are depressed or have other mental disorders are highly vulnerable to drug company marketing.[347] As a result, all countries, except New Zealand and the US, prohibit direct-to-consumer marketing of prescription drugs. People who are suffering often want an easy way out. Taking a pill usually is much easier than getting honest with oneself and changing beliefs and life situations. Citizens also frequently prefer taking drugs because this implies that they have a physical rather than psychological problem. People with psychological problems often are stigmatized. The stigma frequently is lower with physical problems.

Citizens are vulnerable to doctors. People often trust expert medical advice. But doctors are humans, not gods. They mostly know what they learn from medical school, ongoing education, drug and other studies, and experience treating patients. Drug companies heavily influence medical education and drug research. This often causes doctors to be biased toward drug use. They also frequently are biased because they can make more money by prescribing psychiatric drugs than providing psychotherapy.

In addition to knowing what they are taught, doctors know what they experience. But experience with psychological problems often is much different than experience with physical problems. With physical problems, doctors frequently can run tests to ensure that problems actually are resolved. However, psychiatrists often do not know the cause of mental disorders and frequently cannot confirm that they have been resolved. It is not possible to directly and accurately measure brain chemical imbalances. As discussed below, there are no clinical tests for any mental disorder. They are diagnosed through opinion. (One could say that mental disorders are diagnosed through expert opinions. This is true in one sense, but misleading in another. Even experts know nearly nothing about the mind, compared to all there is to know. In this sense, there are no experts on the mind.)

To illustrate the difficulty of assessing treatment effectiveness, a patient might take psychiatric drugs and report that they feel less depressed. But the drugs might be suppressing negative emotions caused by life circumstances. This could remove or weaken motivation to effectively address the actual causes of depression. As these causes are ignored, the person's life probably will get worse over time. In these cases, psychiatric drugs are like the temporary high that people get from taking illegal drugs. The good feeling only is temporary because real problems are not addressed.

Inadequate Drug Trials. This also can promote public deception and overprescription of psychiatric drugs. The multi-step FDA drug approval process can take several years. But actual clinical trials (i.e. Phase 1, 2 and 3 trials) often last for only a few months or up to a year.[348][349] However, most psychiatric conditions are long-lasting. As a result, the effectiveness of treatments should be assessed over the long-term. Short-term drug studies might find that some psychiatric drugs provide statistically significant benefits compared to placebos. While the benefits might be statistically significant, they frequently are clinically irrelevant. An apparent short-term benefit often is largely irrelevant to solving a long-term problem. Clinically relevant drug studies would show that psychiatric drugs relieve or solve psychological problems over the long-term.

But the effectiveness of psychiatric drugs usually declines over time. Many psychiatric drugs become ineffective within one year. Requiring clinically relevant drug studies (i.e. studies that show long-term safety and effectiveness) would severely inhibit psychiatric drug sales. This might be one reason why the heavily business-influenced FDA rarely, if ever, requires proof that psychiatric drugs are safe and effective over the long-term. (One might argue that providing short-term benefits, such as symptom suppression, is clinically relevant. This depends on perspective. If the goal is short-term symptom suppression, this result is relevant. But if the goal is actually resolving psychological problems, short-term symptom suppression, especially when accompanied by adverse effects, is less relevant.)

The emphasis on short-term drug trials in the psychiatric drug area is extremely misleading. As noted, the studies largely are irrelevant from a clinical perspective (i.e. they do not assess whether drugs actually are solving psychological problems). Psychiatric drugs often suppress psychological symptoms. But this does not cure psychological problems, mainly because it does not address causes. Suppressing symptoms frequently makes psychological problems worse over the long-term because actual causes are ignored and psychiatric drugs have many adverse effects.

'Treatment Resistance'. Deceptive descriptions of ineffective drug treatments also facilitate overprescription. When mental disorders are not relieved by psychiatric drugs, patients often are labeled 'treatment-resistant'. This is the type of terminology one would expect from a mental health industry that is heavily dominated by drug companies. Treatment-resistant implies that patients need more, different and/or stronger drugs. However, instead of using the drug company-biased term treatment-resistant, a reality-based system that was focused on the well-being of patients might use the more accurate and honest terminology 'drug treatment not working'.

As discussed above, the reason that most psychiatric drugs are ineffective over the long-term is that the large majority of psychological problems are not caused by physical, neurological issues, and therefore do not require a physical, drug solution. Patients nearly always are 'resisting' drug treatments, not because they need more, different and/or stronger drugs, but because they need no drugs. Psychological problems with nonphysical causes (i.e. nearly all psychological problems) require nonphysical (i.e. nondrug) solutions, such as psychotherapy.

Risk-Benefit Profiles of Psychiatric Drugs. Deceptive risk-benefit profiles also strongly promote overprescription. Benefits often are over-emphasized, while risks are under-emphasized. As noted, psychological problems and treatment effectiveness cannot be clinically measured. They are assessed through opinion. Reported benefits might actually be large negatives (i.e. if symptom suppression removes motivation to address actual causes). In addition, psychiatric drugs often do not outperform placebos. This indicates that the benefit does not come from the drug, but rather from the belief that drugs will be effective. Furthermore, the benefits of psychiatric drugs frequently decline quickly, and then disappear.

While the benefits of psychiatric drugs often are limited, short-term and nebulous, the risks and potential harm frequently are substantial or unknown. We largely do not know all the ways that psychiatric drugs affect the over 100 neurotransmitters and other structures of the brain. Psychiatric drugs often cause known severe adverse impacts in the short-term and largely unknown but probably more severe negative impacts in the long-term. Poor risk-benefit profiles frequently make psychiatric drugs not worth taking. The principle of first do no harm strongly indicates that psychiatric drugs usually should only be used as a last resort or not at all in the large majority of cases.

Promoting the brain chemical imbalance theory and use of psychiatric drugs can make the fields of psychology and psychiatry appear to be more credible. But this is a flawed approach. Rather than promoting a simplistic, discredited and in many ways illogical theory, it would be better to admit that we still do not know how much of the mind functions. Admitting uncertainty and lack of knowledge requires courage. While the mechanics of the mind largely are unknown, we have proven effective methods of addressing psychological problems. Many studies have shown that psychotherapy and some alternative treatments are more effective than psychiatric drugs at treating depression and other psychological problems, while causing few or no adverse effects.[350]

Diagnosis of Mental Disorders

Diagnosis of mental disorders can improve the usefulness and credibility of psychology and psychiatry. In the US, the Diagnostic and Statistical Manual of Mental Disorders (DSM) is the primary reference manual used for classifying mental disorders. The World Health Organization publishes a classification system called the International Classification of Diseases (ICD). It is more widely used in Europe and other parts of the world. The latest version of the DSM (DSM-5-TR) uses ICD codes that have been modified for clinical use in the US (ICD-10-CM).

The DSM is used by mental health service providers, researchers, insurance companies, drug companies and regulators. The manual is important because psychiatric diagnoses based on the DSM are used to select treatments, determine eligibility for benefits and services, allocate resources, and guide legal judgments.

The number of mental disorders listed in the DSM has increased substantially since it was first published in 1952. This is a main factor contributing to extensive psychiatric drug use. Widespread drug use helps drug companies. But as discussed below, it harms society in many ways.

This section discusses problems related to current diagnostic strategies and possible alternatives. Problems relate to pathologizing normal human behavior, diagnostic method, drug company influence, and inadequate psychological and psychiatric training of doctors prescribing psychiatric drugs.

Pathologizing Normal Human Behavior

Many feelings and behaviors that once were considered to be normal aspects of character and temperament now are considered to be symptoms of various mental disorders listed in the DSM.[351] The first edition of the DSM (DSM-1) was published in 1952 and listed 106 mental disorders. DSM-2 was published in 1968. It contained 182 mental disorders. DSM-3 was published in 1980 and listed 265 mental disorders. Homosexuality had been listed as a mental disorder in DSM-2. This was dropped in DSM-3, but many new mental disorders were added.[352]

For example, in 1980 at the beginning of deregulation, the mental disorder Oppositional Defiant Disorder (ODD) was created. Symptoms of ODD listed in the DSM include "often actively defies or refuses to comply with adult requests or rules" and "often argues with adults." Teenagers frequently naturally are rebellious or oppositional. They often are attempting to individuate (i.e. separate from parents and establish themselves as independent persons). This is a normal, natural and many would say sometimes necessary process for maintaining mental health and achieving a successful and satisfying life. As discussed in the Authoritarianism section, young people frequently lead or support opposition to unfairness and injustice in society. This occurred, for example, during the 1960s and 1970s antiwar and civil rights protests.

In the early 1980s, business greatly increased its influence of government and drove large shifts of public wealth from social welfare to corporate welfare. Public deception was a primary factor enabling this theft of public wealth. The main deception strategy was to divide society into debating factions, such as conservatives and liberals. Animosity for the other side often suppresses rational thought. Ongoing theft of the people's wealth and power requires blind faith in economic and political dogma, such as the irrational idea that government is the enemy and must be reduced.

In an increasingly authoritarian society that demands unthinking, blind faith adherence to dogma, opposition from young people could be dangerous and destabilizing. As discussed in the Authoritarianism section, young people have been suppressed in many ways under deregulation since the 1980s. The ODD diagnosis provided justification for drugging and suppressing defiant young people. Rebellious people, such as the Founders of the US, often drive the greatest advances of humanity. But these rebels frequently threaten abusive authorities and systems, such as business control of government.

The US education system is severely flawed and getting worse under education reform. It often is natural and healthy for young people to oppose boring, judgmental education. Rather than drugging children so that they tolerate a flawed education system, we should change the system. Rebelliousness once was considered to be a normal part of youth. Pathologizing this normal behavior justifies the use of powerful psychiatric drugs on young people.

Some people might say that logic requires acknowledging that ODD might be an appropriate diagnosis in some cases. But logic does not require this. As discussed below, ODD or any other supposed mental disorder it is not like a medical problem that can be confirmed with physical or clinical tests. The idea that ODD is a mental disorder is an opinion. There is no biological proof that ODD is a mental disorder that actually exists. Many people are naturally oppositional or confrontational. This is an element of their personalities. Their strategy for learning might include questioning or opposing new ideas at first. If the idea can withstand their scrutiny, it might be accepted. Labeling this aspect of personality as a mental illness is not rational.

An ODD diagnosis often is based on observations of oppositional behavior. But this behavior is normal in some people. The supposed mental disorder ODD might not exist in reality. In other words, all ODD diagnoses might be inappropriate because ODD might not be a legitimate mental disorder. Instead, ODD might only be a pejorative way of describing normal behavior. This opinion enables drug companies, psychiatrists and insurance companies to make more money. It also allows school administrators and business-controlled government to suppress youth who question authority.

If excessive oppositional or rebellious behavior is causing problems for young people, action might be needed. But as discussed below, prescribing psychiatric drugs should be the last resort, not the first treatment option. Harmful oppositional behavior with no obvious cause probably results from psychological factors, such as upbringing, or other factors, possibly including diet or a competitive, dehumanizing educational environment like that expanding in the US. It is highly unlikely that the cause is a neurological problem, such as a brain chemical imbalance. Psychiatric drugs can numb young people and force them to be compliant. But this does not address the cause of oppositional behavior. Instead, the actual cause often is ignored. This combined with the common adverse effects of psychiatric drugs can harm young people and make their lives worse.

The ODD diagnosis is particularly problematic. If a young person resists ODD treatment because they believe that their questioning or opposing authority is appropriate (as it would be in many cases), clinicians might consider their resistance to be a confirmation of the ODD diagnosis. Albert Einstein and many other people who made great contributions to humanity probably could have been diagnosed with ODD. Imagine what human society would be like if the minds of these rebellious innovators had been numbed and suppressed with powerful drugs. Some people might find oppositional, defiant or rebellious behavior in young people annoying and difficult to handle. But we should not label this behavior mental illness simply because it is annoying or inconvenient for authorities.

DSM-4 was published in 1994. It listed 297 mental disorders.[353] Expanding the reclassification of behaviors and feelings from normal to mental disorders caused great harm in many cases, for example, by substantially increasing mental illness diagnoses and subsequent psychiatric drug use. To illustrate, over the past 20 years, there has been a tripling of ADHD diagnoses, 20-fold increase in autism diagnoses, and 40-fold increase in childhood bipolar diagnoses.[354] Rapid growth in mental disorder diagnoses has driven high growth in psychiatric drug use.

Published in 2013, DSM-5 further increases mental disorder diagnoses and psychiatric drug use. Professor and psychiatrist Allen Frances, M.D. was the chairman of the DSM-4 taskforce. He expressed grave concerns about DSM-5. Nearly all of the DSM-5 changes loosened the definitions and diagnosis of mental disorders. Dr. Frances stated that this will cause already excessive diagnoses and psychiatric drug use to become even higher. Loosened DSM-5 diagnoses will result in millions more people taking psychiatric drugs.[355]

Many other clinicians and mental health professional organizations strongly questioned or opposed DSM-5. They stated that it often lacked scientific support and even defied common sense.[356] Dr. Frances strongly advises clinicians and prospective patients to be highly skeptical of changes made in DSM-5, especially if the proposed diagnosis involves taking psychiatric drugs.[357]

He provides several examples of unwise changes made in DSM-5. These include the following. DSM-5 lists a new mental disorder called Disruptive Mood Dysregulation Disorder (DMDD). Due partly to the rapid growth of bipolar diagnoses, DSM-5 seeks to provide a less severe diagnosis for moody children. But DMDD often would classify temper tantrums and other normal behavior as a mental disorder. This will further increase psychiatric drug use among children.[358]

Dr. Frances said that loosened diagnostic criteria in DSM-5 will greatly increase childhood and adult ADHD diagnoses. This will increase the use of stimulant drugs for performance enhancement and recreation. It also will expand the already large illegal market for diverted prescription drugs.[359] DSM-5 only requires 5 of 18 symptoms to be present in people over 17 years old for an ADHD diagnosis (six symptoms are required for childhood ADHD diagnoses). Symptom assessment is highly subjective. The listed symptoms are normal behavior for many people. For example, if someone has difficulty with organization, a tendency to lose things, and frequently is forgetful, distracted and inattentive, they could be diagnosed with ADHD under DSM-5. Many people in the US display these and other ADHD 'symptoms' (i.e. normal behaviors) sometimes. Under the subjective DSM-5 criteria, a large percentage of the US population probably could be diagnosed with ADHD.[360]

DSM-4 noted that experiencing symptoms of depression while grieving the loss of a loved one is normal and not a mental disorder. However, DSM-5 calls extended grief after the loss of a loved one Major Depressive Disorder. This will result in many more people taking psychiatric drugs. Grief is a normal, healthy process. It is not a mental disorder. Grief helps people to accept the limitations of life, become resilient and function effectively in society. In other words, grief often is a beneficial, life-enhancing, though painful process. Suppressing grief with drugs can block psychological healing and degrade life over the long-term, as well as produce the severe side effects that often accompany psychiatric drugs.

Minor Neurocognitive Disorder is another new mental disorder listed in DSM-5. It refers to the normal forgetfulness of old age. Dr. Frances noted that the diagnosis will create false positives for people who are not at risk of dementia. There is no treatment for the condition. As a result, diagnosis of the new mental disorder provides no benefit. Instead, it often will create anxiety, which might be treated with psychiatric drugs.

Dr. Frances also said that DSM-5 will obscure the already fuzzy boundary between Generalized Anxiety Disorder and the worries of everyday life. This could create millions of new anxiety patients and expand the already excessive use of anti-anxiety drugs.[361] Under DSM-5, first-time substance abusers are definitionally grouped with long-term drug addicts, even though the prognoses and treatments for each group are substantially different. This will create far worse stigma for limited or recreational drug users.

Binge Eating Disorder is another new mental disorder listed in DSM-5. This so-called mental illness involves excessive eating at least 12 times in 3 months (about once per week). Additional criteria include eating large amounts of food when not feeling physically hungry, eating until feeling uncomfortably full, and feeling guilty after overeating. As discussed in the Food section, over two-thirds of adults and one-third of children and teenagers are obese or overweight in the US. Probably many, if not most, of these people meet the criteria for Binge Eating Disorder. Through this new mental disorder, DSM-5 effectively states that many more people in the US are mentally ill, and thereby are candidates for taking psychiatric drugs.

Regularly overeating usually is unhealthy. But it is a common behavior among humans, especially when abundant, cheap, tasty food is available, a weak social safety net creates high stress for many low and middle-income citizens, and advertising creates a widespread sense of emptiness and inadequacy in society. Saying that many people who overeat are mentally ill could help drug companies by greatly increasing the use of antidepressants and other psychiatric drugs. But it will severely degrade society.

(As discussed in the Food section, most, if not nearly all, processed, packaged, prepared and restaurant food contains MSG. About 40 ingredients, including natural flavor and spices, always or often contain it. This enables food companies to put MSG in food without showing it on ingredient labels. MSG causes or contributes to obesity, neurological diseases and many other problems. It often makes food with bland, low quality ingredients taste good. It also suppresses the sense of fullness and compels people to eat more than they normally would. Rather than taking a drug or substance that compels people to overeat and then taking psychiatric drugs to suppress overeating, if would be vastly healthier to stop taking the drug that causes overeating (MSG). Even food labeled No MSG can contain MSG. Citizens frequently have no way of knowing if processed, packaged, prepared or restaurant food contains MSG. Therefore, it is safest to avoid these foods to the greatest extent possible.)

DSM-5 also introduced the concept of Behavioral Addictions. This could cause nearly anything that people like doing to be labeled a mental disorder. Dr. Frances notes that Internet and sex addiction could become mental disorders under the Behavioral Addiction concept. This also could substantially increase the use of psychiatric drugs.

As noted, nearly all DSM-5 changes involved loosened diagnostic criteria that will increase mental disorder diagnoses and psychiatric drug use. However, the definition of autism was restricted or tightened in DSM-5. Dr. Frances said that this will reduce autism diagnoses by 10 to 50 percent.[362] But this probably will not substantially lower psychiatric drug sales because autism frequently is not treated with drugs. Autistic children often require additional education services. Therefore, reducing autism diagnoses could placate those who wish to cut funding for public education so that corporate welfare can be increased.

DSM-5 was updated in 2022 with a text revision (DSM-5-TR). The update added new disorders and psychiatric conditions, updated naming conventions and diagnostic criteria, and addressed the impact of racism and discrimination on mental disorders. New DSM-5-TR disorders include Prolonged Grief Disorder and Unspecified Mood Disorder. Prolonged Grief Disorder updates Major Depressive Disorder noted above in relation to extended grief after the loss of a loved one. Unspecified Mood Disorder is discussed in the Antipsychotics and Bipolar Disorder section below.[363]

Pathologizing normal human behavior by redefining it as mental illness is most tragic for children. Children and teenagers often do not have the knowledge or power needed to oppose adults who claim that their normal behavior is mental illness. Sixty years ago, virtually no children were considered to be mentally ill. In 1952, of the 106 mental disorders listed in DSM-1, only one related to children. In 1950, only about 7,500 children in the US were considered to be mentally ill. Most of these children had explicit neurological symptoms.[364]

Being sluggish, hyperactive, moody, sad, inattentive, fragile, pestering and/or defiant were considered to be normal aspects of temperament and character.[365] Children usually grew out of these phases and became normally functioning adults. Childhood and adolescence often are complicated and difficult, especially in today's rapidly changing world. It is normal for young people to have their ups and downs as they develop physically and psychologically. Labeling these normal feelings and behaviors as mental illness is irrational and harmful.

The expanding DSM effectively has redefined childhood. According to the DSM, our children are rife with mental illness. Redefining our healthy, normal children as mentally ill helps drug companies to maximize sales and shareholder returns. But this is an abomination. We are taking away our children's ability to think freely and possibly saddling them with lifelong physical and psychological problems. This benefits authoritarian leaders who will not tolerate any disrespect or opposition from young people. But drugging young people into compliance with authorities is a heinous violation of democracy and freedom.

DSM Diagnostic Method

There are substantial problems with the DSM method of creating and diagnosing specific mental disorder categories. Two of the most frequently cited problems are validity and reliability.[366] Validity involves determining if behaviors labeled as mental disorders actually are disorders. Part of this determination depends on the definition of mental disorder. For example, mental disorders could be defined as collections of psychological symptoms with unknown or unproven causes that produce life problems. Using this definition, mental disorders clearly exist.

However, the term mental disorder often is used in ways that state or imply the existence of a physical brain problem that causes psychological symptoms. This commonly used implied definition of mental disorder is problematic because the existence of physical brain problems usually cannot be proven. As noted, mental disorders are different than medical problems. Medical conditions often can be verified and proven with physical tests. But there are no clinical laboratory or neuroimaging tests that can be used to determine or prove that physically caused mental disorders exist.[367]

There also is no agreed scientific model for mental disorders. As discussed, the brain chemical imbalance model is simplistic, unproven and discredited by many studies. The determination and diagnosis of mental disorders is done through clinical observation and interviews. But the clinical interview process is inherently flawed due to the bias or perspective of the interviewer.

There is a spectrum or spectrums of human behaviors and feelings. The DSM diagnostic approach often imposes discrete categories along these spectrums. But these categories are theories or opinions. Diagnosis of DSM mental disorders frequently involves checking off lists of symptoms. If enough symptoms are present, the mental disorder is assumed to be present. But there are many flaws with this approach.

For example, the DSM diagnostic process usually does not address causes. No causes or biological proof are given for mental disorders. Therefore, it cannot be proven that physically caused mental disorders exist. Some people might say that the presence of symptoms proves the existence of physically caused mental disorders. But it does not. The symptoms could be (and probably usually are) caused by disempowering beliefs and life circumstances, not physical brain problems. DSM diagnosis generally does not consider life circumstances at all or until after the diagnosis is assigned.[368] Ignoring life circumstances in diagnosis is ignoring reality.

Many leaders in the psychiatric field have criticized the DSM. For example, beyond the criticism of DSM-4 taskforce chairman Dr. Frances noted above, Robert Spitzer, M.D., former chairman of the DSM-3 taskforce, criticized later versions of the DSM. He said that, while the DSM could be clinically useful, its failure to consider context or life experiences, such as problems in jobs or relationships, could result in normal human behavior being pathologized (i.e. normal, psychologically healthy people being incorrectly labeled mentally ill). Thomas Insel, director of the National Institute of Mental Health (NIMH), said that the DSM's diagnostic categories lack validity. Partly as a result, the NIMH is re-orienting its research away from DSM categories.[369]

DSM diagnoses suffer from the scientific problem of reification.[370] This involves treating an abstraction as if it had concrete or material existence.

Symptoms and behaviors can be observed. But saying that the existence of these symptoms proves the existence of physically caused mental disorders is reification. Brain/mind research often shows that the brain/mind is more complex than previously imagined.[371] The more we study the brain/mind, the more we realize how little we know about it. We do not even know if the mind is fully contained in the brain.

The causes of behaviors and psychological symptoms often vary from person to person. For example, people frequently react differently to similar events or life circumstances. Grouping uniquely caused behaviors, symptoms and feelings into mental disorder categories is simplistic. Creating mental disorder categories might have some value from a treatment perspective. But this illustrates another weakness of DSM diagnosis – reliability.

Reliability implies that clinicians trained in DSM criteria would agree on diagnoses. But clinicians frequently disagree about diagnoses, and even about whether a person has a mental disorder. This strongly indicates that the DSM is unreliable. A 1973 study showed the unreliability of the DSM. Eight people pretended to be mentally ill by saying that they heard voices. They all tricked clinicians and were admitted to mental hospitals.[372]

To improve reliability, in 1980, DSM-3 added behavior checklists and formal decision-making rules. But many studies have shown that this did not improve reliability. In one study, mental health professionals were given extensive training in DSM diagnosis. Then pairs of clinicians interviewed nearly 600 prospective patients. It was anticipated that the additional DSM training would have produced higher diagnostic agreement than occurs in normal clinical settings. But there was wide disagreement among clinicians on diagnoses. Trained clinicians independently interviewing the same person disagreed about half the time about which mental disorder a prospective patient might have. They also disagreed about half the time about whether a prospective patient had a mental disorder. The study showed that DSM-3 was as unreliable as previous editions of the DSM. No study has found high reliability in any version of the DSM.[373]

The DSM suffers from the reliability related problems of falsifiability and differentiability.[374] Regarding falsifiability, diagnoses cannot be disproven because they are based on opinions about abstract concepts, instead of physical tests. Regarding differentiability, as shown in the above study, diagnoses cannot be indisputably distinguished from one another.

Several factors cause the DSM to be unreliable. For example, many DSM mental disorders share similar symptoms. Therefore, the decision about which mental disorder to assign is based in part on the opinion, bias or prejudice of clinicians. The DSM also is unreliable because diagnoses often fail to account for life circumstances and cultural differences, both of which frequently influence behaviors, feelings and psychological symptoms.

The creation of mental disorder classifications also can cause unreliability. As noted, the DSM frequently attempts to segregate spectrums of feelings and behaviors into discrete categories of mental disorders. The boundaries between categories often have overlap and are based on opinions, rather than a valid scientific model of mental disorders. There also frequently are arbitrary cutoffs between normal and abnormal behaviors.[375] These often arbitrary and unscientific distinctions between mental disorder categories help to explain why clinicians frequently disagree on diagnoses and why the DSM is unreliable.

A major problem with the DSM diagnostic method involves stigma. A mental disorder diagnosis can create social stigma and contribute to discrimination. The stigma is increased because clinicians and the psychiatry field in general often promote or describe mental disorders as actual neurological disorders, instead of acknowledging that they are opinions about largely unknown mechanisms of the mind. Being labeled mentally ill can lower self-esteem, increase psychological symptoms and inhibit recovery.[376]

The definitions and terminology of DSM mental disorders also can inhibit recovery because they frequently are focused on psychopathology and chronicity. The mental disorder label is not focused on recovery. It sometimes implies that people are more mentally ill and less able to recover than they actually are. The mental disorder label often is dangerous because it stigmatizes. It also frequently is unjustified because it implies the existence of an actual neurological problem, when there is no proof that physical problems exist. Psychological symptoms usually are responses to disempowering beliefs and life circumstances.

A more realistic, accurate and beneficial diagnostic approach might focus on spectrums or dimensions of symptoms. It would not use the stigmatizing terms mental disorder or mental illness in most cases. Rather than relying on abstract, opinion-based categories, it might rely more on a complaint-based approach, which integrates life circumstances, disempowering beliefs, culture and other relevant causal factors.

The approach also would acknowledge the vast uncertainty of the mind. For example, it would not establish abstract, unprovable mental disorders, and then create a false sense of certainty by pretending that the disorders are real. Perhaps most importantly, people would be treated like complex, dignified human beings, rather than flawed, mentally ill patients. In reality, we know as little about mental illness as we do about the mind. Therefore, we should not stigmatize and harm people by assigning simplistic, opinion-based, reality-ignoring labels.

Drug Company Influence

Drug company influence of the DSM is strongly indicated by the very large benefits that DSM changes provide to drug companies. Over the past 50 years, the creation of new mental disorder categories and loosening of existing mental disorder definitions caused millions of more people to be labeled mentally ill. This produced millions of new customers for drug companies.

DSM-5 and DSM-5-TR continued this expansion of mental illness diagnoses and psychiatric drug use. Dr. Frances said that millions of people with normal grief, gluttony, distractibility, worries, reactions to stress, temper tantrums of childhood, forgetfulness of old-age and 'behavioral addictions' will be mislabeled mentally ill and inappropriately prescribed psychiatric drugs.[377]

The DSM is published by the American Psychiatric Association (APA). To produce revised editions of the DSM, experts study and recommend revisions, and then the APA Board of Trustees approves them. About 170 panel members suggested revisions for DSM-4. A 2006 study found that

56 percent of the panel members had financial ties to drug companies. In areas where drugs were the first line of treatment for mental disorders, 100 percent of panel members had financial ties to drug companies.[378]

DSM-5 also was heavily influenced by drug companies. Sixty-nine percent of DSM-5 taskforce members had financial ties to them.[379] More than 50 mental health professional organizations petitioned the APA for an outside review of DSM-5. They requested an independent evaluation of supporting evidence and assessment of the balance between risks and benefits. But the APA failed to heed the advice of outside experts. Dr. Frances stated that the APA was "deaf to the repeated and widespread warnings that [DSM-5] would lead to massive misdiagnosis."[380]

The APA claims that an independent review of DSM-5 was conducted. But the organization did not disclose the results of the review or the identities of the people who conducted it before releasing DSM-5.[381] Failing to disclose this information could hide inappropriate influence.

Drug company influence is not the only factor driving DSM expansion. Dr. Frances noted that the specialized experts working on DSM-5 often overvalue their own ideas and theories, want to expand their own areas of research, and inadequately consider the distortions that will occur when DSM-5 theories and abstract ideas are applied in real-world clinical settings.[382]

One factor that possibly indicates drug company influence of the APA and DSM-5 involves statements made by the APA. The APA claimed that DSM-5 is a conservative document that only will have minimal impacts on the rates of mental illness diagnosis and psychiatric drug use.[383] As discussed in the Misleading the Public section, this is the same type of deceptive statement that often is used by publicly traded companies to protect shareholder returns.

Delays and missed deadlines caused the APA to skip DSM-5 field testing.[384] Releasing DSM-5 without assessing risks and benefits in real-world settings is not conservative. Also, DSM-5 is redefining extensive normal behavior as mental illness. Loosened mental disorder definitions and new mental disorder categories will cause extensive new mental illness diagnoses, and thereby produce many new psychiatric drug users.

The statement that DSM-5 is conservative and will not substantially increase mental disorder diagnoses and psychiatric drug use is dishonest. Publicly traded companies are required to protect shareholder returns. If honest communication threatens returns, flawed systems often compel these companies to mislead the public (i.e. lie). As discussed in the Misleading the Public section, if the choice is lie or die, publicly traded companies often will be compelled to lie. The use of public deception strategies that are commonly used by corporations further indicates that drug companies are strongly influencing the APA and DSM-5.

Treatment guidelines represent another area of drug company influence. The APA issues treatment guidelines for specific mental disorders after DSM revisions are made and when substantial new information becomes available. The guidelines usually are developed by committees of experts who often have financial ties to drug companies. These companies also frequently fund the expert committees. The guidelines often suggest treatment with psychiatric drugs.

Medical education is heavily influenced by drug companies. The bulk of psychiatric training and education is focused on the use of psychiatric drugs. Psychiatrists often receive relatively little training in psychotherapy and other nondrug treatments. Medical education and treatment guidelines create strong pressure to prescribe psychiatric drugs. If psychiatrists working at clinics frequently recommend psychotherapy instead of following guidelines that recommend treatment with drugs, they might lose their jobs. If a psychiatrist in private practice recommends psychotherapy, lifestyle changes or other nondrug treatments, instead of following treatment guidelines that call for drugs, and a patient makes a complaint, the psychiatrist might lose their license.

Many factors encourage or compel doctors to prescribe psychiatric drugs. Those who heavily prescribe often receive substantial financial and nonfinancial inducements from drug companies (in effect, bribes). Doctors who fail to prescribe psychiatric drugs frequently risk losing their jobs or licenses.

Inadequate Psychiatric Training

DSM-4 warns that appropriate use of diagnostic criteria requires extensive clinical training. But about 80 percent of psychiatric drugs are prescribed in primary care settings.[385] Most primary care doctors have relatively little training and clinical experience in psychology and psychiatry. In the same way that a foot doctor would not perform brain surgery, a primary care doctor or other doctor with little psychological and psychiatric training should not prescribe psychiatric drugs.

Effective psychological diagnosis and prescription requires an understanding of psychology. Psychiatric drugs often have severe side effects. Before prescribing them, doctors should assess whether life circumstances, disempowering beliefs or other factors are producing psychological symptoms as well as consider the risks and benefits of drugs compared to psychotherapy and other nondrug treatments. But this type of psychological evaluation often is not done in primary care settings. Drug companies give substantial financial and other inducements to doctors. This strongly contributes to excess prescription of psychiatric drugs by doctors who lack the psychological and psychiatric training and clinical experience needed to safely and effectively prescribe the drugs.

Alternative Diagnostic Methods

The DSM diagnostic method implies a level of certainty that does not exist. Behaviors and symptoms can be observed and known. But the causes of these symptoms often are unknown. DSM diagnosis frequently implies that the symptoms are caused by or indicative of neurological mental disorders. But this is a gross oversimplification. The causes of each person's symptoms often are as unique as that person. There are some measurable neurological conditions that produce psychological symptoms, such as brain injury or disease. There also might be other unproven physical causes of psychological symptoms, possibly including brain chemical imbalances. But the large majority of psychological symptoms probably are caused by unique combinations of personality, character, upbringing, life circumstances, disempowering beliefs, and other environmental or nonphysical factors.

Attempting to reduce millions of people's unique combinations of symptoms and causes down to a few hundred DSM mental disorder categories can harm people. It stigmatizes them by saying that they have unproven, abstract mental disorders. It dishonors them by often failing to acknowledge or address life circumstances, disempowering beliefs and other potential nonphysical causes. It also dishonors them by pathologizing or labeling their frequently normal behavior as abnormal, and thereby claiming that normal people are mentally ill. The DSM approach also often physically and psychologically harms people by promoting the use of psychiatric drugs, which frequently cause severe side effects. If one were attempting to develop a psychological diagnostic approach that maximizes the use of psychiatric drugs, it would be difficult to come up with a better strategy than the ever-expanding DSM.

Psychological diagnosis can be a useful tool. But there are alternatives to the DSM. The goal of a diagnostic system should be to maximize the health and well-being of citizens. A system such as this would honor the uniqueness of each person and acknowledge humanity's great lack of understanding about the mind.

Creating categories of people displaying similar symptoms can be useful for treatment. But the current DSM system creates artificial or arbitrary boundaries between categories. Physical or medical problems often can be tested, categorized and effectively treated. But this situation does not exist in the psychological and psychiatric areas. Clinical interviews or checklists of symptoms are not adequate substitutes for physical tests. They often ignore relevant factors, such as life circumstances. Interviews also are inherently biased by the interviewer. As one might expect of an abstract, opinion-based, frequently reality-ignoring diagnostic system, the DSM checklist approach is unreliable.

Psychology was on the right track before it was largely derailed by the unscientific assignment of mental disorders and widespread psychiatric drug use. Psychotherapy does not simplify a person down to a category and give them powerful drugs to suppress symptoms. A good therapist becomes the partner and ally of clients. They venture into the unknown on a process of discovery, awareness, growth and healing with the goal of achieving a truly successful and satisfying life.

The healing and growth process is different for each person. Psychiatric drugs might be useful in some cases. But currently there is large and detrimental overreliance on them. These drugs often block the inner journey of growth and healing by suppressing psychological pain, clouding the mind, and removing the motivation to change.

It might be intellectually comforting to believe that we have successfully rendered psychological problems down to specific categories with identifiable treatments, as occurs in the medical area. But this is a false, simplifying and in some ways dogmatic sense of security. A more effective, reality-based diagnostic approach would integrate life circumstances, disempowering beliefs and other causal factors. At first, it might be less specific, less categorized and more uncertain. But it probably is necessary to step back from the false and harmful sense of security provided by the DSM. We might have to live with uncertainty while more accurate, effective, reality-based diagnostic and treatment approaches are developed.

In many cases, diagnostic labels will not be needed. Each person is different. Therefore, it often would be inappropriate to label and categorize people. Instead, it would be more effective to help them chart their own unique course of awareness, healing and growth through their unique inner and outer life circumstances.

The DSM diagnostic approach often is irrational. Drug company influence is the main reason for this. In the medical area, people usually go to doctors because they have medical problems or symptoms. Doctors usually analyze symptoms, run tests to determine illnesses or causes of symptoms, and then prescribe drugs or other treatments that are proven to relieve symptoms and/or cure illnesses. In other words, doctors frequently use symptoms to determine causes.

But as noted, this step usually is not done at all or until after diagnoses are made under the DSM symptom checklist approach. Under a rational mental health system, when a patient went to a psychiatrist and complained of psychological symptoms or problems, the psychiatrist often would start by asking, is there anything going on in your life that might be causing the symptoms, such as a problematic job or relationship? Examining past and present life circumstances, including diet, lifestyle and other potential causal factors, would reveal that these external factors and disempowering beliefs are the cause of nearly all psychological problems. Using this rational, reality-based diagnostic approach might reduce the use of psychiatric drugs by 75 percent or more.

Publicly traded drug companies are structurally required to attempt to grow forever. As a result, they often would strongly oppose a reality-based diagnostic system. Instead, they would (and do) strongly promote the current irrational, reality-ignoring DSM approach. The approach mainly is irrational because it focuses on symptoms not causes. Drug companies fund studies that attempt to prove physical, neurological causes of mental disorders. But these studies rarely, if ever, prove physical causes and they frequently are refuted by independent studies. Drug company-influenced studies fail to prove physical causes largely because they ignore the reality that most psychological problems are not caused by physical, neurological factors.

When doctors cannot determine the specific cause of physical, medical symptoms, they might use symptoms to estimate or assume a particular cause, and then prescribe treatments that have been proven to effectively address it. However, this generally is not an appropriate rationale for assuming a physical cause to a psychological problem, and then prescribing psychiatric drugs based on this assumption. Nearly all of the research that links physical, neurological causes to psychological problems is influenced by drug companies, and therefore is inherently biased, untrustworthy and unreliable. In addition, assuming a physical cause ignores the obvious fact that most psychological problems are caused by disempowering beliefs and life circumstances.

Further weakening the medical rational for prescribing psychiatric drugs is the fact that most drug studies are short-term. There is little evidence that psychiatric drugs actually solve psychological problems. Instead, they suppress symptoms in the short-term while often ignoring actual causes. As discussed below, there is strong evidence that psychiatric drugs make psychological and physical health worse over the long-term. Given the lack of reliable evidence linking psychological problems to physical causes, the obvious link to nonphysical causes, and the strong evidence that psychiatric drugs often make people worse over the long-term, it generally is not appropriate to prescribe psychiatric drugs.

When doctors check off psychological symptoms and prescribe psychiatric drugs without assessing causes, they are ignoring the 800-pound gorilla sitting in the room (i.e. past and present life circumstances and disempowering beliefs). As discussed in the Misleading the Public section, when rational and honest means fail to maximize shareholder returns, flawed systems often compel publicly traded companies to use dishonest or irrational means. Prescribing drugs based on symptoms largely is irrational. Causes are the relevant factors. They should determine treatments, not symptoms. But as noted, assessing causes, such as life circumstances, would greatly lower the use of psychiatric drugs. Probably as a result, the drug company-dominated DSM largely does not base diagnosis and treatment on causes.

Using a rational, reality-based mental health diagnostic system that maximizes the well-being of society, for example by focusing on actual causes and not overprescribing psychiatric drugs, would not maximize drug company shareholder returns. As a result, drug companies promote the current irrational, dishonest system (dishonest because actual causes often are ignored). The existence of the reality-ignoring DSM diagnostic approach shows the great extent to which drug companies influence the mental health field in the US. Improving psychological diagnoses is further discussed in the Psychiatric Drug Solution section below.

Stimulants and ADHD

The widespread use of amphetamines and other stimulants to treat Attention Deficit Hyperactivity Disorder (ADHD) in children and adults is a major problem. It illustrates how the myopic, reality-ignoring DSM diagnostic approach often causes excessive, unnecessary and harmful use of psychiatric drugs.

The use of ADHD drugs has increased 20-fold over the past 30 years.[386] Over six million school-age children (ages 4 to 17) in the US have been diagnosed with ADHD (15 percent of boys and 7 percent of girls). At the high school level (ages 14 to 17), 19 percent of boys and 10 percent of girls have been diagnosed with ADHD. Two-thirds of those with current ADHD diagnoses take prescription stimulants.[387] Sales of stimulants used to treat ADHD have grown from $4 billion in 2007 to $9 billion in 2012. By loosening the definition and diagnostic criteria for ADHD, DSM-5 is causing many more children and adults to be diagnosed with ADHD.[388]

ADHD is considered to be a mental disorder. It is characterized by difficulty concentrating or paying attention and/or hyperactivity and impulsiveness. ADHD often is treated with stimulants. Adderall and Ritalin are two of the most common drugs used to treat ADHD. Adderall is comprised of four types of amphetamines, including Dexedrine. Ritalin has a similar structure and effect as cocaine.[389] Adderall and Ritalin increase levels of dopamine in the brain. Both drugs can produce euphoria and increased alertness, libido, verboseness and sociability. The drugs also can cause heightened senses of well-being, self-confidence, superiority and grandiosity.[390]

Side effects of the drugs include addiction, irritability, aggression, hopelessness, depression, anxiety, paranoia, psychosis (i.e. loss of contact with reality), insomnia, reduced appetite, anorexia, stunted growth, cardiovascular problems, seizures, heart attack, suicidal thoughts and sudden death.[391] [392] Withdrawal symptoms can include anxiety, agitation, mental fatigue, increased appetite, excessive sleep, depression and suicidal thoughts. These symptoms can last for weeks or months, especially after long-term use.[393] Withdrawal symptoms can create a strong desire to get back on the drugs. The long-term impacts of using stimulants to treat ADHD largely are unknown, in part because it is illegal to test drugs on children and clinical trials usually are short-term. As noted, they rarely last a year or longer. However, long-term animal studies indicate that using stimulants in adolescence can cause problems in adulthood, including memory damage and depression.[394]

Key questions about ADHD include, is it an actual mental disorder with a physical cause? ADHD symptoms (i.e. inattention, hyperactivity and/or impulsiveness) obviously exist. But there is no proof that ADHD is caused by brain chemical imbalances, genetic defects or any other physical, neurological problem.[395] As discussed, there are no clinical tests to determine if ADHD or any other mental disorder exists.

In one sense, mental disorders are created by experts and other groups in society. They create them by deciding which behaviors and feelings are abnormal. But the boundary between normal and abnormal is decided by opinion, not scientific tests. To illustrate, DSM criteria diagnose ADHD at three to four times the rate of ICD criteria used in Europe and other parts of the world.[396] In other words, about 75 percent of people diagnosed with ADHD in the US would not be considered to have this condition in Europe. Psychological diagnosis is based completely on opinion. The business-dominated US draws boundaries between normal and abnormal behaviors in ways that maximize drug company sales. But these boundaries are business-biased opinions. They are not scientific facts.

Drug companies, researchers paid by them, and other allies often strongly promote the theory that ADHD is caused by physical factors, in part because this helps to justify widespread use of prescription stimulants. Drug company influence of researchers, doctors, politicians and regulators contributes to most ADHD research being focused on physical causes.[397] Some studies have shown that children with ADHD symptoms have different neurotransmitter levels and other brain anomalies. But this is the obvious and expected outcome. The brain and behavior are inextricably linked. The existence of brain anomalies does not prove that ADHD is caused by physical, neurological factors.[398] As discussed above, brain chemical imbalances could be the mediating factor between life experience and psychological responses. Recent research shows that life experience influences brain development.

Many studies have shown that diet, abuse, family dysfunction, chaotic living situations, lack of social support, and poor education quality can cause ADHD symptoms.[399] One large study found that innate, neurological anomalies at birth, such as IQ, infant temperament and infant activity level, do not predict ADHD. But environmental factors, such as family situation, are reliable predictors.[400] Several other studies have shown that placebos are as effective as prescription stimulants in treating ADHD.[401] Additional research showed that children without attention problems respond the same to stimulants as children with ADHD.[402] All of these findings strongly indicate that ADHD symptoms are caused by external, psychological or environmental factors, not by physical, neurological problems or defects.

Some studies indicate that genetics play a role in ADHD. These studies greatly benefit drug companies because they imply or state that ADHD is an inherited physical condition that cannot be changed, but can be managed with drugs. But this position is deceptive. Children often emulate parents and assimilate their psychological problems. For example, if parents have psychological issues that make concentrating difficult, such as insecurity and fear, children could adopt these mannerisms or ways of being in the world and also have difficulty paying attention. In these cases, ADHD symptoms would be learned, not passed on through genetics.

Some studies speculate that certain genes might be related to ADHD symptoms, for example, by influencing dopamine levels. This might be true. But it does not prove that ADHD symptoms are caused by inherited genetic factors. If ADHD is a genetic condition, one might ask, why are so many parents with ADHD diagnosed children able to concentrate and succeed in life without taking prescription stimulants?

Each person is different. Everyone has unique interests. Identifying and building one's life around them often produces the most successful and satisfying life. It appears that people frequently have the skills needed to succeed in their true areas of interest and passion (i.e. not those taught or conditioned by society, such as acquiring wealth and possessions). If high ability to concentrate is needed to pursue one's passion, people often will have it. Whether or not this link between skills and life passion exists, variations in the ability to concentrate, like many other human characteristics, are normal. Perhaps there is a genetic link to lower ability to concentrate. But that does not mean that people with less ability in this area are abnormal, mentally ill or genetically flawed.

Humans evolved with a basic ability to pay attention. If we did not have this, we probably would not have survived. Nearly everyone has the ability to pay attention to things that interest them, except for people with brain injuries, diseases or actual physical defects. Inability to focus on something that one is not interested in, such as boring work or education courses, does not mean that people are mentally ill. It is within the realm of normal, expected human behavior.

Beyond psychological causes of ADHD, such as those related to abuse or chaotic living situations, environmental factors, such as toxic chemicals in drinking water, can contribute to or cause neurological and psychological problems. For example, a Harvard study found that fluoride in drinking water increases the rates of ADHD, autism and other psychological problems. Earlier studies found that fluoride can harm the brain and reduce children's IQ. The large majority of countries prohibit fluoride in drinking water. Based on extensive research, reducing toxic chemicals in the environment will reduce ADHD and other psychological problems.[403]

The idea that ADHD results from genetic defects or physiological factors is an unproven theory that helps drug companies to achieve their systemically-mandated requirement to provide ever-increasing shareholder returns. Probably nearly all ADHD symptoms result from nonphysical, environmental or psychological causes. The symptoms might be exacerbated by lower ability to pay attention that falls within the range of normal variations among humans.

Another key question about ADHD is, why do many experts in the US call ADHD a mental disorder with probable physical causes when there are more logical and obvious nonphysical causes and much of the rest of the world considers most of this behavior to be normal? For example, it is obvious and known that environmental factors can cause ADHD and other psychological problems. Abused children often will have difficulty focusing on schoolwork because they are filled with fear and focusing primarily on survival.

The obvious reason that the US diagnoses ADHD at much higher rates than many other countries is that it helps drug companies. These companies strongly influence doctors, politicians, regulators, drug researchers, DSM standards, treatment guidelines and medical education. As a result, they have strong ability to focus the ADHD research agenda on physical causes and promote over-diagnosis of ADHD.

Another possible reason for over-promoting physical causes of ADHD symptoms and ignoring more obvious and logical nonphysical or environmental causes relates to lack of knowledge about the mind. Some people are unwilling to acknowledge that there might be nonphysical components to the mind. This could produce uncertainty and intellectual discomfort. To avoid this, they might irrationally argue that the mind is completely physical and mediated only through physical processes (i.e. irrational because it is impossible to prove this and there is extensive evidence which indicates that there are nonphysical aspects of the mind). This unwillingness to acknowledge the unknown, possibly nonphysical aspects of the mind could cause some researchers and other experts to be biased toward physical causes of ADHD and other mental disorders.

But maximizing the shareholder returns of drug companies and avoiding intellectual uncertainty are poor reasons for over-promoting physical explanations for ADHD and subsequent stimulant use. Adderall, Ritalin and other prescription stimulants have known severe side effects, including increased suicide and sudden death risk. They also probably often have substantial long-term negative effects. The priority should be the well-being of children and society, not the shareholder returns of drug companies.

Before powerful, often harmful stimulants are prescribed, nonphysical, environmental and psychological causes of ADHD symptoms should be assessed and nondrug treatments pursued. This is done in many cases. Many doctors understand the risks of psychiatric drugs and only prescribe them as a last resort. But the high rate of prescription relative to other countries indicates that pursuit of nondrug treatments is inadequate, especially in primary care settings where doctors often have little psychological training and experience.

To illustrate, a 2013 study assessed pediatricians and other doctors who treated four to six-year-old children diagnosed with ADHD. Guidelines issued by the American Academy of Pediatrics state that doctors should treat ADHD in preschoolers with behavioral therapies before prescribing medication. The study found that less than 10 percent of doctors followed the guidelines. Doctors often prescribed stimulants to young children as the first line of treatment, failed to check if behavior therapy was working before prescribing drugs, and/or failed to prescribe the recommended drugs.[404]

A highly deceptive aspect of ADHD and stimulants relates to short-term benefits. Many studies have shown that prescription stimulants are effective at relieving ADHD symptoms in 70 to 80 percent of patients.[405] But this is like saying that drinking alcohol makes 80 percent of people feel better. Inattention and hyperactivity often result from boredom, difficult life circumstances and/or disempowering beliefs. Adderall, Ritalin and other stimulants frequently produce euphoria or other heightened senses of well-being. People often use illegal drugs because they produce good feelings and make life more fun. Legal stimulants frequently do the same thing. By producing euphoria or other good feelings, previously boring activities, such as schoolwork, often become more fun or interesting.

The fact that taking drugs which produce euphoria or other good feelings makes previously boring activities more interesting is the obvious and expected outcome. In effect, stimulants make people better able to focus by creating an altered state of consciousness (i.e. getting them high). For over 50 years, it has been known that amphetamines help people to stay awake and focus on boring or repetitive activities. For example, amphetamines were given to radar operators during World War II.[406]

As with illegal drugs, taking prescription stimulants is not a real solution. The inattention problem is not solved. It simply is temporarily relieved by getting high on amphetamines or cocaine-like drugs. When the drugs wear off, life often seems boring again and difficulty concentrating returns. Prescription stimulants produce short-term benefits by creating a temporarily altered state of consciousness. But no study has shown that taking ADHD drugs provides any long-term benefit, including improved academic performance, better peer relationships or reduced behavior problems.[407]

When people use amphetamines or cocaine illegally, they often are sent to jail. But when drug companies that give money to politicians sell stimulants, we say it's okay. But it frequently is not okay. Before drug company-influenced regulators and doctors allowed and promoted widespread ADHD drug use, children often learned to deal with boredom. The current suboptimal structure of education and society require that nearly everyone do boring work at least sometimes. For example, many students, including good students, find studying for tests difficult and boring. They frequently are unable to concentrate. They might find themselves rereading the same sentence over and over again. But most people force themselves to focus and get the job done, even if it is done imperfectly.

People who cannot focus on studying or other boring tasks often learn the hard way (due to our flawed education system) that these areas are not meant for them. They figure out how to get by and find something that they can focus on and do. This process of learning to concentrate, perhaps by being forced to do so, usually is beneficial. It builds character and resilience.

But ADHD theory and drug treatment often block this character and resilience building. Now young people who have difficulty focusing effectively are told, it's not your fault. You have a physical brain problem. You are mentally ill. As a result, you are allowed to take drugs that make you feel really good. You're relieved of responsibility for not working hard on your studies and you're allowed to legally get high. As an added benefit, you'll now start doing better on tests (provided of course that you continue to regularly get high by using our prescription stimulants). 'High school' should not include allowing millions of students to get high on amphetamines and cocaine-like drugs.

Drug companies and their allies sometimes argue that Adderall, Ritalin and other prescription stimulants do not produce the same euphoria as amphetamines and cocaine. But this is deceptive. There is a large illegal market for diverted prescription stimulants. Many students fake ADHD symptoms to get drugs, and then sell them. About 10 percent of teenagers say they have used prescription stimulants without a prescription (i.e. illegally).[408] Some studies found that about 30 percent of prescription stimulants are given to friends or resold.[409] If these drugs did not produce euphoria or get people high in other ways, they would not be so heavily abused.

Rapidly growing emergency room visits for nonmedical stimulant use (i.e. without a prescription) further indicates widespread illegal use of prescription stimulants. A study by the Substance Abuse and Mental Health Services Administration found that emergency room visits related to stimulants among people aged 18 to 34 increased by about 400 percent from 2005 to 2011. Growth occurred most rapidly among 18 to 25-year-olds. The study analyzed emergency room visits related to prescription stimulants, such as Adderall and Ritalin, and over-the-counter stimulants, such as caffeine energy drinks. Most of the increase in emergency room visits related to illegal use of prescription stimulants. Two-thirds of people misusing the drugs said they got them from a relative or friend.[410]

Adderall is banned in the National Football League because it is a performance-enhancing drug that contains amphetamines. Several NFL players have been suspended for using Adderall without a prescription. However, NFL players can take Adderall if they have a prescription.[411]

As discussed in the Advertising, Media and Culture section, the US has the highest illegal drug use rate in the world. We lost or did not win the war on drugs largely because we did not adequately address the demand-side. We did not ask, what is it about our society that makes so many young people want to escape reality by taking drugs? This would require addressing the disempowering, harmful aspects of advertising and media, the boredom and inadequacy produced by our competitive education system, and the high stress placed on average citizens by putting economic growth and shareholder returns before all else. These factors probably are main causes of ADHD symptoms and many other psychological problems. But addressing these causes would threaten vested interests and disrupt the status quo.

As a result, we delude ourselves into thinking that our children's normal behavior is abnormal. When healthy children respond naturally to our flawed education and other systems, we often label them mentally ill and drug them into compliance. Children and teenagers frequently do not complain because getting high legally and doing better in school often is fun (until the drugs wear off or become ineffective, and side effects, such as depression, set in).

Legal drugs are like illegal drugs. Over time, larger doses are needed to get the same effect. This frequently is the case with stimulants used to treat ADHD. One study found that the benefits of stimulants decline over time. After three years of taking the drugs, there is no benefit. But many young people take stimulants for six years or more. European regulators recommend that people on stimulants stop taking them once per year to see if the drugs still are needed. But this advice frequently is not followed in the US.[412]

Illegal drug users often take drugs occasionally for recreational purposes, in the same way that many people occasionally drink alcohol for recreation. But children and teenagers on Adderall, Ritalin and other prescription stimulants effectively are getting high every day. These drugs are more powerful than marijuana and alcohol in many ways. Until recently, we sometimes put people in jail for occasional marijuana use. But we allow millions of children, teenagers and adults to take much more powerful and harmful drugs. Most parents would not give alcohol or marijuana to young children. But children as young as three years old frequently are given amphetamines and cocaine-like drugs on a daily basis.

This shows the grossly flawed nature of our economic and political systems. As discussed in the Economic Growth section of *Global System Change*, the stated goal of these systems might be to maximize the well-being of society. But that is not the actual goal pursed. The measured and managed priority is that a small group of wealthy people gets continuously wealthier. If giving young people powerful, often harmful drugs facilitates this goal, it frequently is allowed.

It is time to end this insanity. Probably the large majority of young people with ADHD do not have this abstract, so-called mental disorder. As noted, the diagnostic system used in Europe would say that about 75 percent of young people diagnosed with ADHD in the US do not have ADHD. Instead, most young people probably are displaying normal responses to life circumstances, our flawed education system, and other problems in families, communities and society overall.

The strong link between ADHD symptoms and boring, flawed education systems is shown by research summarized in a book by Dr. Bruce Levine, called *Commonsense Rebellion*. The research found that children diagnosed with ADHD performed poorly in learning environments where the work was boring, repetitive and externally controlled. However, when ADHD-diagnosed children were allowed to choose learning activities that they found interesting, their ADHD symptoms disappeared. They were indistinguishable from normal children.[413] Children and teenagers in Waldorf and other schools that provide an interesting and balanced education probably take stimulants and other psychiatric drugs much less frequently. They are not bored or inattentive because their education is not boring.

The flawed US education system is a major cause of rapid growth in ADHD diagnoses. The system causes inattention by being boring and demeaning. Education reform also is causing over-diagnosis or false diagnosis of ADHD. Inattention and hyperactivity often are noticed in the classroom. As a result, teachers frequently encourage parents to have their children evaluated and possibly treated for ADHD. Education reform apparently is causing teachers to make this recommendation to parents more than is necessary.

One study linked education reform and increased accountability to rising ADHD diagnoses. NCLB was implemented in 2001. But 30 states implemented accountability standards prior to this, sometimes as early as the 1980s. These programs often reduced funding or penalized schools in other ways if they failed to improve standardized test scores. The study found that states which penalize schools for low test scores usually had substantially higher ADHD diagnosis rates. ADHD diagnoses of public school students within 200 percent of the federal poverty line increased by 59 percent on average after accountability legislation passed.[414]

These diagnoses help schools to improve test scores and avoid penalties in several ways. For example, stimulants help many students to improve concentration and test scores, regardless of whether they have ADHD. Stimulants can calm disruptive students, and thereby improve scores for the whole class. Also, test scores of students diagnosed with ADHD often are not counted in state assessments. Pressure to increase test scores can compel teachers and school administrators to suggest that many children have ADHD, when they actually do not.

Beyond false ADHD diagnoses, some children with brain diseases and other specific neurological problems might be hyperactive or inattentive due to physical causes. But the vast majority of young people with ADHD almost certainly are not mentally ill. Our shareholder-focused economic, political and education systems are ill and need to be changed. The solution to ADHD symptoms nearly always is not to drug children. In large part, it is to change our systems. But drugging children protects the status quo, in part by inhibiting system change. Labeling normal children as mentally ill and giving them drugs relieves parents, educators and society in general of responsibility for family problems, boring education systems, and other problems in society that almost certainly cause the vast majority of ADHD symptoms.

Beyond system change, another important solution in the ADHD area is to stop overprescribing stimulants. Many leaders in the medical and psychological fields have expressed serious concerns about overprescription. Minor, normal inattention frequently is being labeled as ADHD and treated with stimulants. Drug company marketing to parents often emphasizes how stimulants can help children to do better in school. As a result, many parents pressure doctors to prescribe stimulants.[415]

Dr. William Graf, a pediatric neurologist and professor at the Yale School of Medicine said, "Mild symptoms are being diagnosed so readily, which goes well beyond the disorder and beyond the zone of ambiguity to pure enhancement of children who are otherwise healthy." Dr. Jerome Groopman, a professor at the Harvard Medical School, also said that healthy, normal children too often are being diagnosed with ADHD and prescribed stimulants. He said, "There's a tremendous push where if the kid's behavior is thought to be quote-unquote abnormal – if they're not sitting quietly at their desk – that's pathological, instead of just childhood."[416]

Regarding overprescription of stimulants, Dr. Thomas Friedman, Director of the CDC, said, "misuse appears to be growing at an alarming rate." Dr. James Swanson, professor of psychiatry and a leading ADHD researcher over the past 20 years, also said that stimulants are being greatly overprescribed, in part to help young people do better in school. He said, "There's no way that one in five high school boys has ADHD."[417]

An excellent article by Dr. Richard Saul, called *ADHD Does Not Exist*, suggests that ADHD, as it is currently defined in the DSM, does not exist as a standalone condition.[418] Stimulants have been used to treat ADHD symptoms since 1937. The drugs often effectively suppress symptoms, but do not address causes. Dr. Saul points out that there are many conditions that could cause ADHD symptoms. These include sleep disorders, vision and hearing problems, substance abuse, iron deficiency, allergies, learning disabilities, and other psychological problems, such as depression. In particular, economic and education changes have caused extensive ADHD symptoms. The suppression of labor and focus on shareholder returns frequently compels employees to work harder and longer. Long, difficult, boring jobs almost certainly cause growing inattention, depression and other psychological problems. Education reform often compels students to work harder on core courses. Boring, difficult, competitive education causes extensive inattention and other psychological problems.

Dr. Saul notes that treating ADHD symptoms with stimulants can produce severe side effects, including addiction. As the brain compensates for stimulants, fewer neurotransmitters are produced. As a result, people often require larger doses, as occurs with other addictions. In addition, suppressing symptoms and failing to address the actual causes of ADHD symptoms can exacerbate problems and degrade life.

Dr. Saul suggests that people diagnosed with ADHD fall into two categories: those displaying normal distraction and impulsiveness and those with specific problems that require individualized treatment. For those in the first group, he suggests that people adopt a healthy diet, exercise regularly, get enough sleep, minimize caffeine intake, and most importantly, engage in activities that interest them. Boring work and education often will cause difficulty paying attention. For those in the second category, usually those with more severe inattention, Dr. Saul suggests a thorough evaluation to identify and treat the specific causes of ADHD symptoms.

Addressing causes can be difficult when the cause of ADHD symptoms is flawed economic and education systems. These systems produce widespread boring and difficult work and education environments. They almost certainly are the root cause of ADHD symptoms for millions of children and adults. Individuals acting alone cannot change economic and education systems. However, this does not mean that people should deal with boredom by getting high on stimulants. Prior to widespread stimulant use, people often essentially were forced to learn to concentrate and finish boring tasks. Dr. Saul expressed concern that widespread stimulant use could produce a generation of young people who cannot concentrate without stimulants.[419]

As discussed, Adderall, Ritalin and other stimulants provide short-term benefits by making children feel better. But they provide no long-term benefit. Instead, they often cause short-term and probably long-term harm. Amphetamines and cocaine-like drugs only should be used as a last resort in nearly all cases, or not used at all. But unfortunately, these drugs frequently are quickly prescribed as the first or preferred option.

A leading neuroscientist, Dr. Bruce Perry, also said that ADHD is not a real disease. ADHD describes a broad set of symptoms that could apply to nearly anyone at certain times. He expressed concerns about the overuse of stimulants to treat ADHD. Dr. Perry noted that there is no evidence of long-term benefits. Instead, animal studies show that stimulant use could cause long-term harm. He said, "If you give psychostimulants to animals when they are young, their rewards systems change. They require much more stimulation to get the same level of pleasure. So on a very concrete level they need to eat more food to get the same sensation of satiation. They need to do more high-risk things to get that little buzz from doing something. It is not a benign phenomenon. Taking a medication influences systems in ways we don't always understand. I tend to be pretty cautious about this stuff, particularly when the research shows you that other interventions are equally effective and over time more effective and have none of the adverse effects. For me it's a no-brainer."[420]

Dr. Perry recommends focusing on root causes and using nondrug treatments, including those that help parents. He said, "There are number of non-pharmacological therapies which have been pretty effective. A lot of them involve helping the adults that are around children. Part of what happens is if you have an anxious, overwhelmed parent, that is contagious. When a child is struggling, the adults around them are easily disregulated too. This negative feedback process between the frustrated teacher or parent and disregulated child can escalate out of control. You can teach the adults how to regulate themselves, how to have realistic expectations of the children, how to give them opportunities that are achievable and have success, and coach them through the process of helping children who are struggling."

"There are a lot of therapeutic approaches. Some would use somato-sensory therapies like yoga, some use motor activity like drumming. All have some efficacy. If you can put together a package of those things: keep the adults more mannered, give the children achievable goals, give them opportunities to regulate themselves, then you are going to minimize a huge percentage of the problems I have seen with children who have the problem labeled as ADHD."[421]

Our flawed education system often creates great pressure for students to take stimulants, and for parents to allow their children to take them. The increased focus on standardized testing of core subjects raises pressure to do well in these areas. Students and parents frequently see other students taking stimulants, and then getting better grades. Parents with children who are struggling in school probably often become concerned that their children will fall behind, not get into good colleges, and perhaps not do well in life. Drug company marketing, drug company influence of doctors, and the desire to help children can create great pressure for parents to allow their children to take stimulants. Many students fake ADHD symptoms to get stimulants. In some cases, parents might encourage this, believing that they are helping their children.

But this often is extremely harmful. It is normal to be bored and inattentive in our grossly flawed, competitive, factory-like education system. Giving children powerful amphetamines and other stimulants rarely is the right approach. It often produces severe side effects, and probably causes long-term physical and psychological harm. It teaches young people that they are not responsible for their behavior and performance. They learn to depend on drugs and other crutches to get by in life.

When children are inattentive in school, parents who are able to do so might consider sending their children to schools that provide more interesting and balanced educations, such as Waldorf schools. Parents who cannot afford to take children out of public schools could help them by encouraging them to focus on areas that interest them and complementing children for successes (rather than criticizing them for failure in areas that bore them).

Parents also could speak with and listen to their children in empathetic and nonjudgmental ways. Inattention often is caused by emotional or psychological problems. Helping children to work through these issues can empower them to succeed in school and life. Some struggle in life can be important and beneficial. It can build character and resilience.

Seeing other children do better in school after taking stimulants and speaking with doctors who receive money from drug companies for prescribing them can make it difficult for parents to resist allowing their children to take stimulants. But they often will greatly benefit their children if they remain strong and courageous in these situations. Perhaps their children will not do as well in school as those who take amphetamines and other prescription stimulants. But test scores are not the most important output of education. Learning to deal with adversity and take responsibility for one's behavior and performance often are more important lessons. Children and teenagers who take stimulants for many years might get better test scores in the short-term. But their long-term ability to succeed in life probably will be greatly reduced.

All young people are talented in certain areas. Parents should trust the inner wisdom of their children. It is not a child's fault if they are bored with our grossly flawed education system. Perhaps the child will not excel in what society says is important. But that largely is irrelevant. The factor that truly determines life success and satisfaction is excelling in areas that are important and relevant to the individual. One of the greatest gifts that parents can give to their children is to help them identify their unique interests and passions, and then build their lives around them.

Antipsychotics and Bipolar Disorder

Widespread and rapidly growing childhood bipolar diagnoses and resulting antipsychotic drug use is one of the most dangerous and tragic issues in the mental health area. Bipolar disorder formerly was called manic-depression. It was renamed bipolar in the DSM-3 in 1980. The manic-depression concept or diagnosis has existed since the 1850s. For over 100 years, manic-depression (i.e. bipolar) was rare, occurring about once in every 50,000 people. Bipolar virtually never was diagnosed in pre-teenage children.[422] Pre-teenage bipolar diagnosis continues to be rare in nearly all other countries.[423] But it has been growing rapidly in the US. As noted, childhood bipolar diagnoses increased 40-fold over the past 20 years. Rapidly growing diagnoses have caused over one million children and teenagers to be treated with powerful antipsychotic and other psychiatric drugs.[424]

Many mental health professionals and professional organizations have expressed strong concerns about the rapid growth of childhood bipolar diagnoses and antipsychotic drug use.[425] They often say that children who once were considered to be normal or mildly impaired, and continue to be considered so in virtually all other countries, are being labeled severely mentally ill. This often is used to justify prescription of powerful antipsychotic drugs that are known to frequently cause severe negative physical and psychological impacts.

This section discusses bipolar disorder, antipsychotic drugs, factors driving growing use of these drugs, and alternative approaches for dealing with behaviors labeled bipolar.

Bipolar Disorder

As the name implies, bipolar frequently involves alternating between high and low states or moods. Bipolar states include mania, hypomania, depression and major depression. Mania involves a distinct period of elevated or irritable mood. Symptoms can include euphoria, increased energy, decreased need for sleep, aggression, intolerance, increased libido, anxiety, grandiosity and psychosis. Hypomania involves mild to moderately elevated moods. Symptoms can include increased energy, reduced need for sleep, increased activity and productivity, euphoria, optimism, rapid speech, increased libido and irritability. Symptoms of depression include sadness, anxiety, guilt, anger, isolation, hopelessness, self-loathing, apathy, decreased libido, shyness, irritability and suicidal thoughts. Major depression is characterized by severe, highly persistent depression. It can include the above symptoms of depression plus chronic fatigue, sleep disturbances, psychosis and increased suicide risk.

Bipolar is considered to be a spectrum disorder. There are several categories of bipolar, including Bipolar I (mania, no depression required), Bipolar II (hypomania and major depression) and cyclothymia (hypomania and mild depression). DSM-4 included the category Bipolar NOS (not otherwise specified). DSM-5 replaced this with similar vague categories, such as "Unspecified bipolar and related disorder". DSM-5-TR reestablished a disorder similar to Bipolar NOS under the name Unspecified Mood Disorder. This involves symptoms that are similar to bipolar or depressive disorders, but do not meet the full criteria for them.

This broad range of symptoms and categories gives clinicians wide discretion when assigning bipolar diagnoses. Bipolar in adults is characterized by distinct periods of elevated, depressed or irritable moods that usually last for several days and interfere with the functions of ordinary life. Moods only are required to last for several hours for a childhood bipolar diagnosis.

Bipolar often is difficult to diagnose. As with other mental disorders, there are no physical tests to determine if bipolar exists. In addition, bipolar shares many symptoms with ADHD and other mental disorders. Diagnosis is based on clinical assessment and interviews. A bipolar diagnosis can cause stigma, prejudice and discrimination. Bipolar is considered to be incurable. People with a history of hypomania and depression often are considered to be bipolar, even if their symptoms ended many years ago. This is problematic because hypomania (i.e. increased energy and activity) and mild depression are widespread and frequently not considered to be dysfunctional.[426]

Antipsychotic Drugs

Bipolar often is treated with psychotherapy and/or drugs, including mood stabilizers, antipsychotics and antidepressants. Except for lithium, most mood stabilizers are anticonvulsants that frequently are used to control seizures. However, they also can suppress mania in people diagnosed with bipolar. Several antipsychotics were developed to treat schizophrenia, which is characterized by disorganized speech and thinking, psychosis, paranoia, social or occupational dysfunction, and/or lack of normal emotional responses. Antipsychotics often are used to control psychotic symptoms of bipolar, such as hallucinations and delusions. These can occur during mania or severe depression. Some antipsychotics are used over the longer-term as mood stabilizers. Antipsychotics reduce dopamine levels and probably affect other neurotransmitters and brain structures. The mechanisms of action are not fully understood.[427]

Mood stabilizers and antipsychotics often have severe side effects. Side effects of mood stabilizers include liver and kidney damage, thyroid dysfunction, hair loss, obesity, headaches, birth defects, polycystic ovary syndrome in young women, increased risk of heart disease and diabetes, worsening depression, and suicidal thoughts and behaviors.[428]

Antipsychotics (also known as neuroleptics) strongly inhibit memory, intelligence and brain functioning. They also severely reduce energy, motivation and the ability to feel pleasure. Patients often are not able to work or study while taking antipsychotics. Older antipsychotic drugs, such as Thorazine and Haldol, are known as typical antipsychotics. Newer antipsychotics are called atypicals. They were intended to have fewer side effects and be more effective than typicals. However, several studies have shown that atypicals provide little or no improvement in effectiveness.[429] In addition, atypicals reduce some side effects, such as movement disorders, but increase other adverse effects, such as metabolic syndrome.

Side effects of antipsychotics include life-threatening reductions in white blood cell counts, diabetes, pancreatitis, neuroleptic malignant syndrome (a life-threatening neurological disorder typically characterized by muscle rigidity and cognitive changes such as delirium), rapid body temperature increase, seizures, severe headaches, depression, erectile dysfunction, neuron death in the cerebral cortex, and reduced brain volume.[430][431] Antipsychotics often cause brain atrophy within one year. They also reduce life expectancy by about 20 percent and increase the risk of premature death by about 250 percent.[432]

In addition, antipsychotics frequently cause movement disorders such as inability to initiate movement or remain motionless and Parkinson's disease-like rigidity and trembling.[433] Drug companies often claim that atypical antipsychotics cause fewer movement disorders than typicals. But some studies found that this may be inaccurate. For example, drug trials often found that atypicals cause movement disorders in 5 to 15 percent of patients. However, a real-world clinical study found that 63 percent of bipolar patients taking atypicals had movement disorders.[434]

Tardive dyskinesia is a severe, sometimes permanent movement disorder that is frequently caused by antipsychotics. The disorder often produces involuntary movements of the face, eyes, tongue, mouth, neck, torso, limbs, fingers and toes. It can impair the ability to walk, speak, breathe and swallow. It also can produce distorted body postures, painful muscle spasms, and severely painful neurological symptoms. The risk of getting tardive dyskinesia increases the longer that antipsychotics are used. Antipsychotic drugs can mask initial tardive dyskinesia symptoms and make the disorder difficult to detect. This can make it difficult to stop antipsychotic use before the disorder becomes advanced or permanent. Tardive dyskinesia often becomes permanent, even if antipsychotic use is discontinued. Drug companies frequently claim that tardive dyskinesia rates are lower with atypicals. But the affliction rate remains substantial.[435]

Atypical antipsychotics produce higher rates of metabolic syndrome. This condition is a combination of medical disorders, such as elevated blood sugar, cholesterol and blood pressure, which increase the risk of heart disease and diabetes. Longer-term antipsychotic use causes metabolic syndrome in about 40 to 50 percent of patients.[436]

Antipsychotics also can cause breast development in adolescent boys and men (gynecomastia) as well as lactation in males and females. Antipsychotics suppress dopamine. This can increase prolactin levels. Prolactin strongly influences breast development and lactation. Feminine breasts sometimes remain on boys and men after antipsychotic use is stopped. They also sometimes regrow after surgical removal. Developing large and/or lactating breasts can cause severe embarrassment and social problems for adolescent boys.[437]

Antipsychotics also frequently cause increased appetite and significant weight gain that can lead to morbid obesity and diabetes. Antipsychotic drugs interfere with dopamine and serotonin systems. This strongly inhibits the ability to feel pleasure and initiate activities. With the ability to feel pleasure suppressed, eating may be one of the few sources of enjoyment available to people taking antipsychotics. This could partly explain why antipsychotics often cause obesity.[438]

Many side effects of antipsychotics diminish or end when drug use is stopped. But some negative effects can remain and become permanent. As noted, these include severe movement disorders, male breast enlargement, brain cell death and reduction in brain volume. There also is significant evidence that antipsychotics cause cognitive decline over the long-term.[439] Withdrawal from antipsychotics can cause severe symptoms, including anxiety, agitation, loss of appetite, restlessness, insomnia and psychosis. Psychosis can be mistaken for a relapse of bipolar or trigger a relapse of bipolar symptoms.[440]

Antipsychotics increasingly are being used off-label to treat nonpsychotic disorders, such as ADHD, disruptive behavior disorders such as ODD, autism, depression, anxiety, impulsivity, suicidality and dementia. Off-label means that the FDA has not approved antipsychotic use for these conditions, in part because the drugs have not been shown to be safe and effective in these areas. Several studies have found that off-label use of antipsychotics often is not justified because benefits are limited or nonexistent, while the risks of severe adverse effects are high.[441] For example, a review of clinical trials of antipsychotic use for old age dementia found modest benefits compared to a placebo, but substantial risk of severe side effects. The study concluded that antipsychotics should not be used to treat dementia patients with aggression or psychosis, except in limited cases where there is severe distress or risk of harm to others.[442]

Prescribing two or more antipsychotics and/or high antipsychotic doses is common, even though clinical guidelines usually recommend minimizing doses. Many studies indicate that prescribing multiple and/or high-dose antipsychotics usually is no more effective. But it substantially increases the risk of severe adverse effects.[443] Like other drugs, the brain can become sensitized to antipsychotics. As the brain produces more neurochemicals to compensate for the drugs, larger doses often are needed to avoid psychosis and other symptoms. If drug use is stopped, psychosis can occur that is worse than before treatment began. Antipsychotic use can lead to permanent chemical dependence.[444] A childhood bipolar diagnosis implies lifelong severe mental illness that requires long-term psychiatric drugs use.[445]

Antipsychotics strongly suppress cognitive and emotional functions. This combined with severe side effects cause about two-thirds of patients to stop taking the drugs or refuse to take them.[446] Antipsychotics often produce many moderate to severe side effects in children. As a result, children frequently are prescribed up to eight additional drugs to manage adverse effects. But this often makes the situation worse because each additional drug has its own side effects.[447] Children and teenagers are more vulnerable to the adverse effects of antipsychotics, in part because their brains and bodies are developing rapidly.

Many factors are causing rapid growth in antipsychotic drug use and childhood bipolar diagnoses. The main underlying cause is the systemically-mandated requirement of drug companies to provide ever-increasing shareholder returns. This unintentionally suicidal system flaw plays out through many mechanisms or factors. Several of them were discussed generally. However, in relation to antipsychotics and bipolar, these factors include DSM changes, psychiatric drug use causing mental illness, drug company influence of government, growing off-label use, the non-addictive nature of antipsychotics, suppressing disruptive behavior, growing institutional use, extending patents by finding new uses for drugs, drug company influence of research, drug company influence of doctors, similarity of symptoms between mental disorders, insurance reimbursement practices, prescription of psychiatric drugs in primary care settings, drug company marketing to parents and patients, and inability to successfully sue drug companies.

DSM Changes

DSM changes are a primary cause of rapid growth in bipolar diagnoses and antipsychotic drug use. Prior to DSM-3 being issued in 1980, hospitalization for a manic episode was required for a bipolar diagnosis. At that time, it was estimated that 0.5 to 1 percent of the population had bipolar.[448] Prior to that, bipolar occurrence estimates were even lower.

Bipolar diagnoses increased when bipolar was converted to a spectrum disorder. This greatly loosened definitions and requirements for bipolar diagnosis. It allowed a wide range of behaviors that previously had been considered normal to be labeled bipolar. For example, DSM-4 added irritability to diagnostic criteria. This enabled irritability to be used as a substitute for mania. As a result, being diagnosed with bipolar (i.e. manic-depression) no longer required the manic portion.

Other loosened DSM-4 bipolar criteria included hypomania. As noted, hypomania is a less severe form of mania. The definition of hypomania in adults introduced in DSM-4 includes four days of elevated mood that does not cause occupational or social dysfunction. Using this definition, if a person is very happy or very productive and energetic for a few days, they could be labeled hypomanic. Soft bipolar diagnoses represent a further loosening of bipolar definitions. Soft bipolar does not require four days of hypomania. This enables many people with depression and occasionally elevated moods to be labeled bipolar.

In addition to loosened requirements for mania, requirements for depression were weakened. As a result, if someone was very happy sometimes and sad other times, they often could be diagnosed with bipolar under the cyclothymia category. Bipolar diagnosis sometimes requires that moods negatively affect a person's life or performance, although as noted, this is not required for hypomania. But one could say that sadness, for example, interferes with life. Therefore, life impairment often is not a significant restriction to bipolar diagnoses. Under DSM-5-TR, clinicians have the discretion to label a wide range of bipolar-type moods and behaviors as Unspecified Mood Disorder.

Using the greatly expanded and loosened bipolar definitions in the DSM, some studies now show that over 10 percent of US citizens have bipolar disorder.[449] Obviously, bipolar prevalence has not grown by 1000 to 2000 percent since 1980. This growth in diagnoses largely does not result from clinicians doing a better job of recognizing previously unrecognized bipolar. Probably the large majority of growth in bipolar diagnoses results from labeling normal behavior or mild psychological symptoms as bipolar. Substantial growth in bipolar symptoms probably also results from increased stress in society, increased toxic chemicals in the environment, harmful food ingredients such as synthetic food dyes, and other factors that do not require treatment with psychiatric drugs.

DSM changes are a main cause of rapid growth in childhood bipolar diagnoses. DSM-4 substantially loosened requirements for this diagnosis. Episodes of mania or depression only are required to last for a few hours instead of several days or weeks, as is the case for adult bipolar diagnosis. Also, under the loosened criteria, severe anger in children could be considered mania.[450]

In 1994, when DSM-4 was issued, there were about 20,000 office visits for children and adolescents with bipolar in the US. By 2002, loosened childhood bipolar diagnostic requirements had driven child and adolescent bipolar office visits up to about 800,000.[451] Rapid growth in childhood bipolar diagnoses drove high growth in antipsychotic use among children and teenagers, including young children. For example, use of antipsychotics among privately insured children aged two to five years old doubled between 1999 and 2007. In Florida in 2007, 23 infants less than one year old were prescribed antipsychotics.[452]

DSM changes provided large benefits to drug companies by greatly increasing sales of antipsychotics and other psychiatric drugs. As noted, the majority of experts who recommended changes to DSM-4 and DSM-5 had financial ties to drug companies. These companies also heavily influenced bipolar treatment guidelines that often strongly promote use of antipsychotics and mood stabilizers. In addition, the bipolar spectrum diagnostic scale was developed by a drug company consultant.

Many mental health professionals and parents are concerned about rapid growth of bipolar diagnoses. Resistance to these diagnoses could limit sales of antipsychotics and other drugs. As discussed, DSM-5 created a less severe diagnosis for children with mood swings (DMDD). This will enable temper tantrums and other normal behavior to be labeled mental illness, and thereby facilitate treatment with antipsychotics and other psychiatric drugs. Creation of the DMDD disorder in DSM-5 might reduce certain types of bipolar diagnoses. But this largely is irrelevant from the drug company perspective. The key issue is achieving never-ending growth in drug sales and shareholder returns. DSM-5 will protect drug company shareholders by alleviating some concerns about excess bipolar diagnoses and facilitating even higher growth in antipsychotic and other psychiatric drug sales. This further indicates drug company influence of the APA and DSM.

Psychiatric Drugs Causing Mental Illness

The issue of psychiatric drugs causing or exacerbating mental illness is extensively discussed in an award winning book by Robert Whitaker, called *Anatomy of an Epidemic: Magic Bullets, Psychiatric Drugs, and the Astonishing Rise of Mental Illness in America.*[453] Diagnosed mental illness has been growing rapidly in the US. In 2021, about 26 percent of adults had a diagnosable mental disorder. About 46 percent of adults will have a mental disorder over the course of their lifetimes.[454] From 1987 to 2007, the percentage of US adults receiving federal disability payments for mental illness tripled. The rate among children under the age of 18 grew 35-fold. From 1985 to 2008, sales of antidepressants and antipsychotics grew 50-fold.[455]

Several factors caused rapid growth in mental illness diagnoses. As discussed, DSM changes that redefine normal behavior as mental illness caused substantial growth. Other factors include growing stress in society, reduced stigma about seeking treatment for mental illness, and improved ability to diagnose or recognize mental illness. While much of the growth in mental illness diagnoses was false or artificial (i.e. labeling normal behavior as mental illness), there also was substantial growth in actual mental illness.

Anatomy of an Epidemic provides extensive evidence which shows that much of the growth in actual mental illness was caused by increased use of psychiatric drugs. These drugs frequently provide short-term benefits. This is the main reason why the drugs are widely used and often strongly supported. Robert Whitaker analyzed data in major mental illness categories including depression, anxiety, bipolar and schizophrenia.

Extensive data and evidence showed that, while psychiatric drugs might be effective in the short-term, they increase the likelihood that people will become chronically ill over the long-term. In other words, psychiatric drugs often make people worse over the long-term.[456] Expanding use of psychiatric drugs is a major cause of growing mental illness in the US. A substantial portion of mental illness is iatrogenic (i.e. illness caused by medical treatment). To illustrate, many people take psychiatric drugs for mild psychological symptoms. Then they often have negative reactions to the drugs. This frequently leads to more severe mental illness diagnoses and more extensive drug use.

Anatomy of an Epidemic extensively examines the childhood bipolar epidemic in the US. Prior to the use of stimulants for ADHD and antidepressants for depression, bipolar virtually never occurred in children before puberty. However, stimulants and antidepressants often produce manic and hypomanic reactions in children. This frequently caused them to be diagnosed with bipolar and given antipsychotics and other powerful drugs. Many of these children are expected to be chronically ill and take psychiatric drugs for the rest of their lives. Robert Whitaker estimates that over one million children have been diagnosed with bipolar after being initially treated with stimulants or antidepressants.[457] In other words, it appears that much of the childhood bipolar epidemic in the US was caused by the use of drugs that produce bipolar symptoms.

As discussed above, psychiatric drugs also appear to be increasing depression. Extensive evidence shows that people who stop taking SSRIs often experience worse depression than before they started taking the drugs. As a result, larger doses of antidepressants frequently are required over the long-term to control depression. A World Health Organization study found that long-term antidepressant use is associated with higher rates of long-term depression. Antidepressants frequently make people more depressed than they would have been if they never had been medicated.[458]

A similar situation appears to be occurring with schizophrenia. In the 1950s, two-thirds of patients hospitalized for schizophrenia were released within a year, and most did not require subsequent hospitalization.[459] However, over the past 50 years, schizophrenia has come to be seen as a largely chronic, degenerative disease. Another World Health Organization study found that schizophrenia patients had higher recovery rates in developing countries where antipsychotics were used much less frequently.[460]

Similar results were found in a study published in the Journal of Nervous and Mental Disease. The study assessed 145 patients diagnosed with schizophrenia. After 15 years, 65 percent of patients taking antipsychotics were psychotic, but only 28 percent of unmedicated patients were.[461] Citing long-term research, NIMH director Thomas Insel said that people with schizophrenia and psychosis do better without antipsychotic medication.[462] Once again, psychiatric drugs appear to be causing or exacerbating long-term mental illness.

In the 1950s, depression, anxiety, bipolar and schizophrenia usually were episodic, not chronic. People usually got better over time. Severe, chronic mental illness was rare.[463] However, over the past 50 years, as psychiatric drug use grew rapidly in the US, chronic mental illness also has grown rapidly. This is not surprising. We do not know all of the ways that psychiatric drugs affect neurotransmitters and other brain structures. However, we do know that these drugs often cause severe physical and psychological side effects. Long-term adverse effects frequently are the expected outcome of bathing the brain in strong chemicals that are not meant to be there. Also, it is obvious that most psychological problems are caused by life circumstances, unconscious beliefs and other environmental factors. Psychiatric drugs often suppress emotions and inhibit the ability to address the actual causes of psychological problems. Ignoring or not adequately addressing actual causes can strongly promote long-term mental illness.

Developing lifelong drug customers helps to maximize drug company shareholder returns. Psychiatric drugs often cause or exacerbate more severe mental disorders such as bipolar which require long-term drug use. By providing short-term benefits and frequently promoting long-term mental illness, psychiatric drugs greatly benefit drug companies, but greatly harm society. Drug company leaders obviously do not intend to cause long-term harm and mental illness. Their focus is on maximizing shareholder returns. Long-term harm is an unintended consequence of being compelled to put shareholder returns before all else, including the mental health and well-being of citizens.

Drug Company Influence of Government

The FDA is overseen by politicians who often accept large amounts of money directly or indirectly from drug companies and their owners. Drug companies regularly rotate their employees and consultants in and out of the FDA and inappropriately influence the agency in other ways. Antipsychotics often cause severe negative effects. They have been described as giving someone a chemical lobotomy or placing them in chemical restraints.[464] Use of these frequently harmful drugs should be prohibited among children in nearly all cases. But the business-influenced FDA bases its usage decisions almost completely on studies that are supervised or strongly influenced by drug companies.[465] Drug company influence of the FDA compels the agency to allow frequently harmful antipsychotic drug use.

Growing Off-Label Use

Off-label usage represents one of the most important and harmful examples of drug company influence of the FDA. As noted, off-label use of antipsychotics for non-psychotic mental disorders has been growing rapidly. Off-label prescription involves prescribing drugs for uses that are not approved by the FDA, often because research has not shown the drugs to be safe and effective for these uses. There is a large conflict in the off-label prescription area that strongly indicates drug company influence of the FDA. Drug companies are not allowed to market drugs for off-label uses. But doctors are allowed to prescribe off-label. One might ask, if drug companies are not allowed to market off-label, why are doctors allowed to prescribe this way? Off-label prescription provides billions of dollars of revenue for drug companies. This strongly indicates that drug company influence of the FDA is a main reason why the agency allows off-label prescription.

Other factors also could be driving off-label prescription. For example, off-label uses might be the only option for patients who are not responding to approved drugs. This type of usage potentially could be allowed on a last resort basis. But there should be full disclosure of risks and uncertain benefits. Currently, doctors often prescribe unapproved, off-label drugs as quickly and easily as approved drugs. Regarding antipsychotics, one might ask, if off-label use is not proven to be safe and effective, and antipsychotics frequently have known severe side effects, why would doctors prescribe them off-label? Drug company influence of doctors appears to be a main factor driving off-label prescription.

Requiring long-term safety and efficacy research before off-label prescriptions were allowed often would show that off-label uses are unsafe and/or ineffective. This could substantially reduce drug company revenues. The current system maximizes drug company sales and shareholder returns by allowing doctors to prescribe drugs that are not proven to be safe and effective. As noted above, many independent studies show that off-label use of antipsychotics frequently provides high risks, but little or no benefit. If the FDA were primarily focused on protecting public health instead of drug company shareholders, it usually would not allow off-label usage until it was shown to be safe and effective. Doctors generally would only be allowed to prescribe drugs that are proven to be safe and effective for the conditions being treated. (Limited exceptions might be allowed for last resort or emergency situations.)

Drug companies have paid among the largest fines in US history for illegally marketing antipsychotics off-label. One company agreed to pay a settlement of $2.2 billion for illegal marketing of the antipsychotic Risperdal.[466] The fact that drug companies frequently pay large fines for illegal marketing indicates the highly profitable nature of these drugs. As noted, antipsychotics are the largest segment of the US psychiatric drug market. Use of these drugs often turns people into long-term or lifetime customers. As a result, it appears that it frequently is more profitable to continue illegal off-label marketing, develop long-term customers, and pay relatively small fines. In the above example, Risperdal sales from 1999 to 2010 were about

$30 billion.[467] While $2.2 billion is a large fine, in comparison to Risperdal revenues, it is minor or token.

Rushing Drugs to Market

This situation reflects a common drug company strategy for maximizing shareholder returns. Drug companies often seek to rush drugs to market while they are under patent protection. Lack of competition enables them to charge extremely high prices. (As discussed in the Healthcare section, virtually all other developed countries do not allow drug companies to take advantage of vulnerable patients by charging very high drug prices. But business influence of government in the US frequently enables them to do this.)

As discussed, the multi-step drug approval process can take many years. But the heavily business-influenced FDA generally does not require long-term clinical safety trials before approving psychiatric drugs. Clinical trials often only last a few months or up to a year. From a shareholder perspective, it is important to identify obvious, short-term, substantial adverse effects. Selling drugs with these effects could hurt shareholder returns. But long-term adverse effects frequently are more difficult to identify. In addition, companies often can avoid being held responsible for these effects by inappropriately influencing government and arguing that other factors could have caused harm.

The requirement to maximize shareholder returns frequently compels drug companies to rush drugs to market by exaggerating benefits and hiding risks. After earning substantial profits on patent protected drugs for many years, adverse impacts often emerge. Drug companies frequently pay fines that are small in comparison to profits earned. In several cases, such as with the drugs Vioxx, Fosamax, Paxil and Zyprexa, drug companies apparently suppressed evidence of adverse effects while the drugs were under patent protection and often paid fines for doing so. With many other drugs, such as Lipitor, Seroquel, Levaquin, Topamax and Ambien, adverse effect warnings were increased or not issued until drugs were off or nearly off patent protection.[468][469]

The FDA argues that adverse effects often do not become obvious until thousands or millions of people take a particular drug for many years.[470] But this is deceptive. The failure to identify longer-term adverse effects frequently results from the short-term nature of clinical drug trials, rather than inadequate numbers of study participants. Long-term drug safety testing often is not done. Instead, citizens essentially are used as guinea pigs.

Failing to issue adverse effect warnings until drugs are off patent greatly benefits drug companies. This strongly indicates business influence of the FDA. If the agency were focused on protecting citizens instead of drug company shareholders, it would require long-term safety testing. In some cases, safety testing might be expedited if there were a legitimate, imperative medical need. But patients should be warned that long-term adverse effects are unknown. The priority should be the health and well-being of citizens, not the financial returns of drug company shareholders.

Suppressing Disruptive Behavior

Suppressing disruptive behavior in children with off-label use of antipsychotics is another factor driving rapid growth in antipsychotic sales. A study published in the Archives of General Psychiatry found that, from 2005 to 2009, nearly two-thirds of antipsychotic prescriptions for children aged 13 and younger were written for ADHD, ODD and other disruptive behavior disorders. In addition, one-third of prescriptions for teenagers aged 14 to 20 were written for these disorders.[471]

Several antipsychotics originally were approved to treat schizophrenia. They are not approved to treat ADHD, ODD and several other disorders for which they regularly are prescribed off-label. There is little evidence that antipsychotics are effective for treating these disorders. However, the common, severe effects and side effects of antipsychotics are well known. Antipsychotic use for ADHD can appear to be illogical. Stimulants are approved to treat ADHD. As noted, stimulants raise dopamine levels, but antipsychotics reduce them.

Suppressing disruptive or defiant behavior with antipsychotic drugs should be cause for great concern in a supposedly free and democratic society. Our education, economic and political systems are grossly flawed. Rebellious, defiant or disruptive behavior often is a normal, natural and sometimes justified response to these systems and other conditions in the US. But this disruption or defiance frequently is annoying or inconvenient for authorities. As a result, we often put our children and teenagers into chemical straitjackets by giving them newer versions of Thorazine. Antipsychotics effectively suppress disruptive behavior by putting children and teenagers into a mind-numbing chemical stupor. These actions might make sense in an authoritarian society. But they are horrible and insane in a free society, which the US supposedly is but obviously is not.

Non-Addictive Qualities

The non-addictive nature of antipsychotics strongly facilitates rapid growth in usage. Many stimulants and sedatives, such as Adderall and Valium, produce pleasurable sensations. As a result, people often take them illegally. This causes the US government to aggressively control or restrict illegal usage. But antipsychotics usually have the opposite effect.

These drugs suppress emotions and thought processes. They inhibit or remove the ability to feel pleasure. And they often cause severe, painful side effects. As a result, people frequently resist taking antipsychotics. As noted, about two-thirds of people stop taking the drugs or refuse to take them. The non-addictive, unpleasant nature of antipsychotics greatly reduces concerns about abuse of these drugs. As a result, government oversight is substantially lower than it is for controlled, commonly abused, pleasure-inducing prescription drugs, such as Adderall. This makes it easier for drug companies to promote approved and unapproved (i.e. off-label) uses.

Growing Institutional Use

The growing institutional use of antipsychotics on vulnerable people is another cause of rapid growth in antipsychotic drug sales. Antipsychotics increasingly are being used in institutional settings where people are locked in and can be forced to take drugs. For example, children and teenagers often are forced to take antipsychotics in psychiatric hospitals, juvenile prisons, and foster care homes and facilities. Elderly people in nursing homes also frequently are forced or coerced into taking them. Antipsychotics in institutional settings often are prescribed for off-label uses for which there is little or no evidence that they are safe and effective. Institutions frequently require or force patients and prisoners to take them because the drugs heavily sedate people and make them easier to manage.

More than half of 5 to 12-year-old children in psychiatric hospitals are prescribed antipsychotics. The drugs also are widely used in juvenile prisons, and apparently promoted by drug companies. To illustrate, in 2007, one-third of the psychiatrists hired by the Florida Department of Juvenile Justice to evaluate incarcerated children and teenagers received money from drug companies. These doctors prescribed 54 percent of the antipsychotics used in Florida's juvenile detention facilities.[472]

Antipsychotic usage also is widespread in foster care in the US. Children and teenagers in foster care are three times more likely to be medicated than low-income youth on Medicaid. More than half of medicated children in foster care take antipsychotics. In US nursing homes, 14 percent of residents have been prescribed atypical antipsychotics. Nearly 90 percent of the prescriptions are for dementia, an unapproved off-label use.[473]

Forcing vulnerable people to take antipsychotics is inhumane. Rare usage in cases where people are in severe distress or at high risk of harming themselves or others might be justified. But the large majority of antipsychotic usage in institutional settings does not meet these criteria. The drugs often are used to make people easier to handle. This is inhumane because it essentially takes away people's humanity. Antipsychotics largely inhibit the ability to think and feel. They also often impose severe, sometimes painful and permanent side effects. Forced antipsychotic use is like a form of torture. The body is degraded, and often dies prematurely. The mind or spirit is severely inhibited. The ability to feel emotions and think clearly are essential components of being human. Taking these abilities away through forced antipsychotic usage essentially takes away people's humanity.

Patent Extensions

Extending patents by finding new uses for old drugs can contribute to increased drug sales. Many studies have shown that discovering new drugs to treat a mental disorder, or discovering new uses for old drugs, often substantially increases diagnoses of the disorder. For example, bipolar diagnoses substantially increased after it was discovered that lithium could be used to treat the disorder.[474]

Drug companies usually make far more money by selling patented drugs. This often blocks competition and enables companies to charge very high prices. To protect patents and limit competition from generic drugs, drug companies sometimes seek new uses for old drugs. This occurred with anticonvulsants. As noted, anticonvulsants suppress seizures. Drug companies argued that the drugs also could suppress mania. They renamed anticonvulsants mood stabilizers, even though there is no evidence that anticonvulsants actually stabilize moods.[475] The FDA began approving use of anticonvulsant/mood stabilizers to treat mania in 1995. With new drugs available to treat bipolar, bipolar diagnoses grew rapidly.

The same occurred with antipsychotics. They originally were developed to treat schizophrenia. Once the FDA approved them to treat bipolar, bipolar diagnoses increased further. With a new large market (i.e. the bipolar market) for patent-protected drugs, drug companies heavily marketed mood stabilizers and antipsychotics to doctors and citizens.[476]

Drug Company Influence of Research

Drug companies frequently fund or strongly influence research about the causes of bipolar and the risks and benefits of antipsychotics and other drugs used to treat it. Much of the bipolar research is focused on physical causes, in part because this can support increased drug sales. But as with other mental disorders, there is no proof that bipolar is caused by genetics, brain chemical imbalances or any other physiological factor. Some studies with small sample sizes linked bipolar to genetics. But the results often were not replicated in subsequent studies.[477] Studies that attempt to find other physiological causes of bipolar also frequently are inconclusive.

However, many studies have strongly linked bipolar to environmental factors, such as life circumstances. One-third to one-half of adults with bipolar experienced abuse or trauma as children. On average, people with bipolar report having more stressful events in childhood than those without bipolar.[478] This is the obvious and expected outcome. The mind responds and adapts to life circumstances. Abused children and adults who were abused as children often believe at a deep, unconscious level that they are unworthy and do not deserve a good life. These beliefs could cause them to work hard to compensate for senses of inadequacy (i.e. display mania or hypomania symptoms). At other times, the foundational sense of unworthiness could cause them to be depressed. In other words, child abuse or other negative life circumstances could cause bipolar symptoms.

Regarding antipsychotic research, several studies found that the drugs only are slightly more effective than placebos. However, most antipsychotic research is funded or strongly influenced by drug companies. As a result, there is high potential for this research to be biased in favor of antipsychotics.[479] If truly independent research were conducted, antipsychotics probably often would be no more effective than placebos.

A book by psychiatrist Joanna Moncrieff, called *The Myth of the Chemical Cure*, examined decades of clinical trials. The analysis found that, when placebo and withdrawal affects are taken into account, antipsychotics are not effective over the long-term.[480] Several studies also showed that patients stop taking atypicals at the same rates as typicals. This implies that benefits and side effects are about equal.[481] Other studies found that the effectiveness of antipsychotics declines over time, while the risks of severe side effects substantially increase.[482]

As discussed, DSM-4 substantially loosened the criteria for diagnosis of bipolar in children. The British National Institute of Health and Clinical Excellence said that research does not support the weaker criteria in the DSM. It creates significant risk that children without bipolar will be treated with harmful antipsychotic drugs.[483] Also, patients in the US often are prescribed multiple and/or high doses of antipsychotics, even though guidelines usually recommend minimizing doses. Several studies show that high doses are riskier, but no more effective. Finland has the best long-term results in treating bipolar. Doctors there use antipsychotics in a limited and cautious manner.[484]

A study of bipolar treatment in the 1890s and 1990s found that 81 percent of patients in the 1890s recovered from bipolar, but only 17 percent recovered in the 1990s. The study concluded that mood stabilizing drugs do not work.[485] Bipolar patients do better when they do not take drugs. Some people might argue that bipolar diagnostic methods were worse in the 1890s. This probably is true. But it is less relevant in this case. The study assessed patients who had been diagnosed with bipolar. Having diagnosed bipolar initially, doctors in the 1890s presumably could have diagnosed it again if a relapse occurred.

The strongest evidence indicates that bipolar is caused mainly by environmental factors, such as life circumstances. In support of this, several studies have shown that psychotherapy is the most effective way to treat bipolar. However, dealing with the acute mania of Bipolar I can be difficult. Some therapists stress the importance of building a strong, trusting relationship with clients.[486] This is logical because bipolar often appears to result from child abuse or neglect. This can severely degrade people's ability to trust others, and thereby cause psychological symptoms and life problems. In a safe, supportive therapeutic setting, people can learn to trust others, heal wounds from the past, and improve life satisfaction and functionality.

Children often play by creating fantasy worlds in their minds. Abused children sometimes create fantasy worlds to survive. If their real world is too horrible, they escape into a safe fantasy world. Severe child abuse often causes feelings of self-loathing that can last a lifetime. As adults, the self-loathing can cause negative emotions and life problems. When emotions become too painful, people might escape into a fantasy world, as they did as children. Antipsychotics and mood stabilizers suppress negative emotions, and thereby could reduce the need to escape reality (i.e. psychosis).

In the 1950s, antipsychotics often were referred to as major tranquilizers. The drugs work by heavily sedating people. They frequently produce lethargy, impaired motor control, emotional indifference, detachment and inability to feel pleasure. By heavily suppressing emotions and cognitive ability, the drugs often suppress paranoia, delusions and other psychotic symptoms. There is no evidence that antipsychotics work directly on the symptoms of psychosis.[487] In other words, antipsychotics are not directly antipsychotic. They suppress psychosis through heavy sedation.

As discussed, anticonvulsants were renamed mood stabilizer even though there is no proof that they actually stabilize moods. This protected patents and allowed increased shareholder returns. In the same way, it appears that major tranquilizers were renamed antipsychotics, even though there is no proof that they directly address psychotic symptoms. This renaming facilitated expanded use and increased drug sales. In terms of actual effects, major tranquilizer or sedative remains the more accurate name for antipsychotics. Antipsychotics do not cure people, for example, by fixing some physical flaw in the brain. They essentially are heavy-duty sedatives that suppress emotions. As noted, they have been described as giving people a chemical lobotomy or placing them in chemical restraints.

Suppressing psychological symptoms might enable people to more effectively engage in psychotherapy and address root causes. This might be true in some cases with antidepressants and other psychiatric drugs. But it is less likely that antipsychotics would enable or facilitate psychotherapy. The drugs inhibit people's ability to feel emotions and think clearly. This often would suppress the motivation and ability to engage in psychotherapy and effectively address root causes of psychological problems, such as self-loathing caused by child abuse.

In some cases, the break from reality of psychosis might result from people feeling that the world is unsafe and other people are untrustworthy. Therapists often attempt to build a bridge back to reality for people with psychotic symptoms. By building a safe, trustworthy environment, people can explore trusting others. Negative emotions caused by child abuse or other trauma can provide the motivation to do the hard work of therapy as well as provide raw material for exploration in therapy. Having a clear mind makes it easier to understand the false nature of harmful beliefs learned during an abusive childhood. With the help of an empathetic therapist, people frequently re-educate or re-parent themselves. Doing the life enhancing work of uncovering unconscious disempowering beliefs and changing them can be difficult or impossible if one's mind is clouded and numbed by psychiatric drugs, especially antipsychotics.

While many cases of bipolar appear to be caused by child abuse, children from good, loving homes also could develop bipolar symptoms. As noted, bipolar often appears to result from stress or trauma. Many factors potentially could cause stress and bipolar symptoms, including bullying, disempowering media, judgmental education, environmental toxins and chemical food additives.

Drug Company Influence of Doctors

Influence of doctors contributes to rapid growth in the use of antipsychotics and other psychiatric drugs. Psychiatrists usually can make substantially more money by prescribing drugs than providing psychotherapy. Partly as a result, the percentage of psychiatric office visits that involve psychotherapy has been declining for many years. Less than 30 percent of psychiatric office visits include it.[488]

Drug companies would not give money and other inducements to doctors if it did not increase drug sales. When drug companies influence doctors, there often is an implied, though probably unstated, expectation of reciprocity. Drug companies expect doctors to prescribe more drugs. Doctors should be fully informing patients and parents about short-term and long-term risks and benefits of psychiatric drug use. They also should clarify that there is great uncertainty about long-term negative impacts and how the drugs work.

But this sometimes apparently does not occur. Instead, doctors often appear to quickly prescribe antipsychotics and other dangerous drugs to adults and children.[489] They probably often face great pressure from drug companies to prescribe these drugs because, as noted, once people are placed on them, they frequently become long-term or even lifetime drug company customers. They also often become long-term customers for psychiatrists.

Similarity of Symptoms Between Mental Disorders

The similarity of symptoms between bipolar and other mental disorders also potentially contributes to increased bipolar diagnoses and antipsychotic drug use. Bipolar shares many symptoms with ADHD, schizophrenia and some other mental disorders. As discussed, diagnoses of mental disorders is based completely on opinion. As note above, a major study found that well-trained clinicians disagree about 50 percent of the time about mental disorder diagnoses. The bias or prejudice of clinicians can play a substantial role in diagnosis.

To illustrate, effects and side effects of stimulants are listed above. Several of these could appear to be mania or hypomania. Stimulants and antidepressants often produce bipolar-like symptoms. Similarities between bipolar symptoms, ADHD symptoms, and effects and side effects of drugs used to treat ADHD and depression almost certainly cause substantial increases in bipolar diagnoses and subsequent antipsychotic drug use.

Insurance Reimbursement Practices

Reimbursement practices also cause growing bipolar diagnoses, especially among children. Many studies showed that psychotherapy, behavior management, parent training and other nondrug bipolar treatments are more effective than medication, especially over the longer-term.[490] But medication usually is far less expensive than psychotherapy and some other nondrug treatments.

Publicly traded health insurance companies are structurally required to put the well-being of shareholders before all else, including the health and well-being of citizens. To maximize shareholder returns, they often have reduced coverage for psychotherapy, but provide strong coverage for antipsychotics and other bipolar drugs. This substantially contributes to increased drug use, as well as substantially degrades society, because many, if not the large majority, of bipolar patients would have higher recovery rates with nondrug treatments.

Diagnostic upcoding is another insurance related practice that causes increased bipolar diagnoses and antipsychotic drug use. To illustrate, insurance reimbursement for inpatient treatment of children with behavioral problems requires meeting higher hurdles or standards. Some studies have found that high bipolar diagnosis rates probably result in part from clinicians upcoding children to more severe bipolar diagnoses to get insurance reimbursement.[491]

Prescription in Primary Care Settings

Allowing primary care and other doctors with little psychological and psychiatric training and clinical experience to prescribe antipsychotics and other psychiatric drugs almost certainly is another major factor causing rapid growth in antipsychotic drug use. As noted, about 80 percent of psychiatric drugs are prescribed in primary care settings, often by doctors with no psychological or psychiatric training, beyond the limited training they received in medical school.

This is particularly problematic with bipolar and antipsychotics. Bipolar is a severe, lifelong mental illness diagnosis. Antipsychotics have common, severe negative side effects. Stigmatizing someone for life with a severe mental illness diagnosis and prescribing psychiatric drugs with severe, sometimes permanent adverse effects only should be done by doctors with extensive psychological and psychiatric training and clinical experience. Unfortunately, this often is not occurring. One study found that there is an extreme shortage of child and adolescent psychiatrists in the US. Partly as a result, a growing number of children are being prescribed antipsychotics by pediatricians.[492]

Drug companies strongly influence doctors to increase antipsychotic drug sales. Doctors frequently prescribe antipsychotics without doing adequate psychological evaluations. One study found that nearly two percent of two to five-year-old privately insured children in the US were prescribed antipsychotics. Less than half of these children received a mental health assessment, psychotherapy visit, or visit with a psychiatrist while they were taking drugs.[493] Given the high risks of antipsychotics, prescription should not be allowed by doctors who lack extensive psychological and psychiatric training and clinical experience. Prescription without adequate psychological evaluations and oversight also should be prohibited.

Drug Company Marketing

Marketing to parents and potential patients also is a major cause of increased bipolar diagnoses and antipsychotic drug use. To provide ever-increasing shareholder returns, drug companies aggressively market atypical antipsychotics, with a particular emphasis on expanding antipsychotic use among children and the elderly.[494] As discussed, citizens are highly vulnerable to drug advertising. This is a main reason why every country, except the US and New Zealand, prohibits direct-to-consumer marketing of prescription drugs.

Drug companies often take advantage of loosened DSM criteria that define happiness and sadness as symptoms of bipolar. Ads often create the impression that bipolar is widespread, severe and treatable with drugs. Antipsychotic ads frequently take advantage of parents' natural desire to find a quick solution for unhappy or misbehaving children. Extensive antipsychotic ads often are placed on television, in periodicals and in other locations.

Drug sales require a medical diagnosis. As a result, drug ads frequently suggest that people might have a "medical disorder" (i.e. implying physical, not psychological problem). Ads often encourage consumers to focus on feelings and behaviors, and then discuss them with a doctor.

Drug companies frequently provide online questionnaires. People are encouraged to answer the questions, print out the answers and take them to a doctor. One study found that discussing specific symptoms and a particular drug with doctors greatly increase the likelihood that doctors would prescribe the drug. In effect, drug companies are coaching potential drug consumers on how to get doctors to prescribe drugs.

Drug company online questionnaires often ask questions such as, are there times when you are more talkative, energetic, productive, irritable, sociable or confident than usual? If people answer yes, the drug company websites suggest that people might have bipolar disorder. Probably nearly everyone could answer yes to many or most of the questions on these websites. Variations in moods or performance, and sometimes feeling up or down, are normal parts of life. These drug marketing websites imply that normal feelings and behaviors are mental illnesses that can be managed with drugs.

People who are depressed or experiencing other psychological problems often are highly vulnerable. A simple solution to their problems, like taking a pill, frequently is highly appealing. But most psychological problems result from disempowering beliefs, life circumstances and other environmental factors, not neurological problems. Taking a pill often will suppress the motivation and mental clarity needed to address the actual causes of psychological symptoms and problems.

To protect vulnerable citizens, the US should do what virtually every other country does – prohibit direct-to-consumer marketing of prescription drugs. But the priority of the business-controlled US government is not maximizing the well-being of citizens and society in general, as required by the Constitution. The priority often is to maximize the well-being of businesses and shareholders. As a result, direct-to-consumer drug marketing is allowed.

Difficulty Holding Drug Companies Responsible

Difficulty in bringing lawsuits against drug companies also facilitates increased antipsychotic sales. Antipsychotics cause widespread, severe, sometimes permanent adverse effects and disabilities. These drugs harm many people each year.[495] But relatively few product liability or other lawsuits are brought against drug companies. Several factors make it difficult to bring, much less win, drug company lawsuits. These factors are summarized in an excellent article by Dr. Peter Breggin, called *Antipsychotic Drugs, Their Harmful Effects, and the Limits of Tort Reform*.[496]

As discussed, antipsychotics often effectively give patients a chemical lobotomy. This frequently makes them too apathetic to complain about or recognize abnormal movements or other adverse effects. Also, drug companies spend millions of dollars to defend lawsuits. These lawsuits can last many years. Most people cannot afford the time or money needed to sue drug companies. In addition, many lawyers will not sue drug companies because the chance of winning is very low. Doctors often are unwilling to testify against fellow doctors. This can make it difficult to get expert witnesses.

Also, businesses frequently give money to politicians, who then appoint pro-business judges. These judges often require scientific proof that a particular drug produces a specific adverse effect. It frequently is difficult or impossible to get this proof because drug companies control the majority of drug research. In addition, during lawsuits, drug companies sometimes are able to avoid disclosing drug safety data and research which shows that drugs are harmful by arguing that the data is proprietary.[497]

If the US government were focused on the well-being of society instead of the well-being of business, it would demand that drugs be proven to be safe over the short-term and long-term before use was allowed. It is impossible to prove this with inherently biased drug company-influenced research. The burden of proof should be on drug companies to show that drugs are safe (through independent research), not on citizens to show the drugs are unsafe. Difficulty in winning lawsuits greatly reduces the likelihood that drug companies will be held responsible for the negative impacts of antipsychotics. This strongly facilitates increased sales.

Business influence of government is further indicated by a 2012 Supreme Court decision, *Mutual Pharmaceutical Co., Inc. v. Bartlett*. In the 5-4 decision, the five Republican-appointed justices found that generic drug manufacturers could not be held responsible for harm caused by their drugs because they are required to make copies of brand-name drugs. Dissenting justices argued that FDA approval of a drug should not absolve drug companies of their responsibility to sell safe products.[498]

In this case, the five pro-business justices on the Supreme Court found that generic drug companies could sell drugs that sicken or kill people without penalty. People injured by generic drugs often would seek government healthcare assistance. As discussed on the Corporate Welfare section of *Global System Change*, this situation is similar to one of the largest forms of corporate welfare – limited liability. With limited liability, taxpayers often are compelled to act as the owners of business on the downside (by paying for negative impacts caused by companies) while receiving none of the financial upside. *Mutual Pharmaceutical Co., Inc. v. Bartlett* once again shows how business influence often causes the US government to be more focused on protecting shareholder returns than the health and lives of citizens.

Alternative Approaches

The growing use of antipsychotics for psychotic and non-psychotic mental disorders well illustrates the grossly flawed nature of our economic and political systems. To maximize shareholder returns, drug companies are compelled to promote widespread use that often is unnecessary and harmful. This promotion includes strongly influencing medical education, drug research, regulators, doctors, parents and potential patients. Vera Hassner Sharav, President of the Alliance for Human Research Potential, said, "Antipsychotics, which are being widely and irresponsibly prescribed for American children—mostly as chemical restraints—are shown to be causing irreparable harm."[499]

The widespread use of antipsychotics to treat bipolar in children is a uniquely US phenomenon. No other country diagnoses bipolar in children and prescribes antipsychotics to anywhere near the extent of the US. In reality, US children do not have substantially higher rates of bipolar than children in the rest of the world. Instead, they have a government that is more focused on protecting drug company shareholders than children. This must end. Antipsychotics do not cure bipolar. The drugs often make people severely and permanently worse, physically and psychologically. Once people understand the harmful nature of these drugs and the reasons why they are overprescribed, it can seem unbelievable that We the People would allow such use.

Antipsychotics often are given to vulnerable people who cannot speak up for themselves. The drugs severely inhibit people's ability to feel emotions and think clearly. They frequently cause permanent brain damage, cognitive impairment and terrible physical degradation, including premature death. Forcing vulnerable people to take antipsychotics seems like something from the movie *One Flew Over the Cuckoo's Nest*. Widespread, unnecessary use of antipsychotics severely degrades society. Therefore, the well-being of society demands that this use be substantially scaled back. Drug and any other companies have no right to profit by degrading society.

There often are far more effective treatments for bipolar symptoms than antipsychotics, anticonvulsants and other psychiatric drugs. Many actions are needed to scale back antipsychotic use and more effectively treat bipolar symptoms. Raising public awareness of the following information is one of the most important actions needed.

Psychiatrists and other experts often create the impression among parents and patients that bipolar is well understood and drugs frequently are the best treatment option. This is understandable because medical education often teaches doctors that there is a drug to solve nearly every problem. Biased drug research frequently shows psychiatric drugs to be more effective and safe than they actually are. And psychiatrists and other doctors often accept money and other influence from drug companies.

However, bipolar is not well understood and drugs frequently are not the most effective treatment. Like other mental disorders, experts can observe the symptoms of bipolar, such as mania and depression. But they do not know the specific causes of these symptoms. Strong evidence and common sense indicates that most bipolar symptoms, probably the large majority, are caused by life circumstances such as child abuse, trauma and other stressful life events. These nonphysical causes imply that nonphysical treatments would be most effective.

It is important to help parents and patients understand that a bipolar diagnosis only is an opinion. It is not based on verifiable science, as occurs with many medical diagnoses. Bipolar diagnoses are much higher in the US than in other countries in large part because drug companies strongly influenced the DSM criteria used to diagnose bipolar. These criteria have been expanded to include normal happiness and sadness as symptoms of bipolar. Childhood bipolar criteria have been further loosened. As a result, the large majority of children diagnosed with bipolar in the US probably do not have this disorder. As it is currently defined, bipolar is considered to be an incurable, severe mental illness. Assigning a bipolar diagnosis implies lifelong stigma and possible discrimination. Therefore, parents and patients should be highly skeptical of bipolar diagnoses, especially of children, in the US.

Parents and patients also should be made aware of the benefits and risks of antipsychotics, anticonvulsant/mood stabilizers and other drugs used to treat bipolar. There is no proof that antipsychotics directly address psychosis or other bipolar symptoms. The drugs mainly work by heavily sedating people. This is not a cure. It is temporary suppression of symptoms. This might be acceptable if there were minimal or no side effects. But as discussed, the effects and side effects of these drugs often are severely negative. This causes two-thirds of people to stop taking them. The drugs frequently degrade people physically and psychologically over the long-term. They can cause people to become dependent on drugs for life.

Many historical and current studies show that people who are given no drugs or minimal drugs recover from bipolar much more frequently. As noted, Finland uses antipsychotics sparingly and has the highest long-term success with bipolar treatment. Widespread drug use has largely converted bipolar from an episodic to chronic disorder. Antipsychotics provide short-term benefits by suppressing symptoms, including distressing or annoying behaviors. But the drugs almost certainly will make children worse over the long-term, and possibly ruin their lives. To minimize harm, parents and patients should be given full, honest information about the short-term and long-term risks and benefits of antipsychotics. It should be made clear that the mechanics of action are unknown and there are high risks of long-term physical and psychological harm.

As discussed in *Anatomy of an Epidemic*, widespread prescription of stimulants and antidepressants is a main cause, perhaps the main cause, of the childhood bipolar epidemic in the US. These drugs often cause bipolar symptoms, which frequently drive bipolar diagnoses and prescription of antipsychotic drugs. As a result, if children who are taking stimulants or antidepressants begin to display mania or other bipolar symptoms, they probably often should be taken off of drugs and observed, before being diagnosed with bipolar and prescribed antipsychotics or other bipolar drugs. Taking children off of drugs frequently will end drug-induced symptoms.

Psychiatric drugs often make people worse over the long-term. The solution frequently is to stop taking drugs, rather than taking stronger ones. Symptoms such as inattention, hyperactivity or depression might reappear once stimulant or antidepressant use is stopped. But these symptoms often would be more effectively treated with psychotherapy or other nondrug treatments.

Reversing loosened DSM diagnostic criteria is a critical aspect of addressing the artificial childhood bipolar epidemic in the US (artificial in the senses of calling normal behavior bipolar and prescribing stimulants and antidepressants that cause bipolar symptoms). Bipolar definitions should be based on maximizing the well-being of society, not the well-being of drug companies. Bipolar spectrum definitions probably should be reversed and returned to original definitions. This primarily includes severe mania combined with severe depression. High energy, productivity or happiness combined with sadness or mild depression should not be seen as bipolar. As a result, the cyclothymia bipolar category probably should be eliminated.

The vague category Unspecified Mood Disorder gives clinicians wide discretion to say that people are mentally ill when bipolar-type symptoms do not fit bipolar categories. This facilitates overdiagnosis. These unspecified or vague categories also probably should be reduced or eliminated. In addition, loosened childhood bipolar criteria should be reversed. The American Academy of Childhood and Adolescent Psychology recommends that the same criteria used to diagnose bipolar in adults should be used in children.

The use of antipsychotics to treat bipolar and other mental disorders should be substantially scaled back, and prohibited among preadolescent children. Rather than providing long-term benefits, these drugs often cause severe long-term harm. They should be mostly or only used when patients experience severe distress or are at risk of hurting themselves or others. To minimize the risk of long-term harm, doses and duration of use should be minimized. People should be tapered off the drugs as quickly as possible. Abruptly stopping antipsychotic use can cause psychosis and other severe symptoms. This indicates the powerful impact that antipsychotics have on the brain/mind.

Antipsychotics often are prescribed to young children, sometimes less than one year old. This is insane. Giving antipsychotics to vulnerable children when their brains and bodies are developing rapidly frequently will cause severe, permanent harm. Attempting to diagnose bipolar in an infant is not rational. Doctors who accept money from drug companies might conclude that an infant has bipolar because the child appears to be manic sometimes and depressed at other times. But happiness, overactivity, sadness, moodiness and anger are normal childhood states. It is tragic that vulnerable parents sometimes are encouraged by drug company-influenced doctors to place their infants and young children on antipsychotics. This is a crime. If the US government were focused on protecting children instead of drug company shareholders, this extremely harmful action would not be allowed.

There are many good psychiatrists, psychologists and other experts who understand the risks of antipsychotics and other psychiatric drugs. They prescribe the drugs cautiously and sparingly, and often use them only as a last resort. Through referrals, research and other means, parents and patients should seek out these types of experts. Doctors who quickly prescribe psychiatric drugs with little or no psychological evaluation, such as many doctors in primary care settings, probably should be avoided.

Most bipolar and other psychotic mental disorders result from environmental factors, such as abuse, trauma or stress, rather than from physiological or neurological causes. Given the prevalence of nonphysical causes, it should not be surprising that nonphysical (i.e. nondrug) treatments often provide the greatest long-term benefit. As discussed above, psychotherapy, behavior management and parent training programs have been shown to be more effective than medication when treating children with the behavioral problems associated with bipolar.

Regarding psychosis, there are several nondrug treatment options. People experiencing hallucinations or delusions often should not be medicated, unless their psychosis is causing severe distress, risk of harm, or major dysfunction.[500] Prior to widespread drug use, most people with bipolar, schizophrenia and other psychotic conditions recovered. The mind, like the body, has the ability to heal itself. A temporary break from reality might be the mind's way of avoiding overwhelming emotions and facilitating healing.

The Soteria network illustrates a wiser, nondrug approach to treating psychosis. Soteria provides therapeutic residential environments for people experiencing psychosis and other extreme states. Residents are treated with dignity, respect and compassion. They are encouraged to assume responsibilities in their living environments. Antipsychotics and other drugs are rarely or never used. Drug use always is voluntary.[501] Residents are treated like unique human beings, not sick patients. Part of the respect shown to residents is to assume that hallucinations or delusions mean something.

Carl Jung and many other therapists showed that dreams often contain helpful information that apparently is communicated from a wiser, deeper, unconscious part of the mind. Psychotic episodes could represent a similar phenomenon. Wise therapists frequently assume there is a reason for psychosis. Rather than suppressing it with drugs, they help clients to understand the 'message' of psychosis, and thereby help to heal their lives.

The situation with bipolar, antipsychotics and children is particularly tragic. In *Anatomy of an Epidemic*, Robert Whitaker provides extensive evidence which shows that psychiatric drugs are harming many children. Use of stimulants and antidepressants often produces bipolar symptoms, which leads to antipsychotic drug use. Children start out displaying normal happiness and sadness, enter the drug company-controlled US mental health system, and wind up with severely degraded lives. In discussing the harm done by psychiatric drugs to US children, Robert Whitaker said, "When you think of the millions of children so affected, it makes you want to weep."[502]

The Vulnerability of Children

Protecting children and future generations is a main purpose of *Global System Change*. Children are highly vulnerable in the psychiatric drug area. They are extensively harmed by overprescription. Due to their vulnerability, children deserve and must receive much greater protection from unnecessary and often harmful prescription of psychiatric drugs.

The vulnerability of children is discussed in an excellent article by Dr. Andrew Weiss, called "*The Wholesale Sedation of America's Youth.*"[503] Dr. Weiss points out that, in many ways, children are ideal customers for drug companies. They often are passive and compliant when parents tell them to take a pill. Unlike adults, children frequently are not able to stop taking psychiatric drugs if the drugs cause unpleasant or harmful effects or side effects. Once parents are convinced that drug use is necessary, if children complain, parents can force them to take drugs. Also, children generally do not know how they are supposed to feel. As a result, they are more likely than adults to tolerate or adjust to the effects and side effects of psychiatric drugs.[504]

The vulnerability of children makes childhood drug use an excellent growth opportunity for drug companies. To capitalize on this opportunity, these companies have been aggressively marketing and promoting increased pediatric drug use for over 40 years. Parents are highly vulnerable to drug company marketing and doctors who accept money and other inducements from them. As discussed in the Misleading the Public section, average citizens often do not have the time needed to study complex issues, such as the safety and efficacy of psychiatric drugs. Even if they do study this issue, their lack of expertise frequently makes them unable to identify biased or inaccurate information in drug company-influenced research and marketing materials.

Parents often are overwhelmed with obligations at work and home. Dealing with a disruptive or unhappy child can be extremely difficult. This makes parents highly vulnerable to doctors who suggest psychiatric drug use. Doctors often state or imply that there is evidence that mental disorders are caused by genetic or other physiological factors. They further imply that the condition is not the parent's or child's fault. The child has an illness, just like a medical problem. The implied or stated conclusion is that using psychiatric drugs is the preferred or only option. This relieves the parent and child of responsibility for the child's behavior. The drugs frequently suppress psychological symptoms. This makes life easier for overwhelmed parents.

However, doctors often fail to inform parents that they are receiving money or other inducements from drug companies. They also frequently neglect to mention that the so-called evidence of physical causes usually was developed or influenced by drug companies and does not come close to proof that mental disorders are caused by physiological factors. Doctors probably also sometimes neglect to mention that much stronger evidence indicates that mental disorders usually are caused by environmental factors and more effectively treated with nondrug options. Doctors and drug companies often create the impression that psychological problems are worse than they actually are and unlikely to heal on their own. They frequently neglect to mention that virtually all childhood psychological symptoms once were considered to be normal aspects of childhood and nearly always healed on their own without psychiatric drugs.

As government continues to redistribute trillions of dollars of public wealth through many forms of corporate welfare to the small group of wealthy citizens that controls government, life becomes increasingly difficult for average citizens. Overwhelmed parents often are not able to give children the time and attention they need to grow up well. This is particularly true with troubled children who need extra time and attention.

As business-controlled government continues to cut funding and other support for public education, teachers and other school personnel frequently do not have the time or resources needed to effectively deal with disruptive children. Many schools strongly encourage parents to place their children on psychiatric drugs. Some schools will not allow disruptive children to attend classes unless they are medicated.

Children, especially young children, often are powerless and defenseless. They frequently do not understand how life or society works. They are in the process of learning these things. Dr. Weiss states in the article noted above that an entire generation of young people has been brought up to believe that most psychological problems can be solved with drugs and drug-seeking behavior is rational and respectable. Comforted by assurances from doctors and drug companies, millions of parents take actions that improve short-term behavior, but harm children in the long-term. The ubiquity of psychiatric drugs conditions children to lifelong habits of self-medicating.

Dr. Weiss states that childhood largely has been redefined. Normal variations in character and temperament seem to mean little. Virtually every undesirable impulse of childhood now is considered to be a symptom of mental illness.[505]

Medicating away the normal highs and lows of children is horrible. Throughout human history, high and low moods were a normal part of childhood. These moods, especially low moods, often are teachers. Children have strong survival instincts. They usually naturally learn to deal with the highs and lows of life through experience. This frequently helps them to become stronger, more effective adults. Putting children into drug-induced altered states of consciousness robs them of the normal childhood experience. It often severely inhibits their ability to enjoy childhood, develop into effective adults and prosper in life.

Psychological drugs, especially antipsychotics, also impose terrible side effects, such as movement disorders, metabolic syndrome, obesity, and large or lactating breasts in adolescent boys. Using these harmful drugs on children should be illegal in nearly all cases. But our business-controlled government makes these harmful actions legal.

Finally, and perhaps most importantly, psychiatric drugs often rob children of the ability to freely think and feel like normal human beings. Self-reflective consciousness differentiates humans from animals. This ability is a natural right of humans. Psychiatric drugs should not be used to take this fundamental right away from people, especially vulnerable children.

Psychiatric Drug Solutions

The situation with psychiatric drugs illustrates the need for a whole system approach. Flawed economic and political systems are main causes of overprescription. These systems often compel companies to put maximizing shareholder returns before all else. When they fail to do this, management frequently is replaced, companies get taken over, or they go out of business. Flawed systems essentially force drug companies to oppose anything that threatens shareholder returns, including safe and effective use of psychiatric drugs.

Many children and adults who take psychiatric drugs probably should not be doing so. The risk-benefit profile often does not justify drug use. Drug company-influenced studies frequently show psychiatric drugs to be only slightly more effective than placebos. If study biases were removed and truly independent research was conducted, psychiatric drugs often would be no more effective than placebos.

Psychiatric drugs often provide short-term benefits, such as suppression of undesirable behaviors. But they frequently cause long-term physical and psychological harm. They often increase the risk that people will become chronically ill and drug dependent for life. This maximizes drug company shareholder returns, but gravely harms society. As noted, antidepressants often increase long-term depression. Antipsychotics frequently make psychosis worse, especially if drug use is discontinued. As people become used to drugs, larger doses often are needed. This further helps drug companies, but harms society.

In one sense, giving psychiatric drugs to children is like hitting them. As discussed in the Hitting Children section, physical punishment often provides short-term benefits, such as suppression of undesirable behavior. But no study has shown that hitting children provides long-term benefits. Instead, nearly every study shows that it causes long-term harm. Children become more aggressive when they are hit. They often have more problems as teenagers and adults. Their ability to prosper in life frequently is severely inhibited.

The same often is true with psychiatric drugs. Giving speed (i.e. amphetamines) to children might help them to do better in school. But taking amphetamines daily is not a formula for life success. It frequently will cause long-term physical and psychological harm. We should not be giving children speed so that they are better able to focus on something they have little or no interest in. A better approach would be to improve the education system and help young people to identify and focus on their unique areas of interest and competence.

The main reason that many people with psychological problems should not be taking psychiatric drugs is that most, probably the large majority, of these problems are not caused by physical, neurological factors, and therefore do not require a physical, drug solution. The widespread use of psychiatric drugs implies that most mental disorders are caused by physical, neurological or genetic factors. Drug companies, doctors paid by them and other allies heavily promote this idea. But there is no proof and little credible, independent evidence to show that it is true. Instead, overwhelming evidence, common sense and observations of reality show that most psychological problems are caused by environmental or external factors.

The mind largely is a sensing, processing and adapting mechanism. Things happen around people. Then the mind adapts and produces different behaviors and feelings. For example, abused children often think, feel and behave differently than children who were not abused. Psychological pain and problems usually essentially are signals that something needs to change, such as current life circumstances or disempowering beliefs that resulted from previous life experiences.

Many external factors can cause psychological problems. As discussed in the Chemicals section, pesticides and other synthetic chemicals are ubiquitous in the environment. Every person in developed countries has at least hundreds of these chemicals in their bodies. They often can cause physical and psychological problems. As discussed in the Food section, food additives and other contamination in industrial food can cause physical and psychological problems. For example, many studies have linked ADHD to MSG, aspartame, synthetic food dyes and other food additives. Thousands of children diagnosed with ADHD lost their symptoms and no longer needed medication once they stopped consuming food and beverages containing aspartame.[506]

One study of children diagnosed with ADHD found that symptoms disappeared in two-thirds of children when they were switched from processed foods to whole foods.[507] For over 40 years, many studies have shown that artificial food dyes cause hyperactivity in children. As a result, these additives are restricted in much of Europe. But the business-controlled US government allows them. Other external factors that potentially could cause psychological problems include reactions to vaccines and other drugs and long-term exposure to the ubiquitous electromagnetic radiation of modern society.

One of the main factors causing psychological and other problems in the US is the focus on maximizing economic growth and shareholder returns, instead of maximizing the well-being of society. Business-controlled government transfers trillions of dollars of wealth every year from average citizens to the small group that gives large amounts of money to politicians. This makes life increasingly difficult for low and middle-income citizens. This in turn increases depression and other psychological problems.

Dividing society into debating, often hateful factions, such as conservatives and liberals, produces widespread anger, animosity, intolerance, isolation, unwillingness to help fellow citizens, and many psychological problems. It also severely degrades communities and other support systems that traditionally helped people to deal with family, psychological and other problems.

Spending excessive time in the cyberworld disconnects people from the real world of family, friends and community. It often produces isolation and other psychological problems. Several studies have linked video game playing to ADHD.[508] And our competitive, judgmental and frequently boring education system produces widespread depression, inattention, anxiety, defiance, hyperactivity and other psychological problems.

These external systemic factors combined with normal aspects of human life, such as problems with relationships, work, health and finances, probably cause the large majority of psychological problems in the US. There might be genetic or neurological tendencies toward psychological problems that result from normal variations in humans. But as discussed in the Food section, genetic factors, such as tendency towards cancer, often will not be expressed without some triggering factor, such as creating a cancer-promoting environment in the body by eating animal products. In the same way, even if there is a genetic or neurological tendency to have psychological problems, these problems often will not be expressed if the systemic triggering factors discussed above are not present.

This section discusses many of the actions needed to relieve psychological problems and greatly reduce overprescription of psychiatric drugs.

System Change

System change implemented through a whole system approach is essential for effectively addressing the systemic causes of psychological problems, such as the overemphasis on economic growth, food contamination, and disempowering advertising and media. This type of change often is difficult. Businesses, their owners and business allies frequently will strongly resist changes that threaten ever-increasing shareholder returns.

It often is much easier to suppress psychological problems with psychiatric drugs than to change the factors that cause them. To illustrate, corporate welfare and business control of government make life more difficult for hundreds of millions of US citizens and probably cause extensive depression. But individuals cannot change the economic and political systems that steal their wealth and power. Taking psychiatric drugs often is the easiest, and some might think only, way to relieve depression and other psychological problems.

But this is not a real solution. Antidepressants do not cure depression. They often make it worse over the long-term. The real solution is to end public deception and develop the collective will to change flawed systems. Our grossly flawed, unintentionally suicidal economic and political systems absolutely will change. They are in the process of doing so now. This is indicated by rapidly growing environmental, social, economic and political problems. It will be far better for citizens in the US and other countries if we stop fighting each other, unite and use the overwhelming power of a united public to voluntarily change our systems before they involuntarily change through collapse.

Reversing the widespread and growing use of psychiatric drugs will greatly facilitate system change. These drugs often numb or suppress young people and others who would fight to change our unfair, unsustainable systems. Psychiatric drugs are important tools in authoritarian societies. In the Soviet Union, for example, political prisoners frequently were treated as psychiatric prisoners and forced to take psychiatric drugs. This suppressed their will and ability to oppose abusive government. Putting children on psychiatric drugs often will prevent them from becoming activists who fight for justice and system change. This greatly benefits our increasingly intolerant, authoritarian society. But it is grossly wrong. It severely suppresses democracy and freedom.

Preventing psychological problems is more beneficial to society than treating them. Psychological disorders often are symptoms of problems in society. Therefore, one of the most important solutions is to change the aspects of society that cause or strongly contribute to these problems.

Implementing the system changes discussed throughout *Global System Change* will greatly alleviate psychological problems in the US. These changes include implementing democracy by ending inappropriate business influence of government. Emulating Germany and other countries that successfully retained high-quality jobs, rather than sending them overseas. Improving our competitive, judgmental and often boring education system by implementing the changes discussed below. And using the public wealth to implement a social safety net that is comparable to other developed countries. For example, rather than providing corporate welfare to wealthy people who do not need it, we should use public wealth to help parents who are having trouble raising children with psychological problems.

Another critical system change involves ending the public deception that fractures society into debating factions by creating the illusion that major differences exist. In reality, we all mostly want the same things. Nearly everyone wants a strong economy, good jobs, strong families and communities, a clean environment, good education and healthcare, low crime, good foreign relations, and efficient and effective government. As people see the big picture more, they also will realize that they largely agree on the means to achieve these goals.

Before advertising and media increased the focus on materialism and wealth accumulation, there often were much stronger community and family support structures. Grandparents and other elderly people were far more involved in raising children. Now the wisest people in society (elders) frequently sit alone and neglected in retirement facilities, while children with working parents often sit at home alone watching television and other screens. Ending the conservative-liberal civil war and coming together more in families and communities will provide very large benefits to society. As family networks and communities are strengthened, older people can be much more involved in raising children. This will greatly benefit both groups.

Healthcare Reform

One of the most important system changes needed to reduce psychological problems and more effectively treat them in the US is to improve our grossly flawed healthcare system. As discussed in the Healthcare section, every other developed country uses a not-for-profit, government-owned or government-managed healthcare system. The focus of these systems is on maximizing the health and well-being of citizens and minimizing healthcare costs. The US is the only developed country with a largely for-profit, business-provided healthcare system.

The effectively measured and managed focus of the US healthcare system is maximizing the financial returns of healthcare company shareholders. If there is a conflict between shareholder returns and the well-being of citizens, publicly traded drug, insurance and other healthcare companies often are structurally required to put shareholders ahead of citizens. Maximizing the physical and psychological well-being of citizens and society overall demands that the US healthcare system be refocused on the well-being of citizens.

As noted, many factors often make it difficult for parents, children and patients to avoid overprescription of psychiatric drugs. These include direct-to-consumer marketing of prescription drugs and drug company influence of medical education, drug research, doctors and regulators. By giving money to doctors and politicians who oversee regulators, drug companies strongly influence the US healthcare system. The well-being of society demands that this influence be weakened.

By promoting excessive, unnecessary and often harmful use of psychiatric drugs, drug companies degrade society. This ultimately degrades these companies. For their own good, drug companies must be placed in service of society. They must not be allowed to benefit shareholders by degrading society.

Refocusing the US healthcare system on maximizing the well-being of society mainly requires emulating the not-for-profit healthcare systems of other developed countries that provide far lower costs, far better coverage and frequently superior results. Once this occurs, there will be an important role for drug companies. Under sustainable systems, they will earn reasonable returns, but only by benefiting society. The suicidal requirement to grow forever, regardless of how much this degrades society, will be removed.

The mental health component of the US healthcare system requires major revision. As with healthcare overall, the measured and managed goal of the mental health system is maximizing shareholder returns. But the goal should be maximizing the mental health of citizens. Most psychological problems are caused by psychological or external factors, such as disempowering beliefs and life circumstances. As a result, they often are most effectively treated with psychotherapy and other nondrug approaches.

US health insurance companies frequently provide little coverage for more expensive nondrug treatments and strong coverage for medication because this maximizes shareholder returns. This must be reversed. The most effective treatments should be fully covered. For-profit insurance and other companies must be compelled to focus first on benefiting society. This is the only way they should be allowed to benefit shareholders. The unwillingness of health insurance companies to cover psychotherapy because it might lower profits shows the need to emulate other developed countries and implement a not-for-profit healthcare system.

Beyond failing to adequately cover psychotherapy, the for-profit US healthcare system leaves millions of people without health insurance. Nearly four million people with serious mental illness, psychological distress or substance abuse disorders do not have health insurance.[509] Many of these people wind up in jail, costing taxpayers about $50,000 per person per year. It often would be far less expensive to treat mental illness rather than pay all the costs of leaving it untreated. Providing healthcare to all citizens, as every other developed country does, would greatly alleviate psychological problems in the US.

Improve Psychological Diagnosis

Another major system change needed to improve mental health and reduce overprescription of psychiatric drugs in the US is to substantially revise or essentially replace the DSM method of diagnosing mental disorders. Problems with the DSM diagnostic method and potential solutions were discussed in the Diagnosis of Mental Disorders section above. In summary, the current system is largely flawed, unreliable and often harmful. The entire system is based on a flawed premise. It effectively is trying to put a square peg in a round hole. The DSM model is based on the medical diagnostic model. But psychological problems are vastly different from medical problems. As a result, using the same diagnostic model is incorrect and often harmful.

Medical diagnosis often involves using physical tests to prove causes and specific illnesses. Treatment frequently involves using proven effective drugs or other treatments. These conditions do not exist with psychological diagnosis. Symptoms can be observed. But physical or neurological causes, assuming there are any, are unknown and unproven. The obvious causes in most cases are disempowering beliefs, life circumstances and other environmental, external factors. It is unknown how the brain specifically processes these external factors and produces psychological symptoms. Psychiatric drugs can suppress symptoms. This can appear to be positive. But interpreting the benefits of drug effects often is difficult. As noted, suppressing a symptom might appear to be positive, but actually be negative if it reduces the motivation to address actual causes of psychological problems. The nebulous short-term benefits of psychiatric drugs must be balanced against frequently severe known side effects and long-term physical and psychological degradation.

Physical illnesses often have the same causes, such as a virus or bacterium. With common causes, symptoms and treatments, it is logical to group illnesses into specific categories. Psychological diagnosis assesses symptoms because it cannot measure or prove causes. Unless there is a specific physical condition, such as a brain injury or disease, the causes of psychological symptoms often vary from person to person. Variations in causes and most effective treatments and inability to physically test and confirm conditions often make the medical diagnostic model inappropriate and counterproductive for psychological problems.

The term mental disorder itself is a problem. Most psychological problems are normal reactions to life situations. They are not mental illnesses. But the current DSM diagnostic system frequently redefines normal people as mentally ill and implies that they should take psychiatric drugs. It does not define people as who they are – unique individuals with uniquely caused problems largely requiring unique treatments and solutions.

The DSM diagnostic model has many problems. It implies that the existence of symptoms proves the existence of abstract illnesses that cannot be physically proven. This is reification. The system is based on opinion, rather than on a proven scientific model of mental disorders. The DSM system assigns arbitrary boundaries between normal and abnormal behaviors. It tends to impose distinct categories on spectrums of human behaviors and emotions. The same symptoms frequently exist in different mental disorder categories. Diagnosis is inherently flawed because it is based solely on clinical observations and interviews. The subjectivity or bias of clinicians combined with extensive overlap of symptoms in different mental disorder categories make DSM diagnoses unreliable.

The approach ignores reality by failing to take disempowering beliefs, life circumstances and other external factors into account when assigning diagnoses. This causes many false positives (i.e. normal behavior being labeled mental illness). The approach emphasizes illness rather than recovery. It stigmatizes people and often implies that they are more ill and less able to recover than they actually are. In other words, the DSM diagnostic system is grossly flawed. It requires major revision or replacement.

The DSM is strongly influenced and promoted by drug companies. It maximizes psychiatric drug use and drug company shareholder returns, but severely degrades society. The mental health diagnosis system should be focused on maximizing the health and well-being of citizens, not the financial returns of drug companies. Shifting the focus of mental health diagnosis requires many changes.

A key issue is ending drug company influence of diagnostic methods. Many mental health professionals and professional organizations oppose the ever-expanding DSM and widespread psychiatric drug use. We should listen to them more. The mental health diagnostic system should not be developed and controlled by one private professional organization (the APA) that is heavily influenced by drug companies. Mental health diagnosis is too important (and potentially too harmful if done wrong) to be developed and controlled by one organization. The mental health diagnostic system should be developed with input from many individual researchers, clinicians and professional organizations. Input from drug company representatives or people with ties to drug companies should be severely restricted or prohibited. Drug company input would bias diagnoses in ways that benefit drug companies but often harm citizens, as currently occurs.

In theory, the mental health diagnostic method should be overseen by the people's agent (government). If government were controlled by the people, this would help to ensure that mental health diagnoses were focused on maximizing the well-being of citizens instead of drug companies. But government largely is not controlled by the people. It mainly is controlled by large companies and wealthy business owners. However, government involvement in the mental health diagnostic process could work if it were done with complete openness. This would expose and thereby minimize drug company influence and other inappropriate influence.

A new or revised mental health diagnostic system would be based on honesty and humility. The current system implies a level of understanding of the brain/mind that simply does not exist. Unlike many medical problems, we do not understand the physical mechanics of psychological problems. Most problems are caused by disempowering beliefs, life circumstances and other external factors. The brain probably at least partly mediates these events through physical processes. But we know nearly nothing about them compared to all there is to know. We know even less about nonphysical aspects of the mind, including whether these aspects exist. However, extensive evidence indicates that they probably do exist.

Applying humility means scaling back the illogical and incorrect sense of certainty applied to mental disorders. We must honestly acknowledge that we mostly do not know how the mind works. Splitting the infinite spectrum of human behaviors and feelings into a few hundred categories often causes more harm than good. Psychological symptoms and problems usually have unique causes that vary from person to person. The current diagnostic system frequently looks at symptoms and ignores the most common causes (disempowering beliefs and life circumstances). It places stigmatizing mental illness labels on people. It often implies that they have a physical condition that will not heal, but can be treated with drugs. This nearly always is not the most effective way to address psychological symptoms and problems.

The most effective approach usually is to treat people with psychological problems as unique individuals, in a safe therapeutic setting. Unique causes and solutions to psychological problems are identified and implemented. This approach treats each person with dignity, honor and respect. Good therapists do not place themselves above the person being served. Clients know vastly more about themselves than therapists. The focus of therapy is on helping the client. The client is the expert on the client, even if their self-knowledge mostly is unconscious. The job of good therapists is to help clients find their own inner knowledge, wisdom and strength. They are equal travelers on the client's journey of self-discovery. Carl Jung and many other leaders in the mental health field used this humble and effective approach to therapy.

This humble acknowledgment of huge uncertainty about the mind and the client's vastly superior self-knowledge should form the basis of effective mental health treatment. Diagnosis should not force unique individuals into a box or label. In many cases, no diagnosis is needed. Clients go to therapists and discuss unique problems. Therapists listen and help clients to find effective solutions. Grouping similar symptoms can be useful for therapist training. It also often helps with recommending solutions. But mental health diagnosis probably is not needed to anywhere near the extent it currently is used. Requiring mental disorder diagnosis for insurance reimbursement forces stigmatizing diagnoses that frequently remain in people's medical records for life. This system facilitates psychiatric drug use. But that should not be the purpose of mental health diagnosis.

A healthcare and mental health system that was focused on the well-being of citizens instead of shareholders would not try to force square pegs into round holes. Public and private insurance organizations need information for reimbursement. But this information could be based more on client specific complaints that take actual causes and life circumstances into account. Therapists could assess therapeutic and other needs based on this information and submit it for reimbursement.

Specific diagnoses probably are needed in some cases. But they should be developed with caution. It should be made clear that diagnoses are not identifying specific mental illnesses with common, often physical causes. They should be honestly described as collections of symptoms, mostly with unique causes related to disempowering beliefs, life circumstances and other environmental factors. The term mental disorder is problematic, stigmatizing and usually incorrect. It implies that physically caused mental disorders actually exist. But there is no physical proof that they do.

The term mental disorder also implies that people are mental ill, when they frequently are not. Instead, they are responding normally to stressful life circumstances, disempowering beliefs and other external factors. As a result, in most cases, the term probably should be replaced with a more accurate and less stigmatizing term, such as symptom clusters that frequently resolve themselves over time. Symptom clusters or other more accurate terms should make clear that the only thing known and proven is the existence of symptoms. Causes and even the existence of actual physical problems are unknown, and therefore should not be implied in the label.

Dr. Frances points out that new mental disorder diagnoses are more dangerous than new psychiatric drugs because diagnoses often determine drug use. Therefore, new diagnoses should get at least the same level of scrutiny and field testing as new drugs.

Also, rather than using the reality-ignoring DSM approach of checking off symptoms, mental health diagnosis should be based on reality. Psychological assessments should thoroughly examine all environmental, lifestyle, psychological, life circumstance and other factors that might cause psychological problems. As discussed above, disempowering beliefs are the ultimate cause of nearly all psychological problems.

Assessing symptoms often can be done quickly. But determining psychological causes usually takes more time. Ultimate causes might include unconscious, disempowering beliefs, such as other people are not trustworthy, the world is not safe, or I am flawed and do not deserve a good life. These unconscious beliefs often produce negative emotions, harmful actions and psychological problems. Effective, reality-based diagnosis would go beyond symptom assessment. It would focus on identifying actual causes, such as disempowering beliefs. Therapists then could develop treatment plans that involve helping clients to become aware of unconscious beliefs and change harmful behaviors caused by them.

Analysis of environmental and psychological causes along with evaluation of psychotherapy and other nondrug treatments should be required before psychiatric drugs are prescribed, except perhaps in emergency situations. Psychological diagnosis and treatment should be based on the idea of first do no harm. Psychiatric drugs often produce limited short-term benefits and long-term harm. The unknown mechanisms and frequently severe harm caused by psychiatric drugs usually should make them the last line of treatment, not the first.

A higher standard of safety and caution must be applied when prescribing psychiatric drugs compared to medical drugs. Medical drugs frequently are prescribed for known illnesses with provable causes and proven solutions. These conditions are not present when psychiatric drugs are prescribed. To protect citizens and maximize the likelihood that they recover from psychological problems, extensive analysis of environmental causes and nondrug treatments should be conducted before psychiatric drugs are prescribed. A mental health diagnosis system that is based on checking off symptoms while ignoring environmental and other causes is myopic and harmful. This system should be replaced with a reality-based system.

Require Full Disclosure

Full disclosure about the short-term and long-term risks and benefits of psychiatric drugs should be required. Adult patients and parents of pediatric patients should be required to sign documents that disclose the following. Psychiatric drugs do not cure psychological problems. They only temporarily suppress symptoms. Drug companies generally do not study the long-term effects of psychiatric drugs. However, many independent studies indicate that long-term use of psychiatric drugs increases the risk of chronic illness and long-term drug dependency. It also often causes cognitive, physical and psychological impairment or degradation. Negative side effects of psychiatric drugs also should be disclosed in documents signed by parents and patients.

Doctors prescribing psychiatric drugs should be required to disclose all gifts, payments and other inducements received from drug companies and other types of relationships or involvement with these companies that might create bias towards psychiatric drug use.

Improve Psychiatric Education

Psychiatric education should be changed from emphasizing psychiatric drug use to a more reality-based focus. Psychiatrists should be trained to analyze actual environmental causes, not drug company promoted unproven physical causes. They also should be extensively trained in psychotherapy and other nondrug approaches.

The theme of psychiatric education should be, first do no harm. With this cautious, reality-based approach, psychiatrists will be taught to use psychiatric drugs only as a last resort in nearly all cases. Medical education, drug company influence of doctors and decades of drug use precedent have built a strong drug prescription culture in the psychiatry field. Maximizing the well-being of citizens instead of drug company shareholders demands that this drug use culture be weakened or reversed.

Focus Treatment Guidelines on Non-Drug Solutions

Treatment guidelines for psychological problems also should be changed. As discussed, current treatment guidelines frequently emphasize psychiatric drug use. Doctors often feel negligent or risk losing their jobs or licenses if they do not quickly prescribe psychiatric drugs. This must be changed.

As with mental health diagnosis, drug companies should be prohibited from having any influence on treatment guidelines. Guidelines should suggest first identifying environmental and other psychological causes and using nondrug treatments. Instead of making doctors feel negligent for not prescribing psychiatric drugs, guidelines should clarify that negligence involves failing to fully evaluate environmental and psychological, nonphysical causes and nondrug treatments before prescribing psychiatric drugs.

Restrict Prescription of Psychiatric Drugs

Treating psychological problems with psychiatric drugs is substantially different that treating medical problems with drugs. As discussed, physical causes of most psychological problems, assuming there are any, are theorized, but unknown and unproven. The existence of most psychological problems cannot be clinically tested or proven. The specific mechanisms of action of nearly all psychological drugs are unknown. Psychiatric drugs often have severe adverse effects. Long-term effects largely are unknown, but likely to be more severe with long-term drug use. It is vastly more likely that nearly all psychological problems are caused by nonphysical factors, and therefore should not be treated with physical, drug solutions.

Given the great uncertainty and risks related to psychiatric drug use, thorough evaluation of psychological and environmental causes as well as nondrug treatment options should be conducted before psychiatric drugs are prescribed. Doctors with little or no psychiatric and psychological training and clinical experience are unable to adequately conduct this assessment. Therefore, only doctors with this training and experience, such as psychiatrists, should be allowed to prescribe psychiatric drugs. Prescription in primary care settings generally should be prohibited, unless it is done by psychiatrists.

Restrict Drug Company Marketing

Direct-to-consumer marketing of prescription drugs, including psychiatric drugs, should be prohibited in the US, as it is in every other country except New Zealand. This issue is important because people are highly vulnerable to ads for psychiatric drugs. People who are suffering often want an easy, quick escape from psychological pain. But taking psychiatric drugs rarely is a solution. It temporarily numbs pain, but leaves actual causes unaddressed. As a result, life frequently gets worse. In this sense, taking psychiatric drugs is no different than overeating, taking illegal drugs or engaging in any other addictive activity to escape painful emotions and life circumstances.

The US mental health system should encourage people to take actions that actually solve their problems, such as engaging in psychotherapy or changing life situations. This work can be difficult in the short-term. Willingness to change and get honest with oneself requires courage. But dealing with reality, rather than running away from it by taking legal or illegal drugs, is the most effective way to achieve true life success and satisfaction.

Prohibiting direct-to-consumer advertising and marketing of psychiatric drugs will prevent people from being seduced into solutions that relieve pain in the short-term, but make life worse over the long-term.

Another dangerous aspect of drug company marketing involves increased marketing efforts in non-English speaking countries and developing countries. Publicly traded drug companies are structurally required to seek ever-increasing shareholder returns. Developing new markets for psychiatric drugs can strongly facilitate this. As a result, some drug companies are expanding marketing efforts in developed and developing countries. As discussed, the business dominated US government does not require independent, long-term safety and efficacy research. Psychiatric drugs often relieve symptoms in the short term, but make people physically and psychologically worse in the long-term. Developing countries in particular frequently would not have the resources needed to deal with the long-term negative impacts of psychiatric drugs.

The economic and political system flaws that are making life more difficult for millions of average citizens in the US often are functioning in similar ways in many other developed and developing countries. This is making life more difficult for citizens in these countries. As a result, psychological problems and demand for treatments often are increasing. The availability of psychotherapy frequently is limited in developing countries, in part because people often are focused on survival, mental health issues are not widely discussed, and people cannot afford psychotherapy. Psychiatric drugs frequently are less expensive, have lower stigma, and are much easier to employ than psychotherapy. As a result, as psychological problems increase, some developing countries could represent good marketing opportunities for drug companies.

But as discussed, psychiatric drugs generally do not solve psychological problems. They often degrade life in the long-term. To protect their citizens, developed and developing countries should continue to prohibit direct-to-consumer drug marketing. Also, other countries should require independent, long-term research which shows that psychiatric drugs are safe and effective, rather than using the US government approach of relying on drug company-influenced, short-term research.

Restrict Psychiatric Drug use among Children and Teenagers

Psychiatric drug use among pre-adolescent children should be prohibited in all but emergency or extremely severe cases. Use of psychiatric drugs among teenagers also should be severely restricted. For example, giving young people amphetamines and other stimulants so that they can do better in school should be prohibited. In addition, schools should be prohibited from requiring or encouraging parents to give children psychiatric drugs.

Restrict Compulsory Psychiatric Drug Use

Compulsory use of antipsychotics and other psychiatric drugs also should be prohibited or severely restricted in institutional settings, such as psychiatric hospitals, prisons and nursing homes. Antipsychotics take away people's humanity and often cause severe harm. They should not be used simply because they make patients, prisoners or elderly people easier to handle. No one should be forced to take antipsychotics, except perhaps the criminally insane. It often is easier to force disruptive people to take powerful sedatives, as occurred in *One Flew Over the Cuckoo's Nest*. But we must live up to our name more. We must treat people humanely, especially vulnerable people who are institutionalized or cannot speak up for themselves.

Require Long-term, Independent Drug Research

Long-term, truly independent (i.e. not influenced by drug companies) research of safety and efficacy must be required before psychiatric drugs are approved for use. Drug company conducted or influenced research must not be used to determine public safety and use because this research is inherently biased. As discussed, short-term drug trials often are clinically irrelevant to the treatment of long-term psychological problems. Therefore, research must accurately assess long-term safety and effectiveness.

Failing to require independent, long-term safety and efficacy research before psychiatric drugs are approved for use is extremely dangerous. Many psychological treatments and 'cures' that once were thought to be beneficial, such as lobotomies, electroshock therapy and certain drugs, later were shown to be harmful in many cases. As discussed above, there is strong evidence that many psychiatric drugs currently being used are causing substantial long-term harm. Much of this could have been prevented if independent, long-term research had been required before drugs were approved for use.

Drug research also should quantify the total economic costs of psychiatric drugs. As discussed, these drugs often cause severe long-term physical and psychological degradation. The costs of treating these adverse effects should be determined. Psychiatric drugs frequently appear to be cheaper than psychotherapy or other nondrug treatments in the short-term. But when total costs are assessed, it often will be clear that psychiatric drugs are more expensive, more harmful and less effective than nondrug treatments.

Hold Drug Companies Fully Responsible

One problem with assessing the total costs of psychiatric drugs is that drug companies rarely are held responsible for the adverse effects of their drugs. They are able to externalize these costs onto taxpayers and health insurance policyholders. This illustrates a major system flaw discussed throughout this book – the failure to hold companies fully responsible for negative impacts. This places business in conflict with society. When companies are not held fully responsible for negative impacts, they often maximize shareholders returns by degrading society. Holding them fully responsible makes acting in a fully responsible manner the profit-maximizing strategy. In the prescription drug area, holding companies fully responsible for adverse effects will compel them to develop safer drugs.

In the legal area, the burden of proof should be on drug companies to show that their drugs are safe, not on citizens to show the drugs are unsafe. This burden of proving safety only can be met with independent research. Drug companies often argue in court and other venues that drug use should not be prohibited because there is inadequate evidence to show the drugs are unsafe. As discussed in the Misleading the Public section, this is the wrong perspective. The correct perspective is that drug use should not be allowed until overwhelming, independent evidence shows that it is safe.

Restrict Off-Label Drug Use

Holding drug companies fully responsible will discourage them from promoting off-label uses that have not been shown to be safe and effective over the long-term. In general, off-label prescription should be prohibited, except in rare, perhaps last resort cases where there is full disclosure of risks and uncertain benefits. Doctors usually only should be allowed to prescribe drugs that have been shown to be safe and effective for the conditions being treated.

Emphasize Psychotherapy

One of the most important actions needed to improve mental health and reduce overprescription of psychiatric drugs is to refocus psychology and psychiatry on treatments that have been shown to be most effective over the long-term, primarily psychotherapy. Several aspects of effective psychotherapy have been discussed throughout this Psychiatric Drugs section. In essence, effective psychotherapy is a reality-based approach. Therapists treat clients as unique individuals, rather than focusing on a mental illness diagnosis or abstract, unproven mental disorders. Therapists often consider all factors that might cause psychological problems. For example lifestyle factors might be considered, such as poor diet, lack of sleep, lack of exercise, environmental toxins, and drug or alcohol use. Life histories frequently would be examined. Links between past and current life circumstances and psychological problems would be considered. Disempowering beliefs also might be examined.

For example, as discussed in the Obesity section, obesity often causes depression and other psychological problems, perhaps because obese people frequently cannot enjoy an active, pain-free life. In this case, the cause of psychological problems frequently is overeating, not serotonin deficiencies or other neurological problems. The first attempted solution probably should be to help obese people lose weight, not prescribe antidepressants. The solution might involve teaching them about healthy eating. In addition, therapists might help clients to identify and change disempowering beliefs that create negative emotions and compel people to overeat to suppress the emotions. Suppressing negative emotions with psychiatric drugs instead of food does not solve root problems. It replaces one set of negative impacts (from overeating) with another (the short-term and long-term negative physical and psychological impacts of psychiatric drugs).

Effective therapists also often would help clients to wean themselves off of psychiatric drugs. Therapeutic needs in this area probably are high in the US because millions of people are unnecessarily taking psychiatric drugs. Stopping the use of psychiatric drugs such as antipsychotics can have severe negative consequences. As a result, getting off of psychiatric drugs frequently should be done gradually with the help of a professional. As people wean themselves off of drugs, negative emotions that were suppressed by them often will arise. This can create a desire to go back on the drugs or engage in other types of pain-suppressing addictive or escapist behaviors. It frequently takes great courage to face negative emotions and get honest about disempowering beliefs and life circumstances. Effective therapists provide a safe environment for facing and changing painful emotions, beliefs and life situations.

One of the most important aspects of psychotherapy, perhaps the most important, is empathy. Therapists who truly care about their clients usually are the most effective. Empathy often is more important than superior knowledge of the mind or other factors. Empathetic listening without judging makes it safe for clients to explore painful or shameful aspects of themselves. Making it safe for the whole person to emerge in therapy, the good and the bad, the light and the shadow side, helps people to understand and accept all aspects of themselves, and let go of shame or self-judgment. This facilitates ending harmful behaviors and improving life success and satisfaction.

Illustrating the importance of empathy, empathetic friends or family members who simply listen without judgment can greatly help people to make it through difficult times. This can help them to understand that they are loved and worthy. It can make all the difference. This empathy and understanding among humans is the heart of sustainable human society.

There are many types of psychotherapy. However, a review of hundreds of psychotherapy studies and meta-analyses found that the effectiveness of therapy does not depend on specific techniques. In other words, no type of psychotherapy is generally superior to other types. The review found that the effectiveness of psychotherapy depends primarily on factors such as the quality of the relationship between clients and therapists and clients' faith or confidence in therapy and their therapists.[510] As noted above, finding a truly empathetic therapist, as opposed to one who is primarily interested in revenue, is critical to building the trust and strong client-therapist relationship needed for successful psychotherapy. Also, as discussed in the Placebo Effect section above, believing or trusting that therapy can work is critical to the success of therapy.

While the type of therapy usually is less important than the relationship with the therapist and trust in therapy, having many different therapeutic options benefits clients. Each person is different. Having many options enables people to find the approach that works best for them. Types of therapy include cognitive, behavioral, gestalt, hypnotherapy and psychoanalysis. Additional approaches include cognitive behavioral therapy, which was discussed in the Food section of *Global System Change*. Positive psychology was discussed in the Life Satisfaction section. And Ecopsychology was discussed in the Fascination with Disaster section.

Transpersonal and spiritual psychology involve exploring or expanding the sense of self beyond the individual to higher levels, such as all of humanity. This relates to the concepts of oneness and intuitive wisdom discussed throughout *Global System Change*. Through the intuitive function, we all have access to the essentially infinite wisdom and intelligence seen in nature. As discussed in the Twelve Step Programs section, using intuitive wisdom (or religious people might say the will of God heard within) to guide one's life helps people to reach their fullest potential and produces the highest level of success and life satisfaction.

Our five senses often trick us into thinking that we are separate from each other and nature. But this is an illusion produced from the individual perspective, in the same way that the Earth appears to be flat to the individual. However, from a higher physical level, such as outer space, we see that the Earth is round. From a higher intuitive level, we know in ways that the conscious, limited mind cannot fully understand or explain, that we are one. The virtually infinite beauty, symmetry and cooperation of nature strongly indicate that there is a unifying guiding force. As humanity better understands and operates from this higher level, we also will express the infinite cooperation, beauty, symmetry and sustainability seen in nature. When this occurs, humanity will have reached our fullest potential and created Heaven on Earth.

Expressive therapy is another important and often highly effective form of therapy. The approach involves exploring conscious and unconscious beliefs and feelings through artistic expression. Expressive modes include art, music, dance, drama and writing. As discussed in the Hitting Children section, the most important core believes mainly are formed in childhood through experience and emotions. These foundational beliefs often relate to the safety and trustworthiness of other people and the world. They largely determine the quality of one's life experience. Negative core beliefs are the cause of many, if not most, psychological problems. These beliefs frequently are unconscious and emotionally charged. Some people have difficulty accessing and changing them through intellectual therapeutic approaches, such as cognitive therapy. In these cases, artistic expression therapy often can provide a more effective way to access and transform core beliefs and the emotions attached to them.

Integrative psychotherapy is another important type of therapy. This combines theories and practices from different therapeutic approaches. A main goal is to develop customized approaches that best serve each person.

Effectively Address Addictive and Compulsive Behavior

Extensive research has focused on physical, neurological causes of addictive and compulsive behavior. Many studies indicate that addiction results from triggering of physical, neurological circuits that are reinforced through repetition. Emphasizing physical causes of addiction can help drug companies by implying that physical problems (i.e. suboptimal or damaged neurological circuits) require physical solutions (i.e. psychiatric drugs). But as with other drug company-influenced research, the stated or implied conclusions of this research often are irrational in several ways.

For example, instruments might detect certain areas of the brain that 'light up' when addicts think about or engage in their addictions. But as noted, the mind is massively complex and largely unknown. At our current level of understanding, it probably is impossible to accurately determine what this 'lighting up' means. The addictive response is complex and related to many factors. It probably is impossible to know if the electrical activity in a portion of the brain that occurs during addictive thought or behavior is an actual stored memory or behavior circuit, processing of a circuit that is stored somewhere else, activity that links various memories or processes related to addiction, or something else.

Using common sense and observations of reality, one can see that addictive or compulsive behavior usually results from repeated responses to some type of trigger, such as negative emotions. As the response is repeated, it becomes habituated or automatic. This mechanism of formation (repetition of harmful behavior) indicates the solution (repetition of healthy behavior). As discussed in the Strengthening Healthy Habits subsection of the Food section, the harmful habit or behavior was formed through repetition. Replacing the harmful habit with healthy behavior often requires repetition of healthy behavior.

From a therapeutic perspective (by far the most relevant perspective for treatment and recovery from addiction/compulsion), the physical mechanics of habituated responses largely are irrelevant. The relevant issue is that repeating healthy habits or new behaviors can weaken or replace unhealthy habits or addictions. Physical addictions (i.e. food, alcohol, drugs, tobacco) may have physical components, such as affecting dopamine and other brain chemical levels. But addictive responses to negative emotions and other triggers largely are formed through repetition, and therefore apparently can be 'unformed' or weakened through repetition of different activities.

Taking a pill often is much easier than doing the difficult work of changing habits or examining the frequently painful psychological issues that cause harmful habits. But taking drugs often will not work. It essentially pretends that the psychological issues that cause most addictive or compulsive behavior do not exist. It is an irrational fantasy solution that ignores reality. Rather than helping people, the severe effects and side effects of psychiatric drugs frequently will make them worse.

We should not be putting the financial well-being of drug companies ahead of the well-being of citizens. We should not be pushing physical, often harmful, drug solutions to problems that usually have obvious psychological causes, and therefore require psychological, nonphysical solutions.

Consider Spiritual Solutions

Beyond psychotherapy, there are many other ways to effectively resolve psychological problems. Probably the most common are religious and spiritual practices. Many people find deep meaning in life and alleviate depression and other psychological problems by participating in religion and employing spiritual practices. As discussed in the Twelve Step Programs section, Twelve Step programs have helped millions of people to end harmful behaviors and alleviate the depression and other psychological problems that often accompany these behaviors. The Twelve Step programs are based on core spiritual principles that are common to nearly all religions. This further indicates the importance and effectiveness of using spiritual practices to maximize mental health and well-being.

Establish Support Networks

Extensive support often is needed to help people get off of psychiatric drugs, or avoid taking them in the first place. In addition to support from therapists, support networks like Twelve Step programs should be expanded or established to help in this area. Twelve Step programs are successful in large part because people with similar problems help each other for free. The temptation to begin or continue using psychiatric drugs when life feels difficult can be as strong as the temptation to use alcohol, illegal drugs or other addictions. Having support from people who are dealing with the same temptations and life problems can make all the difference.

Twelve Step and similar self-help groups are autonomously organized by local people seeking to deal with the same problems. Therapists and other professionals usually do not make money on them. The profit motive should not be used to facilitate the expansion of these types of self-help groups. Instead, local government and community organizations perhaps could raise awareness and provide mechanisms that facilitate the establishment of free, autonomous self-help groups. These groups frequently could be based on the proven-effective principles and structures of Twelve Step programs.

Many years ago, strong family, community and other social networks (actual face-to-face networks, not cyber networks) helped people to make it through stressful times and deal with psychological problems. But the disempowering, technology-focused US culture is increasing alienation and isolation in society, while corporate welfare and the emphasis on business well-being is making life more difficult for millions of average citizens. Growing isolation, division, anger and advertising-driven selfishness often weaken family, community and other traditional support networks. Lack of social support contributes to more people relying on psychiatric drugs to deal with psychological problems.

As discussed, people without confidants and other social support are much more likely to be depressed and have other psychological problems. Those with close friends and family, friendly neighbors and supportive co-workers can better withstand the growing stress of society and maintain mental health. Therefore, beyond establishing support groups like Twelve Step groups, an important aspect of treating depression and other psychological problems should involve finding ways to help people improve connections with family, friends, community, co-workers and other social networks. This generally should involve at least some actual face-to-face support, rather than online networks and other cyberworld connections, which often promote isolation.

An organization in the UK (Talk for Health) helps to establish support groups that address mental health problems caused by loneliness. The group trains people on skills that reduce loneliness, such as authentic sharing and empathic listening. After a short training, long-term peer support groups are established where people can connect on a deep level. The groups have been successful at reducing loneliness and improving senses of well-being.[511] In the US, Twelve Step groups such as Emotions Anonymous and Depression Anonymous provide support for people who are dealing with loneliness, depression and other mental health issues.

Expand Parent Support and Training

Another important action needed to maximize mental health and reduce overprescription of psychiatric drugs among children is to give parents more support and training in dealing with unhappy or disruptive children. As noted, giving psychiatric drugs to children is like physical punishment in the sense that it provides short-term benefits (i.e. suppressing disruptive or undesirable behaviors), but often causes long-term harm. The healthcare and education systems frequently pressure or encourage parents to put their children on psychiatric drugs. Parents often trust so-called experts and drug their children. As discussed above, pressure from doctors, educators and others to drug children must be ended.

As with physical punishment, parents often drug their children because they think this is the best or only option. As discussed, when Sweden made physical punishment of children illegal, they provided support and training to parents about alternative methods of discipline. Parents also should be given the support and training needed to effectively help children with psychological problems. Good parenting frequently is difficult and time-consuming, but immensely rewarding. Stressed-out parents often find it easier to hit or drug problematic children. This can relieve short-term problems. But the long-term cost will be far greater than the short-term benefit. Hit or drugged children frequently will have more problems as teenagers and adults. Parents often will watch their children fail to prosper as adults and wonder if they could have done a better job of parenting.

More effort should be made to help parents, especially inexperienced parents, to understand the normal ups and downs of childhood, and the normal variations in character and temperament. Rebelliousness, hyperactivity, sadness or inattention nearly always are not symptoms of mental illness. They are normal aspects of childhood. There are far more effective ways to deal with these behaviors than giving children powerful, mind-altering, frequently harmful drugs. More effective approaches often require that parents give children more time and attention. This usually is more difficult in the short-term, especially in the US were corporate welfare and business control of government makes life increasingly difficult for parents and other average citizens. But the investment made in giving troubled children the love and attention they need will pay large dividends down the road. When children prosper as adults, parents can be proud of the hard work they did when their children were young.

Children with behavior problems or mental disorders are like disabled children. Parents would not deal with them by locking them in a closet. Drugging children, especially with antipsychotics, is like locking them in a chemical closet. Children with psychological problems usually need more attention. The mind is like the body. It often will heal if it is put in a safe, supportive, healing environment.

Parents should seek out experts who can provide effective help with troubled children. As noted, parents should be highly skeptical of doctors who quickly seek to apply a mental illness diagnosis and prescribe psychiatric drugs. Receiving this diagnosis can stigmatize a child for life. The stigmatizing often is not justified because DSM diagnoses are abstract, unproven concepts. They are names that describe groups of symptoms. But there is no proof that an actual mental disorder exists. Symptoms nearly always probably are caused by environmental factors, not neurological problems or mental illness. Through recommendations, research and other means, parents should seek out therapists and other experts who treat their children as unique individuals. They should strive to find experts who understand the risks of psychiatric drugs, and only prescribe them cautiously or as a last resort.

In particular, parents should be highly skeptical of antipsychotic drugs. As noted above, the many severe adverse effects of antipsychotics include potentially shortening life expectancy by 20 percent. In other words, putting children on antipsychotics might shorten their lives by 15 years or more. Parents probably should not allow their children to take these drugs, except in the most extreme circumstances. They probably should rarely or never allow their children to take antipsychotics for off-label uses such as ADHD or ODD. Hyperactivity, inattention and/or defiance are not extreme conditions that warrant the use of these frequently harmful and sometimes life-ruining drugs.

Research and Expand Alternative Treatments

In general, safer and more effective treatments than psychiatric drugs should be researched, developed and promoted. Many practitioners use herbs, supplements, acupuncture and other nonprescription drug treatments to effectively address psychological symptoms and problems. Drug company-influenced regulators and other allies sometimes question or criticize these approaches, partly because widespread use of nondrug treatments could threaten never-ending growth of drug company shareholder returns.

Research of nondrug treatments often has been inadequate because drug companies influence most of the mental health research. Nondrug treatments could substantially lower mental health costs and adverse drug effects, while substantially improving the psychological well-being of citizens. Therefore, through government funding and other mechanisms, research and development of safer, nondrug mental health treatments should be greatly expanded.

Incentivize Recovery, Not Treatment

Incentives for psychiatrists and other mental health practitioners also should be substantially modified. Currently, doctors prescribing psychiatric drugs or using other treatment methods often maximize revenues by promoting long-term treatment, rather than recovery. They generally are not held accountable for results. Financial incentives should be provided to minimize total treatment costs (including the adverse effects of psychiatric drugs) and maximize recovery. Doctors cannot compel clients to recover from psychological problems. But recovery should be monitored and rewarded. This will incentivize therapists to help clients heal as quickly as possible.

However, the incentive system must be used wisely. Mechanisms should be established to protect clients and prevent abuse by drug companies and other parties. The priority of the mental health system should be the psychological well-being of citizens. Cost is a secondary consideration. Psychological problems often are complex. Many people might require long-term psychotherapy or other treatments. Greatly reducing or eliminating corporate welfare will enable the US to establish a mental health system that adequately and compassionately meets the needs of citizens with psychological challenges.

Encourage Following Intuitive Wisdom

As discussed in the Twelve Step Programs section, each person has access to essentially infinite wisdom and intelligence within. Learning to discern or separate this wisdom from the often fear-based mind, and then using it to guide one's life, produces the most successful and satisfying life. One of the most effective ways to do this is to identify unique passions or interests and build one's life around them, or as Joseph Campbell said, to "Follow Your Bliss".

Many people are cut off from wise inner guidance. Instead disempowering beliefs guide or control their lives. As noted, this is the ultimate cause of probably the large majority of psychological problems. There are many ways to find and follow wise inner guidance. Billions of people refer to this guidance as God and use religion to follow it. But as discussed, the name that one places on wise inner guidance ultimately is irrelevant. The key is accessing and using it.

Wise therapists know that it often is more effective to help clients find their own answers, rather than give them the answers. In the psychological area, no one heals anyone else. People ultimately heal themselves, or they do not heal. The wise therapist is a guide and assistant on this process of self-discovery and self-healing. Wise therapists help people to find their own truths and answers within.

Encourage Service and Activism

As discussed in the Causes of Depression section, growing division, anger, intolerance and senses of inadequacy in society are causing many people to feel alienated, isolated, powerless, helpless, hopeless, afraid, bored and/or dehumanized. Dr. Levine said that psychological problems often are inner rebellions against growing injustice and oppression in society. People turn their negative emotions inward in ways that cause psychological problems, such as depression, anxiety, psychosis, hyperactivity or inability to focus.

Rather than destructively turning emotions inward, therapists and others can encourage people to turn their attention outward and do something to address problems in society. Engaging in community service, volunteering, activism or virtually any other effort to address environmental or social problems can be highly empowering and uplifting. Taking action to address problems in society can relieve senses of helplessness, hopelessness and powerlessness. Working with like-minded people on worthy causes can relieve senses of alienation, isolation, loneliness and fear.

As discussed in the Fascination with Disaster section, ecopsychology theorizes that humans are connected to larger systems such as the Earth in ways that are real, but not always obvious. The theory states that humans are aware at deep, often unconscious levels of environmental and social problems, in a similar way that animals frequently seem to know that a storm is coming. According to ecopsychology, psychological problems sometimes result from conscious or unconscious knowledge that the environmental and social systems needed for survival and prosperity are declining. The larger system of which we are apart, in a sense our larger body, is being degraded. At a psychological level, this may be difficult to prove scientifically. But at a physical level, it is obvious and not debatable within the realm of logic. As noted, humans cannot survive in outer space. We are as dependent on the Earth as the hand is on the body. In this sense, the Earth literally and logically is our larger body.

Taking actions to address almost any problem in society that one feels moved to address at any level (local, regional, national or global) is acting on the reality of our interconnectedness. In a very real sense, when each of us takes actions to help improve society, we are counteracting the forces that literally are destroying our home. In this larger sense, activism and other efforts to improve society are the larger body healing itself, in the same way that healthy cells in the human body overcome disease and cause healing. People who are actively working to make the world a better place are much less likely to be depressed or have other psychological problems. Instead, their lives often are rich and energized. They are interacting with other positive, enthusiastic, committed people. Their lives have meaning.

Many studies have shown that people who regularly do kind acts are happier. In a workplace study, people who did acts of kindness for coworkers became more engaged and satisfied with their work. There was a 'Pay It Forward' effect where those who received acts of kindness started helping colleagues more. There also was an inspirational effect where workers who observed acts of kindness began to help colleagues more.[512]

Many studies also have shown that as people become happier, their relationships improve, they become more productive at work, their immune systems become stronger and they become more creative.[513] When people help others or treat them kindly, they are acting on the reality of our interconnectedness. This is a main reason why helping other people enhances happiness and helps to alleviate psychological problems. As noted, helping others is a foundation of Twelve Step programs.

As the mental health field transitions away from drug use and maximizing the well-being of drug companies to maximizing the well-being of society, encouraging citizens to actively contribute to society or help other people in some way should be a key component of mental health strategies. This not only will substantially improve individual mental health, it also will improve the health and well-being of society.

Promote Rational Thought, Not Skepticism

As discussed in the Placebo Effect section, faith or belief that a treatment will work is critical to recovery from depression and many other psychological issues. As a result, skepticism can severely inhibit the ability to recover. Skepticism about a treatment essentially is the belief that the treatment probably will not work. This belief often becomes a self-fulfilling prophecy.

Some people think that skepticism is rational. But this frequently is not true. The priority should be rational, objective thinking based on observations of reality. Skepticism or doubt sometimes is rational. For example, it is rational to say, I am skeptical that elephants can fly. Observations of reality show that elephants cannot fly. Therefore, this skepticism is logical and rational, in this case.

But there are many areas of life where it is not rational to be skeptical. Instead, skepticism in these areas often is harmful and irrational. For example, it generally would not be rational to say, I am skeptical that psychotherapy will work for me. Psychotherapy has worked for millions of people. Therefore, it is not rational to conclude in advance that therapy probably would not work. Skepticism or doubt essentially is the belief that an unpreferred outcome is most likely. The belief that therapy probably will not work frequently produces that outcome. When one considers the importance of faith or belief in the effectiveness of treatment, doubt or skepticism is shown to be irrational.

The great psychologist and philosopher William James (1842 - 1910) suffered from severe depression. It reduced his will to live. Earlier in his life, he was a critical, often skeptical thinker. But he came to realize the benefit of faith or trust, and the often harmful nature of skepticism. William James saw that faith or belief in God, for example, helped many people to improve their lives. Therefore, from a practical, pragmatic perspective (i.e. focusing on what actually works and produces positive results), he determined that faith or belief was rational. He realized that skepticism might kill him. As a result, he came to believe in belief, trust and faith.[514]

People sometimes say that they are skeptical that God exists or that a belief in God could help them. This is irrational in several ways. For example, it is impossible to prove that God or some type of transcendent wisdom or power does not exist. The large majority of people believe that God exists. Billions of people benefit from a belief in God. This belief is practical and pragmatic because it improves many people's lives. Even if people are deluded and God does not exist, their lives often are improved by the belief. Therefore, from a pragmatic, results-focused perspective, the belief in God is rational. Sometimes skepticism results from fear or intellectual arrogance. People are afraid to admit the existence or effectiveness of something that they do not fully understand. But fear and arrogance frequently are not rational or objective.

Global System Change takes the position that each person has access to essentially infinite wisdom and intelligence within, referred to as intuitive wisdom or the wisdom of nature. Observations of reality show the nearly infinite sophistication, complexity and beauty of nature. Many of the US Founders were Deists. They believed that the obvious implied intelligence of nature proves the existence of God or some type of creative power.

It is logical to assume that intuitive wisdom probably exists because many people benefit from discerning it in their minds and using it to guide their lives. As discussed in the Twelve Step Program section, it would be irrational to at least not try accessing and applying intuitive wisdom. Based on the experience of many others, the upside is very large and there is little or no downside.

Choosing positive beliefs and then trusting and acting upon them is critical when addressing psychological problems. Animals always follow instinct. They essentially have no choice. But we have the ability to think, reflect and make choices. The existence of choices indicates that we essentially have different 'voices' in our minds. Unconscious 'voices' might say, I'm unworthy, people will hurt me. But an equally valid 'voice' or belief is, I am worthy, the world is safe. Actually, based on observations of reality, the latter beliefs are far more valid and rational. Unworthiness is a concept created by humans. It is an illusion, opinion or disempowering belief. Nothing in nature is inherently 'unworthy'.

Choosing to believe that psychotherapy will be effective is rational because it greatly increases the chance that it will work. As discussed in the Placebo Effect section, all situations ultimately are neutral. We assign the meeting. Life circumstances ultimately do not cause psychological problems. Beliefs do. Suicide illustrates this. Some people face far more difficult lives than most people who commit suicide. But they do not kill themselves. Perceptions or beliefs about reality, not reality itself, cause nearly all suicides.

Lack of unconditional self-acceptance and love frequently cause life difficulties and psychological problems. Many people are perfectionists. They often believe that they are not good enough. But this frequently is arrogant. It implies that people who are not perfect are less worthy. The key is accepting who we are with all of our flaws, weaknesses and mistakes. This way, no one is above anyone else. We each can grant ourselves unconditional self-acceptance. Once we accept the flawed, imperfect self, it is easier to make changes and become the person we would like to be. Judging the shadow (our perceived flaws and imperfections) locks in the dark side. Loving and accepting the shadow often enables negative aspects of character to transform or improve. This self-acceptance helps people to reach their fullest potential.

The ability to think clearly, rationally and objectively often is critical to relieving psychological problems and attaining a successful and satisfying life. Psychological drugs frequently cloud the mind and suppress emotions. This can severely inhibit the ability to resolve psychological problems.

With a clear, rational, objective mind, and often with the help of an empathetic, wise therapist, people can courageously explore their beliefs and perceptions about life. This not only is the key to resolving psychological problems, it is the key to achieving a successful and satisfying life. While some perceptions are spontaneous, such as perceiving the beauty of nature, ongoing perceptions or beliefs about life essentially are choices. Beliefs often are unconscious. But once they become conscious, we can choose to change them. People frequently cannot change outer circumstances. But they always can change how they perceive circumstances. Once basic needs are met, choices or beliefs about reality largely determine the quality of one's life.

Face Negative Emotions

People often attempt to deal with negative emotions by denying or suppressing them, for example, with overeating and other addictive or compulsive activities. But depression and other negative emotions are survival mechanisms. They warn people that problems exist and actions should be taken to resolve them. In this sense, negative emotions are gifts. An excellent article by Melanie Greenberg, PhD, called five *Reasons It's So Hard to Combat Anxiety and Depression and What You Can Do*, provides several suggestions for dealing with depression and anxiety.[515]

She emphasizes the importance of facing emotions, rather than denying or running away from them. Once faced, emotions often run their course and move on. Denying negative emotions often keeps them locked in place. She also notes that depression can give people a narrow, negative worldview. As a result, Dr. Greenberg suggests stepping back and looking at the big picture. This helps people to see themselves and their lives objectively, adopt a more realistic and positive perspective, and develop more creative solutions. She also emphasizes the importance of getting support from friends, colleagues and family members. Discussing situations with an empathic listener can help people to work through emotions and find effective solutions.

Encourage Meditation

Meditation is a highly effective tool for improving mental health. It provides many benefits, including increased ability to focus the mind, relax and soothe negative emotions. Dr. Brett Atkinson encourages people dealing with relationship and other problems to practice mindfulness and loving-kindness meditation.[516]

Mindfulness meditation increases the ability to relax and soothe negative emotions. Practicing this self-soothing before responding to negative emotions and stressful life situations greatly increases the ability to respond positively and productively. Mindfulness meditation also increases the ability to focus the mind and more effectively analyze and transform disempowering beliefs.

Loving-kindness or compassion meditation increases general feelings of compassion and empathy, strengthens the desire to help other people, and leads to more altruistic actions. This often substantially improves senses of individual well-being and happiness. Meditation enables people to be more effective in relationships and other life areas. It helps to alleviate psychological problems, and thereby reduce the inclination to take psychiatric drugs.

Empower People

The drug company promoted narrative that many psychological problems have physical/neurological causes, and therefore are best treated with psychiatric drugs, disempowers millions of people and severely degrades society. The priority of drug companies is not to help citizens or society. It is to help shareholders. If deceiving millions of citizens into unnecessarily taking psychiatric drugs helps shareholders, drug companies often will face strong pressure to do it.

The narrative that many, if not most, psychological problems have physical/neurological causes disempowers people because it makes them victims. People often are misled into thinking that there is something physically wrong with them that only can be treated by experts. This deception makes the mental health of people dependent on drug companies and doctors.

But the vast majority of psychological problems probably are caused by nonphysical factors, such as disempowering beliefs and life circumstances. This knowledge is highly empowering because it gives people control over their mental health. They can change their beliefs and life circumstances, and thereby eliminate the root causes of psychological problems.

However, changing beliefs and life circumstances can be difficult, especially for people with depression and other psychological problems. This makes them highly vulnerable to drug company marketing. They can be easily misled into believing that drugs will solve their problems. The drugs often make them feel better in the short-term (especially if they are taking euphoria-producing drugs, such as amphetamines). The short-term symptom suppression of psychiatric drugs further increases vulnerability to the deception that people have physical/neurological problems.

Depressed and other vulnerable people are being manipulated to help drug companies make more money. Psychiatric drugs often make people worse physically and psychologically over the long-term. Therefore, it is essential that people be given greater protection from drug company deceptions. Direct-to-consumer marketing must be prohibited, as it is in virtually every other country. The priority of society should be maximizing the well-being of citizens and society overall, not the well-being of drug and other companies. Once again, this shows the need to put business in service of society. Businesses must be prohibited from benefiting shareholders in ways that degrade society, such as by promoting the overprescription of psychiatric drugs.

The mental illness narrative in the US must be changed. The current harmful and dishonest narrative includes, It is not your fault. You have a physical problem. You cannot do anything about it yourself. But psychiatric drugs can help. We must empower citizens by promoting a new and honest narrative. This could be, Your psychological problems almost certainly result from disempowering beliefs and life circumstances. You have strong control over these. You can change your beliefs and often life circumstances, and thereby resolve your psychological problems.

Psychiatric Drugs Conclusion

In conclusion, psychiatric drugs are hugely overprescribed in the US. This severely degrades society. The problem is especially tragic and severe with children because they often are vulnerable, unaware and defenseless. Suicidal systems compel drug companies to see our children as good sources of new revenue and profits. But children should not be seen as little cash dispensers for drug companies. We must protect them from unnecessary and harmful drug use.

We also must protect ourselves and our freedom. The ability to think clearly is a defining characteristic of humanity. Freedom of thought is essential for democracy, prosperity and sustainability. Psychiatric drugs cloud the minds of millions of children and adults in the US and other countries. They often take away their ability to think and feel like normal human beings. As our suicidal systems rapidly degrade society, suppressing children and adults with psychiatric drugs will help to maintain these systems in place.

Authoritarianism is rising as our systems decline. It often seems that we have become unwilling to tolerate children's normal behaviors. Psychiatric drug use can be cruel. We suppress symptoms with drugs without even trying to address causes. This can make children and adults more compliant and easier to manage. It helps authorities who will tolerate no questioning of their irrational dogma. But it severely degrades society. It is an abomination. We must wake up and replace authoritarianism with enlightenment, as the US Founders did long ago.

We must think and act from a whole system perspective. Once we do, the actual causes and most effective solutions to our most pressing problems frequently will become evident. We will see the chains of cause and effect. To illustrate, as noted, one study found that two-thirds of children diagnosed with ADHD lost their symptoms when they stopped eating processed foods. But parents in the US often are not made aware that artificial food dyes can cause hyperactivity in children. As a result, they frequently put their ADHD-diagnosed children on stimulants. These drugs often cause bipolar symptoms, which leads to antipsychotic drug use. This in turn frequently causes severe side effects, long-term physical and psychological degradation, lifetime stigma and lifetime drug dependence.

From a whole system perspective, one sees how truly tragic this situation is. If parents understood this chain of cause and effect, they often would stop feeding their children unhealthy processed foods. This frequently would relieve ADHD symptoms, and thereby stop the progression to physical and psychological degradation and long-term drug use before it begins. As Albert Einstein said, we must think at a higher level if we wish to solve our most complex problems.

Nearly all people go through difficult times. The greatest growth and development in life often occur as people struggle to deal with painful emotions and difficult life situations. Psychiatric drugs might help people to get through difficult times in some cases. But we do not understand the mind nearly as well as the body. We largely do not know how psychiatric drugs affect the brain and mind. As a result, these drugs must be used much more cautiously and sparingly. There frequently are far more effective and much less harmful ways to deal with psychological problems and difficult life situations.

Refocusing the mental health field on the well-being of citizens and society instead of the financial well-being of drug companies, psychiatrists and other doctors will require many changes. Foundational changes include focusing on actual causes of psychological problems, such as disempowering beliefs and difficult life circumstances, rather than deceptive, drug company-promoted physical, neurological causes. More effective, lower risk solutions, such as psychotherapy, also should be emphasized.

As is the case in many other areas of society, drug companies, politicians paid by them and other allies often will vigorously oppose changes that benefit society, but threaten shareholder returns. Psychiatrists might oppose shifting the emphasis back to safer, more effective nondrug solutions because they frequently can earn much money by prescribing psychiatric drugs rather than providing psychotherapy. Psychiatrists and other doctors have been prescribing psychiatric drugs for many years. Shifting the mental health field away from drug use implies that their years of work have been suboptimal, off-target or flawed in some way. Some doctors might hesitate to admit that they have not been providing the most effective mental health treatments for many years.

This problem or resistance to change probably will occur in many areas of society. But the priority is doing what is best for society, especially future generations. Once the people regain control of government in the US and establish democracy, we can figure out practical, minimally disruptive ways to transition the emphasis of the mental health field away from what's best for drug companies to what's best for citizens and society in general.

This Psychiatric Drugs section was included in the larger Education section in part because some schools will not allow disruptive children to attend classes unless they are medicated. As funding for public education declines and schools are less able to deal with disruptive or troubled children, drugging them might seem logical from a myopic perspective. But from a whole system perspective, drugging disruptive or troubled children into compliance with increasingly intolerant, authoritarian systems is shown to be an abomination. It is a gross violation of our obligation to protect and care for our children.

Our education and other systems are grossly flawed. The inattention, hyperactivity, depression and defiance of our children often are rational and justified. These are normal, expected responses to grossly flawed ideas and systems. Human society belongs to the young. We adults hold it in trust for them. We must not stifle and degrade their minds and hearts with psychiatric drugs.

The Psychiatric Drugs section also was included in the Education section because, in a larger sense, education refers to the general upbringing and well-being of children. Children are being continuously educated at home, in schools and everywhere else in society. Advertising and media often teach them violence, anger, division, inadequacy and materialism. Competitive schools reinforce the lesson of inadequacy. Wounded parents sometimes are not able to teach their children what it means to be an empowered, confident, compassionate human being, because they never learned this.

We all collectively have a responsibility to protect and educate our children. Ending inappropriate psychiatric drug use among children only is a first step. But it is critical. Children cannot learn to reach their fullest potential if their minds and emotions are clouded, confused and suppressed with psychiatric drugs.

Children have a right to fully express who they are. They usually do not become troubled or disruptive due to physical brain problems, even though drug companies and their allies work hard to promote this deception. Children usually have psychological problems for logical, nonphysical reasons. Rather than drugging them, we should compassionately listen to them. They deserve this respect as human beings. Children mirror the problems of schools, families and society in general. In this sense, they can be our teachers. If we give them the love and attention they deserve, we will learn what troubles them. This will better enable us to clarify problems in society, fix our flawed systems, and fulfill our obligation to protect children and future generations.

Higher Education

The degradation of public higher education is one of the most tragic and destructive aspects of US society. The world, or at least human society, belongs to the young. Middle-aged and older generations hold it in trust for them. We have an obligation to prepare young people to effectively function in society and rectify the many problems we created and might not be able to fully solve before they take over.

Investing in low-cost or free public higher education is one of the most important, beneficial and cost-effective investments that society can make. As noted, it promotes a highly skilled, competent workforce. It strongly promotes the advancement of science, technology and other disciplines. College graduates earn 65 percent more than high school graduates. This increases demand for products and services and enhances the economy in many other ways. Low-cost higher education strongly promotes equal opportunity by enabling young people from low-income families to attain middle-class or higher status.

One of the most important benefits of low-cost public higher education is the promotion of critical, enlightened, higher-level thinking, like the wise, enlightened thinking used by our Founders to establish the US. Benjamin Franklin, Thomas Jefferson and many other Founders strongly advocated and supported low-cost public higher education.

As discussed throughout this book, the problems facing the US, other countries and global society in general are large and complex. They cannot be solved from the myopic, reductionistic level of thinking that created them. The problems only can be effectively and sustainably solved through higher-level, whole system thinking. Colleges and universities are main places where this type of thinking can and should occur and be taught.

Much of society is focused on the execution of specific tasks, such as manufacturing, healthcare and governance. However, higher education largely is focused on the development, critical examination and study of old and new ideas. Society carves out a realm where students, professors and researchers have the time to examine and develop new ideas. Giving people who are interested in thinking deeply and critically (i.e. intellectuals) the freedom and opportunity to do so greatly benefits all of society. Many of the greatest advances in human society came from or were initiated in academia. Colleges and universities overwhelmingly are our most important 'think tanks'.

There are other think tanks that benefit society. But many of them are funded by corporations and their owners. When one examines the activities and results of these corporate think tanks, it often becomes clear that their actual, though not stated, purpose is to block systemic and other changes that benefit society, but threaten shareholder returns.

During their teens and 20s, before they assume more responsibility in life, young people often have the time, freedom and flexibility to study and get involved with issues they believe are important. Higher education frequently helps young people to see the big picture and critically examine major problems and possible solutions in society. It often empowers them by providing a sense that change is possible and they can be a part of it. Colleges and universities frequently serve as incubators for new ideas and beneficial changes in society. During the 1960s and 1970s, much of the civil rights, antiwar and environmental protection activism was initiated or strongly supported by university and college students.

Many current economic, political and other ideas and systems are severely flawed. Having a strong, robust, independent, well-funded public higher education system will greatly facilitate the rapid evolution of these ideas and systems into sustainable forms. Adequately funding public higher education greatly facilitates resolving the many large, complex challenges facing society.

Developed and developing countries gain substantial benefits by strongly supporting public higher education. For example, many European countries provide inexpensive or free public higher education. China, India, Mexico and other developing countries substantially strengthen their economies and gain numerous other benefits by investing in low-cost public higher education.[517]

But business controls government and society in the US more than in most other countries. As discussed, our unintentionally suicidal economic and political systems demand that the financial returns of the small group that owns most business assets always must grow, regardless of how much this degrades society. This group gives large amounts of money to politicians in both major political parties and inappropriately influences government in other ways. As a result, they often are able to compel government to reduce or remove any programs, regulations or other factors that threaten ever-increasing shareholder returns.

Low-cost, widely available public higher education substantially threatens ever-increasing shareholder returns in several ways. For example, as with many other social well-being enhancement programs discussed in *Global System Change*, using public wealth to support high-quality public higher education limits the amount of taxpayer wealth that can be used for corporate welfare. Partly as a result, many business-influenced politicians in the US have been reducing funding for public higher education for over 30 years. This enables increased corporate welfare and ever-increasing shareholder returns. But it degrades society.

In addition, teaching and encouraging young people to critically examine modern ideas and systems, and giving them the time and opportunity to do so in colleges and universities, threatens the perpetuation of our suicidally flawed economic and political systems. Publicly traded companies essentially are structurally required to oppose anything that threatens ever-increasing shareholder returns. The need to suppress ideas and activities that threaten these returns and the status quo probably is a major factor driving the rapid degradation of public higher education in the US.

Through government influence, large corporations and the small group that owns most of their shares can drive reductions of funding for public higher education. This makes public colleges and universities highly vulnerable to corporate influence. By providing donations that supplement declining public funding, companies often gain substantial influence over higher education.

Reduced public funding and increased corporate influence have facilitated ever-increasing shareholder returns in the short term. But it creates many problems in higher education and society in general. These include rapid tuition growth, high student debt, declining class mobility, bloated university administrations, expanding for-profit colleges, growing online courses, business control of university research, suppression of professors, suppression of critical thinking, limited job opportunities for graduates, and unfair student debt terms.

Rapid Tuition Growth

Higher education tuition costs have risen nearly 600 percent since 1980, increasing much faster than inflation.[518] Reduced funding for public higher education is a major cause of rising tuition costs at public colleges and universities. Prior to 1980, public higher education was inexpensive or free in many states. The average annual tuition and fees at a public university in 1974 was $510. In 2022, the average cost of attending a private US college, including living expenses, was about $58,000. After financial aid, the cost was $33,000 at private universities and $19,000 at public ones.[519]

The US is an outlier on higher education costs. Public university tuition is about $5,000 per year in Canada and Japan, $2,000 per year in Italy, Spain and Israel, and essentially zero in France, Denmark and Germany. Since 2000, college attendance rose by an average of 20 percent in OECD countries. However, high tuition costs drove declining attendance in the US. Since 2016 for example, the number of undergraduates in the UK rose by 12 percent, but fell by 8 percent in the US. As a result, eleven OECD countries now have better educated labor forces than the US.[520]

College graduates earn about 65 percent more than high school graduates. However, high tuition costs lower the value of higher education. Students born before 1980 (i.e. often paid low tuition) have substantially higher wealth than high school graduates. But those born after 1980, facing high tuition and student debt, had only slightly more wealth. Those with postgraduate degrees had essentially the same wealth as high school graduates.[521]

The value of higher education varies by profession. Those pursuing business or STEM (science, technology, engineering, math) degrees have a good chance of increasing wealth compared to high school graduates. But those pursuing most other degrees (e.g. arts, humanities, social sciences) are likely to achieve lower wealth than if they had avoided college. [522]

Discouraging higher education through high tuition and student debt severely harms the US. It will cause shortages in many professions that are essential for the well-being of society (e.g. social workers). One study found that declining college attendance would cause a shortage of 8.5 million college graduates and $1.2 trillion of lost economic output by 2030. [523]

High US college tuition costs reflect the difference between countries that are focused on maximizing the well-being of society versus those that are focused on maximizing the wealth of wealthy citizens. To illustrate, Germany provides free higher education, even for international students. Free college in Germany is seen as an extension of free high school that broadly benefits the economy and society. Germany often provides free tuition to international students because many of them remain in the country after graduation, pay taxes and benefit the economy. The implied myopic US attitude toward college is that college mainly benefits individuals, not society. Therefore, students should pay for higher education. [524]

Public funding of US higher education greatly increased the number of young people attending college. In 1946, about two million young people attended colleges or universities (one of eight college-age people). By 1970, this had risen to eight million (one of three college-age people). However, reduced public funding of higher education prevents many young people from going the college. As a result, for the first time in US history, fewer young people are attending colleges or universities than the previous generation. [525] Indicating that higher education rates are declining relative to other countries, when all adults of working age are considered, the US has one of the most highly-educated populations in the world. However, the US ranks 14th among developed countries in the percentage of 25-34 year-olds with higher education (42 percent). [526]

High Student Debt

From World War II to the 1970s, public higher education often was nearly free. As a result, there was virtually no student debt. However, in the 1980s, funding for public higher education declined and student debt began to rise.[527] High student debt is a major problem in the US. As discussed, business influence of government since the 1980s caused trillions of dollars of taxpayer wealth to be shifted from helping average citizens (social welfare) to helping wealthy citizens (corporate welfare). This reduced public funding of higher education and drove rapid growth of tuition rates. This in turn compelled more students to take on higher levels of debt.

US student debt rose from about $500 billion in 2007 to $1.6 trillion in 2023.[528] This is higher than credit card and auto loan debt. Among consumer loans, student debt outstanding is second only to mortgage debt. In 1993, 46 percent of college and university students graduated with some student debt (average of $9,000). By 2012, 65 percent of students graduated with an average of $27,000 in student debt.[529] When credit card debt is added, the average rises to $35,000.[530]

Many young people are unfamiliar with borrowing. Student loans can seem like free money. As a result, young people often take on more debt than they can handle. About one-third of student loans in repayment (i.e. not in deferred status) are delinquent or in default. About 60 percent of graduates with student debt say that they regret their college financing decisions.[531]

Young people frequently are leaving higher education with levels of debt that once only were incurred through the purchase of a new home. One study found that students with bachelor's degrees take an average of 19 years to pay off their student loans. Total repayment including interest averaged $117,000, with an average monthly payment of $500.[532]

Reducing funding for public higher education and forcing students to take on large amounts of debt hurts young people, the economy and society in general. Many young people say that high student debt has prevented them from buying a home, starting a business or saving for retirement. As a result of high student debt, one survey found that 40 percent of graduates delayed buying a car or saving for retirement, 29 percent delayed buying a home, and 15 percent postponed marriage.[533] Nearly 10 million former students are in default on student loans. This often blocks them from getting ordinary consumer credit and constrains their lives in many other ways.[534]

Reduced public funding and rising tuition costs and student debt levels strongly contribute to the US having the highest college dropout rate among developed countries. More than half of students who enter college fail to earn a degree.[535] The six-year college graduation rate is 51 percent at private schools and 21 percent at state schools.[536] Driven by declining support for low and middle-income students, dropout rates are highest at community colleges and lower-tier public universities.[537] In 2022, to reduce the harm that high student debt imposes on US society, President Biden announced plans to cancel up to $20,000 of student debt for low and middle-income families.[538]

Declining Class Mobility

Declining class mobility is one of the most tragic and economically harmful aspects of the reduced commitment to public higher education in the US. The US once was considered to be a land of opportunity. Low-income people regularly used to advance to the middle class or higher. Low-cost public higher education was one of the most important factors creating equal opportunity in the US. But the US shift in focus from the well-being of society to the well-being of wealthy people who give lots of money to politicians has substantially degraded public higher education and class mobility.

As discussed in the Education Funding section, the US has less equality of opportunity than nearly all other developed countries. For example, the life prospects of a person in the US are more dependent on the income and education of parents than in almost all other developed countries.[539] The US ranks 26th among 28 developed countries on the percentage of young people in higher education if parents did not attend high school. The burden placed on parents and students for funding higher education is higher in the US than in nearly all other developed countries. To illustrate, 38 percent of higher education funding comes from public sources in the US compared to an average of 70 percent among all other OECD countries.[540]

Reduced funding is causing many public colleges and universities to accept fewer students and shift the emphasis of financial aid from need-based to merit-based. As a result, fewer students from low-income families are being admitted. The top public universities are becoming more like Ivy League schools where most students come from wealthier families. For example, at Ivy League schools and the top public universities, 80 percent of students come from the top income quartile, while only two percent come from the bottom quartile.[541]

Failing to adequately fund public higher education creates difficult choices for low and middle-income families and students. Families often must choose between reduced prospects for their children or living on the brink of financial ruin due to high debt and/or using up life savings to send their children to college. Students with families who are unable to help with higher education frequently must choose between reduced income and job opportunities for life or high, severely constraining debt levels that many young people are unable to repay, regardless of how hard they work.

Shifting public funds from social welfare to corporate welfare over the past 40 years of deregulation has caused social mobility to be at the lowest or near the lowest point in US history. The greatest predictor of whether a person will graduate from college is whether their parents graduated from high school. US higher education costs are near the highest in the world.[542] High tuition combined with nearly the lowest level of public funding for higher education and the shift in financial aid away from low-income students often make it difficult or impossible for young people from low-income families to attend college.

From a financial perspective, it is extremely irrational to make it difficult or impossible for low-income families to send their children to college. As noted, college graduates earn substantially more over their lives. The US has near the highest rate of return on higher education in the world.[543]

Providing higher education access to all young people who want it would greatly benefit the US economy and society.

Bloated University Administrations

Bloated university administrations are another problem caused in large part by corporate influence of higher education. This issue and the degradation of public higher education in general are discussed in an excellent article by Deborah Leigh Scott, called *"How Higher Education in the US Was Destroyed in five Basic Steps."*[544] She points out that changes in public higher education are like those that began in the healthcare sector in the 1970s. As discussed in the Healthcare section, prior to 1970, the US healthcare sector largely was nonprofit. Hospitals mainly were managed by doctors. However, with the introduction of health management organizations in the 1970s, the sector quickly shifted to a for-profit basis. This led to frequent price increases, service reductions and denial of claims. Doctors became a managed profession.

In the same way, public universities largely used to be run by professors. But corporate influence and declining public funding caused many colleges and universities to hire professional administrators. They often took over control of budgets, curriculum development and other functions. Schools frequently argued that reduced public funding required cost cutting and efficiency improvement. As a result, new administrators often cut full-time faculty positions and replaced them with graduate students and temporary adjunct professors. Administrators also frequently reduced or eliminated more expensive programs, such as engineering, computer science and nursing.[545]

This cost cutting often did little to lower overall costs. But it substantially degraded the quality of education. Funds frequently were shifted away from education (i.e. professors, academic programs) and towards administration. By 2012, nearly every college and university in the US had more administrators than faculty.[546] Declining public funding often compelled schools to solicit donations from corporations and wealthy citizens. As a result, more money frequently was spent on fundraising, public relations, marketing, consulting and legal services.[547] Professional management often was more appealing to corporate donors. The increased emphasis on administration drove increased salaries and benefits for university presidents and other senior administrators. Administrators often make two to five times more than professors.

The increased emphasis on businesslike practices in public higher education drove many of the same problems seen in the healthcare sector. These include bloated administrative costs (as noted, healthcare administration costs are twice as high in the US as in Canada), frequent tuition increases, reduced course and program offerings, declining quality of education, and more rejected applications for admission. Ironically, the use of professional administrators to lower costs is raising total costs at many schools while severely degrading the quality of education.

Increased accountability and standardized testing were used in the K-12 area to create the perception of a crisis and facilitate sales of business products and services. The same approach is being promoted in higher education. Over 100 colleges and universities are using a standardized test called the Collegiate Learning Assessment (CLA). Standardized testing facilitates cost cutting and creates many business opportunities, such as gathering and utilizing student test data.

As discussed in the Privatization section, a software billionaire partly funded the Common Core standards and efforts that gather and process student test data. The same person is funding the CLA and data gathering efforts in higher education.[548] Producing, gathering and utilizing college standardized test data creates many business opportunities in the software, hardware and related areas.

As in the K-12 area, the stated goal of increased accountability and other businesslike processes is to improve higher education. But the result frequently is to benefit business at the expense of higher education. Increased standardized testing, data gathering and use of businesslike practices in general will create many of the same problems discussed in the K-12 area above. These include increased administrative and other costs, segmented education where lower-income students receive lower quality education, and lower quality education overall, for example, through the reduction of liberal arts and other programs.

Expanding For-Profit Colleges

Expanding for-profit colleges represents another problem caused by reduced public funding of higher education. Publicly traded companies are structurally required to grow. Privatizing government services is an important growth area. Businesses and their owners often give money to politicians and inappropriately influence government in other ways. Politicians then privatize government services or take actions that facilitate privatization. For example, cutting funding for public higher education reduces attendance at public colleges and universities. This in turn drives increased demand for for-profit colleges. Reduced funding of public higher education is driving rapid growth of for-profit universities and vocational schools.[549]

Business obviously can benefit society in many areas. But the suicidal profit motive of publicly traded companies (which requires never-ending growth regardless of how much this degrades society) is incompatible with maximizing the well-being of society in certain areas. Education, including higher education, is one of these areas. The primary focus or goal of public colleges and universities is to provide high-quality education in an efficient, cost-effective manner. But the primary goal of publicly traded school companies is to provide ongoing growth of shareholder returns. This creates frequent pressure to increase revenues and/or reduce costs.

For-profit colleges reduce costs in many ways, including by frequently using remote Internet learning instead of classroom instruction. This substantially degrades the quality of education and contributes to high dropout rates at many for-profit colleges.[550] To increase revenues, for-profit colleges often charge high tuition fees relative to public colleges and universities. In addition, the schools often employ many recruiters. One study found that 30 of the largest for-profit colleges employed about 35,000 recruiters, 4,000 career services staff and 12,000 support services staff.[551]

Heavy recruiting attracts many low-income or minority students who have difficulty gaining admittance to public universities and colleges. High tuition fees often compel students to take on high student debt. For-profit colleges generate over 80 percent of their revenue from government student loans.[552] These colleges represent 13 percent of higher education students, 31 percent of federal student loans, and nearly 50 percent of student loan defaults.[553]

This illustrates how privatization often helps business, but harms society. Taxpayers frequently wind up paying more money for lower quality products or services. They also often wind up paying higher salaries and other administrative costs. To illustrate, the average CEO compensation at a publicly traded college was $7.3 million in 2009.[554] The average compensation of a public university president was $440,000 in 2011.[555]

Graduates of for-profit colleges often have difficulty finding employment. Government funding represents a major revenue source of for-profit colleges. As a result, the federal government has attempted to hold the schools accountable for results and performance, such as postgraduate employment, to ensure that taxpayer funds are used effectively. But for-profit schools frequently use lobbying and legal action to vigorously oppose being held responsible.[556] This is the expected outcome. Publicly traded companies essentially are structurally required to oppose anything that threatens ever-increasing shareholder returns. When conflicts between maximizing education quality and maximizing shareholder returns exist, as they often do, publicly traded school companies frequently are compelled to protect shareholders. This is a main reason why the suicidal profit motive is incompatible with maximizing the quality of education and the well-being of students.

For nearly all of human history, businesses did not labor under the suicidal requirement to grow forever. This requirement mainly was imposed by the financial sector since the 1980s. Businesses that seek reasonable profits while acting responsibly to all stakeholders and society in general can be sustainable. This type of for-profit company potentially could be effectively involved in education and other areas. But this largely is not the type of for-profit entity operating in higher education and most other sectors in the US.

Expanding Online Education

Rapidly expanding online courses could substantially degrade US higher education. Many colleges and universities have offered online courses for several years. In 2019, prior to Covid-19, about one-third of college students in the US were enrolled in at least one online course.[557] By 2020, this rose to 84 percent.[558] Covid-19 accelerated the shift to online education. In-person course enrollment has grown since 2020. But it almost certainly will not return to pre-pandemic levels. Many students and a majority of faculty support expanded use of blended learning that combines in-person and online education.[559]

Regular online courses often have about 25 students and are run by professors who usually have little interaction with students.[560] Newer types of online courses, called massive open online courses (MOOCs), have been implemented more recently. MOOCs usually are free and often have thousands, sometimes hundreds of thousands, of students enrolled. The courses include video lectures and practices employed by social networking websites. MOOCs often have online forums for questions, comments and discussions. Students frequently grade each other's tests.

MOOCs and other online courses provide large cost-cutting opportunities for colleges and universities. Schools can substantially reduce faculty positions and traditional classroom education. Declining public funding and business influence of higher education are driving rapid growth of MOOCs. Hundreds of universities in the US offer MOOCs and millions of students around the world have signed up for them.[561]

But there are many problems with online education, especially MOOCs. Education usually is most effectively achieved through actual human interactions with teachers, professors and other students. Education, especially higher education, generally cannot be standardized, commoditized, mechanized, packaged and delivered over the Internet. Higher education mainly involves developing the higher mind. Learning facts and information is important. But information usually is easily available in today's online world. By far, the most important part of higher education is learning how to process, evaluate and utilize information. In other words, higher education mainly should be about learning how to think, not what to think.

For example, leading business schools usually employ the case method extensively. Through this process, students analyze and develop solutions to complex management and other problems. Then cases are discussed in class. Professors guide the discussion in ways that illuminate leading-edge analyses and solutions. Through classroom lectures and dialogue, along with other face-to-face educational experiences, students learn to collaborate, lead and think critically.

Organizations providing MOOCs utilize advanced online analysis and techniques to simulate classroom benefits. For example, frequently asked questions might be given priority in online forums, lectures might be interspersed with questions and other activities to better engage students, efforts might be made to customize the online education experience for each student, and effectiveness might be tracked so that future delivery and processes can be improved.[562]

However, in spite of these efforts, the online environment, especially in very large courses such as MOOCs, usually is inferior to the classroom experience. Instead of sitting in a room with an instructor and other students, students often are sitting alone staring at a computer screen. They generally are not able to get feedback from instructors. MOOCs attempt to compensate for this by facilitating feedback from other students. But student feedback in online courses frequently is unsophisticated and simplistic. Common feedback includes statements such as "great comment". Student feedback in online forums often is like the blind leading the blind.[563] Student discussions frequently occur in classroom settings. But teachers or professors are present to guide the discussion and point out important ideas and information that students might be missing. This often does not occur in online student discussions, especially in MOOC-facilitated discussions.

Another feedback problem with MOOCs involves grading or evaluating tests and other projects. Multiple-choice and other simple tests can be graded by computers or other students. But essays and other complex, qualitative material generally cannot be adequately evaluated this way. Advocates of MOOCs sometimes argue that rubrics or grading frameworks can be used to evaluate written material. But this is oversimplified. A grading rubric might suggest looking for the presence of certain ideas and connections between the ideas. But evaluating the quality of writing is far more complex than this.

Beyond the presence of ideas and linkages, one often must evaluate the sequence of ideas, logic flow, creativity, clarity, the quality of facts and information, the ability to evoke interest or passion in the reader, and the extent to which writing achieves its objective, such as entertaining or prompting action. Also, rubrics or grading frameworks implicitly make assumptions about the optimal answer or essay. However, creative students might find better ways of achieving the writing goal implied in the rubric. The essay might be the best in the class. But a rubric might grade it the worst if it misses many points in the rubric. High-level evaluation of writing and other complex, subjective work generally cannot be adequately done by students using rubrics to grade other students. Beneficial analysis and feedback usually is best provided by experts, such as course instructors.

Advocates of MOOCs also often argue that students can listen to some of the best lecturers and professors in the world, an opportunity that most students would not otherwise have. But even with outstanding lecturers, the dropout rate for MOOCs is about 90 to 93 percent.[564] This strongly indicates that the vast majority of students find the MOOC delivery method and related engagement processes to be inadequate. If the courses were adequately educating students or benefiting them in other ways, completion rates would be much higher.

People spend extensive time on social networking websites because it often is fun, easy or interesting. However, online education usually requires hard mental work, commitment and tenacity. It frequently is difficult to complete online courses because students do not get face-to-face feedback and support from professors and other students. Based on extremely high dropout rates, most students apparently do not have the tenacity or commitment needed to complete MOOC courses. Generally only the most motivated and committed students complete them.

Beyond MOOCs, smaller online courses also often provide an inferior learning experience. Many studies have shown that students in online courses get lower grades, dropout and fail at higher rates than those in traditional classroom courses.[565] Few studies have shown that online courses provide a superior education compared to traditional classroom courses.

For example, many studies have shown that community college students who enroll in online courses are substantially more likely to fail or dropout than those in traditional courses.[566] In addition, underperforming students who are barely getting by in traditional courses usually fall further behind in online courses. A study of 51,000 students enrolled in community and technical colleges found that those who took more online courses were less likely to graduate or transfer to four-year colleges.[567] A survey of employers found that they were more likely to hire applicants from traditional rather than online education.[568]

Humans are complex and multifaceted. We are not simple machines. We cannot accept information downloads, like a computer. Online education often attempts to treat humans like machines. This is a main reason why the online learning environment often is inferior to traditional classroom learning. Humans evolved to interact face-to-face with other humans. As discussed in the Real World vs. Cyberworld section of *Global System Change*, we frequently find our greatest life satisfaction and success in relationships with other humans or in close proximity to them. Simple online activities that require little or no mental effort can be fun or distracting. But learning often requires hard work and commitment. Successful learning also frequently requires face-to-face interaction and support from instructors and other students.

An excellent article by Emily Wilson, called *The Huge Growth of MOOCs Threatens America's Great Public University System*, points out that many aspects of online education are not new or innovative. For example, lectures by well-known professors have been available on CDs for years. Also, the movement towards online education is like movements to put TVs in classrooms in the 1950s and computers in classrooms in the 1980s. It became clear that students could not be taught effectively by TVs or computers. However, it also was clear that this technology could be used at times in traditional classroom settings to enhance the educational experience.

In the same way, online education often is a poor or ineffective substitute for traditional classroom education. However, in today's online world, online research and other activities can be used in many ways to enhance the traditional classroom learning experience.

For example, adaptive learning software has the potential to improve education performance when used in combination with traditional classroom learning. Based on previous experience using the software, adaptive learning technologies customize lessons and other learning material for each student. This enables students to learn at their own pace, which often could be faster than classroom learning. The technology also gives teachers more detailed information about student progress. This enables teachers to focus on students who are having difficulty. But it also could make teachers' jobs more difficult. Rather than moving the class along at one pace, teachers might have to keep track of 30 students who are moving at different paces. However, regardless of adaptive learning software, good teachers usually are aware of the varying competencies of their students. They frequently attempt to customize assignments and other materials accordingly.

While adaptive learning technologies probably can and will enhance education in some cases, it also generally is not an adequate substitute for human-to-human education. Adaptive learning technologies mainly are focused on knowledge transfer (i.e. downloading information or learning what to think). But as noted, the most important aspect of education, especially higher education, usually is learning how to think, not what to think. Software can analyze objective facts. But it cannot adequately assess students' insights during class discussions, the quality of writing, creativity, critical thinking, complex problem-solving, and dealing with complexity, uncertainty and subjectivity (i.e. the most important components of true higher education). These issues generally must be assessed by experienced humans.[569]

Some students might prefer online courses because it could be more convenient to stay home. Alternatively, some young people feel insecure or have other psychological issues that make them feel uncomfortable around other people. Avoiding human interaction through online education might be more comfortable. But that does not mean that it is more beneficial. Learning often requires hard work and commitment. Social skills such as the ability to cooperate are among the most important qualities needed for success in life. These are learned far more effectively by being in the presence of other people.

In addition, critical thinking and other important aspects of higher education usually are learned much more effectively in classroom settings. Going to class might involve more work or inconvenience. But true success and satisfaction in life often result from doing things that seem uncomfortable or difficult at first. Humans did not evolve to be loners. Life nearly always is more successful and satisfying when it includes interaction with others.

Advocates of online education often attempt to portray adaptive learning and other online technologies as the greatest thing since sliced bread. But there is no denying the fact that students are interacting with machines instead of humans. As discussed in the Economic Growth section, to provide ever-increasing shareholder returns, companies often replace telephone operators with computers. As a result, customers are treated like machines. Being forced to 'talk' to a computer and listen to annoying, time-wasting telephone prompts severely degrades customer service and satisfaction.

The same service degradation is inevitable with online education. The ability to learn from a computer always will be limited. Machines never will replace essentially infinitely more sophisticated human beings. Computers and other machines sometimes can replace humans for simple or repetitive tasks. But educating a human being is one of the most complex tasks in human society. Learning includes emotional, psychological, physical and even spiritual elements, along with intellectual components. It is irrational to think that we can or will develop an adequate nonhuman replacement for human teachers.

Education involves expanding the human mind. As discussed in the Psychiatric Drugs section, we know virtually nothing about the mind, compared to all that there is to know. The idea that we can replace a human teacher or professor with a virtually infinitely less sophisticated machine is not logical. There is a limited role for machines in learning. In nearly all cases, that role is to help human teachers and professors, rather than to replace them.

Using adaptive learning software to customize lessons and other material for each student seems to ignore a more important, bigger picture customization issue. As discussed in the Competitive Grading and other sections, each human being is different. We all have unique interests and passions. But our grossly flawed, myopic education system often attempts to force all students into the same core courses. Many students are not interested in math or other subjects. This is the main reason why performance often varies widely among students. All students need some basic courses. But beyond this, the education system should help each student to identify their unique interests and skills, and then built their lives around them.

Customizing education mainly should focus on guiding students to courses that interest them. If this occurred, there would be less variation in performance in each class, and therefore less need to customize lessons for individual students. As discussed above, most poor academic performance probably results from boredom, lack of interest and/or issues outside of school, such as poverty or family problems. Poor performance mainly does not result from lack of intelligence.

There are several situations where online education might be appropriate or beneficial. For example, when no higher education options are available, perhaps in developing countries, online options are better than no higher education. Developing countries could use online higher education as a transitional strategy until they can afford superior classroom education. Also, for people who cannot attend classes, such as some disabled or handicapped people, online higher education is better than no higher education.

In addition, online education might be appropriate if important new ideas or strategies become available that are not widely known by professors. However, rather than delivering this material through complete online courses, it probably usually would be more effective to deliver it through one or more recorded or online lectures in traditional classroom environments.

Then professors can manage discussions and related projects as well as deliver supplemental lectures.

Advocates of MOOCs and other online courses sometimes argue that online education can relieve professors of the burden of providing repetitive lectures. While this is true in one sense, there also are several problems with this position. For example, professors often do not give the same lecture to the same group of students more than once. Each time a professor gives a particular lecture, the students usually are different. Good lecturers would not simply talk to students as if they were speaking to a wall. They frequently attempt to discern the response or comprehension of students, and adjust their delivery accordingly.

In addition, the most interesting and effective lectures usually involve at least some interaction with students. Delivering a long monologue in person often is boring and ineffective. Lectures frequently are even more boring, intolerable or ineffective when delivered through a computer screen. Even if classroom lecturers are not as dynamic as those recruited by MOOC companies, they still are able to engage with students and customize their talk based on the specific group of students sitting in front of them. Replacing classroom lectures with online lectures often effectively turns professors into teachers' aides. In addition, when courses are moved completely online, rather than relieving professors of the burden of repetitive lectures, they frequently are relieved of the burden of their jobs.

Online education might work in some cases for basic or simple material when learning mainly involves memorization or repetition. However, it probably would be very difficult, if not impossible, to effectively teach true higher-level thinking (i.e. true higher education) online. As discussed, studying liberal arts produces more effective leaders and more empowered citizens. Liberal arts courses teach students to better understand and deal with complexity and uncertainty, think critically, see the big picture more clearly, understand human society, make moral and ethical decisions, and be more effective team players.

Classroom dialogue among professors and students is one of the most effective and beneficial components of true higher-level learning. In classrooms, students immediately see and participate in high-level, complex discussions. There is an energy and engagement in classroom discussions that would be difficult to replicate through online lectures and discussions. In online forums, many people feel marginalized, while a few people often dominate discussions. This strongly contributes to alienation and high dropout rates.

Some advocates of online education suggest that MOOCs and other online courses can be used for remedial education to help students who are having difficulty in traditional classes. But this is not rational. Students who are having difficulty learning usually need the most one-on-one attention, something that generally is not available in online courses. Pushing remedial students into online courses rarely will help them. Instead, they probably will fall further behind and often dropout.

The movement toward online education will create growing inequality and stratification in higher education. Young people from wealthier families will continue to receive high quality, traditional classroom education. But minority students and students from low or middle-income families frequently will be shunted off to lower quality online courses.

Many businesses and financial organizations strongly support the shift of higher education from traditional classrooms to online courses. In addition, increased business influence and reduced public funding compel many colleges and universities to strongly promote MOOCs and other online courses.

Some organizations established to provide MOOCs are nonprofit. But the motivation for providing these courses largely is not altruistic. Many organizations see MOOCs and other online education as an opportunity to substantially increase revenues and profits. While some MOOC organizations are nonprofit, others are for-profit and have substantial venture capital investment. In addition, as discussed above with nonprofit charter schools, there are many profit-making opportunities related to nonprofit MOOC organizations.

While MOOCs generally are free, there are many ways that organizations could make money on these courses. For example, MOOC organizations often charge colleges and universities licensing fees to provide online courses. MOOC courses usually are noncredit. But MOOC organizations potentially could charge students for university credits. They also potentially can charge for mentoring services, career counseling and job placement assistance.

One of the largest potential revenue opportunities related to MOOCs involves gathering and utilizing students' personal information. As discussed in the Privacy section, free Internet services, such as search, email, news and social networking, are not free. Users effectively pay for these services by giving large amounts of personal information to online companies. These companies earn revenues mainly by selling personal user data or utilizing it in other revenue-generating ways.

The data capture opportunities of MOOCs are huge. Students reveal abundant, valuable information about themselves when they participate in online courses. MOOCs and other online organizations can create extensive profiles that reveal student competencies, interests, biases and other factors. This information often would be valuable to potential employers, marketers and other companies, as well as to government.

MOOC and other online organizations sometimes state that student data remains private. But these entities often are under pressure to provide never-ending profit growth. If using student data enhances profits and shareholder returns, as it often would, organizations frequently will face great pressure to use it. As discussed in the Privacy section, like other online organizations, online education companies might claim that student data is kept private. But user agreements sometimes could contain deceptive terms and loopholes that allow MOOC and other online organizations to utilize student data in various revenue-generating ways.

Beyond substantial revenue opportunities, businesses often strongly support MOOCs and other online courses because they enable large reductions in public funding for higher education. As public funding for society-enhancing programs is cut, more public wealth becomes available for corporate welfare. This enables business-influenced politicians to do what they are paid to do – facilitate ever-increasing shareholder returns by transferring ever-increasing amounts of public wealth to the small group of business owners who give the most money to politicians.

Perhaps the main business benefit of shifting higher education online is the greatly increased ability to suppress critical, big picture analysis and other higher-level thinking. This thinking might threaten business control of government, corporate welfare and ever-increasing shareholder returns. As discussed, online courses cannot come close to matching the ability of traditional classroom courses in teaching liberal arts and other subjective areas. These subjects strongly develop the higher mind. They greatly enhance leadership, problem solving and critical thinking skills. Online education is better suited for information delivery. This is more like vocational education. Suppressing critical thinking and true higher education by shifting college and university courses online greatly increases businesses' ability to protect the status quo of business control of government and theft of the public wealth through corporate welfare.

Controlling content is another major business benefit of online education. Some professors might discuss the numerous major flaws of our economic and political systems, describe sustainable alternatives and solutions, and encourage students to promote or pursue them. Helping millions of young adults to understand the suicidal flaws of current systems and strongly work to change them could severely threaten the status quo of extensive corporate welfare and business control of government.

It often is difficult or impossible to control individual professors. One never knows what a professor might say to young people. However, this is not a problem with online education. Moving higher education online enables businesses and their allies to control the information going to students. Lectures, articles, books and other materials and ideas that question or threaten the status quo can be excluded from MOOC and other online courses. Online education enables businesses and their allies to ensure the young people hear only what businesses want them to hear.

Some people argue that shifting higher education to MOOCs and other online courses is inevitable. From the perspective of our current economic and political ideas and systems, this might be true. Our grossly myopic, suicidal systems demand that financial returns to the small group of wealthy citizens who largely control government must take priority over everything else, including the survival of humanity. Any aspect of society that interferes with ever-increasing shareholder returns must be suppressed, according to our suicidal systems. This includes higher education. If funding high-quality traditional classroom public higher education and teaching young people to think critically interferes with ever-increasing shareholder returns, these activities will be suppressed, as they are being suppressed now.

In this sense, higher education is like manufacturing. As discussed in the Labor section, the decline of US manufacturing is not due to labor or unions. It largely is due to the suicidal requirement to put shareholder returns before all else. Protecting jobs in the US by keeping manufacturing here often restricted shareholder returns. As a result, jobs frequently were sent overseas. In the same way, our flawed systems inevitably will cause the defunding and degradation of higher education. Moving higher education online is a primary means of defunding, privatizing and controlling higher education.

Shifting higher education online represents a compromise between cost and quality. But as discussed below, if we end or greatly reduce corporate welfare, public higher education can be fully funded. If this occurred, there would be no need to replace traditional classroom education with lower quality, lower cost online courses. Many colleges and university administrators and professors strongly oppose the movement towards online higher education. However, reduced public funding and increased business influence of higher education often compel them to go along with it.[570]

Shifting higher education online is strongly supported by many Republican Governors and other Republican politicians.[571] This is the expected outcome. As discussed, Republican and Democratic politicians largely are controlled by business because businesses and their wealthy owners usually give politicians the most money and inappropriately influence government in other ways. But Democratic politicians usually at least try (but often fail) to balance business interests with other aspects of society. Republicans, on the other hand, are much more likely to do whatever business wants without restriction or hesitation, and then mislead the public into believing that putting business ahead of society is the best course for society. The fact that business-influenced Republican politicians often strongly support shifting higher education online further indicates that business is the primary force driving this degradation and privatization of higher education.

Businesses and other parties that benefit from online higher education often attempt to mislead the public into believing that this form of education is as good or better than traditional classroom higher education. Misleading the public and inappropriately influencing government are two main strategies used to maintain the status quo and protect ever-increasing shareholder returns.

But rational analysis and common sense show that online higher education usually is inferior to traditional classroom education. Even when some of the best lecturers in the world present material, the courses often have near 100 percent dropout rates. Delivering education online is not like delivering other products online, such as music. Songs are complete products that easily can be transmitted online. But education is not one-way. The goal or product, in a sense, is the developed and enlightened minds of students. This is not a product that can be delivered online. Information can be delivered and online discussions can be facilitated. But true education is much more than this. We are physical beings living in a physical world. We evolved to usually learn best by being in the physical presence of other human beings for at least part of the educational experience.

Shifting higher education online will create inequality and stratification, like that seen in healthcare and many other areas of society. Children from wealthy families will get high-quality education and other services, while average citizens get lower quality services. As discussed below, this is penny-wise, but pound-foolish. Investing in high-quality public education is one of the most cost effective and beneficial investments that society can make. By greatly reducing corporate welfare, the US easily could afford to provide low-cost or free public higher education in traditional classroom settings.

Business owners and others who profit from online higher education often argue that it is as good as traditional education. But many, if not the large majority, of these people probably send their children to traditional colleges and universities. One way to determine if online higher education is as good as traditional higher education is to ask, would wealthy people put their children in online higher education courses? Probably nearly all families who could afford to pay any price for higher education would not put their children in these courses. If online higher education courses are not good enough for children from wealthy families, they are not good enough for any children.

Business Control of University Research

As discussed in the Business Influence of Education section above, growing business control of university research is a major problem. It places society at great risk and causes substantial environmental and social degradation. Taxpayers fund extensive basic scientific research at public and private universities. This research plays an extremely important role in society. Many medical and other scientific breakthroughs resulted from taxpayer-funded research. Traditionally, independent university research protected society, in part by identifying and analyzing risky products and processes, as well as by developing solutions to major environmental and social problems.

However, independent, taxpayer-funded research can threaten ever-increasing shareholder returns in several ways. As a result, publicly traded companies often have strong financial incentives to control or suppress university research. Business-funded or influenced research is inherently biased. Companies have strong incentives to show their products to be safe and effective when negative impacts are not immediate and obvious, they are unlikely to be held responsible (due to strong influence of government), and there are no cost-effective alternatives. This bias means that company-influenced research should not be used by government to determine public safety and use.

Only truly independent research can effectively protect the public. Taxpayer-funded university research is one of the most important sources of independent research. It often shows the dangers of climate change, synthetic chemicals, and many other products and processes. To protect shareholder returns, companies frequently work aggressively to control, influence or suppress university research.

Beyond suppressing research that threatens shareholder returns, companies also often seek to gain access to taxpayer-funded research that could enhance revenues and shareholder returns. A 1980 law enabled universities to patent taxpayer-funded research and license it to companies.[572] As a result, the financial benefits of this research frequently flow mainly to companies instead of taxpayers. This is another major form of corporate welfare.

To offset declining public funding, many public universities are expanding the patenting and licensing of taxpayer-funded research. For example, the University of California established a nonprofit organization that will take over control of much of the taxpayer-funded research at UCLA. Similar structures are being considered at other UC schools. The new research management organization will be run by a board of directors comprised mainly of business executives. The board will at least partly control factors including allocating research funds, patenting taxpayer-funded inventions, and structuring licensing agreements with businesses.[573]

Growing business influence and control of university research must be reversed. Extensive, robust, independent scientific research is essential for protecting the long-term well-being of society. Companies must not be allowed to block the publication and use of research that benefits society, but threatens shareholder returns. Also, universities and companies should not be allowed to retain most or all of the financial benefits resulting from taxpayer-funded research.

Traditionally, taxpayer-funded university research was made widely available. This maximized the number of individuals and organizations that could use and develop it in ways that benefit society. However, since 1980, universities often sought to restrict or patent the taxpayer-funded inventions of their faculty, students and laboratories. This frequently restricts the ability to rapidly develop the research and inventions. Most taxpayer-funded university research, inventions and knowledge should be quickly placed in the public domain, or made rapidly available through noncommercial means.[574]

Failing to do this substantially degrades society in many ways. For example, as discussed in the Property Rights section of *Global System Change*, taxpayers often fund the development of drugs, which are then patented and licensed to drug companies on an exclusive basis. This enables drug companies to charge extremely high prices. It is a main cause of high healthcare costs in the US. If taxpayer-funded drug research were placed in the public domain, drug companies could compete to produce and sell the drugs. This potentially could lower healthcare costs in the US by over $100 billion per year.[575]

Applied across many industry sectors, this approach could substantially lower-income taxes and prices for numerous products, while substantially improving quality of life in the US. The benefits of taxpayer-funded research should flow mainly to taxpayers. The health, safety and financial well-being of citizens demands that university research be independent of business influence and control.

Suppression of Professors

Suppression of professors is another major problem in higher education. An independent, well-funded public higher education system is critical to the well-being of society. Professors and university researchers often devote their lives to analyzing and developing solutions to complex problems. They also teach young people about these problems and potential solutions. Professors are among the leading intellectuals in society. Their innovative, leading-edge ideas and solutions sometimes are controversial and threaten vested interests. Suppressing leading intellectuals and their innovative ideas would severely inhibit society's ability to resolve the many large and growing environmental, social, economic and political problems facing humanity.

For many years, it is been known that university professors and researchers must have the intellectual freedom and job security needed to pursue innovative ideas and approaches without fear of retribution or suppression by powerful vested interests. Tenure provides job security and intellectual freedom, and thereby protects society's ability to resolve major problems.

Professors often teach young people to think for themselves, rather than blindly believe the positions of business and political leaders. Young people are encouraged to critically examine ideas and systems, identify injustice and problems in society, and work to resolve them. During the 1960s and 1970s, many of the efforts to improve civil rights, protect the environment, and end unnecessary military activity were incubated or supported by universities. Professors frequently opened the minds of young people and empowered them to protect their country and fight for what they believed was right.

But teaching young people to question and challenge economic, political and other ideas and systems severely threatened the ability of businesses to continue negatively impacting the environment and society, inappropriately controlling government, and essentially stealing trillions of dollars of wealth from average citizens. As a result, protecting the status quo required the suppression of freethinking, independent professors. This is not to suggest that there was a coordinated effort by business to suppress professors. However, as business influence of higher education grew, professors often were severely suppressed. Whether this suppression was intentional or unintentional largely is irrelevant. The key issue is that suppression of professors severely degrades society. Therefore, this suppression must be ended.

Over the past 40 years, many colleges and universities reduced tenured jobs and increased the use of temporary, part-time adjunct professors. In the early 1980s, about 80 percent of courses were taught by tenured or tenure-track faculty.[576] Currently, less than 25 percent of professors in the US have tenured or tenure-track jobs.[577] About 75 percent are adjuncts.[578]

Adjunct professors have little or no job security. They usually are employed on a temporary basis, often for one semester at a time. Many adjunct professors live at or near the poverty level. In addition, many have PhD's and over $100,000 of student debt. Most adjuncts work at multiple universities in an effort to stay above the poverty line. Adjuncts earn an average of less than $20,000 per year, while tenure-track and tenured salaries range from $80,000 to $140,000 on average.[579]

Adjunct professors usually receive no healthcare or other benefits. They often do not qualify for unemployment benefits when they are unemployed, for example over the summer. Adjunct professors usually have no office to meet with students, no support staff and no university e-mail address. They frequently are not listed in university faculty directories. Adjuncts usually have little or no say in curriculum or courses being taught. They generally do not attend faculty meetings.[580] Adjunct professors usually can be fired for nearly any reason, including criticizing their university, creating controversy in classes, or taking positions that threaten corporate donors.

Communist countries often suppressed intellectuals who threatened abusive leaders by killing them or putting them in jail. But some studies have shown that the US approach to suppressing intellectuals is more effective than incarceration.[581] Unfairly incarcerating intellectuals can generate sympathy and support from citizens. However, impoverishing professors frequently is a more effective way to control and suppress them. Reduced public funding often creates a sense of crisis or fear of losing their poverty-level jobs. This can prevent professors from questioning myopic economic and political systems, business control of government, corporate welfare and other injustices in society.

Working hard for many years to get a PhD, and then being unable to find a tenure-track job often lowers self-esteem. This combined with a desire to remain affiliated with higher education can compel people to take poverty-level adjunct professor positions where they receive no benefits and no respect from universities. Beyond the emotional, psychological and financial strain of being an adjunct professor, the position also apparently frequently causes degraded physical health. The lack of healthcare benefits has contributed to growing medical problems among adjunct professors.[582]

Colleges and universities sometimes argue that reduced public funding compels the reduction of tenured positions and increased use of adjunct professors. But as discussed above, this position is deceptive. Business-influenced colleges and universities often are not reducing total costs. Instead, they are lowering faculty and academic program costs, while increasing administrative costs.

As discussed below, reducing corporate welfare would enable the US to provide high quality, very low cost public higher education. Ending the abuse and exploitation of adjunct professors is a critical element of re-establishing outstanding public higher education in the US. Tenured positions should be greatly increased. College and university professors should receive the pay, benefits and respect commensurate with the very large contributions they make to society.

Suppression of Critical Thinking

The suppression of critical thinking and courses that promote it are substantially degrading higher education in the US. A major purpose of higher education traditionally has been to develop the higher mind by teaching people to see the big picture of human society and think critically and objectively about it. Liberal arts and humanities (a branch of liberal arts focused on the study of human culture) generally were the foundation of higher education. A main goal of liberal arts education is to develop virtuous, knowledgeable and articulate citizens. As discussed, this type of education produces better leaders and strategic thinkers. Many of the US Founders and other great leaders studied liberal arts and humanities. Wealthy families often send their children to liberal arts colleges because this best prepares them to take over the leadership roles of their parents.

However, liberal arts education can threaten business and the status quo. Teaching young people to be open-minded, critical freethinkers will better enable them to identify and oppose injustices in society, such as corporate welfare and business control of government. Also, liberal arts and humanities courses often do not best prepare students for entry-level or lower-level business positions. As a result, as business influence of higher education increased over the past 40 years, colleges and universities frequently de-emphasized liberal arts and other courses that are not directly related to job preparation.[583] Instead, courses related to STEM and business often were emphasized.

This produced a shift in US higher education away from actual higher education towards vocational education. Instead of opening young people's minds and teaching them to think critically, college and university students implicitly often are taught to obey rules, tolerate tedium and not question authority. This produces well-conditioned, obedient employees for our suicidally flawed business structures that put shareholder returns before all else, including the well-being of employees. The severe degradation of faculty discussed above frequently makes it difficult for students to form mentor or advisor relationships with professors. This further lowers the likelihood that students will be encouraged to critically examine society's flawed ideas, systems and structures.

Several Republican governors and other Republican politicians strongly advocate reduced humanities and liberal arts education in public colleges and universities.[584] Being essentially puppets of business, these politicians do what they are paid to do – protect shareholder returns. Eliminating humanities and other liberal arts courses increases the higher education focus on job preparation and suppresses critical thinking that might threaten ever-increasing shareholder returns. Republican politicians also often strongly support the transition of higher education to MOOCs and other online education. This further suppresses liberal arts education because, as discussed, online education cannot teach higher-level, complex thinking nearly as well as traditional classroom courses.

In supporting reduced funding for humanities education, one Republican governor said that he did not think it was in the vital interest of his state to have more anthropologists. Another governor said that the humanities profession was not supported or rewarded by the market.[585] This type of thinking reflects a negative trend discussed throughout this book. During deregulation since the 1980s, the focus of society switched from maximizing the well-being of society to maximizing the well-being of business. The same trend is occurring in higher education.

To illustrate, humanities studies include social sciences, history, cultural studies, philosophy, law and anthropology (the science of humanity). Humanities education often involves analyzing how society has successfully or unsuccessfully dealt with major problems throughout human history. This big picture thinking is essential for solving the many large and growing problems currently facing humanity.

Liberal arts education often produces citizens and leaders who have the wisdom and courage needed to make difficult choices and systemic changes. But these types of freethinkers would severely threaten the status quo. As a result, the business dominated higher education system appears to be suppressing the production of real leaders and increasingly focused on producing puppets who will do as they are told and not question unjust and unsustainable systems.

Objectivism and Atlas Shrugged

A main strategy for suppressing critical thinking in higher education involves promoting blind faith adherence to irrational economic dogma and philosophies. The promotion of Ayn Rand's book *Atlas Shrugged* and the related philosophy of objectivism well illustrates this suppression. *Atlas Shrugged* explains and attempts to justify several aspects of extreme conservative or Republican philosophies. Many people on the far right consider *Atlas Shrugged* to be a 'Bible' of their movement. Businesses sometimes require or suggest that employees read it. As business influence of higher education increased, several business donors to universities made teaching *Atlas Shrugged* a requirement of receiving donations. For example, a business donor to 60 universities required that the schools teach *Atlas Shrugged*. Schools also often were required to ensure that professors teaching the course "had a positive interest in and be well-versed in objectivism".[586]

The philosophy of objectivism claims to be objective and based on reality. However, when core tenets of objectivism and main ideas promoted in *Atlas Shrugged* are critically and rationally examined, many of these ideas are shown to be irrational and not based on reality. *Atlas Shrugged* promotes a dogmatic, irrational worldview, like those promoted during the Dark Ages. The US Founders used enlightened, critical thinking to penetrate dogma and develop new ideas and systems that truly benefited society, such as the US Constitution and government. Promoting objectivism and other dogmatic, irrational philosophies in higher education is like returning to the Dark Ages. The well-being of society demands that enlightened, critical thinking be re-established and strongly promoted in higher education.

The following discussion illustrates how irrational philosophies can be used to suppress critical thinking and mislead the public. It first summarizes basic ideas of *Atlas Shrugged* and objectivism. The discussion then shows how rational, critical thinking can be used to illuminate the irrational, destructive nature of these ideas.

The philosophy of objectivism holds that reality is independent of consciousness. Humans can get objective knowledge by observing reality, and then drawing logical conclusions based on these observations. The philosophy also states that the proper moral purpose of one's life should be the pursuit of one's own happiness or rational self-interest. This code suggests that people should not sacrifice for others or accept sacrifices from other people. The philosophy further suggests or implies that the only social system consistent with this rational self-interest is one that emphasizes individual rights and is based on laissez-faire capitalism (i.e. limited or no government regulations, except those needed to protect property rights).

In the fiction novel *Atlas Shrugged*, the US becomes a government dictatorship. Business leaders rebel. They refuse to be exploited by taxes and government regulations. They go into hiding and shut down major industries. This causes society to collapse. The book essentially divides society into two types of people – heroes and parasites, or looters and non-looters.[587] Heroes are business leaders and other productive, hard-working people. *Atlas Shrugged* describes different types of parasites, including looters and moochers. Looters take wealth from heroes by force. They include bureaucrats and all government officials. Moochers are people with no ability or work ethic. They produce no value. Instead, based on their neediness, they demand and take earnings from hard-working heroes.

Atlas Shrugged discusses the 'Sanction of the Victim'. This occurs when productive people allow parasites to take their wealth. The book suggests that heroes should not allow this theft. *Atlas Shrugged* describes looters and other parasites as proponents of big government, high taxes, big labor, government planning, government regulations and wealth redistribution.[588] As one might recognize, these are common buzzwords and themes of far right economic and political philosophies. This illustrates why many people consider *Atlas Shrugged* to be a 'Bible' of the far right or radical conservative movement.

Many of the ideas promoted in *Atlas Shrugged* and objectivism have been addressed in this book. For example, the idea that useful knowledge results from observations of reality and logical conclusions based on them is rational and widely supported in this book. This is the type of enlightened thinking used by the US Founders. They were not intellectually hobbled by blind faith in dogma.

However, having advocated drawing logical conclusions based on reality, objectivism and *Atlas Shrugged* then violate this idea by espousing several positions that are irrational and shown to be incorrect by observations of reality. For example, objectivism implies that the well-being of individuals and society is maximized when individuals focus on maximizing their own happiness and do not sacrifice for others. The primary flaw of this logic relates to perspective. As discussed throughout *Global System Change*, myopia or failure to see the big picture creates many problems in society. Many ideas appear to make sense at the individual level, but do not make sense at the whole system level, such as Time Value of Money and over-emphasizing economic growth.

It is understandable that some philosophers, economists and other experts would focus on the individual level because they are individuals. Humans naturally think from the individual perspective, in part because we evolved this way. It enables short-term individual survival. However, as discussed extensively in *Global System Change*, the individual perspective is not the relevant or reality-based perspective for maximizing the well-being of individuals and society.

Emphasizing the individual perspective implies that individuals are separate. But this is a fantasy. From the most important perspective (survival), it is not based on reality. Humans cannot survive in outer space. We are as dependent on the Earth as the hand is on the body. Our five senses often trick us into thinking that we are separate. But in the most important sense, we are not. Through breathing, eating, drinking and evacuation, materials constantly are being cycled between our bodies and the environment, our larger body. Like cells in the body, we are parts of one interconnected and interdependent system.

Atlas Shrugged glorifies competition. But as discussed, this is not reality-based. Limited competition can make sense at the individual level. But the overwhelming force in the human body, other natural systems and nature overall is cooperation. If the individual cells in a human body adopted the objectivism philosophy by focusing on their own well-being and not sacrificing or helping other cells, the body quickly would die.

Treating other people with kindness, love and respect and helping the needy are foundational principles of essentially all the world's great religions. Objectivism contradicts these religious ideas. Objectivism is not smarter than the world's religions in this sense. The religious principles of love and service also are implied laws of nature. They are based on the reality of our interconnectedness. Helping others often produces the highest level of joy and deep meaning in life. At the highest level, we are all interconnected parts of one system. Therefore, helping another person ultimately is the same as helping oneself.

As discussed in the Well-Being of Society section of *Global System Change*, developing sustainable human systems requires a hierarchy of focus. The first, most important level of focus is on the whole system or environment. Without a physical environment that is clean and stable enough to support human life, we are dead and all other issues are irrelevant. After the environment, the next level of focus should be on social systems that enable individuals to survive and prosper. This includes systems and laws that protect citizens and their property. Finally, the last, lowest priority focus should be on individual well-being. Paradoxically, making individual well-being the lowest priority enables individuals to reach their highest level of prosperity. This hierarchy of focus protects the environment and social systems that enable individuals to survive and prosper.

Making the well-being of the individual the highest priority, as objectivism and some other philosophies do, often causes the Tragedy of the Commons – the situation we see in the world today. Focusing on the well-being of individual citizens and companies strongly drives degradation of environmental and social systems needed for the survival and prosperity of humanity.

Observations of reality show in a non-debatable manner (within the realm of logic) that humans cannot survive without the environment. Therefore, logic and reality demand that the whole system be the primary or initial focus of humanity. As Einstein said, we must think at a higher level to solve our most complex problems. That higher level is the whole system level. In other words, we must move away from myopia, reductionism and focusing mainly on individual well-being. Instead, we must adopt reality-based thinking by focusing first on the whole system.

As discussed in the Environmental Sustainability Principles and other sections, to become sustainable, we must emulate nature. Nature implicitly functions from a whole system perspective, as indicated by the immense sophistication and coordination seen there that, for example, produces no waste. Thinking from a whole system perspective is a key element of emulating nature. In addition, observations of reality show that the overwhelming force in nature is cooperation. Therefore, another important aspect of emulating nature includes greatly increasing cooperation and wisdom in human society. But objectivism does the opposite of this. It glorifies competition and encourages people to not help or sacrifice for others. In this most important sense, objectivism is not based on reality. It is irrational, unwise and unsustainable.

However, by advocating competition and not sacrificing for others, objectivism and *Atlas Shrugged* promote reduced social welfare programs. This facilitates increased corporate welfare and shareholder returns. These shareholder benefits apparently often cause businesses and their allies to promote the destructive, irrational, dog-eat-dog view of humanity espoused in *Atlas Shrugged*.

Another irrational, childish aspect of *Atlas Shrugged* is the simplistic, black and white segmentation of society into heroes and parasites, or productive people and takers. As discussed, George Washington said that vested interests would use political parties to fracture society into debating, acrimonious, vengeful factions. When the people are divided, they can be easily conquered. This enables large companies and the small group that owns most business assets to essentially steal the people's wealth and power. Businesses and their allies often use *Atlas Shrugged* to imply that liberals and Democrats are looters and parasites who steal wealth from hard-working conservatives and Republicans. They also frequently use the book to argue that liberals and Democrats want big government, high taxes and government regulations.

But these are false divisions. They do not exist in reality. If one were to ask a liberal or Democrat if they wanted big government and high taxes, probably to a person, they would say no. Instead, most probably would say that they want taxes to be as low as possible, government to be efficient and effective, and regulations to not be excessive or counterproductive. Also, the idea that liberals are lazy people who want to live off the hard work of conservatives is irrational. As discussed in the Misleading the Public section, there probably are just as many lazy conservatives as liberals, and just as many hard-working liberals as conservatives. The vast majority of unemployed people are not lazy. They usually want to work, but often cannot find jobs that provide better than poverty-level wages and benefits. As discussed in the Crime section, unemployment is not higher among African Americans because they are lazy. It results from long-term, ongoing oppression and discrimination against African Americans.

By creating false divisions in society and building disdain or hatred for the other side, businesses and their allies can severely suppress rational thought. Animosity for the other side often causes emotions to override or suppress rational thought and logic. Conservatives frequently can be misled into adopting the blind faith, irrational position that liberals and Democrats are stealing their wealth and degrading the country. Rational thought would help conservatives and liberals to see that the vast majority of their wealth and power is being stolen through corporate welfare and business control of government. By suppressing rational thought and replacing it with false, childish segmentations of society, *Atlas Shrugged* helps businesses to protect ever-increasing shareholder returns.

Another extremely irrational, deceptive and destructive aspect of *Atlas Shrugged* is the glorification of business and demonization of government. As discussed in the Misleading the Public section, business and government are man-made entities. They are neutral. Neither is inherently good or bad. They can be designed and managed in ways that produce excellent, terrible or everything in between performance.

In a democracy, government is the expression of the people's desire to work together and pool their wealth and power for the common good. Plants, animals, cells and other living elements of nature are guided by intuition or instinct. This produces essentially infinite sophistication, coordination, efficiency and beauty. However, at our current stage of development, humanity often appears to be unable to harness the intuitive and produce the same virtually infinite sophistication and coordination seen in nature. Perhaps for a period of time, humanity largely is exploring the consciousness of separation. People often do not trust their intuitive guidance, or were not effectively taught how to use it. They sometimes mistake fear-based products of the mind for intuitive wisdom (i.e. the essentially infinite wisdom of nature that each human can access through the intuitive function).

At some point, it probably is the destiny of humanity to establish or re-establish a consciousness of integration or interconnectedness and rely fully on intuitive wisdom. When this occurs, the nearly infinite complexity, coordination and sophistication seen in nature will be manifest in human society. At this point, the need for government or external coordination will be much lower because humans will be coordinated by the implied intelligence that coordinates nature.

However, prior to this greater reliance on intuition and the wisdom of nature, government is needed. At humanity's current stage of development, human society is not possible without it. The illusion of separation produces fear and belief that competition is necessary. Fear and concern that needs might not be met sometimes cause people to harm others or steal their possessions. If people lived on their own in nature without government or society, they often would have to be on guard. Even then, they frequently would be harmed or killed by stronger or unprincipled people who have no concern for others, as often occurred in the Wild West.

For their own protection and well-being, people form governments and establish laws. By working together, they can be much more prosperous and safe. Even indigenous groups usually had hierarchical structures or implied government, often rule by elders. The US Founders designed and established a new, more effective form of government. It enabled the US to become one of the greatest nations in the world. Without the US government, there would be no United States. Virtually all of the great accomplishments of the US and its citizens over the past 200 plus years would have been impossible without government. Without governments, nations and a coordinated human society would not exist.

Therefore, adopting the implied default position that government is inherently bad (i.e. all politicians are looters), and therefore should be minimized, as is done in *Atlas Shrugged*, is grossly irrational. *Atlas Shrugged* and some other conservative philosophies imply that government is an ill-defined, autonomous, evil entity that unfairly steals wealth and abuses citizens in other ways. This also is grossly irrational. Government is comprised of people. In dictatorships, psychologically unbalanced people often abuse citizens. But in a democracy, citizens control government and politicians. However, as discussed extensively, the US largely is not a democracy. A small group of wealthy citizens dominate or control government by giving large amounts of money to politicians from both major political parties and inappropriately influencing government in other ways.

This means that politicians and government in the US mainly are puppets. Government serves average citizens poorly because they largely do not control it. Getting angry at government for not serving average citizens well is not rational. It would be like getting angry at a puppet in a puppet show for using inappropriate language in front of children. Rational parents would not stand in front of the stage and yell at the puppet. They would walk behind the stage and speak with the person controlling the puppet.

To prevent citizens from realizing who is controlling government, people frequently are misled into believing that unions and people on welfare, for example, are controlling it. But believing this deception is not rational. As discussed in the Influencing Government and Elections sections of *Global System Change*, winning elections has become an issue of money. About 90 percent of Congressional elections are won by the candidate who spent the most on their campaign. Most of the wealth in this country is owned by a small group of people. They are the ones who can afford to give large amounts of money to politicians. Nearly all campaign funding comes from the top 10 percent of society, not from unions or any other group or individuals.[589] Money is not given to politicians freely. Large donors generally demand or request something in return. They presumably ask politicians to protect their interests.

Perhaps the best way to identify who actually is controlling government is to assess who is prospering in society. If unions were controlling or strongly influencing government, one would expect that unions, union workers and nonunion workers would be prospering. (As discussed in the Labor section, unions often help union and nonunion workers because they put upward pressure on all wages and benefits.) But unions have substantially declined since the 1980s. However, the small group that owns much of the wealth in the US has experienced rapid income growth, regardless of which political party was in power. These are the people who are controlling both political parties. They are the puppet masters.

As discussed extensively, the small group of wealthy citizens who largely control the US government are no better or worse than anyone else. They largely are good people who do not intend to harm society. But they often are compelled by flawed systems to take harmful actions. In this sense, the ultimate puppet masters or main enemies of society are flawed ideas and systems.

Again, government is neutral. It is as bad as we allow it to be or as good as we demand that it be. Government in the US does a poor job of serving average citizens largely because we have allowed ourselves to be divided and deceived into blindly believing irrational statements, such as government is inherently bad. As long as citizens remain divided by blind faith in irrational philosophies, we will remain conquered and government will continue to do a poor job of serving average citizens.

In the same way that it is irrational to assume that government is inherently bad, it is equally irrational to assume that business is inherently good. Business is a human creation, essentially a machine. It does what it is designed to do. As discussed extensively, most current business structures, especially publicly traded companies, are severely, even suicidally flawed. Two of the main flaws of publicly traded companies are the implied and managed requirement to grow forever and the failure to require fully responsible behavior.

Observations of reality show that nothing physical grows forever in our finite physical world. The suicidal, grossly irrational, reality-ignoring requirement to grow forever ultimately pushes everything else aside, including the survival of humanity. As noted, about 75 percent of the profit growth of S&P 500 companies from 2000 to 2007 resulted from cutting employee wages and benefits. As a result, US labor compensation is at or near a 50 year low relative to company sales and US GDP. The reality-ignoring requirement to seek infinite growth in a finite system will continue to rapidly degrade labor and all other aspects of society until society collapses or we change our suicidally flawed systems.

The other main business structural flaw, the failure to require fully responsible behavior, places business in inherent, structurally-mandated conflict with society. As discussed in *Global System Change*, very generally speaking, businesses can voluntarily mitigate about 20 percent of negative environmental and social impacts in a profit-enhancing or profit-neutral manner. Beyond this point, costs usually increase. If companies continue voluntary mitigation, they often will be taken over or go out of business. Beyond a certain point, voluntary corporate responsibility equals voluntary corporate suicide.

Our flawed economic and political systems unintentionally create a situation where all publicly traded companies must degrade the environment and society to survive. As businesses degrade life support systems and society, they also ultimately degrade themselves. But this is not on the radar screen of our suicidally myopic business structures. They will continue to severely degrade society, and possibly destroy it, if we do not change them soon.

This situation shows the irrational nature of laissez-faire government. It would be far less harmful to remove murder, assault and robbery laws than it would to remove or not implement business regulations. Most individuals would voluntarily not murder anyone if there were no murder laws. But when businesses are not held fully responsible for negative impacts, they often cannot voluntarily stop harming society. Flawed systems compel irresponsible behavior. Individuals can voluntarily act responsibly. But publicly traded corporations cannot do so fully. That is why business regulations are absolutely essential. This is not debatable within the realm of logic. The rational conversation should focus on how to most efficiently and effectively hold companies fully responsible for negative impacts. This removes conflicts between business and society. Under these sustainable systems, companies maximize profits by maximizing the well-being of society.

Another irrational component of *Atlas Shrugged* and some other conservative ideas is the apparent blind faith devotion to 'the market'. The implication in *Atlas Shrugged* and objectivism is that, if government leaves the market alone, it will function well and maximize the well-being of society. When seen from a big picture perspective, this is no more rational than worshiping a stone statue as if it were God. The market is not some magical force that will function perfectly if government leaves it alone. It is irrational to believe this.

The market or a market is created by human interactions. It is a human creation. Markets can be designed and managed in ways that provide great benefit or great harm. The computer concept of Garbage In, Garbage Out is highly relevant to the concept of the market. Markets must have accurate information to function effectively (i.e. in ways that benefit society). If markets receive garbage inputs (i.e. inaccurate prices), they will produce garbage outputs (i.e. environmental and social degradation).

As discussed in the Externalities section of *Global System Change*, producing and using products, for example by burning a gallon of gasoline, imposes many real, relevant, actual costs and negative impacts on society. These costs and impacts would not exist if the products were not produced and used. In this sense, they are direct costs of production and use. When external costs are not included in prices, products and resources, such as fossil fuels, often are over-consumed. As a result, taxpayers frequently wind up paying far more to clean up pollution and other problems than they would have paid to prevent problems.

Failing to include real costs (i.e. externalities) in prices causes gross market distortions. These in turn drive actions among humanity that severely degrade life support systems and society. In the fantasy markets operating in the US and many other countries, high actual cost products, such as fossil fuels, often appear to be low cost, while true low-cost products, such as renewable energy and energy efficiency, frequently appear to be high cost.

Only government can hold companies fully responsible, in part by ensuring that all real environmental, social and economic costs are included in prices. However, holding companies responsible and requiring accurate pricing often would substantially restrict their ability to provide ever-increasing shareholder returns. As a result, companies frequently essentially are compelled to oppose government efforts to hold them responsible.

Main strategies for protecting shareholder returns are inappropriate government influence and public deception. Probably the most important public deception strategy is to divide the public and build animosity for the other side. When this occurs, emotions, such as hatred of liberals or conservatives, often prevent people from thinking rationally and logically. They frequently blindly believe irrational statements, especially if the statements involve negative characterizations of the group they have been conditioned to dislike.

Blocking critical, rational thinking often is essential for protecting shareholder returns. When this occurs, people can be misled into believing irrational statements, such as government and regulations are bad and should be reduced. These are irrational concepts. Society cannot exist without government. Businesses are compelled to degrade society without regulations. These facts are obvious when people think rationally. But it often is easy to mislead non-expert citizens and block rational, critical thinking.

A common irrational idea promoted in *Atlas Shrugged* is that companies are being abused when they are taxed and regulated. The slightest amount of rational thought shows these ideas to be absurd. No one gets wealthy on their own. Companies need infrastructure, resources, laws and many other resources and factors to succeed. In addition, businesses impose many negative impacts on society. When they resist taxation, they effectively are saying that they do not want to pay for the many resources and services that they receive from society. They also implicitly are saying they do not want to pay for the many environmental and social burdens they impose on society.

Rational thought would show that it is impossible for society to prosper, or even survive, without government, regulations and taxes. The rational conversation should focus on how to best employ these tools in ways that maximize the well-being of individuals and society. But this rational conversation often would limit the ability of companies to grow forever. Therefore, it must be prevented. To achieve this, businesses, their paid political servants and other allies frequently attempt to mislead Republican and conservative citizens into believing that government is bad and business is good.

Believing this is like having Stockholm syndrome. The structured focus of business is on shareholder returns. It often must degrade society when returns are threatened. The structured focus of democratic government (when it is not controlled by vested interests) is on maximizing the well-being of society. Having a bias for the entity that often is structurally required to degrade society and against the entity that is structurally required to protect it is not rational. Having the opposite bias is less irrational, but still irrational. The rational bias should be towards maximizing the well-being of society. Government, business and other tools, structures and systems should be used in whatever ways best achieve this.

There are several other irrational components to *Atlas Shrugged*. For example, the book glorifies sex. It portrays sex as the highest celebration of human values. This can be appealing to young people because sex often is an important part of their lives. Sex can be wonderful, especially in loving relationships. But it is not the pinnacle of human activity. Objectivism and *Atlas Shrugged* promote the idea that the highest moral purpose of individuals should be to seek their own happiness. From this selfish and self-centered perspective, sex perhaps could be seen as the ultimate or highest human experience. But as discussed in the Twelve Step section of *Global System Change*, people who make their own happiness the main focus of their lives often wind up depressed, empty and lonely.

For many people, helping others and being of service to society produces the most satisfying and deeply meaningful life, largely because people are acting on the reality of our interconnectedness. This is not to suggest that people should sacrifice their own needs to meet the needs of others, although this type of sacrifice often does produce a deeply meaningful life.

The idea here is not that people should help others out of moral obligation. The most satisfying and successful life virtually always results were following one's wise inner guidance. This usually involves identifying one's unique interests and passions, and then building one's life around them. As people consider how to focus their lives, they often realize that helping others, for example by being a teacher, brings the greatest joy and meaning. People help others, not out of moral obligation, but rather because this is the preferred, most deeply meaningful activity.

Rather than sex being the highest human experience, the actual highest experience often is that which is opposed by *Atlas Shrugged* and objectivism – helping other people. Providing love, kindness and assistance to other people frequently is the most meaningful and memorable life experience. These actions often raise self-esteem. At the end of one's life, people frequently remember the love, kindness and assistance they gave to other people, and the love they received in return. These memories create a sense of peace and satisfaction. It creates the feeling that life was well-lived and worthy.

Beyond the selfish encouragement to focus on one's own happiness and not help others, another moral problem with *Atlas Shrugged* involves adultery. The book implicitly supports adultery because several heroes or main characters regularly engage in it. In *Atlas Shrugged*, adultery is used to celebrate accomplishments or get revenge.

As noted, many people consider *Atlas Shrugged* to be a 'Bible' of Republicans and conservatives. These people often are Christians. But the elevation of sex and adultery in *Atlas Shrugged* and encouragement to not help others strongly conflict with core Christian values. The fact that many conservative Christians support the teaching and study of *Atlas Shrugged* and objectivism shows how easy it frequently is to use emotions, blind faith and division to mislead citizens.

It is not surprising that business donors would require the teaching of *Atlas Shrugged* and objectivism in higher education. The story and philosophy strongly protect shareholder returns by fostering division and animosity in society. This disempowers citizens and makes them easier to mislead. The story promotes a childish, irrational, good versus evil characterization of business and government. This further facilitates public deception, corporate welfare and business control of government.

Critical, rational analysis of *Atlas Shrugged* and objectivism illuminates their many irrational, reality-ignoring components. But this type of critical thinking would threaten ever-increasing shareholder returns. As discussed in the Misleading the Public section, Rule of Dumb approaches often are used to block rational thought and promote irrational dogma. In educational settings, some professors might use Rule of Dumb by arrogantly insulting or making fun of students who question *Atlas Shrugged* and objectivism. They might try to create an Us Versus Them mentality by implying that anyone who questions *Atlas Shrugged* and objectivism must be a parasite, looter or liberal. Teaching ignorant dogma in an arrogant manner might be appropriate for a Dark Ages curriculum. But it has no place in modern higher education.

Atlas Shrugged potentially could be used as a teaching aid in higher education. Many people believe that it is an entertaining and engaging fiction novel. It contains sex, romance, good versus evil, and rebellion against supposed injustice. Students might benefit from reading the novel, but only if they were encouraged to critically evaluate it. For example, many of the logic flaws and reality-ignoring components discussed above could be highlighted and analyzed. The book also could be used to help students understand how vested interests use dogma and philosophies to mislead the public.

Rational assessment of *Atlas Shrugged* might raise the following points. For example, when businesses rebel against taxation and regulation, they effectively are saying they do not want to pay for the many services and resources they receive from government and society or be held responsible for the negative impacts they impose on society. This is not heroic. It is business being a petulant, spoiled child.

Tricking people into blindly believing that government and regulation are bad harms them because these structures are intended to protect citizens. As regulations are removed, individuals and society often are harmed. To illustrate, financial sector regulations imposed after the Great Depression helped the US to become an economic leader and build the largest middle class in the world. But during deregulation occurring since the 1980s, many citizens were tricked into thinking that regulations were bad. One of the most harmful aspects of deregulation was converting defined benefit to defined contribution pension plans.

As discussed in the Finance and Capital Markets section, this made the retirement security of many hard-working citizens dependent on capital market growth. To protect this growth and retirement security, taxpayers often were required to cover the downside of business and investing. This is socialism not capitalism. Converting pensions to defined contribution caused millions of citizens to become cheerleaders for a system that often impoverishes them.

Under deregulation, income for the small group that controls government rose rapidly, while income for the vast majority of citizens rose slowly, stayed flat or declined. Deregulation and the focus on ever-increasing shareholder returns played a main role in converting the US from being the world's largest exporter and creditor in the 1970s to the world's largest importer and debtor.[590] Deregulation was the main cause of the 2008 financial crash, and subsequent bank bailouts. This cost taxpayers as much as $12 trillion. In other words, deregulation (i.e. reducing government) hugely degraded US society and average citizens and greatly increased taxes and national debt. As George Washington implied in his Farewell Address, businesses and their allies easily misled many citizens by dividing them and turning them against government and regulations. This division and deception greatly harmed society.

Atlas Shrugged implies that when society descends to the level of dictatorship, those being abused and impoverished should go on strike. A small group of wealthy business owners largely controls the US government. They effectively have ended democracy and established a business dictatorship. They are like the small group of communist leaders who control the supposed People's Republic of China. The small group that is controlling the US government effectively steals extensive wealth from average citizens through corporate welfare.

Atlas Shrugged criticizes wealth redistribution. It says that government and lazy citizens are stealing wealth from businesses and hard-working people. This helps to trick many citizens into not seeing who actually is stealing their wealth. Massive wealth redistribution is occurring in the US and many other countries. But it occurs in the opposite direction to that discussed in *Atlas Shrugged*. The small group controlling government essentially is stealing trillions of dollars of wealth from hard-working liberal and conservative citizens through many forms of corporate welfare. Large corporations and the small group that owns most of their assets have become the dictators, looters and parasites in the US. These parasites are stealing the wealth and power of hundreds of millions of citizens. Using *Atlas Shrugged* logic, the people of the US should go on strike or rebel against the business dictators and looters.

But this book does not take that position. Business leaders and owners are good people who intend to help, not harm society. It would be incorrect and counterproductive to cast them as evil abusers of society. The enemies are the flawed ideas and systems that compel well-meaning business and political leaders to take actions that harm society.

It also is incorrect and counterproductive to ascribe evil or harmful motives to businesses. They are human creations. Businesses are amoral, like machines. They do what they are designed to do. Calling a company selfish or greedy because it puts shareholder returns before all else would be like calling a washing machine selfish or greedy because it only 'wants' to wash clothes, instead of driving someone to the store to pick up groceries.

Business structures and economic and political systems unintentionally degrade society because they were developed from a reductionistic perspective that ignores much of reality. In a democracy, citizens would not allow the existence of these systems if they were well informed. The fact that they exist shows that leaders and citizens have been misled and often do not see the big picture.

Flawed systems absolutely will change because they are greatly misaligned with reality and nature. If we fail to see the big picture and think critically, systems will change through collapse, great disruption or revolution. A main purpose of this book is to achieve system evolution so that we can avoid revolution and great disruption of society.

Another book by Ayn Rand, *The Fountainhead*, contains ideas that are similar to those espoused in *Atlas Shrugged* and objectivism. Examining ideas from the *Fountainhead* further indicates the myopic, irrational nature of objectivism and *Atlas Shrugged*. The *Fountainhead* and *Atlas Shrugged* portray altruism, working for the common good and helping others as great evils in society.

For example, *The Fountainhead* states, "The 'common good' of a collective - a race, a class, a state - was the claim and justification of every tyranny ever established over men. Every major horror of history was committed in the name of an altruistic motive. Has any act of selfishness ever equaled the carnage perpetrated by disciples of altruism?"[591]

This irrationally implies that people should not work for or protect the common good. But all humans have an interest in promoting the common good of environmental protection because all humans are dead without an environment that is adequately clean and stable. Also, people have an interest in promoting the common good of their countries and communities because strong nations and communities greatly enhance the ability of individuals to prosper.

The quote also irrationally implies that altruistic acts include atrocities such as slaughtering innocent people. It implies that Hitler was a disciple of altruism. But this is a gross misuse of the word altruism. Altruism is an unselfish desire to help others. It is the opposite of selfishness. The Holocaust resulted from Hitler's selfish, evil and insane desire to see a world without Jews. He was a raving lunatic and psychopath, the personification of evil. The Holocaust was not caused by altruism. It is insane to suggest or imply this. Hitler may have thought that he was promoting the common good by eliminating Jews. But he was a lunatic. The Holocaust was caused by insanity and perhaps the greatest evil to ever exist in human society.

Further denigrating helping others, *The Fountainhead* states, "The man who attempts to live for others is a dependent. He is a parasite in motive and makes parasites of those he serves… The nearest approach to it in reality -- the man who lives to serve others -- is the slave… the man who enslaves himself voluntarily in the name of love is the basest of creatures. He degrades the dignity of man, and he degrades the conception of love."

Saying that serving others degrades the dignity of man and conception of love is not rational. The term humanity implies acting humanely and compassionately to others. In the US, people who are willing to work but cannot find adequate jobs often are unable to feed their children without help from society. *Atlas Shrugged*, *The Fountainhead* and objectivism imply that this help should not be provided. Instead the approach implies that unemployed parents and their children should be allowed to starve to death. *The Fountainhead* and *Atlas Shrugged* imply that this would be beneficial because parasites would be removed from society. According to this philosophy, Jesus Christ, Martin Luther King, Gandhi and many of the greatest people to ever live were the 'basest of creatures'. Their motives were parasitic. They made people parasites by helping them.

 The book also states, "In all proper relationships there is no sacrifice of anyone to anyone." According to this idea, it is improper for a parent to sacrifice for a child or a husband to sacrifice for a wife. Benjamin Franklin retired at the age of 42 and devoted much of the rest of his life to helping average citizens and his country. According to the ridiculous *Atlas Shrugged* and *Fountainhead* philosophy, he should not have done this. But if he had not, the US might not exist.

 After George Washington, Benjamin Franklin probably played the most important role in the establishment of the US. He worked for many years in France as a diplomat, largely on a voluntary, unpaid basis. As a result of his work, the French helped the Colonies to win the Revolutionary War. Without Benjamin Franklin's sacrifice for his country, the US probably would have lost the war.

 The Fountainhead also states, "No creator was prompted by a desire to serve his brothers." This implies that productive people and inventors desire only to serve themselves, rather than benefit others and humanity in general. But this is irrational. Helping other people often is the primary motivation for action. As discussed in the Property Rights section, Benjamin Franklin never sought a patent for one of his most popular inventions, the Franklin stove, because he wanted to help citizens and society.

 The Fountainhead further states, "Men have been taught that it is a virtue to agree with others. But the creator is the man who disagrees... Men have been taught that it is a virtue to stand together. But the creator is the man who stands alone." This reflects simplistic, black-and-white, childish thinking. It implies that people should replace rational thought with blind faith in a philosophy. Should a creator (i.e. productive person) disagree with someone who says that two plus two equals four? Should they stand on their own when it would be objectively better to stand together? People should think for themselves and rationally determine when it is best to agree or disagree, stand alone or together, or do anything else. As shown in nature, standing together (i.e. cooperation) usually is the vastly superior strategy.

The Fountainhead also says, "Rulers of men… create nothing. They exist entirely through the persons of others. Their goal is in their subjects, in the activity of enslaving. They are as dependent as the beggar, the social worker and the bandit. The form of dependence does not matter." This irrationally implies that politicians are parasites who add no value. But as noted, society would not exist without government. Politicians essentially are hired by citizens in a democracy to manage the provision of valuable services, such as infrastructure, national security, law enforcement and other essential administrative services. Using this logic, if politicians are parasites who add no value, the same is true of business managers who also produce nothing directly.

Finally, *The Fountainhead* states, "Now observe the results of a society built on the principle of individualism. This, our country. The noblest country in the history of men. The country of greatest achievement, greatest prosperity, greatest freedom. This country was not based on selfless service, sacrifice, renunciation or any precept of altruism. It was based on a man's right to the pursuit of happiness. His own happiness."

This reflects the intense myopia and blatant inaccuracy of ideas promoted in *Atlas Shrugged*, *The Fountainhead* and objectivism. As discussed, the Founders of the US often sacrificed for future generations. During World War II, US citizens made tremendous sacrifices for the common good. Volunteering has been a huge, beneficial component of the US since its founding.

In general, the ideas promoted in *Atlas Shrugged*, *The Fountainhead* and objectivism often are irrational and refuted by observations of reality. But businesses and their allies frequently use them as justifications for lowering social welfare programs. This facilitates increased corporate welfare and shareholder returns.

Libertarianism

Right-wing libertarianism is similar to the ideas promoted in objectivism, *Atlas Shrugged* and *The Fountainhead*. Businesses and their allies often protect shareholder returns by encouraging citizens to replace rational thought with blind faith adherence to libertarian dogma and philosophy. This section illustrates how rational, objective, big picture thinking can be used to expose the irrational, often harmful nature of right-wing libertarianism.

Libertarianism is a political philosophy that emphasizes individual liberty, political freedom and voluntary association. Some branches of libertarianism reject capitalism and private ownership of the means of production. Instead, they advocate common, collective or cooperative ownership and management.[592] This type of philosophy includes theoretical or democratic communism and socialism, where citizens collectively control their destiny. It does not include totalitarian communism, such as that practiced in China and the former Soviet Union. Under this system, a small group of people essentially steals the people's freedom, wealth and power, as occurs in the US.

Right-wing libertarianism emphasizes free market capitalism, private ownership and limited government. The popularity of this philosophy was low or declining in the mid to late 1900s.[593] But like objectivism, it has seen a resurgence in the 21st Century. The philosophy is being strongly promoted by some wealthy business owners and business-funded libertarian think tanks.[594]

As discussed in the Misleading the Public section, publicly traded companies are structurally required to put shareholder returns before all else. If they do not do this, they ultimately will die. Failing to hold companies fully responsible for negative environmental and social impacts creates conflicts between business and society. When companies are not held fully responsible, the requirement to put shareholders first often essentially compels them to degrade the environment and society. Only government can hold businesses fully responsible, and thereby remove conflicts between business and society.

But holding businesses responsible frequently would limit the ability to provide ever-increasing shareholder returns. As a result, our flawed systems essentially compel companies to oppose government efforts to hold them responsible for harming the environment and society. Honestly admitting that they oppose acting responsibly because it would hurt shareholder returns usually would not be an effective way to protect returns. When honesty fails to do this, companies often essentially are compelled to use dishonesty or public deception. Promoting libertarianism is an increasingly important strategy for misleading the public and protecting shareholder returns. (In the following discussion, the term libertarianism refers to right-wing libertarianism.)

Much of the public deception related to libertarianism almost certainly is unintentional. Many advocates, such as those in think tanks, probably sincerely believe that wider application of the philosophy would benefit society. The failure to recognize or acknowledge the harmful nature of libertarian philosophy probably often results from myopia and blind faith. Blindly adhering to the libertarian philosophy frequently suppresses rational, objective assessment of which actions maximize the well-being of society in each situation.

An article called *Key Concepts of Libertarianism* summarizes important principles of right-wing libertarianism.[595] These principles include the rule of law, limited government, individualism, individual rights, spontaneous order, free markets, virtue of production and natural harmony of interests. In a general, theoretical sense, these concepts often are logical, and even obvious. The rational nature of libertarian concepts frequently makes the philosophy more appealing and deceptive. The main problem with libertarianism is not the principles in general, but rather the flawed, myopic or harmful application of them.

Rule of Law

To illustrate, the rule of law not only is a core principle of libertarianism, it is a foundation of civilized free society. The rule of law states that individuals should be free to pursue their own lives so long as they respect the equal rights of others.[596] In other words, people should be free to do whatever they want, provided that they do not harm others. This is the essence of a free, democratic society. The rule of law is strongly promoted throughout *Global System Change*.

Like objectivism, libertarianism states logical principles, and then often fails to abide by them. The failure to support the rule of law probably is the most harmful aspect of libertarianism. The main failure involves applying the rule of law to individuals, but not to business. However, the rule of law should apply to both. Businesses should be free to do what they want, provided that they do not harm individuals or society overall.

As discussed, only government can hold companies fully responsible for negative impacts and harm imposed on society. But this government requirement to act responsibly and cause no harm (i.e. abide by the rule of law) often interferes with the systemically mandated requirement to provide ever-increasing shareholder returns. As a result, flawed systems frequently compel publicly traded companies to oppose acting responsibly and abiding by the rule of law. Admitting that they oppose this because it would hurt shareholder returns usually would not work. Honesty would be ineffective. As a result, dishonesty or deception is required. One of the most effective ways to avoid being held responsible is to turn citizens against government and regulations. Libertarianism does this in many ways.

For example, the above article states, "The rule of law means that individuals are governed by generally applicable and spontaneously developed legal rules, not by arbitrary commands; and that those rules should protect the freedom of individuals to pursue happiness in their own ways, not aim at any particular result or outcome."

This statement is extremely biased and misleading. It apparently is attempting to turn citizens against government and regulations. It implies that little government is necessary because laws will spontaneous arise. But this is ridiculous. Laws do not magically arise out of thin air. Citizens collectively, through their agent government, develop laws. The statement further implies that politicians develop laws and regulations arbitrarily for no reason, except perhaps to justify their existence and restrict people's freedom and happiness. But this is incorrect. In a democratic society, politicians develop laws for the purpose of upholding the rule of law (i.e. preventing harm). The statement also implies that laws and regulations should not have any particular result or outcome. This also is incorrect. Laws always should have a particular result or outcome, such as preventing a specific type of harm.

The statement attempts to mislead people into thinking that government and laws often are arbitrary, counterproductive and freedom restricting. This is highly misleading. Under the rule of law, individuals and organizations do not have the right or freedom to harm others. Therefore, laws and regulations that prohibit causing harm do not restrict freedom or rights because there is no freedom or right to harm others in a civilized society.

This is not to suggest that laws and regulations sometimes are not inefficient, counterproductive or unnecessarily restrictive. They often are. The main reason for this is business control of government. When businesses and their owners give large amounts of money to politicians and inappropriately influence government in other ways, the goal of lawmakers often becomes to protect large corporations and the small group that owns most of their assets, rather than to implement laws that efficiently and effectively protect individuals, small businesses and society.

The primary solution to counterproductive laws and regulations is to end business control of government and return control to the people. The rational conversation about laws and regulations should focus on how to most efficiently and effectively uphold the rule of law – prevent harm. But this logical conversation often would hold companies responsible and restrict their ability to provide ever-increasing shareholder returns. As a result, businesses and their libertarian allies frequently attempt to mislead citizens into blindly believing that government and regulations are bad.

When libertarians argue that business regulations are bad or arbitrary, they often effectively are saying that the rule of law should not apply to business. It is understandable that business-funded libertarians would say this. Business regulations (i.e. the rule of law) limit the ability to grow forever. Libertarians frequently attempt to mislead the public by arguing that businesses are effectively regulated. But as discussed extensively in this book, this statement is grossly inaccurate. Business-controlled government fails to hold businesses fully responsible for negative impacts in many ways, including by relying on inherently biased company-influenced research to determine product use and safety.

Libertarians also attempt to mislead the public by arguing that business regulations often are counterproductive or economy-suppressing. The implied solution is to eliminate business regulations. But this would accelerate already rapid environmental and social degradation. As noted, it is vastly more important to apply the rule of law to businesses than to individuals. Individuals can and usually do voluntarily act responsibly. But flawed systems often compel companies to act irresponsibly when regulations fail to require responsible behavior.

Regarding business regulations, there are different levels of ineffectiveness. High-level ineffectiveness is failing to prevent harm. Low-level ineffectiveness is preventing harm inefficiently. Of course unnecessarily restrictive regulation should be improved. But the vastly more important issue is preventing harm. Failing to fully apply the rule of law to business is driving rapid environmental and social degradation. In other words, failing to hold companies fully responsible for negative impacts is suicidal.

The rule of law perfectly illustrates the irrational and deceptive nature of right-wing libertarianism. The philosophy supposedly honors and promotes the rule of law. But it often neglects to mention or emphasize that the rule of law only can be effectively and fully implemented and enforced by government. Instead, it denigrates government, probably partly because government enforcement of the rule of law against business would restrict ever-increasing shareholder returns. By strongly and irrationally criticizing government, right-wing libertarianism makes it difficult or impossible to fully enforce the rule of law against business. (Libertarian criticisms of government often are irrational because they imply that all government is the same or bad. But there are many types of government. Bad governments that do not serve the people well are worthy of criticism. But good democratic governments often are not.)

Promoting the rule of law while generally denigrating government is dishonest. An honest and accurate characterization of the rule of law would acknowledge that it cannot be implemented effectively without good government. This illustrates a core deception in libertarianism. The philosophy implies that the solution to many problems is to shrink government. This is irrational. It ignores reality. A reality-based characterization would state that the solution is to improve government, for example, by converting it from plutocracy to democracy.

Sometimes improving government might involve shrinking it. But it is irrational to assume this in advance. The optimal solution should be determined through rational, objective analysis of which option maximizes the well-being of society in a particular situation. But again, this rational analysis often would restrict ever-increasing shareholder returns. To protect their business benefactors, libertarians frequently attempt to block rational thought by encouraging citizens the blindly believe that government is innately bad.

Limited Government

The principle of limited government is another highly misleading aspect of libertarianism. Libertarian organizations often attempt to mislead the public into believing that the US government was based on the principle of limited government. For example, a leading libertarian think tank states, "The American system was established to provide limited government". Another conservative think tank states that its purpose is to "defend the principles" of "limited government".[597] The libertarian Key

Concepts article noted above states, "Limited government is the basic political implication of libertarianism".[598]

But as discussed in the Misleading the Public section, the US was not established based on the principle of limited government. The Articles of Confederation provided a weak federal government. As a result, the US was on the verge of falling apart. James Madison and many other Founders knew that a stronger federal government was needed to enable the US to survive and prosper. The main, if not sole, underlying purpose of the Constitutional Convention of 1787 was to strengthen the federal government.

The Preamble states the purpose of the US Constitution and government. The purpose is to form a more perfect union and protect the general welfare. The Preamble makes no mention of limited government. James Madison and other leading Founders knew that saving the union required giving the federal government whatever powers were necessary to promote the general welfare.

As discussed in the Tenth Amendment section of *Global System Change*, Article I, Section 8 of the US Constitution states, "The Congress shall have Power… To make all Laws which shall be necessary and proper… [to] provide for the… general Welfare of the United States." This gives Congress the power to define the general welfare in any way it chooses consistent with the Constitution and implement any law that it believes is necessary to promote the general welfare, provided that these laws do not violate the few explicit and implicit restrictions in the Constitution, such as passing ex post facto laws or violating the Bill of Rights.

As discussed in the Second Amendment section of *Global System Change*, during the Constitutional Convention, there were debates between federalists and anti-federalists. Federalists wanted a stronger federal government. Anti-federalists wanted a weaker one. Robert Yates, an anti-federalist delegate from New York, walked out of the convention in protest. He argued that the "necessary and proper" clause of Article I, Section 8 (i.e. the Elastic Clause) gives the federal government absolute power. He said, "This government is to process absolute and uncontrollable power…

the Constitution or the laws of any state [cannot], in any way prevent or impede the full and complete execution of every power given."[599]

Dissenting delegates to the Pennsylvania ratification convention stated, "The new government will not be a confederacy of states, as it ought, but one consolidated government, founded upon the destruction of the several governments of the states… The powers of Congress under the new constitution, are complete and unlimited over the purse and the sword, and are perfectly independent of, and supreme over, the state governments…"[600]

The Pennsylvania dissenters further noted that the Articles of Confederation supported state sovereignty. But this language was not included in the Constitution. Instead, national sovereignty implicitly was given to "We the People of the United States" in the Preamble. The dissenters also noted that Article VI made the Constitution and federal laws the supreme law of the land.[601]

The federalists won. Leading federalists included James Madison, George Washington, Benjamin Franklin, John Adams, Alexander Hamilton, John Jay and John Hancock. The goal of the US Constitution was not to limit the power of the federal government. That approach was tried with the Articles of Confederation. It failed. Robert Yates was correct. The Constitution gives the federal government the power to make nearly any law it believes is necessary to promote the general welfare. General welfare is a broad term. It includes all aspects of society. Article I, Section 8 gives Congress the power to make nearly any law it believes is necessary to control or protect any aspect of society. This essentially is absolute power. The wisdom of our Founders in giving the US government nearly absolute power has been proven and confirmed by the tremendous success of the United States over the past 230 plus years.

Following the experience with England, the Founders were concerned about abuse of power. To minimize abuse, they divided the federal government into three branches and established checks and balances between them. However, this does not mean that the federal government in total was not given nearly absolute power. There are few limits on Congress's ability to make any law it believes will promote the general welfare.

The ability of the Supreme Court to overturn laws is limited, in part because Congress has the ability to define the general welfare in any way it chooses consistent with the Constitution. Under current judicial review procedures, the Supreme Court usually only can overturn a law if it finds that the law violated the principle of equality or other principles or requirements embedded in the Constitution. For example, the Supreme Court recently struck down a law that said certain adults were not free to marry who they choose, in part because this violated the constitutional principals and natural laws of equality and freedom.

As discussed in the Tenth Amendment section, the Supreme Court could not logically or constitutionally use the Tenth Amendment to strike down laws. The Tenth Amendment refers to powers not delegated to the federal government by the Constitution. But as noted, Article I, Section 8 implicitly delegates all powers necessary to promote the general welfare. The Tenth Amendment essentially is moot because no necessary powers were left undelegated.

But as discussed, *Citizens United*, *Zelman* and many other Supreme Court decisions show that the effectively business-appointed Supreme Court is not bound by rationality, upholding the Constitution or promoting the general welfare. Due to lifetime appointments, the Supreme Court has nearly absolute power. It essentially can do whatever it wants. The people have little recourse. In several cases, the Republican-appointed justices on the Supreme Court used irrational arguments to violate the Constitution and support their strong pro-business bias.

In *Citizens United*, they said that corporations could spend unlimited amounts of money on election campaigns. This obviously violates the principle of equality by giving wealthy citizens much greater influence over government. As discussed in the Public Funding of Religion section, in *Zelman* and *Winn*, the Supreme Court said that public funds could be used to pay for religious education. This clearly violates the intentions of the Founders and the First Amendment.

Through inappropriate influence, businesses effectively paid to appoint pro-business judges to the Supreme Court. These justices might attempt to use the Tenth Amendment or obscure logic to strike down laws that hold businesses responsible for negative impacts. As discussed in the Judicial Branch section, the Constitution does not give the Supreme Court the power to void laws (i.e. judicial review). The Court unconstitutionally gave itself this power in 1803. The Constitution also does not specify that Supreme Court justices are appointed for life. It gives Congress substantial power to define the Judicial branch and restrict its activities. Establishing democracy requires returning control of the Supreme Court to the people. Congress has the power to do this. It can pass laws that impose term limits on the Judicial branch and restrict or rescind its power of judicial review.

In theory, according to our Constitution, the Supreme Court, Congress or government in total does not have absolute power. Only the people have it because they can change government through constitutional amendments and elections. But in reality, as long as businesses and their allies foment the war between conservatives and liberals, the people will remain divided and conquered. They will not be able to work together and get the majorities needed to end business control of government and corporate welfare.

Libertarianism, *Atlas Shrugged* and other irrational dogma stoke division and animosity in society. In this divisive environment, emotions often suppress rational thought. As a result, liberals and conservatives frequently cannot see that they agree on nearly all major issues. Ending the war between liberals and conservatives does not mean that people must agree on everything. It means that people work together in areas of agreement, and then rationally compromise in areas of disagreement, as our Founders did during the Constitutional Convention.

For example, virtually everyone, liberals and conservatives alike, agrees that a small group of wealthy people should not be effectively controlling all three branches of the US government and using this control to essentially steal trillions of dollars of public wealth through corporate welfare every year. Once citizens put rational thought above emotions, they can work together to make the constitutional and other changes needed to end business control of government and theft of the public wealth. Then, like rational, mature adults, they can do their best to work out remaining areas of disagreement. As divisive public deceptions are ended, liberals and conservatives will realize that these areas of disagreement are much smaller and fewer than they previously thought.

According to the US Constitution, the federal government essentially has absolute power to enforce the rule of law, mainly because this is a valid component of promoting the general welfare. In other words, the US government has the absolute power to prohibit businesses from harming the environment and society. But exercising this constitutionally provided power would limit the ability of publicly traded companies to provide ever-increasing shareholder returns.

Two main strategies for protecting shareholder returns are inappropriately influencing government and misleading the public. By strongly influencing or effectively controlling all three branches of government, large businesses and wealthy business owners can prevent government from holding companies responsible for harming society. By promoting right-wing libertarianism, businesses and their allies can mislead the public into believing that the US government was established based on the principle of limited government. But as noted, the US government clearly was not established to have limited powers.

Libertarians sometimes argue or imply that the federal government fails to serve average citizens well because government is too powerful. The solution they state or imply is to weaken or limit the federal government. But this would substantially degrade society. It would enable large businesses to take even more wealth and power from the people. It also would accelerate environmental and social degradation by holding businesses even less responsible for negative impacts. James Madison and other leading Founders were correct. The people's agent, the federal government, must have full power to protect the general welfare, in large part by fully enforcing the rule of law against individuals, businesses and other organizations.

The reason the federal government does not serve citizens well is not because it is too powerful or large. It is because We the People largely do not control the federal government. The solution is not to weaken the federal government. It is to do what the Founders intended – let all citizens equally control government. Once the federal government is controlled by the people, it will focus on serving all citizens well.

As discussed in the Government and Elections section, arguing that weakening the federal government will improve society is like saying that allowing national referendums or other types of direct democracy would improve society. Virtually all Founders, federalist and anti-federalist alike, knew that democracy was an unworkable form of government for more than small groups. That is why the US is not structured as a democracy. The US is based on the principle of democracy (i.e. all citizens equally control government). But functionally, the US is a constitutional republic. Average citizens usually do not have the time to study complex issues like climate change and make well-informed decisions that maximize the well-being of current and future generations. As a result, under the US system of government, citizens delegate their authority to expert politicians who make well-informed decisions, in theory.

But in reality, politicians mainly serve those who give them large amounts of money. Average citizens, being justifiably angry at politicians who do not serve them well, sometimes argue that politicians should be bypassed through referendums. But this would not work. Businesses can easily mislead non-expert citizens. A parent would not perform surgery on their child. They would delegate their authority to a surgeon. In the same way, non-expert citizens should not bypass expert politicians. They should not attempt to decide complex issues when they have no expertise and limited or biased information from vested interests. Instead, they should demand that politicians and government serve all citizens equally. Using the same logic, we should not attempt to limit the constitutionally provided power of government. We should abide by the Constitution and return control of government to the people.

Flawed systems often compel businesses to use deception or any other means necessary to protect shareholder returns. As discussed in the Misleading the Public section, citizens can predict with virtually 100 percent accuracy what publicly traded companies will say on nearly any issue by assessing which actions maximize shareholder returns. If strong government helps shareholders, businesses usually support it. But when strong government restricts shareholder returns, businesses generally oppose it. To illustrate, at the beginning of the US, businesses benefited from having a strong federal government. The Federalist party was established by Alexander Hamilton and other banking and business leaders. But now, the strong federal government provided by our Constitution often limits the ability of businesses to grow forever, mainly by empowering government to enforce the rule of law against businesses.

As a result, since the 1980s, businesses, politicians paid by them and other business allies have weakened regulations and transferred literally trillions of dollars of public wealth from average citizens to wealthy business owners. Programs that promote the general welfare, such as healthcare and education, often increase taxes and restrict shareholder returns. As a result, libertarians and other business allies frequently argue that the federal government should not be involved in these areas. However, the national highway system greatly benefits businesses. Therefore, one rarely hears libertarians or other business allies arguing that the federal government should get out of the interstate highway business.

The near absolute power granted to the Federal government by the US Constitution illustrates the strong need to establish democracy and run the country as the Founders intended. When large corporations and wealthy business owners largely control government, they use the power of the US government to protect and maintain corporate welfare and business control of government. This is illustrated by the bank bailouts, *Citizens United*, and many other examples of inappropriate business influence of government provided in *Global System Change*.

The great power of the US government can severely harm average citizens when it is wielded by a small group of wealthy business owners, as currently occurs. However, once the people regain control of government, they will use the Constitutionally-granted near absolute power of government to place business in service of society and promote the general welfare in other ways. The power of the US government will be used to fairly and equally serve all citizens, as the Founders intended.

Individualism and Individual Rights

The libertarian concepts of individualism and individual rights often are used to turn citizens against government and regulations, and thereby protect shareholder returns. The Key Concepts article noted above states, "Libertarians see the individual as the basic unit of social analysis." This reflects the same myopia seen in objectivism and many other philosophies. The prosperity and survival of humanity demands that the whole system (which includes larger environmental and social systems), not the individual, be the initial focus of analysis. Leading Founders such as Benjamin Franklin and James Madison were highly rational, enlightened men. They realized that individuals could not prosper if the larger systems that support individuals were not stable and thriving. As a result, the focus of the US Constitution is on promoting the common good (i.e. general welfare). As noted, focusing on individual well-being without adequately addressing larger environmental and social systems creates the Tragedy of the Commons (i.e. it is suicidal).

As with objectivism and laissez-faire capitalism, strict libertarians sometimes say that the sole legitimate purpose of government is protecting private property rights.[602] But this is virtually the exact opposite of what is stated in the US Constitution. The clear purpose of the US Constitution and the federal government that it established is to promote the general welfare (i.e. common good). This does not mean that James Madison and other leading Founders believed that property rights and other individual rights were not important. But they believed that the primary focus of the US government should be on the common good, not individual rights or well-being.

James Madison did not think that a Bill of Rights was necessary because the Constitution did not take rights from citizens. The focus of leading Founders was on empowering the US government to protect the common good. As discussed, Article I, Section 8 gives Congress essentially unlimited power to promote the general welfare/common good. The word power is used 43 times in the Constitution. Excluding the Bill of

Rights and later amendments, the word right only was used once (i.e. in Article I, Section 8 to protect patents and copyrights).[603]

No right to own property is stated in the Constitution or Bill of Rights (except for time limited patents and copyrights). Instead, the Fifth Amendment describes the process by which the federal government can take property from individuals. The clear priority is the common good/general welfare. If promoting the common good requires taking private property, the US federal government is empowered to do so. For example, forests are important life support systems. If private forests are being managed in ways that degrade life support capability, the government has the power to compel sustainable management or take the property. In other words, the collective right of the people to survive takes priority over private or individual property rights.

A major flaw of business-funded libertarianism and other conservative philosophies relates to business rights. The common good or general welfare takes priority over individual well-being. The common good takes even higher priority over nonliving human creations, such as publicly traded corporations. As discussed, businesses or any other human creations have no inherent right to exist, as humans do. Business existence is a privilege contingent on not harming society. When businesses cause harm, the well-being of society demands that they be compelled to end harm or eliminated.

Given the way that corporations were restricted in the early US, the Founders obviously did not intend that businesses would have the same rights as citizens. But business-funded libertarianism and other business influences have suppressed government and elevated companies. As a result, businesses often have more rights than citizens. For example, citizens are held liable for harm. But limited liability often allows companies and their owners to avoid being held responsible by transferring liability to taxpayers. As discussed in the Influencing the Supreme Court section, *Citizens United* is one of the most flagrant suppressions of democracy in US history. The irrational and unfair nature of this case shows strong business influence of the Supreme Court. Placing the financial well-being of nonliving businesses and wealthy business owners ahead of the general welfare grossly violates the spirit and letter of the US Constitution.

The myopic libertarian focus on individualism and individual rights misleads the public by de-emphasizing the more important requirement to promote the common good/general welfare (more important because individuals generally cannot prosper unless larger systems that support individuals are prospering). De-emphasizing the critical role of government in upholding the rule of law and promoting the general welfare facilitates not holding businesses responsible for negative impacts, and thereby protects shareholder returns.

Spontaneous Order

Spontaneous order is another libertarian concept that often characterizes government negatively. This can turn citizens against government and regulations, and thereby protect shareholder returns. Regarding spontaneous order, the Key Concepts article noted above states, "It's easy to assume that order must be imposed by a central authority... The great insight of libertarian social analysis is that order in society arises spontaneously, out of the actions of thousands or millions of individuals who coordinate their actions with those of others in order to achieve their purposes... The most important institutions in human society – language, law, money, and markets – all developed spontaneously, without central direction. Civil society – the complex network of associations and connections among people – is another example of spontaneous order; the associations within civil society are formed for a purpose, but civil society itself is not an organization and does not have a purpose of its own."

This is another example of a concept that sounds logical from a myopic perspective. However, when one steps back and looks at the big picture, a major omission becomes obvious. The concept downplays or does not mention the essential role of government in enforcing the rule of law. This omission often causes the concept of spontaneous order to be highly biased and misleading.

As discussed under objectivism and *Atlas Shrugged*, spontaneous order appears to occur in nature. It often seems that plants and animals are acting spontaneously, independently or randomly. However, when one observes the big picture of nature, they see nearly infinite coordination, sophistication and prosperity. Random action usually produces disorder, not order. The essentially infinite order and coordination of nature strongly implies that some force or intelligence is coordinating it. No voice is whispering in a grasshopper's ear saying, take only what you need from nature and produce only recyclable waste. But all plants and animals, except humans, abide by these and other natural laws. Plants and animals are guided by instinct, DNA or other mechanisms that humans do not fully understand.

The rational thought of humans appears to be more sophisticated than the implied cognition of plants and animals. But when one observes reality and results, the implied intelligence of nature essentially is infinitely greater than human intelligence. Perhaps it is the destiny of humanity to fully trust and act on intuitive wisdom (i.e. the wisdom of nature). When or if this occurs, humanity probably will display a similar level of cooperation, coordination and sophistication as that seen in nature.

This state could be defined as Heaven on Earth. Like other creatures, humans will be guided by intuitive wisdom or the wisdom of nature. But unlike other creatures, humans almost certainly would retain the capacity for objective, rational thought. As discussed in the Women's section of *Global System Change*, humanity might reach a state called conscious unity. People might retain the conscious awareness that they are interconnected parts of one larger system.

(Some people might argue that it is not logical to discuss the possibility of humanity evolving to the point where we display the same essentially infinite cooperation, coordination, sophistication and wisdom seen in nature. But logic standards for speculation are much looser. One is speculating about what might be, not discussing what currently exists in reality. Nevertheless, speculation can be irrational. For example, it would be irrational to speculate how humans might sprout wings and fly, because it is extremely unlikely that this would occur. However, it is not irrational to speculate that humanity might someday display the same sustainability, cooperation and wisdom seen in nature, especially when one considers the fact that humans are part of nature. This strongly implies that we have the ability to be as cooperative, intelligent, sustainable and prosperous as nature.)

Humanity might someday display the same immense sustainability and prosperity seen in nature. But at our current level of development, the illusion of separation often produces fear and many negative, harmful actions in society. The libertarian statement about spontaneous order implies that civil society occurs in a vacuum. But it does not. Civil society frequently is defined as the third sector of society, distinct from government and business. It is part of overall or total society.

The libertarian statement implies that positive, productive civil society evolves spontaneously. But it neglects to mention the context. The spontaneous ordering of society occurs within a larger context. One of the most important aspects of this context is the rule of law enforced by government. As shown throughout history, spontaneous actions among humans without the rule of law often produce disorder, anarchy, murder, robbery and other lawless, harmful results. Productive spontaneous order occurs within the context of the rule of law. This vessel suppresses negative, harmful actions, and thereby promotes positive, productive ones.

The libertarian statement about spontaneous order characterizes government in a negative, biased manner by referring to it as a central authority or central direction. This implies that government is an independent, autocratic entity that arbitrarily or capriciously restricts the freedom of individuals and businesses. This negative characterization of government is similar to that used in objectivism and *Atlas Shrugged*. It can turn citizens against government and regulations, and thereby protect shareholder returns.

However, in a supposedly democratic, free society, such as the US, government is not a capricious autocrat. It is supposed to be the agent and servant of the people. In theory, it does not take freedom from the people. It does not tell people where to work or go to college, or which adults can or cannot marry. The appropriate role of government in a free society is to protect society in large part by enforcing the rule of law. As noted, this does not restrict or remove freedom from citizens because citizens and businesses do not have the freedom or right to harm others in a civilized society.

However, describing government in this honest and accurate manner would help people to see that government, laws and regulations not only do not degrade society. They are essential for the prosperity, and even survival of society. This rational discussion of government and regulations would help citizens to see that the rule of law must be enforced against business. But this would restrict business's ability to provide ever-increasing shareholder returns. To protect shareholder returns, business-funded libertarian allies often promote pejorative, dishonest characterizations of government and regulations, such as those implied in the concept of spontaneous order.

The libertarian statement deceptively implies that government or central authority is not necessary because human institutions, such as the legal systems, evolve spontaneously. This is highly irrational. Legal theories might arise spontaneously as individuals develop them. But the legal system does not magically or spontaneously appear out of thin air. Things happen in human society largely because people make them happen. To protect society, the people collectively establish the legal system through their agent government. Implying that little or no government is needed because laws will spontaneously arise is absurd.

The statement also is deceptive because it implies that civil society is a spontaneously evolving entity that has no purpose. But as discussed, at humanity's current level of development, an unconstrained society often would produce disorder, anarchy and harm. To prevent this, a purpose must be articulated and enforced for civil society and society in general. Ideally, that purpose should be to create a society where people are free to do whatever they want and reach their fullest potential, provided that they do not harm anyone else. Without the rule of law, spontaneous society often would not be civil.

Free Markets

The free market is another libertarian concept that sometimes is used to turn citizens against government and regulations, and thereby protect shareholder returns. The Key Concepts article states, "Free markets are the economic system of free individuals, and they are necessary to create wealth. Libertarians believe that people will be both freer and more prosperous if government intervention in people's economic choices is minimized."

Libertarians and conservatives often state or imply that the free market is natural, inevitable and innately wise. They frequently believe that government intervention, for example by setting minimum wages, would disrupt the market and degrade society. Some people might not earn enough money to feed themselves and their children, while others earn billions of dollars. But government should not interfere with this outcome. The market oracle has spoken. The wise market has determined that some people have little value, while others have great value. The oracle implies that it is acceptable for many people to barely survive, or not survive, while a few others have more wealth than they could ever reasonably spend. We should not question this outcome because the free market knows best.[604] [Sarcasm intended]

These ideas about free markets are irrational and deceptive in several ways. As discussed under objectivism, the market is not a magical force that will function effectively if government leaves it alone. The libertarian concept of spontaneous order states that markets arise spontaneously. But this is misleading. The positive, productive markets that people value do not arise spontaneously. They are human creations. Markets contain many rules that enable them to function well. Market rules include patent protections, contract laws and prohibitions on certain sales, such as sales of slaves, children and weapons of mass destruction. As discussed above, markets also need accurate inputs to function effectively. Garbage inputs (i.e. inaccurate prices that do not include real external costs) produce garbage outputs (i.e. environmental and social degradation).

Effective markets are based on the rule of law. If markets did not have rules, companies could sell harmful products, such as food that tastes good, but contains toxic chemicals that sicken and kill people. Without rules, someone could kill their neighbor, steal their goods and sell them on the unrestricted free-market. The concept of a free market without rules or restrictions is an irrational fantasy. It does not exist in reality. Even black markets or illegal markets have implied rules and restrictions. For example, if one attempts to deal unfairly with a drug dealer, the penalty might be more severe than in legal markets.

Effective, society-enhancing markets cannot exist without rules enforced by some type of collective authority, such as democratic government. These rules often protect businesses and enable them to prosper. However, under the rule of law, some market rules and restrictions prohibit businesses from causing harm. These rules frequently restrict the ability to provide ever-increasing shareholder returns. As a result, the requirement to focus primarily on returns often compels companies to oppose rules, laws or regulations that require responsible behavior. Honestly acknowledging that they oppose acting responsibly because it would hurt shareholder returns would not work. As a result, companies frequently are compelled to use deceptive means to avoid abiding by the rule of law.

Libertarian business allies frequently do this (probably often unintentionally) by encouraging people to replace rational, objective thought with blind faith adherence to libertarian dogma or philosophy. For example, libertarians believe that people will be more prosperous if government interference in the economy and market is minimized. Libertarian use of the term "government interference" is biased. It implies that all government rules degrade markets and society. This is not rational. Government rules that prohibit businesses from killing children, for example, do not 'interfere' with the market. They enable prosperous markets and civilized society to exist. Pejoratively characterizing government laws and regulations as 'interference' facilitates not fully applying the rule of law to business. This characterization helps businesses to maximize shareholder returns.

Rational, objective assessment of how to most efficiently and effectively enforce the rule of law against companies often would limit shareholder returns. Therefore, to block this rational assessment, libertarians and other business allies often encourage people to adopt the irrational, blind faith implied position that nearly all government regulations degrade society and freedom. This is hypocritical. Libertarians and other business allies criticize regulations that restrict shareholder returns by holding companies responsible. But they usually are silent about regulations and rules that help shareholder returns, such as patent and contract laws.

Libertarians often attempt to block rational thought by pejoratively characterizing government regulations as arbitrary or autocratic. But in a democratic government, regulations are not arbitrary. They generally are implemented for a specific, beneficial purpose – preventing harm. There are, however, some arbitrary rules in current market systems. One of the most important is the implied requirement that publicly traded companies seek ever-increasing shareholder returns. This is arbitrary and irrational because it is not based on reality. Nothing physical in the finite, physical world grows forever.

This indicates one of the most important and deceptive aspects of free markets – myopia and reductionism. Libertarian theory implies that markets are independent and autonomous. But they are not. Markets are more than just the point of exchange. They include many activities before and after the exchange. Markets are part of the larger economy, which is part of a larger society. This in turn is part of the larger whole Earth system.

As discussed throughout *Global System Change*, reductionism is the foundational problem of humanity – the failure to think and act from a whole system perspective. Developing market theories without adequately addressing larger systems that contain markets (i.e. environmental and social systems) causes unintended consequences, such as environmental and social degradation. Society-enhancing markets do not spontaneously arise. They are human creations. To maximize the well-being of society, we must consciously develop and implement markets and other economic systems that are focused on maximizing the well-being of society.

This indicates perhaps the most important flaw of current market structures. As noted, free, unrestricted markets do not exist. Markets are comprised of rules. In the US, the problem is that these rules mainly are developed or controlled by business because large corporations and wealthy business owners largely control government. Markets can be developed in ways that enable people to be fairly compensated for their efforts and compel those who benefit the most from society to pay their fair share. This would be the fruit of democratic government. But current business-dominated market rules concentrate wealth among a small group of wealthy business owners and create vast, unnecessary hardship for hundreds of millions of citizens. Once the people gain control of government, they can focus markets on maximizing the well-being of society.

(An important distinction should be made between small and large companies. Small business owners might say that business regulations excessively burden and lower, not increase, their wealth. This occurs in part because small business owners usually do not give millions of dollars to politicians and inappropriately influence government in other ways. Market regulations often help large companies by unfairly restricting small companies. This unfairness can be ended when domination of government by large companies and wealthy business owners is ended.)

Virtue of Production

Virtue of production is another libertarian concept that is used to turn citizens against government and regulations, and thereby protect shareholder returns. The concept is based on the rational idea that people should be allowed to keep the fruits of their labor. It then discusses supposedly unfair taking of wealth. The Key Concepts article states, "Libertarians developed a pre-Marxist class analysis that divided society into two basic classes: those who produced wealth and those who took it by force from others... Modern libertarians defend the right of productive people to keep what they earn, against a new class of politicians and bureaucrats who would seize their earnings to transfer them to nonproducers."

These are the same types of childish, irrational, biased and pejorative characterizations as those used in *Atlas Shrugged*. The statement implies that politicians provide no value. Instead, they unfairly live off of taxpayer wealth. It also implies that there is a large group of lazy citizens who also live off of taxpayer wealth by utilizing social welfare programs. These ideas are extremely irrational. The statement seems to imply that essential government services (i.e. infrastructure, laws, national security) magically appear out of thin air. No one is needed to manage or pay for them. This is absurd. Politicians essentially are hired by citizens to manage the provision of services that are essential for the survival and well-being of society. Without politicians and government, there would be no society, or at least no productive, civilized society.

The statement also implies that all or nearly all people who use social welfare programs are lazy parasites. This also is grossly inaccurate. Some people abuse these programs. But the vast majority, probably well over 95 percent, are legitimately using them. Many people cannot find jobs that provide more than poverty-level wages and benefits. Also, many people are legitimately unable to work for physical or psychological reasons.

One might ask, why would libertarians and other conservatives often espouse these pejorative and irrational characterizations of politicians and needy citizens? The answer is obvious. It helps shareholder returns. Rational discussions about the essential need for government and regulations and the legitimate needs of disadvantaged or disabled citizens often would restrict returns. It would show the need to hold companies responsible and require them to pay their fair share for services and benefits derived from society.

Companies cannot rationally oppose these rational requirements. As a result, to protect shareholder returns, libertarians and other business allies implicitly encourage citizens to not think rationally. Instead, they are encouraged to blindly believe the irrational libertarian characterizations of politicians, government, regulations and social welfare recipients.

This public deception is sad for several reasons. Citizens (mostly conservatives) are being manipulated in ways that degrade society and enrich those who deceive them. Turning citizens against social welfare programs degrades society. Civilized society should cooperate and use collective wealth for legitimate purposes, such as helping to feed the children of unemployed parents. But our suicidal economic and political systems often suppress anything that interferes with ever-increasing shareholder returns, including social welfare programs. The systems will continue to steal wealth from citizens and concentrate it in the hands of the small group that controls government until they collapse or are changed. Ongoing degradation of society is inevitable under current grossly flawed systems.

To illustrate, many Republican politicians are seeking to substantially reduce funding for food stamps, while maintaining near historically low taxes for wealthy campaign donors. They apparently believe it would be better to let unemployed citizens and their children go hungry, rather than require wealthy citizens to pay their fair share for the large benefits they receive from society.

The main factor enabling this gross injustice is the vested interest manufactured war between conservatives and liberals. By manipulating conservatives into disliking or hating liberals, emotions often trump logic. Conservatives can be tricked into blindly believing highly irrational characterizations, such as those promoted in the libertarian concept of virtue of production. Citizens are being misled into allowing the unfair transfer of trillions of dollars of taxpayer wealth to the small group that controls government, instead of preventing children from going hungry. This illustrates why it is essential to end the civil war between liberals and conservatives, and strongly promote the increased use of rational thought in society.

Natural Harmony of Interests

Natural harmony of interests is another libertarian concept that sounds logical from a myopic perspective. However, from a big picture perspective, one sees that it downplays and distorts the role of government. This can turn citizens against government and regulations, and thereby protect shareholder returns. The Key Concepts article states, "Libertarians believe that there is a natural harmony of interests among peaceful, productive people in a just society… we all prosper from the operation of the free market… Only when government begins to hand out rewards on the basis of political pressure do we find ourselves involved in group conflict, pushed to organize and contend with other groups for a piece of political power."

The statement implies that people's interests and interactions in the free market naturally will produce a harmonious and just society. This fails to mention the critical need for the rule of law enforced by government. At the current level of human development, a just society will not spontaneously arise. In the absence of the rule of law, an unjust society or anarchy often will occur.

The statement also implies that a free market, unrestricted by government, exists. But it does not. As noted, so-called free, unrestricted markets are a fantasy. They do not exist in reality. Markets are comprised of rules. Without the rule of law enforced by government or some other collective group, large, productive, beneficial markets could not exist.

The statement says that government hands out rewards based on political pressure, and that this causes the formation of conflicting political groups. But it fails to mention that the majority of political pressure, for example in the form of large campaign contributions, comes from large corporations and a small group of wealthy business owners. This group largely controls both major political parties.

The statement is true in the sense that those applying the most pressure, for example through legalized bribery, receive the greatest rewards (trillions of dollars of corporate welfare annually). This leads to conflicts as the vast majority of citizens oppose the theft of their wealth and power. The solution is not to weaken government. It is to convert plutocracy to democracy.

The libertarian concept of natural harmony of interests downplays or ignores the critical role of government in forming a just society and beneficial, productive markets. It also disparages government by implying that it capriciously hands out rewards, and thereby causes conflicts in society. But government does not act autonomously or capriciously. It is a puppet. It does what it is told to do by those who control it. Only government can compel businesses to not harm society by enforcing the rule of law against them. But this cannot occur when businesses control government. By turning citizens against government and regulations, this and other libertarian concepts protect shareholder returns. However, the philosophy also substantially degrades society by helping businesses to avoid being held responsible for negative environmental and social impacts.

Hypocrisy

Libertarianism is a broad philosophy with several branches. It contains many logical concepts, such as freedom of the individual. But myopic, deceptive application of the concepts contributes to the degradation of society. In this larger section on Suppression of Critical Thinking, right-wing libertarianism was emphasized because it often is used to protect shareholder returns by encouraging people to blindly adhere to an irrational philosophy, rather than think for themselves.

The many irrational components of right-wing libertarianism discussed above result in large part from business influence. Think tanks, politicians and other individuals and organizations that accept money and influence from businesses often are compelled to become the allies of business in protecting shareholder returns. Our flawed systems unintentionally imply that financial returns to very wealthy people are more important than the survival of humanity. One could not publicly espouse this position without looking like a fool.

But flawed systems nevertheless demand that businesses and their allies put shareholder returns before all else, including the lives of children and survival of humanity. Myopia prevents many well-intentioned libertarians and other business allies from realizing that they effectively are supporting this suicidal approach. Self-interest also causes many business allies to not look at the big picture, and thereby fail to see the harmful nature of placing shareholder returns before all else. Instead, they blindly believe that right-wing libertarianism and other shareholder return focused approaches will benefit society.

This intentional or unintentional myopia encourages or compels many right-wing libertarians and other business allies to espouse hypocritical positions. To illustrate, right-wing libertarianism, like *Atlas Shrugged*, strongly and loudly opposes totalitarian government. But it often says little about totalitarian business. This is hypocritical and deceptive. Right-wing Libertarians often imply that the US government is totalitarian or autocratic. But this is incorrect. Government is a servant or puppet. It does what it is told to do by those who control it. To average citizens, the US government can seem totalitarian because they largely do not control it and government does not serve average citizens in many ways. However, to those who actually control government, the US government has been a good and faithful servant. This is shown by rapid income growth of the small group controlling government, while the lives of hundreds of millions of US citizens continuously get more difficult.

The US government is not totalitarian or autocratic because it is not independent. It largely is controlled by business. The real autocrats or dictators in the US are large corporations and a small group of wealthy business owners who give large amounts of money to politicians. This group has stolen literally trillions of dollars from average citizens. The people largely have lost control of their supposedly democratic government. Many citizens have allowed themselves to become dependent on large corporations for healthcare, retirement security and other basic needs.

A business dictatorship has been established in the US. Libertarianism helps to sustain this dictatorship by turning citizens against government, the only entity that could place business in service of society, if the people controlled it. By deceptively opposing totalitarian government (i.e. deceptive because the US government is a business-controlled puppet not an autocrat), right-wing libertarianism hypocritically helps to sustain totalitarian business. Ironically, this strongly violates the libertarian philosophy because it takes extensive rights, freedom, wealth and power from individuals. In this sense, right-wing libertarianism is strongly anti-libertarian.

Another hypocritical aspect of right-wing libertarianism involves spontaneous, voluntary, free association. Right-wing libertarianism strongly supports the right of businesses to freely and spontaneously associate. This often leads to monopolies, duopolies and other business associations that suppress competition, eliminate small businesses and increase prices. However, right-wing libertarians often oppose or fail to support the free association of employees when they form unions and use market mechanisms to demand fair compensation for their labor.[605]

This hypocritical posture is the common or inevitable result of strong business influence. Right-wing libertarians, like other business allies, frequently are compelled to support actions that help businesses, even if they are irrational and degrade society. At the same time, they often are compelled to oppose actions that hurt shareholder returns, even if they are rational and society-enhancing. Right-wing libertarians support enforcing the rule of law against individuals, but frequently are hypocritically silent about enforcing it against businesses. In other words, they often oppose government regulations that restrict shareholder returns, but say little or nothing about regulations and laws that protect shareholder returns.

One of the most hypocritical aspects of right-wing libertarianism involves growing authoritarianism in society. Authoritarianism is the philosophical opposite of libertarianism. As discussed in the Authoritarianism section, authoritarianism is growing in US education and the US in general. Zero-tolerance policies in schools teach children to not question or disobey authority. World leading incarceration for nonviolent crimes further reflects the zero-tolerance, authoritarian nature of US society. As discussed in the Privacy section, other authoritarian policies include widespread, gross privacy violations of electronic communications and brutal suppression of groups that oppose corporate welfare and business control of government.

These gross restrictions of freedom and civil rights should be anathema to libertarians. But right-wing libertarians often are hypocritically silent about them. Suppressing dissent, violating privacy, and implementing zero-tolerance education and crime policies facilitate ever-increasing shareholder returns. As a result, right-wing libertarians and other business allies frequently are compelled to support or not oppose these gross losses of freedom.

Think tanks, corrupted governments and other individuals and organizations that accept money and influence from businesses and their owners often essentially are required to support putting shareholder returns before all else, even when it degrades society. This frequently compels right-wing libertarians, politicians and other business allies to adopt hypocritical positions that benefit business or support libertarianism and other conservative philosophies.

Same-Sex Marriage

Decisions by the Republican-appointed Supreme Court justices illustrate this conservative, business-biased hypocrisy and public deception. In 2013, the Supreme Court overturned part of a law that defined marriage as being between a man and a woman, the Defense of Marriage Act (DOMA). But four of the five Republican-appointed justices argued that the law should have been left in place. Their arguments illustrate the common hypocrisy and irrational positions of business allies.

The situation also once again illustrates the danger of lifetime Supreme Court appointments. This essentially gives Supreme Court justices nearly absolute power. They essentially can do whatever they want. As Thomas Jefferson warned, there are no consequences. In this environment, Supreme Court justices are not required to be rational, uphold the Constitution or promote the general welfare. They can, and sometimes do, act like dictators. They can loudly and proudly take obviously incorrect positions, equivalent to two plus two equals five or black is white. Citizens, the supposedly leaders of this country, can do nothing about it.

This shows the extreme importance of placing the Supreme Court under the control of the people by implementing term limits. No other country allows lifetime appointments to their highest court. As discussed in the Judicial Branch section, Congress has clear constitutional authority to limit Supreme Court terms through legislation. A constitutional amendment is not required. The hypocritical and irrational nature of the dissenting opinions in *United States v. Windsor* (the case that partially overturned DOMA) illustrate the danger of allowing essentially business-appointed justices to operate in a consequence-free environment.

In *Windsor*, Edith Windsor, the surviving spouse of a legally married same-sex couple, was denied the federal estate tax exemption because

DOMA defines marriage as being between a man and a woman. A lower court found that DOMA was unconstitutional and ordered the federal government to issue a tax refund. An appeals court affirmed the decision. Some dissenting Supreme Court justices argued that the Supreme Court did not have jurisdiction to hear the case because the lower court ruled in favor of the plaintiff (Windsor) and thereby eliminated the controversy. The majority took a broader view and argued that the Supreme Court had jurisdiction in Windsor because the federal government was refusing to pay the refund and the constitutionality of DOMA was being contested.[606]

The reasoning of the Republican-appointed justices reflects hypocrisy and a pro-business, conservative bias. As discussed in the Influencing the Supreme Court section, in *Citizens United*, the court could have ruled narrowly on the specific case. But instead, it ruled broadly. It used *Citizens United* as an opportunity to effectively strike down state and federal campaign-finance laws that limited the ability of corporations to control government. In other words, the Republican-appointed justices ruled broadly when doing so benefited business. But when conservative values were threatened, they argued that the court should rule narrowly.

In *Windsor*, the Supreme Court majority found that DOMA violates the US Constitution by violating citizens' rights to freedom and equality implied in the Fifth Amendment. The majority noted that the Constitution protects people's moral and sexual choices. It said that DOMA demeans and injures people in same-sex marriages.

However, as noted, some Republican-appointed justices said that the Supreme Court did not have the authority to overturn DOMA. One justice said, "we have no power under the Constitution to invalidate this democratically adopted legislation." This reflects gross hypocrisy and abuse of near absolute power. The minority said that the Supreme Court does not have the power to protect the constitutionally guaranteed rights of freedom and equality by invalidating laws that violate these rights. But the power of judicial review, a power exercised by the Supreme Court for nearly all of US history, gives the Supreme Court the authority to overturn state and federal laws that violate the Constitution.

Reflecting hypocrisy, in *Citizens United*, the five Republican-appointed justices argued that they were required to effectively overturn state and federal campaign finance laws because the equal rights of corporations were being violated. In other words, the justices said they could not overturn laws that violate the obvious, constitutional rights of certain human citizens. But they could overturn laws that violate the non-existent equal rights of non-human corporations.

This shows the extreme pro-business bias of the Republican-appointed justices. As discussed in the Influencing Government section, the Revolutionary War was sparked by abuse from British corporations as well as the British government. The Founders understood that corporations enabled a few citizens to grossly violate the rights of other citizens, for example, by effectively stealing public wealth and inappropriately controlling government. As a result, corporations were severely restricted in the early US. But as Abraham Lincoln warned during the Civil War, once businesses gained influence of government, they used it to get even greater power and influence. Corporations now have more power and rights than citizens in many ways. As noted, individuals are held fully responsible for harm imposed on others. But businesses and their owners often are not. Limited liability frequently enables them to transfer liability and responsibility to taxpayers.

Corporations obviously are not equivalent to human citizens. They are nonliving tools meant to serve humanity. They have no inherent right to exist, as humans do. Giving nonhuman corporations much greater power to influence and control government than average citizens is a gross and obvious violation of the US Constitution. But Supreme Court justices operate in a consequence-free environment. As a result, they can do whatever they want. If they choose to say that black is white by placing nonliving corporations above human citizens, they are free to do so.

In the same way, they are free to violate the Constitution when the case involves a lifestyle that goes against conservative values or philosophy. The rule of law implies that people are free to do what they want, provided they do not hurt others. Same-sex marriage hurts no one. Prohibiting same-sex marriage hurts same-sex couples by taking away their freedom and making them unequal. If the Supreme Court were controlled by the people, justices would uphold the Constitution, even when doing so violated conservative values and beliefs. But business influence and lack of term limits cause the Supreme Court to not be controlled by the people. In this autocratic, consequence-free environment, Supreme Court justices are free to not protect the constitutional rights of citizens who are living a lifestyle that conservatives might oppose.

The dissenting opinion of one of the Republican-appointed justices contained the following comments:

"But to defend traditional marriage is not to condemn, demean, or humiliate those who would prefer other arrangements, any more than to defend the Constitution of the United States is to condemn, demean, or humiliate other constitutions. To hurl such accusations so casually demeans this institution... To question [the majority's] high-handed invalidation of a presumptively valid statute is to... "demean," and "humiliate"... our fellow citizens, who are homosexual. All that, simply for supporting an Act that did no more than codify an aspect of marriage that had been unquestioned in our society for most of its existence... It is one thing for a society to elect change; it is another for a court of law to impose change by adjudging those who oppose it... enemies of the human race."

"... [the majority provided] a lecture on how superior the majority's moral judgment in favor of same-sex marriage is to the Congress's hateful moral judgment against it... In the majority's telling, this story is black-and-white: Hate your neighbor or come along with us. The truth is more complicated. It is hard to admit that one's political opponents are not monsters... A reminder that disagreement over something so fundamental as marriage can still be politically legitimate would have been a fit task for what in earlier times was called the judicial temperament. We might have covered ourselves with honor today, by promising all sides of this debate that it was theirs to settle and that we would respect their resolution. We might have let the People decide. But that the majority will not do... the Court has cheated both sides, robbing the winners of an honest victory, and the losers of the peace that comes from a fair defeat..."

These comments are biased, deceptive and irrational in several ways. For example, the dissenting justices said that the people should decide whether same-sex marriage is allowed. But this would be unfair and incorrect. The only perspective that should be relevant to the Supreme Court is upholding the Constitution. From the perspective of government and the Constitution, marriage is society's recognition and validation that two adults have committed to live together as one family. Same-sex marriage hurts no one. Therefore, citizens or government have no right to interfere with a person's ability to freely marry any adult they choose.

As discussed under the Rule of Dumb deception technique in the Misleading the Public section, some people argue that same-sex marriage degrades the institution of marriage, and thereby causes harm that society has a right to prevent. But from a constitutional perspective, this is incorrect. Some people might feel uncomfortable about allowing same-sex marriage. But this discomfort or harm is not caused by same-sex marriage. It is caused by people's intolerance. Many people felt uncomfortable when slavery was ended and interracial marriage was allowed. But this did not mean that slavery should have been continued or interracial marriage prohibited.

As discussed in the Population section, Thomas Jefferson said, "The legitimate powers of government extend to such acts only as are injurious to others. But it does me no injury for my neighbour to say there are twenty gods, or no god. It neither picks my pocket nor breaks my leg." Allowing same-sex marriage does not interfere with the ability of opposite sex couples to marry and freely live their lives. People often feel uncomfortable with change. But that frequently is the nature of progress.

As discussed in the Elections section, James Madison spoke of protecting the minority from the tyranny of the majority. The Founders strongly intended that people should be free to live according to their own religious or moral values. The government or a majority of citizens have no right to impose their religious or moral views on a minority of citizens. Acceptance of same-sex marriage has grown rapidly in the US in recent years. Several polls have shown that a majority of citizens believe that adults should be free to marry who they choose.[607]

But even if 95 percent of citizens strongly opposed same-sex marriage, that should be irrelevant to the Supreme Court. The job of the Court is to protect the constitutional rights of all citizens. It is required to protect the minority from the tyranny of the majority. In a country that guarantees religious and other freedoms and rights, the Supreme Court is bound to protect the freedom and equality of all citizens, for example, by ensuring that they are free to marry whom they choose.

The dissenting justices implicitly argued that same-sex marriage should be prohibited because marriage traditionally has been between a man and a woman. But historical arguments often are irrational and irrelevant. Using the same logic, one could argue that slavery should have been continued, interracial marriages prohibited, and women kept subservient to men. Once society recognizes that historical or traditional actions violate natural, constitutional rights, such as freedom and equality, progress demands that these actions be ended.

Religious ideas often are used to justify prohibition of same-sex marriage. But as discussed in the Population section, religious dogma should have no impact on government or public policy in a country that guarantees freedom of religion, such as the US. Many ideas in the Bible, for example, are outdated, uncivilized and incorrect. Opposition to same-sex marriage is a cultural or dogmatic idea. It is not an absolute spiritual truth, the way treating others with kindness, love and respect is. Using the Bible to determine public policy might enable someone to stab and kill a man, enslave the man's wife, and keep her chained up in the basement (i.e. Thou shall put men to the sword and take woman as booty, Deuteronomy 20:13-14).

The fact that religious dogma opposes same-sex marriage should be completely irrelevant to government policy. Religious dogma caused much of the atrocities and persecution during the Dark Ages. Our Founders used rational, enlightened thinking to ensure that religious dogma would have no impact on government. The guiding document of the US is the Constitution, not the Bible.

The dissenting comments shown above also illustrate a deception technique discussed in the Misleading the Public section called Biased/

Illogical Characterization. Companies often essentially are compelled to oppose ideas and suggestions that benefit society, but threaten shareholder returns. If an idea or suggestion is logical, it frequently is not possible to rationally challenge it. To protect shareholder returns, companies sometimes distort or mischaracterize an idea in ways that make it appear to be illogical, and then attack distorted ideas that were never said or intended. This was done in several ways in the dissenting comments noted above.

For example, the dissenting justices inaccurately imply that citizens simply were trying to defend their opinion about traditional marriage. But that was not the issue in *Windsor*. Of course, people have a right to defend their opinions. But they do not have a right to impose their opinions on others. This was the main issue in *Windsor*. People do not have a right to impose or enforce their opinions about marriage on other citizens.

The minority also used biased/illogical characterization by putting words in the mouths of the majority, and then attacking words that never were said. For example, the majority did not say that people who oppose same-sex marriage are enemies of humanity or monsters, or that they hate their neighbors. These inflammatory terms were used by the minority, but attributed to the majority.

The minority also said that the majority was taking a high-handed or morally superior position. This also is deceptive and biased. *Windsor* largely is not about morality. The case is focused on upholding the Constitution and natural laws of equality and freedom. By using inflammatory words and an accusatory tone, the minority appears to be attempting to distract attention from the logical, even not debatable essence of the case – the constitutionally guaranteed equality and freedom of each citizen. The minority also irrationally and deceptively implied that the majority won by cheating. But upholding the rights of freedom and equality is not cheating. It is the duty of the Supreme Court.

The minority warned that *Windsor* could be used to overturn state laws that prohibit same-sex marriage. They are correct. Like DOMA, these laws also violate the constitutionally guaranteed freedom and equality of citizens. As a result, the laws should be voided. The natural or constitutional rights of citizens should not be determined by elections. It does not matter if a majority of citizens in a particular state oppose same-sex marriage. The majority does not have a right to take the constitutionally guaranteed rights of freedom and equality from a minority of citizens.

Four of the five essentially business-appointed Supreme Court justices effectively argued that same-sex marriage should be prohibited. As discussed in the Population section, this type of decision largely does not benefit businesses directly. However, it could provide strong indirect benefits. The primary factor enabling ongoing corporate welfare and business control of government is public deception, mainly by dividing citizens into debating factions. When the people are divided, they are conquered. Same-sex marriage, abortion and other controversial issues can be used to stoke division and animosity in society. Prohibiting women from controlling the use of their bodies or people from marrying who they love helps to fracture society. This can benefit business by taking away the people's ability to control government and end the theft of their wealth through corporate welfare.

The above discussion is critical of the dissenting opinions in *Windsor*. As is the case throughout this book, the intention is not to criticize Supreme Court Justices or other individuals. It is to criticize flawed ideas and systems that compel good people to do bad things. As discussed in the Judicial Branch section, Thomas Jefferson said that the priority is not protecting judges' reputations. It is protecting the country and upholding the Constitution.

This case raises the issue of judicial review. As discussed extensively in the Judicial Branch section, the Constitution does not give the Supreme Court the power to interpret the Constitution or void US laws. The Supreme Court unilaterally gave itself this power in 1803. It violated the Constitution and intentions of the Founders by essentially declaring that it was the most powerful branch of government. It set itself above the Executive and Legislative branches by unconstitutionally giving itself the power to irrevocably void the actions of these branches. The Constitution gives Congress far more power to determine if laws violate the Constitution. It also gives Congress the power to restrict or regulate the Supreme Court's authority in nearly all cases, including those involving interpretation of US laws.

In this case, one of the five Republican-appointed justices sided with the four Democrat-appointed justices and overturned DOMA. However, in many cases that more directly affect business, such as *Citizens United*, the Republican-appointed justices gave corporations and wealthy citizens substantial power over average citizens, a clear violation of democracy and the constitutional requirement to promote the general welfare. If Congress removed or restricted the Supreme Court's power of judicial review, an unconstitutional law (DOMA) might not have been overturned.

This is a larger issue that was extensively discussed in the Judicial Branch section. Congress is widely corrupted by business influence of both parties. Implementing the changes discussed in *Global System Change* will greatly reduce or eliminate corruption in government. This will substantially lower the probability that Congress passes laws that violate the Constitution, such as DOMA. As noted, the Constitution gives Congress far greater power to determine the constitutionality of US laws. The people are the highest authority in the US. As a result, it is better to leave the power of judicial review where the Constitution implicitly places it (largely with Congress) because the people have far greater power over a regularly elected Congress than over a lifetime appointed Supreme Court. The Judicial Branch section discusses several ways of amending judicial review in ways that place ultimate interpretation of the Constitution where it belongs – with the people.

In a 2015 case, *Obergefell v. Hodges*, the Supreme Court overturned state bans on same-sex marriage. It found that these bans violated the Due Process and Equal Protection Clauses of the Fourteenth Amendment. The case made same-sex marriage legal throughout the United States and its territories, and required states to recognize same-sex marriages validly performed in other jurisdictions. The majority opinions in *Obergefell* were consistent with those in *Windsor*. The majority found that the Fourteenth Amendment guarantees an individual's right to make personal choices that are central to individual dignity and autonomy. It also found that the right to personal choice in marriage is an essential part of individual autonomy.[608]

Dissenting justices in *Obergefell* continued their opposition from *Windsor*. For example, they argued that the court did not have the authority to overturn the historical definition of marriage as being between a man and a woman. In addition, dissenting justices argued that voiding state laws that prohibited same-sex marriage restricted the people's ability to rule themselves.

One dissenting Justice said, "It is not of special importance to me what the law says about marriage. It is of overwhelming importance, however, who it is that rules me. Today's decree says that my Ruler, and the Ruler of 320 million Americans coast-to-coast, is a majority of the nine lawyers on the Supreme Court... This practice of constitutional revision by an unelected committee of nine, always accompanied (as it is today) by extravagant praise of liberty, robs the People of the most important liberty they asserted in the Declaration of Independence and won in the Revolution of 1776: the freedom to govern themselves."[609]

This reflects the gross hypocrisy of the essentially business-appointed justices. They implicitly argue that the court should not overturn laws that violate constitutional rights to freedom and equality because this restricts the people's freedom to govern themselves. But in *Citizens United* and *McCutcheon*, the justices overturned state and federal laws that protected the people's ability to govern themselves. These rulings clearly removed control of government from all citizens, and largely gave it to the wealthy citizens and corporations that effectively paid to appoint business-biased justices to the Supreme Court. This abuse and flawed reasoning once again shows the critical importance of aligning the Supreme Court with the Constitution by imposing term limits and restricting the power of judicial review, as discussed in the Judicial Branch section.

Public Deception

The above section illustrates the common hypocrisy of right-wing libertarians, Republican-appointed Supreme Court justices and other business allies. In addition to hypocrisy, public deception is a major component of right-wing libertarianism. The requirement to provide ever-increasing shareholder returns frequently compels businesses and their allies to mislead the public.

Comments in the libertarian Key Concepts article noted above illustrate this public deception. The article states, "while our society remains generally based on equal rights and capitalism, every day new exceptions to those principles are carved out in Washington... Each new government directive takes a little bit of our freedom, and we should think carefully before giving up any liberty... Those who claim to believe in liberal principles but advocate more and more confiscation of the wealth created by productive people, more and more restrictions on voluntary interaction, more and more exceptions to property rights and the rule of law, more and more transfer of power from society to state, are unwittingly engaged in the ultimately deadly undermining of civilization." [610]

These biased characterizations protect shareholder returns by encouraging people to replace rational thought with blind faith in an irrational philosophy. For example, the biased term government directive implies that government is an autocrat. This is incorrect. Government is a puppet largely controlled by business. The statement says that each new law or regulation takes our freedom. This also is incorrect. Laws and regulations that prohibit individuals and organizations from causing harm do not take away freedom because there is no freedom to cause harm in a civilized society. The biased statement about confiscation of wealth from productive people is misleading. It implies that people should not be required to pay their fair share for benefits derived from society.

The statement about growing exceptions to the rule of law is ridiculous and grossly misleading. The rule of law involves holding individuals, businesses and other organizations responsible for causing harm. The right-wing libertarian castigation of government and regulations makes it extremely difficult to fully apply the rule of law to businesses. In other words, right-wing libertarianism strongly promotes widespread exceptions to the rule of law.

The statement about the growing transfer of power from society to state also is grossly misleading. The people's power or ability to rule themselves definitely is being transferred or stolen, but not by government. As noted, the US government is a puppet largely controlled by business. By unfairly and unconstitutionally controlling government, large corporations and a small group of wealthy business owners have stolen the People's power to rule themselves, as well as stolen trillions of dollars of public wealth. Strong business influence of government makes government unable to hold businesses fully responsible for degrading environmental life support systems and society in general.

The deadly undermining of society discussed in the article is occurring, but not because of the failure to apply the right-wing libertarian philosophy. This myopic and deceptive philosophy is a major part of the problem. Applying right-wing libertarianism is not the solution. The solution involves using rational thought to objectively determine which actions maximize the well-being of society in each situation. Philosophies or biases for or against government severely impede this rational, objective analysis.

Like objectivism, right-wing libertarianism claims to be more realistic, objective and practical than other approaches. It espouses concepts that are highly practical and necessary for a prosperous society, such as the rule of law and individual freedom. But then it deceptively violates its espoused principles. It strongly facilitates not applying the rule of law to businesses. It also suppresses individual rights and freedom by implicitly condoning (through the failure to oppose) totalitarian business and resulting authoritarianism in the US.

Additional deceptive aspects of right-wing libertarianism relate to harm and 'big government'. The rule of law involves preventing harm. Standards for self-harm are looser than standards for harming others. For example, in a free society, people are allowed to harm themselves by smoking cigarettes and eating junk food (although, severe self-harm, such as suicide, generally should be prohibited). However, harming others must be prohibited in a civilized society.

Some libertarians might argue that libertarianism supports applying the rule of law to businesses, but there should be a bias against doing so, unless harm is clear and proven. This reflects the Wrong Perspective deception technique discussed in the Misleading the Public section. This deception involves implying that business activities and products should be assumed to be safe until they are proven to be unsafe at a high level of certainty. But this is the wrong perspective. The priority is protecting society, not shareholder returns. Therefore, the correct, society-enhancing perspective is to assume that business activities and products are unsafe until they are proven to be safe at a high level of certainty.

The anti-government bias of right-wing libertarianism implies that business harm should not be regulated unless we are nearly certain that harm is occurring. This would be like saying that parents should not put seatbelts on their children unless they are 90 percent certain that an accident will occur. We should not wait for near certainty that businesses are causing harm before preventing it. The well-being of society demands that business harm be prevented when we are perhaps 10 to 20 percent certain that harm is occurring.

Right-wing libertarianism sometimes is referred to as a conservative philosophy. But this is a gross insult to the word conservative. Conservative implies minimizing risks, not maximizing them. Failing to protect life support systems and society in general until we are highly certain that harm is occurring is not conservative. It is grossly irresponsible. Instead of conservative, a far more accurate characterization of right-wing libertarianism and many other so-called conservative philosophies would be radical risk-taking.

The emphasis on small versus big government is another perfect example of how right-wing libertarianism and other conservative philosophies are used to deceive citizens and protect shareholder returns. Right-wing libertarianism, *Atlas Shrugged* and other so-called conservative dogma strongly condemn 'big government'. But big government is an irrational and misleading term. It implies that nearly all government actions are bad. It is unclear what big government means. Would prohibiting companies from killing children be an example of big government, and therefore bad government? One of the main functions of government is preventing harm. This is a rational, even not debatable point (within the realm of logic).

However, rationally considering how government must prevent businesses from harming society would limit ever-increasing shareholder returns.

To protect shareholder returns, the derogatory big government term is used to trick citizens into having the unthinking, knee-jerk response that government and regulations are bad. Citizens implicitly are encouraged to not think rationally. The rational focus should be on the well-being of society, not the size of government. Blindly assuming that minimizing government maximizes the well-being of society is brainless and grossly irrational. Blindly assuming the government is bad and therefore should be 'small' often prevents government from enforcing the rule of law against companies. Also, in many cases, government can provide higher quality services at lower total costs. Therefore, biased, irrational exhortations to keep government small can cause society to pay higher prices for lower quality services, as occurs with US healthcare.

Rationally considering when government is needed to prevent harm and provide higher quality, lower cost services would maximize the well-being of society, but often restrict shareholder returns. Therefore, business allies such as right-wing libertarians frequently encourage citizens to replace rational thought with the irrational, essentially meaningless 'big government' prohibition.

Many years ago, the US broke up large business trusts that were abusing employees, unfairly shutting down small businesses, and degrading society in many other ways. Similar actions are occurring today. But businesses and their allies have become masters at deceiving citizens, and thereby protecting their ongoing theft of the people's wealth and power. The main deception is to fracture citizens into hateful, vengeful factions. In this environment, emotions frequently suppress rational thought. Citizens can be misled into believing irrational concepts, such as the ideas that government and regulations are inherently bad.

This once again shows the extreme importance of re-establishing the Fairness Doctrine. Business-controlled media should not be allowed to mislead the public for the purpose of maximizing shareholder returns. If the media were required to provide balanced coverage and commentary of important issues, business-funded media would not be able to promote irrational concepts, like the evils of big government. Rational rebuttal would show the non-debatable need for government in a civilized society. This would compel commentators to rationally discuss the appropriate role of government in promoting the general welfare. Focusing on the size of government is irrational and misleading. The emphasis, according to our Constitution, should be on maximizing the well-being of society. With this rational emphasis, the size and role of government that most efficiently and effectively maximizes the well-being of society can be logically deduced.

Overall, libertarianism, objectivism, *Atlas Shrugged* and other right-wing dogma severely degrade society by inflaming citizens and strongly suppressing rational thought. Our Founders used enlightened, rational thinking to establish one of the greatest nations in the history of humanity. Like our Founders, we must emerge from the New Dark Age by re-establishing rational, enlightened thinking.

Higher education should be a focal point for critical, enlightened, big picture thinking, and the positive system changes that will result from it. It should not be used to produce compliant drones who do not question irrational, reality-ignoring dogma, such as that espoused in *Atlas Shrugged*, *The Fountainhead*, objectivism and right-wing libertarianism. Instead, we must teach young people to think for themselves and see beyond irrational dogma. Religions and political parties might promote blind faith in dogma. But we should not be promoting it in higher education. The well-being of society demands that young people be taught to think critically, rationally and objectively.

Young people often are more vulnerable to the deceptions promoted in *Atlas Shrugged*, objectivism and right-wing libertarianism. Teenagers and young adults frequently are more inclined to see the world or life in simplistic, black-and-white, good versus evil terms. But as they get older and life experience makes them wiser, people usually better understand the deep complexities and subtleties of life. Many young people find the simplistic segmentations of *Atlas Shrugged* and right-wing libertarianism to be compelling. However, as they get older and wiser, they often better understand the childish and destructive nature of these ideas.

Atlas Shrugged was widely criticized by conservatives and liberals for decades after it was published in 1957. Conservatives often called it Godless. Liberals frequently criticized it for being a homage or devotion to greed and selfishness.[611] But sales of *Atlas Shrugged* have increased substantially over the past several years, in part because businesses often encourage or compel employees and students to read it.[612]

The resurgence of *Atlas Shrugged*, objectivism and right-wing libertarianism strongly indicates the ongoing degradation of society. Flawed systems extract ever-increasing amounts of wealth from the large majority of citizens so that the small group controlling government can make ever-increasing financial returns. As life becomes more difficult for most people, the flaws of our suicidal economic and political systems become more obvious. To prevent citizens from rebelling against systems that steal their wealth and power, stronger public deception is needed.

The main deception is to fracture society into debating, acrimonious factions. *Atlas Shrugged* and right-wing libertarianism strongly promote this by irrationally and childishly segmenting society into heroes and parasites, or producers and takers. Conservatives often see liberals as the parasites. This builds disdain and hatred for liberals. As emotions overwhelm rational thinking, conservatives frequently can be tricked into thinking that liberals are responsible for their declining quality of life.

This shows why childish, irrational philosophies like those espoused in *Atlas Shrugged*, objectivism and right-wing libertarianism are so destructive. They enable vested interests to steal the people's wealth and power. They facilitate the perpetuation of socialism (i.e. compelling taxpayers to cover the downside of business and investing), rising national debt, corporate welfare and business control of government.

Ending these injustices requires that people, especially young people, be taught and encouraged to think critically and rationally. As noted, young people are more vulnerable to the simplistic, destructive ideas promoted in *Atlas Shrugged*, objectivism and right-wing libertarianism. Each year, about 400,000 copies of *Atlas Shrugged* are donated to Advanced Placement high school programs throughout the US.[613] This is equivalent to teaching the Bible or other dogma in public schools. As discussed in the Public Funding of Religion section, probably the only appropriate and constitutional way to study the Bible in public schools would be as part of comparative religious courses that fairly, equally and objectively examine all major religions.

Similar fair and objective approaches should be required if young people are exposed to irrational economic dogma, such as *Atlas Shrugged*, objectivism and right-wing libertarianism. As with comparative religion courses, students should be presented with a wide variety of economic and other ideas, as well as rational criticisms of them. This will teach young people to think for themselves, rather than blindly believe irrational economic and other dogma.

Teaching young people that the ideas in *Atlas Shrugged* and right-wing libertarianism are logical and beneficial is destructive. It teaches them to ignore reality. It takes advantage of their greater tendency to see the world in simplistic, black-and-white terms. If *Atlas Shrugged* and right-wing libertarianism are taught at all in high schools and colleges, it should be done in an objective and rational manner. This will illuminate the irrational, dogmatic and frequently destructive nature of these ideas. *Atlas Shrugged* and right-wing libertarianism illustrate the types of ideas that one should not hold if they wish to have a successful and satisfying life and a sustainable and prosperous society. The well-being of society demands that the suppression of critical thinking in higher education, for example through the promotion of dogma and suppression of liberal arts, be quickly reversed.

Ending the suppression of Liberal arts is important for promoting critical thinking in society. Republican politicians and other business allies sometimes argue that liberal arts are less relevant and useful than business courses. But this is incorrect in many ways. As society becomes more complex and people frequently pursue multiple careers over their lives, liberal arts are becoming more important. As discussed in the Authoritarianism section, liberal arts education strongly promotes the development of critical thinking and other important skills needed in our rapidly changing world. Liberal arts education trains people to speak and write clearly and persuasively, open their minds to alternate worldviews and possibilities, analyze problems and develop effective solutions, understand that failure often is part of the process of success, analyze different sides of arguments or positions, flexibly adapt to change and new challenges, and deeply consider issues rather than accept positions at face value.[614]

Higher education in general is essential for promoting critical thinking. Several studies have shown that people are more likely to vote Democrat as education level increases. To illustrate, among white people in the US with no college degrees, 54 percent identified as Republican and 37 percent as Democrat. Among people with college degrees, Democrats had an eight percentage point advantage over Republicans in the 2008 Presidential election. Among voters with postgraduate degrees, Democrats had an 18 percentage point advantage. Since 2008, lower-income and less educated whites have shifted substantially toward the Republican Party. But white people with higher education degrees have not done so.[615]

Demographics do not favor the Republican Party going forward. Among all voters, more people identify as Democrat (35 percent Democrat, 28 percent Republican, 33 percent Independent). Republicans lead among whites (52 percent Republican, 40 percent Democrat).[616] The advantage for the Democratic Party will increase as the percentage of whites in the US population continues to decline. Possibly as a result, many Republican politicians have been aggressively promoting new voting requirements that primarily suppress Democratic votes, such as voter ID laws.

Raising tuition, lowering public funding and financial aid, and erecting other barriers that reduce the number of young people going to college also potentially could benefit Republicans. This is not to suggest that there is a coordinated or intentional Republican effort to benefit their party by making it more difficult for young people, especially those from low-income families, to go to college. But this result nevertheless is occurring. Republican-promoted policies are making it more difficult for young people to attend college. Lack of higher education can suppress critical thinking, which often benefits Republicans.

The link between higher education and voting tendency is similar to the link between IQ and political philosophy discussed in the Authoritarianism section. As noted, people with lower IQs tend to gravitate to more conservative, right-wing ideologies. IQ partly measures critical thinking and analytic ability. Conservative philosophies and groups often emphasize respecting authorities, resisting change and not questioning dogma or ideologies. These philosophies can appeal to those with lower ability or interest in analyzing the complexities of society. Liberal arts education perhaps most strongly promotes the development of critical thinking skills. But virtually all types of higher education train people to analyze complex issues. This strengthens critical thinking skills.

Republican politicians and other business allies often attempt to mislead citizens into believing that government is inherently bad and high taxes primarily result from social welfare programs. This facilitates removing government regulations and social welfare programs that interfere with ever-increasing shareholder returns. Enhanced critical thinking skills provided by higher education, especially liberal arts education, help people to see through these deceptions. Rational thought shows these positions to be irrational and dishonest.

There are many types of government. The business-controlled US government does a poor job of serving average citizens because low and middle-income citizens largely do not control it. But the government developed by our Founders could do an excellent job of serving citizens. It is irrational to blindly assume that all types of government are bad. The solution to bad government generally is not to reduce it. It is to change government from bad to good, for example, by shifting control from wealthy business owners to all citizens (i.e. by replacing plutocracy with democracy).

Regarding social welfare programs raising taxes, rational thought and observations of reality show that trillions of dollars of public wealth essentially are being stolen from average citizens through many types of corporate welfare. These include limited liability, fractional reserve lending, unfair tax policies, selling resources below market rates, transferring taxpayer-funded research to corporations, bailing out banks and businesses, failing to include external costs in prices, subsidizing sectors and businesses that cause environmental, health and other problems, and not holding businesses fully responsible for negative impacts. Corporate welfare, not social welfare, is the main cause of unfairly high taxes.

Republicans and conservatives often attempt to block rational thought by getting citizens to dislike or hate liberals and Democrats. When this occurs, emotions often trump logic. Citizens blindly believe conservative deceptions without analyzing their irrational nature. Through promotion of analytic and critical thinking skills, higher education helps people to think for themselves, resist emotional manipulation, and see through irrational deceptions. This probably is the main reason why people increasingly vote Democrat as they become more highly educated.

The purpose of this book is not to support Democrats and suppress Republicans. As discussed in the Political Parties section, the Republican and Democratic parties largely are controlled by business. Democrats, like Republicans, usually put business before all else. But they generally at least try (but often fail) to balance the environment, labor and other aspects of society with business. The solution is not to vote Democrat instead of Republican. This might benefit average citizens in the short-term. But the vastly more important solution is to greatly weaken or eliminate the unconstitutional, business-controlled political party system in the US, return control of government to the people, and encourage citizens to think for themselves, instead of tribalistically, irrationally, emotionally and blindly believing political dogma, philosophies and deceptions.

Rational thought helps people to see the immensely destructive nature of putting shareholder returns before all else, including the survival of humanity. But our myopic, ultimately suicidal systems require that anything which threatens shareholder returns, such as higher education, liberal arts and critical thinking, must be suppressed. These suicidal systems definitely will end or change, probably soon. To avoid great disruption, we must evolve our systems into sustainable forms before they collapse. We can greatly facilitate system change by ending the business-driven suppression of critical thinking and liberal arts in higher education.

HIGHER EDUCATION

Limited Job Opportunities for Graduates

Job opportunities for college graduates have increased with the decline of Covid-19. Many Jobs are available in areas including healthcare, technology, legal and finance. But graduates often have difficulty finding high quality jobs that utilize their skills and degrees. For example, in 2022, about 40 percent of college graduates took jobs that did not require a degree.[617] Limited high-quality jobs lowers the value of a college degree. But college still has value. The median annual wage for a full-time worker ages 22 to 27 with a high school diploma is $30,000. For a full-time worker with a bachelors degree, it is $52,000.[618]

The main goal of current adult generations should be to prepare society for young people and future generations. As part of this preparation, we should strive to provide good jobs at all levels, something that implicitly occurs in the infinitely more sophisticated economics and systems of nature. We should help young people to establish a solid foundation early on so that they can raise families and pursue other life goals.

But the US is not focused on the well-being of young people and average citizens. As discussed in the Economic Growth and Well-Being of Society sections, the primary measured and managed focus of the US is on economic growth. This essentially measures the financial well-being of the small group that controls government. The suicidal requirement to put shareholder returns ahead of all else ultimately degrades all other parts of society. This is strongly indicated by stock market growth. This growth has been strong, frequently reaching record highs, while many other aspects of society are declining.

For example, every life support system on Earth is in rapid decline, with some regional exceptions. The quality of life support systems essentially is infinitely more important than economic growth and shareholder returns, because there is no economy, society or life without adequately clean and stable life support systems. But the focus of our myopic, suicidal economic and political systems on never-ending financial growth unintentionally degrades environmental life support systems.

The shareholder-focused economy causes many problems, especially for young people. As noted, about 75 percent of S&P 500 profit growth from 2000 to 2007 resulted from cutting employee wages and benefits. This shows how the shareholder focus often degrades labor and jobs. In some ways, recessions are good for business. Recessions often enable companies to lay off higher paid employees, and then hire lower wage workers shortly afterwards. To illustrate, middle-wage jobs were hardest hit by the 2008 financial crash and the slowest to recover. These are the types of jobs frequently taken by college graduates. Meanwhile, low-wage jobs are the fastest-growing segment of the economy.[619]

The decline of labor and manufacturing, sending jobs overseas and increased use of automation under deregulation since the 1980s often limit the availability of high-quality jobs for college graduates. Only about 27 percent of college graduates take jobs directly related to their majors.[620] Many college graduates take low-wage jobs in retail sales, food service and other low-skill areas because they cannot find better jobs. The wages of college graduates fell by nine percent adjusted for inflation from 2000 to 2012. The percentage of college graduates receiving pension benefits fell from 41 percent in 2000 to 27 percent in 2011.[621]

Nearly half of college graduates take unpaid internships. Only about 37 percent of these internships lead to job offers.[622] Earning low or no pay forces many young people to move back home with parents after graduating. About 28 percent of college graduates live at home with parents.[623]

A shareholder-focused economy unfairly transfers wealth from average citizens to the small group that is controlling government. This occurs through corporate welfare and many other mechanisms. One method of maximizing shareholder returns involves replacing skilled middle-wage jobs with less skilled, low-wage jobs. To illustrate this trend, a US government report projected that only three of the 30 occupations with the highest job growth will require a bachelor's degree or higher. Most job growth will occur in lower skilled positions, such as retail sales, fast food and truck driving, jobs that cannot be easily replaced by computers.[624]

Providing high-quality jobs for young people and all citizens who want them requires adopting a whole system perspective and implementing many of the economic and political system changes discussed in this book. One of the most important system changes is to begin to actually measure the well-being of society, rather than myopically measuring the well-being of business (with GDP) and incorrectly assuming that increased business well-being equals increased social well-being. The well-being of all citizens, especially young people, is vastly more important than the financial returns of wealthy business owners. The measurement and management of society should reflect this reality.

Unfair Student Debt Terms

Severe and unfair terms on student loans strongly reflect society's lack of commitment to young people and future generations. The terms of student debt are more severe than those of nearly all other debt in the US. To illustrate, bankruptcy laws have existed for hundreds of years. A long-standing principle of civilized society is that people who cannot afford to pay their debts deserve a second chance at a fresh start. Prior to these laws, people who could not pay debts often were put in jail or forced into indentured servitude (essentially slavery). In the US, nearly all individuals and companies are allowed to file for bankruptcy. But student debt largely cannot be relieved through bankruptcy.

Prior to 1976, student debt was treated like other debt in the bankruptcy process. A 1976 law prohibited people from discharging student loans in bankruptcy for five years after loans were issued. This was extended to seven years in 1990. In 1998, Congress removed the ability to discharge federal student debt through bankruptcy after seven years.[625] In 2005, pressure from banks compelled government to eliminate the ability to discharge private student loans through bankruptcy.[626] Young people only can get relief from student loans if they can prove undue hardship. But this is a very difficult standard to achieve. For example, inability to find a job that pays enough to cover student debt and basic living expenses generally would not be considered undue hardship.⁶²⁷ Due to the more stringent bankruptcy terms on student debt, young people rarely are able to get bankruptcy relief when they cannot afford to pay student loans.

In addition, most types of debt have statutes of limitations on collections. Statutes of limitations on private student loans vary by state, usually ranging between three to ten years. But about 92 percent of student loans in the US are federal.⁶²⁸ There is no statute of limitations on collections of federal student debt.⁶²⁹ The government uses many private debt collectors to collect delinquent student loans. These collectors can, and regularly do, intimidate and harass student borrowers for as long as debt remains outstanding. Collectors and creditors are allowed to garnish nearly any income source, including wages, tax refunds and Social Security payments. A growing number of senior citizens are entering retirement with student debt.⁶³⁰ Statute of limitations on most debt usually would prevent harassment of elderly people by creditors. But senior citizens with decades-old student debt can be harassed and have Social Security checks garnished by debt collectors.

Disclosure requirements often are lower on student debt than on other types of debt. Lenders usually are required to disclose details such as annual percentage rate. But many types of disclosures that are required on other debt are not required on student debt. Young people usually are unfamiliar with major, complex financial transactions. But financial aid offices often encourage them to take on large amounts of debt. People as young at 18 frequently sign up for the equivalent of first mortgages and receive inadequate advice about the risks involved.⁶³¹ Nearly 30 percent of college students who take out student loans dropout before earning a degree. These people usually have the most difficulty paying back student loans.⁶³²

The US government earns about 36 cents on every dollar it loans to students.⁶³³ In addition, student loans issued by banks often are guaranteed by the government. This frequently provides substantial guaranteed profits to banks.⁶³⁴ But the government and banks should not be profiting on student loans. Instead, we should be investing in low-cost public higher education. This is one of the most cost-effective investments that society can make. As noted, it is estimated that the G.I. bill provided $7 of economic benefit for every $1 invested in the program.

The government often loans money to banks at less than one percent interest. Students should get similar inexpensive financing. Some people argue that loans to banks are less expensive than student loans. But this is myopic. As discussed in the Money Creation section of *Global System Change*, allowing banks to create the US money supply through fractional reserve lending costs taxpayers as much as $500 billion per year. Considering this, the potential $6-12 trillion bank bailouts, and other forms of corporate welfare provided to banks, it becomes clear that taxpayers subsidize banks far more than higher education. Subsidizing higher education provides very large benefits to society. It is an appropriate use of public wealth. However, taxpayers should not be subsidizing banks or other large businesses.

In some ways, implementing unfair terms on student debt is like hitting children. As discussed in the Hitting Children section, hitting people is prohibited in nearly all cases. The only people who are allowed to be hit in the US are those who are the smallest, weakest, most defenseless and vulnerable, least likely to understand why they are being hit, and most likely to be physically and psychologically harmed by hitting. The situation is similar with college and university students. Nearly all people who cannot afford to pay their debts are given a second chance through bankruptcy and protection from debt collectors. But young people who are trying to build good lives by attending college are not given this second chance and protection.

This is irrational for several reasons. First, young people have the least life experience. As a result, they often are the most likely to make mistakes and need a second chance. But our selfish and self-centered society often does not give second chances to young people who need them.

Second, young people will be taking over and running society when the adults currently running it are retired. If we do not change our selfish and myopic ways soon, young people will have to deal with the many severe economic, environmental and social problems caused by middle-aged and older generations. Ensuring that young people are able to establish a solid foundation early on will greatly benefit society. It will enable them to start and raise families and pursue other life goals. Money not spent on student debt often will be used in ways that benefit society, such as buying homes and vehicles, saving for retirement, or starting businesses.

Third, the highest, most important obligations of current adult generations is to protect young people and future generations, in large part by resolving environmental, social and economic problems to the greatest extent possible, and leaving society in a sustainable state for them. As discussed in the Time Value of Money section, the Founders often used the word posterity. In his inaugural address, Thomas Jefferson spoke of preserving the union for the ten-thousandth generation (about 250,000 years). The Founders and previous generations often sacrificed so that future generations could prosper.

But our advertising and media driven selfishness is creating a situation where today's young people are the first generation in US history that will be worse off financially than their parents.[635] It is time to end our childish, selfish, self-obsession and do the right thing, no matter what it costs. As discussed below, there should be little or no need for student debt, at least at public universities and colleges. However, if student debt is needed, it should be issued with the most lenient terms in society, not the most severe.

Currently, people who run up high gambling and other debts can get bankruptcy relief. Corporations can and regularly do use bankruptcy to relieve themselves of pension fund obligations and other obligations to employees. In other words, bankruptcy often is used in ways that harm retired people who dedicated much of their working lives to companies seeking bankruptcy protection. But when our shareholder-focused economy does not provide adequate jobs for college graduates, they often are left to drown in student debt.

From a big picture perspective, one sees that this unfair use of bankruptcy laws is irrational and abusive to those who we are most obligated to support. But from the perspective of our flawed systems, allowing wealthy companies and individuals to escape labor and other obligations, while young people get no relief from student debt, is the obvious and expected outcome. Wealthy business owners give large amounts of money to the politicians who make bankruptcy and student debt laws. But young people and students usually cannot afford to give large legalized bribes to politicians.

Politicians, being essentially business puppets, do what they are paid to do – provide lenient bankruptcy laws that protect the shareholder returns of wealthy campaign donors.

Vested interests sometimes argue that students and young people should be forced to live up to their financial obligations. This position frequently is insincere because many of the wealthy citizens making this point escape their financial obligations through bankruptcy. But the more deceptive aspect of this position is the idea that someone gave or loaned money to students. As discussed in the Money Creation section, this mostly is not true. Citizens have been deceived into giving their right to create the money supply to banks. This is one of the largest forms of corporate welfare.

When banks loan money to government to make student loans or make loans directly to students, the money largely does not come from bank owners or anyone else. It mostly is created out of thin air through fractional reserve lending. Ultimately, the wealth generated through money creation belongs to the people. But citizens have been tricked into giving this public wealth to banks.

This is not to suggest that young people should not be taught to live up to their obligations. Of course they should. But they should be given at least as much leniency and consideration as corporations and older, more established citizens, and probably substantially more.

Authoritarianism is another factor that potentially contributes to abusive student debt terms. As discussed in the Authoritarianism section, young people frequently drive resistance to oppression and injustice in society. If the Occupy Wall Street movement had been allowed to expand, for example, it could have severely threatened corporate welfare, business control of government and the status quo in general. High levels of student debt severely constrain young people. It makes them much less likely to engage in activism and other efforts to fight injustice. If young people were allowed to escape student debt through bankruptcy or other lenient terms, it could increase threats to vested interests and the status quo.

It is unclear if severe debt terms are intended to suppress young people and protect shareholder returns. But since these terms at least partly produce this outcome, one could suspect that suppressing young people is one reason for implementing severe debt terms.

The justification given for hitting children often is that they must learn early on to obey authority. It appears that a similar rationale potentially is being used consciously or unconsciously on young adults. Young people who work hard to get through college often will become the leaders and managers of society. By brutally suppressing young people with abusive debt terms, in the same way that young children are brutally suppressed with physical violence, future leaders can be taught to be obedient. As they climb the corporate ladder, they can be taught to obey flawed ideas and systems, rather than question them.

Higher Education Solutions

Many problems and solutions have been discussed or implied in the preceding assessment of US higher education. This section summarizes important actions needed to re-establish high quality higher education in the US.

Whole System Solution. Effectively resolving virtually every major social, environmental, economic and political problem facing humanity requires a whole system approach. The same is true in higher education. The forces driving the rapid degradation of higher education in the US largely lie outside of the education field. If these forces are not addressed through a whole system approach, it probably will be impossible to halt the decline of higher education. As with virtually all other major problems in society, the solution is not to first address specific problems. It is to consider the larger context within which problems reside.

Regarding higher education, flawed society-level ideas and systems are the ultimate cause of higher education degradation, in the same way that they are the ultimate cause of virtually all other major problems in society. To illustrate, the systemically-mandated requirement to achieve never-ending growth often compels businesses, politicians paid by them, and other business allies to suppress or oppose anything that interferes with shareholder returns.

Higher education threatens ever-increasing shareholder returns in at least two major ways. Public funding of higher education limits the amount of taxpayer wealth that can be used for corporate welfare. In addition, true higher education often produces empowered, wise, freethinking citizens. These types of people are less likely to tolerate injustice in society, such as corporate welfare and business control of government. By suppressing critical thinking and emphasizing vocational education, the higher education system is more likely to produce compliant drones who will not question the status quo.

Resolving higher education problems and nearly all other major problems requires implementing the many economic and political system changes discussed throughout *Global System Change*. One of the most important systemic changes is to implement the government established by our Founders. This means establishing democracy where each citizen has equal influence over government, regardless of wealth, race or other factors. The current system where a small group of wealthy, mostly white citizens largely control government, both major political parties and society in general grossly violates the spirit and principles upon which the US was founded.

Once democracy is established in the US, we can evolve our economy into a form that is focused on maximizing the well-being of all citizens, not just wealthy business owners. This type of economy would provide far more high-quality jobs to college graduates and other citizens who want or need them.

Fully Fund Public Higher Education. Fully funding widespread public higher education is a critical component of re-establishing high quality higher education in the US. Investing in this area is one of the most beneficial and cost-effective investments that society can make. The US could easily afford to fully fund public higher education. The key is to eliminate or greatly reduce corporate welfare. Once democracy is established in the US, the great wealth of this country can be used to fund public higher education and provide other social well-being programs that are taken for granted in most other developed countries. As discussed in the Taxes section of *Global*

System Change, ending corporate welfare would enable the great reduction or possible elimination of individual income taxes on nearly all citizens, while also enabling funding of a stronger social safety net.

Tuition at public universities in the US is estimated to be between $70-100 billion per year.[636] This is a small fraction of the taxpayer wealth used for corporate welfare each year. As discussed, one form of corporate welfare, fractional-reserve lending, potentially costs taxpayers as much as $500 billion per year. Ending this form of corporate welfare would enable full funding of public higher education with enough left over to substantially reduce income taxes.

Fully funding public higher education would benefit society in many ways. For example, it would substantially improve class mobility and provide equal opportunity. Free or low-cost public higher education enables children from low and middle-income families to get college degrees and move up in society. It also would substantially contribute to reduced crime. As discussed in the Crime section, providing equal opportunity to children from low-income families is a key element of reducing crime. High school dropouts are 63 times more likely to be incarcerated than college graduates.[637] It is far more cost-effective to provide high-quality public K-12 and higher education than it is to pay for increased incarceration and the many other problems caused by underfunding public education.

During the 1970s, tuition was free at many community colleges and inexpensive at many public four-year colleges and universities. In addition, grants frequently were provided that covered living expenses. Instead of using taxpayer wealth to unfairly enrich already wealthy people, higher education programs that benefit all citizens should be implemented again. For example, tuition could once again be free at community college and perhaps be capped at $500 per year at public four-year colleges and universities. Grants for college living expenses also should be expanded.

Reduced funding for public higher education can benefit private colleges and universities. Tuition, room and board at private universities often cost over $50,000 per year. Reduced public higher education funding frequently lowers potential enrollment at public schools. This can increase demand for private colleges and universities. Also, reduced funding raises tuition costs at public schools. This lowers the differential with private schools and further increases private school demand. Given potential private school benefits, it is possible that some private schools and their allies might oppose fully funding public higher education. However, once democracy is established in the US, the focus of society will be on fairly and equally benefiting all citizens, rather than unfairly benefiting various vested interests.

Greatly Reduce Student Debt. Fully funding public higher education will greatly reduce new student debt. However, the existing roughly $1.6 trillion of student debt in the US also should be greatly reduced. This debt places a substantial drag on the economy. It prevents young people from making major purchases, saving for retirement, and starting businesses and families.

In addition, extensive student debt largely results from flawed systems and unjust actions caused by these systems. Reduced public funding of higher education is a major cause of rapid growth in student debt. The main cause of reduced funding is business control of government, corporate welfare and the systemically mandated requirement to provide ever-increasing shareholder returns. These are inappropriate and unfair influences of government. If not for these injustices, outstanding student debt would be much lower. In other words, much of the outstanding student debt exists due to immoral, unjust factors. Therefore, it probably should be forgiven.

As discussed in the Finance and Capital Markets section, US taxpayers spent about $6-12 trillion to bailout mainly wealthy speculators during the bank bailouts. Much of this money probably went into offshore accounts, or was used in other ways that did not help the economy, as indicated by slow economic and job growth for several years after the bailouts.

It would be far more economically beneficial and morally appropriate to bail out young people who never should have been required to take out student loans in the first place. Student bailouts would cost a small fraction of the bank bailouts. But it would provide a proportionally much larger economic benefit. Forgiving student debt would greatly increase the amount of money that young people spend or invest in the economy.

Most of the money lent to students did not belong to banks or other lenders. It mainly was created out of thin air. Therefore, forgiving student debt would not be unfairly taking wealth from banks or other parties. Practical and fair arrangements can be made to forgive student debt. But fairness requires recognizing that banks ultimately do not own the money that they create out of thin air. The right to create money belongs to the people. In addition to forgiving current student debt, tax credits or other benefits probably should be provided to those who already paid off student debt.

Going forward, some student debt might be needed, for example, for private colleges and universities. However, severe terms, such as no bankruptcy relief or statute of limitations on collections, should be eliminated. Student debt should issued under the most lenient terms in society, not the most severe.

A recent federal student loan program provides more reasonable and fair debt terms. Some post-2010 federal student loans are issued under terms that protect creditworthiness and ability to meet basic needs. If a borrower's income is less than 150 percent of the federal poverty level, no repayment is required. If income is over this amount, the required payment is 10 percent of the excess. Borrowers who maintain this arrangement for 20 years have any remaining balance forgiven. The interval is reduced to 10 years if borrowers work in a public interest capacity (e.g. military, fireman, charity worker).[638] If student debt is not immediately forgiven, it should be reissued under terms such as these.

Greatly Reduce Business Influence of Higher Education. Independent higher education is critical for the well-being of society. It strongly facilitates effective democracy by helping young people to become empowered, freethinking citizens. Businesses have gained strong influence over higher education in large part through inappropriate government influence. This contributes to reduced public funding, which makes colleges and universities more reliant on business donations and funding. Businesses also often promote privatization of higher education, online courses, and more businesslike practices in higher education administration. These also can directly or indirectly increase business influence of higher education. The mission of higher education should be to broadly promote the well-being of society. But business influence is shifting the mission to narrowly promoting the well-being of business. This is extremely dangerous.

Flawed economic and political systems unintentionally often put business in conflict with society. These suicidal systems frequently compel businesses to degrade life support systems and society. Higher education is the main source of the intellectual horsepower needed to resolve this suicidal situation. An independent higher education system can look at the big picture and develop whole system approaches that practically evolve systems and societal structures into sustainable forms.

But higher education cannot effectively do this if it is the agent of business. Developing and implementing sustainable systems would threaten ever-increasing shareholder returns. To protect returns, businesses can use their influence of higher education to block system change efforts. This is tragic. Companies often cannot voluntarily stop degrading society. The well-being of society, and paradoxically business, demands that higher education be independent of business. This empowers higher education to develop systems that eliminate conflicts between business and society.

Fully funding public higher education will greatly reduce business influence. Establishing democracy also will lower inappropriate business influence of higher education. When politicians no longer are puppets of business, but rather are servants of the people, they will ensure that higher education is focused primarily on the well-being of society.

Ensure that Higher Education Research Is Independent and Benefits Taxpayers. As discussed above, extensive taxpayer-funded research is conducted at public and private universities in the US. This is a main source of independent research. This research is critical to protecting and promoting the well-being of society. There are many threats and problems facing humanity. Independent research protects society by objectively assessing risks and developing solutions.

Business influence of higher education places society at great risk by compromising the objectivity of taxpayer-funded research. This influence harms citizens by enabling companies to suppress research that protects society, but threatens shareholder returns. Business influence also enables companies to compel the production of biased research that falsely shows business products and processes to be safe. In addition, it enables companies to essentially steal the financial benefits of taxpayer-funded research through patents and license agreements.

The well-being of society demands that business influence of university research be greatly reduced or eliminated. Taxpayer-funded research must remain objective and focused on protecting and benefiting society. Universities often patent and license taxpayer-funded research to supplement declining public funding of higher education. But this research does not belong to universities or business licensees. It belongs to taxpayers and society in general. It would be far more beneficial for society to fully fund public higher education and retain ownership of taxpayer-funded research. Giving ownership to universities and businesses often results in extremely high drug and other prices. This increases total costs of society and lowers quality of life. If taxpayers retain control of their research, it could be placed in the public domain or used in other ways that promote increased competition and reduced prices.

There are many cases where businesses can and should work closely with universities. For example, universities, especially business schools, frequently conduct research that is focused on improving management, production, entrepreneurship and other business-related issues. But business involvement with universities should be done through partnerships and other mechanisms that do not compromise the independence and objectivity of university research in any way.

Re-establish the Dignity and Independence of Professors. University professors are among the leading intellectuals in society. They greatly benefit society by developing new, innovative ideas and teaching young people to think critically and objectively. Professors are the heart of strong, independent universities. But the independence and critical thinking of professors often threatens the status quo and ever-increasing shareholder returns. Probably partly as a result, many university faculty positions have been severely degraded under deregulation since the 1980s.

As noted, in the 1980s, about 80 percent of courses were taught by tenured or tenure-track professors. Now, about 75 percent of faculty positions are temporary, adjunct jobs that often provide no benefits. High school dropouts earn an average of about $20,000 per year.[639] Adjunct professors, many of whom have PhD's, earn an average of $22,000 per year. Impoverishing professors severely restricts their ability to promote innovative ideas and systemic changes that benefit society, but threaten shareholder returns.

Providing poverty level wages with no benefits or job security can cause talented intellectuals to seek work in business instead of higher education. But it is essential that many talented intellectuals be drawn to higher education. Universities represent the main independent think tanks of society. Universities and professors can and should play a major role in changing systems and solving the complex problems facing humanity. To ensure that universities can fill this role, the dignity and job security of professors must be quickly re-established.

Fully funding public higher education will help to re-establish the dignity and job quality of professors. Reversing bloated administrative costs driven by business influence of higher education and diverting resources back to faculty and academic programs also will enhance the status and compensation of professors. College and university professors should receive the pay, benefits, job security and respect commensurate with the great contributions they make to society.

Reverse the Trend Toward Online Higher Education. As discussed above, rapid growth of online courses is degrading higher education. Therefore, the trend toward online higher education should be reversed. Instead, traditional classroom education should be provided.

Business influence is the main cause of rapid growth in online higher education. This type of education enables large reductions in higher education costs and public funding. It also facilitates the laying off or suppressing of professors who might teach young people to question the status quo. Online higher education further suppresses critical thinking that might threaten the status quo because critical thinking and true higher education cannot be taught nearly as well online as in traditional classrooms. One of the main business benefits of online higher education is much greater ability to control content. For-profit education and other companies can greatly reduce the likelihood that college students receive information that threatens corporate welfare and business control of government.

Online education provides another example of what happens when shareholder returns and economic growth are given priority over all else. Sooner or later, everything else gets pushed aside. For example, if providing human telephone operators reduces profits, humans often are replaced by computers. This degrades customer service. But that is not the priority. Shareholder returns and profits are. It is the same with higher education. If teaching young people with human beings lowers shareholder returns, human professors often are replaced with computers. This substantially degrades higher education. But that is not the priority when business strongly influences higher education. Shareholder returns are.

In today's online world, there obviously is a role for online activities in traditional classroom higher education. But computers cannot teach young people nearly as well as humans. This is indicated by the high dropout rates of MOOCs. Online courses take much of the human element out of education. This is not surprising because the measured and managed goal of a shareholder-focused economy is not benefiting society in general. It is benefiting shareholders.

Online education often treats students like machines, as if they could be downloaded with information like a computer. But humans are not machines. We are infinitely more sophisticated. We have physical, emotional, psychological and spiritual aspects and needs, in addition to intellectual needs. These cannot be met by online education. Higher education should educate the whole person. Treating students as if they were computers ready to accept information downloads will not work. Human students should be taught by human professors. There is no need to replace professors with computers. We can easily afford to fund traditional classroom public higher education for all young people who want it.

In summary, the trend toward online higher education should be quickly reversed. Instead, we should greatly reduce or eliminate corporate welfare. When this occurs, there will be more than enough funds for classroom higher education taught by well-paid professors.

Reverse the Trend Toward Privatization of Higher Education. Rapid privatization of public education is occurring at the K-12 and college levels. This often substantially degrades educational quality, largely because the measured and managed goal of for-profit education is not to maximize education quality and learning. It is to maximize profits and shareholder returns. If there is a conflict between shareholder returns and education quality, as there inevitably frequently will be, for-profit education companies must put profits and shareholder returns first. If they do not do this, they ultimately will die. In other words, the suicidal requirement to provide ever-increasing shareholder returns inevitably will degrade education quality.

The profit motive can benefit society in many areas, such as manufacturing, but only when it is properly regulated. However, the profit motive is incompatible with maximizing the well-being of society in some areas. Education is one of them. The primary goal of education systems should be to maximize educational quality, not maximize shareholder returns. The highest quality higher education in the US and other countries is not provided by for-profit corporations. It is provided by nonprofit organizations that are structurally focused on maximizing education quality and learning.

Increasing privatization of public services is inevitable in a shareholder-focused economy. Businesses give money to politicians, who then do their master's bidding – privatize public services. The privatization strategy usually involves first defunding public services. This frequently lowers performance, for example, because fewer people are required to do more work, as when teachers are required to teach larger classes. Once reduced funding lowers performance, businesses and politicians paid by them often severely criticize public services and claim that privatization is the best solution. Of course, they frequently dishonestly neglect to mention that the performance of public services often was good to outstanding before defunding. For example, the US was a world leader in K-12 public education when there was adequate public funding and strong teachers unions.

Expanding for-profit colleges, online education and other privatization efforts will continue to degrade higher education. As noted, for-profit colleges heavily market to and recruit low-income students. These colleges make about 80 percent their revenues from government student loans. They account for about 10 percent of students, but 25 percent of student loans. They also account for about 50 percent of student loan defaults.[640]

If we end corporate welfare and use public wealth to benefit all citizens, we can easily afford to provide high-quality public higher education. To maximize education quality, for-profit colleges probably should be quickly reduced. Those that remain should be held accountable. A main public deception related to the privatization of public education involves accountability. As discussed above, holding teachers and public schools accountable is a primary component of education reform. But once schools are privatized, for-profit schools often fiercely resist being held accountable. As noted, for-profit colleges frequently achieve worse performance than traditional nonprofit colleges and universities in areas such as academic performance and postgraduate employment. These colleges often used aggressive lobbying and legal action to avoid being held responsible for this poor performance. But if they receive taxpayer funding, they should be held to the same standards as other taxpayer-funded schools.

However, holding for-profit schools accountable is an interim strategy. The main strategy should be to reverse the privatization of higher education and provide low-cost or free public higher education to all people who want it. Some for-profit colleges might survive in niche markets. But strong public funding of higher education will substantially reduce for-profit colleges.

Restore True Higher Education and Teach Critical Thinking. Business influence of higher education is rapidly transforming higher education into vocational education. Courses that do not directly prepare students for jobs, such as some liberal arts and humanities courses, often are being reduced, while business and other job-related courses are increasing. But the main purpose of higher education is not job preparation. It is higher education. This means teaching young people to be articulate, empowered, freethinking citizens.

The complexity of jobs and many other aspects of society is increasing rapidly. Liberal arts, humanities and other traditional higher education courses often teach young people to deal with complexity more effectively. These courses also teach them to be better leaders, problem solvers and team players. In other words, true higher education frequently prepares young people for jobs more effectively than vocational education. Many work related skills are learned on the job. The most important higher education learning often includes critical thinking and leadership skills.

But teaching young people to be critical, freethinkers might not best prepare them to be obedient, low-level workers. Instead, it often would encourage them to question the status quo and injustices in society. To protect shareholder returns, it appears that empowering young people through true higher education often has been suppressed. This must be reversed. The well-being of society demands that we teach young people to think critically, be independent, and do what they believe is right. These are the types of people who will most effectively address the many complex problems facing humanity.

To restore true higher education, the decline of liberal arts, humanities and other true higher education courses should be reversed. There is an important role for business and other vocational type courses in higher education. But vocational courses should not dominate. The emphasis should be on true higher education courses that more effectively teach critical thinking, self-empowerment, cooperation and leadership.

Education Solutions

In addition to higher education solutions, numerous actions are needed to improve the quality of K-12 education in the US. Many solutions have been discussed throughout this book. To bring them together in one place, this section summarizes previously discussed education solutions and lists several others that were not mentioned. Beyond the higher education solutions discussed above, many of the following education solutions apply to K-12 and higher education, such as teaching whole system thinking and minimizing competitive grading.

In general, two levels of solutions are needed in US education. First, we must end the flawed focus on privatization and accountability. Then, once we are back on track by reaffirming our commitment to public education, we can implement changes that enable the US to pioneer and model a truly effective and sustainable education system. Getting back on track requires being honest about the real purpose of the privatization and accountability movements. They are the expected, even inevitable result of grossly flawed economic and political systems. Suicidal systems require that economic growth and shareholder returns take priority over all else, including the well-being of children.

Privatizing government services is a major component of achieving ever-increasing shareholder returns. The question of whether privatization benefits society largely is irrelevant to flawed systems. They require private sector growth, regardless of whether it benefits or degrades society. Many factors essentially prove that privatization of public education is the wrong approach.

World leaders in education are not using this approach. The US did not use it when we were a world leader in education. Forty years of increasing accountability and twenty years under NCLB/ESSA have not improved academic performance. Common sense and observations of reality show that poverty, not the lack of business processes, is the primary cause of poor academic performance in the US. Common sense and past and present education leaders show that the best way to achieve superior education performance is to implement a strong public education system, an economy that is focused on the well-being of all citizens, and a strong social safety net.

The stated goal of privatization and accountability is to improve academic performance and benefit society. But this is not the measured and managed goal of publicly traded companies. They are structurally required to maximize profits and shareholder returns. To achieve this, inappropriate government influence is used to shift the focus of politicians from promoting the general welfare to promoting business welfare. Public deception is used to mislead many citizens into believing that privatizing public education will benefit children and society.

Many citizens are misled into blindly believing the highly irrational idea that the private sector always is better than the public sector. The private sector can do many things well. But education often is not one of them. The profit motive is incompatible with educating young people well. Children are complex, multifaceted human beings. They are not simple machines that can be processed and molded by for-profit companies. With privatization, taxpayer funds are used to pay for investor returns, high executive compensation, and other expenses that would not be acceptable in the public sector. Charter and private schools often discriminate against disabled, minority and underperforming children, something that is prohibited in public schools.

K-12 education is a public good. Privatizing it will degrade society in many ways. It will create the same high cost and poor coverage seen in US healthcare. Privatizing will produce high-quality education for wealthy families, mediocre education for the middle class, and low quality education for low-income families. This is extremely counterproductive. Providing high-quality education to all children, teenagers and young adults is one of the most beneficial investments that society can make.

Privatization of public education in the US is part of the larger shift from focusing on the well-being of the many to the well-being of the few. We must wake up and end this insanity. Putting the financial well-being of already wealthy people ahead of all else degrades society for everyone, including wealthy people.

While public education is vastly better for society than for-profit education, it is not a panacea. Even leading public education systems can be substantially improved. These systems prepare children to work in flawed economic, political and social systems. They contain many implied assumptions about education and child-rearing that are counterproductive or inaccurate. Flawed implied assumptions relate to purpose, teaching method, focus, discipline, competitive grading, performance measurement, intelligence, intuitive development, social and emotional skills, and the role of business in education. These and other ideas are discussed in the following Education Solutions section.

Clarify Purpose

Clarifying the purpose of education is critical. Purpose should determine nearly every other aspect of education. The overarching purpose of education should be to benefit society, in part by helping young people to reach their fullest potential and achieve successful and satisfying lives. Education follows society. The optimal structure and method of education cannot be defined adequately until the optimal, or at least sustainable, structure of society is clarified. Once this is clear, we can structure education to support the development and maintenance of this preferred, sustainable society.

The current education system contains several explicit and implicit assumptions about the optimal human society and the best ways that education can support it. Many of these assumptions are grossly flawed and inaccurate. As discussed in the Boredom section, the current education system is a legacy of the industrial age and Protestant Reformation. Traditional economic theories often see labor as units of production. In many ways, the current education system apparently seeks to mold young people into effective productive units that help the economy grow. This approach is wrong for several critical reasons. First, it dehumanizes our children. It suppresses their unique interests and abilities by forcing them to spend years learning the same basic subjects. Those who fail to excel in what society says is important are demeaned through competitive grading. They implicitly are told that they are less valuable, and therefore deserve less from life.

The current education system also is flawed because it implicitly prepares young people to work and participate in grossly flawed economic, political and social systems. The measured and managed priority of society should not be to grow the economy. It should be to maximize the long-term well-being of society. These are very different goals. Current systems myopically assume that growing the economy will improve the well-being of society. But the opposite increasingly is true.

If the focus of society were on maximizing long-term social well-being, instead of short-term economic growth and shareholder returns, our society would be structured quite differently. For example, technology often is used to promote the sale of more products and help investors to earn high returns. If the focus of society were on maximizing long-term social well-being, technology and human know-how would be used to restore and protect life support systems and make life easier for citizens so that they can work less and do more of what they love.

As discussed throughout *Global System Change*, our myopic, unsustainable economic, political and social systems are rapidly degrading life support systems and causing vast inequality and unhappiness in the US and around the world. These flawed systems absolutely will change because they are so grossly at odds with reality and nature. It often is difficult to see from our limited perspective, but humans systems are in the process of changing now.

In one sense, education creates society. Society could be defined as the collective actions of all people. When we teach children to think and act in certain ways, we are in a sense creating future society. If we teach young people to do what we are doing now, we will perpetuate rapid environmental degradation and vast unhappiness and unfairness in society. If we want a different future, we must educate our children differently.

Virtually all sane people would agree that the purpose of society should be to create an environment where ideally all people, current and future, are able to reach their fullest joy and potential. The first purpose of society should be long-term survival, which largely involves environmental protection. The next purpose should be to create stable, long-lasting communities and social systems that enable individuals to freely live their lives and reach their fullest potential. As we clarify these purposes of society, we can evolve our education systems into forms that support them.

For example, the current education system attempts to churn out well-conditioned workers for our unsustainable economy and society. As we recognize that the purpose of society (and by extension education) is to benefit individuals and society overall, rather than business and the economy, we will educate our children differently. We no longer will force young people to endure boring, demeaning education. This helps the economy and wealthy business owners by conditioning young people to tolerate lifetimes of boring jobs and control by authorities.

Instead, we will give our children what they deserve – a wonderful, exciting, stimulating early life experience. As this occurs, far fewer young people will run away from reality with drugs and other distractions. Reality will be so exciting and interesting that they will not want to escape from it. We will teach young people through experience what life is meant to be – amazing and wonderful. We will honor young people by encouraging them to find and follow their own unique paths in life.

Young people taught in this way will create a new world. Children are the most precious and important people in society. We must not stifle them, as we currently do with our industrial age education system. This section discusses many actions needed to honor, protect, love and empower our children, and thereby help to create the sustainable and prosperous world that we all want.

Clarify Method

Once the purpose of education is clarified, the optimal method of educating young people can be identified. As noted, the purpose of education should be to maximize the well-being of individuals and society overall, rather than maximizing the well-being of business and the economy. Current systems often degrade the most important skills and traits needed for success in life. This benefits business by producing compliant workers who will tolerate tedium. But it violates the purpose of education.

We should be building our children up, not tearing them down. Since the purpose of education is to help young people, education methods must emphasize the development of critical skills and traits needed for life success. These include self-esteem, social and emotional skills, and critical thinking skills.

Cooperation is another critical aspect of education methods. As occurs in healthy natural systems, a sustainable and prosperous human society will be overwhelmingly based on cooperation, not competition. Current economic and political systems largely are based on competition. This is a main reason why these systems are unsustainable and ultimately suicidal.

As discussed in the Women's section, wisdom largely could be defined as the ability to cooperate effectively. Increased wisdom and ability to cooperate are among the most important requirements needed to achieve sustainability and real prosperity. Current education methods emulate our unsustainable systems by being based largely on competition. The ultimate goal of society should be to achieve long-term survival and real prosperity. This then also should be the ultimate goal of our education system. This implies that education methods must be much more focused on teaching children wisdom and cooperation. Increased cooperation and many other aspects of optimal education methods are discussed in the following sections.

Teach Whole System Thinking and Intuitive Wisdom

Education often focuses on specific disciplines and subject areas without adequate reference to the whole system. Achieving a sustainable and prosperous society require shifting the focus of all levels of education from reductionism to whole system thinking. This section discusses the importance of this shift in education focus.

As discussed in Whole System Perspective section of *Global System Change*, the conscious human mind did not evolve to focus on the whole Earth system (of which human society is a sub-element). It usually focuses on people and things in one's immediate vicinity or life. The conscious mind is not capable of comprehending all the details of the whole Earth system or human society at once. As a result, we break society down into parts, and often study them without adequate reference to the whole system that contains them. This process, known as reductionism, is especially strong in the education area.

Science, economics, governance and other academic disciplines have hugely advanced humanity. They are responsible in large part for the structure of modern society. However, economics and other subjective disciplines often are extremely myopic. As researchers and other experts dive more deeply into the details of particular disciplines, they frequently lose sight of the big picture or whole system. This often causes experts to develop economic and other ideas that sound good in theory, but do not work well in reality. Economic and other theories frequently produce unintended negative impacts because they were developed in a theoretical vacuum that does not exist in reality.

As Albert Einstein implied, the solution to the huge problems caused by reductionism is to think at a higher level. This higher level is whole system thinking. It could be referred to as reality-based thinking. Whole system thinking does not ignore much of reality when developing economic and other theories and strategies, as current research, education and other processes often do. Everything in the whole system of human society is connected. The economic is not separate from the social, political, environmental or even psychological, spiritual or religious. To solve major problems, we must elevate our thinking. Considering everything at once greatly increases complexity. But this is reality. Pretending that we can study economics and other disciplines in isolation is an irrational, destructive and ultimately suicidal fantasy.

The conscious human mind might not be able to comprehend the whole system at once. But fortunately, the human mind is not limited to conscious processes. Humans are surrounded by essentially infinitely greater implied intelligence. Comparing human sophistication and technology to that of nature indicates that we only have reached the tiniest fraction of our potential. People 1,000 years ago compared themselves to people many years before and thought they were more sophisticated. We compare ourselves to people 1,000 years ago and see that we are advanced. Looking backwards can cause us to arrogantly and ignorantly believe that we might be near the pinnacle of human achievement.

We cannot compare ourselves to future people. Nature probably is the best reference point for gauging the level of human development. Humbly looking at the virtually infinitely greater implied intelligence all around us illuminates the true stage of human evolution and development. We probably have not reached one billionth of our potential. If we voluntarily change our ways and avoid the hammer of reality and nature, humanity will survive. Then people in the future will look back on us, the way we look back on others. They will see that what we thought was sophisticated, often was hopelessly myopic, simplistic and destructive.

Just because modern humanity has not been able to adequately consider and operate well in the whole system does not mean that we cannot develop this capacity. We clearly have the ability to understand and effectively operate in the whole system. We are part of nature. Therefore, we implicitly have access to the essentially infinite wisdom and intelligence of nature. The primary means of accessing infinite wisdom and intelligence is through the intuitive function.

Anything that has ever happened in the most brilliant conscious human mind is nothing compared to the essentially infinitely greater wisdom and intelligence available to every human being through the intuitive function. Our education system usually focuses strongly on developing the intellect or conscious human mind. Accessing the intelligence and human potential needed to achieve sustainability and real prosperity requires that we do a much better job of teaching children, teenagers and young adults how to utilize the intuitive.

In terms of focus, the emphasis of education at all levels, from early childhood to post-doctorate, should be strongly shifted from reductionism to the whole system. In other words, it should be shifted from fantasy (i.e.

the ivory tower) to reality. Studying the economy without adequate reference to the whole system within which it resides would be like developing a part for a car without adequately considering that the part must fit in with and enhance the functioning of the car.

The implication of this is that children, teenagers and young adults should be taught about the whole system (i.e. the whole Earth system and its sub-element human society) before they go deeply into the details of specific subsystems or fields of study. The techniques for achieving this will vary greatly from primary to graduate education. But the overall theme is that students should at least generally understand the relation of the major parts to the whole system before studying the parts in detail.

For example, before studying detailed economic concepts, students and researchers should have a general understanding of the environment and society that contain the economy and enable it to exist. Then, economic concepts can be studied and developed with reference to the larger system. This will greatly increase the likelihood that evolving economic ideas will work well in reality while producing few or no unintended negative consequences.

To illustrate, virtually all of the economic and political system flaws discussed in *Global System Change* become obvious when one adopts a whole system perspective. Concepts such as time value of money, limited liability, and seeking ever-increasing economic growth and shareholder returns might seem logical and beneficial from a myopic, reductionistic perspective. But a whole system perspective quickly shows these concepts to be irrational, destructive and ultimately suicidal.

The well-being of society demands that reductionism in the education area be replaced with whole system thinking. Theories and processes developed in the academic area often drive the structure and functioning of society. As a result, maximizing the well-being of society requires that academic theories and processes be grounded in the reality of the whole system. This refers less to true science than to subjective subjects such as economics. Physical sciences, such as geology and climatology, are based on observations and rational assessments of reality. As a result, there is less danger that these subjects will suffer from myopia and produce theories that do not work well in reality.

However, less scientific subjects, such as economics and governance, deal with many subjective issues that are more difficult to quantify and rationally explain, such as human behavior, emotions and philosophies. These subjective factors can be extremely complex. Economics and similar fields often deal with complexity by making oversimplified assumptions about human behavior and other factors. These unrealistic assumptions frequently are the main cause of unintended negative impacts.

Adopting a whole system perspective often increases complexity. But it also can reduce it, for example, by eliminating the need for irrational, simplistic assumptions about human behavior and by providing a much clearer and more accurate view of reality. To illustrate, economic theories frequently trade off environmental concerns with other factors, such as financial returns. This myopia or failure to understand the whole system produces unintended outcomes, such as destruction of life support systems.

By adopting a whole system perspective, one sees that the environment takes priority over everything else in human society. Without an environment that is clean and stable enough to support human life, we are dead and everything else is irrelevant. Trading off environmental factors often is equivalent to trading off human life. This is irrational. A rational, whole system focused, sustainable economic system would not make environmental trade-offs. It would not produce Tragedy of the Commons situations where seeking short-term prosperity reduces the ability of future generations to survive.

Economic theories often produce unintended negative consequences because they make the understandable, but irrational, mistake of focusing on individual well-being, for example, of individual persons, companies or countries. This is understandable because individuals are doing the thinking and theorizing. However, as discussed in the Well-Being of Society section, focusing first on individual well-being is irrational because this is not the relevant perspective for human survival and prosperity.

Ensuring survival and maximizing human well-being requires first focusing on the whole system (mainly the environment). Once environmental protection is guaranteed, the next level of focus should be social structures, such as communities. This enables individuals to prosper. Finally, the last, lowest priority focus should be on individual well-being. Paradoxically, placing the well-being of the individual last allows the highest level of individual prosperity. When environmental and social structures are sustainable and stable, individuals can prosper and reach their fullest potential. When these structures are weak or declining, individual well-being also often declines. (Protecting social structures and systems includes protecting individual rights.)

Adopting a whole system perspective can reduce complexity by providing a clearer view of reality and enabling more accurate assumptions about human behavior. For example, one could assume that all sane people would prefer that they and their children be alive rather than dead. With this basic assumption, sustainable economic systems would limit modification or disruption of life support systems. Once this primary, non-negotiable constraint of environmental protection is established, economic and other researchers can figure out how to meet other critical and noncritical human needs without degrading life support systems.

The situation is similar to that discussed for business throughout *Global System Change*. Holding companies fully responsible for negative environmental impacts will compel responsible behavior. Companies that cannot figure out how to operate without degrading environmental life support systems will cease to exist and be replaced by more competent ones. If we allow some environmental degradation, companies that are structurally required to put shareholder returns before all else often essentially will be compelled to degrade life support systems. In other words, allowing environmental degradation frequently is equivalent to requiring it. This becomes obvious when one adopts a whole system perspective.

If we allow environmental degradation, we effectively will be guaranteeing the degradation and possible destruction of life support systems. Adopting a whole system perspective shows that economic and political systems must be evolved into forms that prohibit environmental/human life trade-offs and degradations. If we demand that society and the economy not degrade life support systems, we will use our great creativity and ingenuity to figure out how to do this.

Environmental considerations provide a perfect example of myopic business and economic approaches. The environment often is seen as an implied sub-element of business and human society. For example environmental protection often is one of many issues that businesses and society overall must address. This is the type of myopic, reductionist thinking that leads to life support and human life trade-offs. The environment is not a sub-element of human society. Human society is a sub-element of the environment. As our Founders explained long ago, there are natural environmental laws by which we absolutely must abide. From the myopic, self-centered, human perspective, it can seem that the environment is one issue that must be balanced against other key issues.

But if we think from the reality-based, whole system perspective, we see that human society simply is one element that the environment or whole system must address. We are not the master. We are the servant or sub-element. The master of life and death (the environment, natural laws) will decide how to deal with human society. If we do not comply with the master's rules, it will eliminate us. From the perspective of the environmental whole system, humans are not important. If we fail to abide by nature's laws, humans will be one more species that became extinct because we could not adapt to nature. (Humans are important to humans. We also are important on a higher spiritual level. But from the physical, environmental perspective, we simply are one species on this planet, no more important than any other species.)

Human survival and prosperity require refocusing education and human society on the whole system. Adopting a whole system perspective can lead to the resolution of long-standing problems and development of more effective approaches in virtually all academic disciplines and other areas.

Sustainability could be seen as the meta-discipline. Every aspect of human society, from the individual to the global collective, is part of sustainability. Sustainability refers to the long-term survival and prosperity of humanity. Prosperity includes art, psychology, spirituality and every other aspect of humanity without exception. In this sense, sustainability is equivalent to whole system thinking.

Sustainability or whole system thinking should be the overarching framework for nearly all types and levels of education. People should be taught the overarching, systemic context before studying specific areas in detail. As part of general K-12 and higher education, students should be given a clear understanding of the whole system and all of its physical and non-physical parts (i.e. environmental, social, economic, political, psychological, spiritual, religious). The degree of whole system focus will vary based on the type and level of education. For example, less whole system focus will be needed for appliance repair and some other types of vocational education. But more whole system focus will be needed in areas such as engineering, product design, medicine, economics and governance.

Many universities have programs related to systems thinking. They often focus on systems theory or certain subsystems in human society. But the relevant system for long-term human survival and prosperity is the whole Earth system and its sub-element human society. We need a much greater emphasis in academia on practically addressing this relevant whole system. We must find more ways of analyzing the whole system as one unit, and then clearly describing it to expert and non-expert citizens. In one sense, there are no whole system experts at a detailed level. No person can fully comprehend at a detailed level all aspects of society. But we can find ways to better understand and describe the whole system in a summary manner.

Global System Change illustrates one way to describe and integrate all major elements of the whole Earth system and its sub-element human society. It strives to provide much of the most important knowledge that people might learn from bachelor's, master's, and doctorate degrees in economic, political, social, environmental, psychological, spiritual and comparative religious areas. A main goal of *Global System Change* is to make complex information clear to non-expert citizens, the ultimate leaders of society. *Global System Change* also is intended to help experts by clarifying sustainable, whole system solutions and illustrating how complex ideas can be communicated to non-experts.

Most high school and many middle school students probably could easily understand *Global System Change* because complex issues are explained in ways that assume little or no prior knowledge. The books strive to provide teenagers and adults with an adequately detailed overview of all major aspects of the Earth/human whole system in a relatively short format (given the large number of issues addressed). Books like this can give people the whole system perspective needed to study, understand and develop more effective solutions in economic, political, environmental and social areas.

There is no one 'correct' way to write a whole system overview such as this. Much more work is needed in this area. Clearly describing and practically addressing the Earth/human whole system should become a major focus of academia. It should become the meta-discipline that guides nearly every other aspect of education. Each person hears and understands things differently. Having many different ways to describe the Earth/human whole system will maximize the likelihood that each person hears the description that works best for them.

There are many holistic ways of describing individuals and helping them. These address all relevant aspects of mind, body and spirit. We need more holistic approaches to the Earth/human whole system. Our whole system also has mind, body and spirit components. The body (physical) aspects are obvious. The mind component could be thought of as conscious individual thoughts and widely held ideas among humanity. The spirit could refer to deeper, wiser, intuitive, often unconscious aspects of humanity. There also may be nonphysical aspects of the Earth/human whole system, such as a collective unconscious perceived through intuition as well as the ability to intuitively sense aspects of the whole system, such as environmental and social stresses and problems.

Whole system thinking gives us a more accurate understanding of prosperity. Humans on Earth essentially are the same as cells in the body. The cell cannot survive apart from the body and the human cannot survive apart from the Earth. We understand that cells seeking to maximize their own well-being without limit and without regard to the prosperity of the larger body quickly would kill the body, and thereby kill themselves. But our limited perspective often makes it difficult to see that individuals seeking to maximize their own well-being without regard to the prosperity of the Earth/human whole system would degrade and possibly destroy overall human society.

Whole system thinking shows that what commonly is referred to as 'rational self-interest' often is destructive and ultimately suicidal. Clearly suicide is not rational. Self-interest that actually was rational (and enlightened) would prohibit actions that benefit individuals in the short-term, but degrade the environment and society.

The cell is happiest when the body prospers. The same is true of humans. Our myopic focus on individual well-being causes humans to act like a cancer on this planet. Seeking individual happiness without regard for the prosperity of larger human society causes widespread unhappiness around the world. This is why teaching children and adults to focus on the whole system is so important. In reality, we are not separate from the child dying of starvation in Africa. The idea that we can be truly happy without trying to help others who are suffering often is an illusion or delusion.

The main commandant or suggestion of virtually all major religions is to treat other people with kindness, love and respect. Why? Because it works. It produces a fulfilling and successful life. Why? Because we ultimately are not separate from other people. Helping others ultimately is the same as helping ourselves. This reality becomes clear when people end fantasy, reductionistic thinking and enter the reality of the whole system perspective. The suggestion here is not that people should not be happy or prosperous unless everyone else is. Rather, the idea is that the greatest happiness and true prosperity frequently result from helping others.

Humans often make the mistake of thinking we are separate from nature and each other because we are at a stage of development where we overly rely in the intellect, and frequently ignore the virtually infinitely greater intelligence and wisdom available through the intuitive function. The five senses often trick us into thinking that we are separate from each other and nature, in the same way that they once tricked us into thinking that the Earth was flat. As we learn to discern and utilize the intuitive function more effectively, the interconnected nature of human society and the whole Earth system will become clearer.

The intellect also often tricks humans into thinking that we are the smartest creatures on Earth. Perhaps we are from an intellectual perspective. But judging by results, nature is nearly infinitely smarter. That is partly because nature implicitly operates from a whole system perspective. The implied ordering intelligence of nature appears to operate through some type of instinctual or intuitive function. Humans bound by the intellect produce vastly inferior results. However, humans operating effectively from the intuitive are capable of producing the same brilliance and immense sophistication seen in nature.

Utilizing the intuitive requires humility and open-mindedness. The arrogant intellect or ego often does not feel comfortable acknowledging that there are aspects of reality that it does not understand. This is why humility is so important. As discussed in the Twelve Steps Programs and other sections of *Global System Change*, the proper role of the ego or conscious mind is to be a servant to infinitely greater intuitive wisdom. This produces the most fulfilling and successful life.

Advancing human society requires a much greater focus on utilizing intuitive wisdom and adopting a whole system perspective. (As noted, many people refer to intuitive wisdom as God. But the label that people put on intuitive wisdom ultimately is irrelevant. The critical component is accessing and using it to guide one's life. If calling intuitive wisdom God enables people to most effectively access and utilize it, they should use this approach.)

The discussion here is not meant to denigrate the intellect, or especially rational reasoning. As discussed extensively throughout *Global System Change*, the well-being of humanity demands that we end irrational, blind faith adherence to destructive economic, political, religious and other dogma. Instead, we must greatly expand the use of rational, enlightened reasoning, as our Founders did during the Age of Enlightenment and Reason.

Rational thought is the worker of humanity. Intuitive wisdom provides the higher command and rational thought figures out how to get the job done. Rational thought alone is very useful, but limited. However, rational thought informed by intuitive wisdom can manifest the brilliance of nature in human society. The intuitive naturally functions from a whole system perspective. As a result, teaching children and adults to utilize the intuitive more effectively will facilitate the adoption of a whole system perspective among individuals and society overall.

As discussed at the beginning of *Global System Change*, reductionism (the failure to adopt a whole system perspective) is the foundational cause of nearly all major problems facing humanity. The current education system could be thought of as Reductionism Central. Reductionistic economic, political and other theories are developed in academia, and then spread out in ways that cause unintended damage in society. As a result, it is critical that the focus of education at all levels be switched from reductionism to whole system thinking.

Teach Critical Thinking

As noted, the US education system is a legacy of the Protestant Reformation and Industrial Age. The goals were and largely still our obedience training and indoctrination. Young people usually are trained to blindly believe prevailing economic, political and other ideas. This strongly facilitates the perpetuation of our grossly flawed, unintentionally suicidal systems.

Achieving sustainability and real prosperity requires that we improve our myopic ideas and systems. Teaching young people to critically examine prevailing ideas and systems will greatly facilitate this. Young people should analyze the flaws of modern systems and consider alternatives. They should be encouraged to think freely, creatively and critically.

Teaching whole system thinking facilitates critical thinking. Whole system thinking clarifies reality by illuminating societal linkages, root causes, key leverage points and optimal solutions. This clarity better enables people to critically examine problems and develop effective solutions.

Teaching young people to obey authorities and blindly believe prevailing ideas greatly benefits vested interests and strongly supports authoritarianism. But it is severely degrades democracy and society. It also is a huge disservice to our children. The human mind is meant to be free. To maximize the well-being of society, we must teach young people to think for themselves.

Whole System Strategy

Reductionism produces flawed ideas and systems, which in turn cause virtually all major problems facing humanity, including those in the education area. As a result, the foundational solution to these problems is to think at a higher, whole system level and improve our ideas and systems. As discussed, the main cause of poor academic performance in the US lies outside the education realm. That is why a whole system approach is mandatory for improving academic performance. Little progress can be made if we only focus on the education system.

Flawed systems are the primary cause of poverty in the US, which in turn is the main cause of poor academic performance. Economic and political systems are focused on maximizing economic growth and shareholder returns. To achieve this, literally trillions of dollars essentially are stolen from low and middle-income citizens every year and given to the small group of wealthy citizens that controls government. This causes poverty and makes life more difficult for millions of average citizens, especially low-income citizens. Poverty is (and has been for over 100 years) the primary cause of poor academic performance in the US.

Therefore, the most important action needed to improve US academic performance is to alleviate poverty. This can be achieved by implementing the many economic, political and social system changes discussed in *Global System Change*. These include ending business control of government, implementing true democracy, ending corporate welfare, and using public wealth to equally and fairly benefit all citizens. These changes will greatly alleviate poverty by enabling the implementation of a strong social safety net and an economy that is focused on serving all citizens well and providing jobs for all who want or need them.

The issue of poverty shows how the failure to implement a whole system strategy often harms children. Poverty inhibits academic performance through many factors, including poor nutrition, sleep deprivation, lack of suitable reading materials and stimulation, parental stress and unsafe physical environments. One study found that poverty reduces brain tissue development in children.[641] The myopic US education reform approach largely ignores these highly relevant factors. Instead, the strategy often apparently is to get tough on children. They are given more difficult tests and essentially told to work harder.

One reform approach, called the "No Excuse" model, teaches students and orders teachers to ignore all factors that are not relevant to a particular academic task, which usually is taking a standardized test.[642] Children should be taught to work hard and overcome adversity. But we should not ignore the huge challenges that flawed economic and political systems place on the millions of children living in poverty. The ignorant, myopic education reform approach implies that if children work hard enough, they can overcome hunger, violent homes and communities, and diminished brain volume. This approach shifts responsibility for dealing with poverty away from politicians, business leaders and citizens who tolerate corrupt government to our children.

A smaller, but perhaps more harmful example of the failure to adopt a whole system strategy relates to school shootings. Since 1999, there have been 331 school shootings that killed 185 people and injured 369.[643] As flawed systems make life more difficult for average citizens, the number of school shootings has been increasing. In response, a growing number of schools practice active shooter drills. In these drills, children often are taught what to do if they are shot or a shooter is in the building.[644] On a percentage basis, school shootings are extremely rare. Requiring children to imagine being shot and having shooters in schools as well as practice how to respond to these situations often will be traumatic and harmful.

A whole system approach would effectively address the factors that cause school shootings. Two main causal factors include the proliferation of guns in the US and growing stress, especially among teenagers. As discussed in the Crime section, the US has weak gun laws that make it easy for criminals and other dangerous people to get guns. The US has the highest gun ownership in the world, by far. Guns kept in the home were used in the large majority of school shootings.[645] Many school shootings would not have occurred if guns were not so easily and readily available.

Regarding stress, teenagers have the highest stress levels of any age group in the US.[646] The increasingly boring, competitive and intolerant US education system plays a major role in high teenage stress levels. High stress creates many psychological problems and greatly increases the risk of school shootings. Teaching children what to do if they get shot partly is shifting responsibility for addressing school shootings away from politicians and adults to children. Children can be taught general emergency drills without having to imagine being shot or having shooters in the school. Myopic education policies largely ignore the actual causes of poor academic performance, school shootings and other problems. Effectively addressing these problems requires looking beyond the education system and implementing a whole system strategy.

End Business Control of Education

The business-focused structure of education reform further illustrates the need for a whole system strategy. In addition to being the main cause of poverty, flawed ideas and systems are the main factors shaping education reform. The current structure of education reform is driven mainly by the paramount systemic requirement to provide ever-increasing economic growth and shareholder returns.

It is no coincidence that nearly all education reform actions being implemented strongly benefit business. These actions include expanding privatization, charter schools, public funding of private schools, standardized testing, performance-based teacher pay, attacks on teachers unions, online education, student data utilization, zero-tolerance disciplinary programs, student monitoring, compulsory psychiatric drug use, and corporate control of education.

When businesses control education, the goal is not to help children and society. It is to help business. Refocusing education on helping children and society requires ending business control of education. As noted, education reform largely has shifted control of education from the local level to the state, federal and corporate levels. This must be reversed. The following suggestions illustrate additional aspects of the business-focused education reform agenda that should be reversed.

Fully Fund Public Education

Business influence largely is driving the defunding and privatization of public education. As discussed in the Privatization section, a manufactured crisis was used to justify these actions. Difficult standardized tests were developed. Experts knew in advance that many students would fail these tests. Once this occurred, schools often were labeled as failing and funding was cut. This lowered academic performance and justified privatization. Growing class sizes indicate that public school funding is being cut in many regions.

Cutting funding for public education helps business in many ways, including by reducing taxes and creating many business opportunities. But it greatly harms society. A strong, well-funded public education system is critical for the short-term and long-term success of society. Investing in public education is one of the most beneficial investments that society can make. For example, investments in public K-12 education create more than twice as many jobs as investing in the military.[647]

The Founders of the US strongly believed in the importance and benefits of public education. President John Adams said, "The whole people must take upon themselves the education of the whole people and be willing to bear the expenses of it. There should not be a district of one mile square, without a school in it, not founded by a charitable individual, but maintained at the public expense of the people themselves."[648]

A report by the Center on Education Policy, called *Why We Still Need Public Schools: Public Education for the Common Good*, summarized six foundational missions and benefits of public education. These missions include: to provide universal access to free education; to guarantee equal opportunities for all children; to unify a diverse population; to prepare people for citizenship in a democratic society; to prepare people to become economically self-sufficient; and to improve social conditions.[649] These missions or purposes of public education have been important since the founding of the US. They remain important today.

Countries that lead the world in education show that providing a strong, well-funded public education system is the most effective way to maximize academic performance and benefit society in many other ways. Maximizing the well-being of children and society overall requires that the US reaffirm our commitment to public education by fully funding it.

The funding issue once again shows the need for a whole system approach. US citizens pay at least several trillion dollars every year in corporate welfare, through higher taxes, reduced quality of life and other means. Eliminating just one form of corporate welfare (fractional reserve lending) potentially could pay for nearly all public K-12 education costs (about $600 billion). Ending or greatly reducing all forms of corporate welfare could pay for all K-12 education expenses, while also substantially reducing federal, state and local taxes.

Public education is a right of all citizens. In the 1954 Supreme Court decision *Brown v. Board of Education*, Justice Earl Warren said, "Today, education is perhaps the most important function of state and local governments. Compulsory school attendance laws and the great expenditures for education both demonstrate our recognition of the importance of education to our democratic society. It is required in the performance of our most basic public responsibilities, even service in the armed forces. It is the very foundation of good citizenship. Today it is a principal instrument in awakening the child to cultural values, in preparing him for later professional training, and in helping him to adjust normally to his environment. In these days, it is doubtful that any child may reasonably be expected to succeed in life if he is denied the opportunity of an education. Such an opportunity, where the state has undertaken to provide it, is a right which must be made available to all on equal terms."[650]

As discussed in the Education Funding section, nearly all developed countries provide equal or more public education funding for children from low-income families. The US should end its ignorant, destructive and fiscally irresponsible policy of providing less education funding for low-income children. To achieve this, the inequitable and unfair program of funding public K-12 education in large part with local property taxes should be ended. As noted, about half of local property taxes in the US are used to fund public K-12 education. As a result, ending this system could cut property taxes across the US by an average of about 50 percent. Funding public education through reductions in corporate welfare would enable this large reduction in property taxes without requiring increases in federal and state income taxes.

Ending the system of partly funding public education with property taxes would greatly benefit many rural communities. Since the 1980s, rural school districts, especially those in the South, Southwest and Midwest, have been closing small schools. As a result, children in small towns usually are required to take long bus rides, often several hours per day, to larger schools.[651] Closing schools in small towns degrades communities in many ways.

Population and real estate values often decline after schools are closed. Young families frequently do not want to move to the towns because the commute to school is too long. Beyond providing local education, schools in smaller towns often are hubs of community activity. The schools frequently hold events that bring community members together, such as plays, concerts and holiday gatherings. They also often provide community services, such as helping elderly citizens. Many small-town people feel that their towns lose their identity when local schools are closed. It frequently is like taking the heart out of a town.[652]

Many small towns in the US are struggling economically and financially. Townspeople often cannot afford to support their local schools through property taxes. As a result, they essentially are forced to vote to close their schools. This frequently hastens the demise of small towns.[653]

Proponents of closing small schools sometimes argue that larger schools can provide better education. But this frequently is not the case. Many studies have shown that smaller schools often have higher test scores, graduation rates and student involvement in extracurricular activities. In small schools, teachers usually can devote more time to each student. As a result, students frequently wind up developing better social, emotional and communication skills.[654] Eliminating corporate welfare, ending property tax funding of public education, and ensuring adequate state and federal funding would protect public schools in small towns and strengthen rural communities.

Funding public education partly through property taxes is a main reason why children in low-income communities frequently receive lower quality education. The US should emulate the majority of developed countries that provide more education funding for low-income students. This would be a highly fiscally prudent investment.

As discussed in the Crime section, the US appears to implement an extremely irrational approach to funding social welfare programs. The vested interest-promoted war between conservatives and liberals breeds anger, hatred and division in society. In this environment, we often appear to be unwilling to spend relatively small amounts to help fellow citizens. But we do not seem to mind spending vastly larger amounts to punish, for example through long-term incarceration. Failing to provide high-quality public education to low-income children greatly increases crime and many other problems. It virtually always is far less expensive to prevent problems than to treat them. Spending a few thousand dollars more per year for 12 years to provide high-quality education to children in low-income communities often will eliminate the need to spend $50,000 per year for 10 to 40 years on incarceration.

Providing more public education funding for low-income children will benefit society in many ways beyond lowering crime and total costs to society. Children from wealthier families have many education and other opportunities that lower-income children do not have. Providing higher funding to educate children from low-income families will help to equalize opportunities for all children. It also will improve the public spirit and enhance the quality of the US workforce.

Fully funding public education means ensuring that public schools have enough funds to provide full and balanced curriculums, full services, well-maintained facilities, adequate computers and other supplies, excellent teachers and small class sizes. In addition to core courses, adequate funding should be provided for physical education, liberal arts, vocational education, shop, music, art and other beneficial courses and activities. Services including counseling, career guidance, nursing and free, nutritious lunches also should be provided.

Fully funding public education also includes providing adequate funding to quickly upgrade the many deteriorating school buildings across the US. As discussed in the Education Funding section, many US public schools are old and dilapidated. Upgrading all US public school buildings to good overall condition would cost about $200 billion.

The dilapidated state of many US public schools truly is tragic. It strongly indicates society's failure to uphold our most important obligation – protecting our children. Forcing children to attend underfunded, old, dilapidated schools tells them that they are not important to us. Instead of giving trillions of dollars of corporate welfare to the small group of wealthy people who control government, we should reallocate it where it belongs – in large part to our children and their education.

The current public education funding structure helps businesses, but degrades society in many ways, including by providing low quality education to low-income students. Refocusing education on the well-being of all children and society in general requires that we fully fund public education.

Fully Fund Preschool and Daycare

Providing publicly-funded daycare and preschool would greatly benefit US children, families and society overall. Many developed countries provide publicly-funded daycare and preschool. For example the UK and France provide publicly-funded preschool for all children over three years old. France also provides inexpensive daycare for infants and toddlers. The business focus of the US government and society causes US citizens to have a weaker social safety net than most other developed countries. Many single and two-parent families in the US cannot afford daycare or preschool. The lack of this public benefit, taken for granted in many other developed countries, increases financial stress and creates other problems for millions of US families.

As with public K-12 education, investing in daycare and preschool is a highly effective use of public funds. For example, children who attend preschool are better prepared for primary school, have lower juvenile delinquency and substance abuse rates, are more likely to graduate high school and go to college, have lower incarceration rates, earn more as adults, have more stable families, and use fewer government services.[655] Preschool prepares children for primary school by teaching them cooperation, attentiveness, politeness and fair play. It gives them experience engaging with peers, adjusting to classrooms, and meeting school expectations. Publicly-funded daycare and preschool help to provide equal opportunity for all children and families. It benefits taxpayers by lowering incarceration, social welfare and other public expenditures. As a result, many business, financial, military and law enforcement groups and leaders support publicly-funded early education.[656]

Opponents of publicly-funded preschool sometimes argue that the academic benefits of preschool decline over time. For example, some studies have shown that children who attend preschool initially perform better academically. But this differential declines after a few years.[657] However, these analyses often ignore the many other benefits of preschool, such as those noted above. While many business and financial leaders support public investment in daycare and preschool, many others oppose nearly any public investment that threatens short-term shareholder returns. Currently, trillions of dollars of public wealth are being provided to wealthy people through corporate welfare ever year. Rather than using taxpayer funds to essentially buy mansions, yachts and luxury cars for billionaires, we should use them to benefit all citizens, for example, by providing publicly-funded daycare and preschool.

Since 1965, the Head Start program has provided early childhood education, health, nutrition and parental involvement services to low-income children and their families. It is one of the longest-running poverty reduction programs in the US. Over 22 million preschool age children have participated in the program. Head Start services usually are provided by nonprofit organizations. But a 1998 law and further changes to the program allowed for-profit companies to participate in Head Start.[658] For-profit companies often face great pressure to increase prices and reduce costs. This frequently leads to reductions in service quality. We should not subject our youngest, most vulnerable children to these forces. Daycare and preschool only should be provided by organizations that are primarily focused on the well-being of children, not the well-being of shareholders.

In the UK and some other developed countries, preschool often is provided by public primary schools. This takes advantage of economies of scale and facilitates the transition from preschool to primary school. In the US, voluntary preschool and possibly daycare could be provided through public primary schools. Whether they are provided this way or through nonprofit organizations, the services should be publicly-funded. This would greatly relieve the financial stress of millions of US families, and greatly benefit the US economy and society.

Hold Charter Schools Accountable

Selective application of accountability shows the hypocritical and paradoxical nature of education reform in the US. As discussed in the Libertarianism and other sections, flawed economic and political systems often force businesses, politicians paid by them and other business allies to oppose actions that benefit society, but threaten shareholder returns. At the same time, businesses and their allies frequently essentially are compelled to support actions that increase shareholder returns, even if they degrade society. This hypocritical and contradictory situation exists with accountability in the education reform movement. Types of accountability that help shareholder returns are supported. But those that threaten returns are opposed.

To illustrate, increasing accountability in public schools helps shareholder returns, and therefore is strongly supported. Standardized tests are used to hold schools and teachers accountable for student test scores. This greatly facilitates privatization of public schools and increased sales of business products and services. However, holding charter schools accountable for meeting the same standards as traditional public schools could severely restrict shareholder returns, and might make the for-profit charter school model untenable. Therefore, holding charter schools accountable in this way often is strongly opposed.

Traditional public schools are required to abide by many standards that strongly benefit children, communities and society overall. For example, traditional public schools must accept all children. They cannot discriminate based on race, family income, physical disabilities, learning disabilities, English language ability, academic performance or most delinquency problems. However, as discussed in the Privatization section, charter schools are allowed to discriminate in many of these areas. They often accept fewer students who are more expensive to educate, such as those with learning or other disabilities. Charter schools also frequently force out students with poor academic performance.

Traditional public schools largely are controlled by and held accountable to local parents and communities. But charter schools frequently are controlled by for-profit companies that are structurally required to put the well-being of shareholders ahead of the well-being of children. Traditional public schools are required to abide by many laws and regulations that protect children and communities, such as union and labor laws. Providing better wages benefits children by attracting more qualified teachers. Charter schools regularly suppress teachers unions, pay lower wages and benefits, and hire inexperienced, minimally trained, transient teachers through TFA.

Traditional public schools effectively are prohibited from using taxpayer funds to pay high executive compensation, other high administrative costs and investor returns. But charter schools routinely use taxpayer funds for these purposes. Traditional public schools often provide full services, such as counseling, health and nutrition. But charter schools frequently do not provide many of the services provided by public schools.

As discussed, most charter schools are being established in low-income communities. The primary goal of charter schools run by for-profit companies is not to improve education quality and help children. It is to provide superior investor returns. These schools often do this by lowering education costs, for example, by using lower paid, less qualified teachers and by forcing children to learn from computers instead of human beings. This focus on cost reduction helps shareholders, but frequently degrades education quality.

These factors illustrate how publicly-funded charter schools are allowed to operate at substantially lower standards than traditional public schools. Charter schools are not held accountable for many standards by which traditional public schools must abide. Why do we hold traditional public schools accountable in many ways, but not publicly-funded charter schools? The answer is obvious. Not holding charter schools accountable helps the shareholder returns of companies that give large amounts of money to politicians. Lack of charter school accountability harms children and society, but enables investors to earn superior returns.

This accountability hypocrisy must end. Taxpayer-funded charter schools should not be allowed to evade the standards and obligations by which traditional public schools must abide. Taxpayer funds should not be used to support schools that are allowed to discriminate. Public funds also should not be used to pay excessive executive compensation and other high administrative costs. Publicly-funded schools should not be controlled by distant corporations. If taxpayers fund schools, local parents and communities should control the schools. Taxpayer funds also should not be used to support schools that are allowed to evade labor and other laws and regulations by which public schools must abide. Perhaps most importantly, taxpayer funds should not be used to support schools that are structurally required to focus primarily on something other than education quality and the well-being of children. The for-profit charter school structure creates frequent conflicts between shareholders and children. In these situations, if companies do not place shareholders ahead of children, they might be taken over or go out of business, or management might be fired.

Public deception has tricked citizens into publicly funding discriminatory, lower quality charter schools that often provide fewer services than public schools. Taxpayer funds should not be used to support substandard, less accountable charter schools. If charter schools wish to receive public funding, they should be held accountable for meeting the same standards as traditional public schools.

Charter school laws have been implemented nearly all states. A report by the Center for Popular Democracy and Integrity in Education (CPDIE) released a report called *Charter School Vulnerabilities To Waste, Fraud and*

Abuse. The study found that "charter operator fraud and mismanagement is endemic in the vast majority of states that have passed charter school laws." It "found fraud, waste and abuse cases totaling over $100 million in losses to taxpayers..." The report noted that charter schools lack the transparency of public schools. As a result, fraud and mismanagement could be much higher than that found in the report. CPDIE noted that the $100 million in taxpayer costs might only be the tip of the iceberg.[659]

There are many problems with charter schools, including discrimination, poor performance and extremely high executive compensation. However, the report focused on one major problem – inadequate oversight. This results partly from the genesis of charter schools. These schools were established to innovate and help public schools. As a result, they were exempted from many regulations. However, charter schools have changed substantially. They frequently are controlled by for-profit companies. Instead of helping public schools, charter schools now often are being used to rapidly shut them down.

The report provided many examples of charter school fraud and mismanagement. These included using public funds illegally for personal gain, illegally using public funds to support other charter operator businesses, mismanagement that puts children in danger, illegally requesting public funds for services not provided, illegally inflating enrollment to boost revenue, and mismanaging public funds and schools. In one case, a charter school CEO embezzled $1.4 million and used it for houses, cars and trips to strip clubs. At the same time, his school lacked funds for supplies, computers and textbooks.[660]

Greater oversight and accountability of charter schools is essential because the mission has changed from helping public schools to competing with them. It is more important to strictly oversee charter schools run by for-profit companies than traditional public schools because the for-profit structure often puts charter schools in fundamental, structurally mandated conflict with the well-being of children. These schools are under constant pressure to increase shareholder returns. This frequently forces them to cut costs and take other actions that degrade education quality and harm children.

The CPDIE report provided a detailed list of suggestions for effectively overseeing charter schools and holding them accountable. It noted that charter schools should be held to the same standards as other schools that receive public funds. Taxpayers have a right to know that their funds are not being stolen or misused. The report recommended that states establish charter school oversight offices that have the power to audit, monitor and initiate criminal prosecution against charter schools. Charter school board members should live near charter schools and be elected at least partly by local parents, teachers and high school students.

It also suggested that critical charter school information, such as financial documents and board meeting minutes, should be made public on websites. Charter school board members should be required to file and make public financial disclosure and conflict of interest reports, as members of traditional school district boards are required to do. Also, vendor or service contracts should not be allowed with any company in which the charter operator or any board member has personal or financial interests. Dealing with affiliates could interfere with competitive bidding and force taxpayers to pay more than is necessary.[661]

As noted, holding charter schools accountable for meeting the same standards as traditional public schools could make many for-profit charter schools untenable. Investors provide funds to charter schools primarily for the purpose of earning superior returns. Charter schools often achieve high returns by being held less accountable than public schools. To protect shareholder returns, many politicians who receive money from charter school companies almost certainly will strongly oppose holding charter schools accountable. But the priority is not protecting the shareholder returns of charter school companies. It should be maximizing the well-being of children and society. As a result, charter schools must be held accountable for meeting the same standards as traditional public schools. We must end the accountability hypocrisy that pervades US education reform.

In many cases, enforcing charter school accountability essentially would mean ending public funding of charter schools. Instead of defunding and degrading public schools by shifting funds to less accountable charter schools, we should improve and fully fund traditional public schools. Using taxpayer funds to pay for two or three sets of schools (i.e. traditional public schools, charter schools, private schools) wastes taxpayer funds by lowering economies of scale. It often creates redundant administrative, facilities and other costs. As discussed, charter schools originally were intended to support and complement traditional public schools, for example, by educating the most problematic or difficult to educate children. In limited cases such as these, it might be appropriate to publicly fund nonprofit charter schools.

Prohibit Public Funding of Religious and other Private Schools

Accountability hypocrisy is even stronger with private schools than with publicly-funded charter schools. Essentially all of the arguments noted above about public funding of less accountable charter schools apply more strongly to private schools. As discussed in the Public Funding of Religion section, religious and other private schools are allowed to discriminate against teachers and students for many reasons. Local parents and communities have even less control over private schools than over publicly-funded charter schools. Private schools often are not required to test students, publish curriculums, or meet many other standards by which public schools must abide. Private schools are held even less accountable than charter schools.

For-profit private schools, such as cyber schools, have the same focus problem as charter schools run by for-profit companies. The primary focus is on benefiting shareholders, not children. This inherent structural conflict between shareholders and children often degrades education quality.

Religious schools pose many problems beyond those noted above for private schools in general. The Founders of the US were strongly against public funding of religion and religious education. The US Constitution prohibits the US government from establishing or favoring a particular religion and from blocking the free exercise of religion. However, through bitterly divided 5-4 Supreme Court decisions, the essentially business-appointed justices on the Supreme Court said that public funds could be used to pay for religious education if the funds were delivered to religious institutions through certain mechanisms, such as vouchers and tax credits. These decisions make a mockery of the US Constitution and the Founders' intentions. Funding mechanisms are distractions and deceptions. Public funds should not be used to pay for religious education under any circumstances.

Religious education frequently suppresses rational, critical thinking. In religious schools, children often are taught that scientifically disproven, irrational religious ideas, such as creationism, are valid, while rational, scientifically proven concepts, such as evolution and climate change, are invalid. Teaching irrational religious dogma, that for example blocks climate change action, helps to protect the shareholder returns of energy and other companies. But protecting shareholder returns should not be the priority or focus of publicly-funded education.

US citizens should not be forced to pay for the teaching of religions that are different than their own. In addition, non-Christian children should not be forced to study the Bible in public schools (unless it is taught as part of comparative religion courses that do not favor any religion). Publicly funding religious schools and requiring children to study the Bible in public schools interfere with citizens' First Amendment right to freely exercise and practice their religion.

Religious school attendance peaked in the 1960s. Publicly funding religious education helps to increase enrollment. Religious education can be beneficial in authoritarian societies, such as the US. In fundamentalist religious schools, young people often are trained to blindly believe dogma, rather than rationally think for themselves. As conditions continue to decline for average citizens in the US, growing public deception will be needed to maintain ongoing theft of the people's wealth and power.

The main public deception is enflaming the war between conservatives and liberals. Training young people to blindly believe dogma rather than think for themselves will make it easier to trick them into hating the other political party. This dumbing down of young people will help to perpetuate authoritarianism and plutocracy in the US. But public funds should not be used to perpetuate the theft of the people's wealth and power, for example, by funding religious education that suppresses rational thought.

In summary, public funding of private schools should be prohibited in part because these schools are not held accountable for meeting the same standards as traditional public schools. In particular, we must obey our Constitution and prohibit all forms of public funding of religious education.

Freedom-Based Education

Maximizing the well-being of children and society requires evolving the current forced education system into a freedom-based approach. This section discusses why a transition to freedom-based education is important and how it could be achieved. As discussed in the Boredom section, the current top-down, classroom model of education is not based on scientific assessments of how children learn most effectively. It is based on history. The current education system is a legacy of the Protestant Reformation and Industrial Age. It was designed to promote indoctrination and obedience training. The competitive learning environment strongly suppresses curiosity and the desire to learn. It causes widespread boredom and psychological problems among children and teenagers.

The historic authoritarian learning model is based on the religious, dogmatic idea that humans are flawed or fallen. According to this view, people are inherently lazy. Without religious or authoritarian guidance, they will waste their lives. The main purpose of education was to break the will or spirit of a child, the way one might break the will of a wild animal. As discussed, these views of children and adults are ignorant and irrational. Like many other dogmatic religious ideas, they are not based on reality. Nothing in nature is inherently flawed. The idea that humans are flawed and lazy, and therefore must be forced to work, is an irrational human creation. It is a fantasy.

Prior to the agricultural revolution, humans lived free, independent, autonomous lives as hunter-gatherers. People were free to do what they wanted. But as humans began to congregate in fixed locations, due to agriculture and the development of cities, authoritarian structures were developed. People often no longer were free to live their own lives. They essentially were controlled by authorities. To survive, people frequently were forced to do things that they did not want to do, such as take jobs that they did not like. Authorities viewing their subjects often would see lack of enthusiasm about work. But this was not because humans were inherently lazy. It was because people were not free to do what interested them and live their own lives.

Religions implicitly colluded with government to develop authoritarian structures that forced people to do what they did not want to do. Promoting the idea that humans were flawed and lazy justified the use of coercive, punitive control policies and mechanisms. Modern education arose from this ignorant, irrational and coercive mindset.

In the book *Free to Learn: Why Unleashing the Instinct to Play Will Make Our Children Happier, More Self-Reliant, and Better Students for Life*, Dr. Peter Gray discusses how current education environments are virtually the exact opposite of those that most effectively promote learning. Extensive research shows that children, teenagers and adults learn most effectively when they are free to explore what interests them and is relevant to their lives. Learning is further promoted in environments that are playful, sociable and noncompetitive.[662]

In his book *The World Until Yesterday: What Can We Learn from Traditional Societies?*, Jared Diamond, PhD, discusses how children learned and were socialized throughout human history.[663] For nearly all of history, humans were hunter-gatherers. Parenting in indigenous societies usually involved abundant nurturing and minimal coercion. Dr. Diamond explained that many hunter-gatherer societies "considered young children to be autonomous individuals whose desires should not be thwarted." This is the opposite view of modern education. As noted, these systems were developed based on the idea that young people are flawed individuals whose unhealthy wills must be thwarted or suppressed. Dr. Diamond concluded that the coercive parenting and education of modern society suppresses traits that we admire.

He said, "Other Westerners and I are struck by the emotional security, self-confidence, curiosity, and autonomy of members of small-scale societies, not only as adults but already as children. We see that people in small-scale societies spend far more time talking to each other than we do, and they spend no time at all on passive entertainment supplied by outsiders, such as television, videogames, and books. We are struck by the precocious development of social skills in their children. These are qualities that most of us admire, and would like to see in our own children, but we discourage development of those qualities by ranking and grading our children and constantly telling them what to do."[664]

As discussed in the Authoritarianism section, an excellent article by Dr. Bruce Levine, called *The More a Society Coerces Its People, the Greater the Chance of Mental Illness*, discusses how widespread coercion in the US and many other countries causes extensive psychological problems.[665] Like Dr. Diamond, Dr. Levine contrasts the coercive nature of modern society with the noncoercive parenting and other aspects of many indigenous societies. He discussed studies which found that mental illness was rare or nonexistent among indigenous societies that had little exposure to Western culture. But as exposure to the coercive Western culture increased, mental illness also increased.[666]

Dr. Levine quoted text from the book *Faery Lands of the South Seas* (1921) that illustrates the noncoercive parenting of indigenous societies. The book states, "There is a fascination in watching these youngsters, brought up without clothes and without restraint... Once they are weaned from their mothers' breasts – which often does not occur until they have reached an age of two and a half or three – the children of the islands are left practically to shift for themselves; there is food in the house, a place to sleep, and a scrap of clothing if the weather be cool – that is the extent of parental responsibility. The child eats when it pleases, sleeps when and where it will, amuses itself with no other resources than its own. As it grows older certain light duties are expected of it – gathering fruit, lending a hand in fishing, cleaning the ground about the house – but the command to work is casually given and casually obeyed. Punishment is scarcely known... [Yet] the brown youngster flourishes with astonishingly little friction – sweet tempered, cheerful, never bored, and seldom quarrelsome."[667]

Doctors Diamond, Levine and Gray point out that, for nearly all of human history, children mainly were raised and educated in highly supportive, noncoercive environments. They largely were free to play and pursue their own interests and desires. These environments strongly promoted the development of the most important qualities needed for success in life – high self-esteem, strong social skills, ability to think for oneself, and empowerment to pursue one's unique interests and passions in life.

As noted, the primary purpose of education should be to benefit society by best preparing children to have successful and satisfying lives. Since the above qualities are the most important requirements for life success, promoting them should be a foundational guiding principle or goal of education redesign efforts. (As discussed in the Clarify Purpose section, another major goal should be to prepare young people to help create and function most effectively in a sustainable and prosperous society.)

In his book *Free to Learn*, Dr. Gray describes an education model that strongly promotes the development of the qualities needed for life success and achieves excellent results, in terms of helping young people to live successful lives. The approach is called Self-Directed Education (SDE). An excellent website (www.AlternativesToSchool.com) provides a detailed description of the SDE process, benefits and results. It also lists many schools that use SDE.[668] The approach is based on the idea that children learn most effectively when they are not forced, coerced or manipulated into learning, for example, with competitive grading and required curriculums.

SDE is a form of freedom-based education. Under these approaches, the natural desire to learn, rather than coercion, is the primary driver of learning. Freedom-based education is based on how humans evolved to learn. Young people are free to choose the focus of their education and study issues to any depth they desire, without being ranked against peers. As noted above, extensive research shows that people learn most effectively when they are free to study issues that they find interesting and relevant to their lives. Freedom-based education is the most effective education approach, in part because it honors the uniqueness of each person. The natural desire to learn is stimulated through freedom, rather than suppressed with coercion.

Children have powerful innate qualities that compel them to learn on their own. These include curiosity, playfulness, sociability, attentiveness to activities around them, the desire to grow up, and the desire to do what older children and adults can do. Children teach themselves to walk, speak and interact with others largely on their own. Their natural desire to learn does not end when they enter school at age five or six. Forced curriculums and grading strongly suppress the desire to learn.[669] As noted in the Boredom section, schools often teach children that learning is work which should be avoided whenever possible.

Forced learning not only inhibits the desire to learn. It inhibits actual learning. Plato said, "Knowledge that is acquired under compulsion obtains no hold on the mind."[670] Education expert Marion Brady suggested that education efficiency would be better measured not by standardized test scores, but rather by what adults recall and use from their education. He estimated that adults only recall about 10 percent of what they learned in high school. Probably the large majority of adults could not pass many of the tests they took in high school.[671]

People often forget most of what they were forced to learn in K-12 education largely because they were not interested in it and the information had no apparent relevance to their lives. Fortunately, students frequently were correct about relevance. The fact that people often forget most of what they learn in K-12 education usually has little to no impact on their ability to survive and succeed in life. This strongly implies that much of the supposedly necessary information forced on young people in K-12 education actually was not necessary for life success.

SDE frequently is used in schools known as democratic schools. In these settings, the natural desire of children and teenagers to learn is the primary driver of learning. Young people are not forced to learn because coercion inhibits learning. Extensive experience shows that the natural desire to learn compels young people to learn all that is necessary to succeed in college and later in life. Under SDE, young people take responsibility for their education. Students ranging in age from four to 18 years old are free to do whatever they want at school, provided that they do not break the rules.

Rules are democratically developed by students and adults. They relate only to keeping the peace and respecting other people, not learning.

Democratic schools provide abundant opportunities for young people to explore and study many different subjects and activities. Courses frequently are offered. But students are not required to take them. Students are not tested or graded because this often inhibits self-motivation, self-esteem and learning. Knowledgeable and caring adults are available as helpers, not judges.[672] Young people freely mix with students of different ages. This substantially enhances learning because younger children learn advanced skills and knowledge from older children. Older children and teenagers learn nurturing skills and gain a sense of their own maturity by interacting with younger children.[673] Education leader Roland Meighan summarized the basis of SDE. He said, "in a democracy, learning by compulsion means indoctrination… only learning by invitation and choice is education."[674]

Benefits of Self-Directed Education

SDE provides many benefits to young people, and by extension, society. One of the most important is greatly enhanced ability to lead a self-directed life. SDE is based on the idea that each person has a right to choose their own path in life, provided that they do not harm anyone else. Each person is in charge of their own life. They are responsible for making the choices that create their life. Everyone has unique interests and deep passions. Identifying them and building one's life around them often is the most important action needed to achieve a successful and satisfying life. Therefore, teaching young people to take responsibility for their lives and make decisions based on their own interests should be one of the most important, if not the most important, outputs or results of education.

Many teachers, parents and schools encourage young people to find and follow their own unique paths in life. But actions speak louder than words. The current education system powerfully implies and teaches that children should not follow their own interests. The system effectively says to children, follow your own interests, except when you are in school. Here in school, your interests do not matter. We will tell you what you must study and learn. If you are not interested in these subjects, too bad. We know what is best for you better than you do.

As discussed below, this may be true in some cases for young children. But it does not justify forcing young people to study material that they find boring and irrelevant. There are far more effective ways to help young people learn what they need to succeed in life. Forcing them to study material that they are not interested in teaches them that their interests do not matter. They learn that they are incompetent or incapable of deciding how to focus and live their lives. These messages are not intended or spoken. Nevertheless, forced education deeply inculcates them in young people.

Forced education has a deadening effect on children and teenagers. It severely impedes their ability to freely choose and follow their own path in life. The Alternatives to School website notes that, "Self-directed eductation greatly increases the probability that the person will be good at making sound, intelligent, self-affirming choices when the stakes are highest. The more practice people get at decision-making, at reading their own minds, feelings, wants and needs when they are young, the more likely they are to grow into mature, sensible, healthy, productive and compassionate adults."[675]

Self-esteem. Enhanced lifelong self-esteem is another major benefit of SDE. As discussed in the Competitive Grading section, ranking and grading young people and forcing them to study subjects in which they have no interest causes many young people to feel inadequate at the most vulnerable and formative time of their lives. Being constantly rated as average or below-average during childhood and teenage years causes many young people to develop lifelong senses of inadequacy. This frequently severely impedes their happiness, success and ability to get along with others. People often spend their lifetimes trying to prove that they are not as stupid as they were made to feel in school. They frequently have difficulty in relationships because they have a constant need to defend their positions and prove they are right.[676]

Forced education compels people to focus on external validation and assessment. It often makes them perfectionists. They excessively try to avoid mistakes. They learned at a young age that making mistakes (i.e. getting low grades) was painful. The low grade was a clear sign that they were a failure, less valuable than those with better grades. In his book *How Children Fail*, John Holt said, "School is a place where children learn to feel stupid."[677] Forced education hobbles young people by disconnecting them from their inner knowledge. Each person knows better than anyone else what is best for them. But forced education teaches young people to not trust their inner guidance. Instead they are trained to seek guidance and validation from external sources.

SDE does the opposite of this. Young people are trained to seek, trust and use their inner guidance and wisdom. They experience vastly more success during childhood and teenage years because they are exploring areas that interest them without being judged for their performance. Validation often comes from knowing that they learned something well, rather than from someone else's opinion of them (i.e. competitive grading). They never are made to feel inadequate by being ranked against peers. Rather than emerging from K-12 education with lifelong senses of inadequacy, young people educated in SDE environments gain lifelong senses of high self-esteem and self-confidence.

Motivation to learn. Enhanced internal motivation and lifelong joy of learning are other benefits of SDE. As discussed in the Competitive Grading section, rewards and punishments such as grades can motivate better performance when tasks are boring. But external assessment and competition substantially lower motivation when tasks are interesting. Forced education and competitive grading reduce the internal motivation to learn. It often makes education boring. It suppresses curiosity and the joy of learning. SDE does the opposite. Allowing young people to guide their own education and focus on subjects and activities that interest them strengthens the internal motivation to learn. Curiosity and the joy of learning are maintained throughout childhood and teenage years, and into adulthood.[678]

Personal responsibility. SDE also strongly increases senses of personal responsibility and self-control. Under SDE, young people take responsibility for their education. This teaches them to focus and control their attention and activities. Under forced education, young people have little control over their education. They are taught to passively do what others tell them to do, even if they have no interest in the activities.

Balanced development. SDE promotes enhanced social, emotional, intellectual and physical development, in part because young people are allowed to engage in unlimited play and other enjoyable activities. All mammals play when young. Humans have more to learn than other mammals, and therefore require more play over more years. During play, young people continuously exercise their imaginations. They also often practice necessary skills, such as reading, writing and using computers.[679]

Creativity. SDE also greatly enhances creativity. Standardized curriculums, on the other hand, substantially restrict it because young people are required to conform to other people's standards. Extensive research shows that rewards and other pressures to be creative stifle creativity. Creativity occurs most frequently and effectively in environments that are playful and noncompetitive.[680] This is exactly the type of environment provided by SDE.

Learning effectiveness. SDE also greatly enhances learning effectiveness. As discussed in the Competitive Grading section, competitive grading stifles learning by shifting the focus from learning to performance. Forcing young people to learn a standardized curriculum at a predetermined pace ignores individual interests and development timing. It substantially lowers learning and the desire to learn. Allowing young people to study what interests them and progress at their own pace greatly enhances learning quality, retention and effectiveness.[681]

Learning opportunities. SDE also provides far greater learning opportunities and ability to study issues in depth. Standardized curriculums severely restrict the number of issues and subjects available for study as well as limit the degree to which each issue can be explored. SDE, on the other hand, offers a nearly unlimited curriculum to young people. They are free to study nearly any issue that interests them (excluding illegal activities) and continue their study to nearly any depth they desire.[682]

Democracy and freedom. A major benefit of SDE taught in democratic schools is that young people learn democracy and freedom through participation in governance. Children vote on rules that govern their schools and serve on juries when rules are broken. They practice free speech, free association and freedom to choose their own activities. By participating in the governance of their schools, young people learn to respect the rights of others and work to help other people be happy and successful. This produces self-confident young people who often have more success and better relationships later in life.[683]

Psychological problems. Another major benefit of SDE is substantial reduction of delinquency, rebelliousness and psychological problems. Forced education produces widespread boredom, alienation and unhappiness among students. Many young people rebel. They act delinquently or defiantly because their needs are not being met and they have no other way of expressing their dissatisfaction.[684] Being forced to study subjects that one is not interested in and being ranked against peers also causes widespread depression, anxiety and inattention. Once again, SDE does the opposite. Young people are not coerced. They are free to pursue their interests in a playful, sociable, nonjudgmental environment. This greatly increases happiness and satisfaction with learning, which in turn greatly reduces delinquency, rebellion and psychological problems.

Bullying. SDE also greatly reduces bullying. Bullying occurs when people are forced into settings where they have no power, such as prisons. Bullying is passed down through the hierarchy in autocratic settings like forced learning environments. However, in noncoercive learning environments, young people are not powerless and helpless. As a result, bullying is rare or nonexistent.[685]

Equal opportunity. SDE also strongly promotes equal opportunity and advancement. Children from low-income families usually have fewer learning opportunities than those from middle-income and wealthier families. As a result, they often come to school knowing less. Frequent failure to perform as well as children who start school knowing more often causes children from low-income families to feel inadequate, and sometimes dropout of school. This strongly suppresses their ability to advance in society. With SDE, young people advance at their own pace. No one is made to feel inadequate. Children and teenagers experience frequent, ongoing learning successes. This empowers them to continue their success beyond school.[686]

Wasted time. As discussed on the Alternatives to School website, one of the most tragic aspects of forced education is wasted time and lost opportunities. Young people spend about 15,000 hours in K-12 education. Much of this time is spent being forced to learn boring material that they quickly forget and do not need later in life. In addition, the forced learning environment degrades self-esteem, social skills, the desire to learn, self-initiative and many other factors that are critical for life success. Imagine the tremendous benefits that would accrue to individuals and society if young people were not forced to learn boring, irrelevant information. Instead, they were allowed to learn information that interested them in an environment that greatly enhances the qualities needed for life success.

Joy. Finally, one of the most important benefits of SDE is joy. Youth is a time when people should fully enjoy life and learning. This teaches young people that life should be joyful, exciting and stimulating. SDE provides this type of joyful, stimulating early life experience. In these empowering environments, the need to escape boredom through drugs and other dangerous activities is much lower. Forced education suppresses joy and deadens the early life experience. Children learn to tolerate tedium and find happiness in escape or distraction. Deadening young people in this way helps business by producing compliant workers who will tolerate tedium. But it severely and tragically dishonors and demeans our children.

The well-being of children and future generations is the most important priority of society (after survival). We have an obligation to give our children wonderful, stimulating early life experiences that best propel them into successful and satisfying lives. Self-directed education does this vastly better than forced education.

Results. Results and research show the effectiveness of SDE. Several studies have shown that students educated in democratic schools using SDE regularly gain admittance to college, including highly selective colleges, and then do well once there. SDE students seeking college admittance routinely study for and take SAT and ACT tests. Follow-up studies also show that young people educated with SDE regularly go on to have successful careers in many fields, including business, medicine, science, arts and skilled trades. Graduates of SDE schools commonly report that they feel well prepared for college, work and life in general due to the strong democratic values, personal responsibility, self-control and zest for learning acquired through their self-directed education.[687]

Several follow-up studies have been conducted on the Sudbury Valley School in Framingham, Massachusetts, one of the oldest democratic SDE schools. Tuition at Sudbury Valley School is about half of that charged at nearby private schools. All children who apply are accepted. About 75 percent of Sudbury Valley graduates pursued higher education and did well in it. Regardless of whether they attended college, as a group, graduates were highly successful in securing employment and prospering in their careers.[688] Another study found that involvement in school government, as occurs at democratic SDE schools, enhances self-esteem, empowerment and motivation to learn.[689]

Concerns about Freedom in Education

People who are unfamiliar with SDE often express concerns about the approach. This is understandable because SDE is very different from how nearly everyone was educated. Standardized curriculum, competitive, classroom education has been the primary model for many generations. As a result, it often is difficult to imagine how SDE might be implemented widely.

Common concerns about SDE include the following. Children will not learn what they need to prosper in life. Children and teenagers do not know what they need to know for life success. Young people will take advantage of the system, for example, by playing video games all day. Abused children, children with learning disabilities and children with other problems will not be able to learn with SDE. Teaching children what they want to know when they want to know it is much harder than teaching all children the same things at the same times. Widespread implementation of a radically different education approach, such as SDE, is not practical. And ending required curriculum education is equivalent to ending education.

Necessary knowledge. When seen from a rational, whole system perspective, many of these concerns are shown to be unfounded. For example, many people believe that young people do not know what they need to know to succeed in life and will not learn these things if they are not forced to learn them. This implies that education experts know better than young people what is needed to succeed in life. Common Core standards are one effort to clarify this supposedly necessary information. However, people forget much of what they learn in K-12 education, perhaps as much as 90 percent. But this usually has little or no impact on their ability to succeed in life. Therefore, much of this supposedly necessary information was not necessary.

Probably the largest logic flaw of the idea that life success requires learning an extensive standardized curriculum is the implication that all children are the same. The idea implies that all children have about the same knowledge needs and learn in about the same way at the same time. This is ridiculous. It obviously is incorrect. Each young person needs different knowledge to most effectively pursue their own unique path to success in life. Also, the optimal learning method and timing varies from person to person.

The idea that all young people should be forced to spend 13 years learning nearly the same standardized curriculum in the same way at the same time is irrational. It ignores wide variations in interests and competencies between individuals. This approach teaches obedience and compels young people to blindly believe prevailing ideas (indoctrination). Questioning prevailing ideas often is punished with low grades. Molding our children into obedient, unthinking automatons is not education. It is child abuse.

There are basic concepts and skills that all young people ideally should learn, such as reading, writing and basic math. Beyond these skills, there are many concepts and subjects that apparently would benefit nearly everyone. For example, citizens are the ultimate leaders in a supposed democracy like the US. Therefore, it often would be useful for young people to learn and understand the principles upon which the US was founded, the intentions of our Founders, the creation of our Constitution, and the structure and functioning of the US government. There also are basic and intermediate ideas in science, writing, psychology, history, computers and several other areas that probably would benefit many young people throughout their lives.

However, there are better ways to teach this material than forcing all young people to learn it in the same way at the same age. Under the SDE approach, classes often are offered that teach this information in a more fun, interesting, practical, hands-on and nonjudgmental manner. Not ranking young people makes learning this material more interesting and enjoyable. Classes can be focused on beginning or intermediate ideas and designed for younger children or older children and teenagers. They also emphasize how material is relevant to young people's current and future lives. In SDE schools, many young people voluntarily attend these types of classes because they are interesting and relevant.

Adults who attended forced education schools might say, I never would have taken many classes if they were not required. But these people usually did not experience freedom-based education. Forced education often is boring and demeaning. As a result, many young people would avoid it if they could. However, freedom-based education is fun, interesting, practical, relevant, hands-on and nonjudgmental. If adults had these options when they were younger, they probably frequently would have chosen to take classes taught on this basis. In general, they probably nearly always would have chosen freedom-based education instead of forced education.

In SDE schools, some young people might choose to not study material that education experts say is important. But this should not be cause for great concern. Empowered young people learn to acquire knowledge when they need it. People can learn necessary information outside of school or later in life. The fact that people forget most of what they learn in K-12 education shows that forced education frequently is not the most effective way to learn supposedly necessary information. Beyond basic skills and knowledge, all young people do not need to learn an extensive standardized curriculum. The only constant in nature at the individual level is diversity. Society is greatly enhanced when people have different skills, interests and competencies. It strongly promotes resilience.

In nature, each plant and animal does what it is guided to do by instinct, DNA or other mechanisms that we do not fully understand. This produces essentially infinite coordination and efficiency. As we evolve human society into sustainable forms and teach young people to follow their hearts or wise inner guidance, there will be someone to do every task and everything will get done, as already occurs in nature. However, humanity will have to evolve through several levels of development before we reach this point. Our demeaning, disempowering education and other systems discourage young people from following their hearts and produce a society where the vast majority of people sacrifice so that small groups of wealthy or powerful people can prosper.

Education experts might say that certain information is necessary for life success. But if young people are not interested in it and do not see the relevance to their lives, they often will forget it. People cannot be forced to remember things. Forcing young people to learn extensive information that they are not interested in often is a waste of time because most of it will be quickly forgotten. Even worse, forced learning degrades the most important qualities needed for life success.

A 7-year-old child might not know what they want to do later in life. But they do know what they want to do in the present moment. It is irrational for experts to discount or invalidate the desired play and activities of children. We must trust the intuitive wisdom of young people more. Allowing them to freely play and choose other activities builds many skills and strengths. As shown in indigenous societies and SDE schools, play, art and other freely chosen activities help to develop imagination, creativity, self-initiative, self-confidence, social skills, mental health and other skills that will be needed for success in life.

Even if the play and freely chosen activities of young children are not directly developing skills and knowledge that might be needed in careers, this largely is irrelevant. There is a vast amount of wasted time in K-12 education. Young people do not need to spend anywhere near 15,000 hours learning the relatively small amount of information that will be retained from K-12 education. Leading education approaches, such as Waldorf, employ more developmentally appropriate learning techniques. Young children do not need do extensive cognitive activities. In earlier grades, children are allowed to engage in extensive play, hands-on learning and outdoor activities. As they get older, more extensive cognitive education occurs. Under this approach, children and teenagers have plenty of time to learn skills and information needed for success in adulthood.

Unfortunately, education reform is pushing early education in the wrong direction. To illustrate, the Common Core standards promote a reading instruction technique for young children known as Close Reading. The approach often involves forcing children as young as six or seven years old to read a nonfiction passage several times, reflect on the meaning of new words, extract key concepts and make inferences based on what they read. This is developmentally inappropriate. At this early age, children usually cannot think at abstract, higher levels. They usually develop this capability at ages 8 to 11 years old. Children often are forced to read information that is too complex or not interesting.[690]

For example, in one close reading exercise, second-grade children were required to read about kidney transplants. Forcing young children to read boring, irrelevant, difficult information makes reading seem like a chore. Establishing an environment where many young children fail in their early reading efforts, for example because they failed to comprehend developmentally inappropriate topics such as organ transplants, will dampen their enthusiasm for reading. Ranking children on forced reading of difficult material greatly reduces the likelihood that children will learn to love reading and become lifelong readers. The far more effective way to build reading competence and lifelong joy of reading is to let young children read interesting, age-appropriate material, as was done before so-called education reform.[691]

One might ask, why would education reform approaches ignore extensive research about how young children learn? The answer partly is that the well-being of children is not the primary focus of privatization and other business-oriented education reform efforts. The primary goal is maximizing the well-being of business. Forcing young children to read standardized, testable material increases sales of business products and services. Making the reading material too difficult for young children to understand increases the failure rate. This could further increase business sales because additional learning materials might be needed to help 'failing' children, such as 7-year-olds who fail to adequately comprehend kidney transplants, even after being forced to read about the procedure several times. Beyond increased business sales, removing joy and freedom from early childhood education suppresses children and makes them more obedient. This benefits business by better preparing young people to work in an authoritarian society.

Valerie Strauss, an experienced early education teacher, described how education reform has degraded early childhood education. She said, "When I first began teaching more than 25 years ago, hands-on exploration, investigation, joy and love of learning characterized the early childhood classroom. I'd describe our current period as a time of testing, data collection, competition and punishment. One would be hard put these days to find joy present in classrooms... The overall effect of these federal and state sponsored programs is the corrosion of teacher morale, the demeaning of teacher authority, a move away from collaborating with teachers, and the creation of an overwhelming and developmentally inappropriate burden imposed on our children."[692]

SDE does not squelch the joy of learning in young people, the way education reform approaches often do. It does not ignore the widely varying development timing of children. Young children are allowed to freely play and progress at their own pace. In freedom-based education environments, it does not matter if some children learn to read or develop other skills later than other children. It is far more important to respect the unique timing and interests of each child. Forcing children to learn at an unnatural rate imposes far greater costs than any potential benefit. In forced education environments, young people who do not keep up with standardized curriculums constantly are made to feel inadequate.

The Alternatives to School website states, "When young people in our culture are granted the freedom and opportunity to educate themselves, outside of the boundaries of traditional school, they generally do so fully and joyfully. Through their everyday engagement with life, and especially through their free play and exploration, they acquire the skills, knowledge and values needed for success in our culture."[693] Young people educated in SDE environments often enter adulthood knowing more than those who were forced to learn. People forget most of what they are forced to learn. However, recall usually is much greater when students freely choose subjects and learning activities.

The Higher Education section discussed how traditional classroom education often is far more effective than online education. This SDE discussion is not meant to denigrate classroom education. SDE often involves nontraditional, hands-on, out-of-classroom learning. But it also frequently involves classroom education. Listening to experts explain information often is the most effective way to learn basic concepts and theoretical material, especially if the explanation is balanced with hands-on, project-based or real-world learning. An enlightened education system would use classroom education when it was the most effective option. But the enlightened, effective classroom environment would be very different from the forced education environment. Information would be presented in an interesting and enjoyable manner. Relevance to students' lives would be explained and emphasized. And students would not be demeaned and discouraged through judgment, ranking and grading.

Process versus content. Process versus content is one of the most important education concepts. Considering this issue helps to show the inaccuracy of the idea that young people will not learn what they need for life success if they are not forced to learn it. People often emphasize the importance of education content. But the most important qualities needed for life success are learned in large part through the education process.

The process of forcing young people to learn a standardized curriculum and ranking them based on performance harms young people in many ways. It often creates lifelong senses of inadequacy and incompetence. It teaches them to seek external validation, rather than trust their own inner guidance. It teaches young people that life is boring. Fun largely occurs outside of school and work. It often harms students who get high test scores by giving them inflated and inaccurate senses of their value in society. It teaches young people who excel in areas outside of standardized curriculums that their unique interests and skills are not valued by society. It inhibits relationships, cooperation and social skills by teaching young people to see peers as obstacles to success. It teaches young people to passively obey authorities, rather than take responsibility and initiative for creating and leading their own lives. And it greatly suppresses or kills the desire to learn. Degrading young people in these ways so that they can learn frequently unnecessary standardized content is not rational.

SDE solves all these problems. It builds young people up rather than tears them down. The SDE process teaches and builds self-esteem, self-confidence, self-initiative and personal responsibility. It teaches young people that their unique interests and skills are valuable and important. The SDE process teaches young people to cooperate and have good relationships. And it teaches them that life is meant to be fun, interesting, stimulating and exciting.

Some people might argue that the benefits of learning the content of a standardized curriculum outweigh the psychological damage caused by forced education. But this position is irrational in some ways. Young people forget most of what they are forced to learn. As a result, the benefits of being forced to learn a standardized curriculum are limited because little actual learning frequently occurs. Also, standardized curriculums assume that all young people have about the same knowledge requirements and development timing. This obviously is incorrect.

An article by Marion Brady discussed in the Boredom section, *Ten Things Wrong with What Kids Learn in School*, explains further problems with the content of standardized curriculums.[694] For example, he points out that, for over 100 years, the main goal of K-12 standardized curriculums was to prepare young people for college. This implies that success without college will be limited. But many young people have no desire or need to go to college, perhaps due to the unique paths they wish to follow in life. Rather than focusing on college admittance, K-12 education should be focused on preparing young people to understand and effectively function in society.

Marion Brady also points out that standardized curriculums are reductionistic. All major aspects of human society are parts of one larger, interconnected whole system. Studying subject areas without showing links to other areas and the whole system makes it difficult or impossible for young people to see how complex issues, such as crime, poverty, political corruption and environmental degradation, could be solved. Providing a whole system perspective makes it easier to understand and remember information. It shows context, relevance and linkages to other areas. This greatly facilitates actual learning and long-term retention of information.

He further points out that standardized curriculums often fail to teach information that is critical for understanding and best navigating modern society, such as differing worldviews or belief systems, public deception by vested interests, and complex moral and ethical issues. Marion Brady also explains that standardized curriculums emphasize information that is easy to test and measure. The emphasis is on what to think, not how to think. Short-term memory retention of facts is easy to measure. But complex qualities of mind, such as how to think critically and analyze information, are much more important for life success.

Another important problem with standardized curriculums is the emphasis on secondhand, rather than first-hand, learning and knowledge. Standardized curriculums force young people to spend nearly all of their time reading and studying concepts (i.e. secondhand learning). There is little time for first-hand or hands-on learning. But most of what people know is learned this way.[695] Play, art, music, shop and other hands-on activities increasingly are seen as less important or unnecessary. Young people are being forced to spend more time sitting in classrooms. They are being isolated from the real world. They are not allowed to learn in the ways that humans evolved to learn. We often say that experience is the best teacher. But forced K-12 education increasingly provides little hands-on learning experience.

There are many ways to teach systems thinking and provide firsthand learning. Marion Brady has developed an outstanding, interdisciplinary course. Intended for middle school students, the course links several different subject areas, including science, social studies and math. Students work in small groups studying the real world, instead of secondhand versions of it in textbooks. They look for patterns and linkages between different areas in society. The course effectively develops important qualities of mind, including critical thinking and analyzing and synthesizing information. During the course, students learn about reality in ways that are far more fun, interesting and relevant than the secondhand learning processes used in traditional, reductionistic courses. The course *Introduction to Systems* can be downloaded for free at www.MarionBrady.com.

Regarding process versus content, the benefits gained from good education process frequently outweigh those of good education content. A young person empowered by freedom-based education will figure out how to get the information needed for life success. But a young person disempowered by forced education often will not have the confidence or motivation needed to pursue true life success, even if they have extensive knowledge.

Given the psychological benefits and costs, SDE clearly is superior to forced education in the process aspect of education. It also often is superior in the content area. SDE students focus on learning information that is interesting and relevant to their lives. As a result, they often have higher retention of information and knowledge that will be critical for life success.

Taking advantage of freedom. Another concern with SDE is that young people will take advantage of the system, for example, by choosing not to study anything or playing video games all day. A large part of this concern probably relates to the false idea that humans are inherently flawed and lazy. They will not do anything productive unless they are forced to do it. As discussed, this is another irrational, incorrect religious idea. Observations of reality show that the opposite is true. Learning is essential for human survival. If humans had not evolved with a strong desire to learn, we would not exist. The lack of interest in learning displayed by many young people does not result from an inherent absence of this desire. It results from the lack of interesting learning opportunities.

Young people in SDE schools could play video games all day if they wanted to do so. But decades of experience with SDE schools shows that this rarely occurs. Instead, young people usually choose to study and learn many things that are interesting and relevant to their lives. This occurs in large part due to the intelligent structure of SDE schools. The schools provide materials and other support needed to learn many issues and subjects, including everything that would be learned under a standardized curriculum. SDE schools provide knowledgeable, caring adults. They help young people to develop the skills and knowledge needed to pursue their unique interests and passions in life.

When switching from forced education to SDE, some students might test their newfound freedom. They might choose to do nothing or play video games for a while to test if adults are serious about letting them pursue whatever interests them. Allowing this could provide an empowering lesson. Young people will learn that what they want matters. They have the freedom and responsibility to direct and create their own lives. As shown in SDE schools, once young people realize that adults are serious about the importance of freedom, they nearly always begin to take advantage of the many interesting learning opportunities all around them. Doing nothing or playing video games all day gets boring after a while, especially when many interesting and fun alternatives are available.

Children with problems. Another SDE concern is that abused children, children with learning disabilities and children with other problems will not learn under SDE. In other words, children with problems often will not voluntarily choose to learn. Therefore, they must be forced to learn. The authoritarian approach being expanded under education reform implies that all children should be forced to learn, even if they do not want to learn. This is an ignorant, heartless and harmful approach to education.

Authoritarianism and education reform are forcing compassion and wisdom out of our schools. Virtually all young people have a natural desire to learn things that interest them. When children do not want to learn, there is a reason for it. With abused children, the reason is obvious. They are frightened and focused on survival, not learning in school. The primary focus of their education is learning how to avoid being abused. In general, lack of interest in learning indicates that there is a problem. The focus should be on compassionately trying to understand what is happening with a child or teenager, and then helping to resolve problems. The authoritarian education reform approach implies that children who do not want to learn are being willful or obstinate. The implied solution is to force them to learn. This is ignorant in the extreme.

One of the main causes of lack of interest in learning is competitive grading and boring, forced standardized curriculums. As discussed in the

Psychiatric Drugs section, in his book *Commonsense Rebellion*, Dr. Bruce Levine cited research which showed that ADHD-diagnosed children performed poorly in learning environments that were boring, repetitive and externally controlled. But when they were allowed to freely choose learning activities which they found interesting, their ADHD symptoms disappeared. The problem was boring, forced education, not inability to focus or other problems in children. This indicates that the solution to lack of interest in learning often is to improve education, not drug or coerce children.

This ADHD research strongly indicates that many young people with problems will do better in SDE environments. The SDE approach honors and respects the uniqueness of each child. This is a form of love and compassion. In our troubled and inequitable society, many children unfortunately are not getting the love and attention that they deserve at home. Expanding their abuse through forced education in school will not heal children. It often will make them worse. SDE provides compassionate, nurturing, respectful learning environments. As a result, SDE often will be the most effective way to educate children with learning difficulties and other problems.

The well-being of young people. Additional SDE concerns relate to the ideas that teaching young people what they want to know when they want to know it would be more difficult than teaching all children the same thing at the same time, implementing a substantially different education approach would be impractical, and ending required curriculum education is equivalent to ending education. From a whole system perspective, the key question is not, why should we do something that is different and difficult? It is, why are we continuing forced education? It achieves poor results in the process and content areas. The process of forcing young people to learn substantially degrades the most important qualities needed for success in life. Content is poorly retained because force is an ineffective way to motivate learning. Humans did not evolve to learn by force.

From a whole system, results-oriented, reality-based perspective, it becomes clear that SDE is vastly superior to forced education in the process area, and frequently superior in content retention. SDE builds young people up. It gives them the psychological qualities needed for life success. It also often results in superior retention of more relevant content because young people freely focus their education on issues and subjects that are interesting and relevant to their lives.

The question of why we continue forced education rather than replace it with a more beneficial approach, such as SDE, can be partly answered by considering the purpose of education. As discussed in the Clarify Purpose section, education follows society. Education largely is structured in ways that benefit society by achieving the goals of society. What gets measured gets managed. Our flawed economic and political systems mainly are focused on economic growth and shareholder returns. We make the myopic and increasingly incorrect assumption that growing the economy enhances the well-being of society. Economic growth largely measures the short-term financial well-being of the small group that own most business assets. While no one intends this, our myopic systems make financial returns to very wealthy people more important than all other issues, including the survival of humanity.

Modern systems have the same basic authoritarian structure as those implemented around the First Agricultural Revolution, although the forms have changed many times. To varying degrees over the past 10,000 years, many citizens were required to sacrifice so that small groups of authoritarian leaders could prosper. Current systems require publicly traded companies to achieve ever-increasing shareholder returns. This frequently is done by extracting wealth from labor and other segments of society.

To achieve this, citizens must be conditioned or misled into tolerating the ongoing theft of their wealth and power. Forced education is a highly effective way to do this. During the psychologically formative years, young people are taught that they are inadequate and must submit to authorities. This produces citizens who will tolerate lifetimes of boring, difficult jobs. Forced education teaches young people to obey authorities and not question injustices in society, such as the ongoing theft of their wealth and power.

The current education system largely is based on the current structure, focus and goals of society. The measured and managed focus of society is on the financial well-being of the small group of wealthy business owners who largely control government. Forced education perfectly complements and supports the suicidal, authoritarian focus of society that largely has existed for millennia.

This illustrates why a whole system approach is necessary to effectively address education and all other major issues in society. Education cannot be substantially improved in isolation. As we evolve economic and political systems, and society overall, into sustainable forms, we also can evolve education into sustainable, more effective forms. Our unfree, coercive schools reflect our unfree, coercive society. As we refocus the economy and society on the well-being of all citizens, we will create systems that produce abundant good jobs and small business ownership opportunities. As a result, people will not be forced to take jobs that they do not like.

As we refocus education on the well-being of all young people, we will create interesting, stimulating education environments. As a result, young people will not be forced to study boring, irrelevant issues. SDE can be an important component of evolving education and other systems into sustainable forms. It will inspire and empower young people to help create and manage a sustainable and truly prosperous society.

Barriers to freedom-based education. Beyond benefits to authoritarian society, there are several barriers to replacing forced education with a more effective approach, such as SDE. For example, many education experts probably sincerely believe that forced education is the best approach. This is understandable because it has been the dominant education model for over 100 years. In addition, many religious and other people probably still believe the incorrect idea that humans are inherently lazy and flawed. As a result, they probably believe that young people will not learn if they are not forced to do so.

Also, education experts often spend their whole careers analyzing and working in current systems. After many years of supporting forced education, it might be difficult to acknowledge that other approaches are more effective. Flawed measurement also can promote forced education. The most important qualities needed for life success are qualitative and difficult to measure. It is much easier to measure short-term memory retention.

Failure to adequately measure and account for the important qualitative benefits of SDE and the substantial qualitative costs of forced education can make forced education appear to be more effective than it actually is.

Beyond myopic measurement, other forms of myopia frequently exist among experts. As noted, as experts dive down into the details of their particular fields, they often lose sight of the big picture. They frequently do not see the larger systems that contain and control education and other subsystems. They frequently fail to see linkages and unintended consequences resulting from myopic theories and approaches.

For example, the industrial age mindset still dominates K-12 education. The focus largely is on standardizing and efficiently processing students, as if they were products in a factory. This approach ignores the fact that each student is an infinitely complex, unique human being. Stamping out the will and uniqueness of each child by forcing them through standardized education mills is unbelievably destructive. When seen from a big picture perspective, this approach to education is unconscionable. But that is the problem. Forced education often is not viewed from a whole system perspective.

An additional factor perpetuating forced education relates to funding. The vast majority of education research has focused on forced education. Relatively little research has been done on SDE and other forms of unforced or freedom-based K-12 and higher education. Research funding from businesses, business-controlled government and business-influenced higher education nearly always is focused on forms of education that help businesses to achieve their structurally mandated objective – maximizing shareholder returns. Forced education greatly benefits business. Large companies and wealthy business owners largely control the US government (through inappropriate influence) and society (through public deception). This can make it difficult to secure funding to study forms of education that benefit society but threaten shareholder returns.

Public deception. Public deception is one of the most important barriers to replacing forced education with more beneficial, freedom-based approaches, such as SDE. Flawed systems compel publicly traded companies to oppose any action that threatens shareholder returns. Forced education, especially in privatized form, greatly benefits business. As a result, education companies, their paid political servants and other business allies often would aggressively oppose replacing privatized forced education with publicly-funded freedom-based education. Admitting that they oppose the transition because it might reduce shareholder returns would not be an effective way to protect returns. As a result, deception or dishonesty frequently would be required. To protect returns, business interests might argue that forced education benefits children and implementing SDE would be difficult, expensive, radical and impractical.

These arguments are deceptive or dishonest for several reasons. For example, forced education benefits young people in the sense that it might be better than no education. But forced education severely degrades young people in many ways and usually produces poor knowledge retention. SDE provides greater benefits while causing none of the degradations of forced education.

Calling SDE impractical, radical, difficult and expensive distracts attention from the most important issue – the well-being of young people. The most important priority and obligation of society (after the survival, but not prosperity, of current generations) is the survival and prosperity of children and future generations. In other words, their well-being takes priority over our well-being. If implementing an empowering, effective education system is difficult and expensive, so be it. We have an obligation to work hard and spend whatever it takes to guarantee the well-being of our children.

Calling SDE radical or impractical is pejorative and biased. The goal often appears to be turning citizens against SDE. To protect shareholders, things that threaten returns frequently are deceptively labeled 'impractical' or 'radical'. Calling SDE impractical essentially is saying that we cannot do what is best for our children because it would be too difficult, inconvenient or expensive. Calling SDE radical implies that we should not make substantial changes when necessary to ensure the well-being of our children.

The idea that implementing SDE will be expensive also is deceptive. As noted, tuition at one of the longest-running SDE schools (Sudbury

Valley School) is about 50 percent lower than surrounding private schools. The Marion Brady article noted above explains that required curriculum education is expensive and wasteful. The approach often requires purchasing expensive technologies and other business products and services. Reductionism is expensive because opportunities to efficiently link and teach multiple subjects in an integrated manner are not utilized. Additional expensive aspects of forced education include high administrative costs, unnecessary testing and test preparation, grade retention caused by inappropriate curriculums, and unreasonable pass-fail cutoff scores on standardized tests.[696] In many cases, SDE would be substantially less expensive than forced education, while also providing far greater benefits.

Transition to Freedom-Based Education

Redesigning and implementing a more effective education system almost certainly will require a collaborative, multi-stakeholder, whole system-focused approach. This section discussed the many problems caused by forced education and the many benefits of freedom-based education. However, families and communities probably should consider their options and decide how they would like to educate their children. If families, communities and society overall decide that freedom-based education is the most appropriate and beneficial in our supposedly free society, we may choose to evolve forced education into an approach like SDE taught in democratic schools.

As with other system change efforts, evolving forced education into SDE would require a practical, whole system transition strategy. Immediately converting forced education schools to SDE probably would not be practical or possible in many cases. Therefore, a phased transition might be most effective. However, the pace of transition should be based on what maximizes the well-being of young people and society, not what maximizes the well-being of business. To protect shareholder returns, businesses and their allies might attempt to slow or block the transition. They probably would use many of the deception techniques described in the Misleading the Public Section.

For example, businesses and their paid political servants might employ the Research Instead of Action deception technique. This involves acknowledging that an approach such as SDE might have merit. But extensive research should be conducted before widely implementing the approach. This is a politically correct or deceptive way of saying yes and meaning no. Common sense alone is enough to show the extensive harm caused by forced education and great benefits of freedom-based education. Decades of SDE experience prove the effectiveness of the approach. Further research would be beneficial. But this should occur during the transition, not be used as an excuse to delay or block it.

Evolving and improving forced education requires assessing the various coercive components of forced education. Forced education includes forced school attendance, forced standardized curriculums and forced competitive grading. As discussed in the Competitive Grading section, competitive grading definitely is not needed to educate children well. It probably is impossible to maximize the learning and well-being of all children if competitive grading is used. Therefore, eliminating competitive grading probably should be one of the first actions during a transition to freedom-based education.

Regarding mandatory standardized curriculums, decades of SDE experience show that forced curriculums are not necessary. They severely degrade the most important qualities needed for success in life. Education reform is increasing standardization with Common Core and other efforts. Standardizing our unique young people is irrational and destructive. The trend toward standardization should be quickly reversed. Standardized required courses should be reduced and elective courses increased.

Elective courses can be provided which teach information that education experts say is important for life success. Many students will voluntarily take these courses if the material is presented in an interesting and nonjudgmental manner and if relevance to students' lives is clearly explained. However, this approach requires more trust. We should trust young people to do the right thing. They might make mistakes, for example, by not taking a class that would have been beneficial later in life. But there is value in trial and error. Young people are exercising and strengthening their discernment and ability to guide their lives successfully. Process is more important than content. If we empower young people with a freedom-based education process, they will figure out how to get any knowledge they need to succeed in life.

Regarding forcing young people to attend school, this is a more complex issue. For their own safety, children, especially young children, sometimes cannot be allowed to do whatever they want. For example, young children should not be allowed to play in busy streets, even if they want to. In addition, our flawed economic system that concentrates wealth at the top of society requires many average citizens to work long, hard, boring jobs to survive. Many parents cannot afford to stay home, raise their children, and perhaps homeschool them. As a result, young people, especially young children, often need places to go during the workday.

During the transition to freedom-based education, school attendance might remain mandatory, at least until larger systems are evolved into forms that provide freedom and equality for all citizens and end the theft of the public's wealth and power. However, mandatory school attendance should be handled on a case-by-case basis with more compassion and wisdom. For example, if children do not want to attend school, parents and school authorities might assess why, help to resolve potential problems, and consider alternatives, such as outdoor schools or apprenticeships.

Enlightened, wise learning approaches, such as Waldorf, Montessori, Reggio Emilia and project-based learning, could be highly effective in facilitating the transition to SDE. Children have strong natural desires to learn. Forced learning only is required when education is boring, judgmental and apparently irrelevant to one's life. Waldorf and other leading approaches motivate learning more effectively. Schools based on these approaches often provide more interesting and enjoyable learning opportunities than traditional public and private schools. Expanding the use of these enlightened learning approaches throughout the education system will reduce the need to force young people to learn. They frequently will voluntarily take elective classes based on these approaches because the classes are fun and interesting and satisfy the natural desire to learn.

In general, structuring classes and other learning opportunities in ways that are fun, interesting, nonjudgmental and relevant to students' lives will encourage (not force) many young people to take these classes. As students, teachers, parents and school administrators get used to some freedom in schools, freedom can be increased, for example, by shifting more courses from required to elective.

Waldorf and other leading approaches generally provide more balanced and effective education, in terms of promoting the development of psychological qualities and intellectual capabilities needed for life success. Schools based on these approaches also often provide students with more freedom to guide their education. However, even leading education approaches such as Waldorf have required curriculums and learning agendas that students are expected to follow. Adults effectively are telling young people what to study and do. As society evolves in ways that eliminate coercion and embrace true freedom for all citizens, these leading approaches also can be evolved to include more freedom-based learning.

Beyond converting more courses from required to elective and more widely implementing leading education approaches such as Waldorf in public schools, the Boredom section discussed several other actions that would make education more interesting, useful and relevant to students' lives. These include reversing the growing emphasis on core courses. Instead schools should provide more balanced and stimulating education by increasing physical education, liberal arts, vocational classes, art, music, shop, hands-on learning, and out of school activities, such as learning in nature, working on farms and community service.

A major aspect of improving education involves shifting the emphasis from what is convenient for adults to what maximizes the learning and well-being of young people. As discussed in the Boredom section, schools often appear to be used as babysitters. Young people are sequestered away in sterile buildings for vastly more time than is necessary to learn the relatively small amount of information that will be recalled from forced K-12 education. Forcing young people to spend much of their lives (15,000 hours over 13 years) sitting still and listening to adults talk to them is unintentionally abusive and harmful. Humans did not evolve to learn this way. This approach largely teaches obedience, indoctrination and subordination of one's unique interests. Redesigning education requires restructuring schools and other learning environments in ways that empower young people and promote actual learning.

In summary, a nearly complete redesign of education is needed to maximize the well-being of children and society. Forced education greatly benefits business and the small group of wealthy citizens who largely control government. But it greatly harms citizens and society. Young people who receive the lowest grades in school often have problems later in life. They frequently are obese, addicted, unemployed, depressed or incarcerated. For nearly all of their childhood and teenage years, they were powerfully reminded that they were flawed and inadequate. Our society told them that they were the least important people, the under-achievers. Parents were made to think that their beautiful children were flawed and would not amount to much in life. These so-called under-achievers were brilliant in certain areas, as all people are. But forced, competitive education effectively told them that their unique interests, skills and competencies were unimportant and nearly worthless.

Imagine how these people might have turned out if they had been educated in environments that did not constantly rank them against peers and allowed them to explore and develop their own interests and competencies. Imagine how much better our society would be if people were not frequently trying to prove that they were not as stupid as they were made to feel during their forced K-12 education.

Schools are like jails. Young people are forced to attend and do things they often do not want to do. Around the world, forced education remains the dominant model. Probably nearly everyone takes it for granted and assumes it is the best approach. But a whole system perspective shows that it is far from the best approach. Children born into slavery adapted to their enslavement. They had no choice. Our children are like slave children. They have no choice. They must submit to forced education. We adapt to this approach because we have no choice or freedom. Forced education trains us to accept authoritarianism and plutocracy.

Forced education is unintentionally harmful, like hitting children. Parents have been hitting children for millennia. As discussed in the Hitting Children section, we are not allowed to hit anyone in society, except those who are the smallest, weakest, most powerless and defenseless, most likely to be psychologically harmed by hitting, least likely to understand why they are being hit, and the ones we say we love the most. Parents often hit children because they think it helps them. But nearly all research shows that physical punishment provides no benefit beyond short-term compliance. Instead, it often causes severe long-term psychological harm.

The same situation exists with forced education. It has existed for a long-time. We often assume that forced education is beneficial. But like physical punishment, it severely harms our children. Hitting and forced education train young people to fear and obey authorities. It creates a cowering, compliant population that can be easily misled and abused by authorities.

Forced education is like child abuse because it trains children to accept less from life. Abused children often tolerate suboptimal, abusive lives. Their early abuse frequently caused them to believe on a deep level that abuse is all they deserve. All children should be honored and respected. This will teach them that they deserve to be treated well. They will not accept less from life. Forced education dishonors and disrespects young people. It often teaches them that their unique interests and passions are irrelevant or bad. Not allowing young people to pursue their safe, legal interests teaches them to accept this abuse and coercion throughout life. It conditions them to tolerate being controlled by authorities and forced to do something they do not want to do for the rest of their lives.

It is time to end this madness. Some people argue that ending forced, standardized curriculum education is equivalent to ending education. This is incorrect. Replacing forced education with freedom-based education means ending indoctrination and obedience training and beginning true, empowering, vastly more effective education.

Forced education is incompatible with a free society. Our Constitution says we are free. We believe we have freedom. But we take away the freedom of young people for 13 of the most important and formative years of their lives. This is not freedom. We tell young people that they are free. But then we teach them with our actions that they are not free. Actions speak louder than words. Forced education has no place in a free society.

Eliminate Competitive Grading

As discussed above, ending competitive grading is an important component of replacing forced education with freedom-based education. However, regardless of the timing of implementing freedom-based education, competitive grading should be reduced or eliminated as quickly as possible. It strongly degrades the most important qualities needed for success in life, including self-esteem, social skills and the motivation to learn. With competitive grading, young people are ranked on standards that someone else said were important. This ignores the unique interests and competencies of each person. All people are equally valuable and important. Everyone deserves a fulfilling and successful life. But competitive grading falsely inflates the value of some people and unfairly degrades the value of others.

Competitive grading mostly measures interest, not competence. People often do well in certain subjects because they find them interesting. Interest makes it much easier to study and learn the subjects. Those with little interest in core subjects often have difficulty studying the subjects, not because they lack intelligence, but rather because it is difficult to study something that one finds boring and irrelevant. Our standardized education system implies that those who do well on core subjects are more valuable and competent. Those who do not do well implicitly are less valuable. This is unfair and inaccurate because poor performance probably often results mainly from lack of interest. Young people with low grades frequently are not being given the chance to study and excel in areas they find interesting.

Competitive grading measures performance on content that is irrelevant to many young people and often is forgotten quickly. The process degrades the most important qualities needed for success in life. This system is irrational (to say the least). As discussed in the Competitive Grading section, there are far more effective and accurate ways to assess student performance. One of the most important is to rank students against themselves, not others. This helps teachers and students to ensure learning is occurring. That should be the only purpose of assessment. Ranking students against each other harms them, but helps businesses, for example, by making it easier to identify potential employees. However, the purpose of education is to help young people, not businesses, colleges or other organizations. These groups can assess applicants through interviews and other means. Grades from schools are not needed.

Ending competitive grading will greatly enhance learning by improving teacher-student relationships. Competitive grading creates inherently adversarial relationships between teachers and students, regardless of the intentions or quality of teachers. Eliminating competitive grading transforms teachers from judges to learning allies.

A key element of improving assessment is replacing competitive grading with qualitative assessments. Competitive grading not only fails to measure the most important aspects of education, it degrades them. Qualitative assessments by experienced professional teachers can measure the essential qualitative aspects of education as well as gauge knowledge retention and learning progress.

Competitive grading dishonors and demeans many young people by ignoring their unique interests and competencies. Instead, young people are ranked against arbitrary standards that often are irrelevant to the unique paths they will follow in life. This authoritarian tool should be eliminated as quickly as possible. We should not treat children and teenagers like standardized machines. They are unique individuals who deserve to be honored and respected. No one intends to harm young people with competitive grading. Once again, the harm results from myopia. Whole system thinking shows the extremely destructive nature of competitive grading. It is time to end this unintentionally destructive practice.

Improve Measurement and Accountability

Effective measurement and accountability are critical for implementing an outstanding education system. Measurement and accountability follow purpose and structure. The optimal measurement and accountability systems cannot be developed until the purpose and optimal structure of education are clarified. Once this occurs, measurement points can be selected. This ensures that measurement is focused on achieving the goals of education. With goals, structure and measurement points clarified, people responsible for achieving these goals can be identified and held accountable.

A main purpose or goal of education is to benefit society by best preparing young people to achieve successful and satisfying lives. The most important qualities needed to achieve successful lives include high self-esteem, strong social skills, ability to think for oneself, and empowerment to pursue one's unique interests and passions in life. Knowledge also is important. But these qualities are more important than virtually any knowledge that students might learn from standardized curriculums. Empowered young people will figure out how to get any knowledge they need to succeed in life.

With the goals of education established, the optimal structure can be identified. Each person is different. They have different interests, competencies and development timing. Maximizing the well-being and life success of each young person largely involves helping them to identify their unique interests and passions, and then built their lives around them. Ranking students against each other does not facilitate this goal. It strongly blocks it and greatly harms young people. Since the goal of education is to help young people succeed, anything that subverts this goal, such as competitive grading and standardized testing, would be prohibited.

The optimal structure of education is one that maximizes the ability of young people to succeed in life. Education should create a vessel, so to speak, within which the most important qualities needed for life success are strongly developed and each young person is encouraged to reach their fullest potential by developing their unique interests and competencies. This optimal structure indicates the need for two broad types of measurement – individual student assessment and assessment of the education environment (or vessel).

Students would not be ranked against each other because each student is unique. Ranking degrades the most important qualities needed for success in life for the purpose of measuring retention of knowledge that often is irrelevant to life success. Major factors are degraded for the purpose of measuring minor, frequently irrelevant factors. This is highly irrational and counterproductive.

To avoid the degradation of ranking, students would be assessed only against their own progress. Teachers could provide qualitative assessments of key psychological qualities, knowledge retention and learning progress. This means that measurement of students largely would be subjective, qualitative, fluid and nonbinding. This is the optimal approach because humans are infinitely complex and unique. It is difficult or impossible to render humans down to a few numbers without causing substantial harm (because more important factors that often cannot be quantified are degraded by ranking students).

Regarding measurement of the education environment, while the optimal student measurement is qualitative, the optimal education environment measurement largely is quantitative. There are several critical quantifiable aspects of the education environment that should be measured and enforced through strict accountability. Aspects of the education environment that maximize the well-being of students include providing excellent teachers, full funding of public schools, small class sizes, balanced curriculums, and prohibition of discrimination.

Measurement systems should focus on ensuring that these and other critical education environment factors are provided. For example, the system should require highly trained, committed teachers. Minimally trained, uncommitted teachers, such as those provided by TFA to schools in low-income communities, should be prohibited. Overall, virtually all quantitative measurement in the education area should relate to the quality of the education environment. Student assessments should be noncompetitive and largely qualitative.

Once the optimal measurement strategy is clarified, effective accountability systems can be developed and implemented. We the People ultimately are responsible for ensuring that our children and teenagers are educated well. Politicians and government are responsible for implementing our desire to provide empowering, optimal education to young people. Therefore, we must hold politicians and government strictly accountable for providing everything necessary for high-quality education. Laws should be established that guarantee optimal learning environments by requiring full funding of public schools, small class sizes, the absence of discrimination, balanced, largely elective curriculums, and well trained, excellent teachers.

Accountability mechanisms should be established for politicians. Any politician who fails to uphold their duty to young citizens, for example by blocking the requirements for excellent education, should be held accountable. This could occur through public disclosure and other mechanisms. We the People must not tolerate elected representatives who put the interests of campaign donors or anything else ahead of children. Politicians ultimately will be held accountable during elections. But we should have strong and clear disclosure and public awareness mechanisms that severely restrict the ability of businesses and corrupted politicians to mislead the public about the education of our children.

In addition to holding politicians and government accountable, schools, school administrators and teachers should be held accountable. As discussed above, charter and private schools that receive public funding should be held accountable for meeting the same standards as traditional public schools. Taxpayer funds should not be used to support schools that are sectarian, allowed to discriminate, controlled by distant corporations instead of local parents and communities, allowed to evade laws and regulations by which traditional public schools must abide, allowed to pay high executive compensation and other high administrative costs, and structurally required to focus on something other than the well-being and education of young people.

Charter and private schools run by for-profit companies often face great pressure to continuously increase prices and/or lower costs so that shareholder returns can grow forever. Under this structure, it probably is impossible to maximize the well-being of young people, especially over the longer-term. Holding charter and private schools accountable for meeting the same standards as traditional public schools probably often means that these schools no longer would receive public funds. In cases where charter and private schools could not survive without public funding, taxpayers might offer to buy these schools out and convert them to traditional public schools, but only when doing so would be less expensive than building new public schools or shifting children to existing local public schools.

School administrators should be held accountable for doing everything in their power to ensure that optimal education environments are provided for young people. Their ability to do this could be restricted if politicians do not provide adequate funding and other resources. Through funding, laws and other mechanisms, politicians largely control the quality of the education environment. That is why the ultimate, most strictly enforced accountability in the education area should be focused on politicians and government in general. (Holding teachers accountable is discussed in the following section.)

In summary, the primary focus of measurement and accountability in the education area should be on ensuring that optimal education environments are provided. Politicians and other parties responsible for providing these environments should be held strictly accountable. Measurement of individual student performance should be qualitative and not strictly enforced. Students only should be held accountable for progress against their own inner goals. No one knows these goals better than individual students. Students have a right to change their goals and preferences at any time. Therefore, there should be no strict measurement of student performance. The education focus should be on providing compassionate, nonjudgmental support and encouragement that help students to achieve their unique goals in life.

This approach is nearly the exact opposite of current measurement and accountability systems. Students essentially are held accountable (through competitive grading) for meeting generalized standards that largely ignore their unique interests and competencies. This severely degrades young people. At the same time, business-influenced politicians are not being held accountable for the substantial degradation caused by education reform.

This is the expected outcome of our flawed systems. Business-controlled government does not intend to harm young people. But when politicians accept money and other inappropriate influence from businesses, they become business servants, instead of public servants. Their primary goal becomes helping large companies to achieve ever-increasing shareholder returns. As a result, education reform policies are implemented that achieve this, while unintentionally harming young people. Standardized testing creates many opportunities for large companies to increase shareholder returns. It facilitates running schools like businesses.

But the goal of education should not be to help businesses make more money. Business essentially is a simple mechanical process involving revenues, costs and profits. It is a tool that can help society in many areas, if it is structured and managed well. But businesses in their current forms largely are too simplistic to effectively deal with the infinitely complex process of educating a human being. (The people running businesses are not simplistic. They often are among the brightest people in society. But the publicly traded corporate structure is grossly flawed. It often forces bright, well-meaning business leaders to put financial returns to wealthy people ahead of everything else, including children and the survival of humanity. These myopic systems frequently force bright people to act harmfully.) Once again, it is imperative that we end business control of education and refocus it on the well-being of young people. Effective measurement and accountability systems can ensure that this occurs.

Honor and Empower Teachers

Caring for our children, in large part by educating them well, is the most important obligation of society. This makes teaching one of the most important jobs, if not the most important job, in society. In many countries that lead the world in education, teaching is seen as a high status job, comparable to being a lawyer or doctor. Providing high status and good pay and benefits enables education leaders to attract excellent teachers who provide outstanding education to young people. Teaching used to be a high status, well-compensated job in the US when we were a world leader in education. But as discussed in the Degrading the Teaching Profession and Teach For America sections, education reform has severely degraded teaching in the US.

Humans have an innate desire to love and care for children. In the right environment (i.e. one that is primarily focused on benefiting children instead of shareholders), teaching is one of the most joyous and fulfilling professions. Many talented young adults would be attracted to the teaching profession if it had not been so severely degraded by education reform. Like for-profit healthcare, the focus of for-profit education is on maximizing shareholder returns, not the well-being of young people. To achieve this, for-profit education often faces great pressure to continuously reduce costs, such as teachers' salaries and benefits. Anything that interferes with ever-increasing shareholder returns, such as teachers unions, must be suppressed.

Business-driven education reform has greatly reduced joy in the classroom. Standardized testing and the increased focus on core courses have made classrooms more boring for teachers and students. These degradations show the suicidal nature of our flawed systems. The requirement to put shareholder returns before all else has and inevitably will continue to degrade the teaching profession, teachers unions, joy in education, and most importantly, our children.

It is time to end business-driven degradation under the deceptive term education reform. Reform implies improvement. The last 40 years of changes in the education area have been driven mainly by business influence of government. These changes largely benefited business at the expense of teachers and children. Using the term education reform to describe the past 40 years of education changes in the US is an insult to the word reform.

It is time to start acting like we care about our children, instead of saying we care, and then taking actions that harm children, such as cutting funding for public education and teachers. Fulfilling our paramount obligation to protect and care for our children requires that we fully fund public education. A major component of this is ensuring that teacher salaries and benefits are funded at a level that reflects the high status of teaching in society. Nothing is more important than our children. This should be reflected in the salaries and benefits of those who teach and care for them during most of their waking lives.

Accountability, including accountability of teachers, is important in education. But accountability has been deceptively used to help shareholders by degrading the teaching profession. As discussed, standardized tests were used to create a false crisis in education. These tests ignored the main causes of poor academic performance (primarily poverty). Teachers are held responsible for factors over which they have no control (i.e. factors outside of school that cause the majority of poor academic performance).

Holding teachers responsible for students' standardized test scores greatly facilitated privatizing public schools, weakening teachers unions, and reducing teacher pay and benefits. When seen from a whole system perspective, holding teachers responsible in this way is irrational. Among students, the system degrades the most important qualities needed for success in life. Among teachers, using standardized test scores to justify lowering teacher pay and benefits degrades the profession that is responsible for educating our children.

Accountability of teachers can and should be vastly improved. The optimal accountability system cannot be defined until the system it seeks to measure and control is clarified. In other words, before deciding how to hold teachers accountable, we must define the optimal or preferred teaching environment and methods. Once this is clear, metrics can be selected and teachers can be held accountable for performance.

As discussed above, the optimal teaching or education environment is one that strongly promotes the development of the most important qualities needed for success in life as well as encourages young people to identify and pursue their unique interests and passions. The optimal teaching method varies from teacher to teacher and student to student. Therefore, teachers must have the flexibility and freedom to teach in the ways that most effectively utilize their unique skills and most effectively serve their unique students.

Another critical aspect of the optimal teaching environment is promoting joy and the desire to learn. As discussed in the Implement Freedom-Based Education section, eliminating competitive grading and standardized curriculums are the most important factors needed to foster the desire to learn. However, providing excellent, committed teachers also is key to promoting the joy of learning.

Small class sizes are another critical aspect of the optimal learning environment. Many studies have shown that the presence of at least one caring adult in a child's or teenager's life can make the difference between success and failure.[697] Small class sizes enable teachers to form supportive relationships with students. As discussed in the Degrading the Teaching Profession section, teaching is as much an art as a science. Effective teachers require compassion and wisdom as much or more than intellectual competence. Children are human beings, not downloadable computers. Many factors affect the quality of young people's lives and their ability to learn.

For example, the brightest child in a class might be failing due to problems at home or other issues. Teachers must have the time and ability to get to know students beyond their test scores. This is particularly important for young people who are not getting the love and attention they deserve at home. One compassionate adult paying attention to a troubled young person can make all the difference. Wise teachers can turn a young person away from a life of crime and failure toward a productive and successful life. But teachers cannot do this if there are 40 or more students in their classes. They also cannot do it when education reform shifts the focus of teaching from compassionately helping each unique child to teaching and grading standardized material.

The most important skills needed for life success largely are psychological. This applies to students and teachers. The optimal education environment encourages the development and expression of teachers' compassion and wisdom. The wise teacher reaches the hearts of students. This is the most powerful and effective aspect of teaching. The young person sees their goodness and potential reflected in the eyes of a compassionate and supportive teacher. This touches the hearts of young people and inspires them to reach their fullest potential.

In summary, key aspects of teaching effectiveness include promoting critical skills needed for success in life, helping students to progress in their unique areas of interest, promoting the joy of learning, and using compassion and wisdom to help each student achieve their fullest potential in life. These are highly complex, largely qualitative factors. As a result, it is not possible to accurately render teacher effectiveness down to a few numbers. The optimal teacher accountability approach is similar to that employed by world leaders, such as Finland. As noted, in Finland, rigorous master's level training and certification are required for teachers. However, once trained, teachers are given much greater flexibility to teach in ways they believe are most effective. The wisdom of this approach is indicated by Finland's world leading results.

Teachers should be periodically assessed, for example, to ensure that students are progressing toward their unique learning goals. Also, assessment should be done to ensure that teachers are promoting the development of critical qualities in students (e.g. self-esteem, social skills, critical thinking skills). Student and parent reviews of teachers also could be used to determine if teachers are creating stimulating and effective learning environments. These and other types of reviews could be used to ensure that teachers are doing their jobs well, and hold them accountable if they are not.

From the perspective of maximizing the well-being of young people, the current teacher accountability system is grossly flawed and counterproductive (although, from the perspective of maximizing the well-being of business, it is highly effective). Nevertheless, accountability advocates correctly point out that there are some bad teachers who should be encouraged to improve or leave the teaching profession.

Probably nearly all adults can remember at least some K-12 teachers who seemed to only be going through the motions. Enthusiasm for teaching was lacking. This often made their classes boring. Attractive pay, benefits and job security probably attracted some people who wanted a good job, but were not interested in teaching. They probably thought of teaching as a civil service job where they put in their time, and then retire with good pensions. This probably is fine in some fields, but not teaching. The obligation to educate children and teenagers well means that we should not tolerate teachers who lack enthusiasm for teaching.

By severely degrading the teaching profession, so-called education reform probably has reduced this problem. People seeking good, secure jobs often avoid teaching. Degrading the teaching profession might force out ineffective teachers, or prevent them from entering the profession in the first place. But it also forces out excellent teachers and prevents talented young people from entering the profession. As the degradations of education reform are reversed and the teaching profession is made attractive once again, prospective teachers should be screened well. Only people with a true passion for teaching and helping young people should be hired. Those primarily seeking a good paycheck should be encouraged to look elsewhere.

However, the requirement for enthusiastic teachers should be implemented with compassion and wisdom. Teachers sometimes get burned out by the competitive, boring, disempowering, standardized learning environments implemented under education reform. Every effort should be made to help these once passionate teachers regain their enthusiasm for teaching. As noted, teachers often should be given time off, perhaps to take a sabbatical. The most important action needed to restore enthusiasm for teaching is to reverse the degradations of education reform. This includes greatly reducing the use of standardized tests, providing attractive teacher pay and benefits, strengthening teachers unions, and prohibiting the use of minimally-trained, weakly-certified, inexperienced, uncommitted quasi-teachers, such as those provided by TFA.

In terms of overall accountability in the education area, the primary accountability should be focused on politicians. They are responsible for guaranteeing the existence of outstanding, effective education environments. As part of our commitment to outstanding education, we should reestablish the status, honor, dignity and respect of the teaching profession. This will attract the most talented people for the most important job in society – teaching our children.

Like students, teachers are infinitely complex human beings. They cannot be rendered down to a few numbers. We can assess their effectiveness and hold them accountable through more qualitative means, such as those discussed above. However, the dominant theme of education for teachers and students should be compassion and wisdom. In the same way that we should honor the uniqueness of each student, we also should honor the uniqueness of each teacher. This will empower them to reach their fullest potential. This in turn will maximize the well-being of young people.

As noted, most people probably can remember at least a few boring K-12 teachers who did not seem interested in teaching young people. Many of these teachers began their careers with a passion for teaching. But competitive grading and standardized curriculums ignore the uniqueness of each teacher and student. Over time, this ignorant education environment often saps the enthusiasm for teaching away from teachers and suppresses the desire to learn in students.

However, most people also probably can remember a few shining stars from their K-12 education. In spite of the boring, standardized, competitive education environment, some teachers made their classes fun and interesting. It was obvious to young people that these teachers enjoyed teaching. Students could sense the concern, and even love, for young people emanating from these excellent teachers. These wise and compassionate teachers often provided the attention and words of encouragement that made a huge difference in many people's lives.

Young people, especially young children, are highly vulnerable and open. Their personalities and life expectations are forming. We must ensure that young people receive only positive, empowering, life-enhancing messages from the education system. Replacing forced education with freedom-based education will end the inadequacy and other negative lessons taught by current systems. Wise, compassionate teaching is another critical component. To empower young people, we must first empower teachers by reestablishing the honor, respect and financial attractiveness of the teaching profession.

Refocus Online Education

As discussed in the Expanding Online Education section, the trend toward online K-12 and higher education mirrors the overall focus of education reform in the US. Replacing traditional classroom education with online education provides large benefits to businesses. But it frequently harms students by degrading education quality in many ways. (Online education includes humans and computers teaching online.)

Online education enables large reductions in public education funding by facilitating the firing of teachers and elimination of more expensive classroom education. Reducing funding for social welfare programs, such as public education, frees up more public funds for corporate welfare. By cutting funding for public education, politicians who accept money and other influence from businesses can help their benefactors to achieve ever-increasing shareholder returns. Also, online education provides very large data collection and revenue-generating opportunities for businesses.

Students are human beings. They usually cannot be taught effectively by machines. The psychological, social and emotional components of K-12 education often are far more important than knowledge retention. Important qualities, such as social skills and self-esteem, are gained far more effectively by interacting face-to-face with human teachers and students, instead of computers. Also, in today's online world, the most important learning involves teaching young people how to think, not what to think. Classroom education is far more effective than online education at teaching critical thinking, qualitative analysis and other higher qualities of mind.

By focusing mainly on data download and retention, online education suppresses critical, freethinking. This further benefits business because young people educated in online environments often will be less likely to critically examine and oppose injustices in society, such as corporate welfare and business control of government.

Online education frequently allows businesses to control curriculums and education content. Independent, freethinking teachers and professors might make students aware of injustices that harm society, but benefit business. Online education greatly increases the ability of businesses to block this type of education. By firmly controlling the information presented to students, businesses often can ensure that young people learn only what they want them to learn. It is much easier to control computers than human teachers. One never knows what a freethinking human might say. But this is not a problem with computers.

One of the most tragic aspects of online education is degradation of children in low-income communities. As discussed in the Charter Schools section, charter schools are being established mainly in low-income communities. These schools frequently cut costs (and increase profits) by using computers instead of human beings to teach children. Children in low-income communities often have the most problems outside of school. As a result, they frequently require the most personalized attention to succeed in school.

But these most needy children are getting the opposite of what they need. Wealthier families often would not tolerate having their children, especially young children, being taught by computers instead of human teachers. But minority children from low-income families frequently are treated as if they are not worthy of having the personalized attention afforded to children from wealthier families. This abomination must end. People who profit from online education often attempt to mislead the public by claiming that online education is as good or better than traditional classroom education. But then they frequently send their children to traditional schools where they are taught by human beings instead of computers.

In the education area, computers never will come close to being as effective as infinitely more sophisticated human beings. Online education often treats students as if they were intellectual, downloadable machines. But humans have emotional, psychological, physical and even spiritual components that frequently are more important to learning and life than intellectual components. The online education approach often implicitly ignores these defining characteristics of humanity.

Online education greatly benefits businesses, but often substantially harms young people. Since the primary purpose of education should be to help young people, the focus and use of online education must be changed. In today's online, high-tech world, computers and online activities obviously can and should play important roles in learning. But the focus of online education must be shifted from replacing classroom education to supporting it.

The use of online education classes should be greatly reduced, especially among low-income children who often need the most personalized attention from human beings. Online education should be used mainly to support classroom education, except in limited cases where it provides the best or only education option, such as educating disabled people who cannot leave their homes. As discussed, if we end or greatly reduce corporate welfare, we can easily afford to provide classroom K-12 and higher education to all young people, while substantially lowering property and income taxes.

Online education represents a gold mine for many education and high tech companies. But our children are not profit opportunities. They are the most sacred and precious beings in society. They take priority over everything else, especially nonliving companies. We should not be degrading our children and their education so that wealthy investors can earn superior returns.

People often are enthralled with technology, computers and artificial intelligence (AI). Some people argue that computers will surpass humans at some point. This position is myopic. It reflects a failure to understand the emotional, psychological, spiritual and social aspects of humans. Computers, like all other human technologies, essentially are infinitely less sophisticated than the human mind and humans in general. Computers are infinitely moronic compared to humans. It is ridiculous to say that these technological dolts could come close to replacing human teachers.

Online education software is written by human beings. But they are not psychics. They cannot anticipate the unique emotional, psychological, spiritual, social or even intellectual issues and questions that might arise while a student is attempting to learn something. Computers might use facial monitoring or other technologies to attempt to discern the level of distraction or emotional states of students. But the response to these states would be something that programmers thought up beforehand. AI might try to learn better responses. But AI still is infinitely less capable than a human being. AI might remember what did or did not work, and thereby respond more effectively in the future. But the response always would be formulaic and rationally deduced.

AI or computers cannot produce the intuitive, inspirational or deep wisdom responses of humans. There is no heart, love, compassion or life present. Computers are lifeless machines that cannot come remotely close to simulating a live human being. How would a computer respond if it sensed depression in a student? Would it be programmed to say in a friendly voice, keep your chin up? Would a mechanical hand extend out from the computer and pat the student on the back?

Dealing with a computer that is trying to act like a human being could be profoundly lonely. Students are not stupid. They know that no life is present. They often will sense that they were not worthy enough to receive attention from a human being. When dealing with emotional or psychological problems that interfere with learning, students frequently would be better off on their own, rather than dealing with a machine that is pretending to be human. The presence of a false human can make problems worse by highlighting the fact that no real human is present to help a struggling child or teenager.

This once again shows why the for-profit model often is incompatible with educating our children. Under the for-profit education model, replacing human teachers with computers helps shareholders, and therefore is encouraged. But when the focus of education is on benefiting young people (where it should be), replacing human teachers with nonhuman, nonliving machines usually would not be allowed because it insults and harms our children.

For the foreseeable future, AI or any other technology never will come remotely close to replicating a human being, in large part because we do not fully understand what a human is. As discussed in the Psychiatric Drugs section, there is extensive evidence which indicates that the mind extends beyond the body. Radios, cell phones and other devices can receive information from electromagnetic radiation sent through the air. It is possible that humans could communicate in similar ways, in part because humans essentially are infinitely more sophisticated than manmade technology.

We do not know how thoughts and inspirations are formed, stored and utilized, perhaps on nonphysical levels. We do not know the full mechanics of how emotions arise and affect us. To replicate human teachers with technology, we must understand how humans function and, for example, provide deep, complex responses, such as love and compassion. While we know a lot about humans, compared to all there is to know, we still know virtually nothing.

However, as discussed extensively throughout this book, humans have access to essentially all knowledge and intelligence through the intuitive function. At the level of the intuitive or heart, we know everything. But the conscious mind often is not able to fully understand what is known in the heart.

AI probably always will be infinitely less sophisticated than actual humans because the human intellect often cannot create what it does not know. It probably is impossible to replicate the unique emotional, psychological, spiritual and social responses and wisdom of humans through an intellectual approach, such as developing AI software, because these responses are not intellectual. It is irrational to think that the intellect could replicate the far more complicated, non-intellectual aspects of humans. It is like the student attempting to replicate the master. The student cannot do this because they do not know what the master knows.

Science fiction sometimes discusses AI becoming more powerful than humans and possibly controlling or even destroying us. It is possible that this could occur if we make the mistake of giving computers the power to launch nuclear weapons or take other actions that could harm humans. But the idea of computers controlling us largely is a projection of fear-based human consciousness. The servant (AI) will not dominate the master (the human mind). The computing power of AI might enable it to sometimes go beyond humans in science and other logic-based areas. But AI never can come remotely close to matching the overall intelligence of humans because AI is not alive. It is human ideas projected onto dead computer chips.

Humans are alive. We are the manifestation of the wisdom of nature. As shown with Buddhist meditation, we can develop extremely refined awareness, capable of sensing the tiniest particles and amounts of energy. We probably also have nearly infinite computing power, vastly more than the most powerful computer, although we have not learned how to consciously use it yet. This is especially true if the human mind is networked into a collective, global or transcendent consciousness, as Carl Jung believed it was, many other brilliant people continue to believe, and many meditators have tangibly experienced.

AI could greatly benefit humanity, for example, by rapidly advancing science through intense computing power. But many scientific advances result from intuitive perceptions that were not obvious to the rational, conscious mind. This type of nonlinear advancement probably is not possible with AI. While expanding artificial intelligence might be beneficial, the vastly more important work involves advancing human intelligence and consciousness. AI is bounded by linear logic. It might perform one trillion computations simultaneously. But each one is a linear logic sequence. However, potential human intelligence is unbounded and infinite.

The highest potential intelligence exploration involves expanding human consciousness. Humanity largely is living in a consciousness of separation. This often produces fear and the belief in the need for competition. But separation is an illusion. As we explore the reality of our interconnectedness, our consciousness will evolve to unity and integration. Instead of fear, reality-based unity consciousness will produce compassion, cooperation, peace, safety, security, love, brother/sisterhood and vastly greater enjoyment of life.

We largely do not realize our potential. Exploring AI could benefit humanity. But exploring the boundaries of human consciousness and intelligence (and discovering that there ultimately are no boundaries) will be vastly more beneficial. Considering the vast, multilevel capabilities of humans shows why it is not logical to think that a computer could effectively teach an infinitely more sophisticated human being.

A compassionate teacher can look into the eyes of a troubled child and communicate far more information than a computer. The compassion of a teacher tells a young person that they are worthy and important. Children and teenagers know on a deep level that they are being seen and understood by a wise teacher. This love and connection with an older human being probably often is the most important learning that occurs in school. It empowers young people to fully express who they are and reach their fullest potential.

Children frequently yearn for attention and validation from adults, especially if they are not getting it at home. The idea that children could get the compassion, attention and validation they need to prosper from computers is irrational. They might as well be talking to a cinderblock. Computers can do many things better than humans. But educating a human being is not one of them, and almost certainly never will be. All young people deserve to be taught by human beings.

Prohibit 'Zero-Intelligence' Discipline

Zero-tolerance discipline is a deceptive and inaccurate term. The term implies that those who oppose zero-tolerance discipline are suggesting that some student misbehavior should be tolerated. This is incorrect. Virtually no opponent of zero-tolerance discipline intends this. Learning how to get along with other people and function well in society (i.e. social skills) is one of the most important lessons learned in school. For their own well-being and the well-being of society, young people must learn to respect authorities.

The extensive discussion of authoritarianism in this book does not imply that young people should not respect authority. But respect is a two-way street. Authorities must respect young people. The best way to teach respect is to model it. Competitive grading and standardized curriculums unintentionally disrespect young people. Children and teenagers frequently are made to feel inadequate for not performing well in areas that do not interest them. Their unique interests and competencies often are not respected. Teachers, administrators, politicians and other leaders do not intend to disrespect or harm young people with competitive grading, standardized curriculums, standardized testing and other approaches. The intention is to help young people. Harm and disrespect mainly result from myopia.

Zero-tolerance discipline does not refer to tolerance, in the sense of tolerating misbehavior. That is why the term is inaccurate and deceptive. The term refers to a method of dealing with misbehavior. As discussed in the Authoritarianism section, zero-tolerance discipline generally means providing swift and harsh punishment for misbehavior, including minor infractions. Under zero-tolerance discipline programs, many schools use suspensions, expulsions, in-school police officers, arrests and the court system to deal with minor, nonviolent behavior, such as dress code violations, having food outside of the cafeteria and talking back to teachers.

In one case, an armed, uniformed police officer was called to a kindergarten class to deal with a 5-year-old child who was having a temper tantrum.[698] In another case, a child was arrested for burping in class and placed in a juvenile detention facility.[699] So-called zero-tolerance approaches are widely used in the US. About three million students are suspended each year.

Extensive research has shown that suspensions, arrests and other zero-tolerance approaches are ineffective at reducing misbehavior and do not improve school safety. Even one suspension substantially increases the risk that a young person will dropout of school or wind up in jail. Suspensions degrade academic performance because students often fall behind while out of school. Zero-tolerance approaches not only are ineffective, they are counterproductive. Instead of helping young people, zero-tolerance discipline harms them, and by extension, harms society.

There are far more effective ways to address misbehavior. Zero-intelligence discipline is a more accurate way to describe the approach commonly called zero-tolerance discipline, because the term clarifies that these approaches are ineffective, and therefore implicitly lack awareness or intelligence. As is the case throughout *Global System Change*, the derogatory term zero-intelligence discipline is not meant to insult anyone who supports or uses these approaches. Zero-intelligence/tolerance discipline harms children. They take priority over everything else. Therefore, anything that harms them must be ended. The pejorative term zero-intelligence discipline is intended to discredit zero-tolerance discipline, and thereby facilitate its replacement with more effective approaches.

A growing number of school districts and cities, including Baltimore, Denver and San Francisco, recognize that zero-intelligence discipline is ineffective. As a result, they are replacing it with more effective approaches. The main problem with zero-intelligence discipline is ignorance, hence the name zero-intelligence. The approach largely ignores the causes of misbehavior. It essentially says to young people, we don't care why you're misbehaving. If you don't toe the line, we will come down on you like a ton of bricks. This approach is ignorant because misbehavior usually cannot be resolved in this way. As with incarceration, students can be isolated from the school environment for a period of time. But when they return, they often will be angry and resentful. Misbehavior frequently will increase, which degrades schools and ultimately society.

More effective ways of addressing misbehavior generally could be referred to as compassionate engagement. These wise approaches attempt to see the whole person. They recognize that each student is a unique person with a life history. Misbehavior virtually always is a reflection of this history. Through compassionate engagement, teachers, administrators, counselors and other caring adults understand and engage with young people. Through empathic, nonjudgmental listening, adults strive to create safe, trusting relationships with young people. This encourages and empowers them to express who they are and discuss any problems they might have. As young people feel heard and understood, their self-esteem often improves. Discussing problems in a safe, supportive environment frequently helps to make solutions obvious. Caring adults become allies in helping to resolve problems.

Supporters of zero-intelligence discipline might argue that adults must behave appropriately in society, regardless of what is happening in their lives. Young people must be taught (i.e. forced) to do the same thing. This once again reflects the irrationality of zero-intelligence discipline. Young people, especially young children, are still developing. They often do not fully understand themselves and society. They frequently do not know how to identify and handle feelings, such as those that might arise from an abusive home. Implicitly telling young people to ignore whatever is happening in their lives and minds, and act in certain ways, is extremely ignorant. Teaching young people to ignore their feelings and who they are will hobble them for life. This reality-ignoring approach does not work. It is an irrational fantasy to think that it could work.

The most effective way to end misbehavior is to treat young people with respect, effectively engage with them by becoming their allies, help them to understand what is going on inside, and help to resolve problems in their lives. This is the most effective approach because it is based on compassion, wisdom and respect. The word discipline often would not be used in this process because it implies punishment and distancing.

Misbehavior reflects an imbalance in a young person's history, possibly caused by messages of inadequacy learned from advertising, media and competitive grading. It usually is the result of earlier harm. Essentially punishing young people for earlier harm done to them might suppress misbehavior in the short-term. But it often will cause more misbehavior over the longer-term and set people up to have unsuccessful and unsatisfying lives. Through compassionate engagement, young people are held responsible for their actions. But this occurs in far more effective and compassionate ways. Ignorant punishment usually does not work.

Restorative justice is one of the most effective alternatives to zero-intelligence discipline. Zero-intelligence (i.e. tolerance) justice is a form of punitive justice, like that used in the US criminal justice system. As discussed in the Crime section, punitive justice does little to help victims. The focus is on punishing offenders. This ineffective approach answers harm with more harm. Restorative justice, on the other hand, is focused on restitution and making victims whole. Offenders are held accountable in ways that aid victim healing and do not impose the harm, humiliation and deprivation of punitive approaches.

Restorative justice is used in Oakland, CA, one of the most violent cities in the US. The approach has been so effective that Oakland replaced zero-tolerance discipline with restorative justice throughout its school system.[700] As used in Oakland, restorative justice asks who was harmed, what are the needs of everyone affected, how can harm be healed, and what lessons can be learned. Oakland schools frequently use restorative justice circles. Under this approach, a symbolic talking piece is passed around. The person holding the talking piece speaks with respect from the heart. Others listen.

The approach has increased graduation rates and test scores. Suspension rates have fallen by over 75 percent in many schools. After going through the restorative justice process, students with multiple incarcerations and failing grades often graduated from high school with high GPAs. Girls who had been long-time enemies became friends after participating in restorative justice circles.[701] The city of Denver also is replacing zero-tolerance discipline with restorative justice. As a result, from 2008 to 2012, suspensions decreased by 44 percent, expulsions by 60 percent and referrals to police by 50 percent.[702]

Positive Behavioral Interventions and Support (PBIS) is another effective alternative to zero-tolerance discipline. Cities, including Baltimore, Chicago and Bridgeport, CT, use PBIS. In Chicago, the approach uses positive reinforcement to motivate desired behaviors. Students are held accountable for misbehavior, but not punished in the traditional sense. Instead, misbehavior is used as a learning opportunity. Students meet with staff and discuss what they did wrong. They often are allowed to develop their own behavior improvement plans. This gives them control, autonomy and responsibility. Suspensions still are used for dangerous activities, such as bringing weapons to school, threats, physical fights and gang activity. But PBIS has been highly effective at reducing nonviolent misbehavior.[703]

Other examples of replacing zero-tolerance discipline with compassionate engagement exist in Los Angeles, San Francisco and Roxbury, MA. Los Angeles banned suspensions for minor misbehavior or willful defiance, such as talking back to teachers, eating in classrooms and dress code violations. Instead, the city is training teachers to deal with misbehavior more effectively. Rather than using suspensions, LA schools take actions such as holding parent conferences and having students meet with school counselors. The approach has substantially increased test scores and reduced misbehavior in many schools.[704]

San Francisco is reducing the use of police in city schools. The responsibility for dealing with misbehavior has been shifted back to schools. Police are used only as a last resort. School-based police officers are required to get training on how to deal with young people more effectively.[705] A K-8 school in Roxbury, MA with poor test scores and widespread misbehavior problems ended severe zero-tolerance policies. The school's principal stopped using security officers in the schools. Instead, funds were used to re-establish art, music and dance programs. The approach substantially improved test scores and reduced misbehavior.[706]

Growing awareness that zero-tolerance discipline is ineffective and excessively applied to African American children led the federal government to issue new guidelines for school discipline. The guidelines emphasize the need for school police training and use of in-school disciplinary practices that limit the use of suspensions and expulsions.[707]

In general, compassionate engagement approaches use many strategies and activities to hold students responsible and minimize misbehavior. Activities include providing social skills training, school counseling, parental involvement, social worker interventions, early intervention in elementary school, and replacing codes of discipline with codes of conduct. This shifts the emphasis from punishment to encouraging positive behavior. The goal is to provide a supportive but firm environment for students who misbehave. Instead of suspensions, penalties might include in-school community service.[708] Many schools use restorative justice peer panels. Under this approach, students tell their side of the story to a panel of peers, who then determine a resolution that seeks to heal harm.[709]

Teacher and staff training are critical for successful use of compassionate engagement programs. Teachers and school administrators often make the mistake of taking student misbehavior or defiance personally. Their egos get involved. With proper training, teachers look at the big picture more. They learn that misbehavior virtually always results from stress or problems in students' lives. This helps teachers to display compassion, which virtually always is more effective than the intolerance of zero-tolerance. Teachers understand that rudeness or defiance might be resulting from anger at an abusive parent, for example. Responding to misbehavior compassionately, but not naïvely, is far more effective.

To illustrate compassionate engagement, three African American girls were harassing a Latina cafeteria worker at a Maryland high school. Under zero-tolerance, the girls might have been suspended. The causes of their misbehavior would have gone unaddressed. They might have fallen behind in school and become more likely to dropout. Under new regulations in Maryland intended to reduce suspensions, the school principal held a restorative justice/mediation session with the three girls and cafeteria worker. The principal explained how African American cafeteria workers had been harassed at the school in the 1960s. As the girls better understood harassment and the cafeteria worker's perspective, they felt bad about their actions. Their punishment involved helping to clean the cafeteria for a short time. But the girls decided to help clean it voluntarily for the rest of the year. This type of learning, growth and maturity would not have resulted from zero-tolerance discipline. Instead, the students would have been harmed.[710]

Another example of compassionate engagement occurred at an Oakland, CA high school. A 14-year-old boy had his head down on his desk. His teacher told him twice to sit up straight. He cursed at the teacher in class and after class. The teacher had been assaulted earlier in the year. After the boy's threatening behavior, she considered quitting teaching. During a restorative justice circle, the boy revealed that his mother, who had been sober, began using drugs again and disappeared for three days. The boy had been staying up most of the night taking care of his two younger siblings. In class, he was hungry, tired and scared. The boy apologized to the teacher and offered to make amends by helping her with after-school chores.

Once the teacher understood the cause of the boy's misbehavior, she felt more compassionate and less afraid. She decided to remain in teaching. The boy's mother also was involved in the restorative justice process. As she better understood the impact of her behavior on her children, she reaffirmed her commitment to drug rehabilitation. Under zero-tolerance approaches, the boy's stressful family life would have been ignored. He would have been suspended. His life would have been degraded. Restorative justice helped the boy, his mother and his teacher.[711]

Overall, compassionate engagement is far more effective than zero-tolerance discipline. It nearly always is more effective at improving academic performance and graduation rates and reducing misbehavior and involvement with the criminal justice system. Also, as discussed in the Authoritarianism section, zero-tolerance discipline is applied much more frequently to African American children and teenagers. Effective engagement approaches usually substantially reduce or eliminate the punishment disparity between African American and white young people.[712]

Given the obvious ineffectiveness of zero-intelligence discipline and the obviously superior effectiveness of alternative approaches, one might ask, why are zero-intelligence discipline approaches still widely used in the US? One reason discussed in the Authoritarianism section is that zero-intelligence discipline approaches often are less expensive. Helping misbehaving young people frequently requires extra time and resources. It often is cheaper and easier to kick young people out of school temporarily or permanently, rather than engage with them and help to resolve problems.

As business-controlled education reform reduces funding for public education, many public schools are cutting guidance counselors, increasing class sizes and reducing teacher training. These and other factors make it more difficult for public schools to help misbehaving young people. Many charter schools use the most strict and intolerant discipline. This is yet another way that charter schools run by for-profit companies reduce costs in an effort to achieve their primary objective – maximizing shareholder returns.

If the goal of education reform were to help children, approaches that harm them, such as zero-intelligence discipline, would be replaced with beneficial approaches, such as compassionate engagement. The stated goal and intention of education reform might be to help children. But this is not the structurally mandated goal of the businesses that largely are driving education reform. These companies are required to put shareholder returns before children and all else. They ultimately will die if they do not do this.

Zero-intelligence discipline helps education and other companies in several ways. As noted, it facilitates reduced public education funding, and thereby frees up more public wealth to be used for corporate welfare. Also, zero-intelligence discipline prepares young people to work in the authoritarian US society. It teaches them that there will be severe penalties for failing to obey authorities. It trains them to tolerate boring, difficult jobs and not complain about the theft of their wealth and power. This type of strict authoritarian training greatly benefits the small group of wealthy citizens who largely control the US government and society.

Another possible reason for widespread use of zero-intelligence discipline relates to religious ideas. As discussed, the modern education system is a legacy of the Protestant Reformation. It is based on the idea that children are flawed and their wills must be broken. Under this ignorant worldview, there is no need to ask why young people are misbehaving. The answer and solution are obvious. Young people misbehave because they are inherently bad and willful. The solution, as discussed in the Old Testament, is to use severe zero-intelligence discipline to break their wills.

Perhaps the most important cause of widespread use of zero-intelligence discipline is growing division, anger and hatred in society. In his farewell address, George Washington warned us that vested interests would use political parties to divide citizens and essentially steal their wealth and power. Businesses and their allies foment the civil war between conservatives and liberals. This divides the public and enables large companies and wealthy business owners to steal the people's wealth and power. Conservative media often misleads many conservative citizens into thinking that lazy African American people abuse social welfare programs and are primarily responsible for high taxes. As ongoing business theft of the people's wealth and power make life more difficult for millions of average citizens, hatred for people on social welfare programs increases. Citizens often are tricked into blaming low-income people for high taxes and other problems in society. Their attention is turned away from major problems (corporate welfare and business control of government) toward minor or false problems.

As discussed in the Crime section, white racists often support the use of the death penalty and long-term incarceration because they believe it is applied mainly to people who they do not like – African Americans. A similar situation appears to exist in the education area. African American students are suspended at about three times the rate of white students. Citizens who have been misled into disliking or hating low-income people often do not care about problems in young people's lives. They are angry and want to punish those who they incorrectly believe are responsible for their difficult lives.

Hatred forces out compassion and wisdom. The apparent goal is not to help young people. If this were the goal, helpful, restorative discipline approaches would be used. The goal appears to be punishment. Misled people often think that low-income people have harmed them, for example, by causing higher taxes. Perhaps unconsciously, they want to return the harm through severe punishment, such are long-term incarceration in the criminal justice area and zero-intelligence discipline in the education area. Severe, harmful punishment soothes the bloodlust for revenge.

As the US Founders understood, it is tragic that non-expert citizens can be so easily misled. The evil hatred that results from the business and media-manufactured war between conservatives and liberals makes our society vastly worse. Many people apparently become unwilling to spend a little to help others. But they seem willing to spend much more to punish. From a total cost perspective, zero-intelligence discipline is extremely expensive, again as the name implies. Failing to help a person when they are young often means that we will be paying $50,000 per year for many years to incarcerate them. It also increases crime and severely degrades society.

This once again illustrates why whole system solutions are needed. Our flawed economic and political systems create widespread, unnecessary poverty. This causes problems in families and communities, which in turn causes poor academic performance and misbehavior in schools. The root cause of much school misbehavior is our flawed economic and political systems. Evolving them into fair and sustainable forms is a main part of the solution.

Whole system solutions to misbehavior in schools also involve improving the education system. Our competitive, boring, standardized education system causes widespread psychological problems and delinquency in schools. These systems disrespect and degrade young people by ignoring their unique interests and competencies and constantly making them feel inadequate. Widespread misbehavior is the obvious and expected outcome of this ignorant, grossly flawed education system. If we suppress young people's natural response to flawed education systems with zero-intelligence discipline we will make them worse. They will carry their stifled senses of adequacy into adulthood and often have unsuccessful and unsatisfying lives.

It is time to end zero-intelligence discipline. This ignorant approach reflects the dark side of humanity. The people who promote it often claim to be Christians. Their blind faith in dogma has closed their minds and hearts to the actual teachings of Jesus. Zero-intelligence discipline harms young people, greatly increases total costs, and severely degrades society.

It is time to replace ignorance and intolerance with compassion and wisdom. Thousands of schools already are doing this and achieving superior results. Widespread use of restorative justice, PBIS and other compassionate engagement approaches will substantially reduce misbehavior, greatly enhance the educational environment, and greatly benefit our children.

Prevent Bullying

Bullying, including cyberbullying, is a major problem in US education. This section discusses bullying impacts, causes and solutions. About 13 million children and teenagers are bullied each year in the US. Approximately 40 to 80 percent of school-age children are bullied at some point during their K-12 education. Bullying can cause depression, other psychological problems and poor academic performance.[713] It also substantially increases suicide risk. Being bullied by peers in the previous 12 months doubles the risk of having suicidal thoughts. Bullying or mistreatment by a parent or caregiver quadruples the risk.[714] Young people are bullied for many reasons, including being overweight, shy, poor or LGBTQ (lesbian, gay, bisexual, transgender, queer/questioning). Bullying can be physical or verbal. It also can occur in person or electronically (i.e. cyberbullying).

Sexual harassment in school is a common and severe form of bullying. During the 2010-11 school year, 48 percent of students in grades 7-12 experienced some form of sexual harassment in person or electronically. Sexual harassment includes unwelcome sexual comments, being called gay or lesbian in a negative way, being touched in an unwelcome sexual way, being shown sexual pictures that one does not want to see, and being the subject of unwelcome sexual rumors. Victims of sexual harassment often feel depressed, ashamed, embarrassed, reluctant to go to school and/or suicidal.[715] Sexual assault triples the risk of having suicidal thoughts.[716]

In the electronic age, cyberbullying is a growing problem. It involves using the Internet, cell phones or other devices to send or post text or pictures that are intended to hurt or embarrass another person. About 20 percent of young people between the ages of 10 and 18 have been victims or perpetrators of cyberbullying.[717] This type of bullying often is more harmful and disruptive than in-person bullying. Traditional bullying frequently happens in school. As a result, victims often feel safe in their homes. However, cyberbullying can happen anywhere at any time. Victims frequently do not feel safe anywhere. Cyberbullying often makes people feel isolated, dehumanized or helpless. It causes depression and other psychological problems. Cyberbullying victims frequently report having headaches, ongoing physical pain, sleeping problems and suicidal thoughts.[718]

A whole system assessment reveals many causes of bullying. These occur at the levels of the education system, family and society. As discussed in the Implement Freedom-Based Education section, forced education strongly promotes bullying. Competitive grading and standardized curriculums frequently make young people feel inadequate and force them to do things they do not want to do. Their power and freedom are taken away. Students are being unintentionally abused by the autocratic forced education system. When people feel abused and powerless, they often pass the abuse down the line to weaker or more vulnerable people. As noted, bullying is rare or nonexistent in education environments where young people are empowered to freely choose the focus of their education.

Problems in the family environment are another major cause of bullying. Learning empathy is critical for life success. Empathy is the ability to identify with another person and imagine what they might be thinking or feeling. This ability facilitates having sympathy or compassion for other people. Empathy is essential for having successful personal, and even business and other types of relationships. Without good relationships, it would be impossible for nearly anyone to have a truly successful and satisfying life.

Children who are neglected or abused verbally or physically often lack empathy. Children learn mainly by example. If parents do not model or display empathy and compassion, children frequently will lack these capacities. Nearly 90 percent of brain growth occurs in the first five years of life. If children do not gain the ability to display empathy and compassion early on, it can hobble them for life. They often will have difficulty feeling or displaying love and compassion later in life.[719]

As discussed in the Hitting Children section, overwhelming research shows that hitting children makes them more aggressive and substantially increases the risk that they will engage in bullying and other violent behavior as they get older. Even simple neglect can increase the risk of bullying. For example, children raised in orphanages usually do not receive consistent, loving attention from the same adults. They are raised by a rotating staff of workers. Their needs for love, compassion and nurturing frequently are not met adequately. As a result, they often have lower IQs, slower physical growth, and problems with human attachment and emotional development.[720]

Abuse or neglect often produces anger, sadness, emptiness and low self-esteem in children. It frequently is not safe to express anger or other negative emotions to abusive parents and other authority figures. As a result, abused or neglected young people often take their anger and sadness out on weaker or more vulnerable people. Through these mechanisms, poor parenting is a major cause of bullying.

Flaws at the societal level also strongly promote bullying. Flawed economic and political systems cause widespread, unnecessary poverty. This produces extensive turmoil and problems in families and communities. As a result, children's needs for love, compassion and attention often are not adequately met. This frequently causes psychological problems, misbehavior and bullying.

Another major societal-level cause of bullying is the business-promoted war between conservatives and liberals. Media companies often hire radical media announcers who provide a nearly nonstop, hate-filled invective against the other side. Using Rule of Dumb approaches, these childish, hate-spewing adults frequently bully or berate liberals or conservatives. They provide horrible role models for our children. They teach young people that bullying not only is acceptable. It is admirable. Angry media announcers teach young people that the superior man or woman insults, bullies and berates those who have different views or are different in other ways.

The primary job of these destructive media personalities appears to be turning citizens' attention away from major issues that harm society but help their employers (i.e. corporate welfare and business control of government). As George Washington warned, dividing the country into hateful factions is a very effective way, perhaps the most effective way to perpetuate vested interest theft of the people's wealth and power. The hateful, divisive speech of angry media announcers and politicians promotes bullying. This strongly contributes to many problems among children and teenagers, including increased suicides.

In the first three months of 2014, over 5,000 children ages 10 to 14 attempted to kill themselves in the US. Bullying was the main cause of attempted suicide in many of these cases. To illustrate the devastating impacts of bullying, in 2014, an 11-year-old boy in North Carolina, Michael Morones, attempted to commit suicide after being bullied frequently in school. Michael was bullied because he was a fan of the cartoon *My Favorite Pony*. He was an energetic and friendly boy. But relentless bullying caused him to hang himself from the side of his bunk bed. Michael suffered extensive brain damage and is unable to communicate. The potential extent of his recovery is unclear. Michael might remain permanently incapacitated for life.[721]

Another tragic example of bullying involves an 11-year-old girl in Ohio, Bethany Thompson. Bethany survived a brain tumor. But the treatment left her with a crooked smile. Extensive bullying in school about her appearance by a certain group of boys caused her to commit suicide in 2016. Bethany killed herself with a loaded handgun kept in her family's home.[722] As discussed in the Crime section, handguns are severely restricted in the UK. As a result, there are virtually no handgun deaths in the UK. But weak gun laws make them easily and readily available in the US. If not for weak US gun laws, Bethany probably would still be alive.

The rude, childish behavior of media commentators also possibly contributed to Bethany's suicide. These childish adults teach children, possibly including the boys who bullied Bethany, that it is manly and cool to disrespect and abuse those who are different or hold differing opinions. As discussed below, schools must not perpetuate the hatred that children learn in divisive media. Instead, they must have zero-tolerance for bullying and teach children to treat all people with kindness and respect.

Another societal level cause of bullying relates to religious dogma. Some Christian groups have opposed anti-bullying laws that prohibit bullying of LGBTQ students. They also have attempted to insert exceptions into anti-bullying laws which allow bullying that is motivated by religious ideas.[723] Some Christians believe that homosexual behavior is wrong because the Bible criticizes it. However, many other Christians believe that Biblical prohibitions against homosexuality are outdated cultural ideas that no longer apply in modern society, in the same way that the Bible's encouragement of slavery no longer applies.

Christians might oppose making it illegal to bully LGBTQ people because this strongly implies that it is okay to be gay. They are correct. Making it illegal to bully LGBTQ people does communicate to young people that these are acceptable lifestyles. This is the rational and loving message that should be communicated in a civilized society. As long as no one is being harmed, citizens have the right and freedom to follow their own inner guidance in sex and other areas. Implicitly arguing that is okay to bully LGBTQ people (by opposing making it illegal) once again shows the frequently unintentionally destructive nature of blind faith in religious dogma.

Once the causes of bullying are identified, effective solutions can be developed. They could be categorized as out of school and in school. Out of school, at the whole system level, evolving economic and political systems into sustainable forms is essential for solving many problems, including bullying. Sustainable systems will greatly reduce or possibly eliminate poverty. This will lower problems in families and communities, which in turn will reduce misbehavior and bullying inside and outside of school.

Educating and better supporting parents is another critical aspect of preventing bullying. The propensity to be or not be a bully largely is established in the first few years of life, usually before children go to school. Abused or neglected children are much more likely to become bullies. Giving children the love, compassion and attention they deserve promotes the development of empathy and compassion for others. This greatly reduces the likelihood that young people will become bullies. As discussed in the Hitting Children section, Sweden and several other European countries provide new parents with support and training in child rearing and non-harmful disciplinary methods. Expanding programs like this in the US would greatly benefit children, in part by reducing bullying.

Out of school solutions should involve community and state level actions. At the community level, children should be safe when playing in their neighborhoods. Coordinated programs could be established that involve parents, police, schools, merchants and neighbors. These groups could watch for bullying in communities and quickly intervene if it occurs. Nearly all states are taking action to reduce bullying. Following several highly publicized bullying tragedies, such as the Michael Morones example given above, 49 states have implemented anti-bullying legislation.[724]

A major whole system aspect of preventing bullying involves ending the civil war between conservatives and liberals. This is the primary public deception in the US and many other countries. Large companies and the small group of wealthy citizens who own most of their assets use divisive media announcers and other means to stoke hatred and division between conservatives and liberals. This largely false division poisons and degrades society. It models bullying and thereby teaches vulnerable, easily influenced young people to be bullies. Implementing the many suggestions discussed throughout *Global System Change* for ending the war between conservatives and liberals (such as requiring honest media by re-establishing the Fairness Doctrine) will greatly benefit society, in part by substantially lowering bullying.

Another important whole system solution to bullying includes improving the education system. The current forced education system is unintentionally abusive. It strongly promotes bullying. Implementing freedom-based education, for example by substantially reducing or eliminating competitive grading and standardized curriculums, will greatly improve the education environment. When coercion and authoritarianism are removed from the education system, young people no longer will feel insulted and degraded by the education process. They no longer will be compelled to take out their frustration and anger on those who are weaker or more vulnerable.

Many actions can be taken in schools to reduce bullying. As discussed in the Prohibit Zero-Intelligence Discipline section, misbehavior in school should be addressed effectively. This especially applies to dangerous, violent or threatening actions, such as bringing weapons to school, physical fights, gang activity, sexual harassment and bullying. The priority is protecting innocent students, teachers and school staff. To achieve this, suspensions, arrests and other strict discipline might be needed at times.

However, these approaches often are myopic, ineffective and expensive over the longer-term. Strict discipline is like the business focus on short-term profits. Companies regularly take actions that reduce costs and increase short-term profits, such as emitting pollution instead of preventing it. But these actions usually increase total costs to society and degrade quality of life. Strict discipline for bullying and other actions often is less expensive for schools. It protects students in the short-term by removing misbehaving young people from schools. But as with the myopic focus on short-term profits, strict discipline frequently shifts problems away from schools to larger society. This raises total costs and degrades society, for example, by making young people worse, increasing crime and raising incarceration costs.

From a whole system, reality-based perspective, addressing bullying and other serious misbehavior through compassionate engagement nearly always is the most effective and least expensive solution (on a total cost basis). As discussed, bullying or other misbehavior usually is related to a young person's history. Bullies often were abused or neglected at home. Suspending bullies ignores the cause of bullying. As a result, young people frequently get worse and engage in more bullying or violent behavior. Compassionate engagement approaches, such as restorative justice, seek to address root causes and help victims. These approaches virtually always are more effective at preventing further bullying and other misbehavior.

From the perspective of schools, preventing bullying is crucial. Effectively addressing bullying once it occurs is important. But in terms of creating safe, productive school environments, preventing bullying and other serious misbehavior is more important. To foster a safe, welcoming environment for all students, schools should train teachers and students about bullying, establish effective policies for preventing and addressing bullying (including cyberbullying and sexual harassment), and hold people accountable for implementing these policies.

Several effective bullying prevention programs are being used in schools. For example, the Roots of Empathy program is used in many elementary and middle schools in the US and Canada. The program helps children to better understand their own feelings and develop empathy. Teachers and school staff often ask bullies how they think bullied children feel. But it frequently is more effective to ask how the bully feels. As children better understand their own feelings, it becomes easier to empathize with others and understand how they feel.

Under the Roots of Empathy program, children watch a visiting parent and infant interact. Students learn that a crying baby is not a bad baby, but rather a baby with a problem. They try to figure out what is going on with the baby. They learn to see the world through the baby's eyes. This helps them to understand what it might be like to have needs, but not be able to express them clearly. Teaching empathy reduces bullying by helping students to understand what it feels like to be bullied. Several studies have shown that the Roots of Empathy program effectively reduces bullying and promotes supportive behavior among students.[725]

A book by Carrie Goldman, called *Bullied: What Every Parent, Teacher and Kid Needs to Know about Ending the Cycle of Fear*, provides extensive information about reducing bullying.[726] The book notes that bullying often is driven by contempt for other people. This often prevents bullies from feeling empathy or shame. Bullies frequently have strong senses of entitlement, are intolerant of others, and feel free to exclude those who they believe are inferior.

This contempt for others often is driven by strong, but unconscious, self-loathing. Child abuse or neglect often produces low self-esteem. Young people who dislike themselves unconsciously frequently project their self-loathing onto others. Compassionate engagement with young people who bully helps them to better understand their own uncomfortable feelings. As this occurs, self-esteem often increases. This helps young people to better understand the consequences of their actions, feel remorse and strive to treat others better. In her book, Carrie Goldman discusses a bullying prevention effort called the Wrap Program. Under this approach, families, schools and communities work together to provide help and support to young people who are at high risk of becoming bullies.[727]

Bullying and violence prevention programs also are offered by the Institute for the Study and Practice of Nonviolence, located in Providence, RI. The Institute works with young men and boys in gangs. It strives to provide the compassion and support that gang members often do not get at home. Caring and supportive mentors are consistently present in young people's lives. Mentors are firm about appropriate behavior. Boys and young men usually accept these constraints because they understand that the restrictions come from a place of love and caring.[728] Compassionate engagement approaches such as these often are highly effective at reducing or eliminating bullying and other misbehavior.

Another important bullying prevention strategy in schools involves promoting social justice and more effective discussions about societal causes of bullying. These include racism, sexism, homophobia and Islamophobia. Schools should strive to create open environments were these and other sensitive issues can be discussed. Emphasizing empathy is a critical component of social justice discussions and education. Empathy helps students to better understand and more effectively address racism and similar issues.

Some Christian and conservative groups criticize social justice issues and efforts. This might occur at times because social justice involves treating minorities and LGBTQ people equally and fairly. As noted, religious dogma sometimes says that homosexuality is wrong. As a result, these groups might oppose social justice efforts that support and protect these lifestyles. But religious dogma should not be allowed to block equality and fairness. About 60 percent of LGBTQ students say that they feel unsafe in school. About 82 percent have been verbally harassed for their sexual orientation.[729] Open discussions about racism, sexism, homophobia and other sensitive issues will help to limit this abusive, bullying behavior.

In general, raising student awareness about bullying is one of the most important bullying prevention actions. Our angry and divided society models and teaches bullying. Angry politicians and media announcers regularly bully and berate those with differing views. These public figures glorify bullying. Young people often admire and seek to emulate politicians and media announcers. Children and teenagers probably frequently feel that they can enhance their image among peers by acting like the childish, bullying leaders they see in media.

As with smoking awareness campaigns, changing the image of bullying can greatly reduce it. Smoking ads often made smoking look cool. But smoking awareness campaigns effectively changed this image. Instead of being cool, people frequently saw smoking as harmful. This substantially reduced smoking in the US. Angry, immature politicians and media announcers often effectively are advertising and promoting bullying. Their actions teach young people that bullying is cool and admirable. Real men act like bullies, these childish public figures imply.

Through presentations, discussions and videos in classrooms and school assemblies, young people should be taught the root causes of bullying. For example, it should be explained that bullies often are abused or neglected by their parents. Being abused by a more powerful person frequently causes bullies to dislike themselves and be filled with fear. Abuse often turns bullies into cowards. They take out their anger and self-loathing on people who are weaker or more vulnerable. Bullying frequently is a cry for help from young people who do not know that they have problems.

Portraying bullies as wounded people who do not like themselves and as cowards who attack weaker people will severely degrade the public image of bullies. Awareness raising will teach students to see bullies as uncool, weak cowards. This could greatly reduce bullying. As noted, students frequently emulate bullying politicians and media personalities because they think it makes them look cool. But once it is widely known that bullying is uncool and cowardly, peer pressure will suppress it. Young people will not want to embarrass themselves in front of peers by acting like bullies.

To further discredit bullies, schools might teach young people why politicians and media personalities often act like bullies. They could explain that flawed economic and political systems require that large companies grow forever, even if it harms society. Promoting division and fighting in society distracts people's attention from the damage being done by these flawed systems. Owners and managers of large companies are good people who mean well. But our flawed systems require them to put shareholder returns before all else. Stoking division and hatred in society enables large companies and their wealthy owners to continuously extract more wealth from labor and all other parts of society. Politicians who accept money from large companies and media personalities hired by them become the servants of these companies. They often act like bullies because this helps their masters to continuously extract more wealth from society.

It often would be more useful to see angry politicians and media announcers as puppets or cartoon characters. They are playing roles. They might believe what they are saying when they criticize liberals or conservatives. But this largely is irrelevant. Angry politicians and media personalities are intentionally or unintentionally promoting division in society and turning citizens' attention away from major problems.

As young people better understand the frequently deceptive and dishonest nature of media communication, they will give it less credence. They will understand that angry politicians and media personalities should not be emulated. Instead, they should be replaced. Politicians should be replaced with people who obey the Constitution by serving all citizens equally and fairly, rather than primarily serving wealthy campaign donors. Media personalities should be replaced with people who act like mature adults and tell citizens the truth, for example, by exposing corporate welfare and other important problems in society.

However, without system change, it often will be difficult to elect politicians who obey the Constitution and hire media announcers who tell the truth. Current systems require nearly all politicians to accept large amounts of money from wealthy business owners. Under this system, it is virtually impossible for politicians to serve all citizens equally and fairly, as the Constitution requires. In addition, business-controlled government does not require media to provide fair, accurate and balanced information. As a result, media companies are free to mislead and divide the public. Divisive media frequently protects large companies by turning citizens' attention away from the most important problems in society, including destruction of life support systems, corporate welfare and business control of government.

Under education reform, large companies increasingly control curriculums and learning materials. As a result, it is unlikely that students will study and learn about major problems and public deceptions that harm society, but help large companies in the short-term. This once again shows the essential need for system change at the education and societal levels.

Raising student awareness about bullying should be done with compassion. The purpose is not to insult or embarrass bullies. This often will make them worse. If awareness raising is done with compassion, people who have bullied or might bully will understand that a main purpose of awareness raising is to help them live better lives.

As shown with the Michael Morones and Bethany Thompson examples above, bullying often is tragic and heartbreaking. Parents frequently feel anger and a strong desire to harm those who bullied their children. This is understandable. But harming bullies is not the answer. This will perpetuate the cycle of harm and increase bullying. Bullies usually harm others because they were harmed in some way. They are returning the harm done to them by parents, forced education, divisive media, and/or flawed economic and political systems. The solution to bullying at the individual level is to effectively hold bullies responsible through compassionate engagement. At the school level, the solution is to raise awareness about the causes of bullying and implement effective bullying prevention programs. At the societal level, the solution to bullying (and nearly every other major problem facing humanity) is to improve our flawed systems.

Prohibit Physical Punishment

As discussed in the Hitting Children section, extensive research shows that hitting children and other physical punishment causes many problems. It increases the likelihood that young people will become bullies, abuse their spouses and children later in life, and engage in violent or criminal activities. Physical punishment causes extensive psychological problems and degrades relationships between parents and children. Hitting children in school also causes many problems, including increased truancy, dropout rates and violent behavior. Hitting and other physical punishment can produce short-term compliance. But this benefit is vastly outweighed by the psychological harm caused by physical punishment.

Hitting smaller, defenseless people is an ignorant and destructive legacy of authoritarian society, as slavery was. Common sense alone shows that we should not be hitting the most vulnerable and defenseless people in society. As discussed, over 100 countries prohibit hitting children in schools. Over 30 countries prohibit physical punishment in all locations, including homes. We should do the same in the US. There are far more effective ways to discipline children. It should go without saying that, when raising or educating children, compassion is vastly more effective than physical violence. Millions of parents never hit their children. They prove that hitting children never is necessary. Children never should be hit.

This is especially true in schools. As noted, 19 states in the US allow children to be hit in schools. It seems unbelievable that this could be occurring in a supposedly enlightened society. We tell students not to bully other young people. But then teachers and school administrators model and teach bullying by hitting weaker, more vulnerable students. It sounds like something out of the Dark Ages.

Insecure teachers and school administrators sometimes get angry at young people who do not give them the respect they feel they deserve. They sometimes attempt to literally beat the willfulness out of children and beat respect into them. Ignorant, insecure adults like this should not be educating or supervising our children. They often will cause vulnerable young people to grow into ignorant, insecure adults, just like the teachers and school administrators who are beating them. Adults who hit children frequently seem to be unable to display compassion, perhaps because they were beaten instead of shown compassion when they were children.

Physical punishment in schools should be ended immediately. It also should be ended as quickly as possible in all other locations, including homes. Physical punishment is a main tool in authoritarian societies. But the US should not be authoritarian. The US Constitution does not establish authoritarianism or plutocracy. It requires democracy. We must not suppress our children with physical violence. Instead, we must empower them with love, compassion and respect.

Prohibit Compulsory Psychiatric Drug Use

As discussed in the Psychiatric Drug section, many schools require that misbehaving students take psychiatric drugs. These drugs are hugely overprescribed in the US. To achieve ever-increasing shareholder returns, drug companies strongly influence doctors, medical education, medical research, politicians, regulators and citizens in ways that drive overprescription. A main strategy for achieving this is to create the largely false and unproven impression that many mental disorders are caused by physical, neurological problems, and therefore require physical drug solutions.

But basic common sense shows that the vast majority of psychological problems are caused by past and present life circumstances. Putting shareholder returns before all else harms millions of average citizens and causes widespread depression and other psychological problems. Forced education insults and degrades young people by largely ignoring their unique interests and competencies. This causes widespread inattention, depression, anxiety and defiance in schools.

Forcing students to take psychiatric drugs so that they will comply with our coercive, deeply flawed education system is a hideous violation of their rights as human beings. Parents are deceived into thinking that something is wrong with their children. But in reality, students frequently are displaying normal, expected responses to our coercive, unintentionally abusive education system. Psychiatric drugs, especially antipsychotics, often cause severe, life degrading physical and psychological impacts. We should not be using these drugs on children so the drug companies can make more money. Instead, we should give young people what they deserve – compassion and attention.

There are several reasons why young people sometimes have psychological problems. Inherent brain chemical imbalances probably rarely are the cause. Physical causes of psychological problems are much more likely to result from eating processed foods that contain synthetic chemicals or exposure to environmental toxins. But the main cause is non-physical factors, such as past and present life circumstances. We must take the time to listen to young people. They will reveal the causes of their problems if we give them love, compassion and attention. Then caring adults can help young people to solve problems. We owe this much to our children. This will help them to grow into physically and psychologically healthy, empowered adults.

As discussed, psychiatric drugs are not like proven effective medical drugs, such as antibiotics. We largely do not know how the mind works or how psychiatric drugs affect the mind. These drugs can suppress symptoms in the short-term. But extensive research shows that they often make people worse physically and psychologically over the long-term. In other words, psychiatric drugs largely are unproven and risky. Therefore, schools should not be allowed to require their use. As business-driven education reform cuts funding for public schools, it often is cheaper to drug disobedient or inattentive students. But we must not allow this abuse of children. We must find the will and resources needed to truly help struggling children and teenagers.

System change is the most important solution to psychological problems and psychiatric drug use in schools. As long as we force young people to study subjects that they find boring and irrelevant and make them feel inadequate with competitive grading, many children and teenagers will have psychological problems, including difficulty paying attention. The solution is not to get them high on amphetamines and cocaine-like drugs so that anything, including boring education, becomes interesting. It is to give them what they deserve – an empowering, interesting and useful education.

Protect Student Privacy

As discussed in the Authoritarianism section, monitoring of students in US schools is widespread and growing. Many schools use GPS, RFID, CCTV and other technologies to track and monitor students. Widespread monitoring violates the privacy and freedom of students. The approach implies that all students are dangerous, dishonest or untrustworthy. But the vast majority are responsible, honest and trustworthy. This should be the default position of education. We should not assume that all students are potential delinquents, and then treat them that way. Extensive monitoring in school conditions young people to accept lifetimes of being monitored and suppressed by authorities. This helps to protect corporate welfare and business control of government. But it greatly dishonors and demeans young people.

Increased school shootings often are used to justify expanded monitoring in schools. But school shootings and similar tragedies are rare. We should not be demeaning all young people to prevent rare, horrible events. Some people argue that children must be monitored in school to ensure their safety, in the same way that parents monitor young children. This is true for young children, but less true as children get older. Also, schools have been effectively monitoring children for centuries without GPS, RFID, CCTV and other technologies.

Children should be trusted and given freedom and independence to the greatest extent possible. Extensive monitoring effectively tells them they are untrustworthy. Expectations often become reality. If we treat children like delinquents, they will be more likely to act delinquently. As discussed in the Privacy section, we can implement security systems that effectively protect children without violating their privacy.

Use of student data is another very large potential violation of student privacy. Gathering and utilizing student data represents a large opportunity for business. Also as discussed in the Privacy section, data brokers and other companies have assembled highly detailed information on nearly all citizens. This supposedly private data routinely is sold to businesses and governments. Gathering student data could enable data brokers or other organizations to begin assembling citizen profiles at much earlier ages.

In addition, profiles could contain far more personal information than is available in current citizen profiles. For example, gathering student data could provide information about intelligence, product preferences, political inclinations and many other factors. Tests can be structured in ways that enable companies to gather nearly any type of personal information from students. It is much more difficult to gather this type of personal information from adults because they usually are not required to take tests that companies can structure and interpret. Instead, data brokers must assemble citizen profiles by evaluating online activities, financial transactions and other information.

As discussed in the Authoritarianism section, under the Common Core, many states are developing student databases that contain extensive psychological and other private, non-academic data. These profiles can contain information about religious affiliations, sexual behavior and attitudes, medical history, family voting status, and other highly private, personal information. The profiles generally are maintained for life. Loopholes frequently enable this data to be shared with private companies and government agencies. Parental consent often is not required to gather this data and parents generally are not informed about how their children's personal information is being distributed and used. These life-long profiles could be used to discriminate against students in work and other areas once they become adults.

Selling student data could enable businesses to improve advertising effectiveness. It also could enable government to more effectively monitor young people who might question or challenge business control of government, corporate welfare and other aspects of the unjust status quo. But this privacy violation should not be allowed. Student academic, psychological and other personal data should be kept private. Corporations should not be allowed to benefit shareholders by violating students' privacy.

Teach the Whole System Mind

The physical body is the foundation of a human life. But the mind guides a person's life and largely determines life success and satisfaction. Many aspects of the mind have been discussed in different sections, including intuitive wisdom, changing harmful habits, consciousness, focus, unconscious beliefs, emotions and social skills. Traditional education often views the minds of young people as empty vessels that must be filled with knowledge. This is an inaccurate and harmful way to think of the mind, in part because it ignores the unique interests and immense capabilities already present there. The human mind is an infinitely complex, powerful tool. Based on the implied intelligence all around us, we only have tapped an infinitesimally small amount of the mind's potential. Discovering and utilizing this vast untapped potential can be done far more effectively through a whole system approach to the mind.

As discussed, reductionism dominates and degrades human society. The same applies to the mind. Different aspects of the mind frequently are studied in isolation. Beliefs, emotions, thoughts, intuition, changing habits, and creating a successful life often are analyzed as separate issues. But it would be more empowering and effective to teach young people about the mind as one interconnected whole system.

The mind is the doorway to all knowledge and wisdom. Exploring the mind usually is the most important journey that people take in their lives. On this journey, they can find indescribable bliss and unparalleled life success. Given the infinite potential of the mind, we should build interest and enthusiasm among young people for exploring it. There are different aspects of the mind and different ways of controlling and harnessing it. Young people should be taught these aspects and techniques in an integrated manner. Aspects of the mind include intuitive wisdom, rational thought, beliefs, emotions, unique interests and preferences, consciousness, and unconscious activity. Awareness and control techniques include meditation, mindfulness, intentional focus and managing emotions.

Contents of the mind. Learning to control and focus the mind is critical for life success. Religions sometimes say that the devil puts negative thoughts and temptations into the mind. Seeking God's guidance and support can help people to overcome temptation, do good works and live good lives. This approach might work well for some people. However, for others, it can be limiting. Ascribing negative thoughts to the devil and positive attributes to God takes away one's power and free will. In reality, people have full control over all aspects of their minds because we have free will. The mind is not controlled by external positive or negative forces. However, beliefs control perceptions and life experience. If people believe that they are controlled by external forces, they often will interpret inner and outer events in ways that convince them that this illusion is true.

Fortunately, there are other ways to think about, manage and utilize the contents of one's mind. Thoughts arise in response to inner and outer stimulation and experiences. Powerful experiences generate emotions, such as joy or fear. These emotions can strengthen thoughts. Thoughts or perceptions can become deep-seated, unconscious beliefs. This occurs, for example, when abuse teaches a child that they are unworthy. Thoughts and emotions can arise from beliefs, past or present experience, and intuition. Intuitive thoughts and ideas might originate from beyond the individual mind, perhaps from a global mind or collective unconscious, as Carl Jung and Joseph Campbell discussed. Conscious and unconscious beliefs, thoughts and emotions, and the behaviors that they cause, are the landscape of the mind. Teaching young people to know their own minds and consciously focus their attention is one of the most important life lessons. The unique interests and passions of each person define the individual. They point the direction to the most successful and satisfying life.

Intuitive wisdom. As part of a whole system approach to the mind, young people could be taught several different skills. Mindfulness meditation is a basic tool for learning to observe and understand consciousness and the mind. Young people also should be taught how to utilize intuitive wisdom. This often involves creating an open and receptive space in the mind. From this place, different actions could be taken. People might ask questions or seek guidance on particular issues, and then consider the responses that inevitably will arise in their minds.

As discussed in the Twelve Step Programs section, discernment is key to using intuitive wisdom effectively. Responses to internal questions might come from fear, inadequacy or limiting beliefs. Discernment should be used to sort useful ideas from those that are limiting or harmful. A useful way to screen intuitive guidance is to ask, is it loving and kind to everyone involved? If it is not, thoughts probably are coming from a place of fear and should not be acted upon. But if the guidance is loving and kind to all, it probably is coming from the wise part of the mind. Acting on this guidance virtually always will be life enhancing.

One of the most important skills needed for life success is learning to listen to the wiser part of the mind. This is greatly facilitated by humility. The fear-filled ego often attempts to control the mind. It sometimes pretends to know everything because the unknown can be frightening. Going on in inner journey requires courage and humility. One explores the inner landscape with openness and a willingness to learn. Humility is appropriate and useful when the limited ego or consciousness encounters unlimited, infinite wisdom and knowledge.

As people diligently practice mindfulness and intentional focus, the mind becomes an extremely fine and productive tool. People gain the ability to clearly understand what is happening in the present moment. Compassion and insight arising from intuitive wisdom help them to see beyond surface events and behavior. They often perceive underlying causes and effective solutions.

Emotional and social skills. Teaching emotional and social skills also is an important part of an integrated approach to the mind. Emotions such as anger and fear often restrict people and cause harmful behavior. Many schools teach emotional and social skills. This greatly benefits young people. Emotions often interfere with learning. Teaching children and teenagers to identify and manage emotions can enhance learning and many other aspects of life. Teaching them how to effectively relate to others (social skills) also enhances life. To teach emotional and socials skills effectively, teachers and other adults frequently must learn to identify and manage their own emotions. As with psychotherapy, the ability to help or teach others often is limited if people are not effectively addressing their own emotions or problems.

Life success. Another aspect of an integrated approach to mind includes teaching the psychology of success. As discussed in the Life Satisfaction and Psychiatric Drugs sections, beliefs are like downloaded software. They largely determine perceptions and responses to life. Disempowering beliefs often create negative emotions, psychological problems, unhappiness, problems in relationships, and lack of success in life.

Bringing these beliefs to consciousness (alone or with the help of therapists, family or friends) gives people the ability to essentially reprogram their minds and lives. Once disempowering beliefs are identified, one can choose more empowering ones and act on them. People essentially define a more preferred version of themselves, and then live according to it. This strongly facilitates the achievement of a successful and satisfying life. As discussed in Life Satisfaction section, people have the ability to instantly change their beliefs and actions. They often can quickly transform an unhappy life if they consistently trust and act upon their new, empowering beliefs.

Rational thought. Teaching how to think rationally is another critical element of a whole system approach to the mind. Rational thought is the worker of humanity. It figures out how to apply intuitive wisdom. Rational thought involves learning to see reality clearly and separating emotions from logic. Emotions, biases, public deceptions, fear and many other factors frequently block or inhibit the ability to think rationally. But as discussed throughout *Global System Change*, rational thought is essential for the success and well-being of individuals and humanity as a whole.

Benjamin Franklin, Thomas Jefferson, James Madison, George Washington and John Adams were leading Enlightenment thinkers. The rational thought of these and other Founders produced the US. During these times of extensive public deception and emotionally-charged divisions in society, we need to elevate rational thought once again, as our Founders did. As noted, it is far more important to teach young people how to think rather than what to think. Rational, objective, critical thinking is essential for life success. Therefore, this skill should be strongly emphasized in the study of the whole mind and education in general. Learning specific knowledge and facts often is important for life success. But we should not teach this information through forced education and other means that suppress the more important ability to think freely, clearly and critically.

Critical thinking helps people to see through public deceptions and misconceptions. For example, it helps young people to see through the lie that happiness comes from having the best possessions, appearances or bank accounts. Rational thought helps them to logically deduce that the definition of success varies from person to person. It empowers young people to identify their own definition of success, and then build their lives around it.

Oneness. One of the most important, empowering and enjoyable aspects of the mind is oneness. We literally are part of one, interconnected whole system. None of us can live in outer space. The concept or reality of oneness implies that helping another person ultimately is the same as helping oneself. Hurting others ultimately is equivalent to harming oneself. Treating other people with kindness, love and respect is the primary commandment of virtually all religions. This is the practical application of oneness. We live in the human community. Treating others well usually brings good treatment in return. This helps to produce a successful and satisfying life. Treating other people poorly usually brings poor treatment in return and produces an unfulfilling life.

From this perspective, whether or not humans literally are one largely is irrelevant. Acting as if we are one (whether we are or not) produces the most fulfilling and successful life. This indicates a major component of the whole mind. Adopting the perspective that we are all one produces higher-level, more effective thinking and action. Oneness is a major aspect of whole system thinking. As discussed extensively throughout *Global System Change*, replacing reductionism with whole system thinking is essential for solving the major challenges facing humanity and achieving sustainability and real prosperity. As part of a whole system study of the mind, the ability to see the big picture and think from a whole system perspective should be emphasized, taught and practiced.

Bliss. In terms of enjoyment, the greatest bliss can be found on the inner journey. Science might not be able to prove that we are one in an energetic or metaphysical sense. However, each person can prove this to themself through their own inner exploration. If one persists with meditation, mindfulness and other inner practices, they often experience the reality of oneness. They learn beyond a shadow of a doubt that we all literally are one. Separation is an illusion or product of the limited mind. Buddhism refers to this awareness and experience of oneness as Nirvana. This awareness is not a mental theory. It is experienced reality. People know through experience that oneness is reality.

Millions of people have attained this awareness and found bliss far beyond any physical or outer worldly pleasure. Attaining this experience of oneness may be the paramount human experience. But it is not necessary for achieving a successful and satisfying life. Acting as if we are one, regardless of whether one experiences this internally, is a key aspect of a whole system approach to the mind.

Collective mind. Another aspect of the whole system mind involves considering whether the individual human mind is connected to or part of a global mind, collective mind, infinite mind, collective unconscious or some other type of transcendent energy or consciousness. Many people have experienced a tangible connection to this larger, collective mind through their inner exploration. It often would be useful for individuals and humanity overall to explore the possible existence of this larger mind and, if it does exist, consider how we could use it more effectively. The conscious individual human mind probably cannot fully understand this larger mind (assuming that it exists). The part cannot fully comprehend the whole.

However, that largely is irrelevant to the individual. Each person is here to explore their own unique path in life. They are not here to explore everything or every path. Therefore, they do not need to know everything. Perhaps human consciousness is limited so that we each can focus on living an individual life and experience learning and newness. Intuitive wisdom may be accessing a larger, collective mind. It might be accessing the implied essentially infinite intelligence that we see all around us in nature. However, from a practical perspective, the source of intuitive wisdom is irrelevant. The key issue is that it exists and is available to everyone who seeks it. Utilizing intuitive wisdom enables people to manifest the beautiful, full expression seen in nature. Remaining open-minded about the possible existence of a collective, infinitely wise mind that individuals can access through intuition could lead to huge leaps forward in science, technology, human relations and many other areas.

Intelligence. Another useful aspect of a whole system approach to the mind is to place IQ measurement where it belongs – in the garbage can. The mind is unlimited. The types of analytic ability measured by IQ are a tiny part of the mind. Through intuition, we implicitly have access to knowledge and wisdom that are infinitely greater than anything present in the conscious mind. Debating who is more intelligent is like two fleas sitting on an elephant arguing about which flea is larger. Each person probably has all the skills and talents they need to pursue their unique interests and passions in life. Ranking people on a tiny part of the mind ignores other often more important aspects, such as emotional, social and spiritual intelligence.

A main goal of education should be to help each young person achieve their unique fullest potential in life. Ranking not only is irrelevant to this, it inhibits life success by often unnecessarily and inaccurately degrading or inflating senses of self-worth. Ranking young people on a portion of the mind that is useful to businesses, but ignoring more important aspects, helps business but harms young people. The primary purpose of education should be to help young people, not business. Therefore, processes that harm young people, such as ignorantly ranking intelligence, should not be done. (IQ ranking is ignorant in the sense that it arbitrarily implies that certain aspects of the mind are more important than others. This may be true for some people, such as those who want to become scientists. But it is not true for others, including those who want to be artists, psychotherapists or parents.)

We do not need to measure the so-called intelligence of young people. They each are infinitely intelligent in ways that humans do not fully understand. Measurement implies that we know the boundaries of performance. But we do not know the upper limits of human potential. The person with the highest IQ might be the dumbest person in the room, in terms of having the knowledge and skills needed to achieve a truly successful and satisfying life. As discussed in the Competitive Grading section, ranking people against themselves can be helpful. It helps them to determine if they are making progress toward important goals. However, ranking against others often does far more harm than good.

Unlimited potential. A whole system approach to the mind teaches young people that their minds have infinite potential. It teaches them how to understand their minds and effectively utilize this unlimited potential. A whole system approach helps people to see the mind as one interconnected system. They understand the linkages between aspects of the mind. They learn how beliefs largely influence thoughts, emotions and actions. Changing beliefs can change perceptions and improve life experience.

Adopting a whole system perspective that shows humans to be parts of one interconnected system leads to more effective and cooperative behavior, which in turn produces a more fulfilling and successful life. Effectively and objectively using the tool of rational thought helps people to penetrate deception or confusion, see reality clearly, and more effectively engage in actions that benefit individuals and society. Learning the causes of emotions (mainly beliefs) and managing emotions effectively helps people to attain inner success (happiness, tranquility) and outer success (good relationships, satisfying work).

Learning to observe inner and outer reality objectively and focus the mind makes the mind a useful tool. The individual becomes the observer. They sit in their mind's control seat. They can call up answers to difficult life questions from intuitive wisdom. They can use rational thought to deduce effective solutions. From the perspective of oneness, they can invoke love and compassion, enhance the lives of those around them, and in so doing, achieve the most successful and satisfying life.

Teach and Model Cooperation

Teaching and modeling increased cooperation is critical for the well-being of individuals and humanity overall. As discussed in the Competitive Grading section, the overwhelming force in healthy natural systems and nature overall is cooperation. The illusion of separation produces fear and the belief in the need for competition. Excessive competition in human society contributes to unhappiness, inequality, environmental degradation and many other problems. Our grossly flawed, unsustainable economic and political systems are based in large part on competition. Increasing cooperation is essential for making systems sustainable. Teaching young people cooperation will facilitate the evolution of human systems and society into sustainable forms.

Eliminating competitive grading is a main component of teaching cooperation and making school environments more cooperative. Teaching whole system thinking also facilitates increased cooperation. This type of thinking illuminates the linkages between different aspects of society and shows the essential need for cooperation. Teaching social skills also enhances cooperation because the main aspect of these skills is learning to cooperate and get along with others.

Teamwork or cooperation is one of the most important lessons learned in competitive team sports. But these sports also can damage young people's self-esteem. As discussed in the Men's section of *Global System Change*, media, advertising and culture often teach boys that real men are aggressive and competitive. This teaches young people to get self-esteem and status from beating others, frequently in sports. Boys who are less athletic often are selected last on teams and embarrassed in other ways.

Sports help people to challenge themselves and reach their fullest physical potential. However, they can be managed in ways that emphasize teamwork and build self-esteem, for example, by not selecting teams in ways that embarrass lower skilled players. Also, there are many fun and interesting games and activities that are based on cooperation instead of competition. An excellent book by Terry Orlick, called *Cooperative Games and Sports, Joyful Activities for Everyone*, describes 150 field-tested cooperative games and activities.[730] A main goal is to improve self-esteem through cooperation, acceptance, inclusion and fun. Young people engage in healthy physical activities. But the purpose usually is to work together to achieve a common goal, rather than beating other people.

Elevating the status of girls and women is a major benefit of teaching and modeling cooperation. As discussed in the Women's section, in our competitive and aggressive society, men often have higher status, in part because they manifest more power, when power is defined as physical strength, competitiveness and aggressiveness (due partly to having up to 20 times more testosterone). In the same way that men innately manifest more power, women innately manifest more wisdom, when wisdom is defined as cooperation, empathy, whole system thinking and relationship skills. The solution to elevating the status of women is not to encourage them to be as aggressive and competitive as men. This dishonors and degrades the unique and important strengths of women.

These strengths are the most important qualities lacking in society. Their absence makes humanity unsustainable. Achieving sustainability and real prosperity largely involves expanding these qualities in society. It should be no surprise that women often are suppressed or undervalued in a world that implicitly values the strengths of men more than those of women.

Our immature culture often honors aggression and competition. This frequently encourages girls and women to act aggressively in an effort to gain status. But power is not more important than wisdom. They both are essential for individual and collective well-being. Power without wisdom is destructive, as shown in modern society. Wisdom without power can do nothing. As society matures, we will give wisdom equal honor and status with power. This naturally will help to elevate the status of women to a position of true equality with men. There are many wise men and powerful women. But on average, women innately manifest more wisdom than men.

An important component of teaching and increasing cooperation is to help young people better understand what it means to be a man. As discussed in the Men's section, advertising and media often implicitly teach that real men are aggressive, competitive and rude. They frequently imply that ignorant power (i.e. power without wisdom) is manly, cool and admirable. As with bullying, changing the image of what it means to be a man will help boys to grow into cooperative, compassionate, productive men, instead of harmful, aggressive children in men's bodies.

Wisdom could be defined mainly as the ability to cooperate. This is the most important requirement for civilization. Therefore, cooperation is the most important aspect of wisdom. Competition is the opposite of cooperation. Teaching young people to be competitive strongly inhibits the development of wisdom and perpetuates the unsustainability of human society.

We must make much greater efforts in education to elevate the status of wisdom and cooperation. Media often implicitly portrays cooperative men or men who avoid fights as weak or not manly. This image must be changed. In reality, rude, aggressive, overly competitive men usually are filled with fear. They doubt their masculinity, and therefore feel they must prove it to others. We should help young people (boys and girls) to understand that rude, aggressive men usually are fearful cowards. They should not be emulated. Real men do not need to prove their masculinity to anyone. Their focus mainly is not on elevating themselves by beating others in school, business and other areas. Real men use their power and strength (physical and psychological) in positive, constructive, often protective ways. They frequently help others and make the world a better place. Real men are wise and cooperative.

As we teach young people about the importance of wisdom and cooperation, those who fail to display these qualities will be seen as weak or wounded in some way. Failure to display them strongly indicates that a person does not like themselves. Portraying wisdom and cooperation as manly and cool will cause boys and young men to hesitate to act in a rude or overly aggressive manner. They will not want to embarrass themselves in front of peers by acting like fearful, childish cowards.

We should teach young people more about the differences between men and women. It generally is easier for men to be aggressive and competitive because that is their inherent nature. In the same way, it generally is easier for women to be cooperative, compassionate and wise because those are their inherent qualities. Men can be wise and women can be powerful. But they often must work a little harder to overcome their inherent natures.

As discussed in the Women's section, men tend to individuate more effectively than women (i.e. establish themselves as separate, autonomous individuals), while women tend to be more effective in relationships. In other words, men are better at separation, while women are better at cooperation and integration. They tend to better understand linkages in society and be better whole system thinkers. To achieve greater integration, balance and prosperity in society, we should encourage young men and women to develop their weaknesses as well as strengths. We should teach and encourage boys and young men to be wise, cooperative and more effective in relationships. At the same time, we should teach and encourage girls and young women to be powerful in the positive sense of standing up for themselves and what they believe in.

In our aggressive and competitive society, boys and men often feel superior to girls and women because they have greater physical strength, aggressiveness and other characteristics that ignorant society overly values. Teaching young people the importance of cooperation and wisdom will enhance the status of girls and women. They will be empowered by the knowledge that their unique strengths and characteristics are just as vital to the well-being of individuals and society as the strengths and characteristics of men.

Effectively teaching and modeling cooperation requires considering all aspects of education and replacing competition with cooperation to the greatest extent possible. Cooperation is far more satisfying than competition. It also is essential for the survival and prosperity of humanity. Therefore, teaching and modeling cooperation should be a major focus of education.

Promote Co-Education

Co-education or mixed-sex education provides many benefits to young people. The real world contains men and women. Learning to understand and relate well to the opposite sex will greatly benefit children and teenagers while they are young and later as adults. A few studies have shown that boys and girls sometimes perform better academically in single-sex settings. For example, girls sometimes perform better and are more engaged in science in all-girls classes. Also, some studies indicate that boys and girls learn most effectively with different teaching approaches. For example, boys sometimes do better with more structure in class, while girls sometimes do better with more opportunities to communicate with other students and voice their opinions. In reality, some boys and girls will perform better in single-sex classes, while others will not.[731]

However, academic performance is not the most important aspect of education. The most important factor is best preparing students to live successful and satisfying lives. This mainly involves fostering the development of qualities and skills needed for life success, including self-esteem, social skills, critical thinking skills and empowerment to follow one's unique path in life. Most information needed to succeed in life is learned in the real world, for example, through hands-on job experience. Much of the knowledge acquired in forced K-12 education is forgotten and not needed for life success. The most important output of education is not students with high test scores. It is confident, empowered, socially adept, freethinking young adults.

The fact that girls sometimes perform better in science in all-girls classes does not mean that girls should be isolated from boys. Science grades are not the most important output of education. Girls often outperform boys on verbal skills, while boys sometimes outperform in math and science. This might result from innate differences between men and women. As discussed in the Women's section, women tend to use both halves of the brain simultaneously. They generally are better at big picture thinking, multi-tasking, cooperation, communications, relationships and empathy. Men tend to use only one side of the brain at a time. They often are better at focusing on and completing tasks. Math and science usually involve working through a logic sequence to complete a task and achieve a solution. The male mind is well adapted to do this. Effective verbal communication of perceptions, feelings and other intangibles often requires more subtle or complex analysis, as well as more empathy. The female mind is well adapted for this.

There are many exceptions to these generalizations. But as discussed in the Women's section, the male mind evolved to support and effectively utilize the greater physical strength of men, while the female mind evolved to support and effectively utilize the greater physical nurturing capacity of women. This enabled humans to survive and prosper. Men and women are meant to live together in the same communities and other settings. They balance each other's strengths and form effective, integrated families and communities. Boys and men can learn greater wisdom, cooperation, empathy and relationship skills from girls and women. Girls and women can learn greater power and assertiveness from boys and men. As noted, the fact that girls sometimes underperform in mixed science classes does not mean that girls should be isolated. It is a good opportunity to empower girls, teach them to speak up for themselves, and teach boys to respect girls.

As we evolve away from the ignorant, authoritarian forced education model to empowering freedom-based approaches, performance relative to peers will become less relevant or irrelevant. The focus will not be on the performance of boys versus girls. Underperformance in math and science probably occurs mainly because girls often are less interested in these areas. Girls who like math and science frequently will do well in these subjects, regardless of whether they are in single-sex or mixed-sex classes. With freedom-based education, young people will not be forced to study subjects that they find boring and irrelevant to their lives. This usually is a waste of time because nearly all of the material studied in these classes will be forgotten and not needed later in life. Even worse, ranking students as inadequate on subjects in which they have no interest degrades self-esteem, which is far more important for life success than test scores.

Communicating with and being in the presence of the opposite sex is one of the most joyful and fulfilling aspects of human life. Men and women are innately drawn to each other. We evolved to enjoy being in the presence of each other. Youth should be a time when young people experience the joy and excitement of life. Being in the presence of the opposite sex is a major part of enjoying life. Co-education teaches young people that life should be fun and stimulating. It compels them to pursue a fulfilling and productive life.

Separating boys and girls for the majority of their childhood and teenage lives separates them from reality. It sometimes is useful and fun for boys to only be with boys and girls only with girls. But there are ample opportunities for this with sports, play and other activities. Males and females should not be separated from each other during the majority of their early lives. Co-education strongly promotes the development of social skills, psychological health and empowerment. It best prepares young people to enter the real world where women and men regularly interact with each other.

Reduce Segregation

Reducing segregation is another important action needed in the education area. African American and Latino students attend schools that are more segregated today than before the Civil Rights movement 60 years ago.[732] A main problem with segregation is that children in lower-income schools with large minority populations often receive inferior education. As noted, schools in low-income communities often have larger class sizes, lower quality facilities and learning materials, fewer college preparatory courses, and many other problems.

The 1964 Civil Rights Act sought to ensure that African American and Latino children had equal education. Desegregation orders were used to integrate schools. In 1963, only one percent of African American children in the South attended schools with white children. By the early 1970s, 90 percent attended desegregated schools. Desegregation orders remain in place in over 300 school districts. But these orders usually have not been enforced for decades. Since the 1990s, the Supreme Court has greatly limited the ability of parents to challenge racial inequality in schools as a way to improve the quality of education for their children. School districts not under Civil Rights Act orders are not allowed to use race to balance schools. Parents in these districts must prove that school officials are intentionally discriminating. This is a difficult standard to prove. Prior to Supreme Court weakening of the Civil Rights Act, parents only had to show that children could be harmed by segregation, without showing intent.[733]

The focus on intent once again shows the biased and often irrational nature of the effectively business-appointed Supreme Court. The priority should be whether children are harmed, not intent. The irrational Supreme Court position essentially says that it is okay to harm children, as long as one does not intend to do so. Intent essentially is irrelevant in this case. The sole focus should be on harm. If children are harmed, action should be taken to end the harm. The focus on intent is irrational. No one intends to harm children, except perhaps severe racists. Intent is a difficult or impossible standard to prove in this case. Shifting the focus from harm to intent greatly reduces the ability to use integration to end segregation and improve education.

Segregation often was enforced by bussing students to schools that were far from their homes. This can be problematic. An alternative solution is to ensure that young people in low-income communities receive the same or better quality education as those in wealthier communities. Instead of bussing students from low quality schools in low-income communities to higher quality schools in wealthier communities, ensure that all schools are high quality. Providing high-quality education to students in low-income communities will reduce total costs to society, lower crime and provide many other benefits. (White parents often did not want their children bussed to lower quality, sometimes more violent schools in African American communities. This is a main reason why desegregation and bussing were greatly reduced.)

Segregated schools result mainly from segregated neighborhoods. People have a right to live near those of the same race. However, much of the segregation in the US is not a result of choice. Housing policies often make it difficult for minorities to move to desegregated neighborhoods. Implementing policies that facilitate desegregation of neighborhoods is one of the most important actions needed to desegregate schools.[734] Some people oppose housing desegregation due to concerns about increased crime. These are legitimate concerns. Therefore, desegregation policies, such as expanding low-income housing, should be done in ways that ensure no increase in crime. As discussed in the Crime section, crime largely is a symptom of problems in society, such as ongoing discrimination against African Americans. Ending discrimination and giving African Americans equal opportunity will substantially reduce crime.

Flawed economic and political systems are a main cause of segregation. These unjust, wealth-concentrating systems make life difficult for millions of citizens. As we evolve systems into sustainable forms, higher-quality jobs and business opportunities can be provided to all people who want or need them. This will enable people to more effectively pursue their unique interests and passions in life. It also will facilitate moving out of segregated neighborhoods when necessary to pursue one's career or life ambitions.

Society naturally will become more integrated as we discuss racism more openly and honestly, eliminate discrimination against African Americans and other minorities, and shift the focus of the economy from maximizing the well-being of wealthy people who give large amounts of money to politicians to maximizing the well-being of all citizens.

Teach Clear Communication

Clear communication is essential during this time of widespread public deception and division. As discussed in the Misleading the Public section, large companies and their allies often protect shareholder returns by misleading the public in many ways. Complex issues frequently are presented in grossly oversimplified and deceptive 30-second soundbites. Citizens often are whipped up into a frenzy about how the other side (liberals or conservatives) is destroying society. As a result, emotions frequently overwhelm logic and people blindly accept vested interest deceptions.

Social media also degrades communication. Young people often use cryptic or truncated communications in social media. They frequently do not get much practice communicating fully, clearly and effectively. To balance vested interest public deceptions and truncated social media communications, schools should strive to teach young people how to clearly communicate in written and oral forms. For example, teachers often tell students to write about certain subjects. But young people sometimes are not taught how to do this effectively. To ensure they can communicate effectively, young people should be taught the specifics of clear written and oral communication. There are many ways to do this.

For business or general nonfiction writing, one strategy is to first step back and look at the big picture. Students should identify the goal of their writing. For example, do they wish to teach people about an issue or convince them to take certain actions? Once the goal is clear, students can develop a rough outline of the logic and information sequence that will most effectively achieve the goal. With goals and structure developed, information needs can be identified and data gathered. As students better understand available information, a more detailed outline can be developed. They can be taught to lay out their information and logic in a sequential manner that builds on itself. Students also should be taught to imagine putting themselves into the minds of readers, anticipating reader questions, and then integrating answers into their writing to the greatest extent possible. Effective outlining and data gathering maximize the probability that writers will achieve their goals. It also minimizes the need for rewriting.

A key aspect of effective writing or public speaking is to discuss subjects that one finds interesting. But forced education often compels young people to study issues that they find boring. It frequently is difficult to write or speak about subjects in which one has little interest. Young people often are forced to write about boring material. This trains them to be boring writers and communicators. Freedom-based education minimizes this problem because young people choose to study subjects that they find interesting.

K-12 and higher education also often inhibit the development of superior writing skills by specifying the length of projects. This frequently compels students to fill papers with fluff (i.e. irrelevant or unnecessary information) so that they can achieve the specified length. Writing specific length articles or papers sometimes is necessary in professional settings. However, in general, students should be taught to achieve the writing objective in the most efficient and effective manner possible. If it is possible to write a compelling article and achieve the writing objective in two pages, students should not be compelled to add eight pages of fluff to meet a ten-page requirement. Writing shorter papers often is more difficult than writing long ones. Teaching young people to meet their nonfiction writing goals with the fewest words possible helps them to become clear, effective communicators.

Another problem with clear communication in education relates to textbooks and courses. As noted, there is a vast amount of wasted time in K-12 education. Young people are forced to spend far more time in school than is necessary to learn the relatively small amount of information that usually is retained from K-12 education. Textbooks and courses often seem to be unnecessarily long and boring. It sometimes appears that they are expanded to fit the time allowed. Forcing students to read boring textbooks or take boring courses teaches them to be boring or poor communicators. More efforts should be made to streamline textbooks and courses and make them more interesting and relevant to students' lives.

The most important aspect of clear communication is clear thinking. This precedes clear writing and speaking. If the writer is unclear about their subject and writing strategy, the reader also will be unclear. The ability to think rationally and critically is essential. Young people should be taught to think for themselves and logically and objectively analyze information and issues. Teaching young people to think critically and rationally will help them to see through the extensive public deception in society. It also will help them to organize their ideas and present them in powerful, interesting and effective ways.

Teach Healthy Living

Habits learned when young often are maintained for life. As a result, young people should be taught the components of healthy living, including diet, exercise and psychological health. As discussed in the Sustainable Food Production and Diet section of *Global System Change*, food companies heavily influence nutrition education in schools, in part by providing free nutrition 'education' (i.e. marketing) materials. These often teach young people that animal products and refined carbohydrates are healthy. But these foods cause extensive chronic disease and premature deaths. Organic vegetables, fruits and whole grains are the healthiest foods that humans can eat. Schools should discontinue use of food company marketing/education materials. Instead, students should be taught that whole plant foods minimize disease and maximize health, vitality, mental clarity, athletic performance and longevity.

Students also should be taught the importance of regular physical activity and exercise, safe and empowering perspectives on sex, and psychological health. In addition to teaching this important information, schools should model and promote it, for example, by providing healthy food, physically active school days, and nurturing, supportive, nonjudgmental learning environments.

Provide Daily K-12 Physical Education

As discussed in the Boredom section, physical education classes have been substantially reduced under education reform. This is extremely irrational and counterproductive. The widespread availability of sugar, salt and fat-laden foods strongly drives obesity. In addition, extensive involvement in the cyberworld promotes sedentary lifestyles. To counteract these trends, schools should be increasing physical education, not reducing it. As noted, many studies have shown that physical education improves concentration and academic performance.

Students in all K-12 grades should be provided with at least one hour per day of physical education. Engaging in daily exercise while young greatly increases the likelihood that students will continue regular exercise as adults. With obesity, chronic disease and healthcare costs rising rapidly, greatly increased regular exercise in society is essential. Providing daily K-12 physical education is one of the most effective ways to achieve this.

Extensive efforts should be made to increase noncompetitive physical activities in physical education classes and school in general. Lower skilled or less competitive young people often will not enjoy competitive activities during physical education. This will reduce the likelihood that they engage in regular exercise as adults. As discussed above, there are many ways to engage young people in fun, cooperative, vigorous physical activities. These types of approaches should be expanded in physical education.

Also, young people could be encouraged to focus on self-improvement (i.e. competing with oneself) rather than competing with others. For example, strength, cardiovascular and other physical performance might be measured. But young people only would be made aware of their own performance, not other students. In this way, young people are encouraged to improve physically, without being made to feel inadequate by being compared to stronger, faster or more physically skilled students. This often might be difficult with team sports. But there are many individual physical activities (i.e. running, swimming, weightlifting) where young people can gauge their own performance and improvement, without being compared to others.

Ensure Adequate Recess

Also as discussed in the Boredom section, many schools have eliminated recess under education reform. This is counterproductive and irrational. Like adults, young people need time to process information after classes and lectures. Providing adequate recess and time between classes enhances student learning and well-being. It also gives students time to interact with each other. This fosters the development of communication and social skills. As noted, Japanese schools provide 10 minutes of free time for every 50 minutes in class. US schools should adopt similar policies.

Increase Outdoor Education

Outdoor education and free time should be substantially increased, especially for young children. Humans evolved in nature. For nearly all of human history, children spent extensive time outdoors playing and engaging in other freely chosen activities. Keeping children indoors for most of the day is unnatural. It causes many psychological problems. One pediatrician noted that ADHD is common in conventional preschool and kindergarten classes. But it rarely or never occurs in outdoor education classes. A preschool study found that children who were allowed more free play time in preschool had fewer suspensions and arrests later in life.[735]

As discussed in the Implement Freedom-Based Education section, play helps children to succeed in school and later in life. It develops higher-order cognitive skills, including planning, organizing and decision-making. Playing, caring for animals and other freely chosen activities in nature strongly promote physical and psychological health and well-being. Being in nature also strongly promotes the desire to protect environmental life support systems. As result, outdoor education and activities in nature should be greatly increased for children and teenagers.

The National Outdoor Leadership School provides outstanding, often life changing, wilderness education experiences for teenagers and young adults. But relatively few young people participate in NOLS, similar programs and outdoor education in general. When they do, the experience frequently only is a small part of their education. All children and teenagers should have the opportunity to learn and be in nature. It should represent a major portion of their education.

Minimize Homework

Students often are forced to study subjects in which they have no interest. This produces widespread boredom, frustration and psychological problems in school. Homework frequently extends this boredom and frustration beyond school hours. Young people should have abundant time for play and other interesting activities. This promotes psychological health, empowerment and enjoyment of youth. Homework cuts into young people's free time. As noted, there is a vast amount of wasted, unnecessary time in K-12 education. School schedules should be redesigned in ways that allow ample time for studying in school and minimize the need for homework.

Extensive research shows that homework provides little to no benefit in enhancing learning or performance in elementary and middle school, and only minor benefits in high school.[736] Education expert Alfie Kohn argues that homework often is worse than useless. It is harmful. Homework frequently is stressful for children and parents, creates unnecessary conflicts about getting it done, and limits children's ability to be with friends and family, play, and engage in other beneficial, age-appropriate activities. Alfie Kohn states, "No research has ever found a benefit to assigning homework (of any kind or in any amount) in elementary school. In fact, there isn't even a positive correlation between, on the one hand, having younger children do some homework (vs. none), or more (vs. less), and, on the other hand, any measure of achievement."[737]

Encourage Civic Responsibility and Community Service

Citizens are the ultimate leaders of society in a democracy. To teach and promote effective citizen leadership, young people should be encouraged to take active roles in their communities and society overall. They should be encouraged to identify issues about which they are passionate, and get involved in them. Young people also should be encouraged to engage in community service and other types of service on a regular basis. These types of activities nearly always are more rewarding, enlightening and beneficial than doing homework.

During activism and community service work, children and teenagers engage with other young people and adults. This often provides enjoyment and builds social skills. It also frequently provides abundant hands-on learning, which is the most effective type of learning. Living a life of service is one of the most important suggestions in nearly all major religions. This promotes the cooperation and strong communities needed to achieve sustainability and real prosperity. Helping others also is one of the most important actions needed to achieve a successful and satisfying life. As a result, young people should be encouraged and provided with abundant opportunities to engage in civic responsibility, activism and community service outside of school. These types of activities also should be structured into school days. This will promote hands-on learning, enjoyment of education and psychological health.

Educate Parents

Parenting is the one of most important and difficult activities in society. Knowledge and wisdom are necessary for effective parenting. Yet parents in the US often receive little parent training. Instead, they frequently rely on experience from their own upbringing. This often is helpful. But sometimes it is not, for example, if parents had abusive childhoods. As noted, many

European countries provide education and support to new parents. Similar policies should be expanded in the US. Parents should understand the basic elements of child psychology, non-harmful discipline and effective parenting.

For example, parents should understand that children largely will emulate and learn what parents do, not what they say. If parents encourage children to be kind and help others, but then act rudely and selfishly, children usually will learn to be rude and selfish. Parents also should understand that hitting and other physical punishment can cause psychological damage and severely impede young people's ability to lead successful and satisfying lives. *Parents* should be taught to monitor and manage their emotions, so that they do not harm their children by taking their anger and frustration out on them. Parents also should be taught alternatives to physical punishment. As discussed in the Hitting Children section, millions of parents never hit their children. There are far more effective forms of discipline than physical punishment.

Parents also should be taught to emphasize the positive instead of the negative. Severely criticizing and shaming a child usually causes them to feel small and worthless. This often leads to more bad behavior and problems later in life. Instead of shaming, parents should speak to children compassionately. They should help children to understand why their behavior was wrong, how it affected others, and how it can be rectified and improved in the future. Parents also should teach their children to identify, discuss and understand their emotions. This will help them to control anger and other negative emotions, minimize misbehavior, and get along better with others.

Many well-meaning parents push their children to learn reading, math and other cognitive skills at an early, often preschool age. They frequently are proud of their children's early cognitive skills. However, these are not the most important requirements for life success. As discussed in the Implement Freedom-Based Education section, the most important and developmentally appropriate activities for young children mainly are play, creative endeavors such as art, outdoor activities and other freely chosen activities. These strongly support the development of high self-esteem, good social skills and ability to think for oneself. These qualities are far more important for life success than learning to read or do math at an early age. As a result, parents should be taught to not force their children to learn cognitive activities too early.

In addition, parents of young children should consider limiting or prohibiting screen viewing (TVs, computers, smart phones, video games). Waldorf schools often encourage parents to not let children view screens until ages 5-8. Children's minds are forming. They sometimes have difficulty differentiating the real world from the cyberworld. Allowing screen viewing during the most important psychologically formative years can inhibit young people's ability to understand and effectively function in the real world. Young children are highly sensory and curious. They should be exploring and touching real objects and interacting with real people. In particular, they should be allowed to spend abundant time outside, ideally in nature, whenever possible.

Some parents worry that, if children do not learn cognitive skills early on, they might fall behind in school, not get into good colleges, and not succeed in life. This illustrates the need to end forced education. Young children should not be made to feel inadequate, through competitive grading and standardized curriculums, if they do not advance as quickly as peers. Freedom-based education allows children to advance at their own pace and focus on subjects that they find interesting and relevant. Students from these schools consistently excel in college and careers. Their self-esteem, social skills and other important qualities were not damaged by forced education.

In general, parents should be taught to nurture and support the development of the most important skills and qualities needed for life success. This includes helping parents to understand the self-esteem and social skill degrading impacts of forced education. Parents should be taught to help mitigate these negative impacts, for example, by deemphasizing grades and praising children for successes in areas that they find interesting. Instead of being proud of children's early cognitive abilities, parents should admire and encourage the development of the qualities and skills that truly determine life success, including self-confidence, social skills, ability to manage emotions, and ability to freely choose and pursue activities that one finds interesting.

Improve Adult Education

Improving adult education is another important action needed in the education area. Many people do not get good educations, especially those from low-income communities. About 14 percent of adults in the US cannot read.[738] Poor education, and especially illiteracy, can limit people for life. Giving adults a second chance to get a good education will greatly benefit families, communities and society overall.

Adult education enables people to pursue their unique interests and find more fulfilling work. It also helps people who lost their jobs to improve qualifications and find better jobs. As discussed in the Higher Education section, the US should provide low-cost or free public higher education, as many other developed countries do. This easily could be funded through reductions in corporate welfare. As part of public higher education, adult education classes should be provided that are convenient for people with jobs and/or families.

Many people educate themselves later in life. Libraries greatly facilitate self-education. They provide substantial benefits to children, teenagers and adults. But library funding is being reduced in many states. Louisiana, for example, has eliminated all state funding of libraries.[739] This is being penny wise and pound foolish. Libraries strongly support a well-educated population. They also provide many learning programs and events for children and adults. Libraries play important roles in many communities. As a result, the decline in library funding should be reversed.

In today's online, information-dense world, libraries and librarians can play important roles in helping people to locate, access and utilize important information. Libraries help children to become lifelong readers. Cutting library funding is a sign that society is becoming less enlightened. As discussed in, a Second Enlightenment is needed to once again elevate rational thought and resolve major problems. Fully funding public libraries and adult education are important components of this Second Enlightenment.

Engage Elderly People in Education

Engaging elderly people in K-12 education could greatly benefit young and older people. As discussed in the Elderly section of *Global System Change*, elderly people represent the greatest repository of wisdom in human society. The highest level of knowledge and wisdom usually is gained through experience. Elderly people have the most life experience, and therefore often have the most wisdom. They frequently learned what is truly important in life and how to best navigate life's most difficult challenges. They often learned that modern society's focus on wealth accumulation and beating others is misguided and counterproductive. It frequently produces emptiness and a sense that life was not lived fully. The elderly often realize that love, friendship, helping others and reaching one's fullest potential are the most important things in life. More than anything else, these produce the richest, most satisfying life.

The elderly are our links to the past. If their historic knowledge and wisdom are not passed on to younger generations, it often is lost. Sadly, this frequently is happening. Many retired, elderly people live lonely, isolated lives. This is a tragedy. They often are not being honored and sought out for advice and guidance. As discussed in the Advertising, Media and Culture section, the portrayal and treatment of the elderly reflects society's level of maturity. Many elderly people are respected in the US and other countries. But media often portrays society's implied heroes as younger, aggressive and wealth-seeking.

Greater wisdom is needed in human society to achieve sustainability and real prosperity. We need new role models. Aggressive, rude, self-seeking men are childish. They should not be emulated. Women innately have more wisdom than men. They can help to model the greater wisdom and cooperation needed in human society. But elderly men and women usually have the most wisdom. As a result, we should seek their counsel and guidance more. More opportunities should be created in K-12 education for elderly people to interact with children and teenagers.

The elderly often could provide the love, nurturing and attention that young children need, especially in underfunded schools with large class sizes. Older children and teenagers could greatly benefit from listening to elderly people. Young people could learn living history lessons. Elderly men and women might discuss what it was like raising a family, going to war, building roads and bridges, traveling abroad long ago, and engaging in many other interesting life adventures. They also might share personal stories of tragedy and triumph. Bringing elderly people into schools (or bringing young people to them) will teach young people to respect the elderly. Young people will learn interesting history and knowledge of how to truly succeed in life.

Engaging elderly people in education also is a great gift to the elderly. Helping others is one of the most fulfilling, if not the most fulfilling activity in human society. Elderly people often enjoy sharing their life histories with younger people. Enabling them to do this more frequently would bring them great enjoyment and satisfaction. The most important obligation of older generations is to help younger and future generations to survive and prosper. Engaging elderly people in education helps them to fulfill their mission of promoting the long-term prosperity of humanity. This can help them to feel at peace when they move on to whatever comes after physical death.

Engage Communities in Education

For nearly all of human history, children were not educated in schools. Humans evolved to learn through play and hands-on experience in families and communities. As discussed in the Implement Freedom-Based Education section, children often were raised by communities in many indigenous societies. Adults in the community helped parents to raise children. This gave adults who did not have children the opportunity to participate in the joy and responsibility of raising children.

Humans evolved largely to live in communities. This often is where we find our greatest joy and reach our fullest potential. Encouraging young people to be active in communities builds social skills. They learn from adults, while adults have opportunities to teach and mentor children and teenagers.

Schools could engage communities in education and thereby facilitate the development of stronger, more cooperative communities. Many schools already bring in professionals from local communities to speak with young people. These interactions could be expanded. Schools also could expand activities where students visit and possibly work on projects at local businesses, governments and nonprofit organizations. Schools could further engage communities by establishing or expanding mentoring programs.

As noted, learning academic knowledge is not the most important aspect of education. It is learning key qualities and skills needed for life success. Young people often gain these qualities and learn these skills by interacting with caring, attentive adults. Young people are surrounded by adults in communities. In the past, communities seemed to be much more involved in looking out for and helping children.

But as discussed in the Advertising, Media and Culture section, people often have become more isolated in the US and many other countries. They frequently spend substantial time in their homes engaged in the cyberworld, rather than interacting with neighbors. Advertising and media contribute to isolation and weakening of communities by compelling people to compete with, rather than help, fellow citizens.

The widespread senses of inadequacy caused by advertising and the anger and division caused by divisive media further promote isolation. Media often focuses on rare, but horrible crimes against children. As a result, many families see unknown adults as risks to their children. All of these factors limit children's opportunities to learn from and engage with communities. Children must be protected from dangerous adults. But the vast majority of adults not only are not threats to children, they are potential teachers, mentors, friends and protectors.

Schools could greatly benefit young people by helping to strengthen links between children and communities. In many families, both parents work. As a result, children and teenagers frequently do not get the love and attention they deserve. Strengthening communities and getting to know neighbors more could help overworked or incapacitated parents. It could give more adults opportunities to care for children. It also could help to give young people the care and attention they need when parents are unable to meet these needs.

The most important obligation of society is to care for children and future generations. In this sense, all of the world's adults are the parents of all the world's children. Ultimately, we all are members of one global community and one global family. This perspective will help us to do whatever is necessary to most effectively educate and care for our children (all children).

Improve Business Education

Business education teaches many important aspects of business, such as how to operate efficiently and effectively. However, business education also often is myopic. The environment and society enable business existence. If businesses degrade these larger systems, they ultimately will degrade themselves. Business education usually is focused primarily on maximizing shareholder value. This is logical when a small group of wealthy business owners largely controls government and society, as occurs in the US. Emphasizing shareholder value makes sense in a plutocracy. But nearly all citizens would agree that the US should not be a plutocracy. The US Constitution establishes democracy, not plutocracy.

Focusing primarily on shareholder value is not logical in a democracy. Under democracy, well-informed citizens would require that business structures and the economy be focused primarily on maximizing the well-being of society. Structures and systems that degrade society would not be allowed. They currently exist mainly because citizens have been misled and divided. Many people have been deceived into blindly believing that maximizing the short-term financial well-being of wealthy business owners is the best way to maximize the long-term well-being of society. This position is obviously incorrect.

Placing short-term shareholder returns before all else often compels companies to degrade the environment and society. This has little to do with management ethics, morals or intentions. Nearly all managers and owners of large companies are good people who intend to benefit society. Environmental and social degradation are caused almost completely by flawed business, economic and political systems. These systems frequently force good, well-intentioned people to take actions that harm society. Criticizing business leaders and owners, and their paid political servants, often is counterproductive. The problem largely is systems, not people.

Ending business degradation of life support systems and society requires looking at the big picture and redefining the purpose of business. In a democracy, the purpose should be to benefit and not harm society. What gets measured gets managed. To ensure that businesses only benefit society, we must measure this. Benefiting society should be the primary purpose of business and the economy. As a result, this should be the primary focus of measurement and management. The degree to which companies maximize the well-being of society largely should determine management bonuses, shareholder returns and other critical factors.

In the business education area, this means that the focus should shift from shareholder value analysis to customer value or societal value analysis. When businesses benefit and do not harm society and manage operations well, shareholders often would receive reasonable returns. Shareholder returns should be a byproduct or result of serving society well, not the primary focus of business. Shifting the focus of business and the economy from benefiting shareholders to benefiting society requires implementing the many system changes discussed in *Global System Change*.

To facilitate system change, business education should take a more holistic or whole system approach. Many young people seek business education partly because they want to benefit society. Rather than focusing primarily on shareholder returns, business students should be taught to focus on all of the positive and negative impacts of business. The goal should be to maximize benefits to society while minimizing or eliminating negative impacts.

Corporate responsibility and sustainability have become mainstream business practices. Nearly all large companies have implemented sustainability strategies. Leaders in this field know from experience that minimizing negative environmental and social impacts often provides substantial business and shareholder benefits. As a result, corporate responsibility and sustainability should be major focus areas of business education, on par with marketing, operations management and finance. Many business schools already do this. But more work is needed. Improving business education requires an increased focus on whole system thinking and system change.

Regarding whole system thinking, business education usually includes the study of economics. As discussed throughout *Global System Change*, prevailing economic theories and systems are grossly flawed and myopic. They largely were developed in a theoretical vacuum that ignores much of reality. As a result, these reductionistic theories and systems produce extensive unintended consequences, such as environmental and social degradation. Business and economics students should spend more time studying the larger environmental and social systems that contain the economy and allow it to exist. This whole system thinking will greatly facilitate the evolution of economic systems and business structures into sustainable forms. It also will enable business school graduates to better help their companies succeed in today's rapidly changing world.

Regarding system change, the most important overarching business-related system change is holding companies fully responsible for all negative impacts. When this occurs, they maximize profits by minimizing or eliminating negative impacts. Currently, businesses often influence government to remove regulations that hold them responsible. This frequently makes negatively impacting the environment and society (i.e. acting irresponsibly) the profit-maximizing strategy. Business students should be taught to work with government and other stakeholders in ways that hold businesses more responsible, not less. This ultimately is the only way that businesses can prosper.

Global System Change discusses many actions needed to achieve systemic changes that are essential for the long-term survival and prosperity of humanity. Business schools should be actively engaged in system change. As business research leaders, business schools can play important roles in the development of system change solutions and mechanisms.

Virtually everyone wants businesses to benefit society. Focusing primarily on maximizing shareholder returns is driving substantial environmental and social degradation. Maximizing the well-being of business and society requires that new business structures and systems be developed. This is an exciting time for business. Business students should be involved in the evolution of businesses into sustainable forms.

The majority of business education probably should continue to be focused on the basics of business, including marketing, operations, product development, human resources, accounting, finance, management strategy, and now corporate responsibility and sustainability. However, time should be allocated for studying, and to the greatest extent possible, engaging in collaborative and other system change efforts. Business can and should be a major driver of systemic changes that ensure the long-term well-being of society and business. Teaching business students how to help companies effectively engage in collaborative system change will strongly benefit business and society.

Optimize Developing Country Education

As developing countries modernize, they often adopt Western or developed country education systems. This frequently causes problems. Western-style education often causes young people in developing countries to become interested in Western products and lifestyles. They frequently lose interest in their own cultures and move away from villages to cities. Once there, they often cannot find jobs and wind up getting into trouble.

Western media, advertising and companies strongly promote Western culture and products in developing countries. This helps companies to meet their structurally required obligation to provide ever-increasing shareholder returns. But it often severely degrades developing countries. These countries frequently have rich cultures and traditions that enabled their citizens to prosper for hundreds of years. Fancy cars, clothes and other Western products can seem more appealing, especially to young people who often lack the wisdom and experience to know what truly provides a successful and satisfying life.

Advertising and media can make Western culture seem appealing. But looking beneath the surface reveals many problems. For example, here in the supposedly prosperous US, we are world leaders in obesity, mental illness, addiction, divorce and illegal drug use. We are degrading life support systems here and around the world. And we have rapidly growing inequality and other social problems. Pulling off the advertising and media-generated Western mask reveals a deeply divided, grossly inequitable and unsustainable society. Western society, with its severe, often suicidal flaws, largely should not be emulated.

The term developing country is misleading. It implies that developed countries are better. They are in some ways. But in the most important ways, they often are not. In terms of environmental degradation, developing countries often are much closer to sustainability than developed countries. Survival takes priority over everything else. In this most important sense, developing countries often are better than developed countries. This indicates that the misleading term development should be replaced with more useful and beneficial terminology, such as pursuing or achieving real prosperity.

Rather than emulating Western style so-called development, developing countries should adopt a customized approach, like the Gross National Happiness strategy used in Bhutan. Developing countries should look at the big picture, consider the strengths of their countries that they wish to retain and promote, select Western technologies and approaches that are useful, and reject the rest.

Education systems should be implemented that support this customized strategy for achieving real prosperity. Young people should learn and understand the cultures and traditions of their countries. They should be taught how these traditions often provide many benefits, such as stable families and communities, low crime and frequently high levels of life satisfaction.

In addition, developing countries could consider implementing some of the suggestions made in this education book. For example, all human beings deserve to be taught through freedom-based rather than forced education.

This honors the uniqueness of each person and empowers them to pursue their own path in life. The Western forced education model primarily teaches indoctrination and obedience. We should not be degrading humans anywhere on this planet with this authoritarian approach to education.

Education follows society. In general, each society should collectively decide how they wish to achieve sustainability and real prosperity. Once this is clear, optimized education systems can be developed and implemented that most effectively achieve the goals of society.

Emulate Finland

Finland is highlighted several times throughout this book. For many years, Finland's education system has been ranked as the best or near the best in the world. The country achieves superior education performance, while spending less on education than many other developed countries. For example, education costs per student, including higher education costs, are nearly 40 percent less in Finland than in the US.[740] With superior performance achieved for a competitive cost, many countries seek to emulate Finland's education system and success. The US should do the same.

Finland's approach to education illuminates the defects of US education reform. In the US, children begin rigorous academic study at a young age, sometimes in preschool. Children and teenagers mainly study core courses, have long school days, do large amounts of homework and take extensive standardized tests. Physical education and recess often are minimized. Teachers and teachers unions frequently are demeaned. Degraded teacher pay, benefits and academic freedom often force good teachers out of the profession or prevent them from entering in the first place. Children frequently endure large class sizes, inadequate facilities and learning materials, constant monitoring and strict discipline, especially in low-income communities. The militaristic US approach to education teaches young people to obey authorities and not question prevailing ideas.

Finland achieves better results for less money by doing nearly the exact opposite of the US. Faced with a weak economy in the 1970s, Finland decided that education was critical to improving the economy and society. The country committed to providing outstanding education to each child. There are no private schools in Finland. All schools, preschool to university, are publicly funded at equal levels. Having all public schools is more efficient and cost-effective. Public and private wealth is not used to fund multiple, often redundant school systems (i.e. public, private, charter). Equal funding means that all children (i.e wealthy, low-income, rural, urban) receive the same high quality education.[741]

The emphasis in Finland's school system is on cooperation, not competition. Schools are not ranked. The focus is on learning, not grading. Children do not begin school until age seven. Nearly all five to seven-year-old children attend free, play-based preschool. This prepares them for classroom education. Children have shorter schooldays and do less homework than in the US. School begins at 8 to 9 AM and ends at 1 to 2 PM. Students do less than one hour of homework per day on average. This leaves young people with abundant time for family, friends and fun.[742]

Finland's schools strive to create an environment that is safe, respectful and highly supportive. Students get 15-minute breaks after each class and 75 minutes of recess. They are encouraged to play outdoors. Students go on many field trips, often in nature. All students are provided with free lunches and access to healthcare, mental health services and guidance counseling.[743]

The high honor and status of the teaching profession is a main reason why Finland's education system is so successful. Teachers, especially at the college and university level, are among the most respected people in society. Primary school teaching is the most sought after profession among college graduates. Finland provides free masters-level training for teachers. Less than 10 percent of applicants to this program are accepted. After rigorous training, teachers are given extensive flexibility to teach in the way they feel is best for students. They are told what to teach generally, but not how to teach. They are encouraged to be creative and think outside the box.[744]

Most teachers remain with the same students for five years. This enables them to get to know students well, better understand their needs, and tailor lessons most effectively. Teachers spend less time in school than US teachers and have more time for lesson preparation and student evaluation.

Students in Finland take only one standardized test at the end of high school. Teachers regularly evaluate students and develop their own tests. Teachers' aides are available to help struggling or immigrant children. The focus on providing outstanding education to each student causes Finland to have the smallest gap between the best and worst performing students.[745]

Finland already has one of the best education systems in the world. But they nevertheless are making it even better. Education experts in Finland argue that the world is changing.[746] Traditional subject-focused, classroom-based approaches used for over 100 years often no longer are appropriate or effective in modern society. As a result, the country is making several changes.

A main change is switching from traditional subject-based learning to topic-based.[747] Rather than studying separate subjects, such as economics, government, history, languages and geography, students might study the European Union, for example, in a way that combines all of these subjects. This whole system approach is more efficient because it simultaneously teaches several subjects. It also is more effective because everything is connected in the real world. A subject-based approach illuminates real world linkages and better prepares young people to function effectively in society.

Another major change is moving from the traditional classroom model where students sit passively, listen to teachers talk and wait to be questioned. Instead, Finland is implementing a more collaborative approach where students work in small groups, solve problems, and improve communication skills. Some teachers who spent many years using subject-based, traditional classroom approaches initially resisted the changes. But small financial incentives encouraged them to go along. Once they tried the new teaching styles, many teachers preferred them and did not want to go back to the old ways. Students also frequently prefer the collaborative, topic-based learning style, as indicated by improved student performance.[748]

Companies that profit from the current US education system, and their paid political and media puppets, often attempt to mislead citizens into believing that an education system like Finland's could not work in the US. One of the most common arguments is to say that Finland's education system works well because they have a homogeneous society. It would not work in the heterogeneous US. But the immigrant population has been growing in Finland for many years. The country's education system focuses on helping all children to succeed, including immigrant children. As a result, these children do as well as other students in Finland.[749]

The idea that it is not possible to implement an education system like Finland's in a heterogeneous society is not logical. The implication is that widespread racial, cultural and socioeconomic diversity make it impractical to provide compassionate, high-quality education to each child. Vested interests seem to imply that some children require a strict, highly standardized education, while others do not. This is irrational. A society being homogeneous or heterogeneous is largely or completely irrelevant to the issue of providing compassionate, high quality education to all young people.

Vested interests imply that children from low-income, middle-income and minority families require a strict, highly regimented education to do well in school. (But apparently it is acceptable for children from wealthy families in the US to get the same compassionate, high-quality education provided to all children in Finland.) The idea that the strict, difficult, competitive US education approach is necessary to do well in school is wrong. Finland proves it wrong.

Children do not need to spend long hours in school and do extensive homework to learn the information usually taught in K-12 education. As noted, children in Finland spend less time in school and do less homework, but learn the material more effectively. Happy children and teenagers, who are given plenty of free time to exercise and play, usually will do better in school, even if they spend less time there. Forcing young people to endure long, boring, difficult, competitive education will not improve education performance. Instead, it will produce what we see in the US – high levels of drug abuse, delinquency, inattention, depression, anxiety and poor academic performance.

Children educated in a respectful, cooperative, highly supportive environment will be happy and successful. They will grow up to be happy, successful adults. This potentially is a main reason for perpetuating the strict, disempowering US education system. Young people who experience joyous, productive, successful childhoods usually will demand the same when they grow up. They will not tolerate boring, difficult, low-paying, low-security jobs for the rest of their lives. Young people who are taught to think for themselves often will question our grossly flawed, unjust economic and political systems and demand that they be changed.

To illustrate, people who were indoctrinated in the authoritarian US education system might blindly believe the idea that outstanding education cannot be provided to each child in a heterogeneous society. But those who are taught to think for themselves would quickly see the irrational nature of this vested interest-protecting deception.

Vested interests also might attempt to mislead citizens into thinking that those advocating implementing an outstanding public education system like Finland's want to eliminate private schools. Once again, critical thinking would reveal the irrationality of this position. Parents should be free to send children to private schools. But citizens should not be compelled to support schools that do not meet the same standards and accountability requirements as traditional public schools. Wealthier parents should support public education, even if they send their children to private schools, because they have an obligation to support the society that enabled them to become wealthy. Supporting excellent public education benefits all citizens by strongly promoting a prosperous society.

The strict, difficult, boring US education system suppresses and demeans young people with competitive grading and standardized curriculums that ignore students' unique talents and interests. Children are taught to obey authorities and indoctrinated to not question prevailing ideas. The authoritarian US education system strongly perpetuates plutocracy. Once We the People wake up from our vested interest-induced division and deception, we will demand the implementation of true democracy and an education system that provides all children with the compassionate, high-quality education they deserve.

While Finland's education system is ranked near the best in the world, a few Asian countries sometimes score better on math and science. But these rankings are deceptive. High test scores are not the most important output of education. The factors that most strongly promote successful individuals and society overall include strong social skills, high self-esteem, and empowerment to build one's life around their unique talents and passions. Finland's supportive, respectful, empowering education system strongly promotes the development of these critical traits. If country rankings were based mainly on these most important outputs of education, Finland probably would be ranked even higher.

All children, be they black, white, rich, poor, urban or rural, deserve a compassionate, outstanding education. Finland provides this. Their system cost-effectively produces happy, confident, successful adults. As a result, Finland's education system is highly worthy of emulation in the US and other countries.

Education Conclusion

This book discussed many education problems in the US and other countries. It also proposed many solutions. The overall suggested strategy is to end the abomination of so-called education reform and implement a truly effective and empowering education system.

The education strategy being implemented in the US since the 1980s appears to be based on magical, irrational thinking. Finland and other countries that achieve world leading education performance utilize strong, well-funded public education systems with honored, well-compensated teachers. This is the strategy that the US employed when we were a world leader in education 50 years ago. And yet, we seem to think that if we do the opposite of what world leaders do (i.e. defund and privatize public education, suppress teachers), we somehow will magically surpass, or at least catch up to world leaders. This strategy makes no sense. It would be laughable if it were not so harmful to young people and society.

From the perspective of educating young people well, the current education 'reform' strategy is irrational. However, the US is not focused on maximizing the well-being of children or society overall (as the Constitution requires). Our flawed systems compel the US to focus on the short-term financial well-being of the small group of wealthy business owners who largely control government. From this perspective, the US education strategy is highly logical. If the overall goal of education is to help a small group of wealthy people to get continuously wealthier, we have implemented the perfect strategy.

Privatizing and standardizing education will increase the short-term financial returns of education and related companies. Degrading children and society through harmful education ultimately will harm business in the longer-term. But the long-term well-being of business (much less society) is not on the radar screen of our myopic economic and political systems. These suicidal systems require that large companies and the economy continuously seek short-term growth, regardless of how much this degrades society.

To achieve never-ending growth, businesses often attempt to take over government services. Many people in the business and financial sectors see privatizing public education as a profitable investment opportunity. They believe that applying business processes to public education will drive down costs and improve efficiency and quality. Standardizing and mechanizing processes often is important when producing products in factories. Standardization, quality control and automation frequently are essential for business success. But human beings are not products and schools are not factories. Humans are unique, infinitely complex living beings. Standardizing products often is useful. But attempting to standardize humans is extremely harmful. Standardization is driving wisdom and compassion out of the education system. This business-like approach to education is grossly irrational.

Providing new investment opportunities is a main reason why public education is being privatized. But an even more important reason might be perpetuating flawed systems. Our economic and political systems require that a small group of wealthy citizens extract ever-increasing amounts of wealth from society. This causes increasingly difficult lives for millions of people. As the pain of citizens grows, greater suppression is necessary to ensure that people do not rise up, work together and end the theft of their wealth and power. Controlling education gives large companies and their wealthy owners strong ability to suppress and control society. Businesses can control the content of education and ensure that young people learn only that which benefits business. In addition, Orwellian strategies are used in education that mirror our larger authoritarian society. Young people are constantly monitored, strictly disciplined, and taught to obey authorities.

From the perspective of maximizing the short-term well-being of business, indoctrination is perhaps the most important part of education. In this sense, the US is similar to the Soviet Union. During the Cold War, we frequently criticized the Soviet Union for indoctrinating or brainwashing their children. Young people in the USSR often were taught that capitalism and the US were bad or evil. They were strongly discouraged from examining, or especially questioning, the flawed policies and programs of the Soviet Union.

We seem to be employing a similar indoctrination program in the US. Young people usually are taught that our economic and political systems are good and admirable. They often are not encouraged to examine the fundamental, suicidal flaws of these systems. They also frequently are not encouraged to explore or promote alternatives to the big business-controlled status quo.

This indoctrination, combined with standardization and strict discipline, severely suppresses the will and freedom of young people. They are not taught to think for themselves and do what they believe is right in life. Instead, they are taught to passively obey authorities. Fear (caused by strict discipline) and shaming (through competitive grading) are used to break the will of young people. Authoritarian education trains children and teenagers to passively and obediently do what they are told to do for the rest of their lives.

The evolution of US education since the 1980s should not surprise anyone. As a small group of wealthy people gained greater control of government and both major political parties, an education system was implemented that perpetuates this abuse of citizens' right to rule themselves. The current education system strongly supports plutocracy. Young people are conditioned to passively accept the ongoing theft of their wealth and power.

At a societal level, public deception is essential for keeping our unfair systems in place. Business-controlled media foments division and hatred in society. As a result, emotions often block rational thought. People are trained to blindly believe irrational ideas, such as liberals or conservatives are responsible for most of the problems in society and government is inherently bad. Rational thought would quickly reveal the illogical nature of these positions. Liberals or conservatives are not degrading society. Main causes of degradation include corporate welfare and business control of government. Government is not inherently bad. It is an expression of the people. The government established by our Founders enabled the US to grow into one of the greatest countries in human history.

CONCLUSION

Business and government are best suited for different activities. For-profit structures often can produce high-quality, innovative, low-cost products. But the business strength of efficiently managing production frequently is not well-suited for managing or caring for humans.

Healthcare provides a good example. As discussed in the Healthcare section, in the 1960s, much of the US healthcare system was run on a not-for-profit basis. As a result, US healthcare costs were comparable to other developed countries. However, once healthcare became largely for-profit, healthcare costs rose substantially, while coverage, quality and results often declined. Now the US has by far the most expensive healthcare system in the world, by far the worst coverage among developed countries, and mediocre results. For-profit healthcare puts the health and lives of citizens in fundamental, systemically-mandated conflict with shareholders. If shareholder returns are not put ahead of citizens, healthcare companies might go out of business or be taken over. This system of seeking never-ending financial return growth inevitably drives ongoing price increases and service quality reductions. It is the main reason why the US has the most expensive, worst coverage healthcare system in the developed world.

The same situation is evolving with prisons. For-profit prisons put the well-being of shareholders in systemically-mandated conflict with the well-being of prisoners. Prison companies give money to politicians and lobby for long-term incarceration for nonviolent offenses. Maximizing incarceration and recidivism helps to maximize shareholder returns, but severely degrades society. The need to provide ever-increasing profits often drives ongoing cost reductions in prisons. As a result, the basic needs of prisoners frequently are not adequately met. The structural requirement to place shareholders ahead of prisoners often compels for-profit prisons to treat inmates like animals or human garbage. This flawed system harms prisoners, lowers rehabilitation, increases recidivism, and thereby increases shareholder returns.

The same is happening in education. For-profit schools place shareholders in fundamental conflict with students. When there are conflicts between shareholders and students (as there frequently are), students often must suffer. Otherwise, for-profit schools might go out of business. For-profit education will create the same results as for-profit healthcare. The US will have the highest education costs, while providing poor education to many students. Children from wealthier families will get high-quality education, in the same way they currently get high-quality healthcare. Children from low-income families often will get lower quality education, in the same way they frequently get low-quality or no healthcare.

Applying business efficiencies to nonliving products often is beneficial. But the current for-profit structure generally should not be used to care for humans. The goal of human-focused activities (i.e. education, healthcare, incarceration) should be to maximize the well-being of humans. Not-for-profit structures, such as government, enable this to be the primary goal. But our flawed systems would not allow the primary focus of a publicly traded for-profit entity to be anything other than profit. Focusing primarily on anything else ultimately often would put the entity out of business.

For-profit structures that are not required to seek never-ending profit growth regardless of negative impacts on society might be able to effectively provide human services. Privately held companies often do not face the suicidal growth requirements of the capital markets. However, in their quest for ever-increasing shareholder returns, publicly traded companies frequently acquire privately held companies and impose their suicidal growth requirements. This makes it virtually impossible for the overall for-profit economic system to provide higher-quality, lower-cost human services than government over the longer-term. Other countries prove and rational thought shows that not-for-profit structures, such as government, often can provide education, healthcare, incarceration and other human services more efficiently and effectively over the mid to longer-term than for-profit entities.

The United States was born in the Age of Enlightenment and Reason. Our main Founders were leading Enlightenment thinkers. They honored rational thought. They used it to illuminate the harmful aspects of religious and political dogma, and then move beyond them. Since the 1980s, we have descended into a New Dark Age. Authoritarianism and fear often compel people to blindly believe irrational and harmful economic, political and religious dogma. We must rise above this, as our Founders did. We need a Second Enlightenment. We must use rational thought to see through irrational dogma and public deception. Rational thought will show that we should not be turning over the care of humans to entities that are structurally required to focus on something that often is in conflict with the well-being of humans.

Most importantly, rational thought and intuitive wisdom will show that we must stand up for our children. They are vulnerable. They have no frame of reference. For example, children in abusive families usually do not understand that their families have problems. They often adapt and survive by assuming that they are flawed and deserve to be abused. It is the same with authoritarian education systems. Forced education frequently makes children feel inadequate and unhappy. They usually do not understand that the education system is flawed. Young people often adapt and survive disempowering education by assuming that they are not as talented or valuable as other students. We must not put our vulnerable children into these unintentionally abusive education environments any longer.

It is time to end business-focused education reform. This abomination has been harming our children and society long enough. This is not said as criticism of those who support privatizing public education. They are good people who mean to help, not harm, children. But they often apparently blindly believe the irrational philosophy that putting business before all else will maximize the well-being of children and society. This obviously is incorrect. Putting business first will maximize the well-being of business. If we want to maximize the well-being of children, we must put children first. Entities that educate our children should be primarily focused on the well-being of children, not the well-being of shareholders. People who support privatizing public education also frequently do so because they are locked into flawed systems. Their companies might go out of business or they might lose their jobs if public education is not privatized.

The slightest amount of rational thought shows the obvious solution. We should emulate Finland and other world leaders in education. We should reestablish strong, well-funded public K-12 and higher education. We also should reestablish the honor, dignity and attractiveness of the K-12 and higher education teaching professions.

Public education is one of the most important and cost-effective investments society can make. It is a public good. Public education hugely benefits society. Privatizing it will severely degrade society. Therefore, we must fully and equally fund public K-12 schools and higher education institutions. No public funding should be provided to schools that do not meet the same standards as traditional public schools. In particular, we must end public funding of religious education. This is an obvious and gross violation of our Constitution.

Once we reestablish the superior strategy (strong public education), we can move beyond it. Even countries that lead the world in education utilize forced education. These systems often degrade the most important qualities needed for success in life – self-esteem, social skills, critical thinking skills and empowerment to pursue one's unique talents and passions in life.

We need a new paradigm in education. The current system teaches indoctrination and obedience. The new system should teach freedom and empowerment. The Higher Education Solutions and Education Solutions sections discussed many aspects of empowering, sustainable education. For example, we should quickly phase out competitive grading, extensive standardized curriculums, zero-intelligence discipline, and pervasive, Orwellian monitoring of children and teenagers. We should build student self-esteem, model cooperation, promote whole system thinking, teach intuitive wisdom, and encourage rational, objective, critical thinking. We should empower and teach young people to identify and build their lives around their unique talents and passions.

Ultimately, we should implement freedom-based education. Our society faces many severe environmental, social, economic and political problems. Suicidal economic and political systems are rapidly degrading life support systems and society. We must not teach young people to passively go along with this destruction. We must empower them to think for themselves and follow their hearts. Freedom-based education will best prepare them to resolve the major challenges facing humanity and live successful and satisfying lives.

This book discusses the need for a Second Enlightenment. The shining light of rational thought will end the New Dark Age. K-12 and higher edu-

CONCLUSION

cation can and should play major roles in nurturing, supporting and developing the Second Enlightenment. The US Founders used rational thought to rise above irrational dogma. Let them inspire us to do the same. It is time to do the right thing for our children.

Endnotes

1. Paul Tough, Americans Are Losing Faith in the Value of College. Whose Fault is That?, www.NYTimes.com, September 5, 2023

2. Keith Olson, The G. I. Bill and Higher Education: Success and Surprise, American Quarterly Vol. 25, No. 5, December 1973.

3. Dr. C. Alonzo Peters, To Hell With Student Loans -- It's Time for College to be Free, www.AlterNet.org, November 18, 2010.

4. Colin Greer, The Rise and Fall of the American Childhood, www.AlterNet.org, July 19, 2012.

5. World Rankings of the U.S. ... Education ... NEHA, Journal of Environmental Health, March 2011.

6. Joshua Holland, Teachers Make Handy Scapegoats, But Spiraling Inequality Is Really What Ails Our Education System, www.AlterNet.org, March 4, 2013.

7. Joseph Stiglitz, Equal Opportunity, Our National Myth, New York Times, February 16, 2013.

8. Same as above.

9. Drew DeSilver, U.S. students' academic achievement still lags that of their peers in many other countries, Pew Research Center, February 15, 2017.

10. Eric Zuesse, America Is Far from #1, www.AlterNet.org, February 7, 2013.

11. World Rankings of the U.S. ... Education ... NEHA, Journal of Environmental Health, March 2011.

12. George Scialabba, How Bad Is It?, www.TheNewInquiry.com, May 26, 2012.

13. Mary Beth Marklein, SAT, ACT: Most high school kids lack skills for college, USA TODAY, September 25, 2012.

14. Marian Wright Edelman, The State of America's Children 2012, www.AlterNet.org, August 7, 2012.

15. Colin Greer, Fighting School Failure Isn't Rocket Science -- We Know What Works, www.AlterNet.org, April 4, 2010.

16. Michael Ventura, Letters at 3AM: The System Ain't the System, www.AustinChronicle.com, August 31, 2012.

17. Dan Lips et. al, Does Spending More on Education Improve Academic Achievement?, www.Heritage.org, September 8, 2008.

18. Melanie Hanson, U.S. Public Education Spending Statistics, Education Data Initiative, June 15, 2022.

19. Same as above.

20. Revenues and Expenditures for Public Elementary and Secondary Education, National Center for Education Statistics. Accessed February 15, 2006.

21. Michael B. Sauter et. al., The 10 Richest -- and Poorest -- School Districts in America, www.AlterNet.org, June 11, 2012.

22. Rebecca Strauss, Schooling Ourselves in an Unequal America, New York Times, June 16, 2013.

23. Eduardo Porter, In Public Education, Edge Still Goes to Rich, New York Times, November 5, 2013.

24. Michael B. Sauter et. al., The 10 Richest -- and Poorest -- School Districts in America, www.AlterNet.org, June 11, 2012.

25. Amy Goodman et. al., Poverty Is the Problem With our Public Schools, Not Teachers' Unions, www.AlterNet.org, August 26, 2011.

26. Jeff Bryant, Public Education's 'Shock Doctrine Summer' Rolls Out Once More, www.AlterNet.org, July 5, 2012.

27. Stan Karp, The Problems with the Common Core, Rethinking Schools, Winter 2013/14.

28. Grace Chen, Decreasing Public High School Elective Programs, www.PublicSchoolReview.com, September 8, 2020.

29. Jeff Bryant, Why Mayor De Blasio Is Right About Charter Schools, www.AlterNet.org, March 17, 2014.

30. Same as above.

31. Colin Greer, 10 Ways School Reformers Get It Wrong, www.AlterNet.org, August 6, 2012.

32. Joseph Stiglitz, Equal Opportunity, Our National Myth, New York Times, February 16, 2013.

33. Colin Greer, 10 Ways School Reformers Get It Wrong, www.AlterNet.org, August 6, 2012.

34. Joshua Holland, Teachers Make Handy Scapegoats, But Spiraling Inequality Is Really What Ails Our Education System, www.Al-

ENDNOTES

terNet.org, March 4, 2013.

35 Colin Greer, 10 Ways School Reformers Get It Wrong, www.AlterNet.org, August 6, 2012.

36 Jeff Bryant, When Being 'For The Kids' Really Isn't, www.AlterNet.org, March 5, 2014.

37 Joshua Holland, Teachers Make Handy Scapegoats, But Spiraling Inequality Is Really What Ails Our Education System, www.AlterNet.org, March 4, 2013.

38 Paul Buchheit, What's Wrong with American Education Policy? It's as Simple as A-B-C, www.AlterNet.org, September 24, 2012.

39 Jeff Bryant, When Being 'For The Kids' Really Isn't, www.AlterNet.org, March 5, 2014.

40 Joshua Holland, Teachers Make Handy Scapegoats, But Spiraling Inequality Is Really What Ails Our Education System, www.AlterNet.org, March 4, 2013.

41 Diane Ravitch, Charter Schools Are a Colossal Mistake. Here's Why, www.AlterNet.org, October 2, 2013.

42 Same as above.

43 Michael B. Sauter et. al., The 10 Richest -- and Poorest -- School Districts in America, www.AlterNet.org, June 11, 2012.

44 Amy Goodman et. al., Poverty Is the Problem With our Public Schools, Not Teachers' Unions, www.AlterNet.org, August 26, 2011.

45 Rebecca Strauss, Schooling Ourselves in an Unequal America, New York Times, June 16, 2013.

46 World Rankings of the U.S. ... Education ...

NEHA, Journal of Environmental Health, March 2011.

47 Alfie Kohn, What No Child Left Behind Left Behind, www.AlterNet.org, December 22, 2015.

48 Same as above.

49 Gregory Korte, The Every Student Succeeds Act vs. No Child Left Behind: What's changed?, USA Today, December 10, 2015.

50 Same as above.

51 Stan Karp, The Problems with the Common Core, Rethinking Schools, Winter 2013/14.

52 Thom Hartmann, Why You Can Kiss Public Education (and the Middle Class) Goodbye, www.AlterNet.org, December 14, 2012.

53 Jeff Bryant, Get Ready For America's Next 'Education Crisis', www.AlterNet.org, December 13, 2012.

54 Same as above.

55 No Child Left Behind Waivers Granted To 33 U.S. States, Some With Strings Attached, The Huffington Post, July 19, 2012.

56 Paul L. Thomas, Ed.D., Obama Won, But Did Educators Lose In the Process?, www.AlterNet.org, November 12, 2012.

57 Paul Buchheit, What's Wrong with American Education Policy? It's as Simple as A-B-C, www.AlterNet.org, September 24, 2012.

58 Paul L. Thomas, Ed.D., What Real School Reform Looks Like, www.AlterNet.org, December 11, 2012.

59 Kristin Rawls, five Ways Louisiana's New Voucher Program Spells Disaster for Public Education, www.AlterNet.org, June 8, 2012.

60 Same as above.

61 Daniel Denvir, How "No Child Left Behind" Unleashed a Nationwide Epidemic of Cheating, www.AlterNet.org, May 25, 2012

62 Diane Ravitch, Charter Schools Are a Colossal Mistake. Here's Why, www.AlterNet.org, October 2, 2013.

63 80 percent of Michigan Charter Schools are For-Profits, www.Forbes.com, September 29, 2011.

64 Jeff Faux, Education Profiteering: Wall Street's Next Big Thing?, www.AlterNet.org, October 15, 2012.

65 Jeff Bryant, Public Education's 'Shock Doctrine Summer' Rolls Out Once More, www.AlterNet.org, July 5, 2012.

66 Paul Buchheit, What's Wrong with American Education Policy? It's as Simple as A-B-C, www.AlterNet.org, September 24, 2012.

67 Jeff Faux, Education Profiteering: Wall Street's Next Big Thing?, www.AlterNet.org, October 15, 2012.

68 David Sirota, Charter Schools Are Not the Silver Bullet, AlterNet.org, March 23, 2012.

69 Paul Buchheit, The four Most Profound Ways Privatization Perverts Education, www.AlterNet.org, January 16, 2014.

70 Jeff Faux, Education Profiteering: Wall Street's Next Big Thing?, www.AlterNet.org, October 15, 2012.

71 Diane Ravitch, Charter Schools Are a Colossal

Mistake. Here's Why, www.AlterNet.org, October 2, 2013.

72 Paul Buchheit, What's Wrong with American Education Policy? It's as Simple as A-B-C, www.AlterNet.org, September 24, 2012.

73 Valerie Strauss, Ravitch: Why states should say 'no thanks' to charter schools, The Washington Post, February 13, 2012.

74 Same as above.

75 Jack Jennings, Proportion of U.S. Students in Private Schools is 10 Percent and Declining, Huffington Post, March 28, 2013.

76 Joshua Holland, Teachers Make Handy Scapegoats, But Spiraling Inequality Is Really What Ails Our Education System, www.AlterNet.org, March 4, 2013.

77 Paul L. Thomas, Ed.D., Obama Won, But Did Educators Lose In the Process?, www.AlterNet.org, November 12, 2012.

78 Pamela Kripke, My Public School Beat-Down, www.AlterNet.org, August 14, 2012.

79 Colin Greer, 10 Ways School Reformers Get It Wrong, www.AlterNet.org, August 6, 2012.

80 Les Leopold, Shocking Report Explodes five Myths About American Education, www.AlterNet.org, September 18, 2012.

81 Paul L. Thomas, Ed.D., Obama Won, But Did Educators Lose In the Process?, www.AlterNet.org, November 12, 2012.

82 Paul Buchheit, What's Wrong with American Education Policy? It's as Simple as A-B-C, www.AlterNet.org, September 24, 2012.

83 Greg Toppo, More teachers green in the classroom, USA TODAY, September 5, 2012.

84 Same as above.

85 Ahiza Garcia, Teach for America applications decline again, www.CNN.com, August 17, 2015.

86 Morgaen L. Donaldson et al., TFA Teachers: How Long Do They Teach? Why Do They Leave?, Education Week, October 4, 2011.

87 Julian Vasquez Heilig et.al., Teach For America: A Review of the Evidence, University of Texas at Austin, June 2010.

88 James Cersonsky, A Challenge to Teach For America's Corporate Orientation, From Those on the Inside, The American Prospect, July 16, 2013.

89 Anna Simonton, How Wall Street Power Brokers Are Designing the Future of Public Education as a Money-Making Machine, www.AlterNet.org, December 5, 2013.

90 Chad Sommer, Teach For America: The International Brotherhood of Corporate Interests?, www.EduShyster.com, January 7, 2014.

91 Same as above.

92 Max Blumenthal, Wealthy Widow Is Pouring Millions into Teach for America, Promoting a Pro-Israel Agenda to Needy and Impressionable Children, www.AlterNet.org, August 29, 2013.

93 James Cersonsky, A Challenge to Teach For America's Corporate Orientation, From Those on the Inside, The American Prospecct, July 16, 2013.

94 Max Blumenthal, Wealthy Widow Is Pouring Millions into Teach for America, Promoting a Pro-Israel Agenda to Needy and Impressionable Children, www.AlterNet.org, August 29, 2013.

95 Julian Vasquez Heilig et.al., Teach For America: A Review of the Evidence, University of Texas at Austin, June 2010.

96 Paul Decker et al., The Effects of Teach For America on Students: Findings from a National Evaluation, Mathematica Policy Research, 2004.

97 Deborah Appleman, PhD, Counterpoint: Why I oppose Teach for America, Star Tribune, June 29, 2009.

98 Same as above.

99 Jessie B. Ramey, Six Questions for Teach for America, www.Yinzercation.wordpress.com, November 8, 2013.

100 James Cersonsky, A Challenge to Teach For America's Corporate Orientation, From Those on the Inside, The American Prospecct, July 16, 2013.

101 Paul L. Thomas, Ed.D., Obama Won, But Did Educators Lose In the Process?, www.AlterNet.org, November 12, 2012.

102 Jeff Faux, Education Profiteering: Wall Street's Next Big Thing?, www.AlterNet.org, October 15, 2012.

103 Same as above.

104 Paul Buchheit, What's Wrong with American Education Policy? It's as Simple as A-B-C, www.AlterNet.org, September 24, 2012.

105 Jeff Faux, Education Profiteering: Wall Street's Next

ENDNOTES

Big Thing?, www.AlterNet.org, October 15, 2012.

106 Same as above.

107 Harold Meyerson, No Class Warfare Here!, The American Prospect, July 15, 2011.

108 Jeff Faux, Education Profiteering: Wall Street's Next Big Thing?, www.AlterNet.org, October 15, 2012.

109 Kristin Rawls, five Biggest Lies About America's Public Schools – Debunked, www.AlterNet.org, October 1, 2012.

110 David Morris, How the Government Blows Away the "Private Sector" in Delivering Services, www.AlterNet.org, February 14, 2014.

111 Same as above.

112 Jessie B. Ramey, The Problem with Choice, Yinzercation, January 29, 2014

113 Sean Coughlan, UK education sixth in global ranking, BBC News, November 27, 2012.

114 Paul Thomas, Whatever Happened to Scientifically Based Research in Education Policy?, www.AlterNet.org, September 12, 2013.

115 Paul Thomas, BOOK REVIEW: "Reign of Error": The Hoax of the Privatization Movement and the Danger to America's Public Schools, www.AlterNet.org, September 17, 2013.

116 Jeff Bryant, Sorry, Michelle Rhee, But Our Obsession With Testing Kids is All About Money, www.AlterNet.org, December 6, 2013.

117 Diane Ravitch, Charter Schools Are a Colossal Mistake. Here's Why, www.AlterNet.org, October 2, 2013.

118 Jeff Bryant, Sorry, Michelle Rhee, But Our Obsession With Testing Kids is All About Money, www.AlterNet.org, December 6, 2013.

119 Paul Buchheit, How Privatizers Are Killing Our Schools, www.AlterNet.org, November 17, 2013.

120 The Common Core Corporate Scam, Rethinking Schools, www.AlterNet.org, October 2, 2013.

121 Paul Thomas, Whatever Happened to Scientifically Based Research in Education Policy?, www.AlterNet.org, September 12, 2013.

122 Anya Kamenetz, The High School Graduation Rate Reaches A Record High – Again, www.NPR.org, October 17, 2016.

123 Same as above.

124 Stan Karp, The Problems with the Common Core, Rethinking Schools, Winter 2013/14.

125 Diane Ravitch, PhD, Why so many parents hate Common Core, www.CNN.com, November 25, 2013.

126 Stan Karp, The Problems with the Common Core, Rethinking Schools, Winter 2013/14.

127 The Common Core Corporate Scam, Rethinking Schools, www.AlterNet.org, October 2, 2013.

128 Same as above.

129 Same as above.

130 Diane Ravitch, PhD, Why so many parents hate Common Core, www.CNN.com, November 25, 2013.

131 The Common Core Corporate Scam, Rethinking Schools, www.AlterNet.

org, October 2, 2013.

132 Same as above.

133 Diane Ravitch, PhD, Why so many parents hate Common Core, www.CNN.com, November 25, 2013.

134 Jeff Bryant, Sorry, Michelle Rhee, But Our Obsession With Testing Kids is All About Money, www.AlterNet.org, December 6, 2013.

135 Diane Ravitch, PhD, Why so many parents hate Common Core, www.CNN.com, November 25, 2013.

136 Erika L. Sanchez, America's Dumbest Idea: Creating a Multiple-Choice Test Generation, The Guardian, November 13, 2013.

137 Diane Ravitch, PhD, Why so many parents hate Common Core, www.CNN.com, November 25, 2013.

138 Same as above.

139 Jeff Bryant, Sorry, Michelle Rhee, But Our Obsession With Testing Kids is All About Money, www.AlterNet.org, December 6, 2013.

140 Same as above.

141 Same as above.

142 Same as above.

143 Same as above.

144 Ruth Conniff, Scathing Report Finds School Privatization Hurts Poor Kids, www.AlterNet.org, April 25, 2014.

145 Same as above.

146 Samantha Winslow, Major Charter School Chain's Classrooms Look Like Cubicles for Telemarketers, www.AlterNet.org, December 16, 2013.

147 Kenneth J. Bernstein, 15

Months in Virtual Charter Hell: A Teacher's Tale, www.AlterNet.org, January 10, 2014.

148 Thom Hartmann, Why You Can Kiss Public Education (and the Middle Class) Goodbye, www.AlterNet.org, December 14, 2012.

149 10 Reasons Why Private School Vouchers Should Be Rejected, Americans United, www.AU.org, February 2011.

150 Susan Jacoby, The Ungodly Constitution: How the Founders Ensured America Would Not Be a Christian Nation, Free Inquiry, June 19, 2012.

151 The First Amendment & Religious Freedom: Statements By Founding Fathers and U.S. Presidents Founding Fathers, Anti-Defamation League, www.ADL.org, Posted November 22, 2011.

152 Same as above.

153 Katherine Stewart, How You End up Paying for Religious Schools Without Knowing It, www.AlterNet.org, April 30, 2012.

154 Same as above.

155 Justice David Souter, Hein v. Freedom From Religion Foundation, Dissenting Opinion, Supreme Court of the United States, June 25, 2007.

156 10 Reasons Why Private School Vouchers Should Be Rejected, Americans United, www.AU.org, February 2011.

157 Nina Totenberg, High Court OKs Ariz. Tax Credit For Religious Schools, www.NPR.org, April 04, 2011.

158 Adam Peck, Louisiana Reps Object to Vouchers for Islamic School, No Problem With Christian Schools, Think Progress, June 13, 2012.

159 Rob Boston, five Sneaky Ways Fundamentalists Are Trying To Slip Christian Creationism Into America's Public Schools, www.AlterNet.org, July 3, 2013.

160 Same as above.

161 Same as above.

162 Deanna Pan, 14 Wacky "Facts" Kids Will Learn in Louisiana's Voucher Schools, www.AlterNet.org, August 10, 2012.

163 10 Reasons Why Private School Vouchers Should Be Rejected, Americans United, www.AU.org, February 2011.

164 Paul Buchheit, How Privatizers Are Killing Our Schools, www.AlterNet.org, November 17, 2013.

165 Adam Peck, Louisiana Reps Object to Vouchers for Islamic School, No Problem With Christian Schools, Think Progress, June 13, 2012.

166 10 Reasons Why Private School Vouchers Should Be Rejected, Americans United, www.AU.org, February 2011.

167 Same as above.

168 Same as above.

169 Same as above.

170 Same as above.

171 Jack Jennings, Proportion of U.S. Students in Private Schools is 10 Percent and Declining, Huffington Post, March 28, 2013.

172 Jessica Meyers, Charter schools with ties to religious groups raise fears about state funds' use, The Dallas Morning News, February 13, 2011.

173 Fred Edwords, What is Humanism, www.AmericanHumanist.org, Accessed January 11, 2013.

174 Katherine Stewart, How evangelicals are making children their missionaries in public schools, www.Guardian.co.uk, September 25, 2012.

175 Same as above.

176 Protecting Religious Freedom, Texas Freedom Network, www.TFN.com, Accessed February 23, 2013.

177 Same as above.

178 K.C. Boyd, How the Religious Right Is Helping De-Educate America's Youth, www.AlterNet.org, February 22, 2013.

179 Protecting Religious Freedom, Texas Freedom Network, www.TFN.com, Accessed February 23, 2013.

180 K.C. Boyd, How the Religious Right Is Helping De-Educate America's Youth, www.AlterNet.org, February 22, 2013.

181 Katherine Stewart, Christians Protest Yoga in Schools -- But Welcome Bible Study, www.AlterNet.org, February 26, 2013.

182 Daniel Denvir, Ayn Rand U? Rich Conservatives -- Not Just the Kochs -- Buying Up Professors and Influence on Campus, www.AlterNet.org, May 24, 2011.

183 Jennifer Medina, Los Angeles Schools, Facing Budget Cuts, Decide to Seek Corporate Sponsors, New York Times, December 15, 2010.

184 Katherine Stewart, The Right-Wing Plot to Undermine Science in Public Schools, wwwAlterNet.org, February 24, 2012.

185 Katherine Stewart, How the Religious Right Is Fueling Climate Change Denial, The Guardian, November 5, 2012.

186 Sabrina Stevens, Inside ALEC's Education Task Force: Private Players Manipulating Public Education, www.AlterNet.org, December 6, 2012.

187 Sara Robinson, How the Conservative Worldview Quashes Critical Thinking -- and What That Means For Our Kids' Future, www.AlterNet.org, May 18, 2012.

188 Bruce E. Levine, eight Reasons Young Americans Don't Fight Back: How the US Crushed Youth Resistance, www.AlterNet.org, July 31, 2011.

189 Sara Robinson, How the Conservative Worldview Quashes Critical Thinking -- and What That Means For Our Kids' Future, www.AlterNet.org, May 18, 2012.

190 Julianne Hing, Florida's School-to-Prison Pipeline is Largest in the Nation, www.Colorlines.com, February 12, 2013.

191 L.A. Schools: We Won't Suspend Kids For Mouthing Off Anymore, www.News.Yahoo.com, May 15, 2013.

192 Dana Goldstein, A Fascinating Way to Put a Stop to the School-to-Prison Pipeline for Black Children, www.AlterNet.org, April 7, 2014.

193 Same as above.

194 Lisa Ann Williamson, Suspension Reform Keeps Students in School, www.Tolerance.org, July 30, 2013.

195 Gara LaMarche, Zero-Tolerance Education Policies Are Destroying Young People's Lives, www.AlterNet.org, April 13, 2011.

196 Annette Fuentes, Should Kids Go To Jail for Skipping School?, www.AlterNet.org, September 7, 2012.

197 Joaquin Sapien, Texas Students Thrown in Jail for Days ... as Punishment for Missing School?, www.AlterNet.org, June 13, 2013.

198 Julianne Hing, Florida's School-to-Prison Pipeline is Largest in the Nation, www.Colorlines.com, February 12, 2013.

199 Same as above.

200 Patricia J. Williams, Full-Body Pat-Downs in America's Schools: How the War on Drugs Is a War on Children, The Nation, February 18, 2013.

201 Steven Hsieh, In Texas, Police in Schools Criminalize 300,000 Students Each Year, www.AlterNet.org, April 12, 2013

202 Patricia J. Williams, Full-Body Pat-Downs in America's Schools: How the War on Drugs Is a War on Children, The Nation, February 18, 2013.

203 Mychal Denzel Smith, It's Time to Close New York's School-to-Prison Pipeline, The Nation, January 2, 2014.

204 Patricia J. Williams, Full-Body Pat-Downs in America's Schools: How the War on Drugs Is a War on Children, The Nation, February 18, 2013.

205 L.A. Schools: We Won't Suspend Kids For Mouthing Off Anymore, www.News.Yahoo.com, May 15, 2013.

206 Paul Armentano, Why on Earth Are Almost a Third of High-Schoolers Getting Drug-Tested in America?, www.AlterNet.org, February 14, 2014.

207 Same as above.

208 Dana Goldstein, A Fascinating Way to Put a Stop to the School-to-Prison Pipeline for Black Children, www.AlterNet.org, April 7, 2014.

209 Jeff Bryant, The Ugly Truth about Charter Schools: Padded Cells, Corruption, Lousy Instruction and Worse Results, www.AlterNet.org, January 10,, 2014.

210 Same as above.

211 Same as above.

212 David Rosen, Kids Tagged With RFID Chips? The Creepy New Technology Schools Use to Track Everything Kids Do -- And the Profit Motive Behind It, www.AlterNet.org, October 5, 2012.

213 NSA Ops 'Walk in Park' Next to Plans to Track Kids, www.WND.com, January 20, 2014.

214 Same as above.

215 Mallory Sauer, Data Mining Students Through Common Core, The New American, April 25, 2013.

216 Perry Chiaramonte, Critics say Common Core includes collecting psych data on kids, Fox News, December 7, 2014.

217 Mallory Sauer, Data Mining Students Through Common Core, The New American, April 25, 2013.

218 NSA Ops 'Walk in Park' Next to Plans to Track Kids, www.WND.com, January 20, 2014.

219 Mallory Sauer, Data Mining Students Through

Common Core, The New American, April 25, 2013.

220 Same as above.

221 NSA Ops 'Walk in Park' Next to Plans to Track Kids, www.WND.com, January 20, 2014.

222 Mark Peltz, The Liberal Arts and Leadership, www.InsideHigherEd.com, May 14, 2012.

223 Juan Cole, How Students Landed on the Front Lines of Class War, www.TruthDig.com, November 22, 2011.

224 Bruce E. Levine, eight Reasons Young Americans Don't Fight Back: How the US Crushed Youth Resistance, www.AlterNet.org, July 31, 2011.

225 Same as above.

226 Same as above.

227 Stephanie Pappas, Low IQ & Conservative Beliefs Linked to Prejudice, www.LiveScience.com January 26, 2012.

228 Report of Platform Committee, 2012 Republican Party of Texas, 2012.

229 Bruce E. Levine, PhD, The More a Society Coerces Its People, the Greater the Chance of Mental Illness, www.AlterNet.org, August 26, 2013.

230 Position Statement Regarding Physical Punishment, American Psychoanalytic Association, www.apsa.org, Accessed February 11, 2013.

231 Bonnie Rochman, Why Spanking Doesn't Work, www.Healthland.Time.com, February 6, 2013.

232 Jamie Gumbrecht, In Sweden, a generation of kids who've never been spanked, www.CNN.com, November 9, 2011.

233 Same as above.

234 Corporal Punishment, National Association of Secondary School Principals, www.nassp.org, Accessed Feb 11, 2013.

235 Yunji De Nies, Should Your Child Be Spanked at School?, www.ABCnews.com, March 16, 2012.

236 Heather Vogell, Violent and Legal: The Shocking Ways School Kids are Being Pinned Down, Isolated Against Their Will, www.ProPublica.org, June 19, 2014.

237 Same as above.

238 Same as above.

239 Position Statement Regarding Physical Punishment, American Psychoanalytic Association, www.apsa.org, Accessed February 11, 2013.

240 Jamie Gumbrecht, In Sweden, a generation of kids who've never been spanked, www.CNN.com, November 9, 2011.

241 Corporal Punishment, National Association of Secondary School Principals, www.nassp.org, Accessed Feb 11, 2013.

242 Position Statement Regarding Physical Punishment, American Psychoanalytic Association, www.apsa.org, Accessed February 11, 2013.

243 Bonnie Rochman, Why Spanking Doesn't Work, www.Healthland.Time.com, February 6, 2013.

244 Same as above.

245 Position Statement Regarding Physical Punishment, American Psychoanalytic Association, www.apsa.org, Accessed February 11, 2013.

246 Dr. Jennifer Shu, Can spanking cause mental illness?, www.CNN.com, July 2, 2012.

247 Position Statement Regarding Physical Punishment, American Psychoanalytic Association, www.apsa.org, Accessed February 11, 2013.

248 Bonnie Rochman, Why Spanking Doesn't Work, www.Healthland.Time.com, February 6, 2013.

249 Yunji De Nies, Should Your Child Be Spanked at School?, www.ABCnews.com, March 16, 2012.

250 Position Statement Regarding Physical Punishment, American Psychoanalytic Association, www.apsa.org, Accessed February 11, 2013.

251 Cole Petrochko, Spanking in Childhood Tied to Adult Obesity and Heart Disease, www.MedPageToday.com, July 15, 2013.

252 Corporal Punishment, National Association of Secondary School Principals, www.nassp.org, Accessed Feb 11, 2013.

253 Bonnie Rochman, Why Spanking Doesn't Work, www.Healthland.Time.com, February 6, 2013.

254 Jamie Gumbrecht, In Sweden, a generation of kids who've never been spanked, www.CNN.com, November 9, 2011.

255 Dr. Jennifer Shu, Can spanking cause mental illness?, www.CNN.com, July 2, 2012.

256 Bonnie Rochman, Why Spanking Doesn't Work, www.Healthland.Time.com, February 6, 2013.

257 Rita Swan, Religious Attitudes on Corporal Punishment, www.ChildrensHealthcare.org, Accessed

February 14, 2013.

258 Jennifer Kahn, Can Emotional Intelligence Be Taught?, New York Times, September 11, 2013.

259 Same as above.

260 John Shindler Ph.D., Transformative Classroom Management: Positive Strategies to Engage All Students and Promote a Psychology of Success, www.CalStateLA.edu, Accessed February 18, 2013.

261 Same as above.

262 Elizabeth Hines, What Happens When Parents Stand Up and Say No to Testing?, www.AlterNet.org, October 30, 2013.

263 John Shindler Ph.D., Transformative Classroom Management: Positive Strategies to Engage All Students and Promote a Psychology of Success, www.CalStateLA.edu, Accessed February 18, 2013.

264 Bruce E. Levine, Why Are Americans So Easy to Manipulate and Control?, www.AlterNet.org, October 11, 2012.

265 Alfie Kohn, The Case Against Grades, Educational Leadership, November 2011.

266 Same as above.

267 Bruce E. Levine, Why Are Americans So Easy to Manipulate and Control?, www.AlterNet.org, October 11, 2012.

268 George Catlin, No contest: the case against competition, Share International, March 1998.

269 Alfie Kohn, The Case Against Grades, Educational Leadership, November 2011.

270 Same as above.
271 Same as above.
272 Same as above.
273 Same as above.
274 Same as above.

275 John Shindler, Ph.D., Transformative Classroom Management: Positive Strategies to Engage All Students and Promote a Psychology of Success, www.CalStateLA.edu, Accessed February 18, 2013.

276 Robert Brooks, Ph.D., How Can Teachers Foster Self-Esteem in Children?, www.GreatSchools.org, Accessed February 18, 2013.

277 Peter Gray, PhD, Free to Learn: Why Unleashing the Instinct to Play Will Make Our Children Happier, More Self-Reliant, and Better Students for Life, Basic Books, 2013.

278 Marion Brady, Ten Things Wrong with What Kids Learn in School, The Washington Post, April 2, 2014.

279 Peter Gray, PhD, Free to Learn: Why Unleashing the Instinct to Play Will Make Our Children Happier, More Self-Reliant, and Better Students for Life, Basic Books, 2013.

280 Rebecca Moss, What Ever Happened to Gym Class? Budget Cuts and the Rise of Childhood Obesity, School Stories, July 4, 2012.

281 Darla M. Castelli et. al., Physical Fitness and Academic Achievement in Third- and Fifth-Grade Students, Journal of Sport & Exercise Psychology, 2007.

282 Is It Just Us, Or Are Kids Getting Really Stupid?, Philadelphia Magazine, November 26, 2010.

283 Bruce E. Levine, PhD, The More a Society Coerces Its People, the Greater the Chance of Mental Illness, www.AlterNet.org, August 26, 2013.

284 Andrew M. Seaman, Pediatricians say kids need recess during school, Reuters, December 31, 2012.

285 Maggie Fox, Bring back PE: Exercise should be 'core' class, report says, NBC News, May 23, 2013.

286 Evelyn Pringle, US Kids Represent Psychiatric Drug Goldmine, www.TruthOut.org, December 12, 2009.

287 Katie McDonough, U.S. Ranks at the Bottom of Child Well-Being, www.Salon.com, April 12, 2013.

288 Andrew M. Weiss, The Wholesale Sedation of America's Youth, Skeptical Inquirer, May 5, 2009.

289 S. E. Smith, Medicating Our Children to Nowhere, www.AlterNet.org, October 26, 2012.

290 Erick H. Turner and others, Selective Publication of Antidepressant Trials and Its Influence on Apparent Efficacy, The New England Journal of Medicine, January 17, 2008.

291 Andrew M. Weiss, The Wholesale Sedation of America's Youth, Skeptical Inquirer, May 5, 2009.

292 Chris Kresser, The "chemical imbalance" myth, www.ChrisKresser.com, June 30, 2008.

293 Same as above.

294 Andrew M. Weiss, The Wholesale Sedation of America's Youth, Skeptical Inquirer, May 5, 2009.

295 Chris Kresser, The "chemical imbalance" myth, www.ChrisKresser.com, June 30, 2008.

296 Same as above.

297 Elizabeth Cohen, CDC: Antidepressants most prescribed drugs in the U.S., www.CNN.com, July 9, 2007.

298 Chris Kresser, The "chemical imbalance" myth, www.ChrisKresser.com, June 30, 2008.

299 Colette Bouchez, Serotonin: nine Questions and Answers, www.WebMD.com, Accessed March 10, 2013.

300 Chris Kresser, The "chemical imbalance" myth, www.ChrisKresser.com, June 30, 2008.

301 Same as above.

302 Same as above.

303 Elliot S. Valenstein, Blaming the Brain: The Truth About Drugs and Mental Health, Simon & Shuster, 2002.

304 Same as above.

305 Bruce E. Levine, Are Antidepressants a Scam? five Myths About How to Treat Depression, www.AlterNet.org, December 5, 2010.

306 Irving Kirsch, Ph.D., Do Anti-Depressants Work? It Very Well Might Be the Placebo That Does the Trick, www.AlterNet.org, March 2, 2011.

307 Irving Kirsch, Ph.D., The Emperors New Drugs: Exploding the Antidepressant Myth, Basic Books, 2011.

308 Bruce E. Levine, Are Antidepressants a Scam? five Myths About How to Treat Depression, www.AlterNet.org, December 5, 2010.

309 Erick H. Turner and others, Selective Publication of Antidepressant Trials and Its Influence on Apparent Efficacy, The New England Journal of Medicine, January 17, 2008.

310 Bruce E. Levine, Are Antidepressants a Scam? five Myths About How to Treat Depression, www.AlterNet.org, December 5, 2010.

311 Same as above.

312 Bruce Levine, Why Psychiatry Holds Enormous Power in Society Despite Losing Scientific Credibility, www.AlterNet.org, January 6, 2015.

313 Amit A. Shah, MD and Thomas E. Finucane, MD, Commercial Influence of Psychiatric Drug Studies, Psychiatric Times, May 1, 2006.

314 Same as above.

315 Same as above.

316 Jamie Doward, Medicine's big new battleground: does mental illness really exist?, www.Guardian.co.uk, May 11, 2013.

317 Irving Kirsch, Ph.D., Do Anti-Depressants Work? It Very Well Might Be the Placebo That Does the Trick, www.AlterNet.org, March 2, 2011.

318 Johan A Den Boer, Looking Beyond the Monoamine Hypothesis, European Neurological Review, 2006.

319 Tami Luhby, Why America's middle class is losing ground, www.CNN.com, March 5, 2013.

320 Paul Buchheit, four Creeping Ways Capitalism Is Killing Us, www.AlterNet.org, November 10, 2013.

321 Bruce E. Levine, Why Life in America Can Literally Drive You Insane, www.AlterNet.org, July 30, 2013.

322 Same as above.

323 Bruce E. Levine, 400 percent Rise in Anti-Depressant Pill Use: Americans Are Disempowered -- Can the OWS Uprising Shake Us Out of Our Depression?, www.AlterNet.org, October 26, 2011.

324 Paul Buchheit, four Creeping Ways Capitalism Is Killing Us, www.AlterNet.org, November 10, 2013.

325 Marlena Fitzpatrick Garcia, Major Study: Suicide Rates in the U.S. Are Soaring, www.AlterNet.org, April 22, 2016.

326 Bruce E. Levine, Why Life in America Can Literally Drive You Insane, www.AlterNet.org, July 30, 2013.

327 Philippa Perry, Loneliness Is Killing Us – We Must Start Treating It Like One of the World's Deadliest Diseases, www.AlterNet.org, February 17, 2014.

328 Bruce E. Levine, Does It Make Sense to Treat Depression with Drugs?, www.AlterNet.org, August 14, 2008.

329 Bruce E. Levine, Why Life in America Can Literally Drive You Insane, www.AlterNet.org, July 30, 2013.

330 Same as above.

331 Same as above.

332 Bruce E. Levine, PhD, The More a Society Coerces Its People, the Greater the Chance of Mental Illness, www.AlterNet.org, August 26, 2013.

333 Andrew M. Weiss, The

Wholesale Sedation of America's Youth, Skeptical Inquirer, May 5, 2009.

334 Bruce E. Levine, Take a Pill, Kill Your Sex Drive? six Reasons Antidepressants Are Misnamed, www.AlterNet.org, July 10, 2012.

335 Liz Szabo, Taking antidepressants during pregnancy linked to increased risk of autism, USA Today, December 14, 2015.

336 Bruce E. Levine, Take a Pill, Kill Your Sex Drive? six Reasons Antidepressants Are Misnamed, www.AlterNet.org, July 10, 2012.

337 Jerome R. Corsi, Ph.D., Top Psychiatrist: Meds Behind School Massacres, www.WND.com, January 22, 2013.

338 Bruce E. Levine, Take a Pill, Kill Your Sex Drive? six Reasons Antidepressants Are Misnamed, www.AlterNet.org, July 10, 2012.

339 Bruce Levine, Why Psychiatry Holds Enormous Power in Society Despite Losing Scientific Credibility, www.AlterNet.org, January 6, 2015.

340 Bruce E. Levine, Take a Pill, Kill Your Sex Drive? six Reasons Antidepressants Are Misnamed, www.AlterNet.org, July 10, 2012.

341 John Horgan, Are Psychiatric Medications Making Us Sicker?, www.ScientificAmerican.com, March 5, 2012.

342 Bruce E. Levine, Take a Pill, Kill Your Sex Drive? six Reasons Antidepressants Are Misnamed, www.AlterNet.org, July 10, 2012.

343 Chris Kresser, The dark side of antidepressants, www.ChrisKresser.com, July 15, 2008.

344 Bruce E. Levine, Take a Pill, Kill Your Sex Drive? six Reasons Antidepressants Are Misnamed, www.AlterNet.org, July 10, 2012.

345 Irving Kirsch, Ph.D., Do Anti-Depressants Work? It Very Well Might Be the Placebo That Does the Trick, www.AlterNet.org, March 2, 2011.

346 Bruce E. Levine, Are Antidepressants a Scam? five Myths About How to Treat Depression, www.AlterNet.org, December 5, 2010.

347 Chris Kresser, The "chemical imbalance" myth, www.ChrisKresser.com, June 30, 2008.

348 Gary G. Kohls, How Psychiatric Drugs Made America Mad, Consortium News, April 22, 2012.

349 John Naish, Ritalin calms hyperactive children and prescriptions are soaring - but experts warn of serious side-effects and it's even being linked to suicide, www.DailyMail.co.uk, May 7, 2012.

350 Bruce E. Levine, Take a Pill, Kill Your Sex Drive? six Reasons Antidepressants Are Misnamed, www.AlterNet.org, July 10, 2012.

351 Andrew M. Weiss, The Wholesale Sedation of America's Youth, Skeptical Inquirer, May 5, 2009.

352 Bruce E. Levine, Why the Newest Psychiatric Diagnostic Bible Will Be a Boon for Big Pharma, www.AlterNet.org, February 8, 2013.

353 Same as above.

354 Allen J. Frances, M.D., DSM five Is Guide Not Bible—Ignore Its Ten Worst Changes, www.PsychologyToday.com, December 2, 2012.

355 Same as above.

356 Same as above.

357 Same as above.

358 Bruce E. Levine, Why the Newest Psychiatric Diagnostic Bible Will Be a Boon for Big Pharma, www.AlterNet.org, February 8, 2013.

359 Allen J. Frances, M.D., DSM five Is Guide Not Bible—Ignore Its Ten Worst Changes, www.PsychologyToday.com, December 2, 2012.

360 Dr. Richard Saul, Doctor: ADHD Does Not Exist, www.Time.com, March 14, 2014.

361 Allen J. Frances, M.D., DSM five Is Guide Not Bible—Ignore Its Ten Worst Changes, www.PsychologyToday.com, December 2, 2012.

362 Same as above.

363 Facts about DSM-5-TR, Psychiatric News, February 24, 2022.

364 Andrew M. Weiss, The Wholesale Sedation of America's Youth, Skeptical Inquirer, May 5, 2009.

365 Same as above.

366 R. Kendell et al., Distinguishing Between the Validity and Utility of Psychiatric Diagnoses, American Journal of Psychiatry, January 2003.

367 What is the "Validity" of the SCID-I?, www.scid4.org, Access April 30, 2013.

368 P. Chodoff, Psychiatric Diagnosis: A 60-Year Perspective, Psychiatric News, June 3, 2005.

369 Bruce E. Levine, Why Life in America Can Literally Drive You Insane, www.AlterNet.org, July 30, 2013.

370 Andrew M. Weiss, The Wholesale Sedation of America's Youth, Skeptical Inquirer, May 5, 2009.

371 Spitzer and First, Classification of Psychiatric Disorders, JAMA, 2005.

372 Bruce E. Levine, Why the Newest Psychiatric Diagnostic Bible Will Be a Boon for Big Pharma, www.AlterNet.org, February 8, 2013.

373 Same as above.

374 Andrew M. Weiss, The Wholesale Sedation of America's Youth, Skeptical Inquirer, May 5, 2009.

375 PK Dalal et al., Moving towards ICD-11 and DSM-5: Concept and evolution of psychiatric classification, Indian Journal of Psychiatry, 2009.

376 How Using the DSM Causes Damage: A Client's Report, Journal of Humanistic Psychology, 2001.

377 Allen J. Frances, M.D., DSM five Is Guide Not Bible—Ignore Its Ten Worst Changes, www.PsychologyToday.com, December 2, 2012.

378 Lisa Cosgrove, Lisa et al., Financial Ties between DSM-IV Panel Members and the Pharmaceutical Industry, Psychotherapy and Psychosomatics, 2006.

379 Bruce E. Levine, Why Life in America Can Literally Drive You Insane, www.AlterNet.org, July 30, 2013.

380 Allen J. Frances, M.D., DSM five Is Guide Not Bible—Ignore Its Ten Worst Changes, www.PsychologyToday.com, December 2, 2012.

381 Katti Gray, Are we over-diagnosing mental illness?, www.CNN.com, March 16, 2013.

382 Allen J. Frances, M.D., DSM five Is Guide Not Bible—Ignore Its Ten Worst Changes, www.PsychologyToday.com, December 2, 2012.

383 Same as above.

384 Same as above.

385 Same as above.

386 Alan Sroufe, Ritalin Gone Wrong, New York Times, January 28, 2012.

387 Alan Schwarz et al., A.D.H.D. Seen in 11 percent of U.S. Children as Diagnoses Rise, New York Times, March 31, 2013.

388 Same as above.

389 Ritalin & Cocaine: The Connection and the Controversy, www.utah.edu, Accessed October 16, 2011.

390 SM Berman et al., Potential adverse effects of amphetamine treatment on brain and behavior: a review, Molecular Psychiatry, February 2009.

391 Benedetto Vitiello, M.D., Understanding the Risk of Using Medications for ADHD with Respect to Physical Growth and Cardiovascular Function, www.ChildPsych.com, April 1, 2009.

392 Chad Stone, Ph.D., Dangerous Side Effects of Ritalin & Adderall, www.LiveStrong.com, March 28, 2011.

393 Dexedrine Addiction, Abuse and Treatment, www.DrugAbuseHelp.com, Accessed May 8, 2012.

394 John Naish, Ritalin calms hyperactive children and prescriptions are soaring - but experts warn of serious side-effects and it's even being linked to suicide, www.DailyMail.co.uk, May 7, 2012.

395 Alan Sroufe, Ritalin Gone Wrong, New York Times, January 28, 2012.

396 Ilina Singh, Beyond polemics: science and ethics of ADHD, Nature Reviews Neuroscience, December 2008.

397 Alan Sroufe, Ritalin Gone Wrong, New York Times, January 28, 2012.

398 Same as above.

399 Same as above.

400 Same as above.

401 John Naish, Ritalin calms hyperactive children and prescriptions are soaring - but experts warn of serious side-effects and it's even being linked to suicide, www.DailyMail.co.uk, May 7, 2012.

402 Alan Sroufe, Ritalin Gone Wrong, New York Times, January 28, 2012.

403 Harvard: Fluoride Can Increase Autism and Attention Deficit Disorder, www.WashingtonBlog.com, March 10, 2014.

404 Rachael Rettner, Preschoolers With ADHD Often Treated Incorrectly, www.LiveScience.com, May 4, 2013.

405 Drug Treatment for ADHD, www.WebMD.com, Accessed April 30, 2013.

406 Alan Sroufe, Ritalin Gone Wrong, New York Times, January 28, 2012.

407 Same as above.

408 Andrew M. Weiss, The Wholesale Sedation of

America's Youth, Skeptical Inquirer, May 5, 2009.

409 Alan Schwarz et al., A.D.H.D. Seen in 11 percent of U.S. Children as Diagnoses Rise, New York Times, March 31, 2013.

410 Sabrina Tavernise, ER visits tied to ADHD drugs quadrupled in six years, www.NBCnews.com, Aug 9, 2013.

411 Brian McIntyre, Richard Sherman: 'Half the league' takes Adderall, www.Yahoo.com, April 10, 2013.

412 John Naish, Ritalin calms hyperactive children and prescriptions are soaring - but experts warn of serious side-effects and it's even being linked to suicide, www.DailyMail.co.uk, May 7, 2012.

413 Bruce E. Levine, Why Life in America Can Literally Drive You Insane, www.AlterNet.org, July 30, 2013.

414 Caroline Miller, The Disturbing Link Between ADHD and Conservative Education Reform, www.AlterNet.org, March 2, 2014.

415 Alan Schwarz et al., A.D.H.D. Seen in 11 percent of U.S. Children as Diagnoses Rise, New York Times, March 31, 2013.

416 Same as above.

417 Same as above.

418 Dr. Richard Saul, Doctor: ADHD Does Not Exist, www.Time.com, March 14, 2014.

419 Same as above.

420 Daniel Boffery, Children's hyperactivity 'is not a real disease', says US expert, The Observer, March 29, 2014.

421 Same as above.

422 Andrew M. Weiss, The Wholesale Sedation of America's Youth, Skeptical Inquirer, May 5, 2009.

423 Evelyn Pringle, An American Phenomenon: The Widespread Psychiatric Drugging of Infants and Toddlers, CounterPunch, April 20, 2010.

424 Bruce E. Levine, Are Prozac and Other Psychiatric Drugs Causing the Astonishing Rise of Mental Illness in America?, www.AlterNet.org, April 28, 2010.

425 J. McClellan, Commentary: treatment guidelines for child and adolescent bipolar disorder, Journal of the American Academy of Child and Adolescent Psychiatry, 2005.

426 W. Mansell et al., The ascent into mania: A review of psychological processes associated with the development of manic symptoms, Clinical Psychology Review, 2008.

427 Antipsychotic Medication for Bipolar Disorder, www.WebMD.com, Accessed April 12, 2013.

428 How is bipolar disorder treated?, National Institute of Mental Health, www.nimh.nih.gov, Accessed April 14, 2013.

429 Typical and Atypical Antipsychotics - The Misleading Dichotomy, www.Karger.com, 2008.

430 Peter Breggin, M.D., Antipsychotic Drugs, Their Harmful Effects, and the Limits of Tort Reform, www.HuffingtonPost.com, October 31, 2009.

431 S. M. Stahl, Stahl's Essential Psychopharmacology: Neuroscientific basis and practical applications, Cambridge University Press, 2008,

432 Adam James, Myth of the antipsychotic, www.Guardian.co.uk, March 2, 2008.

433 M. Mangrella et al., Intensive hospital monitoring of adverse reactions to benzodiazepines and neuroleptic agents, Minerva Medica, 1998.

434 SN Ghaemi et al., Extrapyramidal side effects with atypical neuroleptics in bipolar disorder, Progress in Neuro-psychopharmacology & Biological Psychiatry, March 2006.

435 Peter Breggin, M.D., Antipsychotic Drugs, Their Harmful Effects, and the Limits of Tort Reform, www.HuffingtonPost.com, October 31, 2009.

436 Evelyn Pringle, An American Phenomenon: The Widespread Psychiatric Drugging of Infants and Toddlers, CounterPunch, April 20, 2010.

437 Peter Breggin, M.D., Antipsychotic Drugs, Their Harmful Effects, and the Limits of Tort Reform, www.HuffingtonPost.com, October 31, 2009.

438 Stephen Ray Flora et al., The Bipolar Baboozle, Skeptical Inquirer, October 2008.

439 Bruce E. Levine, Are Prozac and Other Psychiatric Drugs Causing the Astonishing Rise of Mental Illness in America?, www.AlterNet.org, April 28, 2010.

440 SC Dilsaver et al., Antipsychotic withdrawal symptoms: phenomenology and pathophysiology, Acta Psychiatrica Scandinavica, March 1988.

441 A.C. James, Prescribing antipsychotics for children

and adolescents, Advances in Psychiatric Treatment, 2010.

442 Clive G Ballard et al., Atypical antipsychotics for aggression and psychosis in Alzheimer's disease, John Wiley & Sons, Ltd., Accessed 27 July 27, 2012.

443 H. Ito et al., Polypharmacy and excessive dosing: psychiatrists' perceptions of antipsychotic drug prescription, The British Journal of Psychiatry, September 2005.

444 M. Peluso, Extrapyramidal motor side-effects of first- and second-generation antipsychotic drugs, National Institutes of Health, May 2012.

445 Evelyn Pringle, An American Phenomenon: The Widespread Psychiatric Drugging of Infants and Toddlers, CounterPunch, April 20, 2010.

446 A. Bellack, Scientific and Consumer Models of Recovery in Schizophrenia: Concordance, Contrasts, and Implications, Schizophrenia Bulletin, July 2006.

447 Andrew M. Weiss, The Wholesale Sedation of America's Youth, Skeptical Inquirer, May 5, 2009.

448 Stephen Ray Flora et al., The Bipolar Baboozle, Skeptical Inquirer, October 2008.

449 Same as above.

450 Evelyn Pringle, An American Phenomenon: The Widespread Psychiatric Drugging of Infants and Toddlers, CounterPunch, April 20, 2010.

451 Stuart L. Kaplan, Mommy, Am I Really Bipolar?, Newsweek, June 19, 2011.

452 Evelyn Pringle, An American Phenomenon: The Widespread Psychiatric Drugging of Infants and Toddlers, CounterPunch, April 20, 2010.

453 John Horgan, Are Psychiatric Medications Making Us Sicker?, www.ScientificAmerican.com, March 5, 2012.

454 Mental Health Across the Life Stages, www.HealthyPeople.gov, accessed September 5, 2022.

455 John Horgan, Are Psychiatric Medications Making Us Sicker?, www.ScientificAmerican.com, March 5, 2012.

456 Bruce E. Levine, Are Prozac and Other Psychiatric Drugs Causing the Astonishing Rise of Mental Illness in America?, www.AlterNet.org, April 28, 2010.

457 Same as above.

458 John Horgan, Are Psychiatric Medications Making Us Sicker?, www.ScientificAmerican.com, March 5, 2012.

459 Same as above.

460 Same as above.

461 Adam James, Myth of the antipsychotic, www.Guardian.co.uk, March 2, 2008.

462 Bruce Levine, Why Psychiatry Holds Enormous Power in Society Despite Losing Scientific Credibility, www.AlterNet.org, January 6, 2015.

463 John Horgan, Are Psychiatric Medications Making Us Sicker?, www.ScientificAmerican.com, March 5, 2012.

464 Peter Breggin, M.D., Antipsychotic Drugs, Their Harmful Effects, and the Limits of Tort Reform, www.HuffingtonPost.com, October 31, 2009.

465 Same as above.

466 Maria Szalavitz, Antipsychotic Prescriptions in Children Have Skyrocketed: Study, www.Time.com, August 9, 2012.

467 Aaron Kase, Johnson & Johnson $2.2 Billion Settlement Just a Slap on the Wrist, www.AlterNet.org, November 7, 2013.

468 Martha Rosenberg, seven Drugs Whose Dangerous Risks Emerged Only After Big Pharma Made Its Money, www.AlterNet.org, January 2, 2014.

469 Martha Rosenberg, six Drugs Whose Dangerous Risks Were Buried So Big Pharma Could Make Money, www.AlterNet.org, January 15, 2014.

470 Martha Rosenberg, seven Drugs Whose Dangerous Risks Emerged Only After Big Pharma Made Its Money, www.AlterNet.org, January 2, 2014.

471 Maria Szalavitz, Antipsychotic Prescriptions in Children Have Skyrocketed: Study, www.Time.com, August 9, 2012.

472 Maria Szalavitz, Drugging the Vulnerable: Atypical Antipsychotics in Children and the Elderly, www.Time.com, May 26, 2011.

473 Same as above.

474 Stephen Ray Flora et al., The Bipolar Baboozle, Skeptical Inquirer, October 2008.

475 Same as above.

476 Same as above.

477 T. Kato, Molecular genetics of bipolar disorder and depression, Psychiatry and Clinical Neurosciences, 2007.

478 G. Leverich et al., Course of bipolar illness after history of childhood trauma, The Lancet, 2006.

479 S. Leucht et al., How effective are second-generation antipsychotic drugs? A meta-analysis of placebo-controlled trials, Molecular Psychiatry, January 2008.

480 Adam James, Myth of the antipsychotic, www.Guardian.co.uk, March 2, 2008.

481 L. Voruganti et al., New generation antipsychotic drugs and compliance behavior, Current Opinion in Psychiatry, March 2008.

482 S. Leucht et al., How effective are second-generation antipsychotic drugs? A meta-analysis of placebo-controlled trials, Molecular Psychiatry, January 2008.

483 National clinical practice guidelines number 38: Bipolar disorder: the management of bipolar disorder in adults, children and adolescents in primary and secondary care, National Institute of Health and Clinical Excellence, 2006.

484 Bruce E. Levine, Are Prozac and Other Psychiatric Drugs Causing the Astonishing Rise of Mental Illness in America?, www.AlterNet.org, April 28, 2010.

485 Stephen Ray Flora et al., The Bipolar Baboozle, Skeptical Inquirer, October 2008.

486 L. Havens et al., Existential despair and bipolar disorder: The therapeutic alliance as a mood stabilizer, American Journal of Psychotherapy, 2005.

487 Adam James, Myth of the antipsychotic, www.Guardian.co.uk, March 2, 2008.

488 Ronald Pies, M.D., Has Psychiatry Really Abandoned Psychotherapy? Behind the New York Times Story, www.psychcentral.com, April 3, 2011.

489 Peter Breggin, M.D., Antipsychotic Drugs, Their Harmful Effects, and the Limits of Tort Reform, www.HuffingtonPost.com, October 31, 2009.

490 Stephen Ray Flora et al., The Bipolar Baboozle, Skeptical Inquirer, October 2008.

491 Same as above.

492 Maria Szalavitz, Antipsychotic Prescriptions in Children Have Skyrocketed: Study, www.Time.com, August 9, 2012.

493 Evelyn Pringle, An American Phenomenon: The Widespread Psychiatric Drugging of Infants and Toddlers, CounterPunch, April 20, 2010.

494 Brent D. Robbins et al., Conflicts of interest in research on antipsychotic treatment of pediatric bipolar disorder, temper dysregulation disorder, and attenuated psychotic symptoms syndrome: Exploring the unholy alliance between big pharma and psychiatry, Journal of Psychological Issues in Organizational Culture, November 4, 2011.

495 Peter Breggin, M.D., Antipsychotic Drugs, Their Harmful Effects, and the Limits of Tort Reform, www.HuffingtonPost.com, October 31, 2009.

496 Same as above.

497 Same as above.

498 Katie Thomas, In 5-4 Ruling, Justices Say Generic Makers Are Not Liable for Design of Drugs, New York Times, June 24, 2013.

499 Evelyn Pringle, An American Phenomenon: The Widespread Psychiatric Drugging of Infants and Toddlers, CounterPunch, April 20, 2010.

500 Choosing the Right Neuroleptic for a Patient, www.alcouncil.com, 2008.

501 Who are we?, Soteria Network, www.Soteria-Network.org.uk, Accessed May 1, 2013.

502 Evelyn Pringle, An American Phenomenon: The Widespread Psychiatric Drugging of Infants and Toddlers, CounterPunch, April 20, 2010.

503 Andrew M. Weiss, The Wholesale Sedation of America's Youth, Skeptical Inquirer, May 5, 2009.

504 Same as above.

505 Same as above.

506 Dr. Leo Rebollo, Buy Your Poison – Aspartame, Diet Soda, Splenda, www.NaturalNews.com, September 24, 2008.

507 Kristin Wartman, ADHD: It's the food, stupid, www.Grist.org, March 28, 2011.

508 Laura Masi et. al., Video Games in ADHD and Non-ADHD Children: Modalities of Use and Association With ADHD Symptoms, Frontiers Media, March 12, 2021.

509 Michael Ollove, Nearly four Million Seriously Mentally Ill Still Without Insurance, www.AlterNet.org, April 8, 2014.

510 Bruce E. Levine, Are Antidepressants a Scam? five Myths About How to Treat Depression, www.AlterNet.org, December 5,

2010.

511 Philippa Perry, Loneliness Is Killing Us – We Must Start Treating It Like One of the World's Deadliest Diseases, www.AlterNet.org, February 17, 2014.

512 Terrence McNally, Who's Happier — Renter or Owner, Urban or Rural Residents? Uncovering the Myths of Happiness, www.AlterNet.org, February 26, 2014.

513 Same as above.

514 Bruce E. Levine, Are Antidepressants a Scam? five Myths About How to Treat Depression, www.AlterNet.org, December 5, 2010.

515 Melanie Greenberg, PhD, five Reasons It's So Hard to Combat Anxiety and Depression and What You Can Do, www.AlterNet.org, April 2, 2014.

516 Brent Atkinson, PhD, Why People Behave in Self-Defeating, Irrational Ways and How to Really Change, www.AlterNet.org, February 27, 2014.

517 Dr. C. Alonzo Peters, To Hell With Student Loans -- It's Time for College to be Free, The Loop 21, November 18, 2010.

518 Noam Chomsky, Chomsky: How the Young Are Indoctrinated to Obey, AlterNet.org, April 4, 2012.

519 Paul Tough, Americans Are Losing Faith in the Value of College. Whose Fault is That?, www.NYTimes.com, September 5, 2023

520 Same as above

521 Same as above

522 Same as above

523 Same as above

524 Franz Strasser, How US students get a university degree for free in Germany, BBC News, June 3, 2015.

525 Joan Walsh, Do We Hate Our Children? The Insane System That Turns Young Adults into Indentured Servants, Salon, July 1, 2013.

526 Richard Eskow, The Moral Power of Free Universal Higher Education, www.AlterNet.org, March 23, 2014.

527 Les Leopold, The Finance Industry Is Gorging Itself on Your Future—The Trend Lines Will Blow You Away, www.AlterNet.org, December 31, 2014.

528 Paul Tough, Americans Are Losing Faith in the Value of College. Whose Fault is That?, www.NYTimes.com, September 5, 2023.

529 Student debt weighs on overall economy, USA Today, May 19, 2013.

530 Joan Walsh, Do We Hate Our Children? The Insane System That Turns Young Adults into Indentured Servants, Salon, July 1, 2013.

531 Student debt weighs on overall economy, USA Today, May 19, 2013.

532 Joan Walsh, Do We Hate Our Children? The Insane System That Turns Young Adults into Indentured Servants, Salon, July 1, 2013.

533 Student debt weighs on overall economy, USA Today, May 19, 2013.

534 Bill Zimmerman, How to Save the Victims of the Student Loan Crisis, www.AlterNet.org, February 13, 2014.

535 Rebecca Strauss, Schooling Ourselves in an Unequal America, New York Times, June 16, 2013.

536 Christian Exoo et.al., MOOCs: Corporate Welfare for Credit, www.AlterNet.org, October 28, 2013.

537 Rebecca Strauss, Schooling Ourselves in an Unequal America, New York Times, June 16, 2013.

538 U.S. Department of Education Estimate: Biden-Harris Student Debt Relief to Cost an Average of $30 Billion Annually Over Next Decade, U.S. Department of Education, September 29, 2022.

539 Joseph Stiglitz, Equal Opportunity, Our National Myth, New York Times, February 16, 2013.

540 Les Leopold, Shocking Report Explodes five Myths About American Education, www.AlterNet.org, September 18, 2012.

541 Joan Walsh, Do We Hate Our Children? The Insane System That Turns Young Adults into Indentured Servants, Salon, July 1, 2013.

542 Richard Eskow, The Moral Power of Free Universal Higher Education, www.AlterNet.org, March 23, 2014.

543 Same as above

544 Deborah Leigh Scott, How Higher Education in the US Was Destroyed in five Basic Steps, www.AlterNet.org, October 16, 2012.

545 Noam Chomsky, Chomsky: The Corporate Assault on Public Education, www.AlterNet.org, March 8, 2013.

546 Deborah Leigh Scott,

ENDNOTES

How Higher Education in the US Was Destroyed in five Basic Steps, www.AlterNet.org, October 16, 2012.

547 Same as above.

548 James Horn et.al., Public Threat, Private Gain: How Scare Tactics Steer Education Policy to Benefit Corporate Interests, www.AlterNet.org, October 31, 2013.

549 Jeff Faux, Education Profiteering: Wall Street's Next Big Thing?, www.AlterNet.org, October 15, 2012.

550 Andrew Leonard, How the For-Profit Education Business Is a Complete Taxpayer Rip-Off, www.AlterNet.org, July 31, 2012.

551 Same as above.

552 Same as above.

553 Aamer Madhani, New federal rules target for-profit colleges, www.USAtoday.com, March 13, 2104.

554 Andrew Leonard, How the For-Profit Education Business Is a Complete Taxpayer Rip-Off, www.AlterNet.org, July 31, 2012.

555 Blake Ellis, Ex-Penn State president tops highest paid list, www.CNN.com, May 12, 2013.

556 Andrew Leonard, How the For-Profit Education Business Is a Complete Taxpayer Rip-Off, www.AlterNet.org, July 31, 2012.

557 The Trouble With Online College, New York Times, February 18, 2013.

558 84% of All Undergraduates Experienced Some or All Their Classes Moved to Online-Only Instruction Due to the Pandemic, National Center for Education Statistics, June 16, 2021.

559 Jon Marcus, With Online Learning, 'Let's Take a Breath and See What Worked and Didn't Work', New York Times, October 7, 2022.

560 The Trouble With Online College, New York Times, February 18, 2013.

561 Emily Wilson, The Huge Growth of MOOCs Threatens America's Great Public University System, www.AlterNet.org, June 18, 2013.

562 M. Mitchell Waldrop, Massive Open Online Courses, aka MOOCs, Transform Higher Education and Science, Scientific American, March 13, 2013.

563 Emily Wilson, The Huge Growth of MOOCs Threatens America's Great Public University System, www.AlterNet.org, June 18, 2013.

564 Same as above.

565 The Trouble With Online College, New York Times, February 18, 2013.

566 Same as above.

567 Same as above.

568 Jon Marcus, Crazy about 'MOOCs': Are online courses the future of learning or overhyped?, www.NBCnews.com, October 3, 2013.

569 Anya Kamenetz, What If You Could Learn Everything?, www.TheDailyBeast.com, July 14, 2013.

570 Emily Wilson, The Huge Growth of MOOCs Threatens America's Great Public University System, www.AlterNet.org, June 18, 2013.

571 Andrew Leonard, Republicans Declare War on College, www.AlterNet.org, February 22, 2013.

572 Tomales Bay Institute, The State of the Commons, www.OnTheCommons.org, November 2006.

573 Darwin BondGraham, Universities Selling Out Important Research to Corporate Overseers, www.AlterNet.org, June 27, 2013.

574 Same as above.

575 Same as above.

576 Kay Steiger, Adjunct Faculty of America, Unite!, The Nation, July 15, 2013.

577 Tamar Lewin, Gap Widens for Faculty at Colleges, Report Finds, New York Times, April 8, 2013.

578 Kay Steiger, Adjunct Faculty of America, Unite!, The Nation, July 15, 2013.

579 Genevieve Carlton, Adjunct Professor vs. Tenured Professor: How Do They Differ?, www.BestColleges.com, August 10, 2021.

580 Deborah Leigh Scott, How Higher Education in the US Was Destroyed in five Basic Steps, www.AlterNet.org, October 16, 2012.

581 Same as above.

582 Same as above.

583 Andrew Leonard, Republicans Declare War on College, www.AlterNet.org, February 22, 2013.

584 Same as above.

585 Same as above.

586 Daniel Denvir, Ayn Rand U? Rich Conservatives -- Not Just the Kochs -- Buying Up Professors and Influence on Campus, www.AlterNet.org, May 24, 2011.

587 Edward W. Younkins, Ayn Rand's Atlas Shrugged: A Philosophical and Liter-

ary Comparison, Ashgate Publishing, 2007.

588 Same as above.

589 Robert Reich, Be Very Afraid: The American Economy Is Cannibalizing Itself, and We the People Are Going to Pay a Huge Price, www.RobertReich.org, November 3, 2013.

590 Tom Hartman and Sam Sacks, How America Is Turning into a Third World Nation In Four Easy Steps, www.ThomHartmann.com, November 10, 2012.

591 Ayn Rand, The Fountainhead, The Bobbs-Merrill Company, 1943.

592 Peter Vallentyne, Libertarianism, The Stanford Encyclopedia of Philosophy, 2009.

593 R.J. Eskow, 11 Questions You Should Ask Libertarians to See if They're Hypocrites, www.AlterNet.org, September 11, 2013.

594 Same as above.

595 David Boaz, Key Concepts of Libertarianism, Cato Institute, January 1, 1999.

596 Same as above.

597 Jada Thacker, Concept of "Limited Government" Is Right-Wing Bunk: Try to Find Anything Remotely Like It in the Constitution, www.AlterNet.org, July 8, 2013.

598 David Boaz, Key Concepts of Libertarianism, Cato Institute, January 1, 1999.

599 Jada Thacker, Concept of "Limited Government" Is Right-Wing Bunk: Try to Find Anything Remotely Like It in the Constitution, www.AlterNet.org, July 8, 2013.

600 Robert Parry, How GOP Extortion Is Rooted in Southern Slavery, www.ConsortiumNews.com, October 3, 2013.

601 Same as above.

602 Jada Thacker, Concept of "Limited Government" Is Right-Wing Bunk: Try to Find Anything Remotely Like It in the Constitution, www.AlterNet.org, July 8, 2013.

603 Same as above.

604 Robert Reich, Why the Idea of a "Free Market" Is Total BS, www.AlterNet.org, September 16, 2013.

605 R.J. Eskow, 11 Questions You Should Ask Libertarians to See if They're Hypocrites, www.AlterNet.org, September 11, 2013.

606 United States v. Windsor, Supreme Court of the United States, June 26, 2013.

607 Poll: Support for gay marriage hits high after ruling, USA Today, July 1, 2013.

608 Obergefell et al. v. Hodges, Supreme Court of the United States, June 26, 2015.

609 Same as above.

610 David Boaz, Key Concepts of Libertarianism, Cato Institute, January 1, 1999.

611 Harriet Rubin, Ayn Rand's Literature of Capitalism, New York Times, September 15, 2007.

612 Atlas Shrugged Selling in Record Numbers, www.AynRand.org, July 13, 2009.

613 Harriet Rubin, Ayn Rand's Literature of Capitalism, New York Times, September 15, 2007.

614 Susan J. Douglas, Dumbing America Down, Conservative Style, www.AlterNet.org, January 4, 2014.

615 Larry Sabato, The higher the education level, the more likely they are to vote Democratic, www.PolitiFact.com, October 16, 2012.

616 A Closer Look at the Parties in 2012, www.People-Press.org, August 23, 2012.

617 Juliana Kaplan et. al., The class of 2022 is being presented with the most open jobs in history. But they aren't the jobs Gen Zers want., www.BusinessInsider.com, June 12, 2022.

618 Andy Hardy, The Wage Gap Between College and High School Grads Just Hit a Record High, www.Money.com, February 14, 2022.

619 Amber Pace, The Economy is "Recovering" By Creating More Low-Wage Jobs... Increasingly Filled By Graduates, Campus Progress, April 1, 2013.

620 Lynn Stuart Parramore, Class of 2013: All Dressed Up and No Place to Work, www.AlterNet.org, June 10, 2013.

621 Same as above.

622 Lynn Stuart Parramore, Boomerang Babies: Record Numbers of Young Adults Live with Parents at Terrible Cost, www.AlterNet.org, August 5, 2013.

623 Tracy Velt, College Graduates More Likely to Live With Parents in 2018, www.RealTrends.com, May 8, 2018.

624 Hope Yen, one in two new graduates are jobless or underemployed, Associated Press, April 23, 2012.

625 David Dayen, Why Student Loans Are an Even Bigger Sham Than You

ENDNOTES

Know, Salon, June 6, 2013.

626 Bill Zimmerman, How to Save the Victims of the Student Loan Crisis, www.AlterNet.org, February 13, 2014.

627 David Dayen, Why Student Loans Are an Even Bigger Sham Than You Know, Salon, June 6, 2013.

628 Alicia Hahn, 2022 Student Loan Debt Statistics: Average Student Loan Debt, www.Forbes.com, September 19, 2022.

629 David Dayen, Why Student Loans Are an Even Bigger Sham Than You Know, Salon, June 6, 2013.

630 Same as above.

631 Matt Taibbi, We're Saddling College Students with Crushing Debt ... and the Govt. Is Acting Like a Greedy Profiteer, www.AlterNet.org, August 20, 2013.

632 Bruce E. Levine, Why Life in America Can Literally Drive You Insane, www.AlterNet.org, July 30, 2013.

633 Ellen Brown, Why Elizabeth Warren's Plan For Student Debt is an Economic Breakthrough, www.AlterNet.org, June 14, 2013.

634 Bill Zimmerman, How to Save the Victims of the Student Loan Crisis, www.AlterNet.org, February 13, 2014.

635 Tami Luhby, Many millennials are worse off than their parents -- a first in American history, www.CNN.com, January 11, 2020.

636 Dr. C. Alonzo Peters, To Hell With Student Loans -- It's Time for College to be Free, www.AlterNet.org, November 18, 2010.

637 Jason M. Breslow, By the Numbers: Dropping Out of High School, www.PBS.org, September 21, 2012.

638 Bill Zimmerman, How to Save the Victims of the Student Loan Crisis, www.AlterNet.org, February 13, 2014.

639 Jason M. Breslow, By the Numbers: Dropping Out of High School, www.PBS.org, September 21, 2012.

640 David Dayen, Why Student Loans Are an Even Bigger Sham Than You Know, Salon, June 6, 2013.

641 Jeff Bryant, When Being 'For The Kids' Really Isn't, www.AlterNet.org, March 5, 2014.

642 Same as above.

643 Matthew Low, There have been at least 554 school shooting victims in the US since the Columbine High School massacre: report, www.Insider.com, May 24, 2022.

644 Jeff Bryant, When Being 'For The Kids' Really Isn't, www.AlterNet.org, March 5, 2014.

645 Same as above.

646 Same as above.

647 Jaisal Noor, Investing in Education Creates More Than Twice as Many Jobs as Military Spending, www.AlterNet.org, June 10, 2013.

648 Why We Still Need Public Schools: Public Education for the Common Good, Center on Education Policy, January 1, 2007.

649 Same as above.

650 Brown v. Board of Education, www.CivilRights.org, Accessed March 12, 2014.

651 Nona Willis Aronowitz, Class Dismissed, Forever: Rural Schools Face Closures, www.NBCnews.com, June 27, 2014.

652 Same as above.

653 Same as above.

654 Same as above.

655 Jeff Bryant, The Time Is Now To Press For Universal Preschool, www.OurFuture, org, July 2, 2013.

656 Same as above.

657 Same as above.

658 Sarah Garland, A for-profit approach to Head Start, www.HechingerReport.org, May 23, 2011.

659 Paul Rosenberg, Charter Schools are Cheating Your Kids: Report Reveals Massive Fraud, Mismanagement, Abuse, www.Salon.com, May 7, 2014.

660 Same as above.

661 Same as above. s

662 Peter Gray, PhD, Free to Learn: Why Unleashing the Instinct to Play Will Make Our Children Happier, More Self-Reliant, and Better Students for Life, Basic Books, 2013.

663 Jared Diamond, PhD, The World Until Yesterday: What Can We Learn from Traditional Societies?, Jared Diamond, PhD, Viking Adult, 2012.

664 Bruce Levine, PhD, The More a Society Coerces Its People, the Greater the Chance of Mental Illness, www.AlterNet.org, August 26, 2013.

665 Same as above.

666 Same as above.

667 Same as above.

668 Alternatives to School, www.AlternativesToSchool.com, Accessed April 3, 2014.

669 Same as above.

670 Same as above.

671 Marion Brady, Why We Should Consider Letting High Schoolers Pick Their Classes, The Washington Post, January 23, 2013.

672 Peter Gray, PhD, School Is a Prison – And Damaging Our Kids, www.Salon.com, August 26, 2013.

673 Alternatives to School, www.AlternativesToSchool.com, Accessed April 3, 2014.

674 Same as above.

675 Same as above.

676 Same as above.

677 Same as above.

678 Peter Gray, PhD, School Is a Prison – And Damaging Our Kids, www.Salon.com, August 26, 2013.

679 Alternatives to School, www.AlternativesToSchool.com, Accessed April 3, 2014.

680 Peter Gray, PhD, Why Students Learn Better in a Playful Environment, www.AlterNet.org, March 11, 2013.

681 Peter Gray, PhD, Free to Learn: Why Unleashing the Instinct to Play Will Make Our Children Happier, More Self-Reliant, and Better Students for Life, Basic Books, 2013.

682 Alternatives to School, www.AlternativesToSchool.com, Accessed April 3, 2014.

683 Same as above.

684 Same as above.

685 Same as above.

686 Same as above.

687 Same as above.

688 Peter Gray, PhD, School Is a Prison – And Damaging Our Kids, www.Salon.com, August 26, 2013.

689 Alternatives to School, www.AlternativesToSchool.com, Accessed April 3, 2014.

690 Laurie Levy, The Problem with Forcing Young Children to Read Before They're Ready, www.AlterNet.org, April 8, 2014.

691 Same as above.

692 Same as above.

693 Alternatives to School, www.AlternativesToSchool.com, Accessed April 3, 2014.

694 Marion Brady, Ten Things Wrong with What Kids Learn in School, The Washington Post, April 2, 2014.

695 Same as above.

696 Same as above.

697 Colin Greer, Fighting School Failure Isn't Rocket Science -- We Know What Works, www.AlterNet.org, April 4, 2010.

698 Susan Ferriss, San Francisco Takes the Lead in Defining Role of School Police, Sets Limits on Interrogations, Arrests, www.AlterNet.org, February 3, 2014.

699 S.E. Smith, Zero-Tolerance Policies in Schools are Often Destructive, Fueling a School to Prison Pipeline, www.AlterNet.org, December 6, 2013.

700 Fania Davis, Discipline With Dignity: Oakland Classrooms Try Healing Instead of Punishment, YES! Magazine, February 19, 2014.

701 Same as above.

702 Julianne Hing, School Police and Principals Forced to Undergo Trainings in Implicit Racism, www.ColorLines.com, February 25, 2013.

703 S.E. Smith, Zero-Tolerance Policies in Schools are Often Destructive, Fueling a School to Prison Pipeline, www.AlterNet.org, December 6, 2013.

704 L.A. Schools: We Won't Suspend Kids For Mouthing Off Anymore, www.TakePart.com, May 15, 2013.

705 Susan Ferriss, San Francisco Takes the Lead in Defining Role of School Police, Sets Limits on Interrogations, Arrests, www.AlterNet.org, February 3, 2014.

706 Steven Hsieh, Principal Fires Guards, Expands Arts and Sees Test Scores Soar, www.AlterNet.org, May 3, 2013.

707 Susan Ferriss, San Francisco Takes the Lead in Defining Role of School Police, Sets Limits on Interrogations, Arrests, www.AlterNet.org, February 3, 2014.

708 Brian Willoughby, Is It Time to End Suspension as the 'Go-To' Punishment in Schools?, www.AlterNet.org, June 23, 2012.

709 Dana Goldstein, A Fascinating Way to Put a Stop to the School-to-Prison Pipeline for Black Children, www.AlterNet.org, April 7, 2014.

710 Khalil Abdullah, Maryland Abandons Zero-tolerance Approach to School Discipline, New America Media, February 5, 2014.

711 Fania Davis, Discipline With Dignity: Oakland Classrooms Try Healing Instead of Punishment, YES! Magazine, February 19, 2014.

712 Julianne Hing, School Police and Principals Forced to Undergo Trainings in Implicit Racism, www.ColorLines.com, February 25, 2013.

713 Katherine Stewart, The Bully Backlash: How the Christian Right Is Attacking Efforts to Help Kids, www.AlterNet.org, April 4, 2012.

714 Amanda Gardner, Bullying, abuse linked to suicidal thoughts in kids, www.CNN.com, October 23, 2012.

715 Sexual harassment is spreading in schools, www.USAtoday.com, November 7, 2011.

716 Amanda Gardner, Bullying, abuse linked to suicidal thoughts in kids, www.CNN.com, October 23, 2012.

717 Stephanie Chen, In a wired world, children unable to escape cyberbullying, www.CNN.com, October 4, 2010.

718 With cyberbulling, there's no safe place, study finds, www.CNN.com, July 5, 2010.

719 Maia Szalavitz, How Not to Raise a Bully: The Early Roots of Empathy, www.Time.com, April 17, 2010.

720 Same as above.

721 Ryan Buxton, Mom Of Michael Morones, 11-Year-Old Bullied Over 'My Little Pony,' Speaks Out On Son's Suicide Attempt, Huffington Post, April 14, 2014.

722 Jenn Gidman, Girl with 'crooked' smile from cancer kills self, www.USAtoday.com, November 2, 2016.

723 Katherine Stewart, The Bully Backlash: How the Christian Right Is Attacking Efforts to Help Kids, www.AlterNet.org, April 4, 2012.

724 What Will It Take to Make Schools Safe for the LGBTQ Community?, Rethinking Schools, April 25, 2014.

725 Maia Szalavitz, How Not to Raise a Bully: The Early Roots of Empathy, www.Time.com, April 17, 2010.

726 Carrie Goldman, Bullied: What Every Parent, Teacher and Kid Needs to Know about Ending the Cycle of Fear, www.AlterNet.org, September 6, 2012.

727 Same as above.

728 Maia Szalavitz, How Not to Raise a Bully: The Early Roots of Empathy, www.Time.com, April 17, 2010.

729 What Will It Take to Make Schools Safe for the LGBTQ Community?, Rethinking Schools, April 25, 2014.

730 Terry Orlick, Competitive Games and Sports, Joyful Activities for Everyone, Human Kinetics Publishers, 2006.

731 David Chadwell, Single-Gender Classes Can Respond to the Needs of Boys and Girls, www.ASCD.org, Accessed May 9, 2014.

732 Gary Orfield, Reviving the Goal of an Integrated Society: A 21st Century Challenge, The Civil Rights Project, UCLA, January 2009.

733 Nikole Hannah-Jones, Why Has the Federal Government Stopped Enforcing Court Orders to Integrate America's Schools?, ProPublica, May 5, 2014.

734 Richard Rothstein, The Unfulfilled Promise of Brown v. Board of Education, Economic Policy Institute, April 29, 2014.

735 David Sobel, Why Outdoor Schools Make Kids Happier -- and Smarter, www.AlterNet.org, May 16, 2014.

736 Jordan Rosenfeld, Why More and More Parents Are Opting Their Kids Out of Homework, www.AlterNet.org, March 6, 2015.

737 Laurie Levy, My 5-Year-Old Grandson Hates Homework—And I Don't Blame Him, www.AlterNet.org, February 26, 2015.

738 Democrats Ramshield, America is About to Lose One of Its Best Public Resource: Public Libraries, www.AlterNet.org, March 12, 2014.

739 Same as above.

740 Education at a Glance 2012, Organization for Economic Cooperation and Development, 2012.

741 Deva Dalporto, Finland's A+ Schools, www.WeAreTeachers.com, April 1, 2015.

742 Same as above.

743 Same as above.

744 Same as above.

745 Same as above.

746 Richard Garner, Finland schools: Subjects scrapped and replaced with 'topics' as country reforms its education system, www.Independent.co.uk, March 20, 2015

747 Same as above.

748 Same as above.

749 Deva Dalporto, Finland's A+ Schools, www.WeAreTeachers.com, April 1, 2015.

Index

A

accountability 12–17, 40–43, 51, 65–66, 69, 210, 303, 412–415, 440–445, 482–486, 488–492

Adderall 201, 205–209, 213, 231

addictive and compulsive behavior 275–276

Adequate Yearly Progress 12, 38

ADHD 185–186, 200–215, 238, 253–254, 290–291, 469, 546

adjunct professors 321–324

administrative costs 20, 302–305, 441–442

adult education 551

alternative treatments 280

American Psychiatric Association (APA) 193–195

anticonvulsants 153, 217–221

antidepressants 153–154, 159–162, 166, 169–172, 177, 217, 224–225, 246–248

antipsychotics 153, 215–221, 223–228, 230–240, 242–248, 269, 280

art 148–149, 274, 477

artificial intelligence (AI) 495-499

assessment 127–129, 132–133, 136, 137–143, 481–486

Atlas Shrugged 326–346, 389–391

authoritarianism 82–102, 374, 514–515

B

bankruptcy 397–401

bipolar 185, 215–226, 233–235, 238–241, 244–248

boredom 145–152, 456–457, 547

brain chemical imbalance 157–163, 168–169, 174, 177, 181

bullying 456, 509–521, 535

business education 555–558

business influence of education 76–81

business influence of higher education 317, 406–412

C

charter schools 17–20, 23, 26, 34, 52–54, 71, 89, 440–445

civic responsibility 548

class mobility 300–302

class sizes 6, 10, 68–69, 434, 489

clear communication 542–544

climate change 77–79, 446

clinical trials 179–180

co-education 537–539

coercion 99–102, 167–168, 448–451, 515

Common Core standards 14–15, 46–51, 462

community service 282–284, 548

competitive grading 118–144, 453–455, 475, 480–481, 534

corporal punishment 103–117, 521–522

corporate welfare 2–4, 7–11, 153, 255–256, 323, 393, 404, 434–438

creationism 62–63

D

depression 157–179, 224–226, 254–255, 271, 284–285, 287

Diagnostic and Statistical Manual of Mental Disorders (DSM) 181–200, 221–224, 259-265

direct-to-consumer marketing 178, 240–241, 267–268

disempowering beliefs 163, 168, 172–177, 189–193, 259–264, 272

drug company influence of doctors 237–238

drug company influence of government 227

drug company influence of research 234–237

drug company marketing 240–241, 249, 267–268, 289

drug testing 88–89

DSM diagnostic method 181–199

E

education funding 1–11, 301, 404, 434–438

education reform 12–17, 33–39, 45–46, 50–51, 68–69, 129, 136, 146, 148, 183, 210, 432–434, 440, 462–463, 468, 486–491, 506, 566–573

elderly people 257, 552–553

Every Student Succeeds Act (ESSA) 13–16, 33, 43–46

F

Finland 8, 16, 20, 43, 235, 560–566

First Amendment 57–59, 73–74

forced education 447–480, 514, 550

freedom-based education 447–480, 543, 572

free markets 365–368
free public higher education 294–295, 318, 412
full disclosure 228, 265, 271
fully fund public higher education 403–405, 408

G

genetics 203, 234

H

healthy living 544
Hein v. Freedom From Religion Foundation 59
higher education 294–413, 560, 571–572
Hispanic 4, 16, 47
hitting children 103–117, 479, 521–522
homework 146, 547, 560–563
honor and empower teachers 487–493
hopelessness 173–177
hyperactive 151, 153, 154
hypocrisy 372–377, 384, 442–445

I

inadequate drug trials 179–180
incarceration vii, 1, 3, 9, 90–91, 374, 437, 439, 569–570
indigenous religions 118
individualism 359–361
Industrial Age 146, 447
institutional use of antipsychotics 232–233
insurance reimbursement practices 238–239

intellectuals 98–99, 295, 321, 323, 408–409
International Classification of Diseases (ICD) 181–182, 202
intuitive wisdom 273, 281–282, 285, 332, 362, 419–430, 461, 526–529, 531
IQ 97–98, 392–393, 532–533

K

K-12 education 37–38, 147, 415, 434–436, 457, 459, 465–466, 552
KIPP 18, 26, 89

L

laws of nature 56, 64, 329
liberal arts 93–94, 149, 313, 324–326, 391, 393, 412–413
libertarianism 346–375, 385–394
limited government 351–358
low-income communities 6–11, 16, 25, 29–30, 40, 52–54, 89, 437, 494, 540–541

M

manufactured crisis 39–51
measurement 128–129, 471–472, 482–486, 532, 556
meditation 288, 498, 527, 531
mixed-sex education 537–539
MOOC 306–319
mood stabilizers 153, 217–218, 233
motivation 130–131, 140–142, 171, 179–180, 260, 454

multiculturalism 80

N

Nation at Risk report 12
negative emotions 119, 167, 179, 236–237, 272, 275–276, 282, 287–288, 511, 529, 549
No Child Left Behind Act (NCLB) 12–17, 33, 43–48, 210, 414

O

objectivism 326–346
off-label use 220, 227–232
online charter schools 53–54
online education 53, 149, 306–319, 325, 410–411, 493–499
Oppositional Defiant Disorder (ODD) 182–185
outdoor education 546–547
overprescription 154–155, 177–180, 211, 249, 252, 258–259, 271, 278

P

parents 245–247, 249–251, 257, 265, 278–280, 291–293, 511, 513–514, 521–523, 548–550, 553–555
pathologizing normal human behavior 182–189
physical education 148–149, 151–153, 545
physical punishment 103–117, 521–522
placebo effect 172–177
plutocracy 3, 7, 393, 555, 568
poverty 7–9, 15–17, 35–36, 322–323, 431–433, 439, 513
privatization 12–55, 69, 89–90, 138, 305, 406, 410–412, 414–415, 434, 440, 462

INDEX

productivity 131–132, 134–135

Protestant Reformation 145–146, 416, 447, 507

psychiatric drugs 93, 153–293, 522–524

psychological diagnosis 181–200, 202, 259–265

psychological pain 163, 171, 198, 253, 267

psychological problems 87, 145, 150, 153–293, 433, 447, 449, 456, 509–511, 521–523, 546

psychosis 216–221, 226, 236–237, 245, 247–248

psychotherapy 157, 174–180, 195, 197, 235–240, 248, 258–259, 268, 270, 271–274, 281, 284–286

public deception 33–39, 41, 99, 177–181, 183, 195, 255–256, 337, 347, 369, 382, 384–394, 412, 415, 446, 472–474, 514, 542, 544, 568

public funding of religion 56–75, 445

public higher education 1, 294–413

purpose of education 122, 145, 416–419, 447, 470, 481, 495, 532

R

Race to the Top program 14, 46

recess 148, 151, 153, 546, 560–561

relationship problems 165–166, 168, 175–176, 283, 288, 510, 536

religion 56–75, 96–97, 116, 118, 130, 276, 329, 380, 391, 445, 446

religious dogma 56–57, 61–62, 65, 71–72, 75, 79–80, 380, 446, 513, 517

religious principles 56, 64, 329, 428, 548

religious schools 56–75, 115, 445–446

restorative justice 502¬–505, 515

Ritalin 201, 205–209, 213

Robert Whitaker 224–225, 248–249

Rocketship 26, 53

rule of law 347–351, 356, 358, 361, 363–366, 371, 374, 377, 385–388

S

school choice 35–39

screen viewing 95, 550

secular humanism 71, 80, 96

segregation 67, 540–542

self-esteem 120, 121–124, 128–129, 136, 140–144, 176, 339, 452–453, 457–458, 465, 501, 516–517, 534, 549–550, 572

sexual dysfunction 169–170

side effects 155, 169, 172, 196–197, 201, 205, 212, 218, 220–221, 226, 228, 230–231, 235, 238, 249, 251

skepticism 78, 80–81, 284–287

social skills 42, 124–127, 137–138, 141, 311, 449–450, 493, 528–529, 534, 538–539, 554

Soteria network 248

standardized testing 6, 12–13, 16, 28, 40–43, 49–53, 69, 84, 125–126, 128–129, 132, 147, 214, 303, 486–487

STAR*D study 160–161

stimulants 153, 200–215, 225, 230–231, 238, 246, 248, 269, 291

student debt 95, 164–165, 299–300, 305, 397–402, 405–406

suicidal thoughts 170–171, 201, 216, 218, 509–510

suicide 164–165, 170–173, 205, 217, 286, 509, 512–513

support networks 277–278

suppressing disruptive behavior 230–231

suppression of critical thinking 324–394

suppression of minorities 133–134

suppression of professors 321–324

system change 211, 255–257, 259, 431, 474, 519–520, 523, 556–558

T

taxpayer-funded research 319–321, 393, 407–408

teacher-student relationships 132–133, 139, 481

teacher pay 17, 23, 41, 67, 69, 433, 488, 560

teachers unions 8, 22–23, 26, 31, 33, 35, 40–41, 69, 129, 142, 411, 441, 487–488

Teach for America (TFA) 24–33, 69, 441, 483

test and punish 44–48, 51, 69

The Fountainhead 342–346, 389

think tanks 78, 295, 346, 409

treatment guidelines 195, 223, 266

treatment-resistant 180

trigger laws 14

U

unconscious beliefs 107–110, 125–126, 226, 264, 274, 526–527

UN Convention on the Rights of the Child 104

unfair student debt terms 397–402

unity 118, 362, 498

university research 319–321, 408

Unspecified Mood Disorder 188, 217, 222, 246

US education performance 3, 22, 33

V

value-added modeling 14

vocational education 149, 316, 324, 403, 412, 426

voucher programs 14, 41, 56, 66–67, 70

vulnerability of children 249–251

W

whole system solution 402–403, 514

whole system thinking 118, 294, 414, 419–430, 481, 530, 534–535, 557

Z

Zelman v. Simmon-Harris 58–60

zero-tolerance discipline 84–88, 499–509

www.ingramcontent.com/pod-product-compliance
Lightning Source LLC
Chambersburg PA
CBHW011407070526
44586CB00022B/2584